Contents

Preface

This is a revised edition of the authors' two previous publications: Authors of Books for Young People which was published in 1964 and Authors of Books For Young People, First Supplement which was published in 1967.

New entries have been included resulting in a total of 2161 biographies in this book. Other revisions are the inclusion of the publisher and year of publication for each title, and cross references for all pseudonyms.

The factors determining inclusion remain the same as in the previous two volumes:

(1) Information was based on the "author file" which was compiled in the Children's Department of the Free Public Library, Quincy, Illinois. Although the file was used by students of all ages, the majority of the students who used it were between the ages of twelve to fourteen. Frequently the decision to include an author was based on the number of times that this particular biography was requested by a student.

(2) A contemporary author whose biography proved difficult to locate was given preference for inclusion over a well-known author whose biographical information was more readily available.

(3) All recipients through 1970 of the Newbery and Caldecott Medals have been included. The Newbery Medal is given "to the author of the most distinguished contribution to American literature for children. " The Caldecott Medal is awarded "to the artist of the most distinguished American picture book for children. "

The symbols which follow the biographies refer to volumes in which additional author information can be found.

Key to Symbols:

CA 1-20 Contemporary Authors, Vols. 1-20. James
M. Ethridge, ed. (c. 1968). Volumes 11-18
Barbara Kopala and James M. Ethridge,
editors; volumes 19-20 Barbara Kopala,
Carolyn Riley, James M. Ethridge, editors.
Gale Research Company

JBA-1 Junior Book of Authors, The. Stanley J.
Kunitz and Howard Haycraft, eds. (c. 1934)
The H. W. Wilson Company

JBA-2 Junior Book of Authors, The. Stanley J.
Kunitz and Howard Haycraft, eds. (2nd ed.,
rev. 1951) The H. W. Wilson Company

MJA More Junior Authors. Muriel Fuller, ed.
(c. 1963) The H. W. Wilson Company

The basic aim of the authors remains the same: "the
work is intended as an aid for all of those who are interested in literature for young people."

Martha E. Ward
Dorothy A. Marquardt

Authors of Books for Young People

A

ABRAHAMS, Robert David 1905-
Attorney and author, Robert Abrahams has been on
the staff of the Law School at Temple University in
Philadelphia and has also been associated with a
prominent law firm in that city. He has been a
Trustee of the School of Law at Dickinson College
in Carlisle, Pennsylvania. Mr. Abrahams has written prose and verse for magazines, and for young
people he wrote Bonus Of Redonda, Macmillan, 1969.

ACHESON, Patricia Castles 1924-
She was born in New York City and attended Bryn
Mawr College in Pennsylvania. She has been a history
teacher in Boston and has also taught at the Madeira
School in Washington. She and her attorney husband
have lived in Washington, D. C. Her books for young
people include: America's Colonial Heritage, Dodd,
1957; Our Federal Government: How It Works, Dodd,
1969. CA-3

ACKER, Helen
Born in Niagara Falls, New York, she received her
D. A. and M. A. degrees from the University of Min-
nesota. She has taught in Puerto Rico and at the
University of Minnesota. She married Arthur B.
Anderson, and they have lived in Minneapolis. She
wrote Five Sons Of Italy, Nelson, 1950.

ADAMS, Ruth Joyce
Author and teacher, she has made her home in San
Pedro, California. Mrs. Adams has been a music
teacher in the schools of Los Angeles. Her poetry
and stories have been published. Her first book for
children was Mr. Picklepaw's Popcorn, Lothrop, 1965.

ADAMS, Samuel Hopkins 1871-
He graduated from Hamilton College where he

5

introduced football and played on its first team.   As
an authority on the Erie Canal, Samuel Adams has
written books of both fact and folklore. He has lived
near Auburn, New York.   Juvenile titles include:
Chingo Smith Of The Erie Canal, Random, 1958; Erie
Canal, Random, 1953.

ADELSON, Leone   1908-
She has been associated with the School for the Deaf in
New York City and has closely worked with the children
who were nursery school age.   She collaborated with
Lilian Moore to write Old Rosie, Junior Literary Guild
and Random, 1952.   She also wrote Please Pass The
Grass!   (A Junior Literary Guild selection), McKay,
1960.

ADLER, Irving   1913-   Ruth 1915-
Husband-wife team.   Dr. Adler has been an instructor
of mathematics at Columbia University and at one time
was head of mathematics in a New York high school.
Ruth Adler has been a science and art teacher in the
New York school system.   She illustrated: Electronics,
Knopf, 1961; How Life Began, Day, 1957; Magic House
of Numbers, Day, 1957.   Dr. and Mrs. Adler have
taught at Bennington College (Vermont) and have resided
in nearby Shaftsbury.   Together they wrote: The
Earth's Crust, Day, 1963; Insects And Plants, Day,
1962; Oceans, Day, 1962.   CA-7/8

ADLER, Peggy
Author-illustrator, the daughter of authors Irving and
Ruth Adler.   At the age of thirteen she made a drawing
for one of her father's books, and at sixteen illustrated
his children's book Hot And Cold (Day, 1959).   She has
made her home in New Haven, Connecticut with her
husband Jeremy A. Walsh.   She wrote The Second
Adler Book Of Puzzles And Riddles, McKay, 1963.

ADOFF, Arnold
Editor, poet, teacher, native of New York.   He did
advanced study at Columbia University after graduating
from New York City College.   Mr. Adoff taught for
many years in the public schools of Manhattan and
Harlem and has also been a federal projects instructor
at Connecticut College and New York University. Books
which he has edited for young people include: Black
On Black, Macmillan, 1968; I Am The Darker Brother,
Macmillan, 1968.

ADRIAN, Mary see VENN, Mary Eleanor

AGLE, Nan Hayden 1905-
Author, teacher, born in Baltimore, Maryland. Many
of her books have had historical backgrounds. Mrs.
Agle has taught art in Baltimore at the Friends School.
She wrote Kate And The Apple Tree, Seabury, 1965;
Makon And The Dauphin, Scribner, 1961. With Ellen
Wilson she wrote: Three Boys And A Helicopter,
Scribner, 1958; Three Boys And A Lighthouse (A
Junior Literary Guild selection), Scribner, 1951;
Three Boys And Space, Scribner, 1962. CA-4

AHNSTROM, Doris N. 1915-
Writer, editor, born in Muskegon, Michigan. When
she was working on the New York Daily News, she
learned to fly. She has been Managing Editor of
Skyways and was a member of the Aviation Writers
Association. She has also served with the Flight
Safety Foundation. D. N. Ahnstrom wrote The Com-
plete Book Of Helicopters (rev. ed.), World, 1968.
CA-7/8

AIKEN, Conrad Potter 1889-
Poet, novelist, born in Savannah, Georgia. His books
of poetry have received many prizes including: the
Pulitzer Prize, National Book Award, Bollingen Award,
and the Shelley Memorial Award. Mr. Aiken has
lived in Brewster, Massachusetts, New York City, and
Savannah, Georgia. In 1950-51 he was poetry con-
sultant of the Library of Congress. He wrote Cats
And Bats And Things With Wings, Atheneum, 1965.
CA-5/6

AIKEN, Joan 1924-
Author, free-lance writer, editor. She was born in
Rye, Sussex, England, the daughter of Conrad Aiken.
At one time she served as an editor on Argosy
magazine, worked with the London office of the United
Nations, and has been a copywriter for an advertising
firm. The author has enjoyed gardening and painting
in her Petworth, England home. For young people
she wrote: Black Hearts In Battersea (A Junior
Literary Guild selection), Doubleday, 1964; Necklace
Of Raindrops, Doubleday, 1969. CA-9/10

AISTROP, Jack Bentley 1916-
He and his wife have been interested in animals. The
Aistrops have often traveled throughout the world to
zoos where they have studied and photographed various
animals. He has served as Radio-TV Director for
British Information Service in New York. His wife
Josephine Aistrop has shown animals on a weekly television program. Jack Aistrop has been a Fellow of
the Zoological Society. His books for young people
include: Enjoying Nature's Marvels, Vanguard, 1961;
Enjoying Pets, Vanguard, 1955. CA-4

AKERS, Floyd see BAUM, Lyman Frank

AKIYAMA, Kazuo
He was born in Japan and received his education at
the Tokyo University of Foreign Affairs. Mr. Akiyama
has contributed captions and information to guide books.
He has also written articles and short stories for Tabi
(Travel) magazine. He collaborated with Florence
White to write Children's Songs From Japan, Marks,
E. B., 1960.

ALBERT, Marvin H.
Author, editor, born in Philadelphia. He once was a
copyboy for the Philadelphia Record and sold his first
article at that time. He served as Chief Radio Officer
on Liberty ships during World War II. Mr. Albert
has been a magazine editor and television scriptwriter.
He has also worked for Look magazine as a researcher. He has lived on Long Island. For young people
he wrote Long White Road, McKay, 1957.

ALCOTT, Louisa May 1832-1888
Author of Little Women (World, 1969, Tudor, T.,
illus.), born in Germantown, Pennsylvania. She grew
up in Concord, Massachusetts where her childhood
friends were the children of Ralph Waldo Emerson and
Nathaniel Hawthorne. Louisa Alcott started a school
for children in order to earn money for her family.
Juvenile titles include: Eight Cousins, Little, 1927;
Little Men, Little, 1924. JBA-1

ALDERMAN, Clifford Lindsey 1902-
He was born in Springfield, Massachusetts and
graduated from the United States Naval Academy. He
also studied chemical engineering at the Massachusetts

Institute of Technology. During World War II, he was
on the staffs of naval units at Columbia University and
Holy Cross, Millsaps, and Middlebury Colleges. He
has enjoyed studying and writing about American history. His articles have appeared in the Atlantic
Monthly. His home has been in Lynbrook, New York.
Juvenile titles include: Great Invasion, Messner,
1969; The Way Of The Eagles, Doubleday, 1965.
CA-3

ALDIS, Dorothy (Keeley) 1896-1966
Author-poet, born in Chicago, Illinois, the daughter
of newspaperman James Keeley. She married Graham
Aldis and has lived in Lake Forest, Illinois. Mrs.
Aldis has been on the staff of a Chicago newspaper
and has written many books and volumes of verse for
young people. Children have enjoyed her poems because they are about familiar situations, things, and
places. Dorothy Aldis died on July 25, 1966. Juvenile titles include: All Together, Putnam, 1952; Boy
Who Cared, Putnam, 1958; Dumb Stupid David, Putnam, 1965; Everything And Anything, Minton, Balch,
& Company, 1927; Hello Day, Putnam, 1959; Jane's
Father, Putnam, 1954; Lucky Year, Rand McNally
and the Junior Literary Guild, 1951. CA-3, JBA-1,
JBA-2

ALDON, Adair see MEIGS, Cornelia Lynde

ALDRIDGE, Josephine Haskell
She married poet Richard Aldridge, and they have
lived in a two-hundred year old house in Maine near
the village of West Point. Her juvenile titles include:
Fisherman's Luck, Parnassus, 1966; Penny And A
Periwinkle, Parnassus, 1961.

ALEXANDER, Anne 1913-
Born in Shanghai, China, Mrs. Alexander became an
American citizen and has lived in Burlingame, California. She has taught at the College of San Mateo
(where she also received an Associated Arts degree)
and Menlo High and has contributed children's stories
to magazines. She married newspaperman Charles
Alexander. Among her books are: ABC Of Cars And
Trucks (A Junior Literary Guild selection), Doubleday,
1956; Boats And Ships From A To Z, Rand McNally,
1961; I Want To Whistle, Abelard-Schuman, 1958;

Linda (A Junior Literary Guild selection), Doubleday,
1964; Pink Dress (A Junior Literary Guild selection),
Doubleday, 1959. CA-7/8

ALEXANDER, Jocelyn see ARUNDEL, Jocelyn

ALEXANDER, Lloyd Chudley 1924-
He was born in Philadelphia, Pennsylvania and later
made his home in Drexel Hill. He attended colleges
here and also studied at the Sorbonne in Paris. He
served with the Army during World War II. He has
written for both adults and children, and his work has
appeared in such magazines as McCall's and Harper's
Bazaar. In 1969 he was awarded the Newbery Medal
for High King (Holt, 1968). Lloyd Alexander has always been fond of cats and has written books about
them including Time Cat, Holt, 1963. CA-1

ALGER, Leclaire G. 1898-1971
Her pseudonym is Sorche Nic Leodhas. In her book
All In The Morning Early (Holt, 1963), Miss Nic
Leodhas wrote: "the [story] was part of the childhood
of three generations: my grandfather's, my father's,
and my own. In its original form it probably is very
old--certainly one hundred and fifty years and perhaps
a century older." Artist Nonny Hogrogian was awarded
the 1966 Caldecott Medal for her illustrations in Miss
Nic Leodhas' book Always Room For One More, Holt,
1965. She also wrote Laird Of Cockpen, Holt, 1969.

ALIKI see BRANDENBERG, Aliki Leacouras

ALLAN, Mabel Esther 1915-
Author, traveler, born in England. She also has
written books under the names of Jean Estoril and
Anne Pilgrim. Miss Allan has traveled extensively
in Great Britain and Europe and has visited the United
States. Many of her own travel experiences have been
included in her books. Young people have also enjoyed
her mystery stories. Mabel Allan has made her home
in Cheshire, England. Her works include: Ballet
Family, Criterion, 1966; Catrin In Wales, (A Junior
Literary Guild selection), Vanguard, 1961; Mystery In
Arles, Vanguard, 1964; Strangers In Skye, (A Junior
Literary Guild selection), Criterion, 1958. CA-7/8

ALLEN, Adam see EPSTEIN, Samuel and Beryl

ALLEN, Allyn   see EBERLE, Irmengarde

ALLEN, Betsy   see CAVANNA, Betty

ALLEN, Lee 1915-
Author, newspaperman. He has lived in Cooperstown,
New York, the home of the National Baseball Museum
and Hall of Fame. Prior to being the historian of the
National Baseball Hall of Fame and Museum, Lee
Allen was publicity director for the Cincinnati Reds.
He has also written for the Sporting News, Cincinnati
Enquirer, and Times-Star in Cincinnati. His juvenile
books include: Babe Ruth, His Story In Baseball, Put-
nam, 1966; Dizzy Dean, Putnam, 1967.   CA-2

ALLEN, Marie Louise
Teacher, author, born in Cleveland, Ohio. She has
taught in a nursery school, and her experiences provided the material for her book of verses. Upon publication of the book, Marie Louise Allen (Mrs. A. O.
Howarth) received requests for permission to reprint
the verses from people who lived in Canada and New
Zealand. Her book Pocketful Of Rhymes was later
published under the title Pocketful of Poems, Harper,
1957.

ALLEN, Mel 1913-
Author, sports announcer. He has combined his knowledge of baseball and interesting anecdotes to provide
enjoyable reading for baseball fans. It has been said:
"Reading his book is like having a ringside seat during
a field day at Cooperstown's Hall of Fame, with all
the greats swapping yarns and topping each other's
baseball stories . . . " Mel Allen collaborated with
Ed Fitzgerald to write You Can't Beat The Hours,
Harper, 1964.

ALLEN, Merritt Parmelee 1892-1954
Born July 2, 1892, he lived in Bristol, Vermont and
died December 26, 1954. Mr. Allen did extensive
research on the history of the United States and wrote
exciting books for boys and girls on both the Revolu-
tionary and Civil Wars. Juvenile titles include: Battle
Lanterns, Longmans, 1949; Blow, Bugles, Blow, Longmans, 1956; Green Cockade, Longmans, 1942; Johnny
Reb, Longmans, 1952; The Mudhen Acts Naturally,
Longmans, 1955; The Mudhen And The Walrus, Long-

mans, 1950.   JBA-2

ALLEN, Richard J.
    Author, inventor, born in New York City. He has
    lived in Massachusetts, Chicago, and Middleborough,
    Maryland. A graduate of the Illinois Institute of
    Technology (Chicago), he later attended Drexel Insti-
    tute of Technology (Philadelphia) where he received
    his master's degree in electrical engineering and in
    physics. Mr. Allen has worked on electronic projects
    and has patents pending on some of his inventions.
    He has also contributed to technical journals. For
    young people he wrote Cyrogenics (Helen Hale, editor-
    ial consultant), Lippincott, 1964.

ALLFREY, Katherine
    She was born in Westphalia, Germany. Katherine
    Allfrey became interested in Greek history and
    mythology when she lived in Athens after her marriage.
    Later the Allfrey family moved to Bristol, England.
    In 1964 she was the recipient of the German children's
    Book Prize for Golden Island (Delphinensommer; tr.
    by Edelgard von Heydekampf Bruehl), Doubleday, 1966.

ALLISON, Bob
    New Yorker, author, teacher. He left the teaching
    profession in order to work in radio. Bob Allison
    served as a Special Events Officer with the "Voice Of
    America. " His first book for young people was
    written with Frank Ernest Hill and was entitled The
    Kid Who Batted 1,000, Doubleday, 1951.

ALSOP, Reese Fell
    Doctor, writer, nephew of author Mary O'Hara (My
    Friend Flicka, Lippincott, 1941). He was born in
    New York City. He once played the leading role in
    the play "Brother Rat. " The author attended Harvard
    and graduated from Columbia Medical School. Dr.
    Alsop served as a Captain in the U. S. Army Medical
    Corps during World War II. He wrote George And
    His Horse Go West, Dodd, 1952.

ALTER, Robert Edmond 1925-1965
    Prior to his career as a writer, Robert Alter was a
    movie extra, citrus picker, and member of the armed
    services. His home has been in Altadena, California.
    He has contributed stories to such magazines as

ALTSHELER, Joseph A.   13

Argosy and Boys' Life.   His juvenile books include:
First Comes Courage, Putnam, 1969; Red Water,
Putnam, 1968.   CA-3

ALTSHELER, Joseph A.   1862-1919
Author and newspaperman, born in Kentucky. He received his education at Liberty College (Glasgow,
Kentucky) and Vanderbilt University (Nashville, Tennessee). At one time Mr. Altsheler was editor of
the New York World tri-weekly edition. He and his
wife, the former Sarah Boles, made their home in
New York City until his death in 1919. Juvenile contributions include: Apache Gold, Appleton, 1913; The
Guns Of Bull Run, Appleton, 1914; Hunters Of The
Hills, Appleton, 1929; The Lords Of The Wild, Appleton, 1919.   JBA-1

AMERMAN, Lockhart 1911-
He was born in New York City. He attended Haverford College in Pennsylvania, and Princeton and Edinburgh Universities. Mr. Amerman has written poetry
and a history text. His hobbies have included golf,
fishing, and chess. After frequent visits to Scotland,
he wrote Guns In The Heather, Harcourt, 1963.

AMES, Lee Judah 1921-
Author, illustrator, teacher. He was born in New
York City, attended Columbia University, and has
lived on Long Island and in Brooklyn, New York. Lee
Ames has worked in advertising, book and magazine
illustration, and animated films for the Walt Disney
Studios. He has also been a cartoonist. After serving with the Army in World War II, he became a
teacher. He has been listed in Who's Who In American Art. For boys and girls he wrote and illustrated
Draw, Draw, Draw, Doubleday, 1962.   CA-4

ANCKARSVÄRD, Karin 1918-
She was born in Stockholm, Sweden. Although she received her education in Sweden, Mrs. Anckarsvärd
also attended Oxford University. When she married,
her schooling came to an end; however, she continued
her writing which had actually begun when she was
eight-years-old (a story was accepted by a magazine).
Her books for young people include: Aunt Vinnie's
Invasion (tr. by Annabelle MacMillan), Harcourt, 1962;
Aunt Vinnie's Victorious Six, Harcourt, 1964; Boni-

facius And Little Bonnie (tr. by C. M. Anckarsvärd
and K. H. Beales), Abelard-Schuman, 1963; Doctor's
Boy (tr. by Annabelle MacMillan), Harcourt, 1965;
Madcap Mystery (tr. by Annabelle MacMillan), Harcourt, 1962.   CA-9/10

ANDERSEN, Hans Christian 1805-1875
He was born April 2, 1805 in the fishing village of
Odense, near the coast of Denmark. When he was a
young man, he visited Copenhagen where he later met
Chancellor Jonas Collin, a director of the Royal
Theater. Mr. Collin recognized Mr. Andersen's talent and encouraged him to attend school. Later he
passed the entrance examinations to Copenhagen University. The village of Odense has been illuminated
in his honor, and the house where he was born has
become a museum. Juvenile contributions include:
Andersen's Fairy Tales (illus. by Leonard Weisgard),
Garden City, 1956; The Little Mermaid (tr. by R. P.
Keigwin), Platt, 1963; Snow Queen (illus. by George
and Doris Hauman), Macmillan, 1942.   JBA-1, JBA-2

ANDERSON, Clarence W. 1891-1971
Author, artist, sportsman, born in Nebraska. He attended the Chicago Art Institute. His excellent drawings of horses have been enjoyed and studied by boys
and girls for many years. Mr. Anderson has been a
member of the American Society of Etchers and has
exhibited his paintings, lithographs, and drawings in a
one-man show. He and his wife have lived in Mason,
New Hampshire. His books include: Afraid To Ride,
Macmillan, 1957; Billy And Blaze, Macmillan, 1936;
Blaze And The Forest Fire, Macmillan, 1938; Blaze
And The Lost Quarry, Macmillan, 1966; . . . Deep
Through The Heart, Macmillan, 1940; Sketchbook,
Macmillan, 1948.   JBA-2

ANDERSON, Ethel Todd
She was born in Ohio and graduated from Oberlin
College. Ethel Anderson has taught at both Colorado
and Pennsylvania State Colleges. She married Cla-
rence Scott Anderson who has been an exchange pro-
fessor at the University of Hawaii. Mrs. Anderson
has traveled to Mexico, Canada, and South America.
Her books for young people include: Rainbow Campus,
Nelson, 1950; Scarlet Bird, Junior Literary Guild and
Nelson, 1948.

ANDERSON, Neil   see BEIM, Jerrold

ANDERSON, Ruth Irene   1919-
She has been widely recognized as an authority in the
field of business education and has conducted business
workshops at various colleges and universities. Ruth
Anderson was born in Pennsylvania and graduated from
Grove City College in Pennsylvania. She continued her
education at Indiana University where she was also a
graduate teaching assistant. She has been on the staffs
of Texas Christian University and North Texas State
University. She wrote Secretarial Careers, Walck,
1961.

ANDREWS, Roy Chapman   1884-
Author, explorer, scientist, born in Beloit, Wisconsin.
Dr. Andrews has been Director of the American
Museum of Natural History in New York. He has
traveled throughout the world on scientific expeditions
and has been the recipient of many awards given by
scientific societies. He later made his home in
southern California. His books for young people include: All About Dinosaurs, Random House, 1953;
All About Strange Beasts Of The Past, Random House,
1956; In The Days Of The Dinosaurs, Random House,
1959; Quest In The Desert, Viking, 1950.

ANGELO, Valenti   1897-
He was born in Italy. When he was eight years old,
he came with his family to America. He started working at an early age and held various jobs including the
position of confectioner and pastry maker in a San
Francisco hotel. He utilized this experience in writing
The Candy Basket (Viking, 1960). Mr. Angelo also
worked in an engraving firm and later became a free-
lance artist in New York City. He has illustrated
books for other authors (including the 1937 Newbery
Medal winner, Roller Skates, Viking, 1936; by Ruth
Sawyer). He wrote and illustrated: Acorn Tree, Viking, 1958; Angelino And The Barefoot Saint, Viking,
1961; Marble Fountain, Viking, 1951; The Tale Of A
Donkey, Viking, 1966.   JBA-2

ANGLUND, Joan Walsh   1926-
Author-illustrator, born in Hinsdale, Illinois, the
daughter of artists. She studied at the Chicago Art
Institute and at the American Academy of Art. In

1947 Mrs. Anglund illustrated her first book for
children. The New York Times selected her book,
A Friend Is Someone Who Likes You (Harcourt, 1958),
as one of the ten best illustrated books of 1958. Other
books which she wrote and illustrated include: Brave
Cowboy, Harcourt, 1959; Christmas Is A Time Of
Giving, Harcourt, 1961; Cowboy And His Friend, Har-
court, 1961; Cowboy's Secret Life, Harcourt, 1963;
Spring Is A New Beginning, Harcourt, 1963; What
Color Is Love?, Harcourt, 1966. CA-7/8

ANNETT, Cora
She was born in Boston, Massachusetts, and later
lived in California, Nevada, and Texas. She studied
psychology at Boston University. She wrote The Dog
Who Thought He Was A Boy, Houghton, 1965.
CA-17/18

ANNIXTER, Jane   see COMFORT, Jane Levington

ANTHONY, Edward 1895-
Author, newspaperman, publisher. His long and outstanding career in the field of publishing has included
being the publisher of Collier's and Woman's Home
Companion magazines. He has also contributed articles to Good Housekeeping. Edward Anthony and his
family have made their home in Connecticut and New
York City. For boys and girls he wrote Oddity Land,
Doubleday, 1957.

ANTONCICH, Betty (Kennedy) 1913-
Teacher, columnist, author, born in Seattle, Washing-
ton. Before moving to California where she taught in
a high school, Mrs. Antoncich had been a teacher in
Washington. She studied Creative Writing under Max-
ine Shore and at one time was a columnist for the
Peninsula Herald in Monterey. The author has worked
with the Girl Scouts and has been a member of the
American Association of University Women and the
League of Women Voters. For young people she
wrote Mystery Of The Chinatown Pearls (A Junior
Literary Guild selection), McKay, 1965. CA-15/16

APPEL, David
He has been book editor for several newspapers including the Philadelphia Inquirer, Chicago Daily News,
and Cleveland News. David Appel has lived in Bucks

County, Pennsylvania. In addition to his work as a
newspaperman, he has written several books for
children. With Eugene Freeman he edited The Great
Ideas Of Plato, Lantern Press, 1952.

ARASON, Steingrimur
Author and teacher. He was born in Iceland and graduated from Columbia University in New York. Mr.
Arason has taught both children and adults in Iceland
for many years. He has also been on the staff at
Normal College in Iceland. The author has written
textbooks and published a periodical for children entitled Young Iceland. He also organized a Child Welfare society. For boys and girls he wrote Smoky
Bay, Macmillan, 1942.

ARBUTHNOT, May Hill 1884-1969
Author, teacher, born in Mason City, Iowa. She
taught at Western Reserve University and also founded
the University Nursery School. Mrs. Arbuthnot grad-
uated from the University of Chicago and received her
M. A. degree from Columbia University. In 1964 the
Regina Medal was awarded to her by the Catholic
Library Association. Her articles have appeared in
the Elementary English Review, Parents' Magazine,
and the National Education Association Journal. She
wrote Children And Books (Third edition), Scott,
Foresman, 1964. She also compiled The Arbuthnot
Anthology Of Children's Literature (Revised), Scott,
Foresman, 1961. CA-9/10

ARCHER, Jules 1915-
Correspondent, scriptwriter, author, born in New
York City. He studied at City College of New York
and served in the Air Force during World War II.
His articles have appeared in many publications, and
he has written scripts for radio. Jules Archer has
had exciting adventures which have ranged from snor-
keling in the West Indies to a midnight swim across
the Seine in the Bois de Boulogne. He married an
Australian girl, and they have lived in Pine Plains,
New York. For boys and girls he wrote: Extremists,
Hawthorne, 1969; Man Of Steel, Joseph Stalin, Messner, 1965. CA-9/10

ARCHIBALD, Joe 1898-
Author, lecturer, cartoonist, born in Newington, New

Hampshire.   At the age of fifteen he won a prize for
his drawings in the Boston Post.   Mr. Archibald attended the Chicago Academy of Fine Arts.   He has
belonged to the Authors Guild and National Cartoonists
Society and has been on the staff of McClure Newspaper Syndicate and United Features Syndicate.   The
author has lived in Port Chester, New York.   He has
written numerous articles and stories about aviation
and sports for young people.   His books include:
Backfield Twins, Macrae Smith, 1960; Circus Catch,
Macrae Smith, 1957; The Easy Out, Macrae Smith,
1965; Touchdown Glory, Westminster, 1949; Windmill
Pilot, McKay, 1963.   CA-9/10

ARDIZZONE, Edward 1900-
Author-artist, born in Haiphong, Vietnam.   He grew
up in England where he acquired a love of the sea and
of ships.   He also liked to draw when he was a boy.
He later had many one-man shows in London.   He
served as an Official War Artist during World War II.
Mr. Ardizzone was the first recipient of the Kate
Greenaway Medal in 1957 for Tim All Alone (Walck,
1957).   This award is given for the best illustrated
children's book of the year by the British Library
Association.   The author has resided in London.   He
also wrote and illustrated Little Tim And The Brave
Sea Captain, Walck, 1955.   CA-5/6, MJA

ARMER, Laura Adams 1874-
Artist-author, born in Sacramento, California.   She
grew up in San Francisco where she attended the
California School of Design.   Laura Armer has
created paintings inspired by visits to a Navaho Reservation and produced a motion picture of a Navaho
ceremonial entitled "The Mountain Chant. "   In 1932
she was awarded the Newbery Medal for her book
Waterless Mountain (Longmans, 1931) which was also
illustrated by the author and her husband (Sidney Armer).   Her books include: Dark Circle Of Branches,
Longmans, 1933; Forest Pool, Longmans, 1938.
JBA-1, JBA-2

ARMOUR, Richard 1906-
Author, lecturer, professor.   A graduate of Pomona
College, he later attended Harvard where he received
his Ph. D. degree.   He has written both for adults
and children and has contributed prose and verse to

magazines.   Richard Armour has been a college professor and was Balch Lecturer in English Literature
at California's Scripps College.   For children he
wrote: On Your Marks, McGraw, 1969; Year Santa
Went Modern, McGraw, 1964.   CA-1

ARMSTRONG, Richard
He has written stories about the sea, spent many
years on the sea, and has lived in a house near the
English seacoast.   His book Cold Hazard (Houghton,
1956) received first prize in the New York Herald
Tribune Spring Book Festival.   Following World War
I, Richard Armstrong served in the Merchant Service.
He also has served on tankers and liners.   He wrote:
The Big Sea, McKay, 1965; Treasure And Treasure
Hunters, White, 1969.

ARMSTRONG, William H.   1914-
He was born in Lexington, Virginia.   He attended
Augusta Military Academy, Hampden-Sydney College,
and the University of Virginia.   Mr. Armstrong has
written both articles and books on education.   He has
lived in Connecticut where he has taught study techniques and history at the Kent School.   He was a-
warded the 1970 Newbery Medal for his first juvenile
book entitled Sounder, Harper, 1969.   CA-19/20

ARNOLD, Elliott 1912-
He has been a reporter on a newspaper in New York.
When he was on a trip to Europe, he visited the home
of Finnish composer Jan Sibelius which was located
near Helsinki.   As a result of this visit he decided
to write a biography of the composer for young people.
Mr. Arnold told his publisher: "I'd like to write a
book so that . . . [young people] will see what the
music of Sibelius is about and why I think there's
something in Finland that has a meaning for them. "
His book was called Finlandia, Holt, 1941.   He also
wrote Kind Of Secret Weapon, Scribner, 1969.
CA-19/20

ARNOLD, Ralph
He studied in England at Oxford University.   His main
interest was history.   When he retired as chairman
of a London publishing house, he moved to the country
where he studied and wrote books about history.   For
boys and girls he wrote Kings, Bishops, Knights, And

Pawns, Norton, 1964.

ARNOV, Boris 1926–
Author and teacher, born in Los Angeles, California.
He graduated from Rollins College (Florida) and also
attended the Chicago School of Medicine and the Universities of Miami and California. He has done research in ichthyology (branch of zoology that treats
of fishes) at the University of Miami's Marine Laboratory. Mr. Arnov once owned and operated a charter
fishing boat and has also written a weekly column on
fishing. He has lived in Hawaii, Florida, and California. He wrote Secrets Of Inland Waters, Little,
1965. With Helen Mather-Smith Mindlin he wrote
Wonders Of The Ocean Zoo, Dodd, 1957. CA-4

ARTZYBASHEFF, Boris 1899–1965
Author-illustrator, born in Kharkov, Russia. His
father was an author and playwright. When he was
a young man, he took a job on a ship whose destination turned out to be America. In addition to writing
and illustrating books, Boris Artzybasheff has painted
portraits for magazines. For boys and girls he retold and illustrated Seven Simeons, Viking, 1937.
JBA-1, JBA-2

ARUNDEL, Anne see ARUNDEL, Jocelyn

ARUNDEL, Jocelyn 1930–
A graduate of Smith College and the National Cathe-
dral School for Girls, she also attended McGill Uni-
versity in Canada and the Sorbonne in Paris. Jocelyn
Arundel has been associated with the International
Union for Conservation in Brussels. She has also
been a copywriter for the Washington Daily News.
At one time she was a staff writer for the National
Geographic Society. She married David Ord Alexander,
and they have lived in Washington, D. C. where she
was born. Her juvenile books include: Mighty Mo,
Little, 1961; Shoes For Punch, McGraw, 1964. CA-4

ASHFORD, Jeffrey see JEFFRIES, Roderic (Graeme)

ASHLEY, Robert Paul 1915–
Author and teacher. Robert Paul Ashley Jr. studied
at Bowdoin College in Brunswick, Maine and later attended Harvard. A major in the Army Reserve, he

served with both the Army and Navy during World War
II. Major Ashley has been associated with Ripon College in Wisconsin as a Professor of English and Dean
of the College. For young readers he wrote Rebel
Raiders, Winston, 1956. CA-17/18

ASHMEAD, Gordon
Author, designer, editor. He has worked in public
relations at the Douglas Aircraft Company and has de-
signed industrial buildings, homes, and tools. Gordon
Ashmead has edited technical magazines about machin-
ery and architecture. He served with the Federal
Board of Vocational Education during World War I.
Mr. Ashmead has resided in Pacific Palisades, Cali-
fornia. He collaborated with Irwin Stambler to write:
Find A Career In Engineering, Putnam, 1962; Project
Mariner, Putnam, 1964.

ASIMOV, Isaac 1920-
Biochemist, teacher, author, born in Russia. His
pseudonym is Paul French. He came to America at
the age of three. Dr. Asimov graduated from Colum-
bia University and has been Associate Professor of
Biochemistry at Boston University School of Medicine.
He received the Edison Foundation Award and James
T. Grady Award and has also reviewed science books
for the Horn Book magazine (August 1958-October
1967). The author and his family have lived in West
Newton, Massachusetts. His books include: David
Starr, Space Ranger, Garden City, Doubleday, 1952;
The Double Planet, Abelard-Schuman, 1960; Inside
The Atom (Second revised edition), Abelard-Schuman,
1961; Realm Of Numbers, Houghton, 1959. CA-2

ATKINSON, Margaret Fleming
She studied art at college and in 1936 she helped to
organize Cooperative Handcrafts, Inc. , in Puerto
Rico. She has also been a department store's Art
Director. Since her marriage, Mrs. Atkinson has
made her home in Washington, D. C. where she was
born. She collaborated with Nancy Draper to write
Ballet For Beginners, Knopf, 1951. She also wrote
Care For Your Kitten, Greenberg, 1946.

ATWATER, Montgomery Meigs 1904-
Writer, rancher, avalanche control specialist, game
warden, born in Oregon. He attended Phillips Exeter

Academy and Harvard University.   During World War
II, he was an instructor in mountain and winter warfare and served overseas in the 87th Cavalry Recon-
naissance Troop.   Mr. Atwater has been associated
with the United States Forest Service and later was a
private consultant on avalanche problems.   In 1966
he was in charge of avalanche control for the World
Ski Championships (Portillo, Chile).   His books for
young people include: Avalanche Patrol, Junior Literary Guild and Random House, 1951; Cattle Dog, (A
Junior Literary Guild selection), Random House, 1954;
Government Hunter, Macmillan, 1940; The Ski Lodge
Mystery, Random House, 1959; Snow Rangers Of The
Andes, Random House, 1967.   MJA

AUSTIN, Margot
     Author, artist, born in Portland, Oregon where she
     attended St. Mary's Academy and the Emil Jacques
     European Art School.   She continued her studies in
     New York City at the Grand Central Art School, the
     National Academy of Design, and the Art Students
     League.   She married artist Darrel Austin, and they
     have lived in Connecticut.   Juvenile books which she
     has written and illustrated include: Archie Angel,
     Dutton, 1957; Brave John Henry, Dutton, 1955;
     Gabriel Churchkitten, Dutton, 1942; Growl Bear,
     Dutton, 1951; Peter Churchmouse, Dutton, 1941;
     Poppet, Dutton, 1949; The Three Silly Kittens, Dutton,
     1950; Trumpet, Dutton, 1943; William's Shadow, Dut-
     ton, 1954.   CA-9/10, MJA

AVERILL, Esther Holden
     Author, artist, publisher, graduate of Vassar, born
     in Bridgeport, Connecticut.   With Lila Stanley she
     founded (1931) the Domino Press in Paris, France.
     Her company first printed Feodor Rojankovsky's Daniel
     Boone which was later published in America by Harper
     (1945).   She has contributed to the Horn Book and
     the Colophon and at one time worked in the Nathan
     Straus Branch of the New York Public Library.   Juve-
     nile books which she has written and illustrated in-
     clude: The Fire Cat, Harper, 1960; Jenny Goes To
     Sea, Harper, 1957; Jenny's Moonlight Adventure, Har-
     per, 1949.   She also wrote King Philip, The Indian
     Chief, Harper, 1950.   JBA-2

AVERY, Al   see MONTGOMERY, Rutherford G.

AVERY, Gillian Elise 1926–
    She and her husband Anthony Cockshut have lived in
    Manchester, England. She was affiliated with publish-
    ing and met her husband when she worked in Oxford.
    She has been a runner-up for the Carnegie Medal, and
    her stories have at times been compared to E. Nes-
    bit's (see Bland, Edith). Many of her stories have
    taken place in Oxfordshire. She wrote: Call Of The
    Valley, Holt, 1968; Mrs. Ewing, Walck, 1964.
    CA-9/10

AVERY, Lynn see COLE, Lois Dwight

AYARS, James Sterling 1898–
    Editor, author. His boyhood was spent in Michigan.
    Mr. Ayars has been Technical Editor and Head of the
    Section of Publications and Public Relations of the
    Natural History Survey Division of the Department of
    Registration and Education of the State of Illinois. He
    has contributed articles to many magazines including:
    Country Gentleman, Field And Stream, Sports Afield,
    and Successful Farming. He married authoress Re-
    becca Caudill, and they have lived in Urbana, Illinois.
    He wrote The Illinois River, Holt, 1968. CA-5/6

AYRE, Robert Hugh 1900–
    He was born in Manitoba and has been supervisor of
    visual redesign for the Canadian National Railways.
    Mr. Ayre has written an art column for the Montreal
    Star. His interests have included the theatre, and he
    has participated in the Montreal Repertory Theatre
    and the Winnipeg Community Players. He has also
    enjoyed hiking in the mountains, and these experiences
    provided the background for his book Sketco, The
    Raven, Macmillan, 1961. CA-4

B

BACON, Paul 1913–
    Author, editor, teacher, graduate of Columbia Univer-
    sity, born in Maryland. He has made his home in
    New York and California and at one time lived and
    taught in the Near East. Paul Bacon's interest in
    science and scientists led to his writing about Luther
    Burbank. He has also completed research and editing
    for biological papers. For young people he wrote
    Creating New And Better Plants: Luther Burbank,

Encyclopaedia Britannica, 1961.

BAGNOLD, Enid 1889-
Her father was Colonel A. H. Bagnold, a Royal Engi-
neer in the Army. Enid Bagnold attended a school
in England which was conducted by the mother of Pro-
fessor Julian Huxley and Aldous Huxley. During World
War I, she served as a V. A. D. in Woolwich at the
Royal Herbert Hospital. Miss Bagnold married Sir
Roderick Jones, and they have lived in London and
Rottingdean with their four children. Juvenile books
include: Alice And Thomas And Jane, Knopf, 1931;
"National Velvet, " Morrow, 1949.   CA-7/8

BAILEY, Bernadine Freeman 1901-
Editor, writer, born in Mattoon, Illinois. She graduated from Wellesley College and received her master's degree from the University of Chicago. Her
articles have appeared in Coronet, Reader's Digest,
New York Times, and Travel Magazine. Mrs. Bailey
has enjoyed travel and has made several trips around
the world. Her interests have also included the
theatre and outdoor sports. Organizations which she
has joined include: the Society of Midland Authors,
the Mystery Writers of America, the Children's Reading Round Table, the National Woman's Book Association, and the Woman's Press Club of London. Juvenile titles include: Abraham Lincoln, Houghton, 1960;
Carol Carson, Dodd, 1956; Famous Latin-American
Liberators, Dodd, 1960; Forest And Fiords, Beckley-
Cardy, 1952; Picture Book Of Alaska, Whitman, 1959.
CA-5/6

BAILEY, Carolyn Sherwin 1875-
Born in Hoosick Falls, New York, author, editor,
teacher, graduate of Teachers College, Columbia
University. At the age of nineteen her work appeared
in Youth's Companion and St. Nicholas. Miss Bailey
has also taught school and edited magazines for
children. She married Dr. Eben Clayton Hill and has
lived in Temple, New Hampshire which provided the
background for many of her stories including Miss
Hickory (winner of the 1947 Newbery Medal), Viking,
1946. Other juvenile books include: Children Of The
Handcrafts, Viking, 1935; Enchanted Village, Viking,
1950; Finnegan II, Junior Literary Guild and Viking,
1953; Flickertail, Walck, 1962; Little Red Schoolhouse,

Viking, 1957; Merry Christmas Book, Whitman, 1948.
JBA-2

BAILEY, Flora
Teacher, author, camp director, ethnologist. She has
been interested in the Navaho Indians and has spent a
summer of research at the University of New Mexico's
Field School. Her first book was Summer At Yellow
Singer's (Macmillan, 1948) which described the experiences (similar to the author's) of a boy and girl who
had spent their vacation in a Navaho home. She also
wrote Between The Four Mountains, Macmillan, 1949.

BAILEY, John
He was born in Ohio and grew up in Indiana. He has
been an associate editor of Suburbia Today and the
Saturday Evening Post. Many magazines have pub-
lished his stories including: Collier's, Esquire, and
the Reader's Digest. Juvenile titles include: Our
Wild Animals, Nelson, 1965; The Wonderful Dolphins,
Hawthorn, 1965.

BAIN, Edward Ustick
He graduated from the University of Missouri and has
been associated with the Sikorsky Aircraft of Bridgeport, Connecticut. Mr. Bain has been interested in
flying and has been a member of the American Helicopter Society. At one time he supervised a project
involving the delivery of mail by helicopter in several
of our nation's larger cities. He wrote S-O-S Helicopter, Whitman, 1947.

BAKELESS, John Edwin 1894-
Teacher, author, historian, editor, veteran of thirty-
five years of army service (both active and reserve).
Colonel Bakeless was born in Carlisle Barracks,
Pennsylvania and received a Ph. D. degree from Harvard University. He has been assistant military
attaché to Turkey and was Chief of the Military Section of the American Delegation of the Allied Control
Commission in Bulgaria. Colonel Bakeless wrote
The Adventures Of Lewis And Clark (North Star books)
Houghton, 1962. With his wife Katherine Little Bakeless he wrote Spies Of The Revolution, Lippincott,
1962.   CA-5/6

BAKER, Betty 1928-
She was born in Bloomsburg, Pennsylvania. She once

said: "At the age of four I began reading and steadily
exhausting every library I found. My main interests
were books about the woods and outdoors---animals,
woodcraft, and Indian life. " She married Robert Venturo, and they have lived in Tucson, Arizona. Juvenile titles include: Killer-Of-Death, Harper, 1963;
Little Runner Of The Longhouse, Harper, 1962. CA-4

BAKER, Charlotte 1910-
Author, artist, teacher, born in Nacogdoches, Texas.
She graduated from Mills College in Oakland, Califor-
nia, received her M. A. degree from the University of
California in Berkeley, and has been a member of the
Texas Institute of Letters. She married an attorney
Roger Montgomery and they have lived in Nacogdoches.
At one time she was on the staff of the Portland
(Oregon) Art Museum. The author has always been
interested in animals and has been associated with
humane societies and animal welfare work. For
several years she lectured on the care of animals.
Juvenile books which she has written and illustrated
include: ABC Of Dog Care For Young Owners, Mc-
Kay, 1959; The Best Of Friends (A Junior Literary
Guild selection), McKay, 1966; The Green Poodles
(A Junior Literary Guild selection), McKay, 1956.
CA-19/20

BAKER, Laura Nelson 1911-
Author and editor, of Norwegian descent. Laura
Baker was born in Iowa where she grew up on a
farm with nine brothers and sisters. She attended
the University of Minnesota. At one time she was
the editor of the Richfield News (a Minneapolis sub-
urban weekly newspaper). She has been the recipient
of the National Press Women's award. She collaborated with Adrien Stoutenburg to write Snowshoe
Thompson (A Junior Literary Guild selection), Scribner, 1957. She also wrote Cowboy Pete, Lippincott,
1968. CA-5/6

BAKER, Margaret J. 1918-
She was born in Reading, Berkshire, England. When
she was nine, her family moved to London. She sold
her first article to the Guide after she had studied
journalism at London University. During World War
II, Margaret Baker drove a mobile canteen for Cana-

dian and English troops.   Later she lived in an old
house called "The Hare and Hounds" in Somerset,
England. Her stories have appeared in publications
both here and abroad.   Her book Homer The Tortoise
(McGraw, 1949) was selected as an Honor Book in the
1950 New York Herald Tribune Spring Book Festival.
Juvenile books include: Anna Sewell And Black Beauty,
Longmans, 1957; Bright High Flyer, Longmans, 1957;
Castaway Christmas, Farrar, 1963; Four Farthings
And A Thimble, Longmans, 1950.   CA-13/14, MJA

BAKER, Nina Brown 1888-1957
Teacher and writer, born in Galena, Kansas. After
attending the University of Colorado she taught in
Colorado where she used to ride to school on horse-
back. She married Sidney J. Baker and later lived
in Brooklyn Heights, New York. Juvenile contributions
include: Amerigo Vespucci, Knopf, 1956; Big Cata-
logue, Harcourt, 1956; He Wouldn't Be King, Van-
guard, 1941; Henry Hudson, Knopf, 1958; Juan Ponce
De León, Knopf, 1957; Juarez, Hero Of Mexico,
Vanguard, 1942; Nickels And Dimes, Harcourt, 1954;
Pike Of Pike's Peak, Harcourt, 1953; Sir Walter
Raleigh, Harcourt, 1950; Story Of Abraham Lincoln
(Signature Books) Grosset, 1952; Story Of Christopher
Columbus (Signature Books) Grosset, 1952; Ten Amer-
ican Cities, Then And Now, Harcourt, 1949.   JBA-2

BAKER, Rachel Mininberg 1904-
After studying at the University of Minnesota and living in Europe, Rachel Baker began her present writing career. She attributed her interest in biography
to an incident which happened when she was fourteen
in Dickinson, North Dakota. She interviewed a man
who was writing a book about Theodore Roosevelt.
"He told me he was a biographer, and I decided that
someday I would be one too. " She was one of the
founders of the organization known as "Resources
Unlimited. " Juvenile titles include: America's First
Trained Nurse, Linda Richards, Messner, 1959; First
Woman Doctor, Messner, 1944.   CA-5/6, MJA

BAKER, William C. 1891-
He has worked in railroading for many years. Mr.
Baker has been associated with the Baltimore and
Ohio Railroad as Vice President of Operations and
Maintenance. In celebration of the railroad's cen-

tennial, Mr. Baker collaborated with writer Adele
Nathan to produce the anniversary pageant, "The Fair
Of The Iron Horse. " With Mrs. Nathan he has also
co-authored a children's book entitled Famous Railroad
Stations Of The World, Random, 1953.

BALCH, Glenn 1902-
Author, horseman, newspaperman, born in Venus,
Texas. He graduated from Baylor University (Waco,
Texas) and did additional work at Columbia. Mr.
Balch served in the Air Force during World War II.
He has believed that "horses are among the best
friends any young person can have. " Glen Balch has
not only written about horses but has been both a
cavalryman and polo player. He later made his home
in Idaho. Juvenile contributions include: Brave Ri-
ders, Crowell, 1959; Christmas Horse, Crowell, 1949;
Horse In Danger, Crowell, 1960; Indian Fur, Crowell,
1951; Little Hawk And The Free Horses (A Junior
Literary Guild selection) Crowell, 1957; Lost Horse,
Crowell, 1950; Spotted Horse, Crowell, 1961; Squaw
Boy, Crowell, 1952; The Stallion King, Crowell, 1960;
Tiger Roan, Crowell, 1938; White Ruff, Grosset &
Dunlap, 1958. CA-3, MJA

BALDWIN, Arthur H.
Scoutmaster, skipper, author. His grandfather was a
noted shipbuilder (including the last sailing ship built
in Quebec). Arthur Baldwin grew up in East Orange,
New Jersey and spent his summers on Long Island
where he learned to sail. After serving in the United
States Navy as a radio operator, he lived in Vermont
on a farm. He wrote and illustrated Junior Skipper's
Handbook, Random, 1940; and Sou'wester Goes North
(illustrated by Gordon Grant) Random, 1938.

BALDWIN, James 1841-1925
Author, editor, teacher, a native of Indiana. Prior to
being superintendent of the Indiana elementary schools,
Mr. Baldwin had been a teacher. He was awarded an
honorary degree of doctor of philosophy by DePauw
University (Greencastle, Ind.). For many years he
served on the staff of several large publishing houses.
James Baldwin made his home in South Orange, New
Jersey. His books for young people include: Hero
Tales Told In School, Scribner, 1904; John Bunyan's
Dream Story (retold by James Baldwin) American Book

Co. , 1913; Old Greek Stories, American Book Co. ,
1895; The Story Of Roland, Scribner, 1883; Story Of
Siegfried, Scribner, 1882.   JBA-1, JBA-2

BALET, Jan B.   1913-
Illustrator-author, born in Bremen, Germany.   He
studied in Munich at the Arts and Crafts School and
at the Academy of Fine Arts.   In 1938 he left Germany for the United States where he became an
American citizen.   He has been an art director on
both Mademoiselle and Seventeen magazines and has
created advertising sketches for several department
stores in New York.   He wrote and illustrated: Amos
And The Moon, Oxford, 1948; What Makes An Orchestra, Oxford, 1951.

BALL, John   1911-
Author, journalist, pilot.   John Ball (Dudley), Jr. ,
has been interested in the study of Japanese culture.
He has learned to play the samisen (a stringed Japanese musical instrument resembling a banjo) as a
hobby and has also been a member of the U. S. A. Judo
Black Belt Federation.   The author has written about
various subjects including aviation, mystery, sociology,
music, and adventure.   For young people he wrote:
Judo Boy (A Junior Literary Guild selection), Duell,
1964; Operation Springboard, Duell, 1958.   CA-7/8

BALL, Zachary   see MASTERS, Kelly Ray

DANCROFT, Griffing
When he was a young man, he lived in California and
worked with his father, ornithologist Griffing Bancroft
and his stepmother Margaret W. Bancroft.   The Ban-
crofts have had two subspecies of birds named after
them: the Bancroft Screech Owl and the Bancroft
Yellow-Crowned Night Heron.   Mr. Bancroft has
written for the "Voice of America" and has done political commentaries for television.   He was a resource
participant for the Aspen Institute of Humanistic Studies in Aspen, Colorado in the summer of 1969.   He
and his wife, the former Jane Eads, have lived on
Captiva Island, Florida.   He wrote Snowy, McCall,
1970.

BANNON, Laura May   d. 1963
She grew up in Traverse Bay, Michigan and attended

Western Michigan State College. She studied and later
taught at the Art Institute of Chicago. Many of her
books had backgrounds based on her travels both in
this country and abroad. In 1962 Miss Bannon received the annual award of the Children's Reading
Round Table of Chicago. She died December 14, 1963
in Roswell, New Mexico. Included in her children's
books are: The Contented Horse Trader, Whitman,
1963; The Famous Baby-Sitter, Whitman, 1960; Horse
On A Houseboat, Junior Literary Guild and Whitman,
1951; Jo-Jo, The Talking Crow, Houghton, 1958; The
Little Sister Doll, Whitman, 1955; Red Mittens, Houghton, 1946; Twirlup On The Moon, Whitman, 1964.
CA-3, MJA

BARBOUR, Ralph Henry 1870-1944
Author, columnist, rancher, native of Massachusetts.
He attended the Highland Military Academy at Worcester, Massachusetts. His career in the newspaper
field included such positions as cartoonist, court reporter, correspondent, and editor. Known as "the
dean of sport story writers for boys", Ralph Barbour
has written books of lasting popularity. His titles for
young people include: Crimson Sweater, Appleton-Century, 1906; For Safety!, Appleton-Century, 1936; Goal
To Go, Appleton-Century, 1933; Good Manners For
Boys, Appleton-Century, 1937; Half-back, Appleton-
Century, 1899; Mystery Of The Bayou, Appleton-Century, 1943. JBA-1, JBA-2

BARKER, Will 1913-
Author, editor, lecturer. At one time Will Barker
was associated with the U. S. Fish and Wildlife Service
as an editor-writer. He has lectured about natural
history, and his articles have appeared in such magazines as Sports Afield, Natural History, Science Digest,
and American Forests. Mr. Barker has made his
home in Washington, D. C. His juvenile books include:
Familiar Animals Of America, Harper, 1956; Familiar
Reptiles And Amphibians Of America, Harper, 1964.
CA-9/10

BARKSDALE, Lena
Bookseller, literary critic, author. She was born in
Philadelphia, the "City of Brotherly Love." Lena
Barksdale grew up in surroundings associated with
American history. "Talking, reviewing, and selling

books for children" have been her main interests.
She has also enjoyed reading as a hobby. Her juve-
nile books include: First Thanksgiving, Knopf, 1942;
That Country Called Virginia, Knopf, 1945.

BARNES, Eric Wollencott 1907-
Actor, author, teacher, born in Little Rock, Arkansas.
He attended the Universities of California and Paris,
and obtained his doctorate at the Sorbonne.   Dr.
Barnes has appeared on Broadway (as Eric Wollencott)
and has written numerous magazine articles and short
stories.   He has also taught in Windsor, Connecticut
at the Loomis School. He has been Professor of
English at both Dickinson (Carlisle, Pa.) and Russell
Sage (Troy, N. Y.) Colleges. He obtained material
for his first children's book from family papers and
notes kept by his grandfather.   The book was entitled
The War Between The States, McGraw, 1959. He
also wrote Free Men Must Stand, McGraw, 1969.

BARNOUW, Adriaan Jacob 1877-
Dr. Barnouw was born in Amsterdam, Holland and received his education at Leiden and Berlin Universities.
He taught at Leiden University and at the municipal
gymnasium, The Hague until 1919 when he came to
America.   Following his position as associate editor
of the Weekly Review he taught at Columbia University where he later became Emeritus Professor in
1948.   The author has also painted, and his work has
been exhibited in both America and in The Hague.   He
wrote: The Land And People Of Holland (Portraits of
the nations series) Lippincott, 1961; Land Of William
Of Orange, Lippincott, 1944.

BARNUM, Jay Hyde
Author-illustrator, born in Geneva, Ohio.   He studied
art in Cleveland, Chicago, and New York.   His career
as an artist has included illustrations for a newspaper,
fashion posters, and advertising drawings for a department store.   His illustrations have also appeared
in Collier's, Cosmopolitan, and Good Housekeeping magazines.   The first book which he illustrated
was The Kid From Tomkinsville by John R. Tunis
(Harcourt, 1940).   Jay Barnum married the daughter
of author-illustrator Marjorie Flack, and they have
lived in Hastings-on-Hudson in New York.   For young
people he wrote and illustrated: Little Old Truck,

Morrow, 1953; Motorcycle Dog, Morrow, 1958; The
New Fire Engine, Morrow, 1952.

BARR, George 1907–
   He attended New York City College and has been an
   elementary science consultant for the New York City
   Board of Education. He has also been a high school
   science teacher in Brooklyn. Mr. Barr and his family have lived in Laurelton, New York. His juvenile
   books include: More Research Ideas For Young Scientists, McGraw, 1961; Research Adventures For
   Young Scientists, McGraw, 1964.   CA-3

BARR, Jene 1900–
   She graduated from the Chicago Normal School of
   Physical Education and continued her studies at the
   University of Chicago and Northwestern University.
   Jene Barr has been a teacher in the Chicago public
   schools and Educational Consultant for a Chicago pub-
   lishing company.   In addition to her many fine books
   for young children, she has written book reviews for
   a newspaper, articles for Highlights For Children,
   Chicago Schools Journal, Junior Magazine, and adapt-
   ed plays for radio.   Juvenile titles include: Ben's
   Busy Service Station, Whitman, 1956; Big Wheels!
   Little Wheels!, Whitman, 1955; Dan, The Weatherman,
   Whitman, 1958; Fast Trains! Busy Trains!, Whitman,
   1956; Mr. Zip And The U. S. Mail, Whitman, 1964.
   CA-5/6

BARROWS, Marjorie
   Author, compiler, editor.   She was the recipient of
   the Chicago Foundation for Literature award "in recognition of her notable contribution to the literary
   heritage of Chicago through her many years of de-
   votion to and influence upon young readers." Miss
   Barrows has been an editor of Child Life magazine
   and has lived in Illinois.   For young readers she compiled Read-Aloud Poems Every Young Child Should
   Know, Rand McNally, 1957.

BARRY, Katharina 1936–
   Author-illustrator, born in Germany.   She studied at
   the Kunstgewerbeschule in Zurich, Switzerland where
   she met her husband Robert Barry, an American
   artist.   The Barrys lived at one time in San Juan,
   Puerto Rico.   It was in a San Juan printing shop that

Mrs. Barry found some old wooden type which provided the inspiration for her to write A Is For Anything, Harcourt, 1961.   She also wrote Bug To Hug,
Harcourt, 1964 and illustrated Sesyle Joslin's Spag-
hetti For Breakfast, Harcourt, 1965.   CA-9/10

BARRY, Robert Everett 1931-
Author-artist, born in Newport, Rhode Island. After
serving with the Army he studied at the Kunstgewerbeschule in Zurich, Switzerland where he met his
wife, Katharina Watjen.   At one time the Barrys lived
in San Juan, Puerto Rico where Mr. Barry became
associated with Pava Prints.   The New York Times
selected his book This Is The Story Of Faint George
Who Wanted To Be A Knight (Houghton, 1957), as one
of the "Ten Best Illustrated Books of the Year. "
Other juvenile books which Robert Barry has written
and illustrated include: Animals Around The World,
McGraw, 1967; Boo, Houghton, 1959; Mr. Willowby's
Christmas Tree, McGraw, 1963; The Musical Palm
Tree, McGraw, 1965; Next Please, Houghton, 1961.
CA-5/6

BASSETT, John Keith see KEATING, Lawrence Alfred

BATE, Norman Arthur 1916-
Author, illustrator, teacher, born in Buffalo, New
York.   He spent part of his childhood in England.   He
received his education at the Buffalo Art School, University of Illinois College of Fine and Applied Art,
and Pratt Institute.   After serving in the Army during
World War II, he became an art instructor at Pratt
Institute in Brooklyn, New York.   His wife has been
a librarian, and they have lived in Bellow Falls, Vermont.   Juvenile books which he wrote and illustrated
include: Who Build The Dam?, Scribner, 1958; Who
Built The Highway?, Junior Literary Guild and Scribner, 1953.   CA-4

BAUM, Betty
Teacher and author.   A graduate of Hunter College,
she taught in the All Day Neighborhood School Program on Long Island.   When a Negro child told Betty
Baum: "Kids in books aren't interesting.   They don't
act like me.   They don't feel as I do!", she endeavored to answer this request in Patricia Crosses
Town, Knopf, 1965.

BAUM, Lyman Frank 1856-1919
His pseudonyms are: Edith Van Dyne and Floyd Akers.
He was born in Chittenango, New York. Although he
has written many books for boys and girls, he gained
fame as the creator of the "Wizard Of Oz" series.
The Wonderful Wizard Of Oz (Dutton, 1966) was first
published in 1900, became a musical comedy in 1901,
and a motion picture in 1939. Frank Baum died in
Hollywood, California. He also wrote A Kidnapped
Santa Claus, Bobbs, 1969.

BEACH, Stewart 1899-
At the age of seventeen he became a reporter on the
Pontiac (Michigan) Daily Press. After graduating from
the University of Michigan (Ann Arbor), he lived in
Boston and New York. From 1934 to 1939 Mr. Beach
served as managing editor of House Beautiful. He has
written a Broadway play, short stories, and a book for
young people entitled Racing Start, Little, 1941.

BEALS, Carleton 1893-
Author, lecturer, born in Medicine Lodge, Kansas, his
baby sitter was Carrie Nation. He graduated from the
University of California and received his master's degree from Columbia University. He has traveled extensively and lived with the Indians of Guatemala, the
Amazon, and the Andes. At one time Mr. Beals was
asked why he wrote about John Eliot, and he replied,
"I felt that Eliot was one of the few great men of early
colonial times, and his interest in the Indians coincided
with my own interest in the Indian peoples of North and
South America . . . . In John Eliot I saw a kindred
spirit. " For young people he wrote: John Eliot, Messner, 1958; Land Of The Mayas, Abelard, 1966. CA-4

BEATTY, Hetty Burlingame 1907-
Sculptor, writer and illustrator, born in New Canaan,
Connecticut. She attended the Goodyear-Burlingame
School in Syracuse, New York, the Boston Museum
School, and studied sculpture under Charles Grafly and
drawing under George Demetrios. Her work has been
exhibited at the Worcester Art Museum and in New
York. Hetty Burlingame Beatty has lived in Rockport,
Massachusetts. Her books include: Bryn, Houghton,
1965; Moorland Pony, Houghton, 1961; Saint Francis
And The Wolf, Houghton, 1953; Voyage Of The Sea
Wind, Houghton, 1959. CA-4, MJA

BEATTY, Jerome 1918-
Editor, columnist, author. He attended Dartmouth
College in Hanover, New Hampshire. Jerome Beatty,
Jr. , served in the Army and has been associated with
the field of journalism. He has also written a column
for the Saturday Review. His home has been on Cape
Cod. For young people he wrote Matthew Looney's
Invasion Of The Earth, Scott, 1965. CA-9/10

BEATTY, Patricia Robbins 1922-
Teacher and librarian, born in Portland, Oregon. She
became a high school teacher after graduating from
Reed College. She has also been a science and technical librarian and has worked in an explosives department of a large industrial company. She married Dr.
John Beatty, an associate professor at the University
of California. Mrs. Beatty has lived in England,
Idaho, Delaware, and California. Together the Beattys
wrote At The Seven Stars, Macmillan, 1963. Patricia
Beatty wrote Squaw Dog, Morrow, 1965. CA-4

BEATY, John Yocum 1884-
Author, teacher, born and educated in Iowa. He has
been editor of a farm paper and professor of agricul-
tural journalism at the University of Wisconsin in
Madison. The author traveled to California where he
visited the Burbank farms in order to provide authenti-
city for his biography Luther Burbank, Plant Magician,
Messner, 1943. Other titles include: Baby Whale,
Sharp Ears, Lippincott, 1938; Mountain Book, Beckley-
Cardy, 1944; The River Book, Beckley-Cardy, 1942;
Story Pictures Of Farm Foods, Beckley-Cardy, 1935;
What We See In The City, Saalfield, 1933.

BECKER, John Leonard 1901-
Author and correspondent, born in Chicago. At one
time he was associated with the Institute for Juvenile
Research in Chicago and was a correspondent for the
Chicago Daily News. The author has also been director of the John Becker Art Gallery in New York and
Public Relations Adviser of the Council Against Intolerance in America. He married artist Virginia Campbell, and they have lived in Rome. John Becker
collaborated with Georgene Faulkner to write his first
juvenile book Melindy's Medal, Messner, 1945. He
also wrote, and his wife illustrated New Feathers For
The Old Goose (selected by the American Institute of

Graphic Arts as one of the Fifty Best Books of 1956),
Pantheon, 1956.   CA-11/12

BECKHARD, Arthur J.
Author, director, producer, newspaperman. A native
New Yorker, he attended Amherst College and the
School of Journalism at Columbia University.   He
served in both World Wars and was awarded a citation
by the late President Eisenhower for his service with
the U. S. O.   Mr. Beckhard's newspaper career has
included crime reporting, the drama, and editorial
writing.   He has also directed and produced plays on
Broadway and has written films and television shows
for children.   He married singer Esther Dale.   His
many biographies for children include: Albert Einstein,
Putnam, 1959; Story Of Dwight D. Eisenhower, Grosset,
1956.

BEE, Clair Francis 1900-
He has served as basketball coach at Long Island Uni-
versity and as athletic director at New York Military
Academy at Cornwall-on-Hudson.   His articles have
appeared in Parents' Magazine and the Saturday Evening
Post.   For boys and girls he wrote: Comeback Cagers,
Grosset, 1963; Make The Team In Basketball, Grosset,
1963.   CA-4

BEECROFT, John 1902-1966
He was born in Superior, Wisconsin and graduated from
Columbia University in New York City.   Mr. Beecroft
has studied and traveled in Europe.   For many years
he was Editor-in-Chief of the Literary Guild and also
served as editor of the Doubleday Dollar Book Club,
Book League of America, Family Reading Club and the
Mystery Guild.   He has also compiled anthologies.
One of the family cats was the subject and the Beecroft
summer home near Old Deerfield, Massachusetts was
the background for his book Rocco Came In, Dodd,
1959.   CA-5/6

BEELER, Nelson Frederick 1910-
Author, teacher, film consultant, born in Adams,
Massachusetts.   A graduate of the University of Massa-
chusetts at Amherst, he also received degrees from
Columbia and New York Universities.   He has been a
high school science teacher and taught chemistry at
Clarkson College of Technology in Potsdam.   Dr. Beeler

also organized science programs in Indonesia. He and
Franklyn M. Branley have been co-editors of the
science page of Young America. He wrote Experiments In Sound, Crowell, 1961. With Franklyn M.
Branley he wrote: Experiments In Chemistry, Crowell, 1952; Experiments In Optical Illusion, Crowell,
1951; Experiments In Science, Crowell, 1947; Experiments With A Microscope, Crowell, 1957.   MJA

BEHN, Harry 1898-
He was born in McCabe, Arizona which had once been
a mining camp. Harry Behn graduated from Harvard
and later studied in Sweden. He has written for the
movies and has taught at the University of Arizona in
Tucson. He has also operated a broadcasting company.
Mr. Behn and his family later lived in Greenwich,
Connecticut. His juvenile books include: Chrysalis,
Harcourt, 1968; The Faraway Lurs, World, 1963.
CA-7/8, MJA

BEHRENS, June York 1925-
She was born in California and graduated from the
University of California located at Santa Barbara. Her
two daughters have been raised in an academic atmosphere as Mrs. Behrens has taught in the elementary
grades, and Mr. Behrens has been a principal of a
school. She wrote Soo Ling Finds A Way (A Junior
Literary Guild selection), Golden Gate, 1965.   CA-17/
18

BEIM, Jerrold 1910-1957   Lorraine Levey 1909-
Husband-wife team. His pseudonym is Neil Anderson.
He was born in Newark, New Jersey and attended New
York University. Mr. Beim wrote advertising copy
for several department stores until he sold his first
story to Vanity Fair and decided to make writing his
career. Lorraine Beim was born in Syracuse, New
York, and graduated from Syracuse University. She
was very active in sports until a fall from a horse;
however, her period of recuperation provided her with
the inspiring experience of meeting President Franklin
D. Roosevelt at Warm Springs, Georgia. For young
people they wrote Burro That Had A Name, Harcourt,
1939. He wrote: The Boy On Lincoln's Lap, Morrow,
1955; Swimming Hole, Morrow, 1951.   JBA-2

BEISER, Arthur   Germaine
Husband-wife team. He received his Ph. D. degree

from New York University where he has been an Associate Professor of Physics and Senior Research Scientist. Dr. Beiser has also served as vice-president of
Nuclear Research Associates, Inc. Germaine Beiser
graduated from the Massachusetts Institute of Technology and received an M. A. degree in physics from
New York University. Both Mrs. Beiser and her husband have been involved in cosmic-ray research. Together they wrote: The Story Of Cosmic Rays, Dutton,
1962; Story Of The Earth's Magnetic Field, Dutton,
1964.

BEITLER, Stanley 1924-
Editor, author, born in New York City. He was once
a copy boy and wrote a weekly column on religion for
the New York Post. After serving in the Air Force
during World War II, he received his B. A. degree
from New York University and became a research
assistant in journalism at Iowa State University. He
has been a production manager with Home Craftsman
magazine, an associate editor of Popular Science
Monthly, and an associate editor of Astronautics, a
publication of the American Rocket Society. He wrote
Rockets And Your Future, Harper, 1961. CA-5/6

BELDEN, Shirley
Author and librarian, she has lived and worked in New
England. She attended the University of Connecticut
(Storrs) where her interest in drama led to further
study at the American Academy of Dramatic Arts in
New York. Prior to being on the staff of the Hartford
Public Library, Miss Belden had worked in radio and
book stores. She has been interested in photography,
cooking, and surf casting. Two of her books for young
people have been Junior Literary Guild selections:
Sand In My Castle, Longmans, 1958; Star Dust, Longmans, 1956.

BELL, Joseph N. 1921-
He was born in Bluffton, Indiana and attended the School
of Journalism at the University of Missouri. During
World War II, he was a pilot in the Navy Air Corps.
After the war he returned to college and received his
degree. Mr. Bell has worked in advertising and public
relations and at one time was an assistant publicity
man for the St. Louis Cardinals. His articles have

appeared in the Reader's Digest, True, and the Saturday Evening Post magazines. He wrote World Series
Thrills, Messner, 1962.   CA-7/8

BELL, Kensil 1907-
Author, writer, born in Camden, New Jersey. He has
been a copywriter for a large advertising firm and
later owned his own advertising agency. Mr. Bell's
book reviews have appeared in the Philadelphia Inquirer, and he has also written articles for periodicals. During World War II, Lieutenant Bell served
as a "roving historian" aboard United States Coast
Guard ships and planes. The author has made his
home near Valley Forge in Chester Springs, Pennsylvania. He received Honorable Mention in the Boys'
Life-Dodd, Mead Competition for his juvenile book
Jersey Rebel, Dodd, 1951.

BELL, Margaret Elizabeth 1898-
She was born on Prince of Wales Island in Alaska and
has lived on an island twenty-five miles north of Ketch-
ikan in Loring, Alaska. She attended the Annie Wright
Seminary in Tacoma and the University of Washington
in Seattle. During World War II, she worked with the
Red Cross in Canada, Alaska, and the Aleutian Islands.
Her books for young people have reflected the author's
love of nature and her native land. Juvenile titles in-
clude: Danger On Old Baldy, Morrow, 1944; Daughter
Of Wolf House, Morrow, 1957; Enemies In Icy Strait,
Morrow, 1945; Kit Carson, Mountain Man, Morrow,
1952; Ride Out The Storm, Morrow, 1951; Touched
With Fire, Morrow, 1960; Watch For A Tall White
Sail, Morrow, 1948.   CA-2, MJA

BELL, Thelma (Harrington) 1896-   Corydon Whitten 1894-
Husband-wife team. The Bells and their children have
lived on a farm in Sapphire, North Carolina. They
have enjoyed books and music, and Mrs. Bell's hobby
has been gardening. Thelma Bell was the recipient of
the 1961 Dorothy Canfield Fisher Children's Book A-
ward for Captain Ghost (A Junior Literary Guild selection, Viking, 1959). Other books written and illustrated by the Bells include: The Riddle Of Time,
Viking, 1963; The Two Worlds Of Davy Blount (A
Junior Literary Guild selection), Viking, 1962.   CA-1,
CA-7/8

BELLOC, Joseph Hilaire Pierre 1870-1953
Hilaire Belloc was born in France at La Celle, St.
Cloud. His father was a French lawyer. He studied
at the Oratory School and at Oxford. Later he became a British citizen and served for a number of
years as a Member of Parliament. His writings have
included: verse, novels, history, essays, and biography. He wrote The Bad Child's Book Of Beasts,
Knopf, 1965.

BELPRÉ, Pura
Author, storyteller, puppeteer, born and educated in
Puerto Rico. She came to America and worked in the
New York Public Library and also attended Library
School. As an assignment for a storytelling course
given by the late Mary Gould Davis, the author wrote
Perez And Martina (Warne, 1961). Miss Belpré's
Puerto Rican background enabled her to present puppet
shows based on legends of her native land. She
married the late Clarence C. White, composer and
violinist. Her home has been in New York City.
Another juvenile book written by Pura Belpré was
Tiger & Rabbit & Other Tales, Lippincott, 1965.

BELTING, Natalia Maree 1915-
A history professor at the University of Illinois in
Urbana, she has been interested in the French coloni-
zation of North America and in the history of the
Illinois Indians. She has contributed articles to period-
icals and was co-author of a textbook on High School
Curriculum. Her books for boys and girls have been
outstanding examples of an author's study of folklore.
Dr. Belting's The Sun Is A Golden Earring (Holt, 1962)
was a runner-up for the 1963 Caldecott Medal, and her
Calendar Moon (Holt, 1964) was selected as an ALA
Notable Book. She also wrote The Stars Are Silver
Reindeer, Holt, 1966.   CA-1

BEMELMANS, Ludwig 1898-1962
Author and illustrator, born in Meram, Tirol, Austria.
After his arrival in the United States at the age of sixteen, he worked in several New York hotels and studied
painting. Four years later he became an American
citizen. He used his wife's name for his popular
"Madeline" books, and many of the incidents were provided during the author's visit to France. In 1954 he
received the Caldecott Medal for Madeline's Rescue,

Junior Literary Guild and Viking, 1953. Other juvenile books which he wrote and illustrated include: The
Castle Number Nine, Viking, 1937; Hansi, Viking,
1934; The Happy Place, Little, 1952; Madeline In London (A Junior Literary Guild selection) Viking, 1961;
Marina, Harper, 1962. MJA

BENARY-ISBERT, Margot 1889-
She was born in Saarbrücken, Germany and became an
American citizen in 1957. She grew up in Frankfurt
am Main and had her first short story published when
she was nineteen. Prior to her marriage she was a
secretary in the Museum of Ethnology in Frankfurt.
Her first novel for young people was The Ark (published in 1948 in Germany under the title of Die Arche
Noah). The English translation of The Ark was published in 1953 by Harcourt. She and her husband later
lived in California. Many of her books have been
translated from the German by Richard and Clara Winston, and they include: Blue Mystery, Harcourt, 1957;
Castle On The Border, Harcourt, 1956; Long Way
Home, Harcourt, 1959; Rowan Farm, Harcourt, 1954.
CA-7/8, MJA

BENDICK, Robert 1917-   Jeanne 1919-
Husband-wife team. Both were born in New York City.
Robert Bendick attended the School of Engineering of
New York University and the Clarence White School of
Photography. He has worked in both movies and tele-
vision (producer of the "Today" and "Wide Wide World"
shows). Jeanne Bendick attended New York School of
Fine and Applied Art and the Parsons School of Design.
She has written and illustrated numerous children's
books (including many on science). The Bendicks have
lived in New York and California. Together they wrote
Television Works Like This, McGraw, 1965. Jeanne
Bendick wrote, and Robert Bendick illustrated: Elec-
tronics For Young People, McGraw, 1960; The Wind,
Rand, 1964. CA-7/8, MJA

BENENSON, Lawrence A.
Author, architect, a graduate of M. I. T. He has always
had a deep interest in the real estate market and wrote
a book about it. He has also operated a newspaper
which specialized in real estate. For young people he
wrote How A House Is Built, Criterion, 1965.

BENÉT, Laura 1884-
 The daughter of an army officer, she was born at
 Fort Hamilton in New York Harbor on Friday the thir-
 teenth. After graduating from the Emma Willard
 School, she attended Vassar College. Laura Benét
 was a social worker and newspaperwoman prior to her
 career as a writer. Her two brothers, William Rose
 and Stephen Vincent Benét, were each awarded a Pulitzer prize for poetry. For boys and girls Laura Benét
 wrote: Famous American Humorists, Dodd, 1959;
 Famous Storytellers For Young People, Dodd, 1968.
 CA-9/10, JBA-2

BENET, Sula 1903-
 Anthropologist, author. She has been on the faculty
 at both Pratt Institute and Hunter College in New York.
 She collaborated with Carl Withers to compile American Riddle Book, Abelard, 1954. They also wrote
 Riddles Of Many Lands (A Junior Literary Guild selection), Abelard, 1956.

BENNETT, Eve
 Author, columnist, editor, born in Neligh, Nebraska.
 She grew up in Yankton, South Dakota where her father
 served as mayor and newspaper editor. After graduating from Yankton College, the author attended writing
 classes at the Universities of Colorado and Southern
 California. Eve Bennett has lived in Denver, Colorado
 where she has been a columnist and woman's editor for
 the Rocky Mountain News. A champion of young people
 she once said: " . . . Young people of my day and
 age didn't discuss world affairs with the interest and
 grasp that most of the young people today have. " Her
 juvenile books include: April Wedding, Messner, 1960;
 I, Judy, Messner, 1957; Little Bit, Messner, 1961.

BENSON, Mildred W.
 Newspaperwoman and author. She was the first woman
 to receive a master's degree in Journalism from the
 University of Iowa. Her birthplace was Ladora, Iowa.
 Mildred Benson has written for the Scout Program and
 once had a story published in St. Nicholas. She has
 also been on the staff of the Toledo Times and a
 swimming instructor in Cleveland, Ohio. Her interests
 have included golf and swimming. For young readers
 she wrote Quarry Ghost, Dodd, 1959.

BENTEL, Pearl Bucklen
She was born in Pennsylvania. She began writing when she was in high school and later wrote a novel for this age group. She married Charles A. Bentel and lived near Pittsburgh. During World War II, she worked in radio and also was a copywriter in an advertising agency. Her book was Program For Christine, Longmans, 1953.

BERENSTAIN, Stanley Janice
Husband-wife, author-illustrator team. Mr. and Mrs. Berenstain attended the Philadelphia Museum School of Art and have lived in Elkins Park, Pennsylvania. Both have designed greeting cards and have had their work published in McCall's magazine. Their juvenile books include: Bears On Wheels, Random, 1969; The Bike Lesson, Random, 1964.

BERGAUST, Erik
Author, editor, engineer, a native of Norway. He became an American citizen and has lived in Falls Church, Virginia. Erik Bergaust has been editor of the Missiles And Rockets magazine and has written articles about space flight development for various magazines. He has conducted a weekly radio program, "Washington Radio Features" and has been associated with the "Voice of America." Mr. Bergaust has served as president of the National Rocket Club and the American Rocket Society's Washington section. His books for young people include: Birth Of A Rocket, Putnam, 1961; First Men In Space, Putnam, 1960; Rockets Around The World, Putnam, 1958; Rockets To The Moon, Putnam, 1961; Satellites And Space Probes, Putnam, 1959; Saturn Story, Putnam, 1962.

BERGER, Melvin H. 1927-
Violist, teacher, author. He graduated from the Eastman School of Music and studied at the City College of New York. Mr. Berger has been a violist not only performing in solo recitals but also with various symphony orchestras. He has taught music in both elementary and secondary schools. Mr. and Mrs. Berger and their family have lived in Levittown, New York. With Frank Clark he wrote Science And Music, McGraw, 1961. He wrote For Good Measure, McGraw, 1969. CA-5/6

BERGERE, Thea
> She studied at the Corcoran School of Art, the Art Students League, Queens College, and Columbia University. Her husband Richard Bergere has illustrated many of her books, but she has also been an artist. Her husband illustrated, and she wrote: Automobiles Of Yesteryear, Dodd, 1962; Paris In The Rain With Jean & Jacqueline, McGraw, 1963.

BERKOWITZ, Freda Pastor 1910-
> Musician, teacher, author. She spent her childhood in Newark, New Jersey where she also began her study of the piano. She graduated from Philadelphia's Curtis Institute of Music and later was a member of its faculty. Mrs. Berkowitz has also given private lessons in music. She wrote: On Lutes, Recorders and Harpsichords, Atheneum, 1967; Unfinished Symphony, Antheneum, 1963. CA-9/10

BERNA, Paul 1913-
> He was born in Hyeres, France and attended schools in Toulon and Aix. At the end of World War II, Paul Berna accepted a position in Paris with the French Ministry of Communications. Prior to a full-time writing career, the author has held such positions as accountant, insurance man, secretary, and film distributor. Mr. Berna has made his home in Paris. His children's books include: Mule On The Expressway, Pantheon, 1968; Threshold Of The Stars (tr. by John Buchanan-Brown), Abelard, 1960.

BERNSTEIN, Ralph 1921-
> Sportswriter, born in Philadelphia, Pennsylvania. He received a B. S. degree from Temple University in Philadelphia. During World War II, he served with the Coast Artillery. Mr. Bernstein later worked for the United Press and the Associated Press. His articles have appeared in both Sport and Collier's magazines. Not only was he a member of the Baseball Writers Association of America, but he also served as president of the Philadelphia Basketball Writers Association. His book was Story Of Bobby Shantz; As Told To Ralph Bernstein, Lippincott, 1953.

BERRILL, Jacquelyn (Batsel) 1905-
> Author-illustrator, born in South Carrollton, Kentucky. After graduating from the University of Toledo in Ohio,

she attended New York University. She married Dr.
N. J. Berrill who has been a professor of zoology at
McGill University in Montreal, Canada. Their home
has been in Swarthmore, Pennsylvania where Mrs.
Berrill has enjoyed photography and jewelry making as
hobbies. Juvenile books which she has written and
illustrated include: Albert Schweitzer: Man Of Mercy,
Dodd, 1956; Wonders Of Animal Migration, Dodd, 1964;
Wonders Of The Antarctic, Dodd, 1958; Wonders Of
The Monkey World, Dodd, 1967; Wonders Of The Sea-
shore, Dodd, 1951.   CA-19/20

BERRISFORD, Judith Mary 1921-
She has lived near Blackpool, England at Cleveleys.
Miss Berrisford's love of horses and dogs has provided her with ideas for her books. After she saw the
show horse "Ballita" at the Blackpool Tower Circus, she
wrote Sue's Circus Horse, Dodd, 1952. She also wrote
Red Rocket, Mystery Horse, Dodd, 1952.

BERRY, Erick see BEST, Allena Champlin

BERRY, William D.
Artist and author. He has lived in Alaska near Mount
McKinley National Park. William Berry has drawn
pictures of wildlife for museums, Disneyland, and the
National Audubon Society. In addition to his illustra-
tions, Mr. Berry has also written for the Audubon
Society's "Mammal Card" series. For young people
he wrote Deneki, Macmillan, 1965.

BEST, Allena Champlin 1892-   Herbert 1894-
Her pseudonym is Erick Berry. She was born on New
Year's Day in New Bedford, Massachusetts. She
studied at the Eric Pape School in Boston, the Pennsylvania Academy of Fine Arts, and in Paris. Mrs. Best
has had one-man shows in Chicago, Paris, and New
York. Herbert Best was born in Chester, England and
studied at Cambridge. He later served as an administrative officer in Nigeria. She has illustrated many of
her husband's books including Flag Of The Desert (Viking, 1936). She wrote and illustrated: Green Door To
The Sea, Viking, 1955; Harvest Of The Hudson, Macmillan, 1945; Hay-foot, Straw-foot, Viking, 1954.
JBA-1, JBA-2

BEST, Herbert 1894-
Born in Chester, England, he attended Queens College

(Cambridge). He served in the Royal Engineers during World War I, and he later worked as an administrative officer in Nigeria, West Africa. Herbert Best married author and artist Erick Berry. After extensive world travel, the Best family settled in the state of New York near Lake Champlain. He wrote: Desmond And Dog Friday, Viking, 1968; Desmond, The Dog Detective, Viking, 1962. JBA-1, JBA-2

BETHERS, Ray 1902-
Painter, photographer, world traveler, this author-illustrator was born in Corvallis, Oregon. After attending the University of Oregon at Eugene, he went to San Francisco where he studied art at the California School of Fine Arts. He also studied in Paris, France. The author has depicted his travels in paintings, photographs, and wood engravings. The Pennell Purchase Prize of the Library of Congress was awarded to Mr. Bethers for his wood engraving entitled "Still Life With Flowers." Juvenile books which he has written and illustrated include: Can You Name Them?, Aladdin, 1948; The Magic Of Oil, Aladdin, 1949; Nature Invents, Science Applies, Hastings House, 1959; Ports Of Adventure, Hastings, 1963; Story Of Rivers, Sterling, 1957. CA-11/12

BETTINA see EHRLICH, Bettina Bauer

BETZ, Betty 1920-
Author-illustrator, columnist. At sixteen Betty Betz was an Illinois State swimming champion. After attending high school in Hammond, Indiana, she studied at Sarah Lawrence College in Bronxville, New York where she was honored as guest fashion editor for the college issue of Mademoiselle magazine. She has written for magazines and has also conducted a teen-age newspaper column. Miss Betz has helped to organize teen-age recreational centers. She married Frank McMahon and has lived in Canada and New York. Juvenile books which she has written and illustrated include: Betty Betz Career Book, Grosset, 1949; Betty Betz Party Book, Grosset, 1947; Manners For Moppets, Grosset, 1962; Your Manners Are Showing, Grosset, 1946. CA-4, MJA

BEVANS, Margaret
She has been an encyclopedia editor and worked in

book promotion.   She has also been a free-lance artist.   Margaret Bevans has lived in New York City.
She collaborated with the editors of McCall's magazine to write McCall's Book Of Everyday Etiquette,
Golden, 1960.

BEVANS, Michael H.
He was born in New York City.   When he was seven-
teen-years-old, he was a member of Carl Kauffeld's
(Curator of the Staten Island Zoo) expedition to Florida
where they collected reptiles.   His work has appeared
in textbooks and magazines, and he has also done bio-
logical pictures.   He wrote and illustrated: Book Of
Reptiles And Amphibians, Garden City Books, 1956;
The Book Of Sea Shells, Doubleday, 1961.

BIANCO, Margery (Williams) 1881-1944
She was born in London and spent her childhood in both
England and America.   She had that rare gift of creating stories drawn from her own vivid childhood memories.   Her children's book The Skin Horse (Doran,
1927) was based on her brother's toy horse named
"Dobbin. "   After her marriage to Francesco Bianco, she
lived in France and Italy.   Her daughter was noted
artist Pamela Bianco.   For boys and girls she wrote
Velveteen Rabbit, Doran, 1926.   JBA-1, JBA-2

BIANCO, Pamela 1906-
Artist and author, born in London, the daughter of the
late author Margery Bianco.   She grew up in Italy,
England, and France.   She has had one-man shows of
her drawings at many galleries including the Leicester
Galleries in London and the Anderson Galleries in New
York.   Pamela Bianco has lived in Connecticut and
New York City.   Juvenile books which she wrote and
illustrated include: The Doll In The Window, Walck,
1953; Look-Inside Easter Egg, Walck, 1952.   JBA-1,
JBA-2

BIANKI, Vitali
He was born in Russia.   Mr. Bianki has been both a
naturalist and a storyteller.   Interested in animals, he
has written many true and exciting stories about them.
One of his books was Peek The Piper (tr. by S. K.
Lederer), Braziller, 1964.

BICE, Clare
Canadian artist and writer, he has lived in London,
Ontario. He attended the Art Students League and the
Grand Central School of Art in New York after gradu-
ating from the University of Western Ontario. The
author has been a member of the Ontario Society of
Artists and was also an Associate of the Royal Cana-
dian Academy. A well-known landscape artist, Mr.
Bice has also done portrait painting. Juvenile titles
include: Across Canada, Macmillan, 1949; A Dog For
Davie's Hill, Macmillan, 1956; Hurricane Treasure,
Viking, 1965; Jory's Cove, Macmillan, 1941.

BINDER, Eando   see BINDER, Otto Oscar

BINDER, Otto Oscar   1911-
Author and editor. A noted authority about space,
Otto Binder has written numerous adult books and arti-
cles about it. At one time he served as Editor-in-
Chief of Space World. He has been a member of the
National Association of Rocketeers, National American
Rocketeers, and Amateur Rocketry Association. Since
1939 the American Rocket Society has made him an
honorary member. For young people he wrote Riddles
Of Astronomy, Basic Bks. , 1964. CA-4

BISCHOFF, Ilse Marthe   1903-
Illustrator-writer, born in New York City where she
attended Horace Mann School and the Parsons School
of Design. She later studied in Paris and Munich.
Miss Bischoff has been especially interested in wood
engraving and painting, and the Metropolitan, Baltimore, and Boston Museums have bought her prints.
It was in Miss Mabel Robinson's Juvenile Workshop at
Columbia University that Ilse Bischoff wrote Painter's
Coach (Longmans, 1943). She has lived in Vermont
in a brick house which is 150 years old. She also
illustrated Emilie Vinall's Super-market Secret, Crowell, 1945. MJA

BISCHOFF, Julia Bristol
She was born in Michigan but has lived in many parts
of the world including Central America and Europe.
Her husband has been editor of a newspaper, and Mrs.
Bischoff has taught school and written articles for
newspapers. The Bischoffs have lived in Miami,
Florida. She wrote Great-Great Uncle Henry's Cats,

Young Scott Bks. , 1965.

BISHOP, Claire (Huchet)
French author and poet, she became an American citizen and has lived in New York City. She founded the first public library ("L'Heure Joyeuse") for French children in Paris. The author has been the recipient of several book awards. Pancakes-Paris (Viking, 1947) was a prize winner in the New York Herald Tribune Spring Book Festival and a runner-up for the Newbery Medal in 1948. All-Alone (Viking, 1953) was chosen as the best-liked book by the Boys' Club of America and a runner-up for the Newbery Medal in 1953. Claire Bishop has also been children's book editor for the Commonweal. Other juvenile books include: Blue Spring Farm, Viking, 1948; Five Chinese Brothers (with Kurt Wiese) Coward-McCann, 1938; Twenty And Ten, Viking, 1952; Twenty-Two Bears, Viking, 1964. JBA-2

BISHOP, Curtis Kent 1912-
His pseudonyms are Curt Brandon and Curt Carroll. When he attended the University of Texas (Austin), he edited the college magazine entitled the Texas Ranger. He has been a sectional champion in tennis and a pitcher in semi-pro baseball. During World War II, he served in the Foreign Broadcast Intelligence Service. Mr. Bishop has lived in Austin, Texas where he organized a Little League baseball team. Juvenile books include: Field Goal, Lippincott, 1964; Larry Of Little League, Steck Co. , 1953; Little League Heroes, Lippincott, 1960; Little Leaguer, Steck Co. , 1956; Lone Star Leader: Sam Houston, Messner, 1961. CA-11/ 12

BISHOP, Grace
She married author Curtis Bishop. When her three children started to school, Mrs. Bishop began to write. Her daughter requested a book about girls, and the result was Prissy Misses, Steck, 1956.

BIXBY, William Courtney 1920-
Author, teacher, born in San Diego, California. After receiving a degree in engineering, he served in the Signal Corps and the Air Corps. He has written for a magazine and has been an associate editor. Later Mr. Bixby decided on a teaching career. Prior to his

position as physics instructor at New Haven College in
Connecticut, the author had taught in Massachusetts,
Rhode Island, and Vermont.   For young people he
wrote Impossible Journey Of Sir Ernest Shackleton (A
Junior Literary Guild selection), Little, 1960.   CA-3

BLACK, Irma Simonton 1906-
She was born in Paterson, New Jersey, graduated from
Barnard College, and attended New York University.
Irma Black has been associated with the Bank Street
College of Education in New York City as Director of
Publications and the Writers' Laboratory.   Her articles
have appeared in such magazines as Art In America
and Saturday Review.   For children she wrote: Big
Puppy And Little Puppy, Holiday, 1960; Busy Water,
Holiday, 1958; Castle, Abbey, And Town, Holiday,
1963; Hamlet, A Cocker Spaniel, Holiday, 1938.   CA-4

BLACKBURN, Edith H.
Teacher and author, born in Denver, Colorado.   After
graduating from the Colorado State Teachers College
in Greeley, she taught school in her native state and
conducted classes in creative writing.   She has also
contributed serials and short stories to children's
magazines.   Mrs. Blackburn has lived in Glendale,
California.   Her juvenile books include: Land Of The
Silver Spruce, Abelard, 1956; Mystery Of The Glory
Hole Mine, Sterling, 1956.

BLAIR, Walter 1900-
Author and teacher, born in Spokane, Washington.   He
has studied American literature (especially folklore and
humor).   Walter Blair has traveled widely in the United
States and has often visited several states many times
in order to study the folklore of that particular region
of America.   Mr. Blair has been a professor at the
University of Chicago and has served as Chairman of
the Department of English.   For children he wrote
Tall Tale America, Coward, 1944.   CA-5/6

BLAND, Edith (Nesbit) 1858-1924
Her books are found in libraries under the name of E.
Nesbit.   She grew up in London but attended schools
in Germany and France.   She had her first poem published at the age of seventeen.   When she was forty,
her famous "Bastable Books" were published.   Mrs.
Bland made her home in Kent and Warwickshire.   Her

juvenile books include: <u>Five Children And It</u>, Coward, 1949; <u>The Wouldbegoods</u>, Coward, 1931. JBA-1, MJA

BLANTON, (Martha) Catherine 1907-
Born in San Angelo, Texas, she grew up in Arizona on a ranch near Willcox. Miss Blanton has made her home in Tucson. She once said that "the homesteading adventures described in <u>The Gold Penny</u> (Day, 1957) are similar to those of friends who were early settlers. " She also wrote <u>Hold Fast To Your Dreams</u>, Messner, 1955. CA-4

BLASSINGAME, Wyatt Rainey 1909-
Author and teacher, born in Demopolis, Alabama. He graduated from the University of Alabama and did further study at New York University. He served in the Pacific during World War II. He wrote a short story entitled "Man's Courage" which was given the Benjamin Franklin Award (best story of 1956). He has lived on an island called Anna Maria near the coast of Florida. Juvenile titles include: <u>Stephen Decatur</u>, Garrard, 1964; <u>Story Of The United States Flag</u>, Garrard, 1969. CA-4

BLIVEN, Bruce 1889-
Newspaperman, writer. Bruce Bliven, Jr. , has written for the <u>Manchester Guardian</u> and the New York <u>Post</u>. During World War II, he served in the campaigns near Aachen and Normandy (where he received a battlefield promotion and the Bronze Star). He has written articles for many magazines including: <u>Harper's</u>, <u>Reader's Digest</u>, and the New Yorker. Juvenile titles include: <u>From Pearl Harbor To Okinawa</u>, Random, 1960; <u>Story Of D-Day: June 6, 1944</u>, Random, 1956.

BLOCH, Marie Halun 1910-
She was born in the Ukraine and spent her childhood in the United States where she became an American citizen. She received a Ph. D. degree from the University of Chicago. Her husband Don Bloch has collected and sold books in Denver. Juvenile titles include: <u>Aunt America</u>, Atheneum, 1963; <u>Dinosaurs</u>, Coward-McCann, 1955; <u>The Dollhouse Story</u>, Walck, 1961; <u>Marya</u>, Coward-McCann, 1957; <u>Mountains On The Move</u>, Coward-McCann, 1960; <u>Tunnels</u>, Coward-McCann,

1954.   CA-4

BLOUGH, Glenn Orlando 1907–
Author, editor, teacher, born in Michigan. He became a science teacher after graduating from the University of Michigan. He was in the Navy during World
War II. At one time Dr. Blough was associated with
the U. S. Office of Education as a specialist in elementary science. He has also been on the faculty of
the University of Maryland. Dr. Blough has been the
editor of Young People's Book Of Science. His juvenile books include: Bird Watchers And Bird Feeders,
McGraw, 1963; Discovering Dinosaurs, McGraw, 1960.
CA-11/12

BLYTON, Enid
Author and teacher. Most famous of her stories are
the series of the "Famous Five" characters which in-
clude: Castle Of Adventure, Macmillan, 1946; The
Circus Of Adventure, St. Martin's Press, 1953; Five
Go Adventuring Again, Crowell, 1951; Five Go Down
To The Sea, Reilly & Lee, 1961; Five Go To Mystery
Moor, Reilly & Lee, 1963; Five On A Treasure Island,
Crowell, 1950.

BOEGEHOLD, Betty
She was born in New York City, graduated from Wellesley College, and received her master's degree from
Teacher's College at Columbia University. She had a
nursery school of her own at one time and has served
on the staff of the City and Country School of New
York. She also has worked on the Bank Street Reading Series and has been on the staff of the Bank Street
College Writers' Laboratory. Her stories for children
have been published in magazines. Betty Boegehold
has lived in Bronxville, New York. She wrote Three
To Get Ready, Harper, 1965.

BOGAN, Louise 1897–
Poet, born in Maine. A member of the Institute of
Arts and Letters, Louise Bogan has been the recipient
of the Bollingen Prize for poetry. For many years
she was the New Yorker magazine's poetry reviewer.
She collaborated with William Jay Smith to compile The
Golden Journey, Reilly, 1965.

BOGGS, Ralph Steele 1901–
He has taught at the University of Puerto Rico, Uni-

versity of North Carolina, and the University of Miami
where he was director of its American Institute and
International Center. Professor Boggs has been interested in Spanish folklore for many years. Due to
this interest he has made many trips to Latin American countries. It was on a visit to the Dominican
Republic that he met his wife. With Moritz Adolf
Jagendorf he wrote The King Of The Mountains, Vanguard, 1960. He wrote Three Golden Oranges, And
Other Spanish Folk Tales with Mary Gould Davis,
Longmans, 1936.   CA-11/12

BOLTON, Ivy May 1879-
English author and librarian, daughter of historian
Reginald Pelham Bolton. After spending part of her
childhood in Kent and London, she came to America
where she attended Saint Mary's School in Peekskill
and later studied at the University of Chicago. For
many years she was Mistress of Studies at Saint Mary's
School for Mountain Girls in Sewanee, Tennessee. She
has been interested in gardening and stamp collecting.
Her books include: Father Junipero Serra, Messner,
1952; Wayfaring Lad, Messner, 1948.

BONHAM, Frank 1914-
Native Californian, he attended the University of California at Los Angeles. He has written over five hundred short stories and twenty novels. Mr. Bonham
has lived with his wife and three children in La Jolla,
California. He wrote: Burma Rifles, Crowell, 1960;
Deepwater Challenge, Crowell, 1963.   CA-11/12

BONNER, Mary Graham 1890-
She grew up in Halifax, Nova Scotia. Miss Bonner began her career writing for magazines and while still in
her teens was the author of two books of collected
stories for children. Her interests have included baseball, hockey, and swimming. She has traveled throughout Canada and has visited Belgium, England, Honolulu,
Paris, and Scotland. For young people she wrote:
Baseball Rookies Who Made Good, Knopf, 1954; The
Base-stealer, Knopf, 1951; Couriers Of The Sky, Knopf,
1952; Mysterious Caboose, Knopf, 1949; Spray Hitter,
Lantern Press, 1959; Wait And See, Knopf, 1952;
Wonders Around The Sun, Lantern Press, 1957; Wonders Of Inventions, Lantern Press, 1961.

BONTEMPS, Arna Wendell 1902-
  Librarian, teacher, author, poet, born in Alexandria,
  Louisiana. He graduated from Union Pacific College,
  Napa County, California and received his master's
  degree from the University of Chicago. In 1943 he
  became Librarian at Fisk University in Nashville, Tennessee where he later became the first Negro member
  of the Nashville Board of Education. In 1956 his book
  Story Of The Negro (3d ed. Knopf, 1958) was awarded
  the Jane Addams Children's Book Award. Juvenile
  titles include: Famous Negro Athletes, Dodd, 1964;
  Frederick Douglass: Slave-Fighter-Freeman, Knopf,
  1959; Golden Slippers, Harper, 1941; Lonesome Boy,
  Houghton, 1955; Story Of George Washington Carver,
  Grosset, 1954. CA-1, JBA-2

BONZON, Paul-Jacques 1908-
  Author and teacher, born in Sainte Marie, France.
  Mr. Bonzon has taught school in Valence, France.
  The author's children have been the "official" critics
  of his stories for boys and girls. His book The Or-
  phans Of Simitra (tr. by Thelma Niklaus), Criterion
  Bks. , [1962 c1957] received a children's book award
  in France. He also wrote Pursuit In The French Alps,
  Lothrop, 1963.

BORDEN, Charles A. 1912-
  Author, engineer, explorer. Mr. Borden has sailed
  twice around the Horn and numerous times in the South
  Pacific. He has lived in California. In addition to
  studying navigation, Mr. Borden has been very interested in Hawaii and its people. This interest enabled him
  to write Hawaii . . . Fiftieth State, Macrae, 1960.
  CA-7/8

BORG, Inga
  Author and artist, born in Sweden. She has created
  informative picture books depicting the animal life of
  her native land. For children she wrote Plupp Builds
  A House, Warne, 1960.

BORHEGYI, Suzanne Catherine Sims de 1926-
  Anthropologist, author. She graduated from Ohio State
  University and did further study in anthropology at the
  University of Arizona. Since her husband has also been
  interested in anthropology, the de Borhegyis have tra-
  veled extensively. They have lived in New Mexico and

Guatemala and have studied archaeology in Central
America. Mr. de Borhegyi has been Director of the
Milwaukee Public Museum. Her books for young
people include: A Book To Begin On Museums, Holt,
1962; Ships, Shoals and Amphoras, Holt, 1961. CA-
5/6

BORTEN, Helen Jacobson 1930-
Illustrator-author, she attended the Philadelphia Museum
of Art. She once said that a rich cultural background
in art and music is one of the most valuable gifts we
can give a child. With this gift in mind she wrote Do
You See What I See? (Abelard-Schuman, 1959) and Do
You Hear What I Hear? (Abelard-Schuman, 1960). In
1959 the New York Times Children's Book Section re-
commended Do You See What I See? as one of the hundred best books for children. In addition to illustrating
books for other authors, her books include: Copycat,
Abelard-Schuman, 1962; Halloween, Crowell, 1965.
CA-5/6

BOSTON, Lucy Maria 1892-
English writer and poet, born in Southport, Lancashire.
She studied in Paris, attended Somerville, Oxford and
St. Thomas Hospital in London. Prior to World War
II, she returned from the continent to England and pur-
chased Manor House at Hemingford Grey (Cambridge).
Manor House became the background for her "Green
Knowe" stories. A distinguished writer of books for
children, Mrs. Boston has been acclaimed for her
ability to combine the past with the present and to cap-
tivate both an adult and juvenile audience. Juvenile
titles include: The Castle Of Yew, Harcourt, 1965;
Children Of Green Knowe, Harcourt, 1955; River At
Green Knowe, Harcourt, 1959; A Stranger At Green
Knowe, Harcourt, 1961; Treasure Of Green Knowe,
Harcourt, 1958.

BOSWORTH, J. Allan
Author, newspaperman, born in California. He served
as a naval officer (aboard the USS Missouri) during
World War II. Allan Bosworth has been on the staff
of the San Francisco Chronicle. He and his family
have lived in Salem, Virginia. He wrote Voices In The
Meadow (A Junior Literary Guild selection), Doubleday,
1964.

BOTHWELL, Jean
Author and teacher, born in Wayne County, Nebraska.
She attended Nebraska Wesleyan University at Lincoln.
Prior to writing and living in New York City, she was
a high-school history teacher in Nebraska and asso-
ciated with a boarding school in India. Jean Bothwell
has belonged to the American Geographical Society.
In 1945 her first book Little Boat Boy (Harcourt, 1945)
was published. Other titles include: The Borrowed
Monkey, Abelard Press, 1953; Cal's Birthday Present,
Abelard, 1955; Dancing Princess, Harcourt, 1965;
The Emerald Clue, Harcourt, 1961; Little Flute Player,
Morrow, 1949; River Boy Of Kashmir, Morrow, 1946.
CA-2, JBA-2

BOWEN, Betty Morgan 1921-
Author-illustrator. She graduated from Swarthmore
College and studied art at Pratt Institute. She has
worked for a publishing company and was sent to
Europe by the American Friends Service Committee
where she served in reconstruction work. She and her
family have lived in Yorkshire. For young people she
wrote and illustrated For Love Of A Donkey (A Junior
Literary Guild selection), McKay, 1963.   CA-7/8

BOWEN, Elizabeth (Dorothea Cole) 1899-
She was born in Dublin and attended Trinity College.
Elizabeth Bowen was honored in the 1948 Brithday
Honors List as a Commander of the British Empire.
Her first juvenile book was entitled Good Tiger, Knopf,
1965.   CA-17/18

BOWEN, Irene
Author and librarian. After graduating from Smith
College, she attended Carnegie Institute of Technology
where she studied library science. Irene Bowen wrote
mystery stories in answer to the many requests from
boys and girls when she was a children's librarian.
She has been a school librarian and has lived in
Schenectady, New York. Her juvenile books include:
Mystery Of Eel Island, Lippincott, 1961; The Stolen
Spoon Mystery, Lippincott, 1958.

BOWEN, Joshua David 1930-
A graduate of Harvard University, he spent his boyhood in Chicago, Illinois. After college, he worked in
the theater both as an actor and director. He has also

been a newspaperman in Raleigh, North Carolina and
has served with the Foreign Policy Association. He
was editor of the United Fruit Company's Middle
America and has traveled extensively in South America.
His articles have appeared in the National Observer,
New York Times, and Reader's Digest. David Bowen
has lived in New York City. He wrote: Hello South
America, Norton, 1964; The Land And People Of Peru,
Lippincott, 1963.

BOWEN, Robert Sidney 1900-
Pilot, author, editor, born in Boston, Massachusetts.
He has been an editor of Aviation Magazine and Flying
News. Robert Bowen has also served the International
Civil Aeronautics Conference in Washington as Editorial
Director. He was Publicity Director of the American
Society for Promotion of Aviation. The Boys' Clubs of
America have awarded a gold medal and several gold
certificates to Mr. Bowen. He has lived in Hawaii.
His juvenile books include: Ball Hawk, Lothrop, 1950;
Bat Boy, Lothrop, 1962.

BOWMAN, James Cloyd 1880-
At a Southeastern Regional Library Conference Mr.
Bowman once said: "My folklore heroes are upstand-
ing men, but they come from the folk and smell of the
good earth. They are strong in their own right. They
are natural leaders. They are not gangsters or killers
of gangsters. They are too strong and too great for
that sort of thing . . . " (see December 1949 issue of
Top Of The News). He became interested in the folklore of America when he was a graduate student at
Harvard. Mr. Bowman has written many tall tales
for boys and girls. His juvenile titles include:
. . . Mike Fink, Little, 1957; Pecos Bill, Whitman,
1937. JBA-2

BOXER, Devorah
She was born in Troy, New York and graduated from
Pembroke College and Yale University School of Archi-
tecture and Design. She also studied abroad at the
University of Paris and the École Internationale in
Geneva, Switzerland. Devorah Boxer has lived in
Paris. For young people she wrote 26 Ways To Be
Somebody Else, Pantheon Bks., 1960.

BOYLSTON, Helen (Dore) 1895-
Nurse, author, born in Portsmouth, New Hampshire.
She received her training at the Massachusetts General
Hospital nursing school in Boston. She served with
the British Expeditionary Force during World War I.
Following the war she continued to work in Europe
with the American Red Cross. In 1925 her Diary Of
A War Nurse was published in the Atlantic Monthly.
She later made her home in Westport, Connecticut.
Juvenile titles include: Carol Goes Backstage, Little,
1941; Carol On Tour, Little, 1946; Clara Barton, Ran-
dom House, 1955; Sue Barton, Neighborhood Nurse,
Little, 1949.   JBA-2

BOYTON, Neil
He has been a member of the Society of Jesus (Jesuit
religious order). He has written many books for boys
and has also served as a Chaplain for a troop of Boy
Scouts. For young people he wrote That Silver Fox
Patrol, Longmans, 1944.

BRADBURY, Bianca 1908-
The author and her husband have lived in New Milford,
Connecticut in a house which was built over a hundred
years ago. One of her sons has worked in Africa
with the Peace Corps. Mrs. Bradbury has written for
children of all ages, and her books for older girls
have received much praise. Juvenile titles include:
Amethyst Summer, Washburn, 1963; Red Sky At Night,
Washburn, 1968.   CA-13/14

BRADDY, Nella 1894-
Author and editor, born in Georgia. She grew up in
Florida, attended South Carolina's Converse College,
and did graduate work at Columbia University. Nella
Braddy has edited and compiled numerous books and
has contributed articles and book reviews to magazines;
however, her main interest has been biography. She
married Keith Henney, editor and author. For young
people she wrote Rudyard Kipling, Messner, 1941.

BRADFORD, Adam M. D.   see WASSERSUG, Joseph David

BRADLEY, Duane 1914-
She was born in Iowa. She married George Sanborn
who served in the Army during World War II, and they
lived in Rhode Island, Washington, and Delaware. She

and her family later lived in New Hampshire.   At one
time Duane Bradley worked on newspapers in California.   When she wrote her book Electing A President
(Van Nostrand, 1963), she said: "the most important
individual in a presidential election is not the one who
is elected, but the individual voter. "   She also wrote
Meeting With A Stranger, Lippincott, 1964.   CA-4

BRADY, Rita G.
She graduated from Brooklyn College and continued her
studies at New York University and Hunter College.
In 1950 she began her writing career in Bavaria, Germany where her husband was a judge in the Occupation
Courts.   Mrs. Brady has not only taught in a high
school in New York City but has also been a teacher
of a course in children's literature at Russell Sage
College in Troy, New York.   Teaching experiences
provided her with a good background to write career
books for young people.   She wrote: Christine Bennet:
Chemist, Abelard, 1955; Lois Thornton, Librarian,
Abelard, 1959; Vida Prescott: Attorney, Abelard, 1957.

BRAGDON, Lillian Jacot
Author, editor, lecturer, born in New Jersey.   She
attended the University of Lausanne in Switzerland and
has traveled in Italy and France.   She has been a
children's book editor, lecturer, and editorial consultant.   Mrs. Bragdon has lived in Connecticut.   For
young people she wrote: It's Fun To Speak French,
Abingdon Press, 1962; The Land And People Of France,
Lippincott, 1960; The Land And People Of Switzerland,
Lippincott, 1961; Luther Burbank, Abingdon, 1959;
Meet The Remarkable Adams Family, Atheneum, 1964.

BRAND, Oscar 1920-
Psychologist, balladier.   He was born in Winnipeg and
later made his home in Manhattan.   Mr. Brand has
collected folk songs and has often sung them on radio
and television and has also recorded them for young
people.   His recording called "The American Almanac"
was selected as "Best In Children's Records" by the
music critics of New York.   During World War II, he
was a psychologist in the army.   Later he did graduate
work in psychology at Bellevue Hospital.   He edited
Singing Holidays, Knopf, 1957.   CA-4

BRANDENBERG, Aliki Leacouras 1929-
 Her pseudonym is Aliki. She spent her childhood in
 Philadelphia and later studied at the Philadelphia
 Museum College of Art. She has illustrated many
 books for other authors, but she wrote and illustrated:
 George And The Cherry Tree, Dial, 1964; The Story
 Of Johnny Appleseed, Prentice, 1963. CA-4

BRANDON, Curt see BISHOP, Curtis Kent

BRANLEY, Franklyn Mansfield 1915-
 Science teacher, author, born in New Rochelle, New
 York. He graduated from New York University and
 received his M. A. and Ed. D. degrees from Columbia
 University. He has taught at the Horace Mann School
 and Teachers College, Columbia University in New
 York, the State Teachers College in Troy, Alabama,
 New Jersey State Teachers College at Jersey City,
 and at Southwestern Louisiana Institute, Lafayette,
 Louisiana. In 1956 he became Associate Astronomer
 of the American Museum-Hayden Planetarium in New
 York City. His books include: Air Is All Around
 You, Crowell, 1962; The Big Dipper, Crowell, 1962;
 A Book Of Astronauts For You, Crowell, 1963; Ex-
 ploring By Astronaut: The Story Of Project Mercury,
 Crowell, 1961. MJA

BRANN, Esther
 Author-illustrator, born in New York City. She studied
 at the Art Students League, Cooper Union, and National
 Academy of Design. She also attended the Fontainbleau
 School of Fine Arts in France. During her travels
 abroad Esther Brann visited a Spanish convent where
 she met "Lupe" the heroine of Lupe Goes To School
 (Macmillan, 1930). The author married Richard Schorr
 and has lived in Los Angeles, California. Her books
 for children include: Book For Baby, Macmillan, 1945;
 Five Puppies For Sale, Macmillan, 1948. JBA-1,
 JBA-2

BRATTON, Karl H. 1906-
 Choral conductor, music director, singer, graduate of
 Kansas University (Lawrence, Kansas). He received
 his master's degree from Teachers' College, Columbia
 University. He has been Head of the Department of
 Music at the University of New Hampshire in Durham.
 Recipient of several music scholarships and awards, at

one time he studied with Willem van Giesen in Holland.
In addition to writing articles on music, Mr. Bratton
has served as Associate Editor for the Journal Of
Musicology.   He wrote Tales Of The Magic Mirror,
Caxton Printers, 1949.

BRAUN, Kathy
She was born and grew up in New York City.   She
studied at Hunter College.   Kathy Braun has worked
with children both in camps and settlement houses.
When she worked in a toy shop, she thought of the
idea for her book Kangaroo & Kangaroo, Doubleday,
1965.

BRAUN, Saul M.
Author, editor, graduate of Yale University.   Mr.
Braun has been a drama counselor for a children's
camp and a magazine editor.   He also has contributed
to Argosy, Saga, Esquire, and other magazines.   Several of his plays have been produced.   Saul Braun and
his family have lived in New York City.   For children
he wrote Seven Heroes: Of The War In The Pacific,
Putnam, 1965.

BRAUN, Wernher von   1912-
Born in Wirsitz, Germany, he came to the United
States in 1945 and became an American citizen.   An
authority in space exploration, Dr. Wernher von Braun
has supervised the development of U. S. Missiles.   He
has lived in Huntsville, Alabama where he has been
Director of the Army's Guided Missile Development
Division at Redstone Arsenal.   For young people he
wrote First Men To The Moon, Holt, 1960.

BRECK, Vivian   see BRECKENFELD, Vivian Gurney

BRECKENFELD, Vivian Gurney   1895-
She has written under the name of Vivian Breck.   Born
in San Francisco, Mrs. Breckenfeld grew up in Mexico
near mining camps where her father was a mining engineer.   She graduated from Vassar College and received her M. A. degree from the University of California.   The Breckenfelds have lived in Berkeley, California.   She wrote White Water (A Junior Literary Guild
selection), Doubleday, 1958.   CA-5/6, MJA

BREETVELD, Jim Patrick 1925-
Newspaperman and author, born in New York. He
served with the 18th Fighter Squadron during World
War II. Mr. Breetveld has worked on several news-
papers including the New York Daily Mirror and Radio
Daily. He has also written stage and radio scripts
about international affairs. His juvenile books include:
Getting To Know Brazil, Coward, 1958; Getting To
Know The FAO, Coward, 1962. CA-4

BRENNAN, Joseph Gerard
Author and teacher, he has made his home in Honolulu.
He has been both an amateur and professional boxer.
During World War II, he taught boxing and calisthenics
in the Navy. He served in the South Pacific. Follow-
ing the war, Joe Brennan studied journalism and later
taught in Hollywood at the Maren Elwood College of
Journalism. Many of his stories have been published
in magazines. For children he wrote Frog-Suited
Fighters, Chilton, 1964. CA-3

BRENNER, Barbara Johnes 1925-
She married artist Fred Brenner who has taught at
Parsons School of Design. His illustrations have also
appeared in her books. She has written for both adults
and children including lyrics of a musical for boys and
girls. Mrs. Brenner and her family have lived in
West Nyack, New York. Her juvenile books include:
Barto Takes The Subway, Knopf, 1961; Beef Stew,
Knopf, 1965. CA-9/10

BRENT, Stuart
He was born in Chicago and has continued to live in its
suburbs with his family. Mr. Brent has conducted a
television program about books and has operated a
bookshop in Chicago. One of the author's golden re-
trievers provided the subject for his children's book
The Strange Disappearance Of Mr. Toast, Viking, 1964.

BREWSTER, Benjamin see ELTING, Mary

BRICK, John 1922-
Born in Newburgh, New York, he graduated from New
York and Columbia Universities. During World War
II, he was in the Air Force. Mr. Brick has been
managing editor of Export Trade Magazine and secre-
tary to the Chairman of the Academic Board of the

United States Military Academy at West Point. He
has been a member of the Putnam County (New York)
Board of Cooperative Educational Services and the
Council of the Authors Guild. The Brick family has
lived in Mahopac, New York. He wrote: Captives Of
The Senecas, Duell, 1964; On The Old Frontier, Putnam, 1967; Yankees On The Run, Duell, 1961. CA-
13/14

BRIDGES, William 1901-
Author, journalist, born in Indiana. He entered the
field of journalism upon graduation from Franklin College (Indiana). At one time Mr. Bridges was associated with American newspapers in France. He has
also been a reporter for the New York Sun and Curator of Publications for the Bronx Zoo. He has traveled to Africa and Panama (accompanied by 10, 000
earthworms for three duck-billed platypuses destined
for the zoo). The author has lived in Pleasantville,
New York. His books for young people include: Zoo
Doctor, Morrow, 1957; Zoo Expeditions, Morrow,
1954; Zoo Pets, Morrow, 1955.

BRIER, Howard Maxwell 1903-
He graduated from the University of Washington in
Seattle where he later taught journalism. He has also
been a state director of a forest fire prevention program in Washington and for many years worked on
various newspapers including: the Everett Herald,
Everett News, Seattle Times, and the Seattle Post-In-
telligencer. His books for young people include: Cin-
der Cyclone, Junior Literary Guild and Random House,
1952; Phantom Backfield, Junior Literary Guild and
Random House, 1948; Short-stop Shadow, Junior Literary Guild and Random House, 1950. CA-13/14, MJA

BRIGGS, Barbara
Author-illustrator. She grew up in California, graduated from the University of California at Berkeley,
and attended the Los Angeles Art School. She moved
to Chicago after her marriage to advertising art director Dex Briggs and did further study at the Chicago
Art Institute. The Briggs family later returned to
California and have lived in the San Francisco Bay
area. She has enjoyed gardening, rock hunting, and
visiting zoos where she sketched the animals. Juvenile books which she has written and illustrated include:

The Biggest, Whitest Egg, Golden Gate Junior Books, 1966; The Otter Twins, McKay, 1959.

BRINDZE, Ruth 1903-
    Born in New York City, she graduated from Columbia University. She has enjoyed sailing and has written books about boats and the sea. She married a lawyer and has lived in Mt. Vernon, New York. Her juvenile books include: The Rise And Fall Of The Seas, Harcourt, 1964; Story Of The Totem Pole, Vanguard, 1951. MJA

BRINK, Carol Ryrie 1895-
    She was born in Moscow, Idaho where her father served as mayor. Both of her parents had died by the time she was eight so she went to live with her aunt and grandmother. Carol Brink's grandmother told many interesting stories about her own youth, and these stories later furnished the inspiration for the author's Caddie Woodlawn (Macmillan, 1935) which was awarded the Newbery Medal in 1936. Other books include: All Over Town, Macmillan, 1939; Andy Buckram's Tin Men (A Junior Literary Guild selection) Viking, 1966; Anything Can Happen On The River!, Macmillan, 1934; Family Grandstand, Viking, 1952; Magical Melons, Macmillan, 1944; Pink Motel, Macmillan, 1959. CA-2, JBA-2

BROCK, Emma Lillian 1886-
    Author-illustrator, born in Fort Shaw, Montana. After graduating from the University of Minnesota she attended the Minneapolis School of Art and the Art Students League in New York. Miss Brock has been on the staff of the Minneapolis and New York Public Libraries. Juvenile books which she wrote and illustrated include: Drusilla, Macmillan, 1937; The Greedy Goat, Knopf, 1931; Mary's Camera, Knopf, 1963; One Little Indian Boy, Knopf, 1950; Pancakes And The Merry-go-round, Knopf, 1960; Too Many Turtles, Knopf, 1951. CA-5/6, JBA-1, JBA-2

BRODERICK, Dorothy M. 1929-
    Children's librarian, editor, and author. Dorothy Broderick has been assistant professor in the School of Library Science at Western Reserve University. Later she was a doctoral candidate at the Columbia University Graduate School of Library Service. She

has been an editor of Top Of The News and has contributed many articles to the School Library Journal.
She wrote: Leete's Island Adventure, Prentice-Hall,
1962; An Introduction To Children's Work In Public
Libraries, Wilson, 1965.   CA-15/16

BRONSON, Lynn see LAMPMAN, Evelyn (Sibley)

BRONSON, Wilfrid Swancourt 1894-
Born in Illinois, he studied at the Chicago Art Institute.   He accompanied scientific expeditions as a staff
artist, and several of his books were results of these
trips.   At one time he served as assistant to mural
painter Ezra Winter, and their assignments included:
the Eastman School of Music in Rochester, New York,
the Chamber of Commerce in Washington, D. C., and
the Cunard Building in New York.   Juvenile titles include: Beetles, Harcourt, 1963; Pinto's Journey,
Messner, 1948; Cats, Harcourt, 1950; Children Of The
Sea, Harcourt, 1940; Coyotes, Harcourt, 1946; Freedom And Plenty: Ours To Save, Harcourt, 1953;
Goats, Harcourt, 1959.   JBA-1, JBA-2

BROOKS, Anita 1914-
Editor, teacher.   She has been a book editor and has
written for the New Yorker magazine.   At one time
the author traveled to Puerto Rico to work on an educational art project.   She also spent a summer in
France where she was associated with Sarah Lawrence
College.   Her juvenile books include: The Picture
Book Of Grains, Day, 1962; The Picture Book Of Timber, Day, 1967.   CA-19/20

BROOKS, Charlotte
Educator, author.   She has served as Supervising Di-
rector of the Department of English in the public
schools of Washington, D. C. and as an English and
Social Studies Supervisor at the Princeton Institute for
Teachers of the Disadvantaged.   Charlotte Brooks has
also been a consultant for the Office of Education and
Professional Relations Representative for the National
Council of Teachers of English.   She edited The Out-
numbered, Delacorte, 1969.

BROWIN, Frances Williams 1898-
Author, copywriter, editor, born in Media, Pennsylvania.   She attended Swarthmore College.   She has

worked for publishing houses, advertising and government agencies, and magazines. In 1953 she was the
recipient of an award from the Freedoms Foundation
for several of her essays. During the winter months
Frances Browin has lived in Philadelphia and during
the summer at Lumberville (on the Delaware River).
She has always enjoyed American history and has read
"particularly old letters, diaries, newspapers, and
other source materials that help to reconstruct the
past. " For children she has written Looking For Orlando, Criterion, 1961.   CA-19/20

BROWN, Bill 1910-   Rosalie (Gertrude) (Moore) 1910-
Husband-wife team; they have lived in California. In
order to obtain background material for their book
The Boy Who Got Mailed (Coward, 1957) Bill Brown
worked in a post office.   Other books created by this
team have also been based on first-hand experiences.
Children have enjoyed their stories in addition to learning factual material.   They wrote: Big Rig, Coward,
1959; The Department Store Ghost, Coward, 1961.
CA-4, CA-5/6

BROWN, Conrad 1922-
Author, ski instructor, born in Oregon. He graduated
from Brown University (Providence, R. I.).   During
World War II, he served as an Army ski trooper and
ambulance driver.   Conrad Brown has worked in Mad
River Glen, Vermont as a ski instructor and in East
Madison, New Hampshire as co-director of a ski
school.   For children he wrote Skiing For Beginners,
Scribner, 1951.

BROWN, Eleanor Frances 1908-
Author, librarian, teacher, born in Spokane, Washing-
ton. She graduated from the University of Washington
at Seattle, taught English in several states, and was
Librarian of the Deschutes County Library in Bend,
Oregon.   Miss Brown has also been a contributor to
the American Horseman and Popular Horseman.   Her
interests have included horses, books, and photography.
Her book A Horse For Peter (Messner, 1950) was
runner-up in the Ford Foundation Award Contest.
Other juvenile titles include: The Colt From Horse
Heaven Hills, Messner, 1956; Mountain Palomino,
Lothrop, 1956.

BROWN, Helen (Evans)   Philip S.
The Browns have lived in Pasadena, California where
both have enjoyed cooking as a hobby.   Helen Evans
Brown's recipes and articles on cooking have been
published in magazines and newspapers.   Mr. Brown
has been a co-owner of a bookstore.   Together Mr.
and Mrs. Brown wrote Boys' Cook Book, Doubleday,
1959.

BROWN, Jeff
Author, editor, producer, born in New York City.   He
has been a contributor to several magazines and has
been on the staff of the New Yorker.   Mr. Brown has
also worked in the film industry in Hollywood both as
an assistant film producer and a story editor.   He and
his family have lived in New York City.   For children
he wrote Flat Stanley, Harper, 1964.

BROWN, Judith Gwyn
Author-illustrator, born in New York City.   She studied
at Parsons School of Design and graduated from New
York University.   Judith Brown has traveled abroad
and once said of London: "its foggy, slightly gloomy
mists . . . the true enchanted place of a fairy tale. "
She has lived in Manhattan.   For young people she
wrote The Happy Voyage (A Junior Literary Guild selection), Macmillan, 1965.

BROWN, Lloyd Arnold   1907-
Cartographer, born in Providence, Rhode Island, graduate of the University of Michigan (Ann Arbor).   He
has been Librarian at the Peabody Institute in Baltimore and has served as curator of maps at the William
L. Clements Library, University of Michigan.   In
addition to books, Mr. Brown has written articles on
maps and surveys concerning American history and
geography.   He has lived in Maryland.   For young
people he wrote Map Making, Little, 1960.   CA-11/12

BROWN, Marcia Joan   1918-
Author, illustrator, librarian, born in Rochester, New
York.   She attended the State College for Teachers at
Albany and studied art at the Woodstock School of
Painting and the New School for Social Research.   One
of her prints is in the permanent collection of the
Library of Congress.   Miss Brown received valuable
experience from her work with children in the New

York Public Library.   Her first picture book was The
Little Carousel, Scribner, 1946.   She was awarded the
Caldecott Medal in 1955 for Charles Perrault's Cinder-
ella (Scribner, 1954) and again in 1962 for . . . Once
A Mouse (Scribner, 1961).   Other books include: Dick
Whittington And His Cat, Scribner, 1950; Felice,
Scribner, 1958; Henry-Fisherman, Scribner, 1949;
Stone Soup, Scribner, 1947; Tamarindo, Scribner,
1960.   MJA

BROWN, Margaret Wise   1910-1952
Her pseudonym is Golden MacDonald.   She was born
in New York City and grew up on Long Island Sound
where her love for animals and the outdoors was
nourished and later was evidenced in her books for
boys and girls.   Miss Brown attended Hollins College
and Columbia University.   In 1947 her book Little
Island (Doubleday, 1946) illustrated by Leonard Weisgard was awarded the Caldecott Medal.   Five years
later at the age of forty-two she died while she was
on a vacation in Nice, France.   She wrote over fifty
books including: A Child's Good Morning, W. R.
Scott, 1952; Christmas In The Barn, Crowell, 1952;
Country Noisy Book, W. R. Scott, 1940; Dead Bird,
W. R. Scott, 1958; The Golden Egg Book, Simon and
Schuster, 1947.   JBA-2

BROWN, Marion Marsh   1908-
Author and teacher, native of Nebraska.   A graduate
of State Teachers College (Peru, Nebraska), she received her M. A. degree from the University of Nebraska at Lincoln and did further study at the University of Minnesota in Minneapolis.   She began to write
at the age of six when she was awarded a book for a
letter she sent to a newspaper.   Mrs. Brown has
taught night school at the University of Omaha and has
served as president of the Omaha chapter of the
American Association of University Women.   Her books
for young people include: Swamp Fox, Westminster,
1950; Young Nathan, Junior Literary Guild and Westminster, 1949.   With Ruth Crone she wrote The Silent
Storm (A Junior Literary Guild selection), Abingdon,
1963.   CA-4

BROWN, Myra Berry   1918-
She has lived in Los Angeles where she has spoken
before PTA meetings and library groups.   Mrs. Brown

has also written book reviews for the Los Angeles
Times. Her husband Ned Brown has been a literary
agent. Her juvenile books include: My Daddy's Visit-
ing Our School Today, Watts, 1961; Pip Camps Out
(A Junior Literary Guild selection), Golden Gate, 1966.
CA-4

BROWN, Pamela Beatrice 1924-
She was born in Colchester, Essex, England. In addition to writing, she has been interested in the theater
and has acted under the name of Mela Brown. She
also has produced plays on the B. B. C. Children's
Television. Pamela Brown has lived in London, Kent,
and on Majorca. Her books include: As Far As
Singapore, Brockhampton Press, 1959; Back-Stage
Portrait, Nelson, 1958; The Bridesmaids, McKay,
1956; Louisa, Crowell, 1957; Understudy, Nelson, 1959.
CA-13/14

BROWN, Paul 1893-
Author-illustrator, born in Mapleton, Minnesota. He
attended school in New York City. Well-known for
his love and illustrations of horses, Paul Brown has
been a contributor to many magazines. The Brown
family has lived on Long Island in Garden City. Juvenile books which he has written and illustrated include:
Crazy Quilt, Scribner, 1934; Daffy Taffy, Scribner,
1955; No Trouble At All, Scribner, 1940; Piper's Pony,
Scribner, 1935; Silver Heels, Scribner, 1951; Your
Pony's Trek Around The World, Scribner, 1956.
JBA-2

BROWN, Regina Margaret
She attended the Theatre Guild School and studied under many fine directors including Reuben Mamoulian.
Regina Brown has been a storyteller with the New
York Public Library, puppeteer, and director of a
television play which she wrote. She has also been
the director of a radio program and children's theatre.
For boys and girls she wrote Little Brother, Obolensky, 1962.

BROWN, Vinson 1912-
Naturalist, camp counselor, rancher, born in Reno,
Nevada. He graduated from the University of Califor-
nia and obtained his master's degree from Stanford
University in Palo Alto. Following service in the

United States Army, he organized the Naturegraph Com-
pany which made nature records and brochures for
schools and scouts. In addition to writing on the eco-
logy of the West, he has farmed in Santa Clara County,
California. Juvenile contributions include: How To
Explore The Secret Worlds Of Nature, Little, 1962;
How To Make A Home Nature Museum, Little, 1954;
How To Make A Miniature Zoo, Little, 1957; How To
Understand Animal Talk (A Junior Literary Guild se-
lection), Little, 1958.   CA-4

BROWN, William (Louis) see BROWN, Bill

BRUNHOFF, Jean de 1899-1937
French painter and writer. Jean de Brunhoff created
the famous elephant named Babar from stories he and
his wife told to their children. These same stories
were later translated into several languages. He died
at the age of thirty-eight before he could complete his
last two books. His son, author-illustrator Laurent
de Brunhoff, continued writing the Babar stories.
Juvenile books which Jean de Brunhoff wrote and illustrated include: Babar And Father Christmas (tr. by
Merle Haas), Random House, 1949; Babar The King
(tr. by Merle Haas), Random, c1935; . . . The Story
Of Babar, The Little Elephant (tr. by Merle Haas),
H. Smith and R. Haas, 1933.

BRUNHOFF, Laurent de 1925-
French author and painter, son of the creator of the
famed Babar books for boys and girls. He has been
interested in painting since boyhood and later had a
studio in the Montparnasse district of Paris. After
the death of his father, he continued to create the
popular Babar stories. Juvenile titles include: Anatole And His Donkey (tr. by Richard Howard), Macmillan, 1963; Babar And The Professor (tr. by Merle
Haas), Random House, 1957; Babar's Castle (tr. by
Merle Haas), Random House, 1962; Babar Comes To
America (tr. by M. Jean Craig), Random House, 1965;
Captain Serafina, World, 1963.   MJA

BRUSTLEIN, Janice Tworkov
Her pseudonym is Janice. She married author and
illustrator Daniel Brustlein. Together they created
the charming story of the French cat Minette (story
by Janice; pictures by Alain, McGraw, 1959). She

and her husband have lived in New Jersey and France.
Juvenile titles include: Angélique, McGraw, 1960;
Little Bear's Christmas, Lothrop, 1964.   CA-9/10

BRYAN, Joseph 1904-
Author, newspaperman, born in Richmond, Virginia.
He studied at Princeton University. Mr. Bryan has
worked on various magazines and newspapers and was
an associate editor of the Saturday Evening Post. At
one time he spent a month each year traveling with
the circus and contributed articles about his experiences to the Saturday Evening Post, Collier's, and
Life magazines. The author has been a member of
United States Army Reserve, the Naval Reserve, and
the Air Force Reserve. For young people he wrote
World's Greatest Showman, Random House, 1956.

BRYANT, Gertrude Thomson
She was born in East Orange, New Jersey and graduated from Mt. Holyoke College. Gertrude Bryant
has worked in the Office of War Information and in
several publishing companies. Her husband has taught
at Cornell University, and they have lived in Ithaca,
New York. She wrote Two Is Company, Lippincott,
1962.

BUCHANAN, William 1930-
Actor, teacher, author. He studied at Northwestern
University and received his master's degree from the
University of California at Los Angeles. He has been
known to those who have attended the theater as Wil-
liam Buck. He once was a member of a road com-
pany's production of "Inherit The Wind." William
Buchanan has lived in California. He wrote Doctor
Anger's Island, Abelard, 1961.   CA-4

BUCK, Margaret Waring 1910-
Artist, author, naturalist, born in Brooklyn. She grew
up in Tuckahoe, Connecticut and later made her home
in Mystic, Connecticut. Margaret Buck studied at the
Art Students League in New York. She has made
pottery and designed fabrics (during the summer months)
at the art colony in Rockport, Massachusetts. She has
also been recognized as a noted naturalist. Juvenile
titles include: Along The Seashore, Abingdon, 1964;
In Woods And Fields, Abingdon, 1950.   CA-5/6

BUCK, Pearl (Sydenstricker) 1892-
Distinguished novelist, born in Hillsboro, West Virginia, the daughter of missionaries. When she was
quite young, her parents were stationed in China where
they lived for many years. She returned to America
in order to attend Randolph-Macon College and Cornell
University where she obtained a master's degree.
Pearl Buck has been the recipient of many honors including the Pulitzer Prize and the Nobel Prize for
Literature. She also was instrumental in founding
"Welcome House," an organization that finds homes
for Asian-American children. Her husband was the
late Richard J. Walsh, and she has lived in Pennsyl-
vania. Her books for young people include: The
Beech Tree, Day, 1955; Big Wave, Day, 1948; The
Christmas Ghost, Day, 1960; Christmas Miniature,
Day, 1957.   CA-2

BUCK, William Ray see BUCHANAN, William

BUDD, Lillian (Peterson) 1897-
Born in Chicago, Illinois, she lived in different states
and countries as a Navy wife before returning to Illinois to live. At one time she was a secretary to a
fire chief and during World War II, she served as
Chief Clerk of the Selective Service System. The
author has enjoyed antique collecting and gardening as
hobbies. Mrs. Budd has written for both adults and
children. Her books for young people include: Calico
Row, Whitman, 1965; Larry, McKay, 1966; One Heart,
One Way, McKay, 1964; People On Long Ago Street,
Rand, 1964; Tekla's Easter, Rand, 1962.   CA-2

BUEHR, Walter Franklin 1897-
Illustrator, designer, born in Chicago, Illinois. Mr.
Buehr studied art in New York, Philadelphia, and
Europe. In addition to writing, he has also been a
time-and-study man in an automobile plant. He has
spent many summers on his 43-foot cutter and has
lived in Connecticut in a house of his own design.
Juvenile titles include: The Birth Of A Liner, Little,
1961; Bread, Morrow, 1959; Cargoes In The Sky, Putnam, 1958; Chivalry And The Mailed Knight, Putnam,
1963; The Crusaders, Putnam, 1959; The First Book
Of Machines, Watts, 1962; Genie And The Word, Putnam, 1959; Heraldry, Putnam, 1964.   CA-5/6

BUELL, Ellen Lewis
She was born in Marietta, Ohio and graduated from
Marietta College. Prior to her association with the
New York Times, she worked in a bookstore in Bos-
ton. Ellen Lewis Buell was editor of the Children's
Books Department of the New York Times Book Review
and has taught a course in the writing of juvenile liter-
ature at Columbia University. She has also taught a
course in children's literature at the University of
Chattanooga during the summer. She married sculptor
Harold Cash and has lived in Wildwood, Georgia. She
edited Read Me A Poem, Grosset, 1965.

BUFANO, Remo 1894-1948
Author and puppeteer. Remo Bufano endeavored to
create a deep interest in the magic world of puppets
through his books. He introduced English-speaking
puppets to America. Prior to his death in an airplane
accident, many of Mr. Bufano's plays had been produced in Hollywood and New York. He wrote Book Of
Puppetry, Macmillan, 1950.

BUFF, Conrad 1886-   Mary (Marsh) 1890-
Artist and author, husband-wife team. Conrad Buff
came from Switzerland where he attended school before
coming to the United States in 1904. He has enjoyed
painting western landscapes. His paintings and lithographs can be found in the permanent collections of
many museums. Mary Marsh Buff grew up in Ohio
and graduated from Bethany College in Kansas. After
teaching art in Montana and Idaho, she became assistant art curator of the Los Angeles Museum where she
met her husband. Mr. and Mrs. Buff's juvenile books
include: Big Tree, Viking, 1946; Dancing Cloud, Viking, 1957; Dash And Dart, Viking, 1942; Elf Owl (A
Junior Literary Guild selection), Viking, 1958; Magic
Maize, Houghton, 1953.   JBA-2

BUGBEE, Emma
Born in Shippensburg, Pennsylvania, she lived in
Methuen, Massachusetts and studied at Barnard College, Columbia University. When she was a senior
in college, she wrote about campus activities for the
New York Tribune where she later became a member
of the staff. Although Emma Bugbee has reported on
a variety of subjects, her specialty has been writing
about women in politics which led to an assignment in

1933 to cover Mrs. Franklin D. Roosevelt. Her book
for young people was Peggy Goes Overseas, Dodd,
1945.

BULLA, Clyde Robert 1914-
Author and newspaperman, born on a farm in Missouri
near King City.   He has lived in Los Angeles where
he has devoted much of his time to the composition of
songs and the writing of books for boys and girls.   At
one time Mr. Bulla was a newspaper columnist and a
linotype operator.   His travels have taken him to
Europe, Hawaii, and Mexico.   The 1955 Boys' Club of
America Gold Medal was awarded to him for Squanto,
Friend Of The White Men, Crowell, 1954.   Other juvenile titles include: Down The Mississippi, Crowell,
1954; Eagle Feather, Crowell, 1953; Ghost Town Treasure, Crowell, 1957; More Stories Of Favorite Operas,
Crowell, 1965; Old Charlie, Crowell, 1957; Pirate's
Promise, Crowell, 1958; Viking Adventure, Crowell,
1963; White Sails To China, Crowell, 1955.   CA-7/8,
MJA

BULLOCK, L. G.
It has been said that a person was a true "Londoner"
("Cockney") if born within the sound of Bow Bells, and
this author has met the qualifications.   He attended
Alleyn's School, Dulwich, and served in both world
wars.   Mr. Bullock has been associated with the Port
of London.   In 1948 he received the O. B. E.   He has
lived in Kent.   He wrote The Children's Book Of London, Warne, 1960.

BUNCE, William Harvey
Illustrator, author, born in Stillwater, New York.   He
studied at Columbia University and the New York
School of Design.   He was supervising draftsman and
artist on the TVA-WPA archeological survey of Chick-
amauga Basin.   He wrote War Belts Of Pontiac, Dutton, 1943.

BUNTAIN, Ruth Jaeger
Author and teacher, born in Chicago, Illinois.   She
later made her home in Wasco, California.   Ruth Buntain has taught in the elementary grades, and educational journals have published her articles on teaching.
For children she wrote The Birthday Story, Holiday,
1953.

BURCH, Gladys 1899-
    She was closely associated with books about music
    through her position as head of the book department of
    G. Schirmer in New York. Gladys Burch also pos-
    sessed a great reservoir of knowledge concerning music
    and musicians. With John Wolcott she wrote A Child's
    Book Of Famous Composers, Barnes, 1939.

BURCH, Robert Joseph 1925-
    He was born in Georgia. During World War II, he
    served in the armed forces in Australia and New
    Guinea. Following the war, he worked in Japan and
    also visited Africa and Europe. After he became in-
    terested in writing for boys and girls, he was the re-
    cipient of a fellowship in children's literature at the
    Bread Loaf Writers' Conference, Vermont. His juve-
    nile books include: D. J. 's Worst Enemy, Viking,
    1965; A Funny Place To Live (A Junior Literary Guild
    selection), Viking, 1962; Queenie Peavy, Viking, 1966.
    CA-5/6

BURCHARD, Peter Duncan 1921-
    He studied at the Philadelphia Museum School of Art.
    During World War II, Mr. Burchard attended radio
    school in New Orleans and later served as a radio
    operator on a troop transport. He has lived in New
    York with his wife and three children. He illustrated
    Big Rig by Bill and Rosalie Brown, Coward, 1959 and
    wrote and illustrated: The Carol Moran, Macmillan,
    1958; Chito, Coward, 1969.   CA-5/6

BURGESS, Thornton Waldo 1874-1965
    He was the creator of Jimmy Skunk, Reddy Fox, and
    other inhabitants of the forest known to many parents,
    grandparents, and children. His first book was Old
    Mother West Wind (Little, 1960) which was written in
    1910. Mr. Burgess was awarded an honorary degree
    from Northwestern University. He lectured, had a
    radio program, and always loved the out-of-doors.
    He lived in Massachusetts and died at the age of nine-
    ty-one. Juvenile titles include: Along Laughing Brook,
    Little, 1949; Mother West Wind's Children, Little,
    1962.   JBA-1, JBA-2

BURGOYNE, Leon E. 1916-
    A graduate of Western Michigan College, he received
    his M. A. degree in Physical Education from the Uni-

versity of Michigan at Ann Arbor. He has coached
the basketball team of St. Joseph High School in Mich-
igan which won the state championship. During World
War II, Mr. Burgoyne served with the Navy in the
South Pacific. His books for young people include:
Jack Davis, Forward, Winston, 1953; State Champs,
Winston, 1951.

BURKE, Lynn
Swimmer, author, she attended St. John's University
in New York. When she was eighteen, she retired
from amateur swimming; however, she had entered
her first swimming meet at the age of four. Lynn
Burke has been the holder of five world records and
won two Gold Medals in the 1960 Olympic Games.
With Don Smith she wrote The Young Sportsman's Guide
To Swimming, Nelson, 1962.

BURLAND, Brian Berkeley 1931-
He was born in Bermuda and received his education in
England. He has made his home in Essex, Connecticut. The author used his own children's names (Anne,
Susan, and William) when he wrote his first juvenile
book St. Nicholas And The Tub, Holiday, 1964. CA-
15/16

BURLAND, Cottie Arthur 1905-
Author, photographer, art critic, born in London. He
has written both for adults and children. He has been
a member of the Craftsman Potters' Association, a
Fellow of the Royal Anthropological Institute (London),
and a member of the British Museum staff. C. A.
Burland has been a contributor to many European and
American journals and has written art criticism for
the London Arts Review. The Burland family has resided near Hampton Court in Molesey, England. Juvenile titles include: Adventuring In Archaeology, Warne,
1963; Finding Out About The Incas, Lothrop, 1962.
CA-5/6

BURNETT, Constance (Buel) 1893-
Her father was Associate Editor of the Century Maga-
zine (Clarence Clough Buel), and her husband was
Vivian Burnett, the son of author Frances Hodgson
Burnett. Mrs. Burnett studied at the Friends Seminary,
Brearley School (New York City), and the Kent Place
School (Summit, New Jersey). She has lived on Long

Island. Her books for young people include: Captain
John Ericsson: Father Of The "Monitor," Vanguard,
1960; Lucretia Mott, Bobbs, 1951.   CA-5/6

BURNETT, Frances (Hodgson) 1849-1924
Born in Manchester, England, she came to America
at an early age and lived in Tennessee. She became
an American citizen and later lived on Long Island and
Bermuda. Her husband was Dr. Swan M. Burnett.
Mrs. Burnett returned often to England and lived at
Maytham Hall in Kent for over ten years. It was at
Maytham Hall that the author was inspired to write
her most "artistic" book The Secret Garden (Stokes,
1909). Other juvenile books include: Little Lord
Fauntleroy, Scribner, 1886; A Little Princess (pictures
by Tasha Tudor), Lippincott, 1963; The Lost Prince,
Century, 1915; Sara Crewe, Scribner, 1907.   JBA-1

BURNFORD, Sheila 1918-
Her pseudonym is Philip Cochrane Every. She was
born in Scotland, studied at St. Georges and Harrogate College, and married a pediatrician. During the
war she served in Royal Naval Hospitals and later was
an ambulance driver. She has enjoyed flying (she held
a pilot's license) and shooting (she has been known as
a "keen shot"). Her work has appeared in Blackwoods,
Canadian Poetry, Glasgow Herald, and Punch. Her
first book was The Incredible Journey, Little, 1961.
CA-2

BURT, Nathaniel 1913-
This author had the distinction of being born in a log
cabin in Wyoming. His first book was written when
he was at Princeton. His work has been published in
many magazines. He has also written books of fiction,
nonfiction, and verse. For boys and girls he wrote
War Cry Of The West, Holt, 1964.   CA-19/20

BURT, Olive (Woolley) 1894-
Author, historian, teacher. When she was eight-years-
old, some of her verses appeared in the San Francisco
Examiner. She graduated from the University of Utah
at Salt Lake City. At one time she taught in the
schools of Utah and Wyoming. Miss Burt has been an
editor with the Salt Lake Tribune and the Deseret
News. Her juvenile books include: Born To Teach,
Messner, 1967; Brigham Young, Messner, 1956; First

Woman Editor: Sarah J. Hale, Messner, 1960; I Am
An American, Day, 1964; Luther Burbank, Boy Wizard,
Bobbs, 1948; Peter Turns Sheepman, Holt, 1952.
CA-7/8

BURTON, Elizabeth
She was born in Egypt, grew up in Canada, and later
lived in England. Elizabeth Burton has always been
interested in history. She has worked in various fields
which have included: journalism, radio, and advertising. She wrote Here Is England (A Junior Literary
Guild selection), Ariel, 1965.

BURTON, Katherine (Kurz) 1890-
She once was an associate editor of McCall's and Redbook magazines. She also served as woman's editor
of the Sign. Katherine Burton was awarded an honorary degree of Doctor of Letters in 1955 from St. Mary
of the Springs College in Columbus, Ohio. She also
was the recipient of the Christopher Award in 1959.
For young people she wrote The Door Of Hope, Hawthorn, 1963.

BURTON, Virginia Lee 1909-1968
Born in Newton Centre, Massachusetts, she studied
art at the California School of Fine Arts and ballet in
San Francisco. Her drawings have appeared in the
Boston Transcript where she was a member of the
staff for two years. She studied drawing under sculp-
tor George Demetrios whom she later married. They
have lived in Folly Cove, Gloucester, Massachusetts.
Her book The Little House (Houghton, 1942) was a-
warded the Caldecott Medal in 1943. Juvenile titles
include: Calico, The Wonder Horse, Houghton, 1950;
Choo Choo, Houghton, 1937; Katy And The Big Snow,
Houghton, 1943; Life Story, Houghton, 1962; Maybelle,
The Cable Car, Houghton, 1952; Mike Mulligan And
His Steam Shovel, Houghton, 1939.   CA-13/14, JBA-2

BUSBY, Edith
Author, librarian, teacher, born in Terre Haute, In-
diana. She attended Baylor University in Waco, Texas
and studied at the Juilliard School of Music in New
York. After working one summer in the New York
Public Library she decided to become a librarian.
Mrs. Busby has been a children's librarian in the New
York Public Library and a Supervisor of Book Order-

ing in the Brooklyn Public Library.   She has also
taught courses in library science at both Pratt Institute and Columbia University.   Her books for young
people include: Behind The Scenes At The Library,
Dodd, 1960; What Does A Librarian Do?, Dodd, 1963.

BUSH-BROWN, Louise
She has been a member of the faculty of George Peabody College in Nashville, Tennessee and has worked
in Florida as a State Specialist associated with the
U. S. Agricultural Extension Service.   For many years
she was Director of the Pennsylvania School of Horticulture for Women.   She founded (1953) Philadelphia's
Neighborhood Garden Association which brought much
beauty to many unattractive areas of the city.   Mrs.
Bush-Brown has been the recipient of many awards
which have been given by various garden clubs.   She
wrote Young America's Garden Book, Scribner, 1962.

BUSONI, Rafaello 1900-
Artist, author, born in Berlin, Germany.   After leaving school he concentrated on painting and had his
first exhibition in Switzerland at the age of seventeen.
He spent several years in Spain gathering material on
the life of Miguel Cervantes.   Mr. Busoni's father
also had been interested in Cervantes and once owned
fifty-six different editions of Don Quixote.   Juvenile
titles include: Australia, Holiday, 1942; Italy, Holiday,
1950; The Man Who Was Don Quixote, Prentice-Hall,
1958; Mexico And The Inca Lands, Holiday, 1942;
Somi Builds A Church, Viking, 1943; Stanley's Africa,
Viking, 1944.   JBA-2

BUTLER, Beverly Kathleen 1932-
Author and teacher, born in Fond du Lac, Wisconsin.
She graduated from Mount Mary College in Milwaukee
and received her master's degree from Marquette University.   Miss Butler has lived in Milwaukee with her
family and guide dog Heidi.   Besides a writing career
she has also taught courses in writing at Mount Mary
College.   Beverly Butler has received several literary
awards including the Clara Ingram Judson Award for
her children's book Light A Single Candle, Dodd, 1962.
Other juvenile titles include: Feather In The Wind,
Dodd, 1965; Song Of The Voyageur, Dodd, 1955.   CA-2

BUTLER, Hal
  Author and editor. He was born in St. Louis, Missouri and grew up in Detroit, Michigan where he has
  continued to make his home. He took courses in
  creative writing and business after graduation from
  high school. His stories have been published in such
  magazines as Coronet, Sport, and Pageant. He has
  also been an associate editor of a national travel
  magazine Ford Times (published by the Ford Motor
  Co.). He has traveled to Hawaii, the Caribbean,
  Europe, and throughout the United States. For young
  people he wrote The Harmon Killebrew Story, Messner, 1966.

BUTTERS, Dorothy Gilman 1923-
  She was born in New Brunswick, New Jersey. Following her marriage to teacher Edgar A. Butters, Jr.,
  she lived in Lake Hiawatha, New Jersey. At an early
  age the author published a monthly magazine which sold
  at five cents a copy. Her association with the Pennsylvania Academy of the Fine Arts resulted in her receiving a Cresson Traveling Scholarship. Several of
  her books have been Junior Literary Guild selections
  and include: Ten Leagues To Boston Town, Macrae
  Smith, 1962; Witch's Silver, Macrae Smith, 1959.
  CA-4

BYARS, Betsy (Cromer)
  She grew up in Charlotte, North Carolina and graduated
  from Queens College at Charlotte. Her articles have
  been printed in Look and the Saturday Evening Post.
  Mrs. Byars and her family have made their home in
  Morgantown, West Virginia. For children she wrote
  Clementine, Houghton, 1962.

C

CAFFREY, Nancy
  Born in Stamford, Connecticut, she later lived in New
  Canaan. Nancy Caffrey, a skilled equestrienne, has
  been interested in horses for some time. She began
  riding at the age of five and began teaching horsemanship when she was fifteen. She has combined this interest with writing and was a reporter for the Chronicle of Middleburg, Virginia. For young people she
  wrote Horse Haven, Dutton, 1955.

CALDWELL, John Cope 1913-
Born in the Orient, he received his education there
before coming to the United States in order to attend
college.   During World War II, he served fifteen
months behind Japanese lines on the coast of China.
He later was associated with the United States Information Service.   An extensive traveler, his authoritative books on other countries include: Let's Visit
Argentina, Day, 1961; Let's Visit Brazil, Day, 1961;
Let's Visit Ceylon, Day, 1960; Let's Visit China, Day,
1959; Let's Visit Japan, Day, 1959; Let's Visit The
South Pacific, Day, 1963.

CALHOUN, Mary Huiskamp 1926-
Author and reporter, born in Keokuk, Iowa.   After receiving a degree in journalism from Iowa State University she was a newspaper reporter.   She also contri-
buted stories to various magazines for children.   The
author has lived in Rangely, Colorado with her hus-
band, the Reverend Leon Wilkins.   Her books for
young people include: Cowboy Cal And The Outlaw,
Morrow, 1961; Depend On Katie John, Harper, 1961;
High Wind For Kansas, Morrow, 1965; Honestly, Katie
John!, Harper, 1963; Houn' Dog, Morrow, 1959; The
House Of Thirty Cats, Harper, 1965; The Hungry
Leprechaun, Morrow, 1962; Katie John, Harper, 1960;
The Runaway Brownie, Morrow, 1967; Wobble The
Witch Cat, Morrow, 1958.   CA-5/6

CALLAHAN, Claire Wallis 1890-
Her pseudonym is Nancy Hartwell.   This author and
columnist has lived in a house which was built in 1717
in Pottstown, Pennsylvania.   She has written magazine
stories and at one time was the editor of a woman's
page on a newspaper.   Claire Callahan has enjoyed
music and antiques as her hobbies.   Her juvenile books
include: My Little Sister, Holt, 1957; Who Was
Sylvia?, Junior Literary Guild and Holt, 1952.   CA-
7/8

CALLAHAN, Dorothy
Dietician, author, teacher.   She has been Clinic Dieti-
tian at the Cornell Medical Center of New York Hos-
pital and Research Dietitian at Massachusetts General
Hospital.   She also was Nutritionist for the Visiting
Nurse Association in Boston and has been Director of
Cafeterias for the schools of Milton, Massachusetts.

With Alma Smith Payne she wrote Great Nutrition Puzzle, Scribner, 1956.   In 1959 Dorothy Callahan and Alma Smith Payne revised Young America's Cook Book, Scribner, 1959.

CALVERT, James
Submarine officer and writer.   He has made his home in Mystic, Connecticut.   The author has written for both adults and children.   For adults he wrote about his two trips to the North Pole as Commanding Officer of the nuclear submarine, "USS Skate."   Captain Calvert has been Commander of Submarine Division 102 (our country's nuclear submarines in the Atlantic Fleet).   For young people he wrote A Promise To Our Country, McGraw, 1961.

CAMERON, Eleanor (Butler) 1912-
Born in Canada, she later made her home in Los Angeles.   She attended the University of California and Art Center School in Los Angeles.   Eleanor Cameron has worked in research for an advertising agency in addition to her career as a writer.   Many of her books were Junior Literary Guild selections and include: Mr. Bass's Planetoid, Little, 1958; The Terrible Churnadryne, Little, 1959.   She also wrote: The Beast With The Magical Horn, Little, 1963; A Mystery For Mr. Bass, Little, 1960.   CA-4

CAMERON, Polly 1928-
Author, sculptor, painter.   Born in Walnut Creek, California, she studied at Phoenix College and the University of California at Santa Barbara.   Following college she lived in Arizona where she worked in advertising.   Polly Cameron spent several years abroad in Mallorca, French Morocco, and Paris.   She later made her home in Palisades, New York.   The books which she wrote and illustrated include: Boy Who Drew Birds, Coward-McCann, 1959; The Cat Who Couldn't Purr, Coward-McCann, 1957; A Child's Book Of Nonsense, Coward-McCann, 1960; Dog Who Grew Too Much (A Junior Literary Guild selection), Coward-McCann, 1958; The 2 Ton Canary & Other Nonsense Riddles, Coward-McCann, 1965.   CA-17/18

CAMPBELL, Bruce   see EPSTEIN, Samuel

CAMPBELL, Elizabeth A.
   Author and librarian. Mrs. Campbell has worked in
   Norfolk, Virginia as a children's librarian. The lack
   of information about American coins for boys and girls
   resulted in the author writing Nails To Nickels, Little,
   1960. She also wrote Fins And Tails, Little, 1963.

CAMPBELL, Rosemae Wells 1909-
   Librarian and author, a graduate of Elmira College
   and the Brooklyn Public Library Training School. Her
   experience as a librarian helped her when she wrote
   the story of a bookmobile called Books And Beaux
   (Westminster, 1958). Mrs. Campbell has made her
   home in Colorado Springs and has enjoyed gardening,
   photography, and square dancing as hobbies. Her
   books for children include: Drag Doll, Funk, 1962;
   Split Rock Mystery, Westminster, 1960.   CA-13/14

CAMPBELL, Wanda Jay
   Author and newspaperwoman, born in Trent, Texas.
   She graduated from the University of Texas at Austin
   and later attended Colorado Woman's College in Denver.   At one time the author worked on a newspaper
   as a reporter and woman's page editor.   Mrs. Campbell has resided in Austin and has used her personal
   knowledge of Texas in the writing of her books.   Juvenile titles include: The Museum Mystery, Dutton,
   1957; The Mystery Of McClellan Creek, Dutton, 1958;
   Ten Cousins, Dutton, 1963.

CAMPION, Nardi Reeder 1917-
   Born in Honolulu, Hawaii, graduate of Wellesley Col-
   lege, she is the sister of Colonel Red Reeder and
   collaborated with him to write The West Point Story
   (Random House, 1956). Her articles have appeared
   in Collier's, Sports Illustrated, and the New York
   Times Magazine. Mrs. Campion has lived in Bronx-
   ville, New York. She wrote Patrick Henry, Firebrand
   Of The Revolution (A Junior Literary Guild selection),
   Little, 1961.   CA-4

CANDY, Robert 1920-
   Author-illustrator, born in Milton, Massachusetts.
   Prior to attending art classes at the Massachusetts
   School of Art and the Rhode Island School of Design,
   Mr. Candy had studied architecture and engineering at
   the Massachusetts Institute of Technology. During

World War II, he served as a pilot in the Aleutians
and Burma. The author has always enjoyed nature,
but it was due to his son's avid interest in it that led
him to write and illustrate Nature Notebook, Houghton,
1953.

CANNAM, Peggie 1925-
British author and nurse. She grew up in Gloucester,
England and has made her home in Jersey, Channel
Islands (in the English Channel). She has worked in
a children's hospital as a nurse and for three years
served in the Women's Land Army. Miss Cannam's
interests have included travel and horses. Her first
children's book to be published in the United States
was Black Fury, Whittlesey, 1956. CA-13/14

CARDEN, Priscilla
She was born in Boston and attended school at Thayer-
lands, South Braintree. Mrs. Carden graduated from
the University of Chicago. In addition to writing books
for young people she has been a children's librarian.
Her home has been in Riverside, Connecticut. She
wrote Young Brave Algonquin, Little, 1956.

CARDOZO, Lois (Steinmetz) see DUNCAN, Lois

CARLSON, Bernice Wells 1910-
She was born in Clare, Michigan and grew up in Buffalo, New York and Milwaukee, Wisconsin. She graduated from Ripon College in Ripon, Wisconsin and
later married Dr. Carl W. Carlson. Both she and
her husband have worked in the Raritan Valley Unit of
the New Jersey Association for Retarded Children.
For young people she wrote: Act It Out, Abingdon,
1956; Do It Yourself!, Abingdon, 1952; Fun For One -
Or Two, Abingdon, 1954; Junior Party Book, Abingdon,
1948; Listen! And Help Tell The Story, Abingdon, 1965;
Make It And Use It, Abingdon, 1958; You Know What?
I Like Animals, Abingdon, 1967. CA-5/6

CARLSON, Esther Elisabeth 1920-
She was born and raised in Belmont, Massachusetts
and attended Chandler School for Women. She has
been employed in the Probation Office at the Cambridge
Courthouse and has served as secretary to the Belmont
Superintendent of Schools. Her interests have been
folk and square dancing and travel (including a visit to

her parents' native land, Sweden). Esther Carlson's
books include: Milestone, Junior Literary Guild and
Abelard, 1952; Sixes And Sevens (A Junior Literary
Guild selection), Holt, 1960.   CA-5/6

CARLSON, Natalie (Savage) 1906-
She was born in Winchester, Virginia and grew up on
a farm in Maryland. After her marriage to a naval
officer, she lived in many places including Paris
where her husband served with the United States European Command. When her husband Rear Admiral
Daniel Carlson retired from the Navy, she lived in
Newport, Rhode Island. Mrs. Carlson has enjoyed
collecting old French books and "trying to translate
them" as a hobby. She has been the recipient of
several awards including the New York Herald Tribune
Spring Book Festival Prize Book Award in 1955 for
Wings Against The Wind (Harper, 1955). In 1959 The
Family Under The Bridge (Harper, 1958), was a
runner-up for the Newbery Award. Other juvenile
titles include: Carnival In Paris, Harper, 1962;
Sailor's Choice, Harper, 1966. CA-4, MJA

CARMER, Carl Lamson 1893-
Poet, author, editor, teacher, born in Cortland, New
York. He graduated from Hamilton College in Clinton,
New York and received his master's degree from Har-
vard University. He has taught in various colleges
and universities including: Hamilton, Rochester, Syra-
cuse, and Alabama. This distinguished American
folklorist has written many books about his native state
New York. He has lived in Irvington-on-Hudson, New
York with his wife Elizabeth Black Carmer. She il-
lustrated his books: Eagle In The Wind, Aladdin, 1948;
A Flag For The Fort, Messner, 1952. His other
titles include: Henry Hudson, Captain Of Ice-Bound
Seas, Garrard, 1960; The Hudson River, Holt, 1962;
Pets At The White House, Dutton, 1959. CA-7/8

CARMER, Elizabeth (Black) 1904-
Artist and author. She was born in New Orleans,
Louisiana and graduated from Newcomb College where
she studied art. She married author Carl Carmer,
and they have lived in New York in Irvington-on-Hudson. Mrs. Carmer has been a contributor to Theatre
Arts Monthly and Harper's Bazaar. Some of her work
has been included in Irwin Kerlin's collection of chil-

dren's book illustrations. She has also illustrated
several of her husband's books. With Carl Carmer
she wrote The Susquehanna From N. Y. To Chesapeake,
Garrard, 1964.

CARNAHAN, Marjorie R.
Teacher and author.   She attended the Universities of
Kansas and Tulsa. She has been Director of Christian
Education in New Jersey and Pennsylvania and has
worked in St. Louis with the First Presbyterian Church.
At one time Marjorie Carnahan directed church camps,
worked with the Y. W. C. A. , and was a teacher in
mission schools. She collaborated with Dorothy Loa
McFadden to write Which Way, Judy?, Dodd, 1958.

CARONA, Philip Ben 1925-
Author and school principal, Philip Carona had his
first article published (by the Texas Academy of Science) while attending college.   He has contributed to
such magazines as the Instructor and the Texas Outlook.   Mr. Carona has been a grade school principal
in Dickinson, Texas. For young people he wrote:
Things That Measure, Prentice, 1962; The True Book
Of Chemistry, Childrens Press, 1962.   CA-4

CARPENTER, Frances 1890-
She was born in Washington, D. C. , and she has con-
tinued to make her home there.   A graduate of Smith
College, she later served on the college's board of
trustees.   She married diplomat W. Chapin Huntington.
Her juvenile books include: Holiday In Washington,
Knopf, 1958; The Mouse Palace, McGraw, 1964.   CA-
5/6, MJA

CARR, Harriett Helen 1899-
Author, newspaperwoman, born in Ann Arbor, Michi-
gan. She spent her early childhood in North Dakota
but returned to Michigan to complete her education.
Harriett Carr has been a news correspondent and an
assistant director of the Field Service Department of
Scholastic Magazines.   She has lived in New York City.
Juvenile books include: Borghild Of Brooklyn (A Junior
Literary Guild selection), Ariel, 1955; Confidential
Secretary, Macmillan, 1958.   CA-9/10, MJA

CARR, Mary Jane 1899-
She was born in Portland, Oregon and attended St.

Mary's College which is now called Marylhurst.   Miss
Carr has been a newspaperwoman and at one time
worked on the Portland Sunday Oregonian.   Actual dis-
like of history at an early age resulted in the author's
statement: "I liked to write, even in those young days,
and I dreamed of writing books, but I had not the
faintest idea that I should turn to that most distasteful,
difficult subject, history for material for my books. "
Juvenile titles include: Children Of The Covered Wagon, Crowell, 1943; Young Mac Of Fort Vancouver,
Crowell, 1940.   CA-9/10, JBA-2

CARROLL, Curt see BISHOP, Curtis Kent

CARROLL, Lewis see DODGSON, Charles Lutwidge

CARSON, John F. 1920-
Born in Indianapolis, Indiana, he graduated from Butler University, and received his master's degree from
Indiana University.   Mr. Carson has been a biologist,
a staff member of the Indianapolis Children's Museum,
and principal of a high school at North Judson, Indiana.
He has also served as principal of a school in Taipei,
Taiwan.   His juvenile books include: Boys Who Van-
ished (A Junior Literary Guild selection), Duell, 1959;
The Coach Nobody Liked (A Junior Literary Guild
selection), Ariel, 1960.   CA-15/16

CARSON, Julia Margaret (Hicks) 1899-
She studied political science at Ohio State University
and received a law degree from Yale.   She was ad-
mitted to the Connecticut bar and the United States
Supreme Court bar.   Mrs. Carson has been active in
the League of Women Voters.   When she wrote a biography about Patrick Henry, Mrs. Carson felt ". . .
that when readers see public men as individuals, alive
in their times, the significance of their achievement
takes on a more balanced validity. " She wrote Son Of
Thunder, Longmans, 1945.

CARSWELL, Evelyn
Author and teacher.   As an elementary school teacher
in Tucson, Arizona, she was instrumental in the organization of a grade school science program.   Her
husband has been associated with the Tucson Desert
Museum as Curator of Education.   Evelyn Carswell
collaborated with Carroll Lane Fenton to write Wild

Folk In The Desert, Day, 1958.

CARTER, Bruce   see HOUGH, Richard Alexander

CARTER, (William) Hodding 1907–
    In 1946 he was awarded the Pulitzer Prize for editor-
    ial writing.   Mr. Carter has served as editor and
    publisher of the Delta Democrat-Times in Greenville,
    Mississippi.   In addition to books, he has written
    many magazine articles about the South.   For young
    people he wrote Robert E. Lee And The Road Of
    Honor, Random, 1955.   CA-13/14

CARTER, James   see MAYNE, William

CARTER, Phyllis Ann   see EBERLE, Irmengarde

CARTER, William E.
    Teacher, author, Ohioan.   He has lived and taught in
    South America.   William Carter married a girl from
    Bolivia, and they have lived in La Paz.   He has taught
    in an Aymara boys' school.   At one time the author
    traveled from La Paz down the Mamoré, Madeira, and
    Amazon rivers.   He wrote The First Book Of South
    America, Watts, 1961.

CARYL, Jean
    She was born in Mount Vernon, New York and attended
    Mount Holyoke College and New York University.   In
    writing books for boys and girls Mrs. Caryl said that
    her own three children and their friends were "a pri-
    mary source for material."   She has lived in Scars-
    dale, New York.   She wrote Bones And The Smiling
    Mackerel (A Junior Literary Guild selection), Funk,
    1964.

CASE, Elinor (Rutt) 1914–
    Teacher, daughter of a minister.   She was born in
    Sharpsburg, Iowa.   She studied at Creston Junior Col-
    lege in Davenport, Iowa.   She began her teaching
    career in a one-room country school and later taught
    in the Rock Island County Schools.   She has been
    Library Coordinator in the Public School System of
    Moline, Illinois.   Her son has also been a teacher in
    Moline.   She wrote Yankee Traitor, Rebel Spy, West-
    minster, 1961.   CA-4

CASS, Joan
    Teacher, storyteller, author.   She has lectured at
    London University in the Department of Child Develop-
    ment (Institute of Education).   Her stories have been
    heard on the B. B. C. radio program called "Listen
    With Mother. "   At one time Joan Cass was in charge
    of a nursery school in London.   Her books include:
    Blossom Finds A Home, Abelard, 1963; The Cat Thief,
    Abelard, 1961.   CA-4

CASTILLO, Edmund Luis
    He graduated from Northwestern and Boston Universities.
    During World War II, he served in the Pacific aboard
    an attack cargo ship.   He has had a distinguished
    career in the Navy including assignments with Joint
    Task Force 8 (nuclear tests in the Pacific) and the
    Great Lakes Naval Training Center.   He has also
    served in the office of the Assistant Secretary of De-
    fense for Public Affairs.   Commander Castillo and
    his family have lived near Washington, D. C. He wrote:
    All About The U. S. Navy, Random, 1961; The Seabees
    Of World War II, Random, 1963.

CASTOR, Henry 1909-
    This author has written for both children and adults.
    He received his education in Philadelphia.   He served
    in the Army during World War II.   His interests in-
    clude fishing and carpentry.   Mr. Castor and his wife
    have made their home in Marin County, California.
    For young people he wrote America's First World War,
    Random, 1957.   CA-17/18

CATHERALL, Arthur 1906-
    He was born in Lancashire, England, and with his wife
    and two children has lived in Bolton, Lancashire, Eng-
    land.   Boys (and girls) have enjoyed his books of ad-
    venture.   He has traveled extensively in Europe.
    Years ago he and several friends visited the Lake Dis-
    trict in England.   Each one carried fishing equipment,
    enough food for one day, and approximately sixty cents
    in cash.   He later wrote: "It was a wonderful exper-
    ience . . . before the end of our holiday (though we
    were rather sick of the somewhat monotonous fare) we
    were eating as much as we wanted, and had lost the
    fear of going hungry. "   His juvenile books include:
    The Arctic Sealer, Criterion, 1961; Lost Off The Grand
    Banks (A Junior Literary Guild selection), Criterion,

1962.   CA-7/8

CAUDILL, Rebecca 1899-
She was born in Cumberland, Kentucky which has
served as a setting for many of her books. She graduated from Wesleyan College at Macon, Georgia and
received her master's degree from Vanderbilt University in Nashville, Tennessee. She once taught English
at Collegio Bennett in Rio de Janeiro and edited a
girls' magazine. She married an editor named James
S. Ayars and has lived in Urbana, Illinois. Mrs.
Ayars was the recipient of the Wesleyan College Alum-
nae Award for distinguished achievement. Her books
include: The Best-Loved Doll (A Junior Literary Guild
selection), Holt, 1962; A Certain Small Shepherd, Holt,
1965; Saturday Cousins, Winston, 1953.   CA-5/6,
MJA

CAUSLEY, Charles (Stanley) 1917-
Poet and teacher. The Arts Council honored Charles
Causley by naming him as one of fifteen poets from
England and the United States to write a poem for the
1964 Shakespeare Celebration. In the introduction to
Dawn And Dusk (Watts, 1963) he wrote: ". . . Some
poems are best read aloud. Others speak to the in-
ward ear, and answer more clearly to silent reading.
But however poems may differ on the surface, they
have one important quality in common. They remain,
as the painter Pablo Picasso has said of all art, weapons of war against brutality and darkness. " He also
edited Modern Ballads And Story Poems, Watts, 1965.
CA-9/10

CAVANAH, Frances 1899-
Writer and editor. She was born in Princeton, Indiana,
graduated from DePauw University, and has resided in
Washington, D. C. Miss Cavanah has served as an
editor of Childcraft, Child Life, and the World Book
Encyclopedia. In 1952 DePauw University awarded her
a citation for attaining "distinction as a writer and
editor of books for young people. " Juvenile titles include: Abe Lincoln Gets His Chance, Rand McNally,
1959; Adventure In Courage, Rand McNally, 1961; Boyhood Adventures Of Our Presidents, Rand McNally,
1938; Children Of America, Follett, 1935; Children Of
The White House, Rand McNally, 1936; Our Country's
Story, Rand McNally, 1962; The Secret Of Madame

Doll, Vanguard, 1965; Two Loves For Jenny Lind,
Macrae Smith, 1956. CA-15/16, MJA

CAVANNA, Betty 1909-
Her pseudonyms are Elizabeth Headley and Betsy Allen. She was born in Camden, New Jersey and graduated from Douglass College where she majored in
journalism. Betty Cavanna has done publicity work
and also has written for newspapers. Phi Beta Kappa
awarded her an honorary membership for her "outstanding contribution to the field of juvenile literature. "
She married George Russell Harrison who was formerly Dean of the School of Science at Massachusetts Institute of Technology. He and his wife have traveled
extensively and based several books on their experiences including Pepe Of Argentina (photographs by
George Russell Harrison), Watts, 1962. Her books
include: The Country Cousin, Morrow, 1967; Going
On Sixteen, Westminster, 1946; Jenny Kimura, Morrow, 1964. CA-9/10, MJA

CERF, Bennett Alfred 1898-
Noted columnist, lecturer, and panelist on the televi-
sion program "What's My Line. " He was born in New
York and received his education at Columbia Univer-
sity. Bennett Cerf has been president of Random
House. At one time he was a reporter on the New
York Herald Tribune and a clerk on the New York
Stock Exchange. He has written for both children and
adults. In 1964 he received the New York Philan-
thropic League Distinguished Service Award. His
popular "beginner books" for children include: Bennett
Cerf's Book Of Laughs, Random House, 1959; Bennett
Cerf's Book Of Riddles, Random House, 1960; More
Riddles, Random House, 1961. CA-19/20

CHAFETZ, Henry 1916-
During World War II, he was a navigator in the Air
Force. Prior to serving in the Air Force he was
associated with the New York City Board of Child Welfare. Later he was a partner in a second-hand bookstore in New York City. He has written for newspapers, magazines, and television. The first book
which he wrote for boys and girls was The Lost
Dream, Knopf, 1956. He also wrote Legend Of Befana, Houghton, 1958. CA-1

CHALMERS, Audrey 1899-
    Canadian writer and teacher. She has lived in New
York where she studied kindergarten work after graduating from Havergal College in Toronto. Her experiences as a teacher and mother inspired her to begin
a career in writing. She wrote and illustrated High
Smoke (Junior Literary Guild and Viking, 1950), her
first book for older boys and girls. Other juvenile
books which Audrey Chalmers wrote and illustrated
include: Birthday Of Obash, Oxford University Press,
1937; Hundreds And Hundreds Of Pancakes, Viking,
1942; The Lovely Time, Viking, 1955; Mr. Topple's
Wish, Viking, 1948.

CHALMERS, Mary (Eileen) 1927-
    Illustrator-author, born in Camden, New Jersey. She
received her training in art from the School of Industrial Art (Philadelphia Museum School) and the Barnes
Foundation. Charlotte S. Huck and Doris A. Young
wrote in Children's Literature In The Elementary
School (p. 107, Holt, 1961): "Kevin (Harper, 1957)
and George Appleton (Harper, 1957), written and illustrated by Chalmers are both childlike and diminutive."
Other juvenile titles include: Be Good, Harry, Harper, 1967; Cat Who Liked To Pretend, Harper, 1959.
CA-5/6

CHAMBERLAIN, Elinor 1901-
    She was born in Muskegon, Michigan, graduated from
the University of Michigan, and received her M. S. degree in Library Service from Columbia University.
She has traveled extensively in the Far East. Following her graduation from college, she taught at the
University of the Philippines in Manila. She married
a correspondent from the United Press and lived in
Peking. She later lived in Fort Lauderdale, Florida.
Her hobbies have been ballroom dancing and dress-
making. For boys and girls she wrote Mystery Of
The Jungle Airstrip, Lippincott, 1967. CA-15/16

CHAMBERLIN, Jo Hubbard
    Author and teacher, a graduate of the University of
Michigan. He received his master's degree from New
York University and was awarded a Riggs Fellowship
at the University of London. Mr. Chamberlin has
taught at Columbia and New York Universities. He has
also been associated with the Nutrition Foundation and

has written articles for many magazines. The author
and his family have lived in Palisades, New York.
He wrote Careers In The Protective Services, Walck,
1963.

CHAMBERS, Robert Warner
He was born in Oakland, California, and received his
doctor's degree from the University of California. Dr.
Chambers has been interested in the study of nucleic
acids which play an important role in digestion and
metabolism. He has been on the staff of the New
York University College of Medicine. With Alma
Smith Payne he wrote From Cell To Test Tube, Scribner, 1960.

CHANDLER, Caroline Augusta 1906-
Doctor, teacher, writer. She received her education
at Mt. Aloysius Academy (Cresson, Pa.) and Yale
Medical School. Dr. Chandler has been an instructor
at John Hopkins University School of Medicine, Department of Preventive Medicine. She has also done
work in research with the Children's Bureau (Washington) and the Army Meningitis Commission. Her own
experiences have provided material for her children's
books which include: Famous Men Of Medicine, Dodd,
1950; Famous Modern Men Of Medicine, Dodd, 1965.
CA-17/18

CHANDLER, Edna Walker 1908-
Born in Kansas, she spent her childhood on a farm.
She attended Friends University in Kansas and grad-
uated from Sacramento State College. Mrs. Chandler
has lived in California. She wrote: Cowboy Andy,
Random, 1959; Popcorn Patch, Whitman, 1969.   CA-4

CHANDLER, Ruth Forbes 1894-
She was born in New Bedford, Massachusetts and received a degree in Education from Boston University
after attending the Bridgewater, Massachusetts Teachers College. She has taught school and at one time
served as a school principal. She has enjoyed gardening, music, writing, and cooking as hobbies. Her
titles for young people include: The Happy Answer,
Abelard-Schuman, 1957; Middle Island Mystery, Abelard-Schuman, 1961; Too Many Promises (A Junior
Literary Guild selection), Abelard-Schuman, 1956;
Triple Test For Trudy, Abelard-Schuman, 1964. CA-4

CHANDLER, Thomas 1911-
    Born in Los Angeles, he graduated from Virginia Uni-
    versity in Charlottesville. He was a teacher until
    World War II when he entered naval aviation. At the
    war's end he did graduate work at Claremont College
    in California. He started a coeducational day school
    in 1950. He wrote Learn To Ready By Seeing Sound,
    Children's Press, 1958.

CHAPIN, Henry
    He has been interested in the study of oceanography
    and has written several books on this subject. He
    also has written about dolphins. With Peter Throck-
    morton he wrote Spiro Of The Sponge Fleet, Little,
    1964.

CHAPMAN, John Stanton   Mary Ilsley
    Husband-wife team who have written under the pseudo-
    nym of Maristan Chapman. John Chapman was born
    in London and served in the Air Service of the British
    Army Reserve as an aeronautical engineer. He came
    to America in 1917. Mrs. Chapman was born in
    Chattanooga, Tennessee and has been an engineering
    technician, missionary, and lecturer. They have writ-
    ten for both adults and children. The Southern moun-
    tains have provided most of the settings for their
    books. For young people Maristan Chapman wrote:
    Mountain Mystery, Appleton-Century, 1941; Mystery
    Of Burro Bray Canyon, Winston, 1958, and Jane Sel-
    kirk (pseudonym) wrote Mystery Of The Hectic Holi-
    days, Dodd, 1944.

CHAPMAN, Maristan see CHAPMAN, John Stanton

CHAPMAN, Mary Ilsley see CHAPMAN, John Stanton

CHARLIP, Remy
    Author-illustrator, born in New York. He graduated
    from Cooper Union School of Art and Architecture.
    Mr. Charlip founded and directed a children's theatre
    group known as "The Paper Bag Players". He was
    awarded the Ingram Merrill Foundation award "for
    the development, experimentation, and creation of
    plays and literature for children." He had the added
    distinction of having a library in Greenville, Delaware
    named after him. He wrote and illustrated: Dress
    Up And Let's Have A Party, Scott, 1956; Fortunately,

Parents, 1964.

CHASE, Alice Elizabeth 1906-
Author, lecturer, professor. She received her education at Radcliffe College and Yale University. She has
been Director of Education at the Brooklyn Museum.
The author has also been Curator of the Art Gallery
at Yale University and Assistant Professor of Art.
Alice Elizabeth Chase has conducted lectures and tours
at Yale and in various art museums. Her juvenile
titles include: Famous Artists Of The Past, Platt,
1964; Famous Paintings, Platt, 1962. CA-11/12

CHASE, Mary (Coyle) 1907-
Playwright and author. She wrote the play "Harvey"
which won the Pulitzer Prize in 1945. Her husband
Robert Chase has been managing editor of the Rocky
Mountain News. Mary Chase has also worked on newspapers. Mr. and Mrs. Chase have lived in Denver,
Colorado. Boys and girls have enjoyed her book Lor-
etta Mason Potts, Lippincott, 1958 and her play entitled Mrs. McThing, Oxford, 1952.

CHASE, Mary Ellen 1887-
Author and teacher, born in Blue Hill, Maine. She
received her M. A. and Ph. D. degrees from the University of Minnesota after graduating from the University of Maine. Miss Chase has received honorary degrees from Bowdoin, Goucher, Smith, and Wilson Colleges and from Northeastern University. She taught
in the English Department at the University of Minnesota before going to Smith College as Professor of
English Literature. The Atlantic Monthly, New York
Herald-Tribune, New York Times, and Yale Review
have published her reviews and stories. The author
has lived in Northampton, Massachusetts. Her juvenile books include: The Fishing Fleets Of New England, Houghton, 1961; Recipe For A Magic Childhood,
Macmillan, 1952. CA-15/16

CHAUNCY, Nan Masterman
She grew up in Tasmania (the smallest state in Australia) and has continued to live in the house which was
built by her father. Nan Chauncy has been a scriptwriter and radio announcer for the Australian Broadcasting Commission. She and her husband have created
a wildlife refuge on their land, and it has been called

the "Chauncy Vale Wildlife Sanctuary. " Her children's
books include: Devil's Hill (A Junior Literary Guild
selection), Watts, 1960; The Secret Friends, Watts,
1962.   CA-3

CHENEY, Cora 1916-
She married B. W. Partridge, Jr. , a Navy Commander, and they have lived in the Far East and the Philippine Islands.   Her own experiences have provided
ideas for many of her books.   After a visit to a doll
exhibit and an auction in Vermont, Cora Cheney wrote
Doll Of Lilac Valley, Knopf, 1959.   Other books include: The Christmas Tree Hessian, Holt, 1957; Fortune Hill, Holt, 1956.   She also collaborated with her
husband to write Rendezvous In Singapore, Knopf, 1961.
CA-3

CHERRYHOLMES, Anne   see PRICE, Olive M.

CHESTER, Michael (Arthur) 1928-
Author and scientist.   He has been a scientist in the
missiles and space division of an aircraft corporation.
Since his work has involved interplanetary travel, he
had an excellent background in order to write space
books for boys and girls.   He has lived in Sunnyvale,
California.   His juvenile books include: Let's Go To
A Rocket Base, Putnam, 1961; The Mystery Of The
Lost Moon, Putnam, 1961.   CA-3

CHILDS, John Farnsworth
A graduate of Trinity College, he obtained his M. B. A.
from the Harvard Graduate Business School before
working on Wall Street as a security analyst.   Later
he studied law at night at Fordham Law School in New
York City.   After he had received his commission in
the United States Naval Reserve, he attended Gunnery
School at the Great Lakes Naval Training Center.   For
young people he wrote Navy Gun Crew, Crowell, 1943.

CHIPPERFIELD, Joseph Eugene 1912-
This author grew up on a farm in England (Cornwall)
and later lived in Surrey.   He has been a newspaperman and a writer for a magazine which specialized in
dogs.   Mr. Chipperfield has traveled throughout Ireland and England.   He has enjoyed nature and dogs.
His juvenile books include: Dog To Trust, McKay,
1964; Windruff Of Links Tor, McKay, 1951.   CA-9/10

CHORON, Jacques 1904-
Author and philosopher, born in Russia. Jacques
Choron graduated from the University of Leipzig (re-
named Karl Marx University by the communists after
World War II). He also attended the New School for
Social Research and later became a staff lecturer
there. Mr. Choron has resided in New York City.
For young people he wrote The Romance Of Philosophy,
Macmillan, 1963. CA-9/10

CHRISMAN, Arthur Bowie 1889-1953
Born on a farm near White Post, Virginia, he studied
electrical engineering at Virginia Polytechnic Institute.
When he was writing a story about an Oriental character, he became friends with a Chinese shopkeeper
which led him to an intensive study of Chinese history.
His book Shen Of The Sea (Dutton, 1925) was awarded
the Newbery Medal in 1926. He also wrote: Treasures Long Hidden, Dutton, 1941; The Wind That
Wouldn't Blow, Dutton, 1927. JBA-1, JBA-2

CHRISTENSEN, Gardell Dano 1907-
Author, artist, naturalist, born in Idaho. He studied
at the Art Students League and the Career Art School
in New York. He has worked in the Museum of Natural History in New York and also was Curator of Exhibits in the Schenectady Museum. His illustrations
have appeared in Nature Magazine, the Animal Kingdom, and Audubon Magazine. When he lived in Wilmington, Delaware, he wrote several books about
animals for children. He wrote and illustrated:
Buffalo Horse, Nelson, 1961; The Buffalo Robe, Nelson, 1960. CA-9/10

CHRISTIE, Agatha (Mary Clarissa) 1890-
Agatha Mary Clarissa Miller was born in Torquay,
Devon, England. She served in the Voluntary Aid
Detachment (V. A. D.) during World War I and did hospital work in the second World War. Agatha Christie
became famous for her creation of the detective Her-
cule Poirot. It has been said that her "masterpiece"
was The Murder Of Roger Ackroyd (Dodd, 1926), in
which the late Charles Laughton portrayed the famous
character on the London stage. Her juvenile books
include: Surprise! Surprise!, Dodd, 1965; Thirteen
Clues For Miss Marple, Dodd, 1966; 13 For Luck!,
Dodd, 1961. CA-19/20

CHRISTOPHER, Matthew F. 1917–
  Next to a career in writing Matt Christopher's interest
  has been baseball. He has been both a professional
  and semiprofessional player. The Christophers have
  lived in Ithaca, New York with their daughter and three
  sons. The author has written many sport stories including: Baseball Flyhawk, Little, 1963; Baseball
  Pals, Little, 1956. CA-2

CHRYSTIE, Frances Nicholson 1904–
  She was born in New York and graduated from the
  School of Journalism of Columbia University. She has
  been a manager of F. A. O. Schwarz's book department.
  Juvenile titles include: First Book Of Jokes And Fun-
  ny Things, Watts, 1951; First Book Of Surprising
  Facts, Watts, 1956; Riddle Me This (compiled by F.
  N. Chrystie), Oxford, 1940.

CHUKOVSKY, Kornei (Ivanovich) 1882–
  Author and translator. A noted literary historian and
  critic, many of this writer's books have been published in Russia for preschool children. He also has
  been known as a specialist in children's literature in
  the Soviet Union. He wrote From Two To Five; tr.
  and ed. by Mariam Morton (with foreword by Frances
  Clarke Sayers), University of California Press, 1963.
  CA-7/8

CHURCH, Alfred John 1829–1912
  He studied at King's College in London and at Lincoln
  College, Oxford. He taught Latin at the University
  College, London and served as headmaster of Henley
  Grammar School. He wrote reviews for the Spectator,
  translated, and had over thirty volumes of his works
  published. He enjoyed fishing, cricket, and golf which
  he took up when he was over seventy. His titles in-
  clude: Odyssey For Boys And Girls Told From Homer,
  Seeley, 1918; Stories From The Greek Tragedians,
  Dodd, 1879. JBA-1, JBA-2

CHUTE, Marchette Gaylord 1909–
  Author-illustrator, member of a literary family. Marchette Chute was born in Wayzata, Minnesota, graduated from the University of Minnesota at Minneapolis,
  and has resided in New York. In 1950 she won the
  Author-Meets-The-Critics award for the best in the
  field of non-fiction, and in 1954 she was the recipient

of both the Secondary Education Board and the Poetry
Chap-Books Awards.   Her juvenile books include: A-
round And About, Dutton, 1957; Innocent Wayfaring,
Dutton, 1943; Jesus Of Israel, Dutton, 1961; Rhymes
About The City, Macmillan, 1946; Rhymes About The
Country, Macmillan, 1941; Stories From Shakespeare,
World, 1956.   CA-4, MJA

CIARDI, John Anthony 1916-
He has lectured extensively and has taught at Rutgers
and Harvard Universities.   In addition to his position
as director of the Bread Loaf Writers' Conference Mr.
Ciardi has been poetry editor of the Saturday Review.
He has also received recognition for his translations
of Dante, volumes of adult poetry, and poems for boys
and girls.   His books for young people include: I Met
A Man, Houghton, 1961; The Man Who Sang The Sillies,
Lippincott, 1961; The Monster Den, Lippincott, 1966;
Reason For The Pelican, Lippincott, 1959; Scrappy
The Pup, Lippincott, 1960; You Know Who, Lippincott,
1964.   CA-7/8

CLAGETT, John (Henry) 1916-
Author, teacher, born in Kentucky.   He graduated
from the United States Naval Academy in Annapolis,
Maryland.   During World War II, he served aboard a
PT boat.   He began his writing career while recuper-
ating in a hospital from injuries received during the
war.   Mr. Clagett has been an English professor at
Middlebury College in Vermont.   For young people he
wrote Gunpowder For Boonesborough, Bobbs, 1965.
CA-7/8

CLARE, Helen see CLARKE, Pauline

CLARK, Ann Nolan 1898-
She was born in Las Vegas, New Mexico.   She has
been an educational supervisor with the Bureau of Indian Affairs and has lived and worked closely with the
Indians.   In addition she has written textbooks for Indian children to be used in the classroom.   Mrs.
Clark's long association with the Indians and their
customs resulted in her writing books for them and
not about them.   In 1953 she was awarded the Newbery
Medal for Secret Of The Andes, Viking, 1952.   Her
books include: Bear Cub, Viking, 1965; Blue Canyon
Horse (A Junior Literary Guild selection), Viking,

1954; The Desert People, Viking, 1962; In My Mother's
House, Viking, 1941; Little Navajo Bluebird, Viking,
1943; Medicine Man's Daughter, Farrar, Straus, 1963.
CA-5/6, JBA-2

CLARK, Denis d. 1950?
At the age of eighteen he became manager of a planta-
tion in the Far East and later worked on a farm in
East Africa. During World War II, he served in the
Royal Air Force and was awarded the Distinguished
Flying Cross. After his marriage he lived on Corsica.
His wife Stephanie wrote in the Foreword to Black
Lightning (Junior Literary Guild and Viking, 1954) that
her husband learned as a young man ". . . there lies
a deep trust and harmony between mankind and those
great kings of the jungle, some of whom also hunt and
kill, as men do, but themselves obey in innocence the
law of nature. " He also wrote Boomer, Viking, 1954.

CLARK, Frank (James) 1922-
Teacher, musician, author. He has played with various orchestras and has written a book about the trum-
pet. Mr. Clark attended New York and Columbia Universities. He also studied at the Ernest Williams
School of Music. He has lived in Hicksville, New
York. With Alan Vorwald he wrote Computers! (rev.
ed.), Whittlesey, 1964, and with Melvin Berger he
wrote Science And Music, McGraw, 1961.   CA-13/14

CLARK, Margaret Goff 1913-
Author, poet, teacher, born in Oklahoma City. She
attended schools in New York State. At the age of
nine she began to write (poetry was her main interest).
After she had a family of her own, she decided to
write for young people. Mrs. Clark has also taught
creative writing in Adult Education Classes. Niagara
Falls has been her home. She wrote The Mystery Of
The Buried Indian Mask, Watts, 1962.   CA-3

CLARK, Ronald William
He served as a war correspondent during World War
II. Mr. Clark has been interested in the history of
mountaineering and has collected many photographs
pertaining to this subject. He also has written many
articles for magazines. For young people he wrote
Great Moments In Battle, Roy, 1960.

CLARKE, Arthur Charles 1917–
Science editor, writer, born in Somerset, England.
He attended King's College and the University of Lon-
don. He was a radar specialist in the R. A. F. during
World War II. Mr. Clarke has been chairman of the
British Interplanetary Society, a member of the Under-
water Explorers Club, and a Fellow of the Royal As-
tronomical Society. His home has been in Ceylon.
Juvenile titles include: The Challenge Of The Sea,
Holt, 1960; Dolphin Island (A Junior Literary Guild
selection), Holt, 1963; Indian Ocean Adventure, Harper, 1961; Islands In The Sky, Winston, 1952.   CA-4

CLARKE, Pauline
Her pseudonym is Helen Clare. She was born in Not-
tinghamshire, England and studied at Somerville College, Oxford. The author has lived in Norfolk, England. In 1962 she received the Carnegie Award in
England for her book The Twelve And The Genii,
called (in America) The Return Of The Twelves, Coward, 1964.

CLEARY, Beverly Bunn 1916–
Author and librarian, born in McMinnville, Oregon.
After receiving her degree from the University of California at Berkeley, she graduated from Washington
University's School of Librarianship at Seattle. She
has been a children's librarian in Yakima, Washington,
and during World War II, she was a librarian in an
army hospital at Oakland. She married Clarence T.
Cleary, and they have lived in Berkeley. In 1958
Beverly Cleary was the recipient of the Dorothy Canfield Fisher Children's Book Award for Fifteen, Morrow, 1956. Other juvenile titles include: Beezus
And Ramona, Morrow, 1955; Ellen Tebbits, Morrow,
1951; Henry And Beezus, Morrow, 1952; Henry Hug-
gins, Morrow, 1950; The Luckiest Girl, Morrow,
1958; Ribsy, Morrow, 1964.   CA-1, MJA

CLEAVER, Vera   William
Husband-wife team. She was born in Virgil, South
Dakota and grew up in Perry, Florida. He was born
in Seattle, Washington. They have written stories for
McCall's and Woman's Day in addition to their books
for boys and girls. Bill Cleaver has served in the
Air Force. They have lived abroad and in North
Carolina and Florida. Their titles include: Ellen

Grae, Lippincott, 1967; Grover, Lippincott, 1970;
Where The Lilies Bloom, Lippincott, 1969.

CLEMENS, Samuel Langhorne 1835-1910
His pseudonym is Mark Twain. He was born in Florida, Missouri and spent his boyhood in Hannibal, Missouri. When his father died, Samuel Clemens left
school and became a printer's apprentice. Later he
was a river pilot on the Mississippi River. When he
became a newspaper reporter, he signed his name as
"Mark Twain" which meant "two fathoms deep." His
books have been enjoyed by children and adults throughout the world. These include: Adventures Of Huckle-
berry Finn, (Children's Catalog-1956: Harper; First
published in 1885); Adventures Of Tom Sawyer, (Children's Catalog-1956: Harper; First published in 1876);
Prince And The Pauper, (Children's Catalog-1956:
World; First published in 1881).   JBA-1

CLEMENTS, Frank
He was born in Devonshire, England, and has served
as Mayor of Salisbury in Southern Rhodesia. He also
was the editor of an agricultural paper called Rhodes-
ian Farmer. Mr. Clements has been interested in the
theater both as an actor and a writer. For young
people he wrote Getting To Know Southern Rhodesia,
Zambia And Malawi, Coward, 1964.

CLEWES, Dorothy (Mary) 1907-
English writer for both children and adults. An enthusiastic traveler, Mrs. Clewes has often visited the
United States. Her writing career began at the age
of fifteen. She has lived in Kent, England. For boys
and girls she wrote: Adopted Daughter, Coward, 1968;
The Runaway (A Junior Literary Guild selection), Coward, 1957.   CA-5/6

CLYMER, Eleanor Lowenton 1906-
She was born in New York City, attended Columbia
and New York Universities, the Bank Street College of
Education, and graduated from the University of Wisconsin. She has always enjoyed writing and was a
contributor to her high school paper. Mrs. Clymer
has lived in Katonah, New York. During her long
writing career she has written many books for children including: Chipmunk In The Forest, Atheneum,
1965; Country Kittens, McBride, 1947; Latch Key

Club, McKay, 1949; Mr. Piper's Bus, Dodd, 1961;
Search For A Living Fossil (A Junior Literary Guild
selection), Holt, 1963; Trolley Car Family, Junior
Literary Guild and McKay, 1947.

COATSWORTH, Elizabeth Jane 1893-
Born in Buffalo, New York, she graduated from Vassar
and received her master's degree from Columbia University. She has written poetry in addition to books
for boys and girls. She married writer Henry Beston,
and they have lived in Maine. The 1931 Newbery
Medal was awarded to Elizabeth Coatsworth for her
book The Cat Who Went To Heaven, Macmillan, 1930.
Juvenile titles include: Captain's Daughter, Macmillan,
1950; Hide And Seek, Pantheon, 1956; Lonely Maria,
Pantheon, 1960; Poems, Macmillan, 1957; The Secret,
Macmillan, 1965; The Sparrow Bush, Norton, 1966.
CA-7/8, JBA-1, JBA-2

COE, Douglas see EPSTEIN, Samuel and Beryl

COFFIN, Geoffrey see MASON, Frank W.

COGGINS, Herbert
Teacher, executive, author. Mr. Coggins has been
president of a machine company in San Francisco. He
has also taught a course in ornithology at the University of California. He has written magazine articles
and contributed to "Accent On Living" in the Atlantic
Monthly. For boys and girls he wrote Busby & Co.,
McGraw, 1952.

COGGINS, Jack Banham 1911-
Author-illustrator, born in London. He came to America in 1923 and studied art. During World War II, his
battle pictures appeared in such magazines as Life and
in the Army weekly Yank. Jack Coggins and his wife
have lived on a farm in Pennsylvania. With the late
Fletcher Pratt he wrote: By Space Ship To The Moon,
Random House, 1952; Rockets, Jets, Guided Missiles
And Space Ships, Random House, 1951. Jack Coggins
also wrote By Star And Compass, Dodd, 1967. CA-
7/8, MJA

COIT, Margaret Louise 1922-
Born in Norwich, Connecticut, she grew up in Greensboro, North Carolina where she later graduated from

the Woman's College.   Following graduation she became a newspaper reporter in Massachusetts.   Her
book John C. Calhoun, American Portrait (Houghton,
1950) won the 1951 Pulitzer Prize.   Margaret Coit
has taught history and English at Fairleigh Dickinson
University and has lived in Rutherford, New Jersey.
Her first book for young people was The Fight For
Union, Houghton, 1961.   She also wrote Andrew Jackson, Houghton, 1965.   CA-1

COLBY, Carroll Burleigh 1904-
Author-illustrator, war correspondent.   He was born
in Claremont, New Hampshire, graduated from the
School of Practical Art in Boston, and has lived in
Briarcliff Manor, New York.   C. B. Colby was a war
correspondent during World War II.   The author has
been a member of the Outdoor Writers Association of
America, the Civil Air Patrol, and the Adventurers
Club of New York.   Mr. Colby has written and illus-
trated a newspaper column "Adventure Today" and has
been camping editor of Outdoor Life.   His juvenile
books include: America's Natural Wonders, Coward-
McCann, 1956; Annapolis, Coward-McCann, 1964; Big
Game, Coward-McCann, 1967; Helicopters To The
Rescue, Coward-McCann, 1958; Jets Of The World,
Coward-McCann, 1952; Night People, Coward-McCann,
1961; Strangely Enough!, Sterling, 1959.   CA-4, MJA

COLE, Davis see ELTING, Mary

COLE, Lois Dwight 1902-
Her pseudonym is Nancy Dudley.   She also wrote under the name of Lynn Avery.   She was born in New
York City and studied at Smith College in Northampton,
Massachusetts.   Nancy Dudley has worked in publishing
firms both in Atlanta and in New York.   She married
a newspaperman, and they have lived in New York.
The author's daughter provided the inspiration for her
books about "Linda" which include: Linda Travels
Alone, Coward, 1955; Linda's First Flight, Coward,
1956.   CA-2

COLE, William (Rossa) 1919-
Native New Yorker, distinguished editor and compiler
of poetry anthologies.   In an introduction to his book
The Birds And The Beasts Were There (World, 1963),
the author wrote: "One of the great things a poet can

do, which no writer of prose really can, is to celebrate the animals, to praise their grace, their beauty,
and the honesty of their instincts.   As Walter de la
Mare said, 'Animals glorify the earth. '   And so do
poets. "   William Cole compiled: Beastly Boys And
Ghastly Girls, World, 1964; A Book Of Nature Poems,
Viking, 1969.   CA-9/10

COLEMAN, Pauline Hodgkinson
She was born in Long Beach, California and graduated
from the University of California.   Mrs. Coleman has
been City Librarian of San Mateo, California.   Her
book . . . The Different One (Dodd, 1955) was the
winner of the first Dodd, Mead Librarian Prize Competition.   The Colemans have enjoyed traveling which
has included visits to Mexico, Canada, and Hawaii.
Juvenile titles include: Beau Collector, Dodd, 1957;
Preposterous Voyage, Dodd, 1958.

COLLIER, Edmund
Author, editor.   His ancestors were from New England, but he moved West at an early age.   His knowledge of the western frontier enabled him to write
books with authentic backgrounds.   Numerous magazines have published Edmund Collier's articles about
cowboys and western life.   At one time he was the
editor of West magazine.   Mr. Collier has also served
in the army and Forestry Service.   His books for
young people include: The Story Of Annie Oakley,
Grosset, 1956; The Story Of Buffalo Bill, Grosset,
1952.

COLLIER, Ethel
She married a journalist and has written for newspapers.   When she read Strange Lives Of Familiar Insects (Dodd, 1962) by Edwin Way Teale, she decided
to write a book for boys and girls about the familiar
insect known as a ladybug.   She once said: "What
child, chanting to a ladybug, could not be pleased at
the news that a half-acre field, infested with aphids,
can be rescued by just one ounce of ladybugs. "   She
wrote Who Goes There In My Garden?, Scott, 1963.

COLLIN, Hedvig
Danish author and illustrator.   She studied at the
Royal Academy of Art in Copenhagen and at the École
des Beaux-Arts in Paris.   Hedvig Collin has exhibited

her work in Copenhagen, Paris, and Reykjavik, Iceland.
She has lived in Holte, Denmark. Juvenile titles in-
clude: The Good-Luck Tree, Viking, 1954; Young Hans
Christian Andersen, Viking, 1955.

COLLINGS, Ellsworth
Author and rancher. He has been Dean of the School
of Education at the University of Oklahoma. Mr. Collings has written several professional books; however,
from his own experiences as a rancher he wrote a
book for boys and girls entitled Adventures On A Dude
Ranch, Bobbs, 1940.

COLLINS, Henry Hill 1907-1961
He graduated from Princeton University where he won
honors in geology. Before his death, Henry Hill Collins, Jr. lived in Scarsdale, New York. He served in
the Army during World War II. Both adults and children have enjoyed his books. For young people he
wrote: Junior Science Book Of Turtles, Garrard, 1962;
The Wonders Of Geology, Putnam, 1962.   CA-17/18

COLLODI, C.   see LORENZINI, Carlo

COLMAN, Hila
She wrote a cookbook with her husband, and they have
lived in Bridgewater, Connecticut. Her articles and
stories have been published in such magazines as Mc-
Call's and Redbook. Since the start of her career as
a writer, Mrs. Colman has written one book each
year. She received the Child Study Association of
America award for her book The Girl From Puerto
Rico, Morrow, 1961. Other books which she wrote
include: The Boy Who Couldn't Make Up His Mind,
Macmillan, 1965; Claudia, Where Are You?, Morrow,
1969.   CA-15/16

COLT, Martin   see EPSTEIN, Samuel

COLUM, Padraic 1881-
Author, dramatist, poet, and storyteller. He was
born in Ireland, grew up in Dunleary, and came to
America when he was thirty-three. At the age of
twenty, Mr. Colum had his first play published. In
1961 he was the recipient of the Catholic Library Association's Regina Medal for his "continued distinguished
contribution to children's literature. " He was also

honored by the American Academy of Arts and Letters in 1964. His juvenile books include: The Children Of Odin, Macmillan, 1920; The Children Who Followed The Piper, Macmillan, 1922; Forge In The Forest, Macmillan, 1925; The King Of Ireland's Son, Macmillan, 1962. JBA-1, JBA-2

COLVER, Alice Mary (Ross) 1892-
She graduated from Wellesley College and has lived in Tenafly, New Jersey and Stockbridge, Massachusetts. Alice Ross Colver began writing when she was twelve; however, her first book was written following graduation from college. Both children and adults have enjoyed her books. She has been interested in: "making rockgardens, swimming, traveling, the theatre, hills, trees, sincerity, courage---and young people." Juvenile titles include: Joan Foster, Junior, Dodd, 1949; Joan Foster, Senior, Dodd, 1950; Joan, Free Lance Writer, Messner, 1948; Susan, Hospital Aide, Dodd, 1964.

COLVER, Anne 1908-
She has always been interested in history and once said: "I am always charmed to discover that people - and especially children - of other generations are so exactly like myself and my own family." Her keen interest in Archibald Willard's famous painting "The Spirit of '76," resulted in her writing Yankee Doodle Painter (Knopf, 1955). Anne Colver and her husband S. Stewart Graff have made their home in Irvington-on-Hudson in New York. For young people she wrote: Abraham Lincoln: For The People, Garrard, 1960; Borrowed Treasure, Knopf, 1958; Florence Nightingale: War Nurse, Garrard, 1961; Lucky Four, Duell, 1960; Nobody's Birthday, Knopf, 1961; Old Bet, Knopf, 1957; Secret Castle, Knopf, 1960.

COMFORT, Jane Levington 1903-
Many of the books listed in libraries under the name of J. L. Comfort were actually written by a husband-wife team (Jane and Paul Annixter). She was born in Detroit and married writer Paul Annixter (Howard A. Sturtzel) who was born in Minneapolis. This team has written numerous short stories for magazines. Prior to living in southern California, the authors have traveled through Canada, Mexico, and the United States. Together they wrote: The Runner, Holiday, 1956;

Wagon Scout, Holiday, 1965.   CA-2

COMMAGER, Henry Steele   1902-
Historian, educator, born in Pittsburgh, Pennsylvania.
He graduated from the University of Chicago.   Mr.
Commager has been a professor of history at Columbia
University and Amherst College.   In addition to his
books he has written for many periodicals.   His books
for young people include: Chestnut Squirrel, Houghton,
1952; Crusaders For Freedom, Doubleday, 1962; First
Book Of American History, Watts, 1957; The Great
Constitution, Bobbs, 1961; The Great Proclamation,
Bobbs, 1960.

COMMINS, Dorothy Berliner
Musician, author, she has lived in Princeton, New
Jersey.   She has given many lectures on music for
the Board of Education of New York City.   Mrs. Commins has been a composer and concert pianist.   Her
juvenile books include: All About The Symphony Orchestra And What It Plays, Random, 1961; Lullabies
Of Many Lands, Harper, 1941.

CONE, Molly Lamken   1918-
Her pseudonym is Caroline More.   She was born in
Tacoma, Washington, attended the University of Washington, and has made her home in Seattle.   Mrs. Cone
has listed her family's main hobbies as clamdigging,
fishing, and skiing.   In 1962 the New York Times selected Molly Cone's book Mishmash (Houghton, 1962),
as one of one hundred outstanding books for young
readers.   Other juvenile titles include: Crazy Mary,
Houghton, 1966; Mishmash And The Sauerkraut Mystery,
Houghton, 1965; Only Jane (A Junior Literary Guild
selection), Nelson, 1960; A Promise Is A Promise,
Houghton, 1964.   CA-4

CONGER, Marion
She was born in Indiana (the Hoosier State) and re-
ceived her education at Rosemary Hall and Vassar
College.   After her marriage to a newspaperman she
traveled abroad.   The Conger family has resided at
Hastings-on-Hudson.   Besides writing for children,
Mrs. Conger has also been associated with the Toy
Guidance Council.   Several magazines have published
her stories and verses.   For young children she wrote
Rosie, The Rhino, Abingdon, 1948.

CONKLIN, Gladys (Plemon) 1903-
　　Author, librarian, naturalist. She has worked in the
　　Los Angeles and New York City public libraries and
　　has been children's librarian at Hayward, California.
　　She has also contributed book reviews to the School
　　Library Journal. As a naturalist she helped to estab-
　　lish the Hayward Library Bug Club, and the enthusi-
　　asm of its members resulted in her writing I Like
　　Butterflies (A Junior Literary Guild selection), Holi-
　　day, 1960. She also wrote If I Were A Bird (A
　　Junior Literary Guild selection), Holiday, 1965.   CA-
　　2

CONKLING, Fleur
　　Teacher, writer, she received her education at New-
　　burg Academy. She has been a staff writer for a
　　publishing company and has also worked in the editor-
　　ial office of Walt Disney in California. She has con-
　　tributed to song books, and her poems and stories
　　have been published in magazines. With Vardine
　　Moore she wrote Billy Between, Westminster Press,
　　1951.

CONRAD, Sybil
　　During her school years Sybil Conrad's interests in-
　　cluded: the piano, working on the school paper, and
　　designing clothes. She attended Columbia University
　　and the University of Michigan where she became in-
　　terested in radio work. She married a dentist and
　　has made her home in Scarsdale, New York.   Mrs.
　　Conrad has been associated with NBC and has also
　　been a fashion copywriter for an advertising firm.
　　Her juvenile books include: Enchanted Sixteen, Holt,
　　1957; Sorority Rebel, Holt, 1958.

CONWAY, Helene
　　She was born in Roxbury, Massachusetts, graduated
　　from Manhattanville College of the Sacred Heart in
　　New York, and later made her home in Boston.   At
　　one time she was associated with the McCall Publish-
　　ing Company, the Russell Sage Foundation and the Wel-
　　fare Council of New York City.   Her aunt is writer
　　Katherine E. Conway.   For young people Helene Con-
　　way wrote A Year To Grow, Longmans, 1943.

COOK, Fred James 1911-
　　Newspaperman, born in Point Pleasant, New Jersey.

He studied at Rutgers University in New Brunswick.
Fred Cook has been a reporter, city editor, and feature writer. Writing for young people provided him
with an opportunity to write about his favorite subject:
history. The Newspaper Guild of New York has presented Mr. Cook with several awards. Juvenile titles
include: Golden Book Of The American Revolution
(adapted by Fred Cook), Golden Press, 1959; Rallying
A Free People: Theodore Roosevelt, Kingston House
distributed by Lippincott, 1961. CA-9/10

COOK, Gladys Emerson 1899-
Author-illustrator, born in Haverhill, Massachusetts.
She graduated from Skidmore College and the University of Wisconsin, and attended the Art Students League
in New York. She has always enjoyed animals and
circuses and began to draw at the age of eight. Miss
Cook has been a costume designer in the motion picture industry and has had one-man exhibits of her
drawings. Her lithographs have been included in the
permanent collections of the Library of Congress,
Metropolitan Museum of Art, and Cincinnati Museum.
She has made her home in New York City. For young
people she wrote and illustrated Circus Clowns On
Parade, Watts, 1956. CA-9/10

COOK, Joseph J. 1924-
Author and school principal. After graduating from
Drake University at Des Moines, Iowa and State University College in New Paltz, New York, he did further study at Columbia University. Mr. Cook has
been a school principal in Long Island (Island Trees
School District) and a reading analyst for a publishing
firm. He collaborated with William L. Wisner to
write The Phantom World Of The Octopus And Squid,
Dodd, 1965. CA-3

COOK, Marion Belden
She was born in Brooklyn and graduated from Packer
Collegiate Institute. Besides a writing career, Miss
Cook has also worked in advertising and has lectured
on children's literature throughout the country. For
boys and girls she wrote Five Cents To See The Monkey, Knopf, 1956.

COOK, Olive Rambo 1892-
She was born in Avalon, Missouri and attended busi-

ness college in Chillicothe, Missouri. At one time she
taught in a state school for girls and has also been
associated with the Campfire Girls. Mrs. Cook has
lived in Mountain View, California where she has enjoyed horseback riding, photography, and swimming as
hobbies. For young people she wrote: Coon Holler
(A Junior Literary Guild selection), Longmans, 1958;
Sign At Six Corners, McKay, 1965.   CA-13/14

COOK, Sherman R.
Industrial engineer, teacher, author. He graduated
from Columbia University and later was engineering
supervisor of shopwork at Robert College in Constan-
tinople, Turkey. He has also taught in the schools of
Chicago and has been associated with the Chicago
Board of Education as a member of the Bureau of
Curriculum. He wrote Electrical Things Boys Like
To Make, Bruce, 1954.

COOKE, Barbara
She was born in Shanghai, China and later lived in
Burlingame, California. Mrs. Cooke has been a news-
paper columnist and a teacher of juvenile writing.
Taking trips with her children and grandchildren pro-
vided the inspiration for her to write My Daddy And I,
Abelard-Schuman, 1961.

COOKE, David Coxe 1917-
Born in Wilmington, Delaware, he attended New York
University. He has written many books and articles
on aviation. At one time he was Aviation Editor for
North American Newspaper Alliance. Also he has
been interested in writing about Indians. Mr. Cooke
has been made an honorary member of the Cherokee
and Chickasaw tribes. Juvenile titles include: Apache
Warrior, Norton, 1963; Behind The Scenes At An Airport, Dodd, 1958.   CA-2

COOKE, Donald Ewin 1916-
Author-illustrator, native Pennsylvanian. He was born
in Philadelphia, graduated from the Philadelphia College of Art, and has resided in Havertown. At one
time Mr. Cooke was associated with the Philadelphia
Museum School of Art as assistant instructor of illustration under American artist Henry C. Pitz. He has
also worked in business and industry as president of
a printing firm. The author served as editor of Yank

(Caribbean Edition) during World War II. His books
for young people include: Atlas Of The Presidents,
Hammond, 1964; Marvels Of American Industry, Ham-
mond, 1962; Silver Horn Of Robin Hood, Winston, 1956;
Valley Of Rebellion (A Junior Literary Guild selection),
Winston, 1955.   CA-4

COOLIDGE, Olivia Ensor 1908-
Born in London, her father was Sir Robert Ensor who
wrote for English newspapers. She graduated from
Oxford University and later taught at the Winsor School
in Boston. Her husband Archibald Cary Coolidge was
also a teacher (Landon School, Bethesda, Maryland).
She wrote: Caesar's Gallic War, Houghton, 1961;
Edith Wharton, 1862-1937, Scribner, 1964; The King
Of Men, Houghton, 1966; Men Of Athens, Houghton,
1962; Trojan War, Houghton, 1952; Winston Churchill,
And The Story Of Two World Wars, Houghton, 1960.
CA-5/6, MJA

COOMBS, Charles Ira 1914-
Pilot, athlete, writer. A native of Los Angeles, he
graduated from the University of California at Los
Angeles. He first wrote stories about sports since
he had been interested in athletics in school. Charles
Coombs was the third civilian to make his first supersonic flight in formation with the famed Thunderbirds
of the U.S. Air Force. He has become well-known
for his magazine articles and books about aviation and
space. In 1958 he was the recipient of the Boys'
Clubs of America Book Award for Rockets, Missiles,
And Moons, Morrow, 1957. Other juvenile titles include: Aerospace Pilot, Morrow, 1964; B-70, Mon-
arch Of The Skies, Morrow, 1962; Gateway To Space,
Morrow, 1960; Lift-Off, Morrow, 1963; Project Mercury, Morrow, 1960; Sleuth At Shortstop, Lantern
Press, 1955.   CA-5/6

COOMBS, Chick see COOMBS, Charles Ira

COONEY, Barbara 1917-
She was born in Brooklyn, graduated from Smith Col-
lege, and attended the Art Students League in New
York City. Barbara Cooney and her husband (Dr. C.
Talbot Porter) have lived in Pepperell, Massachusetts.
In 1959 her adaptation of Geoffrey Chaucer's Chanti-
cleer And The Fox (Crowell, 1958) was awarded the

Caldecott Medal. She illustrated Walter De La Mare's
Peacock Pie, Knopf, 1961 and The Courtship, Merry
Marriage, And Feast Of Cock Robin and Jenny Wren,
Scribner, 1965. She also illustrated and adapted The
Little Juggler (A Junior Literary Guild selection),
Hastings House, 1961.   CA-5/6, MJA

COOPER, James Fenimore   1789-1851
He was born in Burlington, New Jersey and grew up
in Cooperstown, New York (a village founded by his
father).   James Fenimore Cooper attended Yale College and later served in the Navy.   One of his most
popular books was The Spy, Houghton (written in 1821-
22).   His other books include: The Deerslayer, Scribner, 1925; The Pathfinder, Putnam, 1928.

COOPER, Lee   1926-
She was born in Oklahoma.   Lee Cooper has enjoyed
traveling and once spent several months in Germany
in order to write the book Fun With German (Little,
1965).   She has also visited Cuba and Mexico.   Prior
to living in Fredericksburg, Virginia, she lived in
California.   With Clifton McIntosh she wrote Fun With
French, Little, 1963.   She also wrote Fun With Spanish, Little, 1960.   CA-5/6

COPELAND, Frances Virginia
Librarian, teacher, writer.   She developed a great interest in the Middle East when her father was a
teacher at the American University of Beirut, Lebannon
where she later taught in the American Community
School.   After she had obtained her M. A. degree in
library science in the United States, Frances Copeland
returned to Beirut as librarian and elementary school
supervisor until 1956.   She has been an elementary
school librarian in Bellevue, Washington and has made
her home in Seattle.   For young people she wrote
Land Between: The Middle East, Abelard-Schuman,
1958.

COPELAND, Paul W.
Author, architect, teacher, born in New York.   At the
age of twelve his family moved to Washington where he
later graduated from Whitman College at Walla Walla.
He also attended the University of Washington where
he received a master's degree in history.   He has
been an English teacher in Beirut, Lebanon at the

American University and a high school teacher in Seat-
tle.   Paul Copeland also taught in Aleppo, Syria when
the Department of State awarded him a Smith-Mundt
Grant in 1952.   His juvenile books include: The Land
And People Of Jordan, Lippincott, 1965; The Land And
People Of Syria, Lippincott, 1964.

COPPOCK, Charles 1906-
He was born in Kerrville, Texas and has lived in San
Francisco.   He attended Rice Institute (now known as
Rice University) at Houston, Texas.   Mr. Coppock has
been a contributor to Story Parade magazine and has
been connected with the Writers' Program of California.
He wrote Luck Of A Sailor, Dutton, 1942.

CORBETT, James Edward 1875-
Big game hunter and author.   He has lived in Naini
Tal, India and attended an English boys' school there.
During World War II, Jim Corbett trained British sol-
diers in jungle fighting techniques.   He was commision-
ed a Lieutenant Colonel. For boys and girls he wrote:
Man-Eaters Of Kumaon, Oxford, 1946; Man-Eating Leo-
pard Of Rudraprayag, Oxford, 1948.

CORBETT, Scott 1913-
Author and teacher.   Mr. Corbett has written for both
children and adults.   He acquired authentic material
for his books through his travels.   He visited Italy and
Greece, the setting for his book The Cave Above Del-
phi (Holt, 1965).   In 1962 he received the Edgar Allan
Poe Award (given for the best mystery story for children by the Mystery Writers of America) for his book
Cutlass Island (Little, 1962).   Scott Corbett and his
family have lived in Providence, Rhode Island where
he has also taught school.   He also wrote The Limerick Trick (A Junior Literary Guild selection), Little,
1964.   CA-3

CORBIN, William   see McGRAW, William Corbin

CORCOS, Lucille 1908-
Artist and author, born in New York City.   She met
her husband (artist Edgar Levy) at the Art Students
League in New York.   Her paintings have been exhibited in Europe, Great Britain, South America, and
the United States.   The Museum of Tel Aviv (Israel)
and the Whitney Museum (New York) have her paintings

in their collections. She has illustrated fairy tales and
other children's books and has also contributed to Fortune, Holiday, Life, and Vogue magazines. For boys
and girls she wrote From Ungskah, 1, To Oyaylee,
10, Pantheon, 1965.

CORMACK, Maribelle 1902-
Born in Buffalo, New York, she graduated from Cornell University and received her master's degree from
Brown University. She also studied at the University
of Vienna, Austria and at the University of Geneva at
Bourg-Saint-Pierre in Switzerland. Maribelle Cormack
has been associated with the Park Museum at Providence, Rhode Island. She has been interested in astronomy and has taken several Brown University Skyscrapers eclipse expeditions to Manitoba and Brazil.
Her books include: First Book Of Stones, Watts, 1950;
Road To Down Under, Appleton-Century, 1944; Timber
Jack, Watts, 1952; Wind Of The Vikings, Appleton-
Century, 1937.   JBA-2

COSGROVE, Margaret (Leota) 1926-
Born in Sylvania, Ohio, she studied at the Chicago Art
Institute and the University of Chicago. She has worked closely with boys and girls in a New York Sunday
School and in the Good Neighbor Community Center in
East Harlem. Margaret Cosgrove has also been associated with a New York hospital as a medical artist.
She wrote and illustrated: The Strange World Of Animal Senses, Dodd, 1961; Strange Worlds Under A
Microscope, Dodd, 1962.   CA-9/10

COSTAIN, Thomas Bertram 1885-1965
Historian, author, Canadian-American. He was born
in Brantford, Ontario and began writing books when he
was fifty-four. He has written many historical novels
for adults. At one time he served as editor of a
newspaper, magazine (Chief Associate Editor of the
Saturday Evening Post), and publishing company. The
University of Western Ontario awarded him an honorary degree in 1952. His books for young people include: Mississippi Bubble, Random, 1955; William
The Conqueror, Random, 1959.   CA-5/6

COTTRELL, Leonard 1913-
Archeologist, author, born in Wolverhampton, England.
He has been a commentator, writer, and producer for

the British Broadcasting Corporation. During World
War II, Mr. Cottrell was stationed in the Mediterranean with the R. A. F. as a war correspondent. His
juvenile titles include: Crete: Island Of Mystery,
Prentice, 1965; Dig And Diggers, World, 1964. CA-
5/6

COURLANDER, Harold 1908-
Writer of folk tales, he received an A. B. degree from
the University of Michigan. Later he did graduate
work there and at Columbia. Mr. Courlander has
been associated with the United Nations and has traveled
extensively. Also he has been editor of a series of
music albums which were made by the Ethnic Folkways
Library. His folklore for children includes: The
Piece Of Fire, And Other Haitian Tales, Harcourt,
1964; Terrapin's Pot Of Sense, Holt, 1957. CA-11/
12, MJA

COUSINS, Margaret 1905-
Author and traveler. She was born in Munday, Texas
and attended the University of Texas. She was honored
with a Citation of Achievement in 1957 by the Ex-Stu-
dents Association of the University of Texas. Miss
Cousins' short stories have appeared in magazines here
and abroad, and she has contributed to the media of
movies and television. Margaret Cousins has been
Managing Editor of Good Housekeeping magazine. She
has lived in New York. Her juvenile books include:
Ben Franklin Of Old Philadelphia, Random, 1952; We
Were There At The Battle Of The Alamo (Historical
consultant: Walter Prescott Webb), Grosset, 1958.
CA-4

COWELL, Frank Richard
This scholar has interpreted the classics to young
people in such a way that his readers have enjoyed
learning about the daily life of the ancient Romans.
Dr. Cowell did not limit his writing to a particular
period of Roman history or class of Roman society.
He also used many quotations from Roman writers in
order to provide additional authority for his text. He
wrote Everyday Life In Ancient Rome, Putnam, 1961.

COX, William Robert 1901-
He was born in Peapack, New Jersey and attended
school in Newark where he later worked on a newspa-

per.   Prior to working in television, he wrote many
(over a thousand) stories for magazines.   He has always enjoyed sports both as an active participant and
in later years as an avid spectator.   Mr. Cox has
lived in California.   Juvenile titles include: Big League Rookie, Dodd, 1965; Five Were Chosen, Dodd,
1956.   CA-11/12

COY, Harold 1902-
Author and newspaperman.   He was born in La Habra,
California, received his A. B. degree from the University of Arizona in Tucson, and has lived in Connecticut
and Mexico.   At one time Mr. Coy was a reporter on
the New York Daily News and the St. Louis Star.   He
has been a member of the Authors Guild and his main
interest has been history.   In 1959 he received the
Thomas Alva Edison Foundation Award for The Americans, Little, 1958.   His other books include: First
Book Of Congress, Watts, 1956; The First Book Of
Hospitals, Watts, 1964; The First Book Of The Presidents (Revised), Watts, 1966; The First Book Of The
Supreme Court, Watts, 1958.   CA-7/8

CRAIG, M. Jean
She married sculptor Martin Craig and has lived in
New York City.   The Craigs spent seven years in
France where their two daughters were born.   Mrs.
Craig grew up in New Brunswick, New Jersey.   Her
book The Dragon In The Clock Box (Norton, 1962) was
first published in the Ladies' Home Journal and later
was printed in twelve foreign countries.   She also
wrote What Did You Dream? (A Junior Literary Guild
selection), Abelard, 1964.

CRANE, Alan 1901-
Artist, writer, born in Brooklyn.   He attended Pratt
Institute and the Winold Reiss Studio.   Alan Crane's
illustrations have appeared in magazines and he has
designed scenery for the theater.   He has won many
honors and awards for his art work.   His lithographs
have been exhibited throughout the country, and his
prints have hung in the Corcoran Art Gallery and the
Library of Congress.   Mr. Crane has been a member
of the Philadelphia Water Color Club, the Art Association of Rockport, Massachusetts, and the Salmagundi
Club.   For boys and girls he wrote Gloucester Joe,
Nelson, 1943.

CRANE, Florence
    At the age of five her parents died, and she lived in
    an orphanage in St. Louis, Missouri. She later lived
    with a family in St. Louis. Her writing career began
    in Peoria, Illinois after her marriage to a former
    classmate, Irvin Crane. For young people she wrote
    Gypsy Secret, Random, 1957.

CRANE, Irving
    He has been an expert in the game of billiards. As a
    boy he made up his mind to become a champion pocket
    billiards player. His ambition was fulfilled, and he
    won the championship in 1945, 1946, and 1955. He
    has given many lectures to young people on the game
    of billiards. Mr. Crane has lived in Rochester, New
    York. With George Edward Sullivan he wrote The
    Young Sportsman's Guide To Pocket Billiards, Nelson,
    1964.

CRARY, Margaret Coleman 1906-
    She was born in South Dakota and grew up in Sioux
    City, Iowa. She graduated from Morningside College
    in Sioux City and was later (1965) awarded an honorary
    degree from the college. Her husband Ralph W. Crary
    has been a Judge of the District Court. Her daughter
    Nancy Crary Veglahn wrote The Tiger's Tail (Harper,
    1964) for children. Mrs. Crary's juvenile books in-
    clude: Jared And The Yankee Genius, McKay, 1965;
    Pocketful Of Raisins (A Junior Literary Guild selec-
    tion), McKay, 1964. CA-7/8

CRAVEN, Thomas 1889-
    Art critic, author. Mr. Craven was born in Kansas
    and has traveled throughout America and Europe meet-
    ing artists and studying their works. It has been said
    that "this constant contact with the makers of great
    art and with their works has given him an insight un-
    equaled in modern art criticism . . . and this deep
    knowledge of their aims and achievements is reflected
    in his writing. " For young people he wrote Rainbow
    Book Of Art, World, 1956.

CRAWFORD, Thelmar Wyche 1905-
    Born in Longview, Texas. She has been interested in
    history since she was a little girl and heard her grand-
    father relate his experiences in the Civil War. During
    World War II, she was employed in San Diego, Cali-

fornia. After her marriage to Californian Don Crawford, they built a home (which they called "Melody
Hill") overlooking the sea at Solana Beach. Mrs.
Crawford decided to write a book about California
after talking with the children who visited the Library
where she was employed. She wrote Terror Wears A
Feathered Cloak, Westminster, 1969.   CA-4

CRAZ, Albert G. 1926-
Author and teacher, born in New York City. A grad-
uate of Middlebury College in Vermont, Mr. Craz has
taught English in North Tarrytown, New York and once
taught the children of the American armed forces in
Germany. During the time which he spent in Germany
Albert Craz studied music at the Conservatory in
Mainz. He also received honors in the Bavarian
Schützenfeste (shooting match) for markmanship. For
young people he wrote: Getting To Know Italy, Co-
ward, 1961; Getting To Know The Mississippi River,
Coward, 1965.   CA-17/18

CREDLE, Ellis 1902-
Illustrator, author, teacher. She was born in North
Carolina, attended Louisburg College, and taught in
the Blue Ridge Mountains. Later she lived in New
York where she studied art. Ellis Credle painted the
murals for the Brooklyn Children's Museum. She
married photographer Charles de Kay Townsend, and
they have lived in Mexico. She wrote and illustrated:
Big Doin's On Razorback Ridge (A Junior Literary
Guild selection), Nelson, 1956; Down, Down The Moun-
tain, Nelson, 1934; Here Comes The Showboat!, Junior
Literary Guild and Nelson, 1949. She also wrote
Johnny And His Mule (photographs by Charles Town-
send), Oxford University Press, 1946.   CA-15/16,
JBA-2

CRESPI, Pachita 1900-
Author-illustrator. Born in Costa Rica, she later
lived in New York. Pachita Crespi often returned to
her native land to write and illustrate stories of Central America. She collaborated with Zhenya Gay to
write her first book Manuelito Of Costa Rica, Messner, 1940. She also wrote Wings Over Central America, C. Scribner's Sons, 1947.

CRESSWELL, Helen 1934–
Native of Nottingham, England, she studied at Kings
College, London and received a degree in English.
Following college, she worked for an author who was
writing a book on Van Gogh, in the B. B. C. television
studios at Bristol, and also taught school in Nottingham. She married L. B. Rowe. Her interests have
included: collecting antiques, walking, and visiting
the seashore. Juvenile titles include: Jumbo Spencer,
Lippincott, 1966; The Piemakers, Lippincott, 1968;
The White Sea Horse, Lippincott, 1965.   CA-17/18

CRISS, Mildred 1890–
She was born in Orange, New Jersey and attended
schools in Paris and Geneva, Switzerland. When she
lived in Paris, she became acquainted with Madame
Charles Mercier and Abbé Ernest Dimnet. She later
traveled with Madame Mercier and her family and
wrote a book based upon her experiences. The author
and her son designed a house similar to a French
Normandy cottage in Whitefield, New Hampshire where
she has made her home. Her books for young people
include: Book Of Saints, Dodd, 1956; Jefferson's
Daughter, Dodd, 1948.

CRIST, Eda (Szecskay) 1909–   Richard Harrison 1909–
Husband-wife team. Mrs. Crist, the daughter of a
poet, was an actress. At one time she received the
Pittsburgh Drama League award for best actress.
Later Mrs. Crist devoted her time to her family and
to writing. Richard Crist served in the Navy during
the war. He has taught art, and many of his paintings
have received awards. Books written by this team
and illustrated by Mr. Crist include: The Cloud-
Catcher, Abelard, 1956; Mystery Of Broken-Horse
Chimneys (A Junior Literary Guild selection), Abelard,
1960.

CRONE, Ruth 1919–
She was born in Lincoln, Nebraska and graduated from
Nebraska State College. She received her master's
degree from George Washington University and her
doctor's degree from New York University. Ruth
Crone has taught in the Omaha public schools and has
also been on the staff of several colleges. At one
time she held government positions in Seoul, Korea
and Shanghai, China. With Marion Marsh Brown she

CROSBY, Alexander L.   121

wrote The Silent Storm (A Junior Literary Guild selection), Abingdon, 1963.   CA-9/10

CROSBY, Alexander L.
He was born in Maryland, graduated from the Univer-
sity of California, and has made his home in New York
and Pennsylvania.   Mr. Crosby has been a book editor
and newspaperman and has always been interested in
wildlife.   He married author Dr. Nancy Larrick, and
they collaborated to write Rockets Into Space, Random
House, 1959.   His other juvenile books include: The
Colorado, Mover Of Mountains, Garrard, 1961; Junior
Science Book Of Canada Geese, Garrard, 1966; Junior
Science Book Of Pond Life, Garrard, 1964; Rio Grande:
Life For The Desert, Garrard, 1966; Steamboat Up
The Colorado, Little, 1965; World Of Rockets, Ran-
dom, 1965.

CROSBY, Phoebe
Author and teacher.   She grew up in Maryland and
graduated from Bryn Mawr College.   Miss Crosby has
been an elementary school teacher and has been on the
faculty of Carson Valley School near Philadelphia.   She
has also been a member of the Writers' Laboratory in
New York at the Bank Street School.   Her home has
been in Flourtown, Pennsylvania.   Juvenile titles include: Junior Science Book Of Rock Collecting, Garrard, 1962; Junior Science Book Of Stars, Garrard,
1960.

CROSS, John Keir   1914-
He was born in Lanarkshire, Scotland and has lived in
Devon, England.   John Keir Cross has been a radio
announcer and scriptwriter.   One of his books was
made into a radio serial.   He married Audrey Blair,
an English radio actress.   For children he wrote:
Angry Planet, Coward, 1946; Red Journey, Coward,
1954.

CROUSE, Russel 1893-   Anna (Erskine)
Her father was the late author John Erskine.   She has
been a production assistant for several playwrights and
has written scripts for the "Metropolitan Opera Audi-
tions of the Air. "   Her articles have appeared in Good
Housekeeping and Redbook magazines.   Russel Crouse
has been a reporter, columnist, and playwright. With
Howard Lindsay he wrote: "Life With Father, " "Call

Me Madam, " and the play which won the Pulitzer Prize in 1946 "State Of The Union. " Mr. and Mrs. Crouse have lived in New York City. For young people they wrote Peter Stuyvesant Of Old New York, Random, 1954.

CROUSE, William Harry 1907-
Born in Anderson, Indiana, he studied at Purdue University. He has been editor of technical books for a publishing company and Service Engineer and Director of Field Service Education for the Delco-Remy Division of General Motors Corporation. Mr. Crouse has been a member of the American Society for Engineering Education and the Society of Automotive Engineers. He has written many books on science including: Science Marvels Of Tomorrow, McGraw, 1963; Understanding Science (Revised), McGraw, 1963.   CA-7/8

CROWE, Bettina Lum   see LUM, Peter

CROWNFIELD, Gertrude 1867-1945
Born in Baltimore, Maryland, she began teaching when she was quite young in Ohio. Miss Crownfield later came to New York City where she graduated from nursing school. After obtaining employment during her mornings in the office of a nerve specialist, she devoted her free afternoons to writing. A devoted writer of accurate historical novels for young people, she died at the age of seventy-eight in New York City. She wrote Proud Lady, Lippincott, 1942.   JBA-1, JBA-2

CROWTHER, James Gerald
Author, scientific journalist, lecturer. His lecture tours have included Canada and the United States. He has also spoken at Harvard University. He has made several trips to the U. S. S. R. and has written books about Soviet science. When he was a correspondent (scientific) with the Manchester Guardian (1928-48), James Crowther's job was reporting about the discoveries made in the beginning of the atomic age. For young people he wrote Radioastronomy And Radar, Criterion, 1961.

CRUICKSHANK, Helen (Gere) 1907-
Author and photographer. She married ornithologist Allan D. Cruickshank and has lived in Maine and Flo-

rida. She has traveled in Canada and Mexico. An ardent bird watcher, Mrs. Cruickshank's photographs and articles have appeared in magazines. She received the Burroughs Award for excellence in nature writing. For young people she wrote Wonders Of The Reptile World, Dodd, 1959. CA-13/14

CRUMP, Irving 1887-
Editor, author, born in Saugerties, New York. He studied at Columbia University. Irving Crump has worked on newspapers, was an editor of Boys' Life magazine, and has been managing editor of Pictorial Review. At one time he also wrote for radio. His juvenile books include: Og, Son Of Og, Dodd, 1965; Our Marines, Dodd, 1944. JBA-1, JBA-2

CUMMINGS, Edward Estlin 1894-1962
American poet who signed his name: e e cummings. He was born in Cambridge, Massachusetts and graduated from Harvard University. He gave a series of lectures at Harvard in 1952 and called them "i: six nonlectures. " In addition to books, e e cummings wrote plays, volumes of poetry, and also painted. For boys and girls he wrote Fairy Tales, Harcourt, 1965.

CUMMINGS, Richard
Native of Washington, he has been interested in puppets since boyhood. Mr. Cummings has conducted a weekly puppet series on television in Seattle. He and his wife have also lived in Spain (Balearic Islands) where their daughter was born. He wrote and illustrated: 101 Hand Puppets, McKay, 1962; 101 Masks, McKay, 1968.

CUNNINGHAM, E. V. see FAST, Howard Melvin

CUNNINGHAM, Julia (Woolfolk) 1916-
Author and bookseller. Born in Spokane, Washington, her family later moved to Charlottesville, Virginia where she attended art school. Two years in France provided the author with the inspiration to write The Vision Of François The Fox (Houghton, 1960). Julia Cunningham has combined her career as a writer with that of a bookseller in Santa Barbara, California. Her juvenile books include: Candle Tales, Pantheon, 1964; Dear Rat, Houghton, 1961; Dorp Dead, Pantheon, 1965; Macaroon, Pantheon, 1962; Onion Journey, Pantheon,

1967.   CA-9/10

CUNNINGHAM, Mary see PIERCE, Mary Cunningham (Fitzgerald)

CUNNINGHAM, Virginia 1909-
    Born in Dayton, Ohio, she graduated from Ohio State
    University and obtained her master's degree from
    Northwestern University. She once taught school and
    served on the editorial staff of a publishing house.
    Concerned about the lack of material on her home
    town's noted author, Paul Laurence Dunbar, she spent
    several years doing research and wrote Paul Laurence
    Dunbar And His Song, Dodd, 1947.

CURRY, Jane Louise 1932-
    Teacher and writer, born in East Liverpool, Ohio.
    She attended college in Pennsylvania and did graduate
    work at UCLA and Stanford University. In 1962 she
    was awarded a Fulbright fellowship to the University
    of London where she did research in Medieval English
    poetry. Miss Curry began her career as a storyteller
    and writer when she was associated with the Girl
    Scouts and Girl Guides. She has taught at Stanford
    University in Palo Alto, California. For young people
    she wrote: Change-Child, Harcourt, 1969; Down From
    The Lonely Mountain, Harcourt, 1965.   CA-17/18

CURTIS, Alice Bertha
    Author and teacher. She grew up in Iowa and grad-
    uated from the University of Iowa in Iowa City. She
    did further study at Columbia, Oxford, and the Univer-
    sity of Chicago. Miss Curtis has been on the teaching
    staff at Colorado State College. For young readers
    she wrote Winter On The Prairie, Crowell, 1945.

CURTIS, Alice (Turner) 1860-1958
    She was born in Sullivan, Maine. Her home was near
    a shipyard on the coast of Maine, and she used to
    watch the building and launching of schooners when she
    was a little girl. At the age of thirteen, she wrote
    verses which appeared in Ellsworth American and
    made up her mind to write books other girls would
    enjoy reading. She wrote the "Little Maid" series
    which include: A Little Maid Of Boston, Knopf, 1954;
    A Little Maid Of Bunker Hill, Knopf, 1952.

CUTLER, Ann
    A member of the National Science Writers of America
    and author of medical and scientific articles, Ann Cut-
    ler traveled to Zurich, Switzerland where she visited
    the Trachtenberg Mathematical Institute.   At the Insti-
    tute she studied the mathematical system which had
    been created by Professor Jackow Trachtenberg.   Miss
    Cutler returned to the United States and collaborated
    with Professor Rudolf McShane on a book about mathe-
    matics.   For children she wrote Instant Math, Double-
    day, 1962.

D

DAHL, Borghild   1890-
    Author and educator, of Norwegian descent.   She was
    born in Minneapolis and graduated from the University
    of Minnesota.   She obtained her M. A. degree from
    Columbia University.   Borghild Dahl was the first
    foreign-born woman to become a Norsk Akademiker
    at the University of Oslo and the first woman to be
    granted a fellowship from the American-Scandinavian
    Foundation to Norway.   The King of Norway awarded
    her the St. Olaf medal.   The author has been a
    teacher and principal in South Dakota and Minnesota
    and was Professor of Literature and Journalism at
    Augustana College in Sioux Falls, South Dakota for
    thirteen years.   She wrote This Precious Year, Dut-
    ton, 1964.   CA-3

DAHL, Roald   1916-
    He married actress Patricia Neal (winner of an Aca-
    demy Award) and has lived in England.   Mr. Dahl has
    written for both adults and children.   Two of his adult
    books were on the best-seller lists.   His books for
    children include: Charlie And The Chocolate Factory,
    Knopf, 1964; James And The Giant Peach (his first
    children's book), Knopf, 1961.   CA-1

DALE, Ruth Bluestone
    She spent her childhood on Long Island and later lived
    there with her husband and two children.   Mrs. Dale
    has been a teacher.   For boys and girls she wrote a
    book about two basset hounds entitled Benjamin--And
    Sylvester Also, McGraw, 1960.

DALGLIESH, Alice 1893-
Author, editor, teacher. She grew up in the West Indies and England. Later she became an American citizen. Miss Dalgliesh attended Pratt Institute and graduated from Columbia University's Teachers College. She has been a kindergarten teacher and a book editor of a publishing firm. She also taught a course in children's literature at Teachers' College. Alice Dalgliesh has reviewed children's books for Parents' Magazine and has lived in Connecticut and New York. For young people she wrote: Adam And The Golden Cock, Scribner, 1959; America Begins, Scribner, 1938; Columbus Story, Scribner, 1955; Courage Of Sarah Noble (A Junior Literary Guild selection), Scribner, 1954; The Davenports And Cherry Pie, Scribner, 1949; Little Angel, Scribner, 1943; The Young Aunts, Scribner, 1939. JBA-1, JBA-2

DALY, Maureen 1921-
She was born in Ireland, grew up in Fond du Lac, Wisconsin, and graduated from Rosary College. She has been an editor on the Ladies' Home Journal and a reporter on the Chicago Tribune. Her book Seventeenth Summer (Dodd, 1942) was awarded the Dodd, Mead Intercollegiate Literary Fellowship. This book has continued to be popular with young people throughout the years. She married writer William McGivern and has lived in Pennsylvania. Juvenile titles include: Moroccan Roundabout, Dodd, 1961; Patrick Takes A Trip, Dodd, 1960; Patrick Visits The Library, Dodd, 1961; Sixteen And Other Stories, Dodd, 1961; Spanish Roundabout, Dodd, 1960. CA-11/12, MJA

DALY, Sheila John 1929-
Author, columnist, and sister of authors Maggie and Maureen Daly. She went to school in Fond du Lac, Wisconsin, but she has lived in New York City with her husband and children. Sheila Daly was a teen-age columnist for the Chicago Tribune. Many of her stories have appeared in magazines and newspapers. Her books for young people include: Personality Plus!, Dodd, 1964; Questions Teen-Agers Ask, Dodd, 1963.

DANIEL, Anita
She was born in Rumania, attended schools in France, and later became an American citizen. As a freelance writer, Mrs. Daniel has worked for newspapers

and magazines including: Christian Science Monitor,
New York Times Magazine, and This Week. She often
visited the late Albert Schweitzer and has interviewed
artists, kings, statesmen, and writers during her extensive travels. For boys and girls she wrote Story
Of Albert Schweitzer, Random, 1957.

DANIELS, Jonathan 1902-
Author, historian, scholar, born in North Carolina. In
1931 he received a Guggenheim Fellowship in creative
writing to study in Europe. At one time he was Assistant Director of Civilian Defense and press secretary
to the late President Franklin D. Roosevelt. Later
Jonathan Daniels became editor of the News And Observer in Raleigh, North Carolina. His books for
young people include: Mosby, Gray Ghost Of The Con-
federacy, Lippincott, 1959; Stonewall Jackson, Random,
1959.

DANNAY, Frederic 1905-
Born in Brooklyn, he later lived in Larchmont, New
York. He has collaborated with his counsin Manfred
B. Lee to write mysteries under the pen name of
Ellery Queen. Young people have enjoyed the mysteries
written by Ellery Queen, Jr. The first Ellery Queen
novel was published in 1929. Prior to writing full-
time, he worked in advertising as an art director,
copywriter, and account executive. Mr. Dannay's
hobbies have been stamp and book collecting. Books
for young adults written by Ellery Queen, Jr., include:
The Brown Fox Mystery, Little, 1948; The Purple Bird
Mystery, Putnam, 1966. CA-1

DARBY, Ada Claire 1883-
Native of St. Joseph, Missouri, she spent the summers
of her childhood at her grandfather's home called "Oak-
wood" in Fayette, Missouri. Her illustrious ancestors
included: a President of Harvard College, a chaplain
to George Washington, and an early Governor of Massachusetts Bay Colony. Miss Darby's books for young
people have indicated this author's interest in our
nation's history. Juvenile titles include: Columbine
Susan, Stokes, 1940; Gay Soeurette, Stokes, 1933;
Island Girl, Lippincott, 1951; Jump Lively, Jeff!,
Stokes, 1942; Pull Away, Boatman, Lippincott, 1953.

DARBY, Raymond 1912-   Patricia (Paulsen)
Husband-wife team.   Their home has been in California
near Los Angeles.   He was born in Edmonton, Alberta,
Canada and attended schools there and in Winnipeg.
His career as a writer began at the age of sixteen.
He has written documentaries and dramas for the radio.
In 1947 he came to the United States and was associated
with the Columbia Broadcasting System (New York) as
a writer.   Mr. Darby's career has included both adult
and children's books, plays, magazine articles, and
television scripts.   He won a Christopher Award for a
series of short subjects while associated with the Walt
Disney Studio.   Patricia Darby has been a physical
therapist.   Her experience combined with her husband's
talent as a writer enabled them to collaborate on the
book Your Career In Therapy (A Junior Literary Guild
selection), Messner, 1969.   CA-17/18

DAREFF, Hal
Author, editor.   He has lived in Westport, Connecticut.
Mr. Dareff has been editor of Children's Digest, editor
of juvenile books at a publishing house, and once
created a series of paperbacks.   It was announced in
the February 16, 1970 issue of Publishers Weekly that
Hal Dareff had resigned as vice-president and publisher
of Greenwood Press and Negro Universities Press in
order to do free-lance writing.   His juvenile titles include: Fun With ABC and 1 2 3, Parents, 1965; Jacqueline Kennedy, Parents, 1965.

DARLING, Lois (MacIntyre) 1917-   Louis 1916-1970
Husband-wife team.   Mrs. Darling was born in New
York City and has studied zoology at Columbia University.   She has been a free-lance illustrator and has
been associated with the Audubon Society.   Louis Darling was born in Stamford, Connecticut.   He attended
the Grand Central School of Art in New York and also
studied under Frank Reilly and Frank V. DuMond.   Mr.
Darling was a commercial artist and a photographer
with the Air Force.   The Darlings lived in Westport,
Connecticut prior to Louis Darling's death on January
21, 1970.   Juvenile books written and illustrated by
this team include: Before And After Dinosaurs, Morrow, 1959; The Science Of Life, World, 1961.   CA-
5/6, CA-7/8

DAUGHERTY, Charles Michael 1914-
Born in New York City, the son of famed author and
illustrator James H. Daugherty. Charles Daugherty
attended Yale University and the Art Students League
in New York. He has made his home in Westport,
Connecticut. His juvenile books include: The Great
Archaeologists, Crowell, 1962; Searchers Of The Sea,
Viking, 1961; Wisher (A Junior Literary Guild selec-
tion), Viking, 1960. He also wrote and illustrated
Let 'Em Roll, Junior Literary Guild and Viking, 1950.

DAUGHERTY, James Henry 1889-
Artist-author. He was born in Asheville, North Carolina and grew up in Indiana, Ohio, and Washington,
D. C. He later made his home in Westport, Connecti-
cut with his wife, author Sonia (Medvîedeva) Daugherty.
He attended the Corcoran Art School, the Philadelphia
Art Academy, and also studied in England. In 1940
he received the Newbery Medal for Daniel Boone, Vik-
ing, 1939. Other juvenile books which he wrote and
illustrated include: Abraham Lincoln, Viking, 1943;
Andy And The Lion, Viking, 1938; Landing Of The Pilgrims, Random, 1950; Magna Charta, Random, 1956;
Picnic (A Junior Literary Guild selection), Viking, 1958;
Poor Richard, Viking, 1941.   JBA-1, JBA-2

D'AULAIRE, Ingri (Mortenson) 1904-   Edgar Parin 1898-
Husband-wife team. She was born in Kongsberg, Norway, and he was born in Campoblenio, Switzerland.
They met in Paris where both were studying art. In
1929 they arrived in America. The d'Aulaires had
worked separately on their art until they met the late
Anne Carroll Moore who suggested that they combine
their talents and create picture books for boys and
girls. Their books have been distinguished ones including the winner of the Caldecott Medal in 1940
(Abraham Lincoln, Doubleday, 1939). They have lived
in Wilton, Connecticut. Other juvenile titles are:
Animals Everywhere, Doubleday, 1940; Benjamin Franklin, Doubleday, 1950; Buffalo Bill, Junior Literary
Guild and Doubleday, 1952; Ola, Doubleday, 1932.
JBA-1, JBA-2

DAVENPORT, Marcia (Gluck) 1903-
Born in New York City, the daughter of a noted singer,
the late Alma Gluck. Violinist Efrem Zimbalist was
her stepfather. She attended schools in the United

States and Europe. Marcia Davenport has written arti-
cles for many magazines including McCall's and the
Saturday Evening Post. She has lived in New York and
Italy. She wrote Garibaldi, Father Of Modern Italy,
Random, 1957.

DAVID, Eugene
He has been interested in science and has conveyed his
knowledge and appreciation of it to boys and girls.
His books on science have been based on experience
and research. Mr. David has lived in New York City.
His juvenile books include: Spiders And How They
Live, Prentice, 1964; Television And How It Works,
Prentice, 1962.

DAVIDSON, Bill
He was born in Jersey City, New Jersey and graduated
from New York University. He has written for radio
and magazines. In addition to being an associate editor on Collier's magazine, Bill Davidson has also been
contributing editor of Look and the Saturday Evening
Post. He has received many awards including the
Sigma Delta Chi Award for magazine reporting and the
Albert Lasker Award for medical journalism. Mr.
Davidson has lived in New York City. For young people he wrote President Kennedy Selects Six Brave Pres-
dents, Harper, 1962.

DAVIS, Burke 1913-
Newspaperman and author. Born in Durham, North
Carolina, he has made his home in Williamsburg, Virginia with his wife, the former foreign correspondent
Evangeline McLennan. He attended Duke University
and graduated from the University of North Carolina
with a degree in journalism. His newspaper career
has included being a reporter and sports editor. Burke
Davis has been a member of the Authors Guild. For
young people he wrote Appomattox (ed. by Walter Lord),
Harper, 1963. CA-1

DAVIS, Clive Edward 1914-
Author and pilot, born in Chenango County, New York.
Prior to his work in radio and television, he attended
the School of Journalism at Syracuse University. Clive
Davis has always been interested in flying and served
with the Far East Air Force as aviation engineer during World War II. He acquired a commercial pilot's

license, and his flying enthusiasm has been shared by
his wife and children. Mr. Davis has been associated
with radio and television stations in California. For
young people he wrote Man And Space, Dodd, 1960.
CA-17/18

DAVIS, Lavinia (Riker) 1909-
Her pseudonym is Wendell Farmer. Born in New York,
she grew up in Red Bank, New Jersey where she spent
many hours riding and writing. She once said: "Riding and writing are the best of the three R's." Prior
to devoting all of her time to writing books, she was a
research editor for Fortune magazine. The author has
made her home in Connecticut. Juvenile books include:
Donkey Detectives (A Junior Literary Guild selection),
Doubleday, 1955; Fish Hook Island Mystery, Doubleday, 1945; Melody, Mutton Bone, And Sam, Doubleday,
1947; Round Robin (Revised), Scribner, 1962; Sandy's
Spurs, Junior Literary Guild and Doubleday, 1951;
The Secret Of Donkey Island, Junior Literary Guild
and Doubleday, 1952. JBA-2

DAVIS, Mary Gould 1882-
Author, librarian, editor, born in Bangor, Maine.
Her early childhood was spent in the Cumberland Moun-
tains in Kentucky. Mary Gould Davis began her career
as a librarian at the Brooklyn Public Library. She
later became a member of the staff of the New York
Public Library. She retired in 1945 but continued her
work with the Saturday Review as editor of Books for
Young People. She collaborated with Ralph Steele
Boggs to write Three Golden Oranges, And Other Span-
ish Folk Tales, Longmans, 1936. She compiled Girl's
Book Of Verse, Lippincott, 1952. JBA-1, JBA-2

DAVIS, Reda
Author and librarian, born in San Francisco, California. She received her library degree from the University of Chicago Library School after graduating from
the University of California at Berkeley. Miss Davis
has been a children's librarian in California. She
wrote Martin's Dinosaur, Crowell, 1959.

DAWSON, Mitchell 1890-
He often told stories to his children when they were
small, but he actually put the words down on paper for
his son Greg who was away at camp. The author once

said: ". . . He (Greg) was away at summer camp at
the time and wanted me to continue his bedtime serial
by mailing it to him in installments, which I did. "
The book was called Magic Firecrackers, Viking, 1949.

DEAN, Graham M. 1904-
He was born in Lake View, Iowa and later lived on a
ranch near Reno, Nevada. Mr. Dean studied at the
University of Iowa. While he was at the University,
he served as managing editor of the Iowa City Press-
Citizen and achieved the unusual honor of becoming the
youngest managing editor of a U. S. daily newspaper.
He was later publisher of the Western Horseman. He
has enjoyed flying and has been a member of the
Nevada Wing of the Civil Air Patrol. Juvenile titles
include: Bob Gordon, Cub Reporter, Doubleday, 1935;
Dusty Of The Double Seven, Viking, 1948.

DEAN, Nell (Marr)
Author, newspaperwoman, librarian. She was born in
Tulsa, Oklahoma and attended the University of Okla-
homa. Her work on the Tulsa Tribune was the main
factor in her decision to become a writer. She has
also been a librarian on such newspapers as: the
Oklahoma News, the Great Falls, Montana, Tribune,
Sacramento Bee, and the San Francisco Chronicle.
She married George Dean who later became associate
editor of the Sacramento Bee, and they have lived in
California. For young people she wrote: Flight Nurse,
Messner, 1963; Nurse In Vietnam, Messner, 1969.

DE ANGELI, Marguerite 1889-
Author-illustrator, born in Lapeer, Michigan. After
her marriage to John de Angeli she studied drawing
and in 1934 began to illustrate stories which she had
written. In 1950 her book The Door In The Wall
(Junior Literary Guild and Doubleday, 1949) was a-
warded the Newbery Medal. The de Angelis have
lived in Philadelphia. Juvenile titles include: Black
Fox Of Lorne (A Junior Literary Guild selection),
Doubleday, 1956; Henner's Lydia, Doubleday, 1936;
Jared's Island, Junior Literary Guild and Doubleday,
1947; Marguerite de Angeli's Book Of Favorite Hymns,
Doubleday, 1963.   CA-5/6, JBA-2

DE ARMAND, Frances Ullmann
Editor and author, born in Springfield, Missouri. She

graduated from Wellesley College in Massachusetts.
She has been editor of Calling All Girls and PTA Magazine. Mrs. DeArmand has also been managing editor
of the Encyclopedia Of Child Care And Guidance. She
has served as Executive Editor of the Junior Literary
Guild. Her home has been in New York City. For
young people she wrote A Very, Very Special Day (A
Junior Literary Guild selection), Parents, 1963. She
edited When Mother Was A Girl (A Junior Literary
Guild selection), Funk, 1964. CA-7/8

DE BORHEGYI, Suzanne Catherine Sims see BORHEGYI,
Suzanne Catherine Sims de

DE CAMP, Lyon Sprague 1907-
Mr. DeCamp has written for both adults and children.
Several science fiction books and books about science
have been co-authored by him. Lyon DeCamp attended
the Institutes of Technology in California and Massachusetts. For boys and girls he wrote The Heroic Age
Of American Invention, Doubleday, 1961. CA-2

DECKER, Duane Walter 1910-
His pseudonym is Richard Wayne. He was born in
Bridgeport, Connecticut, attended Bridgeport and Colgate (Hamilton, N.Y.) Universities, and has resided
in Westport, Connecticut. At one time he was a reporter and magazine writer. He served as combat
correspondent of the Marine Corps publication Leatherneck during World War II. Duane Decker has been a
member of the Authors Guild. Some of his interests
have included: jazz, fishing, and travel. For young
people he wrote: Big Stretch, Morrow, 1952; The
Catcher From Double-A, Morrow, 1950; Good Field,
No Hit, M. S. Mill Co., 1947; Rebel In Right Field,
Morrow, 1961; Switch Hitter, Morrow, 1953; Third-
Base Rookie, Morrow, 1959. CA-7/8

DE GERING, Etta Fowler 1898-
She was born on a ranch in Nebraska and spent her
childhood in Idaho. She studied at Walla Walla College
in Washington. After her marriage, she lived in Canada. Both she and her husband have been teachers.
They have also edited Braille magazines for the blind
in Lincoln, Nebraska. This work resulted in Etta
DeGering's book Seeing Fingers (A Junior Literary
Guild selection), McKay, 1962. CA-9/10

DE GRUMMOND, Lena (Young)
Dr. Lena De Grummond has resided in Baton Rouge,
Louisiana. A graduate of Southwestern Louisiana Institute, she later attended Louisiana State University
where she received her Ph. D. degree. Mrs. De
Grummond has been active in the Louisiana and American Library Associations. She has also served as
State Supervisor of Louisiana's School Libraries. The
author collaborated with her daughter Lynn De Grummond Delaune to write: Babe Didrikson: Girl Athlete,
Bobbs, 1963; Jeb Stuart, Lippincott, 1962.   CA-4

DE JONG, David Cornel 1905-1967
He was born in Holland and arrived in America when
he was twelve years old. Mr. DeJong has written
poetry, articles, and books. For boys and girls he
wrote: Alexander The Monkey-Sitter, Little, 1965;
The Happy Birthday Egg, Little, 1962.   CA-5/6

DE JONG, Dola 1911-
Born in Holland, she later became an American citizen
and has lived in New York. In addition to her books
for boys and girls, she has also written for adults.
Dola DeJong has served with the United States Informa-
tion Agency. Her books for young people include: The
House On Charlton Street, Scribner, 1962; The Level
Land, Scribner, 1943; Picture Story Of Holland, Rey-
nal, 1946; Return To The Level Land, Scribner, 1947.
CA-5/6, MJA

DE JONG, Meindert 1906-
He was born in Wierum, Friesland, the Netherlands.
At the age of eight he came to America and lived in
Grand Rapids, Michigan where he later graduated from
Calvin College. He also attended the University of
Chicago. Mr. DeJong was an official historian with
the U. S. Air Force in China during World War II. He
later made his home in Mexico. The author won the
1955 Newbery Medal for The Wheel On The School (Harcourt, 1954), the International Hans Christian Andersen Award in 1962, and the National Book Award in
1969. Juvenile titles include: Along Came A Dog,
Harper, 1958; Bible Days, Fideler, 1948; Far Out The
Long Canal, Harper, 1964; The Journey From Pepper-
mint Street, Harper, 1968; The Singing Hill, Harper,
1962.   CA-15/16, MJA

DE LA CROIX, Robert
French poet and journalist, born on the Breton coast
of France. He received his education at the University of Paris. As a merchant marine officer, Robert
De La Croix acquired a background that later enabled
him to write about navigation history. For young people he wrote Ships Of Doom (tr. from the French by
Edward Fitzgerald), Day, 1962.

DE LA MARE, Walter, John 1873-1956
English poet, compiler, author. He was born in Kent,
England and attended St. Paul's Cathedral Choir School
in London. He lived in Twickenham until his death at
the age of eighty-three when he was buried in the
crypt of St. Paul's Cathedral. Walter De la Mare was
the founder of his school's paper the Choristers' Journal. He later worked for an oil company, contributed
to magazines, and compiled anthologies. He was a-
warded the Order of Merit by Queen Elizabeth II in
1953. His juvenile books include: Down-Adown-Derry,
Holt, 1922; Mr. Bumps And His Monkey, Winston, 1942;
Peacock Pie (illus. by Barbara Cooney), Knopf, 1961;
Rhymes And Verses, Holt, 1947.   JBA-1, JBA-2

DE LA TORRE, Lillian 1902-
Her pseudonym is Lillian Bueno McCue. She was born
in New York and studied at Radcliffe and Columbia University. At one time she was a high school English
teacher. She and her husband have lived in Colorado
Springs where he has been on the staff of Colorado
College. Her interests have included: the theatre,
travel, and cooking. Alfred Hitchcock produced one of
her plays on television. Interested in the 18th century,
she wrote The Actress, Nelson, 1957.   CA-2

DELAUNE, (Jewel) Lynn (De Grummond)
Author and librarian, the daughter of writer Lena De
Grummond. She was a librarian in Japan at the time
of her marriage. Mrs. Delaune received a degree in
Library Science from Louisiana State University. She
has made her home in Columbus, Georgia. She collaborated with her mother Dr. Lena De Grummond to
write: Babe Didrikson: Girl Athlete, Bobbs, 1963;
Jeb Stuart, Lippincott, 1962.   CA-4

DE LEEUW, Adèle Louise 1899-
She was born in Hamilton, Ohio and has lived in Plain-

field, New Jersey. At one time she was an assistant
librarian at the Plainfield Public Library. In 1958 she
and her sister, author Cateau DeLeeuw, were honored
for their high standards of writing by the Library
Association of Ohio. Adèle DeLeeuw's books have been
transcribed into braille and translated into foreign languages. Her juvenile titles include: Blue Ribbons For
Meg, Little, 1950; Career For Jennifer, Macmillan,
1941; Clay Fingers, Macmillan, 1948; Curtain Call,
Macmillan, 1949; Doll Cottage, Macmillan, 1939; . . .
Donny, Little, 1957; Miss Fix-It, Macmillan, 1966;
Sir Walter Raleigh, Garrard, 1964   CA-4, JBA-2

DE LEEUW, Cateau 1903-
Her pseudonyms are: Jessica Lyon, Kay Hamilton.
Artist-author. She lived in Ohio and New Jersey be-
fore she came to New York to study portrait painting
at the Metropolitan School of Art and the Art Students
League. In 1958 she and her sister, author Adèle
DeLeeuw, received jointly a citation for the Ohioana
Library Association for their "successful efforts to
blend edification and entertainment in a mixture that
has proved palatable to countless readers." Her books
include: Determined To Be Free, Nelson, 1963; Fear
In The Forest, Nelson, 1960; Give Me Your Hand (A
Junior Literary Guild selection), Little, 1960; The
Proving Years, Nelson, 1962; The Turn In The Road,
Nelson, 1961.   CA-4

DEL REY, Lester 1915-
Author, editor, literary critic, born in Saratoga, Minnesota. At the age of sixteen he entered George
Washington University (Washington, D. C.), and at twenty-two his first story was published. He has done bib-
liographical and editorial work. Lester del Rey's interests have included: electronics and nuclear and
space physics. Concerning his writing he once said:
". . . giving young readers a better knowledge of the
world - its past as well as the possibilities of its
future - is the most important job an author can under-
take. '" For young people he wrote: Moon Of Mutiny
(A Junior Literary Guild selection), Holt, 1961; Outpost
Of Jupiter, Holt, 1963; Rocket From Infinity, Holt,
1966; Rockets Through Space (Revised), Winston, 1960;
The Runaway Robot (A Junior Literary Guild selection),
Westminster Press, 1965.

DEMING, Dorothy 1893-
Nurse, author, graduate of Vassar College. She studied
at the School of Nursing of the Presbyterian Hospital
located in New York City.   She has served as staff
nurse and supervisor in the Henry Street Settlement
Nursing Service.   Dorothy Deming has also been gene-
ral director of the National Organization for Public
Health Nursing and consultant for the American Public
Health Association.   Her varied and interesting nursing
experiences provided the inspiration for her books
which include: Baffling Affair In The County Hospital,
Dodd, 1962; Penny Marsh, R. N. , Director Of Nurses,
Dodd, 1960; Trudy Wells, R. N. , Pediatric Nurse,
Dodd, 1957.

DENISON, Carol
Author and teacher.   She has traveled throughout the
United States and Europe.   At one time Carol Denison
taught school, worked in a Massachusetts art museum,
and wrote and produced classroom films.   During
World War II, she wrote training films for the U. S.
Navy.   For young people she wrote: Part-Time Dog
For Nick, Dodd, 1959; What Every Young Rabbit Should
Know, Dodd, 1948.

DENISON, Muriel (Goggin)
She was born in Winnipeg, Manitoba, Canada and attended schools in Toronto, Nova Scotia, London, and
France.   She graduated from Toronto University and
the Toronto Conservatory of Music.   Her childhood experiences riding horseback with the North West Mounted
Police in Canada later provided the material for her
stories for boys and girls.   She wrote Susannah Rides
Again, Dodd, 1940.

DENMAN, Frank
The author's former occupation of advertising executive
enabled him to tell a great deal of information with an
economy of words.   Frank Denman's books have often
proved helpful to the busy young reader in his studies.
His books for young people include: The Law, It's On
Your Side, Macmillan, 1952; Television: The Magic
Window, Macmillan, 1952.

DENNIS, Morgan 1893-1960
Illustrator-author, born in Boston, Massachusetts.   He
studied at the New School of Design in Boston and with

several leading artists both here and in England. He
created a trademark (a pair of Scotties) for a gasoline
company and a series of Christmas cards. His brother
was Wesley Dennis who illustrated many books about
horses. He and his wife lived in Key West, Florida
in the winter and in Shoreham, Long Island during the
summer. Morgan Dennis died in a bookshop in New
York in October of 1960. He wrote and illustrated
Burlap, Viking, 1945. MJA

DENNIS, Wesley 1903-
He was born in Falmouth, Massachusetts, and he
studied at the New School of Art in Boston. The
brother of Morgan Dennis, he has illustrated many
books. One of these books was Marguerite Henry's
King Of The Wind (Rand, 1948) which was the 1949
Newbery Medal winner. He married Dorothy Schiller
Boggs, and they have lived in Virginia. He wrote and
illustrated A Crow I Know, Viking, 1957. He edited
and illustrated Palomino And Other Horses, World,
1950. MJA

DE OSMA, Lupe
She was born and raised in Costa Rica. Later she
studied at the University of Kansas where she received
her A. B. and M. A. degrees. She also attended the
Corcoran School of Art in Washington, D. C. Miss De-
Osma married an economist, Dr. Keith W. Johnson,
and they have lived in San Mateo, California. From
childhood she has enjoyed hearing and collecting folk
tales. For boys and girls she wrote and illustrated
Witches' Ride, And Other Tales From Costa Rica,
Morrow, 1957.

DE REGNIERS, Beatrice Schenk (Freedman) 1914-
Editor, author, born in LaFayette, Indiana. She grew
up in Crawfordsville, Indiana, graduated from the University of Chicago, and obtained her master's degree
from the Winnetka Graduate Teachers College. Mrs.
de Regniers has served as Educational Materials Director for the American Heart Association and has also
been editor of Scholastic Book Services' Lucky Book
Club. She wrote May I Bring A Friend? (A Junior
Literary Guild selection, Atheneum, 1964) which won
the Caldecott Medal in 1965 for illustrator Beni Montresor. The author and her husband have lived in
Manhattan. Juvenile titles include: The Abraham Lin-

coln Joke Book, Random, 1965; Cats, Cats, Cats, Cats, Cats, Pantheon, 1958; Child's Book Of Dreams, Harcourt, 1957.   CA-13/14, MJA

DERLETH, August William 1909-
Born in Sauk City, Wisconsin, he began writing when he was thirteen years old.   Mr. Derleth has written many books about Wisconsin.   Also he has written essays, reviews, short stories, and poems.   Titles for young people include: Concord Rebel, Chilton, 1962; Prince Goes West, Meredith, 1968.   CA-1

DESMOND, Alice (Curtis) 1897-
The wife of former Senator Thomas C. Desmond (N. Y.), she was born in Southport, Connecticut and has made her home in Newburgh, New York.   In 1946 she received an honorary degree of Doctor of Letters from Russell Sage College and was also made an honorary Fellow of the Rochester Museum of Arts and Sciences.   An extensive traveler, Mrs. Desmond has written books of authenticity for young people.   Her articles and stories have appeared in magazines and newspapers.   Her interests have included photography and painting.   For young people she wrote: Feathers, Macmillan, 1940; Jorge's Journey, Macmillan, 1942; Lucky Llama, Macmillan, 1939; The Sea Cats, Macmillan, 1944; Your Flag And Mine, Macmillan, 1960.   CA-4

DE WITT, James see LEWIS, Mildred D.

DICK, Trolla Lamson 1889-
Native of Nebraska, teacher, author.   She was awarded the Charles W. Follett Award in 1953 for her book Tornado Jones (Wilcox & Follett, 1953).   Mrs. Dick attended the University of Nebraska.   Following her marriage she lived in Idaho, Oregon, and Washington. Juvenile titles include: The Island On The Border (A Junior Literary Guild selection), Abelard-Schuman, 1963; Tornado Jones On Sentinel Mountain, Follett, 1955; Tornado's Big Year, Follett, 1956.   CA-7/8

DICKENS, Charles 1812-1870
He was born at Landport, Portsmouth, England.   As a boy of ten he began working in a warehouse, and at nineteen he became a reporter in the House of Commons.   His own unhappy childhood provided him with

many of the ideas which were later used in his books.
He died at Gadshill near Rochester, England in a house
which he had picked out as a boy that he eventually
wanted to own. Boys and girls have enjoyed his Captain Boldheart, The Magic Fishbone, Two Comedies
(pictures by Hilary Knight), Macmillan, 1964.

DICKSON, Marguerite (Stockman) 1873-1953
She was born in Portland, Maine, grew up in Massachusetts, and later lived in New York. At one time
Mrs. Dickson was a teacher, secretary, and dance
school registrar. Although her first book was published when she was in her twenties, her first book
for young people was written when she was in her
seventies. These include: Bramble Bush (A Junior
Literary Guild selection), Longmans, 1954; Only Child,
Longmans, 1952; Turn In The Road, Nelson, 1949.
MJA

DIETZ, Betty Warner
Author and teacher, a graduate of Northwestern University. She received her doctor's degree in education from New York University. The author has taught
in public schools and has also been an assistant professor at Brooklyn College. In 1952-53 she was a
member of the American Education Mission to Korea
and has served as educational consultant to the Ameri-
can-Korean Foundation. Her articles have appeared
in Childhood Education and the School Library Journal.
Folk Songs Of China, Japan, Korea (Day, 1964) was
edited by Betty Warner Dietz and Thomas Choonbai
Park. With Michael Babatunde Olatunji she wrote
Musical Instruments Of Africa, Day, 1965.

DIETZ, Lew 1907-
He attended schools in New Jersey and New York and
later lived in Maine. He has enjoyed hunting and has
been an amateur naturalist. Mr. Dietz has held a
license as a guide for the state of Maine. He married
painter Denny Winters who illustrated his book Full
Fathom Five, Little, 1958.   CA-5/6

DIGGINS, Julia E.
Author and teacher. She attended Trinity College in
Washington, D. C. , and she obtained an M. A. degree
in psychology at the Catholic University of America.
Julia Diggins also studied at Boston College, the Uni-

versity of Maryland, and Rutgers University. She has
been associated with the University of Maryland's
Mathematics Project in the formation of a new curriculum and has taught mathematics to teachers in the
elementary grades. She wrote String, Straightedge,
And Shadow, Viking, 1965.

DILLER, Angela
Author, teacher, music educator. She was a co-foun-
der of the Dessoff Choirs in New York and the Diller-
Quaile School of Music. In 1953 she was the recipient
of a Guggenheim Foundation Award. The Diller Key-
board was her invention, and she received the first
Mosenthal Fellowship in Composition at Columbia Uni-
versity. At one time she studied in Dresden with
Johannes Schreyer. She wrote The Splendor Of Music,
Schirmer, 1957.

DILLON, Eilís 1920-
She was born in Galway, Ireland. She has lectured
both in Ireland and in the United States. Her husband,
Cormac O'Cuilleanáin, has been a professor at the
University of Cork. Eilís Dillon has written books in
Irish and adult novels and mysteries. Her books for
young people include: A Family Of Foxes (A Junior
Literary Guild selection), Funk, 1965; Under The
Orange Grove, Meredith, 1969. CA-9/10

DINES, Glen 1925-
He was born in Casper, Wyoming and grew up in the
state of Washington. Mr. Dines studied at the Univer-
sity of Washington in Seattle, the Art Center School in
Los Angeles, and received his A. B. and M. A. degrees
from Sacramento State College. When he served in the
Army, he was Staff Artist for the Pacific edition of
Stars And Stripes and Art Director for the Ernie Pyle
Theater in Tokyo. He has lived in Sacramento, Cali-
fornia. His books for young people include: Fabulous
Flying Bicycle, Macmillan, 1960; Mysterious Machine,
Macmillan, 1957. CA-9/10

DITMARS, Raymond Lee 1876-1942
He was born in Newark, New Jersey and graduated
from Barnard Military School. He was assistant curator of entomology at the American Museum of Natural
History and curator of reptiles at the New York Zoological Park (Bronx Zoo). Raymond Ditmars was made

honorary curator of reptiles at the Bronx Zoo, and in
1930 Lincoln Memorial University (Harrogate, Tenn.)
awarded him an honorary degree of Doctor of Letters.
The biography Raymond L. Ditmars (Messner, 1944)
was written by Laura N. Woods. Mr. Ditmars' juvenile books include: The Book Of Insect Oddities, Lippincott, 1938; Book Of Living Reptiles, Lippincott,
1936. JBA-1, JBA-2

DIXON, Marjorie 1887-
For many years she was secretary to the Foreign Editor of the London Times. During the last months of
World War I, she was reader of the foreign press at
the British War Office. Following her marriage, she
and her husband lived in Ireland. In later years they
made their home on a farm in Surrey, England. She
wrote The Forbidden Island, Criterion Books, 1960.

DOANE, Pelagie 1906-
Author and illustrator. She studied interior decorating
and attended art school. She began her career designing greeting cards. Later her illustrations appeared
on book jackets and in magazines. She married Warren Hoffner and has lived in New Jersey. Her first
book was A Small Child's Bible, Walck, 1946. Other
juvenile titles include: The Big Trip, Walck, 1958;
Book Of Nature, Oxford, 1952; The Boy Jesus, Oxford,
1953; First Day, Lippincott, 1956; God Made The
World, Lippincott, 1960; Story Of Moses, Lippincott,
1958; Understanding Kim, Lippincott, 1962. CA-4,
MJA

DOBBS, Rose
Author and editor. She grew up in New York City.
In an introduction to her book More Once-Upon-A-Time
Stories (Random, 1961), she wrote: "When I was a
child, storytelling was a part of every day living. Almost every adult in my world was a storyteller. "
Stories provided amusement for the children as well
as lessons in behavior, manners, and morals. She has
been children's book editor for a publishing firm. For
children she wrote Michael's Friends, Coward, 1953.

DODGE, Bertha Sanford 1902-
Author and teacher. She received degrees from Radcliffe College and the Massachusetts Institute of Technology at Cambridge. She has taught chemistry at

DODGE, Mary (Mapes)   143

City Hospital in St. Louis to student nurses. Her
trips to Central and South America provided material
for her book Plants That Changed The World (A Junior
Literary Guild selection), Little, 1959. She also wrote
The Story Of Nursing (New ed.), Little, 1965.

DODGE, Mary (Mapes) 1831-1905
Author, editor, born in New York City. For thirty
years she was editor of the renowned St. Nicholas
magazine. She married lawyer William Dodge. When
he died, she lived with her two small sons in New Jersey. Her summers were spent at a cottage ("Yarrow")
in the Catskill Mountains. Generations of children
have enjoyed Mary Mapes Dodge's book Hans Brinker,
Scribner, 1915 (first published in 1865). JBA-1

DODGSON, Charles Lutwidge 1832-1898
His pseudonym is Lewis Carroll. He was born in
Daresbury, England. At the age of thirteen he wrote
poetry for his brothers and sisters. He studied at
Rugby Preparatory School and Christ Church College,
Oxford where he later was a professor of mathematics.
Charles Dodgson never married and died two weeks
before his sixty-sixth birthday in Surrey, England. It
was during a boat ride in 1862 with the three small
Liddell sisters that he told a story which became
Alice's Adventures In Wonderland, Macmillan, 1865.
He also wrote Through The Looking Glass, And What
Alice Found There, Macmillan, 1871. JBA-1

DODWORTH, Dorothy L.
Children's librarian and author. She has entertained
boys and girls with stories, chalk talks, and marionette shows. For young readers she also wrote and
illustrated Mrs. Doddlepunk Trades Work, Scott, 1957.

DOHERTY, John Stephen
He went to high school in Sunnyside, Long Island, graduated from Syracuse University, and did additional
study at Yale University. He served in the Field
Artillery and was an Intelligence Officer in Korea. He
has been editor of Saga magazine. Boating has been
his hobby, and he has visited the Bahamas in his own
24-foot sloop. For young people he wrote The Mystery
Of Hidden Harbor, Doubleday, 1963.

DOLBIER, Maurice 1912-
Author, columnist, editor, born in Skowhegan, Maine.
An early interest in the theatre led to his enrollment
at Boston's Whitehouse Academy of Dramatic Arts.
Maurice Dolbier has been a radio announcer and pro-
gram director, playwright, and a book reviewer on the
staff of the New York Herald Tribune. The author and
his family have lived in Providence, Rhode Island.
His juvenile books include: The Magic Bus (original
title was Jenny, The Bus That Nobody Loved), New
Wonder Books, 1948; Paul Bunyan, Random, 1959;
Torten's Christmas Secret, Little, 1951. MJA

DOLIM, Mary Nuzum 1925-
Nurse and writer. She was born in Timberhill, Kansas, spent her childhood in St. Petersburg, Florida,
and has lived in California. The author has also lived
in Japan and Hawaii. Her interest in writing began in
high school when she served as the editor of the school
newspaper. Mrs. Dolim has written for both adults
and children and has been a member of the California
Writers' Club. She collaborated with Gen Kakacek to
write Four Hands For Mercy (A Junior Literary Guild
selection), Van Nostrand, 1965. CA-19/20

DOMANSKA, Janina
Artist and author, born in Warsaw, Poland. She
married writer Jerzy Laskowski, and they have lived
in Valley Stream, New York. Her illustrations have
appeared in many books including The Coconut Thieves
(adapted by Catherine Fournier, Scribner, 1964) which
was a Prize Book in the 1964 Children's Spring Book
Festival. Her work has also been published in the
Reporter and Harper's magazine. Many galleries have
exhibited her paintings. For boys and girls she wrote
and illustrated Why So Much Noise?, Harper, 1965.
CA-17/18

DOMJAN, Joseph 1907-
He was born in Budapest, Hungary and studied at the
Budapest Academy of Arts. He has received wide re-
cognition for his work in woodcuts. Mr. Domjan was
awarded the Kossuth Prize in Hungary. The title
"Master of the Color Woodcut" which is awarded once
every hundred years in China was bestowed upon him.
For boys and girls he wrote Hungarian Heroes And
Legends, Van Nostrand, 1963. CA-9/10

DONAHEY, William   1884-1970
Creator of the "Teenie Weenies," he was born in Ohio
and studied at the Cleveland School of Art.   He mar-
ried author Mary Dickerson, and they have lived in
Chicago.   Mr. Donahey was on the staff of the Cleve-
land Plain Dealer before his association with the
Chicago Tribune.   His "Teenie Weenie" books include:
Teenie Weenie Land, Beckley, 1923; Teenie Weenie
Town, Whittlesey, 1942.

DONALDS, Gordon   see SHIRREFFS, Gordon Donald

DONNA, Natalie   1934-
She has written advertising copy and has also created
several board games and quizzes for boys and girls.
The author has worked in Boston and New York.   Her
interest in Africa led her to write Boy Of The Masai,
Dodd, 1964.   CA-11/12

DONOVAN, Frank Robert   1906-
Film producer, writer, born in New York City.   After
working as a copy-writer, he became owner of an advertising agency.   Prior to his position as Vice-President in Charge of Production for Pathé News, he had
been a scriptwriter.   Mr. Donovan was also Business
Manager of the Magazine Of Wall Street.   He has lived
in Weston, Connecticut.   His books for young people
include: The Cutter, Barnes, 1961; Famous Twentieth
Century Leaders, Dodd, 1964.   CA-4

DOSS, Helen (Grigsby)   1915-
She was born in England, grew up in Illinois, and has
lived in California.   Mrs. Doss studied at Santa Ana
College and received her degree from the University
of Redlands.   She married a minister, and they have
adopted twelve children.   Helen Doss has been interested in Biblical history.   Her juvenile books include: All The Children Of The World, Abingdon, 1958;
Friends Around The World, Abingdon, 1959.   CA-9/10

DOUGHTIE, Charles
The author was born in Virginia.   He attended the Virginia Episcopal School and both Virginia and Michigan
Universities.   He has worked in the advertising field.
Mr. and Mrs. Doughtie and their children have lived
in New Canaan, Connecticut.   For young readers he
wrote Gabriel Wrinkles, Dodd, 1959.

DOUGLAS, John Scott
    He attended the University of Washington and did grad-
uate work at Harvard. He has traveled in Alaska,
Europe, both Central and South America, and the West
Indies. John Douglas once said: "I am convinced that
no amount of research an author can do will give him
material as vital as that picked up first hand. " His
many hobbies and his adventures at sea have provided
ideas for his books. He won the Boys' Life-Dodd,
Mead Prize Competition for The Secret Of The Under-
sea Bell, Dodd, 1951. He also wrote Northward The
Whalers Go, Dodd, 1952.

DOUGLAS, William Orville 1898-
    Author, teacher, associate justice of the Supreme
Court, born in Maine, Minnesota. After graduating
from Whitman College in Walla Walla, Washington, he
received his degree in law from Columbia University.
Justice Douglas has taught at both Columbia and the
Yale Schools of Law. At the age of forty-one he was
appointed an associate justice of the Supreme Court by
President Franklin D. Roosevelt. For young people
he has written: Exploring The Himalaya, Random,
1958; Muir Of The Mountains, Houghton, 1961. CA-
9/10

DOWDEN, Anne Ophelia 1907-
    She has illustrated and researched articles for Natural
History, Life, and House Beautiful under the name of
Anne Ophelia Todd. She graduated from Carnegie In-
stitute of Technology and studied in New York at the
Beaux Arts Institute and the Art Students League. She
has been on the staff of Manhattanville College and has
taught at Pratt Institute. She wrote and illustrated
Look At A Flower, Crowell, 1963. CA-11/12

DOWDS, Gertrude
    She was born in Dublin. She has written books about
her native country of Ireland and about Canada where
she has made her home (Toronto). She wrote The
Mysterious Round Tower, Bobbs, 1964.

DOWNER, Marion
    She studied art in the Spokane, Washington high school
under Josephine Guilbert and continued her education at
the Chicago Art Institute. She did further study in
London, New York, and Paris. Her books for children

include: Discovering Design, Lothrop, 1947; Long Ago
In Florence, Lothrop, 1968.

DOWNEY, Fairfax Davis 1893-
The major part of Fairfax Downey's army career was
spent in the Field Artillery which also provided the
background for several of his books.   He has been on
the staff of several newspapers including the Kansas
City Star and the New York Sun.   Many of his stories
and verses have been published in magazines.   He also
has written songs and created scripts for radio.   Juvenile titles include: Cats Of Destiny, Scribner, 1950;
Cavalry Mount, Dodd, 1946.   CA-2

DOYLE, Sir Arthur Conan 1859-1930
Creator of detective Sherlock Holmes, he was born in
Edinburgh, Scotland and graduated from the University
of Edinburgh.   The author once practiced medicine on
ships (Portsmouth, England) and was a physician at a
field hospital during the Boer War.   He was knighted
by King Edward VII in 1902.   He wrote The Boys'
Sherlock Holmes (A selection from the works of A.
Conan Doyle arranged with introduction by Howard Haycraft), Harper, 1961.   JBA-1

DRAPER, Nancy
Author and ballet instructor, born in New York.   She
studied in Paris and attended the School of American
Ballet.   After her marriage she made her home in
San Francisco.   Mrs. Draper has operated a school of
ballet.   With Margaret F. Atkinson she wrote Ballet
For Beginners, Knopf, 1951.

DRUMMOND, Walter see SILVERBERG, Robert

DU BOIS, Theodora (McCormick) 1890-
She has lived in Connecticut and on Staten Island.   A
grandson interested in the sport of scuba diving ap-
proved her references to the sport in Rich Boy, Poor
Boy (A Junior Literary Guild selection, Farrar, 1961).
Mrs. DuBois has also written books for adults.   For
young people she wrote Tiger Burning Bright, Ariel,
1964.

DU BOIS, William Sherman Pène 1916-
Author-illustrator.   His father was painter and art
critic Guy Pène du Bois.   He was born in Nutley, New

Jersey and attended Mrs. Barstow's School in New
York and the Lycée Hoche in Versailles, France.   Mr.
du Bois served with the Coast Artillery during World
War II.   He married stage designer Willa Kim and
has lived in New York City.   Besides his many book
illustrations, he was the designer of the 1950 Book
Week poster "Make Friends With Books. " William du
Bois received the 1948 Newbery Medal for The Twenty-
One Balloons, Viking, 1947.   Other juvenile books
which he wrote and illustrated include: Bear Party,
Viking, 1951; The Giant, Viking, 1954; The Horse In
The Camel Suit, Harper, 1967; The Lion, Viking, 1956;
Otto In Africa (A Junior Literary Guild selection), Vik-
ing, 1961; Three Policemen, Viking, 1938.   CA-5/6,
JBA-2

DUCAS, Dorothy 1905-
    She was born in New York City and graduated from
    Columbia University where she was awarded a Pulitzer
    Traveling Scholarship.   She has been a reporter for
    newspapers both in London and New York, an editor
    of McCall's magazine, and was Chief of the Magazine
    Bureau of the Office of War Information.   Dorothy
    Ducas has also served as a special consultant to the
    Surgeon General of the U. S. Public Health Service.
    She married James B. Herzog and has lived in South
    Salem and New York City.   She wrote Modern Nursing,
    Walck, 1962.   CA-5/6

DUDLEY, Nancy see COLE, Lois Dwight

DUGGAN, Alfred Leo 1903-
    Born in Buenos Aires, he studied at Eton and Balliol
    College, Oxford. Alfred Duggan has traveled exten-
    sively including a visit to the Galápagos Islands where
    he collected specimens for the British Museum.   His
    interest in archaeology also led him to Constantinople
    and the excavation site of Constantine's palace.   He
    has lived in Herefordshire in a house which was built
    in the sixteenth century.   Juvenile titles include:
    Arches And Spires, Pantheon, 1962; Falcon & Dove,
    Pantheon, 1966.

DUKERT, Joseph Michael 1929-
    Author and newspaperman, born in Baltimore, Mary-
    land. He graduated magna cum laude from Notre Dame
    University and did graduate work at George Washington

and John Hopkins Universities. He served with the
U. S. Air Force (psychological warfare officer) during
the Korean War. Mr. Dukert has been a Director of
Public Relations for the Martin Company's Nuclear
division. He has contributed articles to such magazines as Catholic Digest, Labor Law Journal, and
Space Aeronautics. For young people he wrote Atom-
power, Coward-McCann, 1962.   CA-5/6

DUNCAN, Lois 1934-
She has called Sarasota, Florida her home although she
was born in Philadelphia. She attended Duke University. Her writing career began at the age of thirteen
when she sold her first story to Calling All Girls
magazine. Successive stories appeared in such magazines as: American Girl, McCall's, Reader's Digest,
and Seventeen (she won this magazine's short-story
contest three times). Her poetry was published in the
Saturday Evening Post. For young people she wrote:
Giving Away Suzanne, Dodd, 1963; They Never Came
Home, Doubleday, 1969.   CA-3

DUNLOP, Agnes Mary Robertson
Her pseudonyms are Elisabeth Kyle and Jan Ralston.
She was born in Ayr, Scotland and studied journalism
in Glasgow. At one time she was a correspondent for
the Manchester Guardian. Her interests have included:
travel, music, and antiques. Juvenile books include:
The Captain's House (Elisabeth Kyle, pseud.), P.
Davies, 1952; Girl With A Pen (Elisabeth Kyle, pseud.),
Holt, 1964; Maid Of Orleans, The Story Of Joan Of
Arc (Elisabeth Kyle, pseud.), Nelson, 1957.   CA-15/
16

DUPUY, Trevor Nevitt 1916-
Author, soldier, historian. The son of Colonel R.
Ernest Dupuy, he graduated from West Point and served
with distinction in World War II. He was awarded the
Distinguished Service Order by the British Government
for action in Burma. Retired Colonel of the U. S. Army, Trevor Dupuy's career has enabled him to write
informative and exciting military histories for boys and
girls. These include: The Air War In The West,
Watts, 1963; First Book Of Civil War Land Battles,
Watts, 1960.   CA-4

DURANT, John 1902-
    Athlete and author.   He was born in Waterbury, Con-
necticut, graduated from Yale University, and has resided in Islamorada, Florida.   He was a member of
the Yale track team and later ran for the New York
Athletic Club.   His articles have appeared in such
magazines as Outdoor Life, Saturday Evening Post,
and Sports Illustrated.   Mr. Durant's interests have
included fishing and camping.   For young people he
wrote: The Heavyweight Champions, Hastings House,
1960; Highlights Of The World Series, Hastings House,
1963; The Sports Of Our Presidents, Hastings House,
1964.   CA-9/10

DURELL, Ann
    Editor and author.   She was born in New Jersey and
graduated from Mt. Holyoke College in South Hadley,
Massachusetts.   She also attended St. Andrews University in Scotland.   Her stories have appeared in many
magazines.   Ann Durell has lived in New York City
where she has been an editor in a publishing firm.
For boys and girls she wrote My Heart's In The Highlands, Doubleday, 1958.

DURLACHER, Ed
    Teacher, square dance caller.. He has lived in Free-
port, Long Island.   Mr. Durlacher has been a caller
for square dances throughout the United States.   When
square dances were held in the city parks of New
York, he called for over 4000 people.   His book for
young people was Honor Your Partner, Devin-Adair
Co. , 1949.

DURRELL, Gerald Malcolm 1925-
    He was born in Jamshedpur, India and attended schools
in France, Greece, Italy, and Switzerland.   Gerald
Durrell has been interested in zoology.   He has worked
in zoological institutions in Great Britain and made
several collecting trips to South America and West
Africa.   Brother of writer Laurence Durrell, he has
also been a broadcaster, lecturer, and writer for the
British Broadcasting Company.   He has operated a
private zoo on the island of Jersey.   He wrote The
New Noah, Viking, 1964.   CA-7/8

DUVOISIN, Roger Antoine 1904-
    Author-illustrator.   Born and educated in Geneva,

Switzerland, he became an American citizen in 1938.
He has made his home in Gladstone, New Jersey with
his wife, writer Louise Fatio. A distinguished illustrator of children's books, Roger Duvoisin received
the 1948 Caldecott Medal for White Snow, Bright Snow
(Lothrop, 1947) written by Alvin Tresselt. Prior to
illustrating books, he designed stage scenery and worked in ceramics and textiles. Juvenile books which he
wrote and illustrated include: And There Was America,
Knopf, 1938; Lonely Veronica, Knopf, 1963; Petunia, I
Love You, Knopf, 1965; Spring Snow, Knopf, 1963.
CA-13/14, JBA-2

DYNELY, James see MAYNE, William

E

EAGER, Edward McMaken d. 1964
He was born in Toledo, Ohio and studied at Harvard.
His first book for young people resulted from reading
stories to his young son Fritz. Mr. Eager has also
written for radio, stage, and television. He lived in
Connecticut prior to his death on October 23, 1964.
Juvenile titles include: Half Magic, Harcourt, 1954;
Knight's Castle, Harcourt, 1956; Magic By The Lake,
Harcourt, 1957; Magic Or Not?, Harcourt, 1959; Mouse
Manor, Pellegrini & Cudahy, 1952; Seven-day Magic,
Harcourt, 1962.   MJA

EAMES, Genevieve Torrey
She was born in Pasadena, California and has lived in
London, Paris, and the New England states. An animal lover, she has raised both horses and dogs and
has won several first prize awards (for her dog "Ard-
shiel Wendy") at the New York Dog Show. The author
has contributed articles to such magazines as Adventure
Trails and Story Parade. Her juvenile books include:
Flying Roundup (A Junior Literary Guild selection),
Messner, 1957; Good Luck Colt, Junior Literary Guild
and Messner, 1953; Handy Of The Triple S, Messner,
1949; Pat Rides The Trail, Messner, 1946.

EASTMAN, Philip D.
He has been associated with the film industry not only
during his service in the army but also as a member
of the Hollywood studio that created the cartoon film
"Gerald McBoing-Boing" (also a book by United Pro-

ductions of America, Simon & Schuster, 1952). He al-
so has written for television and has created visual
education film scripts. P. D. Eastman has lived in
Westport, Connecticut. His beginning readers include:
Go, Dog. Go!, Beginner Bks. , 1961; Sam And The
Firefly, Random, 1958.

EASTWICK, Ivy (Ethel) Olive
She has been a member of the British Foreign Service.
Her occupation has taken her to many countries in-
cluding Persia, Russia, and the United States. Miss
Eastwick's poetry has appeared in magazines, news-
papers, and anthologies. Her juvenile books include:
Cherry Stones! Garden Swings! Poems, Abingdon, 1962;
Deck The Stable, McKay, 1960.   CA-5/6

EATON, George L. see VERRAL, Charles Spain

EBERLE, Irmengarde 1898-
Author and editor. Her pseudonyms are Allyn Allen
and Phyllis Ann Carter. She was born in San Antonio,
Texas, graduated from Texas State Women's College
(Denton), and has made her home in New York City.
She married Arnold W. Koehler. In addition to writ-
ing for both children and adults, she has been a textile
designer and magazine editor. She has also been asso-
ciated with the New York Herald Tribune as a reviewer
of books for children. Irmengarde Eberle has received
many book awards, and her work has been translated
into several foreign languages. Juvenile titles include:
Apple Orchard, Walck, 1962; The Bands Play On (by
P. A. Carter, pseud.), McBride, 1942; Bears Live
Here, Doubleday, 1966; A Chipmunk Lives Here (A
Junior Literary Guild selection), Doubleday, 1966;
Evie And Cookie, Knopf, 1957; Robins On The Window
Sill, Crowell, 1958.   CA-4, JBA-2

EBERSTADT, Frederick   Isabel (Nash) 1934?-
Husband-wife team. Mr. Eberstadt graduated from
Phillips Exeter and Princeton University. He has been
a professional photographer. He married Isabel Nash,
the daughter of poet Ogden Nash, in 1954. For young
readers they wrote: What Is For My Birthday?, Little,
1961; Who Is At The Door? (A Junior Literary Guild
selection), Little, 1959.

EBY, Lois Christine 1908-
Her pseudonym is Patrick Lawson. She grew up on
an orange ranch in California where she acquired a
deep love and knowledge of horses. As a young girl
she was impressed with the beauty of the Arabian
horse and later did extensive research about him for
her book Star-Crossed Stallion (Dodd, 1954), winner of
the Boys' Life-Dodd, Mead Prize Competition. Lois
Eby has written mystery books, and her stories of adventure have appeared in newspapers. For children
she also wrote Star-Crossed Stallion's Big Chance,
Dodd, 1957.

ECONOMAKIS, Olga
Born in San Francisco, California, she studied at the
University of Lausanne in Switzerland. She has been
a member of the Foreign Service of the State Department. She met her husband in Cairo, Egypt, and they
have lived in Athens, Greece. For boys and girls she
wrote Oasis Of The Stars (A Junior Literary Guild selection), Coward, 1965.

EDELMAN, Lily
Born in California, she graduated from Hunter College
and received her master's degree from Columbia Uni-
versity. Mrs. Edelman has served as an editor in the
Department of State's Overseas Information Program
and as educational director of Pearl Buck's East and
West Association. She later was associated with B'nai
B'rith's Department of Adult Education. Her titles for
young people include: Hawaii, U. S. A., Nelson, 1954;
Israel, Nelson, 1958.

EDMONDS, Richard W.
Author and columnist. He had planned to become an
engineer, but he became a writer instead. At one
time Mr. Edmonds wrote a newspaper column. When
he read about Captain Joshua Barney in a history book,
the author decided to search for additional material
about him, and the result was Young Captain Barney,
Macrae, 1956.

EDMONDS, Walter Dumaux 1903-
He was born in Boonville, New York, attended Choate,
and graduated from Harvard. Following the publication
of his first story in Scribner's, his work has appeared
in Harper's, the Atlantic Monthly, and the Saturday

Evening Post. In 1942 he was awarded the Newbery
Medal for The Matchlock Gun, Dodd, 1941. Other
juvenile titles include: Cadmus Henry, Dodd, 1949;
Corporal Bess, Dodd, 1952; They Had A Horse, Dodd,
1962; Wilderness Clearing, Dodd, 1944. CA-7/8,
MJA

EDWARDS, Cecile Pepin 1916-
Author, librarian, teacher, born in Medfield, Massachusetts. She attended Boston's Wheelock College and
the University of New Hampshire at Durham. Mrs.
Edwards has made her home in Wrentham, Massachusetts. At one time she served as children's librarian
at the Walpole, Massachusetts Public Library. In addition to books for young people the author has also
written poetry. Her juvenile books include: John Alden: Steadfast Pilgrim, Houghton, 1965; Horace Mann:
Sower Of Learning, Houghton, 1958; Roger Williams,
Defender Of Freedom, Abingdon, 1957. CA-5/6

EHRLICH, Bettina Bauer 1903-
Her pseudonym is Bettina. She was born in Vienna,
Austria and attended Wiener Frauenerwerb-Verein and
Kunstgewerbeschule in Vienna. When she was young,
she spent a great deal of time on the island of Grado
in the northern Adriatic Sea. Grado has provided
much of the inspiration for Bettina's work. She married sculptor Georg Ehrlich and has lived in London.
In 1937 she was awarded a Silver Medal for hand-
painted silks at the International Exhibition of Arts and
Industries in Paris. Juvenile titles include: Castle In
The Sand, Harper, 1951; Goat Boy, Norton, [1966
c1965]; Trovato, Ariel, 1959; She also illustrated Virginia Haviland's Favorite Fairy Tales Told In England,
Little, 1959. CA-13/14, MJA

EIFERT, Virginia Louise (Snider) 1911-
Native of Springfield, Illinois, she has been editor of
the magazine the Living Museum which was published
by the Illinois State Museum. In order to write about
the rivers of our country she has traveled thousands of
miles aboard towboats and steamboats on the Illinois,
Ohio, Cumberland, Tennessee, and Mississippi Rivers.
She married a teacher, Herman D. Eifert. Her books
for young people include: Delta Queen, Dodd, 1960;
George Shannon: Young Explorer With Lewis And Clark,
Dodd, 1963; Mississippi Calling, Dodd, 1957; New Birth

Of Freedom, Dodd, 1959; Three Rivers South, Dodd, 1953.   CA-1

EINSEL, Walter
He married an illustrator and designer.   Mr. Einsel has been the recipient of several awards in the field of advertising design.   He and his wife and two daughters have lived in New York.   He wrote Did You Ever See?, Scott, 1962.

EISENBERG, Azriel Louis   1903-
Graduate of New York University, he received his doctor's degree from Columbia.   He also studied at the Teachers' Institute of the Jewish Theological Seminary. The author has been filmstrip director and Executive Vice President of New York's Jewish Education Committee.   He has also been editor of the "Junior Hebrew Library" and a director of the Bureau of Jewish Education.   For young people he wrote Great Discovery, Abelard-Schuman, 1956.

ELKIN, Benjamin   1911-
Born in Baltimore, teacher, principal, author.   He graduated from Lewis Institute and received both his master's and doctor's degrees from Northwestern University.   In addition to being principal of the Rogers School in Chicago, he has lectured at Roosevelt College. In 1965 the National Association for Gifted Children paid special recognition to Mr. Elkin for "his contributions to quality education through curriculum enrichment."   His juvenile books include: Al And The Magic Lamp, Harper, 1963; Gillespie And The Guards (A Junior Literary Guild selection), Viking, 1956; Lucky And The Giant (A Junior Literary Guild selection), Childrens Press, 1962; Why The Sun Was Late, Parents Mag. Press, 1966.   CA-4

ELKINS, Dov Peretz
During 1962-63, Mr. Elkins traveled to the Middle East for a year's study.   He has been associated with the field of education and interested in the study of archeology.   With noted educator Dr. Azriel Louis Eisenberg he wrote Worlds Lost And Found, Abelard, 1964.

ELLEN, Barbara   1938-
She has studied at the High School of Art and Design

and has been a member of the Art Students League in
New York. Barbara Ellen has been a commercial
artist and has lived in Brooklyn, New York. With
John Todaro she wrote Philip The Flower-Eating Phoenix, Abelard, 1961. CA-7/8

ELLIS, Harry Bearse 1921-
He has been associated with the Christian Science Monitor, and his assignments have included: Paris Chief of
Bureau and staff correspondent in Bonn, West Germany.
He also was a correspondent in the Middle East. Wesleyan University in Middletown, Connecticut awarded
Harry Ellis an honorary degree (Doctor of Humane Letters) in 1959. He wrote The Common Market, World,
1965. CA-1

ELLSBERG, Edward 1891-
Commander Ellsberg was born in New Haven, Connecti-
cut, grew up in Colorado, and later lived in Maine.
He graduated from the United States Naval Academy at
Annapolis and received a master's degree from the
Massachusetts Institute of Technology. Commander
Ellsberg received the Navy's Distinguished Service
Medal when the sunken Submarine S-51 was brought to
the surface under his command. His first story ap-
peared in Youth's Companion. Since then his books
for young people have included: "I Have Just Begun
To Fight!", Dodd, 1942; Spanish Ingots, Dodd, 1936;
Thirty Fathoms Deep, Dodd, 1930; Treasure Below,
Dodd, 1940. CA-7/8, JBA-1, JBA-2

ELMER, Irene (Elizabeth) 1937-
She grew up on a farm in Oregon and later lived in
Berkeley, California. She graduated from Mills College (Oakland, California) with a B. A. degree in English and received her master's degree from Smith
College (Northampton, Massachusetts). Irene Elmer
decided to become a writer at the age of twelve. She
has written short stories and has been a free-lance
writer. Her first book for children was entitled Benjamin, Abingdon, 1961. CA-4

ELTING, Mary 1909-
Her pseudonyms are Campbell Tatham and Benjamin
Brewster. She was born in Creede, Colorado and
graduated from the University of Colorado. She also
studied in France at the University of Strasbourg.

Mary Elting has been associated with Golden Book and
Forum magazines. She married writer Franklin Folsom. The Folsoms have lived in Roosevelt, New Jersey. Her juvenile books include: The Answer Book,
Grosset, 1964; Hopi Way, Evans, 1969. With her husband Franklin Folsom she wrote The Story Of Archeology In The Americas, Harvey, 1960.   CA-9/10,
MJA

ELWELL, Felicia Rosemary
English author and teacher. Miss Elwell has written
about science for television and radio and has been
associated with the British Broadcasting Company as
a producer of school science programs. She has also
been a science instructor. For young people she wrote
Atoms And Energy, Criterion, 1961.

EMBERLEY, Edward Randolph 1931-
He was born in Malden, Massachusetts and graduated
from the Massachusetts College of Art. Following ser-
vice in the army he studied advertising design at the
Rhode Island School of Design. The Emberleys have
lived in Massachusetts. In 1968 he was awarded the
Caldecott Medal for his illustrations in Drummer Hoff
(adapted by his wife Barbara), Prentice-Hall, 1967.
Other juvenile titles include: Cock A Doodle Doo,
Little, 1964; The Parade Book (A Junior Literary Guild
selection), Little, 1962; Rosebud (A Junior Literary
Guild selection), Little, 1966; The Wing On A Flea,
Little, 1961.   CA-5/6

EMERSON, Caroline Dwight 1891-
Teacher and writer, born in Amherst, Massachusetts.
She received her early education in Northampton, Massachusetts and Evanston, Illinois. After graduating
from Columbia University's Teachers College, she
taught school for many years in New York City. Miss
Emerson made her home in Holland, Massachusetts.
Her juvenile books include: New York City, Old And
New, Dutton, 1953; Old New York For Young New Yorkers, Dutton, 1932; Pioneer Children Of America, Heath,
1950.   CA-17/18

EMERY, Anne Eleanor McGuigan 1907-
She was born in Fargo, North Dakota and graduated
from Northwestern University. She also attended the
University of Grenoble in France. Mrs. Emery's father

was a university professor, and she also was a teacher
at one time.   She married John Emery and has lived
in Evanston, Illinois.   Juvenile titles include: Dinny
Gordon, Sophomore, Macrae Smith, 1961; First Love,
True Love, Westminster Press, 1956; First Orchid
For Pat, Westminster Press, 1957; High Note, Low
Note, Westminster Press, 1954; Senior Year, West-
minster Press, 1949; Sorority Girl, Westminster Press,
1952; Sweet Sixteen, Macrae Smith, 1956; Vagabond
Summer, Westminster Press, 1953.   CA-3, MJA

EMERY, Russell Guy 1908-
    Author and teacher, born in Minnesota.   He graduated
    from the United States Military Academy at West Point
    and studied law at the University of Virginia.   During
    World War II, Colonel Emery served overseas with
    an Infantry Division of the Third Army and was injured
    in the Battle of the Bulge.   He later returned to West
    Point and taught law.   He has contributed many arti-
    cles about sports to magazines.   His books for young
    people include: Adventure North, Macrae Smith, 1947;
    Gray Line And Gold, Macrae Smith, 1951; High, In-
    side!, Macrae Smith, 1948; Relief Pitcher, Macrae
    Smith, 1953; T-Quarterback, Macrae Smith, 1949;
    Warren Of West Point, Macrae Smith, 1950.

ENGEMAN, John T. 1901-
    Photographer and author.   He graduated from the Unit-
    ed States Naval Academy and later taught there.   Mr.
    Engeman has created many picture stories for maga-
    zines and has been a member of the National Press
    Photographers Association.   His juvenile books include:
    Airline Stewardess, Lothrop, 1960; U. S. Air Force
    Academy, Lothrop, 1962.

ENGVICK, William
    He was born in Oakland, California and graduated from
    the University of California at Berkeley.   He has writ-
    ten the lyrics for many songs which have been used in
    television shows.   He also wrote the lyrics for Res-
    pighi's music for "Sleeping Beauty In The Woods" pro-
    duced on "Omnibus. "   Mr. Engvick has lived in Stony
    Point, New York.   For boys and girls he edited Alec
    Wilder's Lullabies And Night Songs, Harper, 1965.

ENRIGHT, Elizabeth 1909-1968
    Writer-illustrator, born in Chicago.   She studied at the

Art Students League in New York and continued her
studies in Paris. She was an illustrator before she
became a writer of books for boys and girls. Her
book Thimble Summer (Farrar, 1938) was awarded
the Newbery Medal in 1939. She married Robert Gill-
man. Juvenile titles include: Gone-Away Lake, Harcourt, 1957; . . . Kintu, Farrar, 1935; The Melendy
Family, Rinehart, 1944; Spiderweb For Two, Rinehart,
1951; Tatsinda, Harcourt, 1963; Zeee, Harcourt, 1965.
JBA-2

EPSTEIN, Samuel 1909-   Beryl (Williams) 1910-
Husband-wife team. Their joint pseudonyms are Adam
Allen and Douglas Coe. His work has appeared under
the names of Charles Strong, Martin Colt, and Bruce
Campbell. Samuel Epstein was born in Boston, Massa-
chusetts, graduated from Rutgers University, and served
with the Army during World War II. Beryl Williams
Epstein was born in Columbus, Ohio, graduated from
Douglass College (New Jersey College for Women), and
at one time was a newspaper reporter and editor. The
Epsteins have lived in Southold, Long Island. Together
they wrote: All About Prehistoric Cave Men, Random
House, 1959; All About The Desert, Random House,
1957; First Book Of Codes And Ciphers, Watts, 1956;
Great Houdini, Magician Extraordinary, Messner, 1950;
Medicine From Microbes, Messner, 1965.   CA-7/8,
CA-9/10, MJA

ERDMAN, Loula Grace
She was born in Missouri and graduated from Central
Missouri State College at Warrensburg. She also
studied at the Universities of Southern California and
Wisconsin and received her master's degree from
Columbia University. Miss Erdman has taught in the
Sam Houston Junior High School at Amarillo and later
was on the faculty of West Texas State College at
Canyon. Her books for young people include: Good
Land, Dodd, 1959; Life Was Simpler Then, Dodd, 1963;
Room To Grow, Dodd, 1962; The Wide Horizon (jacket
design was painted by the author's niece, Elizabeth Ann
Erdman), Dodd, 1956; . . . The Wind Blows Free,
Dodd, 1952.   CA-7/8, MJA

ERICKSON, Phoebe 1907-
Author-illustrator, born of Swedish parents on a farm
in Wisconsin. As a child she listened to stories told

by her father and "covered yards of brown paper or
birchbark with drawings of strange looking horses and
even stranger looking people. " Miss Erickson studied
at the Chicago Art Institute. Her work has been exhibited both at the Whitney and Metropolitan Museums
in New York. She married Arthur Blair and has lived
in Connecticut and Vermont. Juvenile books which she
wrote and illustrated include: Black Penny, Knopf and
Junior Literary Guild, 1951; Daniel 'Coon, Knopf, 1954;
Double Or Nothing, Harper, 1958; True Book Of Animals Of Small Pond, Childrens Press, 1953; Who's In
The Mirror?, Knopf, 1965.   CA-1

ERICSON, Walter   see FAST, Howard Melvin

ERLICH, Lillian (Feldman) 1910–
Born in Johnstown, Pennsylvania, she studied at Cornell University and also at Columbia. Following her
marriage she lived in New York. She has always enjoyed music and had the good fortune to be related to
a semi-professional jazz pianist (an uncle) and a per-
former in amateur minstrel shows (her father). At
one time she wrote for newspapers and magazines.
Her first book was Modern American Career Women
(A Junior Literary Guild selection, Dodd, 1959) written
with Eleanor Clymer. She followed this with What Jazz
Is All About, Messner, 1962.   CA-4

ERNEST, Brother, C. S. C.
Teacher and writer, born in Elyria, Ohio. He entered
the Holy Cross Congregation in 1918. Brother Ernest
graduated from Notre Dame University, the Catholic
University of America (Washington, D. C.), and Portland University. He later returned to all three of
these universities as an instructor. He has also taught
in high schools. The author has written books for
young people since 1923. Some of his titles include:
A Story Of Saint Agatha, Dujarie, 1960; A Story Of
Saint Benedict The Negro, Dujarie, 1960; A Story Of
Saint Hyacinth, Dujarie, 1960; A Story Of Saint Paschal Baylon, Dujarie, 1960.

ESTES, Eleanor 1906–
She was born in West Haven, Connecticut (". . . It is
the town of Cranbury in my books. "). Following high
school she worked in the Children's Department of the
New Haven Public Library. She was awarded the

Caroline M. Hewins scholarship and attended Pratt Institute library school. At Pratt she met another student, Rice Estes, whom she married. Mr. Estes
became librarian at Pratt and Secretary of the Institute. Their daughter Helena provided the inspiration
for many of the author's later books. In 1952 she
was awarded the Newbery Medal for Ginger Pye, Harcourt, 1951. Other juvenile titles include: The Alley,
Harcourt, 1964; Hundred Dresses, Harcourt, 1944; A
Little Oven, Harcourt, 1955; The Moffats, Harcourt,
1941. CA-2, JBA-2

ESTORIL, Jean   see ALLAN, Mabel Esther

ETS, Marie Hall 1895-
Author-illustrator, born in Milwaukee, Wisconsin. A
graduate of the University of Chicago, she also attended Columbia University, Parsons School of Design,
and the Chicago Art Institute. She has done social
work in Chicago and once spent a year in Czechoslovakia where she helped to establish a child-health program. After the death of her husband Harold Ets in
1943, Mrs. Ets made her home in New York City.
She collaborated with Aurora Labastida to write Nine
Days To Christmas (Viking, 1959) which won the 1960
Caldecott Medal for her illustrations. Mrs. Ets also
received an Honor award from the International Jury
for the Hans Christian Andersen Medal for her book
Play With Me, Viking, 1955. Other books which she
wrote and illustrated include: Bad Boy, Good Boy,
Crowell, 1967; Just Me, Viking, 1965; Mister Penny,
Viking, 1935. CA-3, JBA-2

EVANS, Edna (Hoffman) 1913-
She graduated from Florida State University at Talla-
hassee. She has been photography editor of Nature
Magazine and has written articles for other periodicals.
She also has written for the St. Petersburg Times.
When she moved to Arizona in 1948, she became interested in brands. She later collected branding irons
in Mexico, Florida, and Canada. Miss Evans has
taught a course in children's literature at Phoenix College in Arizona. She wrote Written With Fire, Holt,
1962.

EVANS, Eva (Knox) 1905-
Teacher and writer, born in Roanoke, Virginia. Upon

graduation from college she taught in rural schools,
city classrooms, and migrant labor camps. She also
taught at the University of Atlanta (Georgia) in the
demonstration school for Negro children. The author
and her husband, the late Boris Witte, made their
home in New Hampshire. Her books for young people
include: Araminta, Minto, Balch & Co. , 1935; Home
Is A Very Special Place, Golden Press, 1961; People
Are Important, Capitol, 1951; Sleepy Time, Houghton,
1962; The Snow Book, Little, 1965; Why We Live
Where We Live, Junior Literary Guild and Little, 1953.
MJA

EVANS, Julia (Rendel) see HOBSON, Polly

EVANS, Katherine (Floyd) 1901-
Born in Sedalia, Missouri, she studied at the Chicago
School of Design, Chicago Art Institute, Provincetown
(Massachusetts) Art School, and in Paris. She was
instrumental in establishing the Artists' Market in
Evanston, Illinois which later became the Evanston
Art Center. Mrs. Evans has traveled extensively in-
cluding trips to Mexico, Ethiopia (she once exhibited
her paintings in Addis Ababa), Spain, and Morocco.
In addition to illustrating books for other authors, her
books include: A Bundle Of Sticks, Whitman, 1962;
A Camel In The Tent, Whitman, 1961; Little Bear Bum-
ble, Whitman, 1956.   CA-5/6

EVANS, Patricia Healy 1920-
She was born in Milwaukee, Wisconsin and later lived
in Berkeley, California. She has spent many years
collecting the language and folklore of children and has
written several booklets about it. Her husband has
operated a bookshop in San Francisco. She wrote
Rimbles; A Book Of Children's Classic Games, Rhymes,
Songs, And Sayings, Doubleday, 1961.

EVERS, Alf 1905-
Author and folklorist. His books have been enjoyed by
both small children and older boys and girls. A noted
authority on the folklore of New York State, he has
often lectured and written about it. Alf Evers and his
family have lived in Woodstock, New York. He collaborated with his wife Helen to write: Copy-Kitten,
Rand, 1937; The Happy Hen, Farrar, 1933; The Plump
Pig, Rand, 1938. Alf Evers also wrote: Abner's

Cabin, Watts, 1957; Baldhead Mountain Expedition,
Macmillan, 1959; The Colonel's Squad, Macmillan,
1952; There's No Such Animal, Lippincott, 1958; Three
Kings Of Saba, Lippincott, 1955; Treasure Of Watch-
dog Mountain, Macmillan, 1955.

EVERSON, William Keith 1929-
He was born in Yeovil, England. He has been associated with the film industry both in England and the
United States. Mr. Everson has been a publicity
director, a theater manager, and a research director
for several television series. He wrote The American
Movie, Atheneum, 1963. CA-4

EVERY, Philip Cochrane see BURNFORD, Sheila

EWEN, David 1907-
He has written about music and musicians for both
adults and children. His books have been translated
into several languages, and the "Voice of America"
has broadcast his series on the history of American
popular music. Time magazine once described him
as "music's interpreter to the American people." Mr.
Ewen has made his home in Miami, Florida. His
juvenile titles include: The Cole Porter Story, Holt,
1965; The Story Of America's Musical Theater (rev.
ed.), Chilton, 1968. CA-3

F

FABELL, Walter C.
Landscape architect and writer. As a landscape architect, Mr. Fabell combined talent with his love of
nature to create the beautiful garden of his Connecticut
home (which once was a windmill). He and his wife
have collected material about nature for his books.
Prior to being published in book form, his writing on
nature first appeared in newspapers. For children he
wrote Nature Was First!, McKay, 1952.

FABER, Doris (Greenberg) 1924-   Harold 1919-
Both native New Yorkers, and both have been reporters.
She attended Goucher College and graduated from New
York University. Mr. Faber, Editorial Director (Book
and Educational Division), of the New York Times
studied at the City College of New York. For young
people he wrote Soldier And Statesman: General George

C. Marshall (Farrar, 1964). The Fabers have lived
in Pleasantville, New York. They collaborated to
write American Heroes Of The 20th Century, Random,
1967. Her books include: Behind The Headlines, Pantheon, 1963; Clarence Darrow: Defender Of The People, Prentice-Hall, 1965; Petticoat Politics, Lothrop,
1967; Printer's Devil To Publisher (A Junior Literary
Guild selection), Messner, 1963.   CA-15/16, CA-17/
18

FALL, Thomas
    Of Cherokee descent, he grew up in Oklahoma and at-
    tended the University of Oklahoma. He began his
    literary career after World War II. Mr. Fall has
    made his home in New York City. His wife's child-
    hood experience with a fledgling sparrow hawk was the
    basis for his book My Bird Is Romeo, Dial, 1964. He
    also wrote Edge Of Manhood, Dial, 1964.

FALLS, Charles Buckles 1874-
    He was born in Fort Wayne, Indiana and has lived in
    Falls Village, Connecticut. He began his career in
    art with the Chicago Tribune and later moved to New
    York City where he achieved success as a poster
    artist. C. B. Falls has also won recognition as an
    etcher and mural painter. His murals have been seen
    in the State Office Building in Albany, New York and
    and the American Radiator Building and Players Club
    in New York. Many other writers have had their
    books for children illustrated by him. His ABC Book
    (Doubleday, 1923) was written for his daughter Bedelia
    Jane. Mr. Falls also wrote and illustrated The First
    3000 Years: Ancient Civilization Of The Tigris, Eu-
    phrates, And Nile River Valleys, And The Mediter-
    ranean Sea, Viking, 1960.   JBA-1, JBA-2

FARGO, Lucille Foster 1880-
    Author, librarian, teacher. Born near Madison, Wis-
    consin, she grew up in South Dakota and later attended
    Yankton College. She also studied at Whitman College
    in Walla Walla, Washington and received her library
    training from New York State Library School. Miss
    Fargo has been an Associate Professor of Library
    Science at Western Reserve University in Cleveland,
    Ohio and has worked with the American Library Asso-
    ciation in Chicago. The author has enjoyed swimming
    and hiking as hobbies. Her juvenile books include:

Come, Colors, Come, Dodd, 1940; Marian-Martha, Dodd, 1936; Prairie Chautauqua, Dodd, 1943.

FARJEON, Eleanor 1881-1965
Born in London, England, her father was writer B. L. Farjeon, and her grandfather was American actor Joseph Jefferson. She began reading and writing at a very early age and at sixteen had written an opera ("Floretta"). Miss Farjeon has been honored with many book awards. She received the Carnegie Medal in England, the Regina Medal from the Catholic Library Association, and the Hans Christian Andersen Award from the International Board on Books for Young People. Miss Farjeon had written more than eighty books (poems, books, plays) when she died in Hampstead, London. Juvenile titles include: Cherrystones, Lippincott, 1944; Glass Slipper, Viking, 1956; Mrs. Malone, Walck, 1962.   CA-11/12, JBA-1, JBA-2

FARLEY, Walter 1915-
He was born in Syracuse, New York and attended the University of Columbia where he wrote The Black Stallion (Random, 1941). At one time the author worked in an advertising firm, and he wrote for Yank magazine during World War II. Following the war, he lived on a farm in Pennsylvania where he raised horses. Walter Farley has traveled throughout this country, Central and South America, Hawaii, and Mexico to gather material for his books. These include: The Black Stallion And Flame, Random, 1960; Blood Bay Colt, Junior Literary Guild and Random, 1950; The Great Dane Thor, Random, 1966; Island Stallion's Fury, Random, 1951; Little Black, A Pony, Random, 1961; Man O'War, Random, 1962.   CA-19/20, JBA-2

FARMER, Penelope 1939-
English author, teacher. She was born in Westerham, Kent and studied at St. Anne's College, Oxford. She later did graduate work at Bedford College, London University. Miss Farmer once wrote about her job experiences: "In the intervals of being educated I have worked as a mother's help, a charwoman, a waitress, an office clerk, a postman, and a teacher." She has written stories for adults and a play which was produced on television in England. Her first book published in the United States was The Summer Birds, Harcourt, 1962.   CA-15/16

FARMER, Wendell   see   DAVIS, Lavinia (Riker)

FARRINGTON, Selwyn Kip   1904-
    Author, fisherman, railroad enthusiast.   S. Kip Far-
    rington, Jr. has held several world records for salt
    water fishing and has written both books and magazine
    stories about it.   Mr. Farrington was one of the de-
    signers of the emergency fishing equipment used by
    our Armed Forces.   His great interest in trains and
    railroads resulted in Giants Of The Rails, Garden
    City, 1944.

FAST, Howard Melvin   1914-
    His pseudonyms are E. V. Cunningham and Walter
    Ericson.   Born in New York, he studied at the Nation-
    al Academy of Design.   He once worked in a library
    and was a bean-picker in the Everglades.   One winter
    he lived on an Oklahoma Indian reservation.   He has
    lectured and written articles for magazines.   Juvenile
    titles include: Goethals And The Panama Canal, Mess-
    ner, 1942; Haym Salomon, Son Of Liberty, Messner,
    1941; Lord Baden-Powell Of The Boy Scouts, Messner,
    1941; Tall Hunter, Harper, 1942.   CA-2

FAULKNER, Anne Irvin   see   FAULKNER, Nancy Irvin

FAULKNER, Georgene   1873-
    She was born in Chicago, Illinois and studied at Ken-
    wood Institute, National Kindergarten College, and the
    University of Chicago.   She was known as "The Story
    Lady" due to the many storytelling programs which she
    conducted for boys and girls.   She has also been an
    editor on the Ladies Home Journal.   With John Becker
    she wrote Melindy's Medal, Messner, 1945.   She also
    wrote White Elephant, And Other Tales From Old India,
    Wise-Parslov, 1929.

FAULKNER, Nancy Irvin   1906-
    Historian, teacher, writer.   She was born in Lynch-
    burg, Virginia, graduated from Wellesley College and
    received her master's degree from Cornell University.
    The author has worked in both radio and television and
    has been an editor of Recreation Magazine.   At one
    time she taught history at Sweet Briar College in Vir-
    ginia.   Miss Faulkner later lived in New York City.
    Many of her books have been Junior Literary Guild
    selections and include: Mystery At Long Barrow House,

Doubleday, 1960; Pirate Quest, Doubleday, 1955; The
Sacred Jewel, Doubleday, 1961; The Secret Of The
Simple Code, Doubleday, 1965; Tomahawk Shadow,
Doubleday, 1959; The Traitor Queen, Doubleday, 1963.
CA-4

FEAGLES, Anita Rae   1926-
Born in Galesburg, Illinois, she studied at Knox College, and received her master's degree from City College of New York.   Anita Feagles and husband and
children have lived in Chappaqua, New York.   She
wrote The Tooth Fairy (Young Scott, 1962) after she
had heard her daughters, Wendy and Priscilla, discuss
Wendy's collection which she had saved for the "Tooth
Fairy." She also wrote: Casey, The Utterly Impossible Horse, Young Scott, 1960; Sea Rock, Bobbs, 1968.
CA-4

FELLER, Robert William Andrew   1918-
Born in Iowa, he displayed athletic ability at an early
age.   His father taught the game of baseball to him
when he was seven.   He pitched a game for the Cleveland Indians when he was seventeen.   During World
War II, Bob Feller served in the Navy.   It was in
1946 that he achieved the record of striking out 348
men breaking the forty-two year old record of Rube
Waddell.   His juvenile books include: How To Pitch,
Barnes, 1948; Strikeout Story, Barnes, 1947.

FELLNER, Rudolph
Author, musician, teacher.   He has received degrees
in musicology from universities in America and Austria.   Rudolph Fellner has been associated with the
Chicago, Montreal, NBC, and San Francisco Opera
companies as a member of their conductorial staffs.
He has also taught in New York at the Mannes College
of Music (Opera Department).   For young people he
wrote Opera Themes And Plots, Simon, 1958.

FELLOWS, Muriel H.
Teacher, author.   She studied anthropology at the University of Pennsylvania and has taught school in Philadelphia.   In the foreword to her book about the stone
age Little Magic Painter (Winston, 1938) N. C. Nelson,
Curator of Prehistoric Archaeology, American Museum
of Natural History wrote: ". . . The kind of life we
must imagine these cave people to have lived is well

told by Miss Fellows. " Mr. Nelson hoped that her
book would provide an incentive for boys and girls to
visit museums in order to learn more about these
ancient peoples.   She also wrote and illustrated The
Land Of Little Rain, Winston, 1936.

FELSEN, Henry Gregor 1916-
His pseudonym is Angus Vicker.   Born in Brooklyn,
New York, he attended the State University of Iowa,
and later made his home in Des Moines.   He served
with the Marine Corps as a drill instructor and later
was editor of Leatherneck magazine during World War
II.   Mr. Felsen has written for and about teen-agers.
Many of his stories have appeared in national magazines.   His books for young people include: Anyone
For Cub Scouts?, Scribner, 1954; Boy Gets Car, Random, 1960; Crash Club, Random, 1958; Hot Rod, Dutton, 1950; Street Rod, Random, 1953; To My Son In
Uniform, Dodd, 1967.   CA-4, JBA-2

FELTON, Harold William 1902-
He was born in Neola, Iowa.   He graduated from the
University of Nebraska, and has practiced law in New
York.   Mr. Felton has been interested in "tall tales"
since he was a boy and used to hear them from his
father.   He and his wife have lived in Jackson Heights,
New York.   His books include: Big Mose, Garrard,
1969; John Henry And His Hammer, Knopf, 1950.
CA-3, MJA

FENNER, Phyllis Reid 1899-
Librarian and teacher, born in Almond, New York.
She studied at Mount Holyoke College and received her
library degree from Columbia University.   For many
years she was librarian at Plandome Road School in
Manhasset, Long Island.   When she retired in 1955,
she made her home in Manchester, Vermont.   She has
compiled many anthologies including: Adventure, Rare
And Magical, Knopf, 1945; Brother Against Brother,
Morrow, 1957; Circus Parade, Knopf, 1954; Ghosts,
Ghosts, Ghosts . . . , Watts, 1952; Giggle Box, Knopf,
1950; Horses, Horses, Horses, Watts, 1949; Open
Throttle, Morrow, 1966.   CA-5/6

FENTON, Carroll Lane 1900-   Mildred Adams 1899-
Husband-wife team, both were born in Iowa, graduated
from the University of Chicago, and have been univer-

sity professors. He has been an editorial consultant
for a publishing firm and has conducted workshops in
nature writing. She has served as critic, photographer,
typist, and later was a co-author of her husband's
books. The Fentons have collected geological material
which has been exhibited in museums. Their home has
been in New Brunswick, New Jersey. Their juvenile
books include: In Prehistoric Seas, Doubleday, 1962;
Land We Live On, Doubleday, 1944; Our Changing
Weather (A Junior Literary Guild selection), Doubleday,
1954; Riches From The Earth, Day, 1953; Rocks And
Their Stories, Doubleday, 1951; Worlds In The Sky,
(rev. ed.), Day, 1963.   CA-1, MJA

FENTON, Edward 1917-
Born in New York, he attended Amherst College in
Massachusetts, and later lived in Italy and Greece
where he met and married a Greek child psychologist
(Sophia Harvati). Upon their return to the United
States, the Fentons made their home in Washington,
D. C. He translated Alki Zei's Wildcat Under Glass,
Holt, 1968. He also wrote: Fierce John, Holt, 1969;
Matter Of Miracles, Holt, 1967.   CA-9/10

FERAVOLO, Rocco Vincent 1922-
School principal, author, fencer, graduate of Montclair
State College. He has also continued his studies at
Rutgers University. In 1957 he was the recipient of
the Science Teacher Achievement Recognition Award.
Mr. Feravolo has served as principal of a Morristown,
New Jersey elementary school and has been a science
instructor in the Newark State College's Extension Di-
vision. His science books for young people include:
Junior Science Book Of Heat, Garrard, 1964; Junior
Science Book Of Light, Garrard, 1961; Junior Science
Book Of Weather Experiments, Garrard, 1963; Wonders
Of Mathematics, Dodd, 1963; Wonders Of Sound, Dodd,
1962.   CA-1

FERMI, Laura Capon 1907-
She was born in Rome, Italy and attended the University of Rome. Following her marriage to the late
Enrico Fermi, noted physicist and nuclear scientist,
she said: "After I married, the only true vacation
from physics that I ever had was the wartime period
of secrecy. At the end of the war, the vacation was
over." Laura Fermi was the recipient of a Guggen-

heim Fellowship in 1957 and has been a historian with
the Atomic Energy Commission. She attended the
First International Conference on the Peaceful Uses of
Atomic Energy in 1955. Mrs. Fermi has resided in
Chicago. For young people she wrote The Story Of
Atomic Energy, Random, 1961.   CA-2

FERRIS, Helen Josephine 1890-1969
Editor, author, born in Nebraska, the daughter of a
clergyman. She graduated from Vassar College. For
many years she was editor-in-chief of the Junior Literary Guild. She has also served as editor of the American Girl, the Guardian, and the children's book review department of the Atlantic Monthly. Helen Ferris
has been a trustee of the North Salem Free Library
which was near the summer home of the author and
her husband, Albert B. Tibbets. With Virginia Moore
she wrote Girls Who Did, Dutton, 1927. Juvenile
books which she compiled include: Girls, Girls, Girls
(A Junior Literary Guild selection), Watts, 1957;
Love's Enchantment, Doubleday, 1944.   JBA-1, JBA-2

FIELD, Eugene 1850-1895
He has been called the "poet of childhood." He was
born in St. Louis, Missouri, the son of the lawyer
who defended Dred Scott (first trial of famous Dred
Scott case). Eugene Field attended Williams and Knox
Colleges and the University of Missouri. He worked
on newspapers in Missouri and Colorado, and he also
had a column ("Sharps and Flats") in the Chicago Daily
News. Eugene Field loved children, and his own family consisted of eight children. A statue stands in his
memory in Lincoln Park in Chicago, Illinois. He
wrote Poems Of Childhood, Scribners, 1904.   JBA-1

FIELD, Rachel Lyman 1894-1942
Author, playwright, poet. She was born in New York
City and attended Radcliffe College in Cambridge.
Rachel Field was a contributor to St. Nicholas maga-
zine. She and her husband Arthur Pederson and their
small daughter Hannah lived in Beverly Hills, Califor-
nia. She wrote for both adults and children, and her
poetry has been enjoyed by all ages. In 1930 Rachel
Field received the Newbery Medal for Hitty: Her First
Hundred Years (Macmillan, 1929). Her book Prayer
For A Child (Macmillan, 1944) was awarded the Caldecott Medal in 1945 for its illustrations created by

Elizabeth Orton Jones.   Other juvenile titles include:
Calico Bush, Macmillan, 1931; Christmas Time, Mac-
millan, 1941; Polly Patchwork, Doubleday, 1928; Rachel
Field Story Book, Doubleday, 1958.   JBA-1, JBA-2

FINGER, Charles Joseph 1871-1941
He was born December 25 in Willesden, England. He
studied at King's College in London and at Frankfort-
on-the-Main, Germany.   He had been an editor, director of a music school, and manager of a railway before
he became a writer at the age of fifty.   He and his
family lived on a farm in Arkansas.   The author was
awarded the Newbery Medal in 1925 for Tales From
Silver Lands, Doubleday, 1924. He also wrote: Cape
Horn Snorter, Houghton, 1939; Courageous Companions,
Longmans, 1929; A Dog At His Heel, Winston, 1936.
JBA-1

FINNEY, Gertrude Elva (Bridgeman)
Born in Indiana, her childhood was spent in the mining
district (Harrison) of Idaho.   She married a doctor and
later lived in Spokane.   One of her books Sleeping
Mines (Junior Literary Guild and Longmans, 1951) was
based on her memories when she was a little girl living near the mines in Harrison.   Another story was
created from her grandmother's pioneering adventures
in Indiana.   She also wrote Is This My Love (A Junior
Literary Guild selection), Longmans, 1956.   CA-15/16

FISHER, Aileen Lucia 1906-
She was born in Iron River, Michigan.   She attended
the University of Chicago and received a degree in
journalism from the University of Missouri.   After
working in Chicago Miss Fisher moved to Colorado
where she has continued her writing career.   Many of
her stories, poems, and plays have been published
both in books and magazines.   Her juvenile titles include: Clean As A Whistle, Crowell, 1969; Summer
Of Little Rain (A Junior Literary Guild selection), Nelson, 1961.   With Olive Rabe she wrote Patriotic Plays
And Programs, Plays, 1956.   CA-5/6, MJA

FISHER, David
Author and artist who has lived in Glasgow, Scotland.
He has been associated with the film industry and has
worked in London, Johannesburg, and Paris.   Mr.
Fisher has written several books based on stories

which he told to his children. His oldest daughter provided him with ideas for the main character in his
first book Tilly Ballooning, Abelard, 1961. He also
wrote and illustrated The Criminal Career Of Vinegar
Tom, Abelard, 1963.

FISHER, Leonard Everett 1924-
    Illustrator-author, born in New York City. He attended
    Brooklyn College, the Art Students League, and grad-
    uated from the Yale Art School. He has been the re-
    cipient of the Weir Prize, Winchester Fellowship, and
    Pulitzer Traveling Fellowship in Art. He has been
    Dean of the Whitney School of Art in New Haven, Con-
    necticut. Leonard Fisher's work has been shown in
    numerous exhibitions. His home has been in Westport,
    Connecticut. He wrote and illustrated: A Head Full
    Of Hats, Dial, 1962; Potters, Watts, 1969.   CA-3

FISHER, Margery (Turner) 1913-
    Teacher, reviewer, writer. She studied at Somerville
    College, Oxford. She has reviewed books for boys
    and girls for a magazine and has been interested in
    courses on reading which have been organized for
    the National Federation of Women's Institutes. She
    married naturalist James Fisher and has lived near
    Northampton. She wrote: Intent Upon Reading, Brock-
    hampton, 1961; John Masefield, Walck, 1963.

FITCH, Clarke see SINCLAIR, Upton Beall

FITCH, Florence Mary 1875-1959
    Teacher, writer, daughter of a minister. Born in
    Stratford, Connecticut, she grew up in Buffalo, New
    York, and has traveled throughout Europe and the Far
    East. She graduated from Oberlin College (Ohio) where
    she later returned as a teacher and Dean of Women.
    The author received a Ph. D. in philosophy from the
    University of Berlin and did advanced study at Union
    Theological Seminary and the University of Chicago
    Divinity School. During her travels to other countries
    Miss Fitch studied religious customs and gathered
    factual material for her books. These include: Book
    About God, Lothrop, 1953; Child Jesus, Lothrop, 1955;
    One God, Lothrop, 1944; Their Search For God, Loth-
    rop, 1947.   MJA

FITZGERALD, Edward E.   1919-
Author and editor.   Prior to being editor of the Liter-
ary Guild, Ed Fitzgerald was Sport magazine's editor.
In addition to his own books, he collaborated with Yogi
Berra and Althea Gibson to write books for children.
With Mel Allen he wrote You Can't Beat The Hours,
Harper, 1964.   His juvenile books include: Champions
In Sports And Spirit, Farrar, 1956; College Slugger,
Barnes, 1950.

FITZHARDINGE, Joan Margaret   1912-
Her pseudonym is Joan Phipson.   Born in Warrawee,
New South Wales, Australia, she has lived on a sheep
ranch at Mandurama.   A distinguished writer of chil-
dren's books, she has been a member of the Australian
Society of Authors.   Her book The Family Conspiracy
(Harcourt, 1964) received the Book-of-the-Year prize
presented by the Australian Children's Book Council
and the New York Herald Tribune Children's Spring
Book Festival Award.   Other titles by Joan Phipson
include: Birkin, Harcourt, 1966; The Boundary Riders,
Harcourt, 1963; Cross Currents, Harcourt, 1967;
Threat To The Barkers, Harcourt, 1965.   CA-15/16

FITZHUGH, Louise
Author and artist, born in Memphis, Tennessee.   She
attended the Art Students League, Bard College, and
Cooper Union.   Prior to locating in New York City,
Miss Fitzhugh had lived in France, Italy, and Washington, D. C.   The Banfer Gallery in New York has exhibited her paintings.   Her first book illustrations appeared in Sandra Scoppettone's Suzuki Beane, Doubleday, 1961.   She wrote and illustrated: Bang, Bang,
You're Dead, Harper, 1969; Harriet The Spy, Harper,
1964; The Long Secret, Harper, 1965.

FITZSIMMONS, Robert
Author and baseball player.   He was born in Newark,
New Jersey, attended Seton Hall, and has lived in
Greenwich Village in Manhattan.   His career has included: ghost writer, public relations adviser with a
chemical firm, and baseball player in the minor leagues.   His son Riley posed for the pictures in his
book How To Play Baseball (written with Martin Iger),
Doubleday, 1962.

FLACK, Marjorie 1897-1958
Author-illustrator, born and raised in Greenport, Long
Island. She studied at the Art Students League in New
York where she met her husband Karl Larsson. Their
daughter Hilma later married artist Jay Hyde Barnum.
Marjorie Flack was later married to poet William
Rose Benét and lived in Massachusetts. Juvenile titles
include: Angus And The Ducks, Doubleday, 1931; Ask
Mr. Bear, Macmillan, 1932; New Pet, Doubleday,
1943; The Story About Ping, Viking, 1933; Wag-Tail
Bess, Doubleday, 1933; Wait For William, Houghton,
1935.   JBA-1, JBA-2

FLANDERS, Michael (Henry) 1922-
Author and singer. His popular recordings resulted
from successful musicals which he did with Donald
Swann. These have included: "At The Drop Of A
Hat, " "At The Drop Of Another Hat, " "Bestiary Of
Flanders And Swann. " Michael Flanders has made
his home in London. He wrote Creatures Great And
Small, Holt, 1965.   CA-7/8

FLEISCHMAN, Albert Sidney 1920-
Author and magician, born in Brooklyn. He spent his
childhood in San Diego, California. At seventeen he
wrote his first book about magic, and he traveled with
a magic show in order to pay for two years at San
Diego State College. Sid Fleischman completed his
college education after World War II. He has been a
reporter on the San Diego Daily Journal and a writer
for motion pictures (for one of his own adult novels).
He and his family have lived in Santa Monica, California. His juvenile book By The Great Horn Spoon (A
Junior Literary Guild selection, Little, 1963) was selected by the Boys' Clubs of America as the best book
for older boys in 1963. He also wrote The Ghost In
The Noonday Sun, Little, 1965.   CA-3

FLEMING, Alice (Mulcahey) 1928-
She was born in New Haven, Connecticut, graduated
from Trinity College in Washington, D. C. , and re-
ceived her master's degree from Columbia University.
She married Thomas J. Fleming, a writer, and they
have lived in New York City. She wrote: Doctors In
Petticoats, Lippincott, 1964; Senator From Maine:
Margaret Chase Smith, Crowell, 1969.   CA-4

FLEMING, Elizabeth P.
She was born in Morioka, Japan, the daughter of missionaries. She received her education in America and graduated from Teachers College in Fredonia, New York. She has enjoyed an unusual and very rewarding hobby of creating animal quilts for boys and girls who have been hospitalized. Mrs. Fleming has lived in Oak Park, Illinois. She wrote The Takula Tree, Westminster, 1964.

FLEMING, Ian (Lancaster) 1908-1964
Adult mystery writer, born in England. He studied at the University of Geneva and the University of Munich. During World War II, he was in the Intelligence Service, and the experience provided him with a good background in order to write thrilling stories about his popular hero, James Bond. He has been Vice President for Europe of the North American Newspapers Alliance, foreign manager for the Kemsely Newspapers, Ltd., and foreign manager for the London Sunday Times. For young people he wrote Chitty Chitty Bang Bang, Random, 1964. CA-7/8

FLETCHER, Beale
Dancer and writer, born in Asheville, North Carolina. When he attended the University of North Carolina, he became a member of the "Carolina Playmakers." He later was a dance instructor in New York and also performed in night clubs. During an engagement in Montreal he met his future wife, and they became known as "The Dancing Fletchers." The author and his wife returned to his native Asheville where they operated the Fletcher School of Dancing. This school became one of the largest dancing schools in the South. For young people he wrote How To Improve Your Tap Dancing, Barnes, 1957.

FLETCHER, Charlie May (Hogue) see SIMON, Charlie May (Hogue)

FLETCHER, Helen Jill 1911-
She has written for both radio and television and has been responsible for several record albums for boys and girls. Many of her articles have appeared in such magazines as the Instructor, Junior Arts And Crafts, and Parents' Magazine. Her juvenile books include: Adventures In Archaeology, Bobbs, 1962; For Junior

Doctors Only, Bobbs, 1961; Would You Believe?, Platt, 1969.   CA-9/10

FLOETHE, Louise Lee 1913-
Daughter of an artist, she also married an artist. She and her husband Richard Floethe have lived in Sarasota, Florida. Mrs. Floethe has been an actress and has also directed children's plays. Mr. Floethe's prints and water-colors have been in the collections of museums. She wrote, and he illustrated: Blueberry Pie, Scribner, 1962; The Fisherman And His Boat, Scribner, 1961; The New Roof, Scribner, 1965; Sea Of Grass, Scribner, 1963.   CA-1

FLOHERTY, John Joseph 1882-1964
He attended the Art Students League in New York and later served in an executive capacity for a publishing firm. The author has been called "The Star Reporter for American Youth" due to his authentic books for young people based on personal observations and experiences. With Mike McGrady he wrote Youth And The FBI (Lippincott, 1960) for which J. Edgar Hoover wrote the forward. Other juvenile books by John Floherty include: Aviation From The Ground Up (rev. ed.), Lippincott, 1957; Behind The Silver Shield, Lippincott, 1948; Deep Down Under, Lippincott, 1953; Forest Ranger, Lippincott, 1956; Get That Story (rev. ed.), Lippincott, 1964; Sons Of The Hurricane, Lippincott, 1938.   JBA-2

FOLEY, Daniel Joseph 1913-
Author, editor, lecturer. He has been called a "Christmas historian" because of the many books he has written about Christmas. Daniel Foley has made radio and television appearances, given lectures, and contributed to magazines and newspapers in addition to writing books for young people. He has also been interested in gardening and was editor of Horticulture (1951-57). For children he wrote Christmas The World Over . . ., Chilton, 1963.   CA-7/8

FOLLETT, Helen (Thomas)
This author has made her home in New York. She has sailed on a schooner in the South Seas where she collected material for some of her books. Her book Ocean Outposts (Scribner, 1942) was illustrated with maps drawn by Armstrong Sperry, winner of the 1941

Newbery MedaL   Helen Follett also wrote Islands On
Guard, Scribners, 1943.

FOLSOM, Franklin (Brewster) 1907-
Teacher, journalist, author, born in Colorado.   He
married writer Mary Elting, and they have lived in
Roosevelt, New Jersey.   Mr. Folsom was a Rhodes
Scholar at Oxford University.   He was also awarded
the Harriet Monroe Memorial Award for poetry.   The
author has been interested in conservation and the
Rocky Mountain area.   For young people he wrote:
Famous Pioneers, Harvey, 1963; The Forest Fire Mystery, Harvey, 1963.   With his wife Mary Elting he
wrote The Story Of Archeology In The Americas, Harvey, 1960.   CA-3

FOLSOM, Michael Brewster 1938-
He was born in New York City, the son of authors
Franklin Folsom and his wife, Mary Elting.   Michael
Folsom graduated from Antioch College (Yellow Springs,
Ohio) and received his master's degree from Rutgers
University (New Brunswick, New Jersey).   He also
studied at Leeds University in England and did gradu-
ate work at the University of California at Berkeley.
He has taught at the Massachusetts Institute of Tech-
nology in Cambridge, and his wife, the former Marcia
McClintock, has been on the faculty of Boston College
in Newton.   With his mother Mary Elting, he wrote
The Secret Story Of Pueblo Bonito, Harvey House,
1963.

FORBERG, Ati
Artist, illustrator, editor.   Her home has been in
Brooklyn, New York.   She has also traveled extensive-
ly throughout Europe.   Her illustrations have appeared
in numerous books for children including Phyllis Mc-
Ginley's Boys Are Awful (Watts, 1962).   She also
edited and illustrated On A Grass-Green Horn, Old
Scotch And English Ballads (her first book for children),
Atheneum, 1965.

FORBES, Esther 1894-1967
She was born in Westborough, Massachusetts, graduated from Bradford Academy, and studied at the University of Wisconsin.   She once was a member of the
editorial department of a publishing company.   Her
book Paul Revere & The World He Lived In (Houghton,

1942) won the Pulitzer Prize in 1943, and her book
for boys and girls Johnny Tremain (Houghton, 1943)
was awarded the Newbery Medal in 1944. She also
wrote America's Paul Revere, Houghton, 1946.   CA-
13/14, MJA

FORBES, Katherine (Russell)   d. 1956
She was born on a farm in New Hampshire and later
lived in Marblehead, Massachusetts.   Mrs. Forbes
once wrote of her writing career: "Always when I
could get together a knot of small children I have told
stories, first to my four brothers and sisters, then
to my three sons; and now I am making a quiet living
by writing books for six grandchildren. "   For children
she wrote Dog Who Spoke To Santa Claus, McKay,
1956.

FORMAN, Brenda-Lu   1936-
A graduate of Barnard College, she was born in Hollywood, the daughter of author Harrison Forman.   She
spent her childhood in Port Washington, New York and
later lived in Manhattan.   Miss Forman has studied
music and piano.   With her father she wrote The Land
And People Of Nigeria, Lippincott, 1964.   CA-9/10

FORMAN, Harrison   1904-
Author, correspondent, lecturer.   He has traveled
throughout the world.   During his many years as a
foreign correspondent, Mr. Forman was on the scene
during many crucial periods in world history including
the bombardment of Shanghai (1937) and Warsaw (1939).
He has been a lecturer on both radio and television
and has contributed to such magazines as Harper's,
Holiday, Life, and Reader's Digest.   With his daughter
Brenda-Lu Forman he wrote The Land And People Of
Nigeria, Lippincott, 1964.   CA-5/6

FORD, Lauren   1891-
Born in New York City, the daughter of Simeon Ford
(owner of Grand Union Hotel in New York) and Julia
Ellsworth Ford (author and founder of the Julia Ellsworth Ford Foundation).   Lauren Ford received her
education at Rye Seminary, Académie Colarossi, and
the Art Students League.   Private collectors as well
as the Metropolitan Museum of Art in New York and
the Corcoran Gallery of Art in Washington, D. C. have
hung her paintings.   She has lived on a farm near

Bethlehem, Connecticut. Juvenile titles include:
Lauren Ford's Christmas Book, Dodd, 1963; The Little
Book About God, Doubleday, 1934.

FORD, Nancy K.
Her plays, stories, and verses have been published in
children's magazines. She has been on the staff of
Jack And Jill magazine as an associate editor. Nancy
Ford has lived in a farm house (one hundred-years-
old) near Harrisburg, Pennsylvania and also has had
an apartment in Philadelphia. She wrote: Baba Yaga
And The Enchanted Ring, Lippincott, 1960; Baba Yaga
And The Prince, Lippincott, 1961.

FORMAN, James 1932-
Attorney and author, born in Mineola, New York. He
attended Princeton University and Columbia Law School.
Mr. Forman and his family have made their home in
Port Washington, New York. For young people he
wrote: The Cow Neck Rebels, Straus, 1969; Ring The
Judas Bell (A Junior Literary Guild selection), Bell,
1965.   CA-9/10

FORREST, Sybil see MARKUN, Patricia (Maloney)

FORRESTER, Frank H.
Meteorologist, writer, native New Yorker. He has
been weather observer and forecaster for training units
in the U. S. Marine Air Corps and has been a meteorologist for an airline company at La Guardia Airport.
At one time Mr. Forrester worked in New York's
Hayden Planetarium as "deputy manager" which included teaching and creating promotional material for
the news media. He has been a member of the A-
merican Meteorological Society and the New York
Academy of Sciences. The author and his family have
lived in Jacksonville, Florida. For young people he
wrote The Real Book About The Weather, Garden City,
1958.

FORSYTH, Gloria
She graduated from Bennett Junior College and Stanford
University. Gloria Forsyth has worked in a radio
station in San Francisco and on a newspaper in Santa
Barbara. She and her husband have edited This Week
In Santa Barbara. At one time she attended a Univer-
sity of Connecticut Writers' Conference and was for-

tunate in having Newbery Medal winner Elizabeth Yates
(Amos Fortune, Free Man, Aladdin, 1950) as her
teacher. She wrote Pelican Prill, Dutton, 1956.

FOSDICK, Harry Emerson 1878–
This noted Protestant clergyman was born in Buffalo,
New York. He graduated from Colgate University and
attended Union Theological Seminary and Columbia University. At one time he taught at Union Theological
Seminary in New York City. He preached at the non-
denominational Riverside Church until 1946. His titles
for young people include: Jesus Of Nazareth, Random,
1959; The Life Of Saint Paul, Random, 1962; Martin
Luther, Random, 1956.

FOSS, William Otto 1918–
Author and newspaperman, born in Boston, Massachusetts. He received his education in Norway and Milton, Massachusetts. His home has been in Virginia
Beach, Virginia. William Foss joined the Navy and
has worked for the Navy Times and served as trans-
lator-researcher for the Central Intelligence Agency.
He has also been associated with the U. S. Department
of Commerce as a writer, and he has been a member
of the United States Naval Institute. With Erik Bergaust he wrote: The Marine Corps In Action, Putnam,
1965; Skin Divers In Action, Putnam, 1965. CA-19/20

FOSTER, Genevieve (Stump) 1893–
Illustrator and author, born in Oswego, New York. She
grew up in Wisconsin and graduated from the University of Wisconsin. She also studied at the Chicago
Academy of Fine Arts. Prior to writing books, Mrs.
Foster illustrated books for children. Her juvenile
books include: Abraham Lincoln's World, Scribner,
1944; Andrew Jackson, Scribner, 1951; Year Of The
Pilgrims: 1620, Scribner, 1969. CA-5/6, JBA-2

FOSTER, George Allen 1907–
He studied at Dartmouth College and graduated from
the Eastman School of Music. Mr. Foster has been
interested in the study of the Civil War and in politics
where he has been both a spectator and a participant.
In addition to being an author, he has been an instructor in a college. For young people he wrote: Eyes &
Ears Of The Civil War, Criterion, 1963; Road To The
White House, Criterion, 1969. CA-9/10

FOSTER, Marian Curtis 1909-
Her pseudonym is Mariana. Author and illustrator,
born in Atlanta, Georgia. She received her education
in New Orleans (Sophie Newcomb Art School), New
York (Art Students League), and Paris (Académie de
la Grande Chaumière). She has lived in New York during the winter months and on Long Island (Wainscott)
in the summertime. Juvenile books which she has
written and illustrated include: Doki, The Lonely Pa-
poose (A Junior Literary Guild selection), Lothrop,
1955; The Journey Of Bangwell Putt, Lothrop, 1965.

FOX, Dorothy
She was born in Oak Park, Illinois. Dorothy Fox has
been manager of the Photo and Print Department of
the National Audubon Society. She has been recognized
as an authority not only on old editions of Audubon
prints but also on modern Audubon print editions. With
Maie Lounsbury Wells she wrote Boy Of The Woods,
Dutton, 1942.

FOX, Mary Virginia
She began writing at an early age and had many short
stories published. The author attended Northwestern
University where she majored in art. After her
marriage, Mary Fox traveled to New York where a
visit to the Statue of Liberty inspired her to write
Apprentice To Liberty, Abingdon, 1960. She also
wrote Ambush At Fort Dearborn, St Martins, 1962.

FOX, William Wellington 1909-
Born in Ontario, Oregon, he graduated from the University of California and has been associated with the
Soil Conservation Service, United States Department
of Agriculture. Mr. Fox has also lectured and served
as Principal Museum Paleontologist at the University
of California and has been General Chairman of the
California Writers Conference. He and his wife, a
librarian, have lived in Berkeley, California. His
books for young people include: Rocks And Rain And
The Rays Of The Sun, Walck, 1958; Careers In Bio-
logical Sciences, Walck, 1963. CA-4

FRANCIS, Henry S. 1925-
He was born in Cambridge, Massachusetts and graduated from Harvard University. Henry Francis, Jr.,
has been associated with the National Science Founda-

tion's Antarctic Program. During the International
Geophysical Year he worked with the U. S. program in
Little America. He has lived in Washington, D. C.
With Philip M. Smith he wrote Defrosting Antarctic
Secrets, Coward, 1962.

FRANK, Josette 1893-
Author, lecturer, native New Yorker. She has served
on the Advisory Editorial Board of National Comics
Publications. For many years Josette Frank worked
with the Children's Book Committee of the Child Study
Association of America. She has written articles for
many magazines including: McCall's, Child Study, and
Parents' Magazine. Juvenile books include: What
Books For Children?, Doubleday, 1937; Your Child's
Reading Today (rev. ed.), Doubleday, 1969.

FRANKEL, Edward
Lecturer, teacher, author. He graduated from the
College of the City of New York, received his master's
degree from Columbia University, and obtained a Ph. D.
degree from Yeshiva University. He has taught at the
Bronx High School of Science and has been associated
with the New York City Board of Education's Bureau
of Educational Research. Edward Frankel has also
been chairman of the Yeshiva University High School's
Science Department. He wrote DNA, Ladder Of Life,
McGraw, 1964.

FRASCONI, Antonio 1919-
Artist and author, born in Uruguay. In 1945 he came
to the United States on a scholarship to the Art Students League. He also attended the New School for
Social Research. He has received many awards which
have included a grant from the National Institute of
Arts and Letters in 1954 and two Guggenheim Inter-
American Fellowships. Antonio Frasconi has held
many one-man shows, and much of his work can be
found in museums and private collections. He married artist Leona Pierce, and their home has been in
South Norwalk, Connecticut. His juvenile books include: . . . House That Jack Built, Harcourt, 1958;
See Again, Say Again, Harcourt, 1964; . . . See And
Say, Guarda E Parla, Mira Y Habla, Regarde Et Parle,
Harcourt, 1955; . . . The Snow And The Sun, Harcourt, 1961.   CA-1

FRASER, Beatrice   Ferrin
Husband and wife team.   Both attended high school in
Lockport, New York.   She studied at the Eastman
School of Music at the University of Rochester, and
he went to Columbia University.   Following graduation,
she traveled to Europe, and they were married in
Paris.   When they returned to the United States, Mrs.
Fraser started a Music School, and Ferrin Fraser con-
tinued his career in writing and publishing.   Both have
enjoyed golf as a hobby.   Together they wrote A Song
Is Born, Little, 1959.

FRAZER, Andrew   see   LESSER, Milton

FRAZIER, Neta (Lohnes)   1890-
Author and teacher.   She was born in Owasso, Michi-
gan, graduated from Whitman College in Walla Walla,
Washington and has lived in Spokane.   The author has
been a teacher in a high school at Waitsburg, Washing-
ton and a newspaper editor.   She married Earl C.
Frazier, a teacher that she met in Waitsburg.   Her
juvenile books include: Five Roads To The Pacific,
McKay, 1964; The General's Boots, McKay, 1965;
The Magic Ring (A Junior Literary Guild selection),
Longmans, 1959; Sacajawea, McKay, 1967; Young Bill
Fargo (A Junior Literary Guild selection), Longmans,
1956.   CA-2

FREDERICKS, Arnold   see   KUMMER, Frederic Arnold

FREEDMAN, Russell (Bruce)   1929-
He was born in San Francisco, California and graduated
from the University of California at Berkeley.   He
served in the Counter Intelligence Corps in Korea and
later was an Associated Press reporter.   Mr. Freedman has also written publicity for television and material for an encyclopedia.   He has lived in New York
City.   His books for young people include: Jules
Verne: Portrait Of A Prophet, Holiday, 1965; Teen-
Agers Who Made History, Holiday, 1961.   CA-19/20

FREEMAN, Don   1908-
Born in San Diego, California, he attended Principia
College and the Art Students League.   His drawings
of the theater have appeared in the New York Herald
Tribune and the New York Times.   He met his wife
while attending school in San Diego.   Mr. and Mrs.

Freeman collaborated to write Pet Of The Met, Junior
Literary Guild and Viking, 1953. He also wrote and
illustrated: Dandelion, Viking, 1964; Tilly Witch, Viking, 1969.

FREEMAN, Eugene
He attended Ohio State University and the University of
California at Los Angeles. The author received his
doctorate from the University of Chicago. Dr. Free-
man has been on the staff of the Illinois Institute of
Technology as an instructor of philosophy. Eugene
Freeman has lived in Wilmette, Illinois. With David
Appel he edited The Great Ideas Of Plato, Lantern,
1952.

FREEMAN, Godfrey
Born in Oxfordshire, England, his father was a clergyman. Mr. Freeman studied at St. Edward's, Oxford.
He was a glider pilot during World War II and was
captured by the Germans at Arnhem. Following the
war, he lived in Iran. Mr. Freeman, an English
schoolmaster, has lived near Oxford. He wrote about
the adventures of Till Eulenspiegel in The Owl And
The Mirror, Duell, 1960.

FREEMAN, Ira Maximilian 1905-   Mae (Blacker) 1907-
Husband-wife team. Both are photographers. Dr.
Freeman has been a science consultant to UNESCO, an
associate professor of physics at Rutgers University,
and a member of the Educational Testing Service's
Physics Committee. Mae Blacker Freeman has collaborated with her husband to write science books for
boys and girls. After living in Princeton where they
became acquainted with Albert Einstein, Mrs. Freeman
wrote Story Of Albert Einstein (Random, 1958). Her
interest in the ballet resulted in Fun With Ballet, Random, 1952. Together the Freemans wrote: Fun And
Experiments With Light, Random, 1963; You Will Go
To The Moon, Random, 1959; Your Wonderful World
Of Science, Random, 1957. Ira Freeman wrote: All
About Electricity, Random, 1957; All About Light And
Radiation, Random, 1965; All About Sound And Ultra-
sonics, Random, 1961. MJA

FREEMAN, Serge Herbert
He was born in Los Angeles, California and graduated
from the University of Southern California. He has

been a high school coach and a physical educational
instructor at El Camino College. He also served as
varsity baseball coach at the college. Mr. Freeman
and his family have lived in Redondo Beach, California. For young people he wrote Basic Baseball Strat-
egy, Doubleday, 1965.

FRENCH, Dorothy Kayser 1926-
She received her degree in journalism from the University of Wisconsin. She has written articles for
both newspapers and magazines. Mrs. French's husband has been a patent attorney for a petroleum company, and they have lived in Bartlesville, Oklahoma.
Her first book was The Mystery Of The Old Oil Well,
Watts, 1963. She also wrote Swim To Victory, Lippincott, 1969.   CA-9/10

FRENCH, Marion Flood
She graduated from the Bangor Theological Seminary
and later worked throughout the state of Maine with
young people. Miss French has written for publications in the field of religious education and has also
been a proofreader on a newspaper. She wrote Mr.
Bear Goes To Boston, Follett, 1955.

FRENCH, Paul see ASIMOV, Isaac

FREUCHEN, Peter 1886-1957
Born in Denmark, he studied at the university in Copenhagen in order to become a doctor. The sea changed
his mind for him, and he took many trips to the
Arctic. He wrote about Eskimos and his adventures
in the Arctic. During World War II, he was captured
by the Nazis and later escaped from a German concentration camp. In the United States he was a winning
contestant on the television program "The $64,000
Question." He contributed: Peter Freuchen's Story
About Life In The Seven Seas (by Peter Freuchen with
David Loth), Messner, 1959; Peter Freuchen's Story
About Treasures Of The Seven Seas (by Peter Freuchen
with David Loth), Messner, 1959.

FREWER, Glyn 1931-
Born in England, he has traveled throughout his native
land and in Europe. He has been interested in ornithology. Mr. Frewer has been associated with a London advertising firm and has resided in Surrey. For

boys and girls he wrote Adventure In Forgotten Valley
(A Junior Literary Guild selection), Putnam, 1964.
CA-15/16

FREY, Shaney
    She was born in Baltimore, Maryland and studied art
    at the Maryland Institute of Fine Arts.   Shaney Frey
    has enjoyed skin diving and underwater photography.
    She married a physicist who took many of the photo-
    graphs which appeared in the author's book The Com-
    plete Beginner's Guide To Skin Diving, Doubleday, 1965.

FRIBOURG, Marjorie G.   1920-
    Author and teacher, born in Chappaqua, New York.
    After graduating from Columbia University she became
    a teacher.   She has been interested in American his-
    tory and enjoyed the study of it through reading her
    husband's law books and spending a great deal of time
    in research at the Library of Congress.   Mrs. Fri-
    bourg has been active in literary and civic organiza-
    tions.   With her husband (a trial examiner with the
    Federal Power Commission) she has lived in Washing-
    ton.   Her juvenile books include: Dear Valentine,
    Sterling, 1957; The Supreme Court In American His-
    tory, Macrae, 1965.   CA-3

FRIEDMAN, Estelle (Ehrenwald) 1920-
    She has lived in Nashville, Tennessee where she has
    conducted surveys for a public opinion firm.   Mrs.
    Friedman graduated from Vanderbilt University where
    she studied philosophy.   She has also been interested
    in archaeology.   For boys and girls she wrote: Ben
    Franklin, Putnam, 1961; Digging Into Yesterday, Put-
    nam, 1958.   CA-5/6

FRIENDLICH, Dick 1909-
    Author and sportswriter.   Richard J. Friendlich began
    his newspaper career with the Associated Press at the
    age of seventeen.   He attended Stanford University.
    His work as a sportswriter on the San Francisco
    Chronicle was interrupted only by World War II and by
    European travel.   Young readers have enjoyed his
    authentic books which include: Backstop Ace, West-
    minster, 1961; Fullback From Nowhere (A Junior Liter-
    ary Guild selection), Westminster, 1967.   CA-15/16

FRIERMOOD, Elisabeth (Hamilton) 1903-
Author and librarian, born in Marion, Indiana. She
attended Northwestern University and the University of
Wisconsin. For many years she was a children's
librarian in Marion, Indiana and Dayton, Ohio. The
author married her high school sweetheart, Harold T.
Friermood. Dr. and Mrs. Friermood and their daughter have lived in Pelham, New York. For young people she wrote: Candle In The Sun (A Junior Literary
Guild selection), Doubleday, 1955; Pepper's Paradise,
Doubleday, 1969. CA-1, MJA

FRISBEE, Lucy Post
Her husband has been a Colonel in the Air Force, and
they have lived in McLean, Virginia. When she wrote
John F. Kennedy: Young Statesman (Bobbs, 1964) for
young people, she not only contacted many of the late
President's friends and associates in order to achieve
authenticity, but she also created a realistic background
in the book drawn from her own personal experiences
when she lived in Boston and spent summers on Cape
Cod. She also wrote John Burroughs, Boy Of Field
And Stream, Bobbs, 1964.

FRISCH, Otto Robert 1904-
Physicist, lecturer, writer. He was born in Vienna
and attended schools there. In 1939 he interpreted the
work of physical chemists Otto Hahn and Fritz Strass-
mann on the pheonomenon of nuclear fission with physicist Lise Meitner. Professor Frisch has also served
as editor of Progress In Nuclear Physics (an annual
review). He has been associated with the Cavendish
Laboratory as head of its nuclear physics department
and with the University of Cambridge as Jacksonian
Professor of Physics. For young people he wrote
Atomic Physics Today, Basic Bks., 1961. CA-11/12

FRISKEY, Margaret (Richards) 1901-
Her pseudonym is Elizabeth Sherman. She was born in
Newton, Massachusetts and has made her home in
Phoenix, Arizona. Margaret Friskey wanted to be a
writer from her earliest school days. Her many books
for children include: Cave Man To Space Man, Chil-
drens, 1961; Indian Two Feet And His Horse (A Junior
Literary Guild selection), Childrens, 1959; Mystery Of
Rackety's Way, Childrens, 1969. CA-5/6

FRITZ, Jean Guttery 1915-
    She was born in Hankow, China, the daughter of mis-
    sionaries. When she was thirteen, her family returned
    to the United States and lived in Hartford, Connecticut.
    Mrs. Fritz studied at Wheaton College (Norton, Massa-
    chusetts) and Columbia University. She married
    Michael Fritz and has lived in California and New
    York. At one time Jean Fritz served as Children's
    Librarian in Dobbs Ferry. She has also done book
    reviewing, research, and editing. Several of her
    books have been A. L. A. Notable Book Selections. Ju-
    venile titles include: Brady, Coward-McCann, 1960;
    The Cabin Faced West, Coward-McCann, 1958; Early
    Thunder, Coward-McCann, 1967; How To Read A Rab-
    bit, Coward-McCann, 1959; Late Spring, Coward-Mc-
    Cann, 1957.   CA-4

FROMAN, Robert (Winslow) 1917-
    He was born in Montana, grew up in Caldwell, Idaho,
    and later lived in Garnerville, New York. Mr. Fro-
    man has been a contributor to magazines, a ghost-
    writer, and an editor. His ideas about the intelligence
    of dolphins resulted in a Junior Literary Guild selec-
    tion, Quacko And The Elps, McKay, 1964. He also
    wrote: Great Reaching Out, World, 1968; Wanted:
    Amateur Scientists (A Junior Literary Guild selection),
    McKay, 1963.   CA-4

FRY, Christopher 1907-
    English playwright, translator, author. He was born
    in Bristol and has made his home in London, England.
    His verse plays ("A Phoenix Too Frequent," "The
    Lady's Not For Burning, " "Venus Observed") have
    established him as a noted playwright. Christopher
    Fry has translated such works as "Ring Round The
    Moon" (Jean Anouilh) and "Tiger At The Gates" (Jean
    Giraudoux). He has also written film plays. For boys
    and girls he wrote The Boat That Mooed, Macmillan,
    1965.   CA-17/18

FRY, Rosalie Kingsmill 1911-
    She was born in Vancouver, British Columbia and grew
    up in Hertfordshire, England and South Wales. She re-
    ceived her education at St. Margaret's School in Swan-
    sea, South Wales and the Central School of Arts and
    Crafts in London. Rosalie Fry has contributed many
    drawings and stories to children's magazines in Great

Britain. She served as a Cypher Officer during World
War II. Juvenile books which she has written and illustrated include: A Bell For Ringelblume, Dutton,
1957; The Echo Song (A Junior Literary Guild selection), Dutton, 1962; Gypsy Princess, Dutton, 1969.
CA-9/10

FRYATT, Norma R.
She has been a member of the staff of Horn Book and
has edited books for a publishing company. Norma
Fryatt has been interested in book design and illustrators of picture books. She edited A Horn Book Sampler, Horn Bk. , 1959.

FRYE, Dean
Teacher and author, he has lived in Montreal, Canada.
He attended Cornell University, obtained his B. A. and
M. A. degrees at New York University, and received
his Ph. D. degree from the University of Wisconsin.
Dr. Frye has been Assistant Professor of English at
McGill University in Montreal. His juvenile books in-
clude: Days Of Sunshine, Days Of Rain, McGraw,
1965; The Lamb And The Child, McGraw, 1963.

FULLER, Alice Cook
She was born in South Dakota and has lived in Berkeley, California. She grew up in the mining district
of the Black Hills and has also lived on a cattle ranch
in Colorado. She wrote her first story when she was
eleven years old. For boys and girls she wrote Gold
For The Grahams, Messner, 1949.

FULLER, Edmund
Teacher, editor, actor, author. He once edited Theatre
Workshop Magazine and has been an editor for a publishing firm. Edmund Fuller has also taught playwrit-
ing at the New Theatre School and in the Dramatic
Workshop of the New School for Social Research. He
married Ann Graham, and they have lived in Nyack
(Rockland County), New York. For young people he
wrote Poems Of Henry Wadsworth Longfellow, Crowell, 1967.

FULLER, Raymond Tifft 1889-
He has always lived in the state of New York and has
always been a nature lover. When he lived near the
Catskills in Winterton, he planted thousands of trees

near his 150-year-old house. His articles have appeared in many publications including: <u>Good House-
keeping</u>, <u>Nature Magazine</u>, <u>North American Review</u>,
and <u>Travel.</u> Raymond Fuller has also been a playwright. For young people he wrote <u>Nature Quests And
Quizzes</u>, Day, 1948.

G

GAER, Joseph 1897-
He was born in a region in southeastern Europe called
Bessarabia. At the age of sixteen he journeyed to
Winnipeg, Canada where he went to school. Mr. Gaer
also studied at the University of Minnesota and at the
University of Southern California. He married a sculp-
tor and painter named Fay Ratner. Juvenile titles in-
clude: <u>Fables Of India</u>, Little, 1955; <u>Holidays Around
The World</u>, Little, 1953. CA-9/10, MJA

GÁG, Flavia 1907-
Illustrator and author, born in New Ulm, Minnesota.
She was the youngest of seven children which included
another author-illustrator of children's books, Wanda
Gág who died in 1946. Flavia Gág has illustrated
many books besides her own. She has lived in New
York and Florida. Juvenile books which she wrote
and illustrated include: <u>Four Legs And A Tail</u>, Holt,
1952; <u>Fourth Floor Menagerie</u>, Holt, 1955; <u>The Melon
Patch Mystery</u>, McKay, 1964; <u>Tweeter Of Prairie Dog
Town</u>, Holt, 1957; <u>A Wish For Mimi</u>, Holt, 1958.
CA-7/8, MJA

GÁG, Wanda 1893-1946
Author, illustrator, teacher, born in New Ulm, Minnesota. When her parents died, Wanda Gág, the oldest (fourteen years) of seven children, assumed many
family responsibilities. She attended art schools in
Minnesota and the Art Students League in New York.
After a career in commercial art, one of her rejected
juvenile manuscripts was accepted by a publisher. It
was <u>Millions Of Cats</u> (Coward, 1928) which has been
read by generations of children. She married Earle
Humphreys and lived in New Jersey. She wrote and
illustrated: <u>The Funny Thing</u>, Coward, 1929; <u>Nothing
At All</u>, Coward, 1941. JBA-1, JBA-2

GAGE, Wilson see STEELE, Mary Quintard (Govan)

GAGLIARDO, Ruth
   She grew up in Kansas and graduated from the University of Kansas. Mrs. Gagliardo has been very interested in children's reading and has served on many
   committees for both the American Library Association
   and the National Parent-Teacher's Association. She
   has also taught courses in children's literature. The
   Gagliardos have lived in Lawrence, Kansas, and Mr.
   Gagliardo has taught at the University of Kansas. She
   wrote Let's Read Aloud, Lippincott, 1962.

GALDONE, Paul
   He was born in Budapest, Hungary and studied at the
   Art Students League in New York. He was with the
   United States Army Engineers during World War II.
   Mr. Galdone has worked in the art department of a
   publishing house and has painted portraits and land-
   scapes. He has illustrated many books for both adults
   and children. The Galdones have lived in New City,
   New York. He wrote: The Monkey And The Crocodile,
   Seabury, 1969; Paddy The Penguin, Crowell, 1959.

GALL, Alice (Crew)
   She was born in McConnelsville, Ohio and returned
   there to live after spending many years in New York.
   Her brother Fleming H. Crew has collaborated with
   her on many books for boys and girls. They both have
   always enjoyed the outdoors, and their numerous childhood hiking trips later provided both the inspiration and
   information for their books. Together they wrote:
   Each In His Way, Oxford, 1937; Flat Tail, Oxford,
   1935; Little Black Ant, Oxford, 1936; Ringtail, Oxford,
   1933; Splasher, Oxford, 1945; Wagtail, Oxford, 1932;
   Winter Flight, Oxford, 1949.   JBA-2

GALLANT, Roy Arthur 1924-
   He was born in Portland, Maine and graduated from
   Bowdoin College and Columbia University. Following
   graduation he became a writer for Science Illustrated
   magazine. Mr. Gallant has written articles on science
   for Boys' Life and Science World. Juvenile titles include: Man Must Speak, Random, 1969; Man's Reach
   Into Space, Garden City, 1959.   CA-7/8

GANNETT, Ruth Stiles 1923-
   She graduated from Vassar and later served on the
   Children's Book Council. Her father was book critic

of the New York Herald-Tribune, Lewis Gannett who
married illustrator Ruth Chrisman. Ruth Chrisman
Gannett illustrated her stepdaughter's My Father's Dra-
gon (Random, 1948). Ruth Stiles Gannett married ar-
tist Peter Kahn. Her books for children include:
Dragons Of Blueland, Junior Literary Guild and Random
House, 1951; Elmer And The Dragon, Random House
and the Junior Literary Guild, 1950; Katie And The
Sad Noise, Random, 1961; Wonderful House-Boat-Train,
Random, 1949.   MJA

GARD, Joyce
    She graduated from Oxford University where she ob-
    tained a degree in English Language and Literature.
    She has taught school, worked for a literary agent, and
    has made pottery. During World War II, she was in
    economic intelligence in London and was later assigned
    to Versailles and Frankfurt Am Main. She wrote:
    Smudge Of The Fells, Holt, 1966; Talargain, Holt,
    1965.

GARD, Robert Edward
    Novelist, playwright, teacher. He was born in Kansas
    and later lived in Canada. He has been Director of
    the Wisconsin Idea Theatre and has taught at the Uni-
    versity of Wisconsin. For boys and girls he wrote:
    America's Players, Seabury, 1967; Scotty's Mare,
    Sloan, 1957.

GARDNER, Dic
    He was born in Seattle, Washington and attended Wash-
    ington State College at Pullman. The author lived in
    various American cities prior to making his home on
    Ibiza (Balearic Islands) near the coast of Spain. For
    young people he wrote The Bridge (A Junior Literary
    Guild selection), Day, 1963.

GARDNER, Lillian Soskin 1907-
    Author and Scout leader. The scouting program in
    Maplewood, New Jersey furnished the background for
    several of her books. With the publication of her
    seventh book Sal Fisher At Girl Scout Camp (Watts,
    1959), Lillian Gardner began her seventh year as a
    Girl Scout leader. She has also worked with the Boy
    Scout program and served as a Den Mother when her
    son was a Cub Scout. Other juvenile titles include:
    Exactly Like Ben's (A Junior Literary Guild selection),

Watts, 1956; The Oldest, The Youngest, And The One
In The Middle (A Junior Literary Guild selection),
Watts, 1954.

GARELICK, May 1910–
Author and editor. The author has been an editor for
a publishing firm. She married writer Marshall (Mike)
McClintock, and they have resided in Washingtonville,
New York. Her juvenile books include: Double Trouble, Crowell, 1958; What Makes A Bird A Bird?, Follett, 1969.

GARNETT, Eve C. R.
Author, illustrator, painter. She was born in Worcestershire, England, attended schools in Devon and
Worcester, and has lived in Sussex. She studied
painting at the Royal Academy Schools where she was
awarded the Cheswick Prize and Medal. London art
galleries have exhibited her work. In 1937 Miss Garnett was the recipient of the Carnegie Gold Medal for
her first book The Family From One End Street, And
Some Of Their Adventures, Vanguard, 1938. Other
juvenile books which she wrote and illustrated include:
Further Adventures Of The Family From One End
Street, Vanguard, 1956; Holiday At The Dew Drop Inn,
Vanguard, 1963. CA-4

GARRETT, Helen 1895–
She grew up in Massachusetts. She was a teacher in
New York prior to her position as State Education
Supervisor in the Elementary Division of the State
Education Department in Albany, New York. In des-
cribing her work she once wrote: ". . . I start writ-
ing with someone, not too clear cut to be sure, as
prototype for each of my people, only to have them
begin to depart and become increasingly themselves."
For young people she wrote: Brothers From North
Bay, Westminster, 1966; Rufous Redtail, Viking, 1947.

GARRISON, Frederick see SINCLAIR, Upton Beall

GARST, Doris Shannon 1899–
She was born in Ironwood, Michigan, grew up in Denver, Colorado, and later taught school in Oregon. The
author married an attorney, and they have lived in
Wyoming. She contributed stories to juvenile magazines
prior to writing books for young people. When the

author wrote Annie Oakley, Born August 13, 1869, Died
November 3, 1926, (Messner, 1958), the research
proved especially interesting since there is a collection
of Oakley memorabilia in the Darke County Museum,
the building which formerly belonged to the Garst family.   She also wrote: Amelia Earhart, Heroine Of The
Skies, Messner, 1947; Cowboy Boots, Abingdon-Cokesbury, 1946; Red Eagle (A Junior Literary Guild selection), Hastings House, 1959.   CA-4, JBA-2

GARST, Shannon   see GARST, Doris Shannon

GARTEN, Jan
New Yorker, teacher, author.   She graduated from
Fairleigh Dickinson University and has lived in Morristown, New Jersey.   She has been a teacher in a nursery school.   With her neighbor Muriel Batherman
(who illustrated the book) she wrote Alphabet Tale (A
Junior Literary Guild selection), Random, 1964.

GASS, Irene
Writer and music teacher.   Her family was very musical, and she was taught to sight-read when she was
quite young.   When she was fifteen-years-old, she began her formal education in music.   Miss Gass has
written about music and has become well-known in
England as both a teacher and a publisher of music.
She collaborated with Herbert Weinstock to write
Through An Opera Glass, Abelard, 1958.

GARTHWAITE, Marion (Hook) 1893-
Librarian, author, native Californian.   She was born
in Oakland, graduated from the University of Califor-
nia, and has made her home in Menlo Park.   She re-
ceived her library training at the Riverside Library
School and has been both a high school and children's
librarian.   Mrs. Garthwaite's stories have appeared in
American Girl, Jack and Jill, and other magazines.
Her first book Tomás And The Red Headed Angel
(Messner, 1950) received both the Julia Ellsworth Ford
Award and the Commonwealth Award.   Other juvenile
books include: Coarse Gold Gulch (A Junior Literary
Guild selection), Doubleday, 1956; Holdup On Bootjack
Hill, Doubleday, 1962; The Locked Crowns (A Junior
Literary Guild selection), Doubleday, 1963; Mystery Of
Skull Cap Island, Doubleday, 1959; Shaken Days, Mess-
ner, 1952; The Twelfth Night Santons, Doubleday, 1965.

CA-5/6

GATES, Doris 1901-
Author and librarian, born near San Jose, California
in the Santa Clara Valley. During her childhood Doris
Gates received a small gray burro which later was the
inspiration for her first book Sarah's Idea (Viking,
1938). Her experiences as a children's librarian in
the San Joaquin valley resulted in her second book
Blue Willow (Viking, 1940). She married William H.
Hall, an attorney. She wrote: The Cat And Mrs.
Cary, Viking, 1962; Elderberry Bush, Viking, 1967.
CA-4, JBA-2

GATTI, Attilio 1896-   Ellen Morgan
Explorer, author, born in Italy. He served in World
War I. During the years following the war Mr. Gatti
organized many scientific expeditions to Africa. He
married Ellen Morgan who was born in Springfield,
Missouri. Mr. and Mrs. Gatti have lived in a house
on the Vermont-Canadian border and at one time in
New York. They wrote Here Is Africa, Scribner, 1943.
Attilio Gatti wrote Kamanda (illustrated with photographs
taken by Commander and Mrs. Attilio Gatti), McBride,
1941.   JBA-2

GAUL, Albro T.
Entomologist, native of Brooklyn. Mr. Gaul has served
as an officer of the Brooklyn Entomological Society and
has been associated with the Department of Parks in
New York City. He later worked in the United States
Department of Agriculture. He wrote Picture Book Of
Insects, Lothrop, 1943.

GAULT, William Campbell
He was born in Milwaukee, Wisconsin and later made
his home in Santa Barbara, California. Besides his
books for young people, he has also written many stor-
ies for magazines. He served in the Infantry during
World War II. The author has enjoyed golf as a hobby.
William Gault's many books for young people include:
Backfield Challenge, Dutton, 1967; The Checkered Flag,
Dutton, 1964; Drag Strip, Dutton, 1959; The Lonely
Mound, Dutton, 1967; Long Green, Dutton, 1965; Road-
Race Rookie, Dutton, 1962; Two-Wheeled Thunder, Dut-
ton, 1962; Wheels Of Fortune, Dutton, 1963.

GAY, Zhenya 1906–
    Author-illustrator.   She studied with sculptor Solon
    Borglum and artist Winold Reiss.   Miss Gay has tra-
    veled in Central America, Europe, and Mexico.   She
    lived in New York before moving to a house located
    near the Catskill Mountains.   Books which she has
    written and illustrated include: Bits And Pieces, Vik-
    ing, 1958; The Dear Friends, Harper, 1959; I'm Tired
    Of Lions (A Junior Literary Guild selection), Viking,
    1961.   MJA

GEIS, Darlene Stern
    She grew up in Chicago, Illinois, studied at Connecticut
    College for Women, and received her degree from
    Northwestern University.   Mrs. Geis has designed
    dresses in addition to writing books for boys and girls.
    Her juvenile titles include: Dinosaurs, Grosset, 1959;
    Let's Travel In The Holy Land, Childrens, 1965.
    CA-1

GEISEL, Theodore Seuss 1904–
    His pseudonym is Dr. Seuss (his mother's maiden
    name).   He was born in Springfield, Massachusetts
    where his father served as Superintendent of Parks.
    After graduating from Dartmouth College, he studied
    at Oxford.   Dr. Seuss had planned to become a history
    teacher but instead he made history in the field of
    children's books.   His famed Cat In The Hat (Random,
    1957) launched a new type of children's books which
    were designed for the beginning reader.   During World
    War II, he was a lieutenant colonel in the Army Signal
    Corps.   He married Helen Manon Palmer whom he met
    at Oxford, and they have lived in La Jolla, California.
    Juvenile titles include: And To Think That I Saw It
    On Mulberry Street, Vanguard, 1937; Green Eggs And
    Ham, Beginner Bks. distributed by Random House,
    1960.   CA-15/16, MJA

GEORGE, Jean Craighead 1919–
    Author-illustrator.   She was born in Washington, D.C.,
    graduated from Penn State College, and has lived in
    Chappaqua, New York.   She was a reporter with the
    International News Service in Washington during the
    war.   She wrote: Gull Number 737, Crowell, 1964;
    My Side Of The Mountain, Dutton, 1959; The Summer
    Of The Falcon, Crowell, 1962.   With John George she
    wrote: Dipper Of Copper Creek, Dutton, 1956; Masked

Prowler, Dutton, 1950; Vision, The Mink, Junior Literary Guild and Dutton, 1949; Vulpes, The Red Fox, Dutton, 1948.   CA-7/8, MJA

GEORGE, John Lothar 1916-
He was born in Milwaukee, Wisconsin, graduated from
the University of Michigan School of Forestry and Conservation, and served in the U. S. Navy during World
War II. After the war he received his Ph. D. and was
a professor of ecology and conservation at Vassar College. With Jean George he wrote: Dipper Of Copper
Creek, Dutton, 1956; Masked Prowler, Dutton, 1950;
Vison, The Mink, Junior Literary Guild and Dutton,
1949; Vulpes, The Red Fox, Dutton, 1948.   CA-7/8

GERSON, Noel Bertram 1914-
Newspaperman and author, born in Chicago, Illinois.
He graduated from the University of Chicago. Noel
Gerson has contributed articles to magazines and has
written documentaries and plays for radio and television. He was an Army Military Intelligence officer
during World War II. The author has resided in Connecticut and has enjoyed gardening and swimming. For
young people he wrote: Edict Of Nantes, Grosset,
1969; Rock Of Freedom, Messner, 1964.

GIANAKOULIS, Theodore
Author, journalist, poet, born in Greece. He grew
up in America, attended school in Ohio, and has lived
in New York City. At one time he was known as the
"Voice of America" to Greece. His love and understanding of the Greek people and their country resulted
in his juvenile book The Land And People Of Greece
(rev.), Lippincott, 1965.

GIBBS, Alonzo (Lawrence) 1915-
He was born in Brooklyn, New York and has lived in
Long Island, New York. He has been interested in
history and once said: "The more rapidly we expand,
the more important I think it is for us to have a con-
sciousness of the past. " His first book for young people was entitled The Fields Breathe Sweet, Lothrop,
1963. He also wrote The Least Likely One, Lothrop,
1964.   CA-5/6

GIDAL, Sonia (Epstein) 1922-   Tim Nahum 1909-
Husband and wife team. Sonia Gidal was born in

Berlin, and came to the United States in 1948.   Tim
Gidal, the photographer of this team, was born in
Munich, Germany.   He attended the universities in
Munich, Berlin, and Basle.   He has been on the staff
of the London Picture Post and has been a contributor
to Life magazine.   Dr. and Mrs. Gidal have often traveled abroad in order to acquire facts and photographs
for their "My Village" books.   Their home has been
in Westchester and North Bergen, New Jersey.   Juvenile books include: Follow The Reindeer (A Junior
Literary Guild selection), Pantheon, 1959; My Village
In Ghana, Pantheon, 1969.   CA-5/6, CA-7/8

GILBERT, Helen Earle
She has lived in Connecticut.   The author's home has
been the same house in Hebron that her grandfather
(who was a doctor) occupied.   His office has been re-
tained in the house, and this office was similar to the
one portrayed in Helen Gilbert's book Dr. Trotter And
His Big Gold Watch, Abingdon, 1948.   She also wrote
Mr. Plum And The Little Green Tree, Abingdon, 1946.

GILL, Richard Cochran 1901-
He was born in Washington, D. C. Following graduation
from college he worked in South America and later
lived on a ranch near the Andes.   In order to discover
more about curare he visited the jungles of Ecuador
and lived among the Indians.   At one time Mr. Gill
was paralyzed, and following his rehabilitation he returned to the jungles for additional curare to be used
in medical research.   He wrote Manga, Stokes, 1937,
and with Helen L. Hoke he wrote Paco Goes To The
Fair, Holt, 1940.

GILLELAN, George Howard 1917-
He attended Johns Hopkins University in Baltimore,
Maryland where he was born.   He also studied at Cornell University in Ithaca, New York.   He has continued
to make his home in Baltimore.   His interest in the
bow and arrow led him not only to hunt moose in Newfoundland but also in hunting sharks in the Caribbean.
Howard Gillelan has written a monthly column for Outdoor Life.   He gave archery lessons to his four children and then decided to write a book on archery for
boys and girls entitled The Young Sportsman's Guide
To Archery, Nelson, 1962.   CA-2

GILMORE, Horace Herman 1903-
Author, painter.   A graduate of Syracuse University
(New York), he has operated his own model ship building business and has designed and manufactured construction sets which were sold in Eastern department
stores.   Horace Gilmore has illustrated children's
books and painted pictures of ships for magazine covers.
He has lived in a replica (which he designed) of an old
Dutch house in New York.   Books for boys and girls
which he wrote and illustrated include: Model Boats
For Beginners, Harper, 1959; Model Rockets For Beginners, Harper, 1961.

GILMORE, Iris
She has worked with young people as a director of both
a Children's Theater and a marionette troupe.   Iris
Gilmore has also written scripts for radio and taught
at the University of Denver.   She was awarded the
1956 Boys' Life-Dodd, Mead Prize Competition with
her co-author Marian Talmadge for the book Pony Express Boy, Dodd, 1956.   Both authors also wrote:
Let's Go To A Truck Terminal, Putnam, 1964; Six
Great Horse Rides, Putnam, 1968.

GIPSON, Federick Benjamin 1908-
He grew up in Texas and has continued to live there
with his wife and two sons.   Mr. Gipson's book Re-
collection Creek (Harper, 1959) was the winner of the
Texas Institute of Arts and Letters for the best Texas
novel.   In addition to writing books and managing his
ranch, he has contributed many articles to magazines.
He wrote: Old Yeller, Harper, 1956; Savage Sam,
Harper, 1962.   CA-3

GIRVAN, Helen (Masterman) 1891-
A New Yorker since she was six, she was born in
Minneapolis, Minnesota, studied art, and attended
secretarial school.   At one time she held a secretarial
position with Vogue magazine.   She married Colin Girvan and has made her home in Connecticut.   Her books
for young people include: The Frightened Whisper,
Westminster Press, 1963; Hidden Pond, Dutton, 1951;
The Missing Masterpiece, Westminster Press, 1965. MJA

GITTINGS, Jo (Grenville) Manton see MANTON, Jo

GLEICK, Beth Youman
   She was born in New York and attended Connecticut
   College at New London. Prior to her marriage to a
   lawyer, Beth Youman Gleick did art work for a com-
   pany which specialized in greeting cards. She has
   also worked on magazines. The Gleicks have lived in
   New York City. For boys and girls she wrote Time
   Is When, Rand, 1960.

GLUBOK, Shirley (Astor)
   Teacher, author, native of St. Louis, Missouri. She
   graduated from Washington University and received her
   master's degree from Columbia. Shirley Glubok was
   an A. A. U. backstroke swimming champion. She has
   been a teacher in New York City and has given gallery
   talks to children at the Metropolitan Museum of Art.
   Her juvenile books include: The Art Of Ancient Egypt,
   Atheneum, 1962; Art Of India, Macmillan, 1969.   CA-
   5/6

GODDEN, Rumer 1907-
   Born in England, Rumer Godden also spent part of her
   life in India. She attended school in England and later
   conducted a ballet school in Calcutta. She married
   Laurence S. Foster. Her interests have included gardening and the opera. For boys and girls she wrote:
   Candy Floss (A Junior Literary Guild selection), Viking, 1960; Dolls' House, Viking, 1947; Operation Sip-
   pacik, Viking, 1969.   CA-7/8, MJA

GOETZ, Delia 1898-
   Teacher, translator, writer, born in Wesley, Iowa.
   She graduated from Iowa State Teachers College. After
   she had been an instructor at the State Normal School
   of Albion, Idaho, Miss Goetz taught in Guatamala, the
   Panama Canal Zone, and in North Dakota. She later
   held a government position in Washington, D. C. Her
   books for young people include: Arctic Tundra, Mor-
   row, 1958; Deserts, Morrow, 1956; Half A Hemisphere,
   Harcourt, 1943; Islands Of The Ocean, Morrow, 1964;
   Letters From Guatemala, Heath, 1941; Mountains,
   Morrow, 1962.

GOLDBERG, Martha 1907-
   Author and teacher, born in New York City. She spent
   her childhood in San Francisco where she later taught
   school. Her teaching career has included both college

and nursery school. She has also been a ballet instructor. The author has enjoyed rock collecting as a
hobby. Her juvenile books include: Big House, Little
House, Macmillan, 1960; The Twirly Skirt, Holiday,
1954.

GOLDFRANK, Helen Colodny 1912-
Her pseudonym is Helen Kay. She attended Columbia
and New York Universities. Her work ("observant
lady from Thornwood") has appeared in the New Yorker
magazine. In addition to writing books for boys and
girls, she has been an editor for trade papers and a
researcher for Fortune and Time magazines. She
married a chemist and has lived in Thornwood, New
York. Juvenile titles include: City Springtime, Hastings House, 1957; An Egg Is For Wishing (A Junior
Literary Guild selection), Abelard, 1966; A Duck For
Keeps, Abelard, 1962; Henri's Hands For Pablo Picasso, Abelard, 1966; The House Of Many Colors, Abelard, 1963.   CA-2

GOLL, Reinhold Weimar 1897-
Teacher and author, born in Philadelphia. Reinhold
Goll received his B. S. and M. S. degrees from Temple
University in Philadelphia and his Ph. D. degree from
the University of Pennsylvania. He has been a school
principal in Philadelphia. Dr. Goll has written arti-
cles on education in addition to several science fiction
books for young readers. These include: Through
Space To Planet T, Westminster, 1963; The Visitors
From Planet Veta, Westminster, 1961.   CA-7/8

GOLLOMB, Joseph 1881-1950
Teacher, reporter, author. He was born in Russia
and came to America at the age of ten. A graduate
of New York City College, the author received his
master's degree from Columbia University. Joseph
Gollomb was the first American reporter permitted to
make an intensive study of Scotland Yard from the inside. His stories and articles have been published in
the Atlantic Monthly, Collier's, Cosmopolitan, and New
Yorker. He made his home in New York. For young
people he wrote: Albert Schweitzer: Genius In The
Jungle, Vanguard, 1949; Tiger At City High, Harcourt,
1946; Up At City High, Harcourt, 1945.   JBA-1,
JBA-2

GORDON, Dorothy (Lerner) 1893-
She has been known to boys and girls as the "Song and
Story Lady. " Dorothy Gordon has been associated with
many radio shows including: "Yesterday's Children, "
"Youth Views The News, " and "The Children's Corner. "
She has been the receipient of many awards for her
work in radio.   Juvenile titles include: Around The
World In Song, Dutton, 1930; You And Democracy, Dut-
ton, 1951.

GORDON, Stewart see SHIRREFFS, Gordon Donald

GORHAM, Michael see FOLSOM, Franklin

GOSSETT, Margaret
She grew up in a nautical family and has always been
interested in boats.   After her marriage to a Navy
man Margaret Gossett traveled throughout the world
and continued her interest in the sea.   She wrote:
First Book Of Boats, Watts, 1953; Real Book Of Jokes,
Watts, 1954.

GOTTLIEB, Gerald 1923-
Author and editor. He was born in New York City and
received his education there. He served with the
Eighth Air Force during World War II.   Gerald Gottlieb
returned to France (the place he visited during the war)
and became an editor and author.   His juvenile books
include: Adventures Of Ulysses, Random, 1959; First
Book Of France, Watts, 1959.   CA-5/6

GOTTLIEB, Robin (Grossman) 1928-
Born in New York City, she attended Friends Seminary,
Vassar College, and graduated from Barnard College.
She was once employed in the juvenile department of a
publishing company.   Mrs. Gottlieb and her husband,
who is also a writer, have lived in Switzerland, France,
New York, and Connecticut.   Juvenile titles include:
Mystery Of The Forgotten Diamond, Funk, 1962; Mys-
tery Of The Marco Polo Ring, Funk, 1968.   CA-4

GOTTLIEB, William P.
Photographer, producer, author. He was an aerial
photo officer in World War II. He has been president
of a company which produces sales, training, and educational filmstrips.   His articles and photographs were
published in many periodicals, and his portraits of jazz

musicians were reprinted throughout the world. Mr.
Gottlieb and his family have lived on Long Island.
Juvenile contributions include: Jets And Rockets And
How They Work (A Junior Literary Guild selection),
Garden City Bks., 1959; Real Book About Photography,
Garden City Bks., 1957; Space Flight And How It
Works (A Junior Literary Guild selection), Doubleday,
1963; Table Tennis, Knopf, 1954; Photography With
Basic Cameras, Knopf, 1953.

GOUDEY, Alice E. 1898-
Born in Kansas, she has lived in New York and in
Maine. Her husband has been Chairman of the Science
Department of the Bronxville Public School and has
provided a great deal of help for her books about na-
ture. Her picture books, The Day We Saw The Sun
Come Up (Scribner, 1961) and Houses From The Sea
(Scribner, 1959) have been ALA Notable Books selec-
tions. Alice Goudey is also the author of the popular
"Here Come" books for young readers which include:
Here Come The Bears!, Scribner, 1954; Here Come
The Bees!, Scribner, 1960; Here Come The Cotton-
tails!, Scribner, 1965. She also wrote: Graywings,
Scribner, 1964; Red Legs, Scribner, 1966.

GOUDGE, Elizabeth 1900-
She spent her childhood in Wells, Somersetshire, England and later lived in Devonshire. When she began
her career in writing, she created several short stories; however, her first success came with a Sunday-
night performance in London of a play which she had
written. Later she wrote novels. Her books for boys
and girls include: I Saw Three Ships, Coward, 1969;
Linnets And Valerians, Coward, 1964. CA-7/8

GOULD, Jean Rosalind 1909-
She was born in Greenville, Ohio and later made her
home in New York. Jean Gould studied at the University of Michigan and also at Toledo University. When
Robert Frost was Poet in Residence at the University
of Michigan, she served as Poetry Editor on her high
school paper and heard him speak. In 1962 she discussed poetry with Frost in Ripton, Vermont. Miss
Gould not only has been friends with leading contemporary poets, but she also has enjoyed writing poetry. Her
books for boys and girls include: Robert Frost, Dodd,
1964; That Dunbar Boy, Dodd, 1958; Young Mariner

<u>Melville</u>, Dodd, 1956.   CA-5/6

GOVAN, Christine (Noble) 1898-
Born in New York City, she attended the University of
Chattanooga.   She has lived in Tennessee since she
was four-years-old.   She married a writer who has
been librarian of the University of Chattanooga.   Both
of her daughters (Emily and Mary) have also been
authors.   Mary's husband, W. O. Steele, has written
many books for boys and girls.   Christine Govan has
been a teacher, librarian, and book reviewer in addition to writing books.   Her juvenile titles include:
<u>The Delectable Mountain</u>, World, 1962; <u>Phinny's Fine
Summer</u>, World, 1968.   With her daughter Emmy West
she also wrote <u>Mystery At Fearsome Lake</u>, Sterling,
1960.   CA-4

GRAFF, Stewart
A graduate of Harvard College and Law School, he was
born in Pennsylvania.   He has been an attorney and
executive secretary of a professional association.
Stewart Graff married author Anne Colver, and together they wrote <u>Squanto: Indian Adventurer</u>, Garrard,
1965.   He also wrote <u>George Washington</u>, Garrard,
1964.

GRAHAM, Al 1897-
A native of Newburyport, Massachusetts, he has lived
both in Boston and New York City.   Al Graham's work
has been published in such magazines as the <u>Saturday
Evening Post</u> and the <u>New Yorker</u>.   At one time he
contributed to the late Franklin P. Adams' column
"The Conning Tower."   His books for young people in-
clude: <u>Down With Dinosaurs!</u>, Duell, 1963; <u>Songs For
A Small Guitar</u>, Duell, 1962; <u>The Rhymes Of Squire
O'Squirrel</u>, Duell, 1963; <u>Timothy Turtle</u>, Welch, 1946.

GRAHAM, Alberta (Powell)
Composer, teacher, author.   She was born in Harrington, Delaware, grew up in Ottumwa, Iowa, and later
lived in Washington, D. C.   Mrs. Graham graduated
from the American Conservatory in Chicago and also
studied at Northwestern, Columbia, and Cornell Universities.   She has been a Music Supervisor in Iowa
schools and has had many of her songs published.   One
of the author's hobbies has been the study of United
States history.   Her books include: <u>Christopher Colum-</u>

bus, Discover, Abingdon-Cokesbury, 1950; Great Bands
Of America, Nelson, 1952; Strike Up The Band!, Nelson, 1949; Thirty-Two Roads To The White House,
Nelson, 1949.

GRAHAM, Clarence Reginald 1907-
Author and librarian. He has lived in Louisville, Kentucky where he has been head librarian of the Public
Library. Mr. Graham has served as president of the
American Library Association and of the Kentucky and
Southeastern Library Associations. He has written
articles on library science and educational films for
magazines. For young readers he wrote First Book
Of Public Libraries, Watts, 1959.

GRAHAM, Frank 1925-
Native New Yorker, Frank Graham, Jr., attended
Columbia University. His writing career started when
he was a student at Columbia and worked as a copy
boy for the New York Sun. His articles have appeared
in the New York Times Magazine and Sports Illustrated.
Mr. Graham has lived in Europe, Maine, and New York
City. His father was author Frank Graham who wrote
Lou Gehrig: A Quiet Hero, Putnam, 1942. Frank
Graham, Jr., wrote: Austria, Macmillan, 1964; Great
Hitters Of The Major Leagues, Random, 1969. CA-
11/12

GRAHAM, Helen Holland
She was born in Springtown, Arkansas and attended
Harding College at Searcy. Mrs. Graham has also
lived in Washington, D. C., and Portland, Oregon. She
and her family moved to the West Coast at the end of
World War II when her husband was discharged from
military service. She collaborated with Barbara A.
Huff to write her first book for children entitled Taco,
The Snoring Burro, Abelard, 1957.

GRAHAM, Shirley 1907-
The daughter of a Methodist minister, she was born in
Indiana. She graduated from high school in Spokane,
Washington and received her B. A. and M. A. degrees
from Oberlin College in Ohio. Miss Graham attended
school in Paris, France when her father was assigned
to Liberia as head of a Mission School. In 1947 she
received the Julian Messner Award ("the best book
combating intolerance in America") for her book There

Was Once A Slave, Messner, 1947. Other juvenile
books include: Booker T. Washington, Messner, 1955;
Story Of Pocahontas, Grosset, 1953. MJA

GRAHAME, Kenneth 1859-1932
He was born in Edinburgh, Scotland. After the death
of his parents he lived with relatives in Berkshire,
England. When he was a young man, Mr. Grahame
became a clerk for the Bank of England where he enjoyed a successful career. In 1899 he married Els-
peth Thomson, and he later wrote The Wind In The
Willows (Scribner, 1923) for their son Alastair. Alastair died an accidental death when he was twenty, and
Mr. Grahame died at seventy-three at Pangbourne,
England. His juvenile books include: Bertie's Esca-
pade, Lippincott, 1949; Dream Days, Dodd, 1931; The
Golden Age, Dodd, 1929. JBA-1

GRAMATKY, Hardie 1907-
Author-illustrator. He was born in Dallas, Texas, attended Stanford University (Palo Alto) and Chouinard
Art School (Los Angeles), and has lived in Westport,
Connecticut. Mr. Gramatky has worked in animation
for the Walt Disney Studios and has designed magazine
covers. He has received many water color awards,
and his work can be found in the permanent collections
of museums and the Chicago Art Institute. Hardie
Gramatky has been an Associate of the National Academy and a member of the Society of Illustrators.
From his studio overlooking New York's East River he
wrote and illustrated his famous Little Toot, Putnam,
1939. Other juvenile books which he wrote and illustrated include: Bolivar, Putnam, 1961; Hercules, Putnam, 1940; Little Toot On The Thames, Putnam, 1964;
Loopy, Putnam, 1941; Sparky, Putnam, 1952. CA-2,
JBA-2

GRAMET, Charles
He graduated from the City College of New York and
obtained his master's degree from Columbia University.
Charles Gramet has been a fellow of the American
Association for the Advancement of Science. He has
taught science in New York City and has been a principal of a junior high school. In addition to writing
books on science, he has produced science films. His
books include: Light And Sight, Abelard, 1963; Your
Health And You, Lothrop, 1968. CA-3

GRANT, Bruce 1893-
      He was born in Wichita Falls, Texas, studied at the
      University of Kentucky, and later lived in Illinois. He
      served in the Artillery during World War I and was a
      war correspondent and chief of his paper's (Chicago
      Times) London Bureau during World War II. He has
      written and collected books on the War of 1812. Juve-
      nile contributions include: American Forts, Yesterday
      And Today, Dutton, 1965; American Indians, Yesterday
      And Today, Dutton, 1958; Cyclone, World, 1959; Davy
      Crockett, American Hero, Rand, 1955; Star-Spangled
      Rooster, World, 1961.   CA-1

GRANT, Madeleine Parker 1895-
      She graduated from Simmons College and received both
      her master's and doctor's degrees from Radcliffe.   Dr.
      Grant has been Professor Emeritus of Biology at Sarah
      Lawrence College.   She has enjoyed writing, traveling,
      and teaching.   Radcliffe gave her the Whitney Fellow-
      ship, and she received the Margaret Snell Fellowship
      from the American Association of University Women.
      She wrote Wonder World Of Microbes, McGraw, 1956.

GRAVES, Charles Parlin 1911-
      He was born in Apalachicola, Florida and later made
      his home in New York. He graduated from the Uni-
      versity of Florida. During a summer vacation he once
      worked as a deckhand aboard a freighter bound for
      Europe.   During World War II, he served in both the
      Aleutian and Philippine Islands.   He has written radio
      scripts, advertising copy, and newspaper articles.
      Juvenile titles include: Colony Leader: William Brad-
      ford, Garrard, 1969; John F. Kennedy: New Frontiers-
      man, Garrard, 1965.   CA-5/6

GRAVES, Robert 1895-
      Critic, historian, poet. He was born in England, at-
      tended Oxford University, and has resided in Spain.
      During World War I, he was a captain with the Royal
      Welch Fusiliers.   At one time the author occupied the
      Chair of English Literature at Cairo, Egypt's Royal
      University.   His main interest has always been poetry,
      and he received both the gold medal of America's Na-
      tional Poetry Society and England's Foyle Award for
      Collected Poems, Doubleday, 1961.   Robert Graves al-
      so wrote: Ann At Highwood Hall, Doubleday, 1966;
      Greek Gods And Heroes, Doubleday, 1960; The Penny

Fiddle, Doubleday, 1960.   CA-5/6

GRAY, Alice
She has lived in Connecticut but has worked in New
York City at the American Museum of Natural History.
Her interest has been the study of insects and at the
Museum of Natural History Alice Gray has been em-
ployed in the Department of Insects and Spiders.   Her
work at the Museum has included: the planning of ex-
hibits, answering questions about insects, and often
the care of live insects.   She wrote The Adventure
Book Of Insects, Capitol, 1956.

GRAY, Elizabeth Janet 1902-
Her books can be found under the name of Elizabeth
Gray Vining.   She was born in Philadelphia, graduated
from Bryn Mawr, and obtained her library training
from the Drexel Institute of Library Science.   She
began her first book for girls during the year that she
taught in New Jersey.   She later worked in the library
of the University of North Carolina where she met and
married Morgan Vining.   Following her husband's un-
timely death in an automobile accident, the author made
her home in Pennsylvania.   In 1946 she became a
tutor to the Crown Prince of Japan.   Her book Adam
Of The Road, Viking, 1942 was awarded the 1943 Newbery Medal.   She also wrote: Cheerful Heart, Viking,
1959; Fair Adventure, Viking, 1940; I Will Adventure,
Viking, 1962.   CA-7/8, JBA-1, JBA-2

GRAY, Patricia (Clark)
She has always been interested in horses and at one
one time rode in rodeos and fairs in California.   She
married a doctor (Gerald Gray), and they have lived
on a ranch in Walnut Creek, California.   Her daughter
Celia won the Van Sinderen Award which was given for
western horsemanship by the American Horse Show
Association in New York.   Juvenile titles include:
Horse In Her Heart, Coward, 1960; Star Lost, Norton,
1965.

GRAYSON, Marion (Forbourg) 1906-
Author and teacher, born in New York City.   Her career as a teacher began when she was fifteen, and she
organized a summer play-school in her home in Westchester.   She later operated a private nursery school.
The author has lived in Washington, D. C.   She has

been a consultant to parent-teacher groups and has
worked with children at the National Child Research
Center.   Her experiences as a teacher and mother in
the use of fingerplays resulted in her book Let's Do
Fingerplays, Luce, 1962.   CA-5/6

GREEN, Margaret 1926-
Editor and writer, born in Lawrence, Massachusetts.
She studied art before going to college, and after her
marriage Mrs. Green attended the University of Hawaii.
Her main interests have been reading and writing.   She
sold her first article to Yankee magazine.   Margaret
Green has lived in Virginia near Washington, D. C.
She compiled and edited The Big Book Of Animal Stor-
ies, Watts, 1961.   She wrote Paul Revere: The Man
Behind The Legend, Messner, 1964.   CA-2

GREEN, Mary McBurney
Author and teacher, she has lived in Connecticut.   Her
position as director of a college nursery school, and
her work in schools and camps has provided the author
with a background which has proved advantageous for
her writing career.   She has also conducted an Arts
Workshop for boys and girls.   Her juvenile books include: Everybody Has A House, Scott, 1964; When
Will I Whistle?, Watts, 1967.

GREEN, Roger Gilbert Lancelyn 1918-
English writer and editor, he graduated from Oxford
University.   From the age of ten his favorite storyteller was Andrew Lang.   He later selected Lang as
the subject of his thesis.   His main interests have
been history, Greek and Egyptian myths and legends.
Mr. Green has resided in the family ancestral home
at Poulton-Lancelyn in Cheshire, England.   For young
people he wrote: Ancient Egypt, Day, 1963; Tales Of
Ancient Egypt, Walck, 1968.   CA-4

GREENAWAY, Kate 1846-1901
English illustrator and writer, born in London.   Her
father was an engraver.   Kate Greenaway began to
study art at the age of twelve and attended the Slade
School of Art.   Her exquisite water colors of children
and flowers have become very familiar to all of those
who have been associated with children's books.   In a
booklet written by Anne Carroll Moore was a quotation
from Kenneth Grahame who referred to the work of

Kate Greenaway in this way: "Once in a hundred years I like to think the golden key to the kingdom of childhood unlocks the door for a rare creative spirit, who, in pictures or words, records what is seen and felt with a truth and beauty that defy time and space. " Her juvenile titles include: The Kate Greenaway Treasury, World, 1967; Under The Window, Warne, 1878. JBA-1, JBA-2

GREENE, Carla 1916-

She was born in Minneapolis, Minnesota and has made her home in Los Angeles, California. Prior to a writing career, Miss Greene had worked in advertising. She has written for both adults and children and for magazines and radio. Her interests have included the ballet and the theater. Her own travel experiences provided authenticity for her "Trip" books which include: A Trip On A Bus, Lantern Press, 1964; A Trip On A Jet, Lantern Press, 1960; A Trip On A Ship, Lantern Press, 1958; A Trip On A Train, Lantern Press, 1956. Other juvenile books include: Doctors And Nurses, Harper, 1963; How To Know Dinosaurs, Bobbs, 1966; I Want To Be A Farmer, Childrens Press, 1959; I Want To Be A Librarian, Childrens Press, 1960; Let's Learn About The Orchestra, Harvey House, 1967. CA-4

GREY, Elizabeth 1917-

She has lived in England with her husband Garry Hogg, also a writer. They have often traveled abroad to obtain material for books, articles, and radio scripts. Both have enjoyed music, reading, and walking. For boys and girls Elizabeth Grey has written: Friend Within The Gates, Houghton, 1961; Story Of Journalism, Houghton, 1969. CA-7/8

GRIFFIN, Ella

A native of New England, she has worked in various parts of the world with UNESCO. With her assistance texts have been written in Arabic, Hindi, Creole, and several African languages. She has also written books ("easy-to-read") for the U. S. Office of Education. Her books for boys and girls include: Continent In A Hurry, Coward, 1962; Getting To Know UNESCO, Coward, 1962.

GRIFFIN, Gillett Good 1928-
He was born in Brooklyn, New York and studied painting at the Yale School of Fine Arts. Mr. Griffin has served as Curator of the Graphic Arts Foundation of the Princeton University Library. He has been interested in juvenile books which were published in New England prior to 1846 and has an outstanding collection of them. During his fourth year at Yale the author wrote and illustrated a children's book which was selected as one of the Fifty Books of the Year (1952) entitled A Mouse's Tale, Abelard, 1952.

GRIFFIN, Velma
Author, accordionist, and teacher. She has been associated with Ringling Bros. and Barnum & Bailey Circus. Prior to being the leader of her own quintette called the "Griffin Accordion Gypsies," Mrs. Griffin had toured throughout North American with chautauqua associations. She has taught in Dellroy, Ohio where she and her husband have made their home. The author has written many magazine articles. For young people she wrote Fair Prize, Westminster, 1956.

GRIGSON, Geoffrey 1905-
English poet, born in Cornwall. He studied at Oxford University. He was founder and editor of the publication entitled New Verses. He has also compiled anthologies of poetry and written several volumes of poetry. His work has appeared in several British magazines including: the Listener, the Spectator, the Times Literary Supplement, and Encounter. For boys and girls he edited The Cherry Tree, Vanguard, 1959.

GRIMM, Jakob Ludwig Karl 1785-1863   Wilhelm Karl 1786-1859
Both were born in Hanau, Germany, attended the University of Marburg, and became professors at Kassel and Berlin Universities. Their first volume of folk tales was published in 1812. The tales have been translated into many languages, and generations of children have enjoyed them. Their many titles include: Fisherman And His Wife, Pantheon Bks., 1957; The Four Musicians, Doubleday, 1962; The Good-For-Nothings, Harcourt, 1957; Goose Girl, Doubleday, 1964; Hansel And Gretel, Golden Press, 1954; Rapunzel, Harcourt, 1961; Snow White And The Seven Dwarfs,

Coward, 1938; Tales From Grimm, Coward, 1936; Traveling Musicians, Harcourt, 1955.

GRINGHUIS, Richard H. 1918-
Dirk Gringhuis has created murals for Fort Michilimackinac (which means "place of the great turtle spirits") and for Fort Mackinac on Mackinac Island. He has described a frontier fort's reconstruction in his book The Big Dig, Dial, 1962. Other books which he has written and illustrated for boys and girls include: The Big Hunt, Dial, 1962; In Scarlet And Blue, Dial, 1963.   CA-2

GRINNELL, David see WOLLHEIM, Donald Allen

GROCH, Judith (Goldstein) 1929-
Born in New York City, she attended Vassar College and graduated from Columbia University. She has always been interested in literature and medicine. Mrs. Groch has studied the problems of depth perception at the Mayo Clinic, and has also translated medical and scientific articles for the library there. Her short stories have appeared in such magazines as American Girl, McCall's, and Seventeen. The author has continued to live in New York City where she has enjoyed music, sewing, and horseback riding as hobbies. For young people she wrote You And Your Brain, Harper, 1963.   CA-9/10

GRONOWICZ, Antoni 1913-
He was born in Poland. When he received a literature award from the Polish government in 1938, he traveled to America in order to make a study of our country for writing purposes. He has lectured throughout the United States. His poems and novels have been published in Czechoslovakia and France, and he has written plays. His books for young people include: Chopin (rendered in English by Jessie McEwen), Nelson, 1943; Paderewski, Pianist And Patriot (rendered in English by Jessie McEwen), Nelson, 1943.

GROVER, Eulalie Osgood 1873-
Author and teacher, born in Minnesota. Her father was a Congregational minister. Prior to European travel and study and her career as a teacher, Miss Grover attended school in Vermont at St. Johnsbury Academy. Her main interest has been writing for

young people. She has enjoyed flower gardening and
collecting old and rare children's books as hobbies.
The author has made her home in North Carolina and
Florida.   For boys and girls she wrote Robert Louis
Stevenson, Teller Of Tales, Dodd, 1940. She also
arranged and edited Mother Goose (The Volland ed.),
Volland, 1915.

GROVES-RAINES, Ralph Gore Antony 1913-
    Author-artist. He has made his home in County Down,
    Northern Ireland. American boys and girls were in-
    troduced to the illustrations of Mr. Groves-Raines in
    John Langstaff's book On Christmas Day In The Mor-
    ning!, Harcourt, 1959. He also wrote and illustrated
    The Tidy Hen, Harcourt, 1961.

GRUENBERG, Sidonie (Matsner) 1881-
    Author and editor. She was born in Austria, attended
    Columbia University, and has lived in New York. She
    married author and educator Benjamin C. Gruenberg.
    At one time she was a Director and Special Consultant
    for the Child Study Association of America. Her in-
    terest in child development and parent education has
    resulted in extensive travel throughout the country.
    Mrs. Gruenberg has also contributed to such maga-
    zines as Family Weekly and Redbook. For young peo-
    ple she wrote Wonderful Story Of How You Were Born,
    Hanover House, 1952. She also edited: . . . All Kinds
    Of Courage (A Junior Literary Guild selection), Double-
    day, 1962; . . . Let's Read A Story (A Junior Liter-
    ary Guild selection), Garden City Bks., 1957.   CA-
    15/16

GRUMBINE, E. Evalyn 1900-
    She was born in Chicago, graduated from the Univer-
    sity of Illinois, and married a Chicago doctor, Andrew
    McNally, Jr. Mrs. McNally has worked in advertising
    and once served as an advertising director and assis-
    tant publisher. She and Andrew McNally wrote This
    Is Mexico, Dodd, 1947.

GUDMUNDSON, Shirley M.
    Author and teacher, born in England. Shirley Gud-
    mundson once served as an assistant to a doctor in a
    remote section of the Missouri Ozarks. She has also
    taught school in a one-room schoolhouse on an island.
    The author married an architect, and they have lived

in a hillside home in St. George's, Grenada. Her
juvenile books include: Getting To Know The British
West Indies, Coward, 1962; Hurricane, Brazillier,
1966.

GUILLOT, René 1900-
French writer and teacher, graduate of the University
of Bordeaux, and a resident of Vincennes. He has
been a high school teacher in Dakar, Africa and a
professor at the Lycée Condorcet in Paris. René
Guillot has been the recipient of many literary awards,
and his stories for children have been translated into
several languages. Juvenile titles include: Fofana (tr.
by Barbara Seccombe), Criterion, 1962; Grishka And
The Bear (tr. by Gwen Marsh), Criterion, 1959; The
King Of Cats (tr. by John Marshall), Lothrop, 1963;
Mokokambo, The Lost Land (tr. by John Marshall),
Criterion, 1961. MJA

GULICK, Peggy 1918-
She grew up in Montana and later made her home in
Ventura, California. Peggy Gulick and her sister
Elizabeth Dresser have created educational filmstrips
used by the beginning reader. Together they wrote
Hurrah For Maxie (A Junior Literary Guild selection),
Lothrop, 1959.

GULLAHORN, Genevieve
Born in Lithuania, she came to the United States at
the age of eight. When she was twelve, her first
story for boys and girls was published in the Baltimore Sunday Sun. Mrs. Gullahorn was awarded a
scholarship in journalism at the University of Southern
California where she served as women's editor on the
school paper. Following graduation, she worked on
several newspapers. Later she and her family lived
in Illinois. A family pet became the subject of her
book for boys and girls Zigger, The Pet Chameleon,
Abelard, 1956.

GUNTHER, John 1901-1970
Author, radio commentator, reporter, foreign correspondent, lecturer, born in Chicago, Illinois. He graduated from the University of Chicago. Mr. Gunther
has been a member of the Century Club, Bucks Club,
the New York Council on Foreign Relations, and the
Association of Radio News Analysts. He has lived in

New York City.   John Gunther has made many trips
abroad to collect material for his "Meet The World"
books.   His books for young people include: Julius
Caesar, Random, 1959; Meet The Congo And Its Neighbors, Harper, 1959.   CA-11/12

GURNEY, J. Eric 1910-   Nancy (Jack)
Canadian-born, husband-wife team.   Eric Gurney was
born in Winnipeg and attended the Ontario College of
Art in Canada.   He was associated with the Walt Disney Studios for a number of years.   In 1962 Mr. Gurney was the recipient of the National Cartoonists Society's Silver Plaque as Best Advertising and Illustration Cartoonist.   Nancy (Jack) Gurney was born in
Montreal, Canada and began her writing career in
Toronto.   Together they wrote The King, The Mice
And The Cheese, Random, 1965.   CA-4

GUSTAFSON, Elton T.
Author, teacher, editor.   He attended the Universities
of California, Columbia, New Hampshire, and New
York.   At one time he was a college professor and
has edited and written medical articles.   Mr. Gustafson has also been an Assistant Editor of several medical journals on the West Coast.   He married author
Sarah Regal Riedman and collaborated with her to
write Portraits Of Nobel Laureates In Medicine And
Physiology, Abelard, 1964.

GUTHRIE, Anne 1890-
She was born in San Diego, California, graduated from
Stanford University (Guthrie House on the campus was
named after her), and has resided in New York City
since 1947.   Anne Guthrie worked for many years with
the Y. W. C. A. in South America and the Far East.
Since her return to this country her main interest has
been the United Nations.   Miss Guthrie has attended
the meetings of the General Assembly and has served
as Vice Chairman of the Speakers Research Committee.
Her friendship with Mrs. Pandit of India which began
in 1941 resulted in her book Madame Ambassador, Harcourt, 1962.   CA-5/6

GWYNNE, John Harold 1899-
Minister and writer, native of Pennsylvania.   An or-
dained minister, Dr. Gwynne received degrees from
the College of Wooster (Ohio) and the Theological

Seminary and Graduate College of Princeton University.
He has written devotional meditations and articles,
books about Christian living, and subject matter for
worship programs.   For young people he wrote Rainbow Book Of Bible Stories, World, 1956.

H

HABBERTON, William
Native of Illinois, teacher, author.   He has taught in
high schools and universities.   Dr. Habberton has been
Professor Emeritus of History, Division of General
Studies, at the University of Illinois.   He has lived in
Illinois but has spent his winters in St. Petersburg,
Florida.   In addition to textbooks he has also written
a children's book called Russia, Houghton, 1965.

HABER, Heinz   1913-
Author and scientist, born in Germany.   He graduated
from the University of Berlin where he received de-
grees in physics and astronomy.   Dr. Haber came to
the United States in 1947 and was associated with the
Air Force School of Aviation Medicine.   He has been
honored as the co-founder of space medicine.   He has
written magazine articles, scientific papers, and books.
The author has been on the staff of the University of
California at Los Angeles and has worked with the
Walt Disney Studio.   His juvenile books include: Stars,
Men And Atoms, Golden, 1962; The Walt Disney Story
Of Our Friend The Atom, Simon, 1956.

HACKETT, Albert   Frances (Goodrich)
Husband-wife team, actors and writers.   Born of the-
atrical parents, Albert Hackett appeared on the stage
at six years of age and studied at the Professional
Children's School.   He has been associated with the
theater as an actor, director, and writer.   Mrs.
Hackett attended Vassar and the New York School of
Social Service.   She met her husband when he was in
a stage play called "Whoopee," and she was in "The
Show-Off. "   As a writing team, they have achieved
great success as Broadway playwrights ("Bridal Wise, "
"The Great Big Doorstep, " "Up Pops The Devil") and
screen writers ("Father Of The Bride, " "Easter Parade, " "Seven Brides For Seven Brothers, " "The Virginian").   Together they dramatized The Diary Of
Anne Frank, Random, 1956.

HADER, Berta (Hoerner)   Elmer 1889-
    Husband-wife team. Berta Hoerner was born in Mexi-
    co, attended the University of Washington and the Cali-
    fornia School of Design. She married artist Elmer
    Hader whom she met in New York. The Haders have
    spent a lifetime together creating distinguished picture
    books for boys and girls. Mr. Hader who was born
    in Pajaro, California attended an art school in San
    Francisco and continued his studies in Paris. The
    Haders have lived in a stone house which they built
    themselves in Nyack, New York. In 1949 the Calde-
    cott medal was awarded to them for their book The
    Big Snow, Macmillan, 1948. They also wrote and il-
    lustrated: Big City, Macmillan, 1947; Friendly Phoebe,
    Macmillan, 1953; Little Antelope, Macmillan, 1962;
    Lost In The Zoo, Macmillan, 1951.   JBA-1, JBA-2

HAGER, Alice (Rogers) 1894-
    Author and newspaperwoman, born in Peoria, Illinois.
    She received her degree from Stanford and did graduate
    work at the University of California at Berkeley. She
    has lived in Arlington, Virginia. Her versatile career
    has included: writing for both adults and children,
    serving as president of the Woman's National Press
    Club, and an Information Officer in the Foreign Ser-
    vice at the American Embassy in Brussels. She re-
    ceived a War Department Citation for her work as a
    correspondent during World War II. As a reporter,
    Mrs. Hager has flown over half a million miles and
    has written books about aviation. For young people
    she wrote: Canvas Castle (recipient of the Julia Ells-
    worth Ford Foundation award for children's literature),
    Junior Literary Guild and Messner, 1949; Washington,
    City Of Destiny, Macmillan, 1949.   CA-5/6

HAHN, Emily 1905-
    Author, reporter, born in St. Louis, Missouri. She
    received her degree in Mining Engineering from the
    University of Wisconsin and continued her studies at
    Columbia and Oxford Universities. She married Charles
    R. Boxer who has been a Professor and has lived in
    Hertfordshire, England. Her articles have appeared
    in the New Yorker. Juvenile titles include: First Book
    Of India, Watts, 1955; Francie, Junior Literary Guild
    and Watts, 1951; June Finds A Way (A Junior Literary
    Guild selection), Watts, 1960; Leonardo da Vinci, Ran-
    dom, 1956; Mary, Queen Of Scots, Random, 1953. CA-3

HALACY, Daniel Stephen 1919-
Author, editor, teacher, born in South Carolina. He
has made his home in Glendale, Arizona. He graduated from Phoenix College and Arizona State University. Daniel S. Halacy, Jr., was a member of the
Air Force during World War II and the Korean Conflict. He has been associated with Convair, AiRe-
search, Motorola, and Goodyear Aricraft. The author
has written both fiction and technical books and has
taught at Phoenix College. His books for young people include: Beyond Tomorrow, Macrae, 1965; Bionics,
Holiday, 1965.   CA-7/8

HALE, Arlene 1924-
She was born on a farm in Iowa and later lived in New
London, Iowa. She has written both books and short
stories for children. Her main interests have been
farming and travel, and her ambition has been to
write about Midwest farm life. Miss Hale visited
many ghost towns in order to acquire material for her
book Ghost Town's Secret, Abelard, 1962.   CA-1

HALE, Helen see MULCAHY, Lucille Burnett

HALL, Adele 1910-
Teacher and author, born in Philadelphia, Pennsylvania.
She taught school after graduating from the State Teachers' College at Glassboro, New Jersey. Her hobbies
have included antiques, boating, gardening, and swimming. Adele Hall has been on the Hostess Committee
at the Miss America Pageant for many years. Her
books for young people include: Beauty Queen, Messner, 1957; Seashore Summer, Harper, 1962.   CA-4

HALL, Donald Andrew 1928-
Donald Hall, Jr. was born in Connecticut and studied
at Harvard and Oxford Universities. He has written
both prose and poetry which has appeared in such
magazines as Horizon, the New Yorker, Poetry, Encounter, and the New Statesman. For seven years
Mr. Hall was the poetry editor of the Paris Review.
He has also taught at the University of Michigan. For
children he wrote Andrew The Lion Farmer, Watts,
1959, and he edited A Poetry Sampler, Watts, 1962.
CA-7/8

HALL, Elvajean 1910-
Author and librarian, born in Hamilton, Illinois. A
graduate of Oberlin College (Ohio), she attended library
school at the University of Wisconsin and did further
study at Columbia. She has made her home in Boston,
Massachusetts. Miss Hall has been head librarian at
Stephens College in Columbia, Missouri, supervisor of
library services for the public schools in Newton,
Massachusetts, and a library consultant of Hong Kong's
New Chinese University (Chung Chi College). The author has contributed to educational and library publications, and her drawings have appeared in Library Journal and ALA Bulletin. Her juvenile books include:
Hong Kong, Rand, 1967; Land And People Of Argentina,
Lippincott, 1960; The Land And People Of Czechoslo-
vakia, Lippincott, 1966; The Volga: Lifeline Of Russia,
Rand, 1965.   CA-15/16

HALL, Esther Greenacre
She was born in Colorado and studied at Stanford University. She and her husband have lived in a 175-
year-old farmhouse in Armonk, New York where Mrs.
Hall has been instrumental in starting a public library.
Collecting antiques has been the author's hobby.   Her
book for young people was Mario And The Chuna, Random, 1940.

HALL, Gordon Langley
He was born in England and later became an American
citizen.   Mr. Hall has owned houses in both England
and America.   The house in Sussex was built by a
Spanish Gypsy ancestor, and its location was near the
place where William the Conqueror landed.   He bought
the Dr. Joseph Johnson House in Charleston, South
Carolina and restored it to its pre-Civil War period.
Mr. Hall received his education in England and began
writing at an early age.   At the age of nineteen he
taught in the Gull Bay Ojibway Indian reservation at
Ontario, Canada.   He wrote: Osceola, Holt, 1964;
William Father Of The Netherlands, Rand, 1969.   CA
-2

HALL, James Norman
He was born in Colfax, Iowa and later lived on Tahiti.
Mr. Hall attended Grinnell College (Iowa).   During
World War I, he met his co-author Charles Bernard
Nordhoff in the Lafayette Flying Corps.   They edited

a history of the Corps.   Mr. Hall has also written
poetry.   For boys and girls he collaborated with
Charles Bernard Nordhoff to write: Falcons Of France,
Little, 1929; Mutiny On The Bounty, Little, 1932.
JBA-1

HALL, Marjory (Yeakley) 1908-
   Author, columnist, editor.   She graduated from Wellesley College and later studied creative writing at Harvard and Columbia.   Marjory Hall has served on the
   editorial staff of the Ladies' Home Journal and at one
   time was "teen" columnist for the Boston Transcript.
   She has also been an advertising executive and a travel and resort editor for Yankee Magazine.   The author and her husband, a lawyer, have lived at Swamp-
   scott, Massachusetts.   Books which she has written
   for young people include: Another Kind Of Courage,
   Westminster, 1967; Hatbox For Mimi (A Junior Literary Guild selection), Funk, 1960.   CA-3

HALL, Rosalys Haskell 1914-
   Born in New York, she studied in Tunisia and Paris,
   and attended New Jersey College.   She obtained a New
   York teacher's certificate and taught school.   It was
   after she took a course in children's writing from May
   Lamberton Becker at Columbia University that she sold
   her first story.   Rosalys Hall once worked in a book
   shop as an assistant to Lena Barksdale and later became an associate editor in the juvenile department of
   a publishing company.   Her books include: Bertie And
   Eddie, Oxford, 1956; Bright And Shining Breadboard,
   Lothrop, 1969; Young Fancy, Longmans, 1960.   CA-
   11/12, MJA

HALL, William Norman 1915-
   Author and editor.   He graduated from St. John's College in Annapolis, Maryland.   He and his family have
   lived in Oceanport, New Jersey.   Prior to his position
   as editor of children's books in a publishing firm, Mr.
   Hall wrote speeches for a political campaign and did
   publicity work.   His juvenile books include: Telltime,
   The Rabbit, Crowell, 1943; Winkie's World, Doubleday,
   1958.

HALLER, Adolf 1897-
   Swiss writer and teacher, born in the district of Aargau.   He received his education at Bern, Geneva, and

HALL-QUEST, Edna Olga (Wilbourne)   221

Zurich Universities. Mr. Haller has been a high
school teacher and a superintendent of schools in Switzerland. The author has been the recipient of an
honorary degree from Aargau (1957), the Swiss Children's Book Prize (1947), and the Swiss Schiller Foundation Prize (1944). For boys and girls he wrote He
Served Two Masters, Pantheon, 1962.

HALL-QUEST, Edna Olga (Wilbourne) 1899-
Author and teacher, born in Texas. She graduated
from Columbia and New York Universities, and has
lived in New York City. A former teacher in San
Antonio, Texas, Mrs. Hall-Quest has also taught in
Dobbs Ferry, New York. She and her husband have
visited many national parks and monuments throughout
the United States. Her juvenile books include: Guar-
dians Of Liberty: Sam Adams And John Hancock, Dutton, 1963; Powhattan And Captain Smith, Ariel Bks. ,
1957.   CA-7/8

HALSELL, Grace
She spent her early years in Lubbock, Texas and later
made her home in Hyde Park, New York. As a newspaper correspondent and columnist, she has done extensive travel. She has visited many Latin American
countries and once bicycled throughout the British
Isles. In order to acquire authentic backgrounds for
her "Getting To Know" books, the author made return
visits to Colombia, Peru, Honduras, and Guatemala.
She has also traveled to Japan, Hong Kong, Malaysia,
Turkey, and Saudi Arabia. Her books for young people include: Getting To Know Guatemala And The Two
Honduras, Coward, 1964; Peru, Macmillan, 1969.

HALSMAN, Philippe
Author, photographer, playwright. He once had the
distinction of creating more Life magazine covers than
any other cameraman. In addition to photography, Mr.
Halsman devoted some of his time to writing plays and
books during his stay in Europe. His first book to be
published in America was in 1949. He invented the
character "Piccoli" for stories which he told to his
daughters and later assembled them into a juvenile
book Piccoli, A Fairy Tale, Simon and Schuster, 1953.

HAMBLETON, Jack
Author and newspaperman. He began his newspaper

career as a teletype operator and later held various
editorial positions. Mr. Hambleton has been associated
with such newspapers as the Toronto Star, the Globe
and Mail. He also was the director of the Ontario
Travel and Publicity Bureau which he founded in 1934.
The author has worked with the CBC's Sportsman's
Show, contributed numerous articles to magazines and
newspapers, and traveled over 500, 000 miles on newspaper assignments in addition to his writing career.
For boys and girls he wrote: Charter Pilot, Longmans, 1953; Young Bush Pilot, Longmans, 1949.

HAMBLIN, Dora Jane
Author and magazine correspondent, born in Bedford,
Iowa. She graduated from Coe College in Cedar Ra-
pids (Iowa) and received a Master of Science degree in
journalism from Northwestern University in Evanston,
Illinois. Miss Hamblin has contributed articles to
Life magazine, worked in London as a correspondent
for Life, and served as its bureau chief in both Rome
and Paris. Her work has also appeared in Harper's
Bazaar, Reader's Digest, Sports Illustrated, and Euro-
pean magazines. Her first book for young people was
Pots And Robbers (A Junior Literary Guild selection),
Simon, 1970.

HAMIL, Thomas Arthur 1928-
Painter, author. The American Institute of Graphic
Arts selected Tom Hamil's book Brother Alonzo (Mac-
millan, 1957) for its exhibit of outstanding children's
books. He has lived in California. He also wrote
Hans And The Golden Flute, Macmillan, 1958 and il-
lustrated Patricia Miles Martin's book Calvin And The
Cub Scouts, Putnam, 1964.

HAMILTON, Kay see DE LEEUW, Cateau

HAMILTON, Russel
He has lived in Greenfield, Massachusetts. Mr. Hamilton's interest and hobby has been railroading. He
has built railroad models, studied books on the subject, and has traveled many miles on railroads. Although he has worked in the advertising profession, he
once claimed that "he is one of the many thousand
Americans whose chief disappointment is that they have
never been locomotive engineers. " For boys and girls
he wrote First Book Of Trains, Watts, 1958.

HAMILTON, Virginia
She was born in Yellow Springs, Ohio and attended An-
tioch College. Her first book for young people was
Zeely (Macmillan, 1967). In the June 1969 issue of
Top of the News ("Profile of an Author---Virginia
Hamilton") Miss Hamilton told about her writing:
". . . I suppose I'm writing for myself at the very
onset of a book idea. I solve whatever problems a-
rise in the plotting in the way my instincts tell me is
the right way . . ." She, her husband, and daughter
have lived in New York City. She also wrote: The
House Of Dies Drear, Macmillan, 1968; The Time-Ago
Tales Of Jahdu, Macmillan, 1969.

HAMMOND, Ralph see HAMMOND-INNES, Ralph

HAMMOND-INNES, Ralph 1913-
His pseudonym is Ralph Hammond. Prior to World
War II, he wrote for the London Financial News. Following his service in the artillery he became a full-
time author. Several of his books have been published
in serial form in the Saturday Evening Post. He has
been both a yachtsman (owner of British ocean racer
"Triune of Troy") and a writer of sea stories. His
titles for young people include: Cocos Gold, Harper,
1950; Cruise Of Danger, Westminster, 1954. CA-5/6

HANDFORTH, Thomas Schofield 1897-1948
He was born in Tacoma, Washington, attended art
school in New York, and later studied in Paris. His
work has been exhibited in the Chicago Art Institute,
the Metropolitan Museum of Art, and the Fogg Art
Museum in Cambridge, Massachusetts. Mr. Handforth
once lived in Peking where his neighbors became the
subjects in his 1939 Caldecott award winning book Mei
Li, Doubleday, 1938. JBA-2

HANNA, Geneva R.
Author and teacher, born in Paynesville, Minnesota.
A graduate of Hamline University in St. Paul, Minnesota, she later received her M. A. and Ph. D. degrees
from Northwestern University. Geneva Hanna has been
a teacher in the high schools of Illinois, Iowa, Ohio,
and Minnesota. She has also been an associate professor at the University of Texas, College of Education. She collaborated with Mariana K. McAllister to
write Books, Young People, And Reading Guidance,

Harper, 1960.

HANNUM, Sara
    She was born in Moundsville, West Virginia and grad-
    uated from Radcliffe College.   She also studied at
    Columbia University and the Sorbonne.   Sara Hannum
    has not only been an assistant editor on a magazine
    but also was Assistant Editor of the Book Of Knowledge.
    With Gwendolyn E. Reed she compiled Lean Out Of The
    Window, Atheneum, 1965.

HANO, Arnold 1922-
    Teacher, newspaperman, editor.   Mr. Hano has lived
    in Laguana Beach, California.   He has written many
    magazine articles and several books about sports.   In
    1963 he was selected as Magazine Sportswriter of the
    year by twenty-two magazine editors.   For boys and
    girls he wrote: Roberto Clemente, Putnam, 1968;
    Sandy Koufax, Strikeout King, Putnam, 1964.   CA-9/
    10

HANSEN, Harry 1884-
    Editor, correspondent, author, born in Davenport, Iowa.
    Mr. Hansen studied at the University of Chicago.   At
    one time he served as a correspondent in Europe and
    literary editor for the Chicago Daily News.   The au-
    thor has also been literary editor of the New York
    World-Telegram and New York World, and editor of
    the World Almanac.   He has belonged to the Illinois
    State Historical Society.   His juvenile books include:
    Old Ironsides: The Fighting "Constitution, " Random,
    1955; The Story Of Illinois, Garden City, 1956.

HARKINS, Philip 1912-
    Sports enthusiast and writer, born in Boston, Massa-
    chusetts.   He attended France's Grenoble University
    and the School of Political Science in Paris and has re-
    sided in Weston, Connecticut.   He spent several years
    abroad and was a hockey player and news reporter.
    The author served with the Merchant Marine and the
    United Seamen's Service during World War II.   His
    first book to be published for boys and girls was
    Coast Guard, Ahoy!, Harcourt, 1943.   Other juvenile
    titles include: Big Silver Bowl, Morrow, 1947; Bom-
    ber Pilot, Harcourt, 1944; Double Play, Holiday, 1951;
    Fight Like A Falcon, Morrow, 1961; Knockout, Holiday,
    1950; No Head For Soccer, Morrow, 1964; Road Race,

Crowell, 1953; Young Skin Diver, Morrow, 1956.
MJA

HARLOW, Alvin Fay 1875-
Born in Sedalia, Missouri, he graduated from Franklin
College in Indiana. Prior to living in New York, Mr.
Harlow lived in Indiana and Tennessee. He has enjoyed
hiking as a special interest. The author has contri-
buted numerous articles to adult reference books. His
juvenile books include: Joel Chandler Harris (Uncle
Remus) Plantation Storyteller, Messner, 1941; The
Ringlings, Messner, 1951.

HARNETT, Cynthia Mary
Author-illustrator. She was born in London, England
and studied at the Chelsea School of Art. In 1951 she
won England's Carnegie Medal for her book Nicholas
And The Wool-Pack (Putnam, 1953). When she was
ten, she wrote a historical novel for her own magazine. The author has lived in Henley-on-Thames,
England. She wrote and illustrated Caxton's Challenge,
World, 1960. CA-9/10

HARPER, Wilhelmina 1884-
Librarian, teacher, compiler. She was born in Farmington, Maine and later made her home in Palo Alto,
California. Miss Harper attended New York State
Library School and Columbia University. She has been
both a children's librarian and head librarian in New
York and California. She has also taught courses in
library science and contributed to educational and library publications. At one time Wilhelmina Harper was
associated with the Y. M. C. A. in France and the American Red Cross. Books which she compiled for young
readers include: Easter Chimes (New, rev. ed.), Dutton, 1965; Flying Hoofs, Houghton, 1939; Ghosts And
Goblins (New, rev. ed.), Dutton, 1965; The Harvest
Feast, Dutton, 1938; Merry Christmas To You!, Dutton, 1935; Yankee Yarns, Dutton, 1944. CA-17/18

HARRINGTON, Lyn (Evelyn) Davis 1911-
She married a photographer and has traveled extensively with her husband on assignments. She was born in
Ontario, Canada. Lyn Harrington attended the University of Toronto Library School and has been a children's librarian in Toronto. She wrote Ootook, Young
Eskimo Girl (photographs by Richard Harrington),

Abelard, 1956.   CA-7/8

HARRIS, Joel Chandler   1848-1908
Storyteller, journalist, author, born in Georgia. At
an early age he began a newspaper career as a type-
setter.   When he became editor of the Atlanta Constitution, Joel Chandler Harris wrote his first "Uncle
Remus" story.   All of the famous "Uncle Remus" tales
were stories the author had heard as a boy from the
Negroes.   Joel Chandler Harris has been called the
"Hans Christian Andersen of America. "   His home
"Wren's Nest" in Atlanta, Georgia, was made into a
public shrine.   Juvenile stories include: On The Plantation, Appleton, 1919; Told By Uncle Remus, McClure,
Philips & Co. , 1905.   JBA-1

HARRIS, Leon A.   1926-
Leon A. Harris, Jr. , was born in New York City and
grew up in Dallas, Texas.   He spent the summer
months in France.   He graduated from Phillips Academy and Harvard College.   Prior to a full-time writing career, he was in the department store business.
He has contributed articles to magazines in addition to
writing books.   The author married French ballerina
Marina Svetlova, and they have lived in Dallas.   His
juvenile titles include: The Great Picture Robbery,
Atheneum, 1963; Young Peru, Dodd, 1969.   CA-9/10

HARRISON, C. William   1913-
He was born on a farm near Indianapolis, Indiana and
later made his home in Redlands, California.   When
he finished school, he worked for two summers at
Yellowstone National Park.   At one time Mr. Harrison
was an advertising copywriter, editor of a house organ,
photographer, and radio continuity director.   His stories have appeared in anthologies, magazines, movies,
and on television.   Many of his novels have been translated into different languages.   For boys and girls he
wrote: Conservation, Messner, 1963; Forests, Messner, 1969.

HARSHAW, Ruth Hetzel
She has been educational director for a Chicago department store.   With Dilla MacBean she conducted a
weekly radio program "The Battle of Books. "   This co-
author also originated and was the conductor of the
radio program known as "The Hobby Horse Presents. "

With Dilla MacBean she wrote What Book Is That?,
Macmillan, 1948.

HARTE, Bret   1836-1902
He was born in Albany, New York.   When he was eighteen, he went to California and became interested in
journalism and fourteen years later was made the first
editor of the Overland Monthly.   After his story "The
Luck Of Roaring Camp" was published in the Overland,
Bret Harte became famous.   He later wrote for the
Atlantic Monthly.   In 1878 he became United States
commercial agent at Krefeld, Germany and continued
to live in Europe for the remainder of his life.   He
wrote: Queen Of The Pirate Isle (Illustrated by Kate
Greenaway), Warne, 1931; Stories Of The Early West,
Platt, 1964; Stories Of The Old West (selected by Wilhelmina Harper and Aimee M. Peters), Houghton, 1940.

HARTWELL, Nancy   see   CALLAHAN, Claire Wallis

HARWIN, Brian   see   HENDERSON, Le Grand

HATCH, Alden   1898-
He has written articles on politics and sports for many
magazines including the Saturday Evening Post, Collier's, and Harper's.   When he wrote a book about
President Dwight D. Eisenhower, he talked with many
of the former President's friends and relatives and in
addition completed research in San Antonio, Kansas
City, and Abilene, Kansas.   He also wrote George Pat-
ton, General In Spurs, Messner, 1950.   His book about
President Eisenhower for young people was Young Ike,
Messner, 1953.

HAUFF, Wilhelm
Storyteller of the nineteenth century, Wilhelm Hauff
died at the age of twenty-five.   His stories have become as familiar as those of Hans Christian Andersen
to the children of Germany.   In the preface of Dwarf
Long-Nose; translated by Doris Orgel and winner of the
Lewis Carroll Shelf Award (Random, 1960), Phyllis
McGinley wrote: ". . . There is something about the
robust and earthy quality of primitive folktales which
seems to defy imitation.   That Hauff managed it is a
tribute to his odd talent and perhaps only his extreme
youth accounts for his ability to create stories as art-
less and spellbinding as if they had been handed down

to him from generations of cottagers. " He also wrote
<u>Monkey's Uncle</u>, Farrar, 1969.

HAUGAARD, Erik Christian 1923-
    He was born in Denmark. As a young man he traveled
to the United States and Canada and also visited Spain,
Italy, and England. When he wrote <u>Hakon Of Rogen's</u>
<u>Saga</u> (Houghton, 1963), he took a camping trip along the
fiords of Norway and met several people who were natural born storytellers and who discussed the Viking
heroes with him. He has written poetry and a play
("The Heroes") which was given at Antioch College in
1958. Erik Haugaard married a writer, and they have
lived in Denmark. He also wrote <u>Rider And His Horse</u>,
Houghton, 1968. CA-7/8

HAUTZIG, Esther (Rudomin) 1930-
    She was born in Vilno, Poland and lived in Siberia,
Poland, and Sweden. When she came to America, she
attended Hunter College. She has been associated with
children's books not only as an author but in the publishing and promotion of them. She married a concert
pianist and has lived in New York City. She wrote:
<u>In School</u>, Macmillan, 1969; <u>Let's Make Presents</u>, Cro-
well, 1962. CA-2

HAVIGHURST, Marion (Boyd)
    Teacher and writer, born in Marietta, Ohio. A grad-
uate of Smith College, she received her master's degree from Yale and has taught English in Oxford, Ohio
at both Western College and Miami University. With
her husband, professor and author Walter Havighurst,
she wrote . . . <u>Climb A Lofty Ladder</u>, Winston, 1952.
She also wrote <u>Sycamore Tree</u>, World, 1960. CA-13/
14, MJA

HAVIGHURST, Walter 1901-
    Teacher, scholar, author, born in Appleton, Wisconsin.
He received degrees from Columbia and Denver Universities and also attended King's College (University of
England) in London. He joined the Merchant Marine
and traveled around the world. Mr. Havighurst married author Marion Boyd, and together they wrote
. . . <u>Climb A Lofty Ladder</u> (Winston, 1952). The
Havighursts have lived in Oxford, Ohio where he has
been a Professor of English at Miami University. His
juvenile books include: <u>Buffalo Bill's Great Wild West</u>

Show, Random, 1957; First Book Of Pioneers: Northwest Territory, Watts, 1959; Life In America: The
Great Plains, Fideler, 1951; The Northeast, Fideler,
1952; Proud Prisoner, Holt, 1964.   CA-3, MJA

HAWES, Charles Boardman 1889-1923
He was born in Clifton Springs, New York and grew up
in Bangor, Maine.   He was class poet and editor of the
paper at Bowdoin College.   Charles Hawes later served
in an editorial capacity for both Youth's Companion and
the Open Road magazines.   He and his wife, the daughter of author George W. Cable, lived in Gloucester.
He died at the age of thirty-four and was awarded the
Newbery Medal posthumously in 1924 for his book The
Dark Frigate, Little, 1923.   JBA-1

HAWKES, Hester 1900-
Storyteller and writer.   She settled in Cambridge, Massachusetts after spending several years in the Far East.
It was from the Orient that she gathered material for
her book Three Seeds (Coward-McCann, 1956) which
was based on actual shipment of "Seeds for Democracy"
to the Filipino people in 1950.   She also wrote Ning's
Pony, Coward-McCann, 1953.

HAWKINS, Quail
She was born in Spokane, Washington, the oldest in a
family of seven children.   Miss Hawkins studied at the
University of California and later was associated with
the University of California Press in Berkeley.   She
also gained valuable experience with books for young
people through her work at the Sather Gate Book Shop
in Berkeley.   Juvenile books include: The Aunt-Sitter,
Holiday, 1958; Mountain Courage, Doubleday, 1957;
Puppy For Keeps, Holiday, 1943.

HAWKINSON, John Samuel 1912-   Lucy (Ozone) 1924-
Husband-wife team, artists, authors.   Born in Chicago,
John Hawkinson has been both an artist and a teacher.
He once said: ". . . Anyone who can write can learn
to use a brush.   Observation is what really makes an
artist. " He served in the U. S. Army and was awarded
the Bronze Star.   He married Lucy Ozone, and they
have written and illustrated their own books.   Born in
California, she studied at the Chicago Academy of Art.
At one time she worked for a publishing firm.   The
Hawkinsons have lived in Chicago.   Their illustrations

have appeared in many books by other writers. Together they wrote and illustrated: Birds In The Sky,
Childrens, 1965; Little Boy Who Lives Up High, Whitman, 1967.   CA-5/6

HAWTHORNE, Hildegarde
    She was born in New York City, the daughter of writer
    Julian Hawthorne. Her grandfather was Nathaniel Haw-
    thorne. At the age of six weeks, she made her first
    trip abroad. Miss Hawthorne has contributed to maga-
    zines and has served on the staff of the New York
    Times and St. Nicholas magazine. She married writer
    John M. Oskison and lived in California and Connecti-
    cut. Her books for children include: Born To Adven-
    ture, Appleton-Century, 1947; Give Me Liberty, Apple-
    ton-Century, 1945; The Miniature's Secret, Appleton-
    Century, 1938; Ox-Team Miracle, Longmans, 1942;
    Phantom King, Appleton-Century, 1937; The Poet Of
    Craigie House, Appleton-Century, 1936.   JBA-1,
    JBA-2

HAYCRAFT, Howard 1905-
    He was born in Madelia, Minnesota and graduated from
    the University of Minnesota. He married the daughter
    of writer Thomas Costain and has lived in New York
    City. Mr. Haycraft has served as president of the
    H. W. Wilson Company and has edited may books for
    young people. He also was instrumental in founding
    the Mystery Writers of America. He edited: Boys'
    Book Of Great Detective Stories, Harper, 1938; Boys'
    Second Book Of Great Detective Stories, Harper, 1940;
    The Boys' Sherlock Holmes (New and enl. ed.), Har-
    per, 1961. With Stanley Jasspon Kunitz he edited
    Junior Book Of Authors (2d ed., rev.), Wilson, 1951.

HAYES, Florence (Sooy) 1895-
    Traveler and writer. She studied creative writing at
    Columbia University where a short story assignment
    later provided the ideas for her juvenile book Hosk-ki
    The Navajo (Random, 1943). Extensive travel through-
    out Central America, Mexico, and Alaska has provided
    authentic backgrounds for her books about people of
    other races. Mrs. Hayes' books have also been pub-
    lished in other countries, and two of her stories were
    produced as serials on radio. Her books for boys and
    girls include: The Boy In The 49th Seat, Random,
    1963; Burro Tamer, Random, 1946; Good Luck Feather,

Houghton, 1958; Skid, Houghton, 1948.

HAYES, William Dimitt 1913-
Author and illustrator, born in Goliad, Texas. He
grew up in Arizona, attended Arizona State University,
and the Art Students League in New York City. He
graduated from the University of Missouri. Mr. Hayes
has been a staff artist for Scholastic Magazines. He
married author Kathryn Hitte, and they have lived in
New York. Juvenile books which he wrote include:
Hold That Computer, Atheneum, 1968; Project: Genius,
Atheneum, 1962. CA-7/8

HAYS, Hobe
Author, illustrator, teacher. He and his family have
made their home on Long Island. Prior to his writing
career, Mr. Hays was an art instructor in a college
in Kansas. When the author decided to create a story
for his young son, it resulted in his first book to be
published for children entitled The Adventure, Westminster, 1965.

HAYS, Wilma Pitchford 1909-
Distinguished author and teacher, she has made her
home in Orleans, Massachusetts. Mrs. Hays has writ-
ten several historical fiction books for young readers.
As a teacher and mother she has endeavored to portray
characters which boys and girls have found realistic.
Her juvenile titles include: Abe Lincoln's Birthday,
Coward, 1961; Little Lone Coyote (A Junior Literary
Guild selection), Little, 1961; Naughty Little Pilgrim,
Washburn, 1969. CA-1

HAYWOOD, Carolyn 1898-
Author-illustrator, born in Philadelphia. She graduated
from Philadelphia Normal School and attended the Pennsylvania Academy of Fine Arts. She once studied with
three former students of the distinguished illustrator
Howard Pyle: Violet Oakley, Elizabeth Shippen Green
Elliott, and Jessie Willcox Smith. In addition to writing books for boys and girls she has been a portrait
painter. Her first book "B" Is For Betsy (Harcourt)
was published in 1939. Miss Haywood has made her
home in Philadelphia. Books which she wrote and illustrated include: Back To School With Betsy, Harcourt, 1943; Betsy And Billy, Harcourt, 1941; Betsy
And Mr. Kilpatrick, Morrow, 1967. CA-7/8, JBA-2

HAZELTINE, Alice Isabel 1878-
Editor and compiler, she has been a faculty member of
the School of Library Science at Columbia University.
At one time she was in charge of children's work at
the public libraries in St. Louis and Pittsburgh. Alice
Hazeltine's experience and deep interest in children's
literature has qualified her to edit and compile books
for young readers. Juvenile books which she has compiled and edited include: Children's Stories To Read
Or Tell, Abingdon, 1949; Hero Tales From Many Lands,
Abingdon, 1961.

HAZLETT, Edward Everett 1892-
He was born in Kansas, graduated from Annapolis, and
made his home in Chapel Hill, North Carolina upon retirement from the Navy. He served as a submarine
commander in World War I and was an instructor at
Annapolis during World War II. He also was in charge
of the U. S. Naval training programs at North Carolina
University. Captain Hazlett's work has appeared in the
Naval Institute Proceedings and the Encyclopaedia Britannica. For young people he wrote "He's Jake!",
Dodd, 1947.

HEADLEY, Elizabeth see CAVANNA, Betty

HEADSTROM, Birger Richard 1902-
Author and teacher, he has lived in West Medway,
Massachusetts. He has been associated with the Wor-
cester Museum of Natural History as Curator of Ento-
mology. The Audubon Society has published his work
for many years. Richard Headstrom has also written
numerous articles about literature, philosophy, and
science. He has also taught science in a high school.
For boys and girls he wrote and illustrated Adventures
With A Hand Lens, Lippincott, 1962. He also wrote
Adventures With Freshwater Animals, Lippincott, 1964.
CA-4

HEAPS, Willard Allison 1909-
Librarian, teacher, author. He has taught at Columbia
University, State Teachers College in Pennsylvania, and
at Arizona State. Mr. Heaps was chief of readers' services at the UN Headquarters Library and was assistant librarian at UNESCO in Paris. He wrote: Assas-
sination, Meredith, 1969; The Wall Of Shame, Duell,
1964.

HEGARTY, Reginald Beaton   1906–
  He has been associated with the New Bedford (Massachusetts) Free Public Library as curator of its Mel-
  ville Whaling Room.   He went to sea at the age of
  two, and eight of his first twelve years were spent
  aboard whaleships.   Reginald Hegarty attended high
  school in New Bedford and gained a valuable education
  and vivid experiences from the "school of the sea. "
  He wrote The Rope's End, Houghton, 1965.   CA-15/16

HEIDERSTADT, Dorothy   1907–
  Librarian, author.   Born in Geneva, Nebraska, she
  has been a children's librarian at the Bethlehem, Pennsylvania Public Library and a branch librarian in the
  Kansas City, Missouri Public Library system.   She
  graduated from the University of Kansas and received
  her library degree from Simmons College.   Dorothy
  Heiderstadt has been interested in Indians and Indian
  lore and once visited Bacone College where she heard
  an Indian choir and saw them use sign language for the
  23rd Psalm.   She has been a member of the Oklahoma
  Historical Society.   Her juvenile books include: A
  Book Of Heroes, Bobbs-Merrill, 1954; Frontier Leaders
  And Pioneers, McKay, 1962; Knights And Champions,
  Nelson, 1960.   CA-4

HEINLEIN, Robert Anson   1907–
  He was born in Butler, Missouri and graduated from
  the United States Naval Academy at Annapolis.   During
  World War II, he served as an engineer at the Philadelphia Naval Air Material Center.   Although he and
  his wife have made their home in Colorado, part of
  each year has been spent in travel.   The author has
  received the Hugo Award several times for his science
  fiction books.   Juvenile titles include: Between Planets,
  Scribner, 1951; Citizen Of The Galaxy, Scribner, 1957;
  Podkayne Of Mars, Putnam, 1963; The Rolling Stones,
  Scribner, 1952; The Star Beast, Scribner, 1954.   CA-
  2, MJA

HELFMAN, Harry   Elizabeth (Seaver) 1911–
  Husband-wife team, teachers.   Born in New York City,
  Harry Helfman graduated from the American Artists'
  School.   He has been an artist and teacher in Brooklyn
  and at one time taught in various sections of the United
  States.   Born in Pittsfield, Massachusetts, Mrs. Helf-
  man graduated from Mt. Holyoke College and received

a master's degree from Radcliffe. Her work has appeared in magazines, and she has worked in New York City with the Bank Street College of Education. Mr. and Mrs. Helfman have made their home in Brooklyn, New York. Together they wrote Strings On Your Fingers, Morrow, 1965. CA-5/6

HENDERSON, Le Grand 1901-
Author-illustrator. His pseudonyms are Le Grand and Brian Harwin. He was born in Torrington, Connecticut, attended Yale University, and has resided in Camden, Maine. Experiences which he enjoyed through travel provided the author with ideas for his many books. His first story in the popular "Augustus" series Augustus And The River (by Le Grand pseud., Bobbs, 1944) resulted from a trip down the Mississippi. Other juvenile books which he wrote and illustrated include: The Amazing Adventures Of Archie And The First Hot Dog (by Le Grand pseud.), Abingdon, 1964; Augustus And The Desert (by Le Grand pseud.), Bobbs, 1948; Augustus Flies (by Le Grand pseud.), Bobbs, 1944; Cap'n Dow And The Hole In The Doughnut (by Le Grand pseud.), Abingdon-Cokesbury, 1946; Cats For Kansas (by Le Grand pseud.), Abingdon-Cokesbury, 1948. CA-5/6, JBA-2

HENRY, Marguerite (Breithaupt) 1902-
Born in Milwaukee, Wisconsin, the author graduated from the Milwaukee State Teachers College. After her marriage to Sidney Crocker Henry, she made her home near Wayne, Illinois. Mrs. Henry has been the recipient of many book awards and honors including the Newbery Medal in 1949 for King Of The Wind (Rand, 1948). She also was given the Junior Scholastic Gold Seal Award and the Award of the Friends of Literature for Justin Morgan Had A Horse (Follett, 1945). Her book Misty Of Chincoteague (Rand, 1947) was made into a movie. Other juvenile titles include: All About Horses, Random, 1962; Always Reddy, McGraw, 1947; Benjamin West And His Cat Grimalkin, Bobbs, 1947; Born To Trot, Winston, 1945; Mustang, Rand, 1966; Sea Star, Rand, 1949. CA-19/20, JBA-2

HENTOFF, Nat 1925-
Born in Boston, Massachusetts, he later graduated from Northeastern University. He continued his studies at Harvard and attended the Sorbonne in Paris on a

Fulbright fellowship. At one time he was co-editor of
the Jazz Review and associate editor of Down Beat
magazine. Nat Hentoff has often lectured on jazz, originated radio jazz programs, and has been a staff
writer for the New Yorker magazine. He has lived in
New York City. For young people he wrote: I'm Really Dragged But Nothing Gets Me Down, Simon, 1968;
Jazz Country, Harper, 1965.   CA-2

HERBERT, Don
Science experiments conducted on television brought
fame to the author as the man called "Mr. Wizard. "
His program was the recipient of many awards including four First Awards from the Ohio State University
Institute for Education by Radio-Television. Other a-
wards include the Thomas Alva Edison Foundation National Mass Media Award and the Peabody Award. His
science newsletter has been read by thousands of children each month. For boys and girls Don Herbert
wrote Mr. Wizard's Science Secrets, Popular Mechanics, 1952.

HEREFORD, Robert A. 1902-
Newspaperman and author, born in the Philippine Islands. He graduated from the School of Journalism
at the University of Missouri. The author has been
Bureau Manager of the International News Service in
St. Louis. He has also worked in radio. For young
readers he wrote Old Man River, The Memories Of
Captain Louis Rosché, Pioneer Steamboatman, Caxton,
1942.

HERZOG, Emile 1885-
André Maurois is his pseudonym. French writer and
lecturer, he was born at Elbeuf, Normandy. A noted
biographer, he has also written essays and novels.
He served in both World Wars. The author has been
a member of the French Academy (Académie Françoise).
The election to the Academy is considered by French-
men to be the highest honor to be achieved by a French
writer. His juvenile books include: French Boy, Sterling, 1957; Lafayette In America, Houghton, 1960.

HEUMAN, William 1912-
He was born in Brooklyn, New York. Prior to writing,
Mr. Heuman was an office clerk. His stories have
appeared in Sports Illustrated and Collier's magazines.

He has been interested in guns, antique weapons, and
sports.   The Heumans have lived in Huntington, New
York.   His titles for young people include: <u>Famous</u>
<u>American Athletes</u>, Dodd, 1963; <u>Hillbilly Hurler</u>, Dodd,
1966; Rookie Backstop, Dodd, 1962.   CA-7/8

HEWES, Agnes (Danforth)
She grew up in Syria.   Her father and grandmother
were both missionaries.   The author attended Radcliffe
and Elmira College.   Her husband was writer and noted
engineer Dr. Laurence I. Hewes.   Mrs. Hewes has
lived in San Francisco, California.   Her juvenile titles
include: <u>Anabel's Windows</u>, Dodd, 1949; <u>Boy Of The</u>
<u>Lost Crusade</u>, Houghton, 1923.   JBA-1, <u>JBA-2</u>

HEWETT, Anita
English author and teacher, born in Somerset, England.
A kindergarten teacher in the schools of England, she
later conducted her own kindergarten school at Shirley
Hall, Kingston-upon Thames.   Stories which she told
to her pupils later helped Anita Hewett in her writing
career.   Many of her stories have been used on the
"Schools Programs" of the British Broadcasting Company.   Her juvenile books include <u>Mr. Faksimily And</u>
<u>The Tiger</u>, Follett, 1969.

HEYLIGER, William   1884-
Newspaperman and writer, born in Hoboken, New Jersey.   At an early age he began his newspaper career
as a reporter on Hoboken's <u>Hudson Observer</u>.   He
spent twenty years in the newspaper field before writing full-time for boys and girls.   His juvenile books
include: <u>Gasoline Jockey</u>, Appleton, 1942; <u>Son Of The</u>
<u>Apple Valley</u>, Appleton, 1940; <u>SOS Radio Patrol</u>, Dodd,
1942; <u>Steve Merrill</u>, Engineer, Appleton-Century, 1935;
<u>Top Lineman</u>, Appleton-Century, 1943.   JBA-1

HICKOK, Lorena A.
Born in East Troy, Wisconsin, she attended Battle
Creek, Michigan High School and the University of Min-
nesota.   Following college Lorena Hickok worked on
the Minneapolis <u>Tribune</u> and later wrote articles for the
Associated Press.   She was a close friend of President
Roosevelt and his wife and lived near the Roosevelts in
Hyde Park, New York.   Her hobbies have included:
gardening, history, and sports.   Juvenile titles include:
<u>The Road To The White House</u>, Chilton, 1962; <u>Story Of</u>

HICKS, Clifford B.

Franklin D. Roosevelt, Grosset, 1956.

HICKS, Clifford B. 1920-
He was born in Marshalltown, Iowa, graduated from
Northwestern University, and has lived in Elmhurst,
Illinois. He served in the Marine Corps during World
War II. Mr. Hicks has been Associate Editor of Pop-
ular Mechanics magazine. His books for young people
include: Alvin Fernald, Foreign Trader, Holt, 1966;
Alvin's Secret Code (A Junior Literary Guild selection),
Holt, 1963; First Boy On The Moon, Winston, 1959;
World Above, Holt, 1965. CA-5/6

HIGHTOWER, Florence Cole 1916-
She was born in Boston, spent her childhood in Concord, and graduated from Vassar. Her husband James
Robert Hightower has been a member of the faculty of
Harvard University. Prior to World War II, the High-
towers lived in Peking. Later they lived in Massachusetts. Her books for young people include: Dark Horse
Of Woodfield, Houghton, 1962; Fayerweather Forecast,
Houghton, 1967; Ghost Of Follonsbee's Folly, Houghton,
1958; Mrs. Wappinger's Secret, Houghton, 1956. CA-
4

HILL, Frank Ernest 1888-
Poet, historian, author. He has lived in New York
City but has spent his summers in Hampton Bays on
Long Island. Mr. Hill has translated Chaucer and also
has been a critic of poetry. With Joseph Auslander he
compiled Winged Horse Anthology, Doubleday, 1929.
He also wrote Famous Historians, Dodd, 1966.

HILL, Lorna 1902-
British author, born in Durham, England. She received
her education at the University of Durham and has lived
in Keswick, Cumberland, England. When her daughter
attended Sadler Wells Ballet School, Mrs. Hill used the
school as the background for her book Veronica At Sadler's Wells, Holt, 1954. She also wrote The Little
Dancer, Nelson, 1957. CA-9/10

HILL, Margaret (Ohler) 1915-
She has lived in Laramie, Wyoming. Mrs. Hill has
worked with the Wyoming mental health program and
has written many articles for various publications. She
has also directed P. T. A. radio programs. Margaret

Hill has been a member of the National Federation of
Press Women, and this organization has given several
awards to her in recognition of her work. Books
which she has written for young people include: Goal
In The Sky, Little, 1953; Senior Hostess, Little, 1958.
CA-4

HILL, Ralph Nading 1917-
A native of Vermont, he has written for both adults and
children. He graduated from Dartmouth College in
Hanover, New Hampshire. Ralph Nading Hill served
as an intelligence officer during World War II. As
president of a steamboat company, Mr. Hill toured
Lake Champlain and later wrote Robert Fulton And The
Steamboat, Random, 1954. He also wrote Doctors Who
Conquered Yellow Fever, Random, 1957. CA-4

HILL, Robert W. 1919-
Editor, author, pilot. Robert Hill received his education in Washington, D. C. at the Landon School and at
Haverford College in Haverford, Pennsylvania. He and
his family have lived in Wilton, Connecticut. Mr. Hill
has edited a number of books about aviation including a
handbook on rocketry and an anthology of flight. He
wrote What The Moon Astronauts Will Do All Day, Day,
1963. CA-9/10

HILLCOURT, William 1900-
Scientist, Boy Scout executive, writer. Mr. Hillcourt
received a degree in pharmacy; however, his main interest has been writing about nature. An extensive
traveler, he has studied flora and fauna of both Europe
and North America. He has also served on the editorial staff of Boys' Life magazine and has been a member of the National Staff of the Boy Scouts of America.
He wrote Field Book Of Nature Activities, Putnam,
1950.

HILLES, Helen (Train) 1905-
She was born in New York, the daughter of author
Arthur Train. Mrs. Hilles has enjoyed traveling and
once lived in Germany. She married an attorney, and
they have lived in New York. She wrote a book about
Germany for boys and girls entitled Rainbow On The
Rhine, Lippincott, 1959.

HILLMAN, May see HIPSHMAN, May

HILLYER, Virgil Mores 1875-1931
He was born in Weymouth, Massachusetts and graduated
from Harvard. At the age of twenty-four he became
headmaster of the Calvert School in Baltimore. He has
written textbooks and at one time conducted a correspondence school. As a dedicated teacher, the author
lived in accordance with his family's motto: "Let
There Be Light." He collaborated with E. G. Huey
to write A Child's History Of Art, Appleton, 1951.
Mr. Hillyer also wrote Child's Geography Of The World,
Appleton, 1951.   JBA-1, JBA-2

HINCKLEY, Helen 1903-
Author and teacher, born in Provo, Utah. She mar-
ried English Professor Ivan C. Jones and has lived in
Altadena, California. She graduated from Brigham
Young University and did further study at Columbia and
Stanford Universities. She also attended the University
of California at Berkeley and Hughes Hall in Cambridge,
England. In 1962 Helen Hinckley and her family visited
Persia and stayed in the home of Najmeh Najafi who
had become the author's close friend ("temporary daughter") when she was a student in America. For boys
and girls she wrote The Land And People Of Iran, Lippincott, 1964.   CA-7/8

HINE, Al 1915-
After graduating from Princeton University he worked
in the advertising field. During World War II, Al
Hine was on the staff of Yank magazine and later became its managing editor. He has also worked for
Holiday magazine and been a film producer. The author has resided in Connecticut. He wrote the narrative of D-Day, The Invasion Of Europe, American Heritage, 1962 and edited This Land Is Mine, Lippincott,
1965. Al Hine also wrote From Other Lands, Lippincott, 1969.   CA-1

HINKINS, Virginia
Author and editor. An early interest in horses and
riding led to a career in farming. She graduated from
Ambler, Pennsylvania's School of Horticulture for Wo-
men and managed the Spengler Hall Farm (Strasburg,
Va.) for a number of years. At one time the author
also served as contributing editor of a farm publication.
She married Dr. John F. Cadden and has lived in
Front Royal, Virginia. For young people she wrote

Gently Now, McGraw-Hill, 1963.

HINKLE, Thomas Clark 1876-1949
Physician, Congregational minister, author. He grew
up in Junction City, Kansas, and one of his favorite
memories was the day he saw the horse "Comanche"
(all that remained alive from Custer's Last Stand at
Little Big Horn) at Fort Riley. Dr. Hinkle's titles for
young people include: Dapple Gray, Morrow, 1950;
Tan, A Wild Dog, Morrow, 1951; Vic, A Dog Of The
Prairies, Morrow, 1949; Wolf, A Range Dog, Morrow,
1948.

HIPPEL, Ursula von
Teacher and writer, born in Germany. After coming
to the United States she made her home in Boston
where she graduated from the School of the Museum of
Fine Arts. At one time the author was a kindergarten
teacher and has also been interested in puppetry. For
boys and girls she wrote and illustrated Craziest Hal-
lowe'en, Coward-McCann, 1957. She also wrote The
Story Of The Snails Who Traded Houses (after a story
by Gertrud von Hippel), Coward-McCann, 1961.

HIPPOPOTAMUS, Eugene H.   see KRAUS, Robert

HIPSHMAN, May 1919-
Her pseudonym is May Hillman. In a biography about
people of the ballet which May Hillman co-authored
with Margaret F. Atkinson was written: ". . . No
two ballet fans anywhere would agree on a list of the
world's greatest dancers . . . and the book has been
confined to a cross section of the leading ballerinas
and premier danseurs of the United States, England,
and France. " She collaborated with Margaret F. Atkinson to write Dancers Of The Ballet, Knopf, 1955.

HIRSHBERG, Albert S. 1909-
He was born in Boston and studied at Boston University.
Al Hirshberg wrote sports stories for the Boston Post
and later traveled with the Boston Red Sox as a baseball writer. In 1952 he became a free-lance writer,
and his articles have appeared in many publications including: Look, Reader's Digest, and Sports Illustrated.
His home has been in Brookline, Massachusetts; however, he has spent summers on Cape Cod and the baseball spring training season in St. Petersburg, Florida.

Juvenile titles include: Baseball's Greatest Catchers,
Putnam, 1966; Basketball's Greatest Stars, Putnam,
1963; The Man Who Fought Back: Red Schoendienst,
Messner, 1961.   CA-4

HITTE, Kathryn
Author and librarian, born in Illinois.   A graduate of
Illinois College at Jacksonville, Illinois, she later be-
came a young adult librarian.   She married author
William D. Hayes, and they have lived in New York
City.   Her juvenile books include: Boy Was I Mad!,
Parents, 1969; Lost And Found, Abingdon, 1951.

HOAG, Edwin
He has served on the staff of Tulane University in New
Orleans and later became medical news editor for the
Tulane School of Medicine.   Mr. Hoag has also worked
on newspapers not only as a resporter but also as
columnist and city editor.   He has lived in Metairie,
Louisiana.   He wrote: American Cities, Lippincott,
1969; American Houses: Colonial, Classic And Contemporary, Lippincott, 1964.   CA-15/16

HOBAN, Russell (Conwell) 1925-   Lillian
Husband-wife team.   They attended the Philadelphia
Museum School of Art and met at the Graphic Sketch
Club located in Philadelphia.   Russell Hoban was an
illustrator before he decided to become a writer.   Prior
to being an illustrator, Lillian Hoban was a dance instructor.   The Hobans and their four children have
lived in Wilton, Connecticut.   Together they wrote London Men And English Men, Harper, 1962.   Books which
he wrote, and she illustrated include: A Baby Sister For
Frances, Harper, 1964; Ugly Bird, Macmillan, 1969.
CA-7/8

HOBART, Lois Elaine
Author, editor, photographer.   She was born in Minneapolis, Minnesota and graduated from the University of
Minnesota.   She married painter-designer Harold Black
and has lived in Guanajuato, Mexico.   At one time she
served as an associate editor of Coronet, Esquire, and
Glamour magazines.   Provided with a grant from the
National Foundation for Infantile Paralysis, the author
visited many physical therapy and rehabilitation centers
in order to provide authenticity for her book Laurie,
Physical Therapist (Messner, 1957).   Her photos have

appeared in such magazines as Life and U. S. Camera.
Juvenile books include: Katie And Her Camera, Messner, 1955; Mexican Mural, Harcourt, 1963.   CA-5/6

HOBSON, Polly 1913-
English author and painter. She was born near London,
studied in France, graduated from Oxford, and has
lived in Sussex, England. At one time she studied
painting in Paris in the studio of "Primavera." Polly
Hobson was with the W. R. N. S. during World War II,
and was stationed in London, Glasgow, and Dover.
She wrote The Mystery House, Lippincott, 1964.   CA-
15/16

HODGE, Jane Aiken 1917-
Born in America, the daughter of poet Conrad Aiken
and sister of author Joan Aiken. She has lived in England with her editor husband Alan Hodge and two daughters. Mrs. Hodge received degrees from both Oxford
University and Radcliffe College. Her stories have
appeared in Ladies' Home Journal and other magazines.
She wrote Maulever Hall, Doubleday, 1964.   CA-7/8

HODGES, Carl G. 1902-1964
He was born in Quincy, Illinois, the son of the late
McClelland and Fredericka Lepper Hodges. He later
lived in Springfield, Illinois. Mr. Hodges was instrumental in organizing the Springfield Civil War Round
Table and once served as its president. Prior to his
retirement, he worked as director of departmental reports for Illinois and also at one time was a research
analyst in the state division of highways. His books
for boys and girls include: Baxie Randall And The
Blue Raiders, Bobbs, 1962; Benjie Ream, Bobbs, 1964;
Dobie Sturgis And The Dog Soldiers, Bobbs, 1963.
CA-7/8

HODGES, Cyril Walter 1909-
English writer and illustrator, born in Beckenham,
Kent, England. He attended London's Dulwich College
and studied art at the University of London. His professional career began in the theatre as a designer of
costumes and scenery. Mr. Hodges has also designed
book jackets and painted murals. His home has been
in Sussex, England although he has lived in France and
Spain and once visited America. Juvenile books which
he has written and illustrated include: The Marsh King:

A Story Of King Alfred, Bell, 1967; The Namesake,
Coward-McCann, 1964; Shaespeare's Theatre, Coward-
McCann, 1964; Sky High, Coward-McCann, 1947.   CA-
15/16

HODGES, Elizabeth Jamison
Librarian and writer, born in Atlanta, Georgia. She
has lived in China, Japan, Manchuria, Puerto Rico,
and the United States.   Miss Hodges received her education at Radcliffe College and Simmons College of
Library Science (Boston, Mass.).   Her main interests
have been painting, people, politics, international
peace, and poetry.   She wrote The Three Princes Of
Serendip, Atheneum, 1964.   CA-11/12

HOEHLING, Mary (Duprey) 1914-
Born in Worcester, Massachusetts, she attended Wheaton College in Norton, Massachusetts.   She married a
writer, and they have lived in Washington, D. C.   The
Hoehlings have traveled extensively, and at one time
lived for six months abroad.   In addition to writing
books for boys and girls, she has prepared scripts for
the Puppet Theater at the Stamford, Connecticut Museum.   She also wrote articles for the New York
Times, Chicago Tribune, and the Christian Science
Monitor.   Juvenile titles include: Girl Soldier And Spy,
Messner, 1959; The Real Sherlock Holmes: Arthur
Conan Doyle, Messner, 1965.

HOFF, Sydney 1912-
Cartoonist, author, illustrator.   Born in New York
City, he has made his home in Miami Beach, Florida.
He attended the National Academy of Design, and his
first cartoon was published in the New Yorker.   Since
that time his cartoons have appeared in many publications including the Saturday Evening Post and Esquire.
Mr. Hoff has also conducted a daily cartoon feature
entitled "Laugh It Off."   Juvenile books which he wrote
and illustrated include: Albert The Albatross, Harper,
1961; Chester, Harper, 1961; Danny And The Dinosaur,
Harper, 1958; Grizzwold, Harper, 1963; Hello Muddah,
Hello Fadduh!, Harper, 1964; Irving And Me, Harper,
1967; Mrs. Switch (A Junior Literary Guild selection),
Putnam, 1967; Stanley, Harper, 1962.   CA-5/6

HOFFMAN, Gloria
Author and photographer, born in St. Louis, Missouri.

The author attended Hunter College and the School of
Modern Photography.   She has held various jobs which
have included: selling, public relations, and fashion
advertising.   Her work as a free-lance photographer
has appeared in such magazines as Look and Today's
Woman.   In 1949 she was awarded the first prize in
the 3rd Annual Art and Photography Contest of the
Conde Nast Publications, Inc.   During a visit to Mexico, Miss Hoffman photographed and wrote her children's
book Primitive And His Dog, Dutton, 1949.

HOFFMANN, Margaret Jones   see   HOFFMANN, Peggy

HOFFMANN, Peggy 1910-
She was born in Delaware, Ohio and graduated from
Miami University at Oxford, Ohio.   She continued her
studies at the Chicago Theological Seminary at the
University of Chicago.   Her husband Arnold E. Hoffmann
has been State Supervisor of Music in the public schools
of North Carolina.   The Hoffmanns have lived in Raleigh.   Juvenile titles include: Sew Easy, Dutton, 1956;
Sew Far! Sew Good! (A Junior Literary Guild selection), Dutton, 1958; Miss B's First Cookbook, Bobbs,
1950; Shift To High! (A Junior Literary Guild selection),
Westminster Press, 1965.   CA-5/6

HOFFNER, Pelagie Doane   see   DOANE, Pelagie

HOFSINDE, Robert 1902-
Author-illustrator, born in Denmark.   He studied at the
Royal Art Academy in Copenhagen before coming to the
United States at the age of twenty.   He continued his
education in Minnesota at the Minneapolis School of Art.
The author has made his home in Monroe, New York.
His interest in American Indian culture began when he
rescued a Chippewa Indian boy in the forests of Minne-
sota and was made an honorary member of the Chippe-
wa tribe.   Mr. Hofsinde and his wife have taught
Indian crafts and lore and have interpreted Indian dances
and songs.   He has contributed articles on Indian lore
to such magazines as Popular Mechanics and Popular
Science.   Juvenile books which he wrote and illustrated
include: Indian Warriors And Their Weapons, Morrow,
1965; Indian Beadwork, Morrow, 1958; Indian Games
And Crafts, Morrow, 1957; The Indian Medicine Man,
Morrow, 1966.

HOGAN, Inez   1895-
  Teacher, author, artist, born in Washington, D. C.,
  and attended Wilson Teachers College. Although she
  became a teacher, she pursued her interest in art and
  attended several art schools including: the National
  Art School, Corcoran Art School, and the Cape Cod
  School of Art in Provincetown, Massachusetts. Miss
  Hogan has written over forty books for boys and girls.
  These include: A Bear Is A Bear, Dutton, 1953; Dino-
  saur Twins, Dutton, 1963; Eager Beaver, Dutton, 1963;
  Fraidy Cat, Dutton, 1962; Giraffe Twins, Dutton, 1948;
  Littlest Satellite, Dutton, 1958; Nicodemus And His
  Little Sister, Dutton, 1932.   CA-4, MJA

HOGEBOOM, Amy   1891-
  She was born in New York and studied at the Albany
  Girls' Academy and the Chase School of Art.   Prior to
  writing and illustrating books for children, she was on
  the staff of several New York newspapers.   The author
  has been interested in birds, painting, and the theatre.
  Her juvenile books include: Boats And How To Draw
  Them, Vanguard, 1950; Dogs And How To Draw Them,
  Vanguard, 1944.

HOGG, Beth (Tootill)   see   GREY, Elizabeth

HOGNER, Dorothy (Childs)   Nils   1893-1970
  Husband-wife team.   She was born in the East and grew
  up on a farm in Connecticut.   At one time she was a
  teacher.   Nils Hogner was born in Whitinsville, Massa-
  chusetts.   He attended Denmark's Rhodes Academy in
  Copenhagen and Sweden's Royal Academy of Arts in
  Stockholm.   He later studied at the Boston School of
  Painting and the School of the Museum of Fine Arts
  (Boston).   Like his wife, Mr. Hogner has also been a
  teacher.   The Hogners have lived in New York and
  Connecticut.   Juvenile books which she wrote and he
  illustrated include: The Bible Story, Oxford, 1943;
  Butterflies, Crowell, 1962; The Cat Family, Oxford,
  1956; Moths, Crowell, 1964.   Nils Hogner wrote and
  illustrated: Farm For Rent (A Junior Literary Guild
  selection), Abelard-Schuman, 1958; Molly The Black
  Mare, Walck, 1962.   JBA-2

HOGROGIAN, Nonny
  She was born in New York and graduated from Hunter
  College.   She studied wood-cutting under Antonio Fras-

coni and has also been a pupil of Hodaka Yoshida. She
was the recipient of the 1966 Caldecott Medal for her
illustrations in Sorche Nic Leodhas' book Always Room
For One More, Holt, 1965. She also illustrated Gaelic
Ghosts (by Sorche Nic Leodhas), Holt, 1964.

HOKE, Helen L. 1903-
Her pseudonym is Helen Sterling. She has edited and
written many children's books. During her school
years and vacations, Helen Hoke wrote articles for her
father's newspaper and also set type. For boys and
girls she wrote First Book Of Dolls, Watts, 1954.
She also edited Arctic Mammals, Watts, 1969.

HOLBERG, Richard A. 1889-1942   Ruth (Langland) 1891-
Husband-wife team, illustrator and author. Both were
born in Milwaukee, Wisconsin. Richard Holberg illustrated the books which his wife wrote. He also created
illustrations for magazines. Both the Holbergs painted
in Europe before they settled in Rockport, Massachusetts. Her poetry has been published in newspapers
and magazines. Ideas for some of her books were
provided by older people's tales of long ago. Together
they wrote Gloucester Boy, Doubleday, 1940. She
wrote, and he illustrated Mitty On Mr. Syrup's Farm,
Doubleday, 1936. Ruth Holberg also wrote Luke And
The Indians, Hastings, 1969. CA-5/6, JBA-2

HOLBROOK, Stewart Hall 1893-
Author and newspaperman, born in Vermont. During
World War I, he served with a field artillery unit in
France. Prior to his work as a newspaper reporter,
Mr. Holbrook worked in the logging camps of the
Northwest. He has lived in Portland, Oregon. Juve-
nile books which he has written include: The Columbia
River, Holt, 1965; The Golden Age Of Railroads, Ran-
dom, 1960. CA-9/10

HOLDEN, Raymond (Peckham) 1894-
Writer, poet, born in New York, he studied at Princeton University. Mr. Holden has published several books
of poetry and a biography of Lincoln. During World
War I, he served in the Cavalry. His home has been
in New Hampshire. For young people he wrote Famous
Scientific Expeditions (A Junior Literary Guild selection), Random, 1955. CA-7/8

HOLDING, James
He was born in Pennsylvania and graduated from Yale
University.   When he was twelve years old, he wrote
some verses which were bought by Country Gentleman
magazine.   Prior to making writing a full-time career,
Mr. Holding was vice president and copy chief for the
advertising firm of Batten, Barton, Durstine and Os-
born in Pittsburgh.   Juvenile titles include: The Mystery Of Dolphin Inlet, Macmillan, 1968; Sherlock On
The Trail, Morrow, 1964.

HOLLAND, Marion 1908-
Author, illustrator, born in Washington, D. C.   She
married college professor and economist Thomas W.
Holland.   Mrs. Holland graduated summa cum laude
from Swarthmore College in Pennsylvania.   The author
has become well-known in the Washington area for her
chalk talks.   Books which she has written and illustrated for boys and girls include: A Big Ball Of String,
Random, 1958; Billy's Clubhouse, Knopf, 1955; Teddy's
Camp-Out, Knopf, 1963.   She also wrote: Muggsy,
Knopf, 1959; No Room For A Dog, Random, 1959.

HOLLANDER, John 1929-
Author and poet, born in New York City.   He graduated
from Columbia University where he received his B. A.
and M. S. degrees.   He later obtained a Ph. D. degree
from Indiana University (Bloomington, Ind.).   John
Hollander has been an Assistant Professor of English
at Yale University, and he has been a teacher at Connecticut College for Women.   He has also been a Junior
Fellow at Harvard in the Society of Fellows (1954-57).
In 1958 he was the recipient of the Yale Younger Poets
Award for A Crackling Of Thorns, Yale University
Press, 1958.   For children he wrote A Book Of Various Owls, Norton, 1963.   With Harold Bloom he edited
an anthology of poems for young people entitled The
Wind And The Rain, Doubleday, 1961.   CA-4

HOLLANDER, Paul
He graduated from Columbia University and has lived
in Riverdale, New York.   Although he once wrote a
great deal of science fiction, Mr. Hollander later
wrote nonfiction paperbacks and books for boys and
girls.   He wrote: The Labors Of Hercules, Putnam,
1965; Sam Houston, Putnam, 1968.

HOLLING, Holling Clancy 1900-
Born in Michigan, he attended the Chicago Art Institute
where he met his wife Lucille Webster.   Later they
worked in an art colony near Taos, New Mexico where
they became interested in the Pueblo Indians.   He has
also served on the staff of the Chicago Museum of
Natural History and once studied anthropology under
Dr. Ralph Linton.   He wrote and with his wife illustrated: Book Of Cowboys, Platt, 1936; Pagoo, Houghton, 1957.   His books include: Minn Of The Mississippi, Houghton, 1951; Paddle-To-The-Sea, Houghton,
1941; Seabird, Houghton, 1948; Tree On The Trail,
Houghton, 1942.   JBA-2

HOLM, Hannebo
Norwegian author and children's librarian.   She has always enjoyed telling stories to children.   Mrs. Holm
has lived in Norway near Oslo and has been a tutor in
a library school.   The author's experiences as a contestant in a beauty pageant in the United States resulted
in her writing Beauty Queen (tr. by Patricia Crampton),
Abelard, 1961.

HOLMAN, Felice 1919-
Poet and author, she attended Syracuse University in
New York.   Her work has appeared in anthologies.
She married Herbert Valen and has lived in a converted
barn in Westport, Connecticut.   Felice Holman has
been an advertising copywriter in New York in addition
to being an author of books for young people.   Her
books include: The Blackmail Machine, Macmillan,
1968; Holiday Rat And The Utmost Mouse, Norton, 1969.
CA-7/8

HOLME, Bryan 1913-
Publisher and editor of art books.   Both his father and
grandfather were associated with the publishing business.   The author's grandfather was Charles Holme
who founded Studio magazine.   In 1955 Eastern Arts
Associates presented Bryan Holme with a certificate
which testified that he had given "twenty years of service contributing to art education in the public schools. "
For young people he compiled and edited: Drawings To
Live With, Viking, 1966; Pictures To Live With (A
Junior Literary Guild selection), Viking, 1959.

HOLMES, Marjorie Rose 1910-
She was born in Storm Lake, Iowa and graduated from
Cornell College in Mount Vernon, Iowa. Her stories
have appeared in many magazines. She has said that
her four children have provided "much background
material" for her stories. The author has lived in
Washington, D. C. Her juvenile books include: Love
Is A Hopscotch Thing, Westminster, 1963; Saturday
Night (A Junior Literary Guild selection), Westminster,
1959. CA-3

HOLSAERT, Eunice
She has wide experience in working with children. At
one time she was a book reviewer, psychologist, and
a teacher. Eunice Holsaert also originated and pro-
duced an educational television program for children.
Two of her juvenile books were edited by Herman and
Nina Schneider and include Life In The Arctic, Harvey
House, 1957. With Robert Gartland she wrote Book
To Begin On Dinosaurs, Holt, 1959.

HOLSINGER, Jane Lumley
She was born in Woodstock, Illinois and attended writing classes at both Indiana and California Universities.
She married Arthur Holsinger and has lived in Wonder
Lake, Illinois. At one time the author was a dental
assistant and telephone operator. Her mystery stories
have appeared in newspaper serials. Her first book
for young people was The Secret Of Indian Ridge,
Bobbs, 1963.

HOLT, Margaret
Author and librarian, born in Buffalo, New York. A
graduate of Elmira College (Elmira, N. Y.) she later
attended Simmons College (Boston, Mass.) in order to
study for a master's degree in library science. Miss
Holt has been a children's librarian at the Public Library in Boston and an editorial assistant for a publishing company. For children she wrote David McChee-
ver's 29 Dogs, Houghton, 1963. CA-17/18

HOLT, Stephen see THOMPSON, Harlan H.

HOLTON, Leonard see WIBBERLEY, Leonard (Patrick
O'Connor)

HONNESS, Elizabeth (Hoffman) 1904-
She was born in Boonton, New Jersey and attended
Skidmore College in Saratoga Springs, New York. At
one time she served as managing editor of American
Girl magazine. She married J. A. McKaughan and has
lived in Philadelphia. In addition to writing books for
boys and girls, she has enjoyed painting. Juvenile
titles include: Mystery In The Square Tower, Lippincott, 1957; Mystery Of The Auction Trunk, Lippincott,
1956; Mystery Of The Hidden Face, Lippincott, 1963;
Mystery Of The Pirate's Ghost, Lippincott, 1966; Mystery Of The Wooden Indian, Lippincott, 1958.

HOPKINS, A. T.   see TURNGREN, Annette

HOPKINS, Clark 1895-
Archaeologist and author. His pseudonym is Roy Lee.
His work has appeared in journals. One of his books
for young readers was written for his son Cy. This
writer has combined both science and imagination in
creating his books for boys and girls. He wrote Cyrus
Hunts The Cougar, Little, 1954.

HOPKINS, Lyman see FOLSOM, Franklin

HORGAN, Paul 1903-
This author has been the recipient of both the Pulitzer
and Bancroft Prizes in History. In the acknowledg-
ment of his children's book Citizen Of New Salem (Farrar, 1961), Mr. Horgan wrote: "In honor of the cen-
tennial of Abraham Lincoln's first inauguration, the
Editors of the Saturday Evening Post asked me to write
this essay in biography . . . It is published as a book
by their kind permission." He has written many novels
about the Southwest for adults. For boys and girls he
also wrote Toby And The Nighttime, Ariel, 1963.
CA-13/14

HORNBLOW, Leonora (Schinasi)
She was born in New York City and has continued to
make her home there. She married film producer
Arthur Hornblow. Mrs. Hornblow has written for newspapers and magazines. Rivers have always interested
her. Her childhood was spent near the Hudson River;
she and her husband have lived in an apartment overlooking the East River, and she has written a book for
boys and girls with a background of the Nile. It was

Cleopatra Of Egypt, Random, 1961.

HOUGH, Richard Alexander 1922-
His pseudonym is Bruce Carter. Journalist, book editor, and writer, born in Brighton, England. He attended Frensham Heights co-educational school and served
with the R. A. F. during World War II. Richard Hough
has written for both adults and children and has also
been a naval historian. A racing car enthusiast, Mr.
Hough has often attended the Grand Prix and has reported on the event for a London newspaper. His
books for young people include: Airfield Man, Coward,
1966; Fast Circuit, Harper, 1962; Four-Wheel Drift,
Harper, 1959; Speed Six!, Harper, 1956. CA-5/6

HOUGHTON, Eric 1930-
English author. He has enjoyed painting, cricket, table
tennis, and chess. He has played chess for the Essex
County Team. He has also been interested in history
which has resulted in his writing several books for
young people. Mr. Houghton has resided in London.
He wrote: Mystery Of The Old Field, McGraw, 1964;
White Wall, Whittlesey, 1962. CA-4

HOUSTON, Joan 1928-
Author and horsewoman, native of New York. She received her education at Chatham Hall and Barnard College. Her summers were spent in Vermont where she
learned horsemanship at an early age. The author has
appeared in many horse shows including the National
Horse Show finals in New York at the age of nine. For
boys and girls she wrote Crofton Meadows, Crowell,
1961. CA-19/20

HOVELL, Lucille A. (Peterson) see HOVELL, Lucy A.
(Peterson)

HOVELL, Lucy A. (Peterson) 1916-
Author and poet, born in Grafton, Illinois. She grew
up in Philadelphia and New York City. She married
inventor Victor Edward Hovell, and they have lived in
Cranford, New Jersey. Lucy Hovell has written poetry,
greeting card verse, and stories. She collaborated
with Sara A. Temkin to write Jinny Williams, Library
Assistant, Messner, 1962. CA-7/8

HOWARD, Elizabeth 1907–
	Author and teacher, born in Detroit, Michigan. The
	author graduated from the University of Michigan and
	studied library science at Wayne State University in
	Detroit. Prior to writing books for young people,
	Elizabeth Howard Mizner taught in a college in Georgia.
	Her juvenile books include: Candle In The Night, Mor-
	row, 1952; Winter On Her Own, Morrow, 1968. CA-
	13/14, MJA

HOWARD, Vernon Linwood 1918–
	Playwright, author, lecturer. He has given many talks
	to various organizations in the southern California area.
	Vernon Howard has written books about self-improve-
	ment, the art of pantomime, and monologues. His
	titles for young people include: Holiday Monologues,
	Sterling, 1956; Pantomimes, Charades, And Skits, Ster-
	ling, 1959.

HOYT, Edwin Palmer 1923–
	Author, newsman, editor, publisher. Edwin P. Hoyt,
	Jr., was born in Portland, Oregon and studied at the
	University of Oregon. He served as a war correspon-
	dent during World War II. Mr. Hoyt has been associ-
	ate editor of Collier's, editorial writer for the Denver
	Post, assistant publisher of American Heritage, and
	editor and publisher of the Colorado Springs Free
	Press. He has also worked in television. His books
	for young people include: Andrew Johnson, Reilly &
	Lee, 1965; Zeppelins, Lothrop, 1969. CA-3

HOYT, Mary Finch
	She was born in Visalia, California and studied at San
	Jose State College, the University of California at Los
	Angeles, and American University in Washington, D. C.
	She has served on the staff of the Historical Evaluation
	and Research Organization (HERO) in Washington, D. C.
	She wrote American Women Of The Space Age (A Junior
	Literary Guild selection), Atheneum, 1966.

HUBBELL, Harriet Weed 1909–
	Author, painter, born in Buffalo, New York. She at-
	tended Grand Central Art School in New York after she
	graduated from Buffalo Seminary. Besides writing,
	Mrs. Hubbell has painted murals and portraits. For
	children she wrote: The Friendship Tree (A Junior
	Literary Guild selection), Nelson, 1962; Surprise

Summer, Westminster, 1958.   CA-7/8

HUGHES, (James) Langston 1902-
Poet, author, lecturer.   Born in Joplin, Missouri, he
grew up in Kansas and Cleveland, Ohio.   He attended
Columbia University and graduated from Lincoln University in Pennsylvania.   Langston Hughes has been
the recipient of numerous awards and fellowships including a Guggenheim Fellowship, a Rosenwald Fellowship, an American Academy of Arts and Letters Grant,
and the Ainsfield-Wolfe Award.   Books which he has
written for young people include: Don't You Turn Back,
Knopf, 1969; Famous American Negroes, Dodd, 1954.
CA-1

HUME, Ruth (Fox) 1922-
Author and teacher, born in New York.   She attended
the College of New Rochelle (N. Y.) where she took
pre-medical courses.   Her interest in medicine later
led to the writing of Great Men Of Medicine (Random,
1961).   She married Paul Hume, a music critic, and
they have lived in Washington, D. C.   Mrs. Hume
taught chemistry at a school for girls and has also
been a Latin teacher at the Catholic University of A-
merica.   She also wrote St. Margaret Mary, Apostle
Of The Sacred Heart, Vision, 1960.

HUNGERFORD, Edward Buell 1900-
He grew up in New England.   During World War II, he
was in the United States Navy and served in the Pacific.   Mr. Hungerford has lived in Kenilworth, Illinois
and has taught English at Northwestern University.
His books for young people include: Emergency Run,
Wilcox & Follett, 1948; Escape To Danger, Wilcox &
Follett, 1949; Forge For Heroes, Wilcox & Follett,
1952.

HUNT, George Pinney 1918-
Author and editor, born in Philadelphia, Pennsylvania.
He graduated cum laude from Amherst College in Massachusetts.   He served overseas with the Marine Corps
during World War II and was awarded the Silver Star
and the Navy Cross.   After the war, Mr. Hunt was an
editor of Fortune magazine and later became co-editor
of Life magazine's Military Affairs Department.   For
young people he wrote Story Of The U. S. Marines,
Random, 1951.

HUNT, Irene 1907–
Native of Illinois, she grew up on a farm near Newton.
She has received degrees from the Universities of Illinois and Minnesota and continued her studies in psychology at the University of Colorado. Miss Hunt has
been a teacher at the University of South Dakota and
in Oak Park and Cicero, Illinois. Her book Across
Five Aprils (Follett, 1964) was the recipient of the
Follett Award, and she was awarded the Newbery Medal in 1967 for Up A Road Slowly, Follett, 1966. She
also wrote No Promises In The Wind, Follett, 1970.
CA-19/20

HUNT, Kari
Her interests in sculpture and drama resulted in the
author's creation of masks and the study of mask making. Her masks were often seen on television during
the show called "Masquerade Party." Kari Hunt has
made a study of masks found in museums both in this
country and abroad. For boys and girls she collaborated with Bernice Wells Carlson to write Masks And
Mask Makers, Abingdon, 1961.

HUNT, Mabel Leigh 1892–
Children's librarian, author, born in Coatesville, Indi-
ana. She grew up in Greencastle, Indiana, studied at
DePauw University, and received her library training
at Western Reserve Library School. Prior to devoting
full-time to writing, she was on the staff of the Indianapolis Public Library. The first book which she wrote
was Lucinda, Stokes, 1934. Her other titles include:
Benjie's Hat, Stokes, 1938; Double Birthday Present,
Lippincott, 1947; John Of Pudding Lane, Stokes, 1941;
Johnny-Up And Johnny-Down, Lippincott, 1962; Little
Grey Gown, Stokes, 1939; Miss Jellytot's Visit, Lippincott, 1955; Sibby Botherbox, Lippincott, 1945. CA-
9/10, JBA-2

HUNTER, Evan 1926–
His pseudonym is Ed McBain. He was born in New
York and has continued to live there at Pound Ridge.
He graduated from Hunter College and served with the
U. S. Navy during World War II. Evan Hunter has
written for both adults and children. His first juvenile
book The Remarkable Harry (Abelard, 1960) was se-
lected as an honor book in the 1961 Children's Spring
Book Festival sponsored by the New York Herald Tri-

bune.   This book was illustrated by his three sons.
The National Father's Day Committee conferred the
honorary title of "Literary Father of the Year" on him.
Boys and girls have also enjoyed his book The Wonderful Button, Abelard, 1961.   CA-7/8

HUNTER, Kristin (Eggleston) 1931-
She was born in Philadelphia and graduated from the
University of Pennsylvania.   She has been an advertising copywriter and also a member of the staff of the
Pittsburgh Courier.   In the January 1970 issue of Top
Of The News Kristin Hunter said: "Through the good
offices of a columnist aunt, I was invited to write a
youth column for a weekly Negro newspaper at age 14.
The column continued for six years and soon allowed
me to sound off on any subject I wished, not just the
social activities of local youth. " Her home has been
in Philadelphia.   For young people she wrote The Soul
Brothers And Sister Lou, Scribner, 1968.   CA-13/14

HUNTER, Mollie
Scottish writer, she spent her early years in the Low-
lands of Scotland and later made her home near Inver-
ness.   Her husband (a member of the Clan Donald) and
two teen-age sons have often given technical advice to
the author.   She has been interested in: the theater,
Scottish folklore, travel, and young people.   Her books
include: The Ghosts Of Glencoe, Funk & Wagnalls,
1968; The Lothian Run, Funk & Wagnalls, 1970.

HUNTINGTON, Harriet Elizabeth 1909-
The daughter of a clergyman, she was born in Ormond
Beach, Florida.   She has traveled around the world
and has made her home in Los Angeles, California.
An assignment in a child psychology class at Whittier
College provided Harriet Huntington with the incentive
to write . . . Let's Go Outdoors (Doubleday, 1939).
The author has enjoyed listening to records of classical
music as a hobby.   Her books include: Aircraft U. S. A. ,
Doubleday, 1951; Let's Go To The Brook, Junior Liter-
ary Guild and Doubleday, 1952; Let's Go To The Seashore, Doubleday, 1941; Praying Mantis, Doubleday,
1957; The Yosemite Story, Doubleday, 1966.   CA-7/8,
MJA

HURD, Clement 1908-   Edith (Thacher) 1910-
Husband-wife team.   Her joint (with Margaret Wise

Brown) pseudonym is Juniper Sage. He was born in
New York City and graduated from Yale University.
Following college he studied art in Paris.   Edith Thacher Hurd grew up in Kansas City, Missouri and later
studied for a year in Switzerland. She attended Radcliffe College.   Although summers have been spent in
Vermont, the Hurds have made their home in Mill
Valley near San Francisco. She wrote, and he illustrated: The Blue Heron Tree, Viking, 1968; Christmas Eve, Harper, 1962; Come And Have Fun, Harper,
1962; Johnny Lion's Book, Harper, 1965.   CA-13/14,
MJA

HURLEY, Leslie
Author and teacher, he attended Hussen College in
Bangor, Maine. He has been a skiing instructor in
addition to teaching first-aid instructors for the Ameri-
can Red Cross. Mr. Hurley has also been on the
staff of Norwich University in Northfield, Vermont as
assistant ski coach and physical education instructor.
He served with the 10th Mountain Division during World
War II.   With William Osgood he wrote Ski Touring,
Tuttle, 1969.

HUTCHINS, Ross Elliott 1906–
Entomologist, photographer, author.   Born in Montana,
he spent his early years on a cattle ranch near Yellowstone Park.   The author studied at Montana State College and received his Ph. D. degree from Iowa State
College.   His articles and pictures have appeared in
many publications including Life and National Geographic.   Ross Hutchins has been a resident of Mississippi
where he was head of the Department of Zoology and
Entomology at Mississippi State University.   He has
also been Entomologist and Executive Officer of the
Mississippi State Plant Board.   His juvenile books include: Adelbert The Penguin, Rand, 1969; This Is A
Flower, Dodd, 1963.   CA-9/10

HYDE, Margaret Oldroyd 1917–
She received her master's degree from Columbia University and has been Science Consultant at the Lincoln
School of Teachers College.   The author has served as
the head of the Science Department of the Shipley School
in Bryn Mawr, Pennsylvania and has also lectured at
Temple University.   Her book Animal Clocks And Com-
passes (McGraw, 1960) received the Edison Award. She

also wrote: Animals In Science, McGraw, 1962; Earth
In Action, McGraw, 1969.   CA-1

HYLANDER, Clarence John 1897-
Teacher and author, born in Waterbury, Connecticut.
Dr. Hylander received his Ph. D. degree from Yale
University and has been on the staff of Colgate University in Hamilton, New York. His home has been in
Bar Harbor, Maine. He served with the U. S. Navy
during World War II. A noted botanist, Clarence Hylander has written many books about nature for young
people. These include: Animals In Fur, Macmillan,
1956; Fishes And Their Ways, Macmillan, 1964; Flowers Of Field And Forest, Macmillan, 1962; Insects On
Parade, Macmillan, 1957; Sea And Shore, Macmillan,
1950; Trees And Trails, Macmillan, 1953.   CA-7/8

HYNDMAN, Jane Lee see WYNDHAM, Lee

I

ICENHOWER, Joseph Bryan 1913-
He was born in Parkersburg, West Virginia, and graduated from the United States Naval Academy. During
World War II, Captain Icenhower was a commanding
officer on submarines. He received the Navy Cross,
the Bronze Star, the Silver Star, and the Gold Star.
Following the war, he was stationed in Philadelphia at
the Damage Control Training Center. Juvenile titles
include: First Book Of Submarines, Watts, 1957; First
Book Of The Antarctic, Watts, 1956.   CA-7/8

IK, Kim Yong
Korean author and teacher. He studied English in Ja-
pan where he attended college. Between 1948 and 1957
Kim Yong Ik received degrees from Florida Southern
College and the University of Kentucky. He has been
an English teacher at the University of Korea. Juve-
nile books include: The Happy Days, Little, 1960;
Love In Winter, Doubleday, 1969.

ILIN, M. see MARSHAK, Ilia IAkolevich

IMMEL, Mary Blair 1930-
Born in Wichita, Kansas, she graduated from Chapman
College and received her master's degree from Purdue
University. Prior to becoming assistant to the curator

of the Tippecanoe County Historical Association and
Museum, Mrs. Immel taught school. Married to a
minister (Daniel M. Immel), she has often served
with her husband as a counselor in camps for young
people. They have lived in Lafayette, Indiana. Her
book for young people was Call Up The Thunder, Bethany Press, 1969.   CA-15/16

INGALLS, Leonard
Newspaperman, author, born in Lowell, Massachusetts.
He studied at Columbia University. Since his father
owned several newspapers on Long Island, Mr. Ingalls
has been interested in all phases of the newspaper profession since boyhood. He actually began his career
with the United Press International and later served as
a correspondent with the New York Times. He wrote:
Getting To Know Kenya, Coward, 1963; Getting To
Know South Africa, Coward, 1965.

IPCAR, Dahlov (Zorach) 1917–
Author and illustrator, the daughter of artists William
and Marguerite Zorach. She was born in Windsor,
Vermont and attended Oberlin College in Ohio. This
artist has had many one-man shows in New York, and
her work has been included in the collections of the
Metropolitan and Whitney museums. Mrs. Ipcar and
her family have lived on a farm in Robinhood, Maine.
Books which she has written and illustrated include:
I Love My Anteater With An A, Knopf, 1964; Warlock
Of Night, Viking, 1969.   CA-19/20

IRVING, Nancy see SEVERN, Bill

IRVING, William see SEVERN, Bill

IRWIN, Grace
Artist and author. She was born in New York City,
grew up in Arlington, New Jersey, and attended Columbia University. Grace Irwin's art lessons began at
nine years of age and continued later at Columbia. The
author once said: ". . . In drawing and writing for
children, I am doing the pleasantest kind of work, for
boys and girls are the grandest, most appreciative
audience in the world!" For young people she wrote
Trail-Blazers Of American Art, Harper, 1930.

ISH-KISHOR, Sulasmith
She was born in London, England. At the age of five
she began to write, and when she was ten some of her
poetry was published. After her arrival in the United
States, Miss Ish-Kishor attended high school and college (Hunter). Her articles have appeared in magazines. For children she wrote: A Boy Of Old Prague,
Pantheon, 1963; Our Eddie, Pantheon, 1969.

IVAN, Gustave   Martha Miller Pfaff   1909-
This husband-wife team has written books under the
name of Gus Tavo. Her pseudonym has also been
Martha Miller. The late Gustave Ivan was born in
Budapest. After coming to America, he painted murals
and later was an art instructor at Kilgore College in
Texas where his wife served as chairman of the Eng-
lish Department. Mrs. Ivan later became Director of
Guidance and Counseling at the college. She was born
in St. Louis, Missouri and did graduate work at the
University of Texas after receiving degrees from Texas
Technological College. The Ivan family has lived in
Kilgore. Gus Tavo wrote Hunt The Mountain Lion,
Knopf, 1960. Martha Miller wrote Ride The Pale Stal-
lion, Knopf, 1968. CA-19/20

IWAMATSU, Jun   1908-
His pseudonym is Taro Yashima. He was born in Ka-
goshima, Japan and attended Tokyo's Imperial Art Academy and the Art Students League in New York. His
illustrations have appeared in magazines, and he has
had several one-man shows in the United States. He
also created a mural for the Long Beach, California
Bayshore Library. Mr. Iwamatsu married an artist,
and they have lived in Los Angeles, California. Juvenile titles include: The Golden Footprints (with Hatoju
Muku), World, 1960; Crow Boy (A Junior Literary
Guild selection), Viking, 1955; Umbrella (A Junior
Literary Guild selection), Viking, 1958; Village Tree,
Junior Literary Guild and Viking, 1953.

J

JABLONSKI, Edward   1922-
Author and columnist. Born in Bay City, Michigan, he
later made his home in New York. He attended Bay
City Junior College and received his B. A. degree from
the New School for Social Research in New York. He

did graduate work in anthropology at Columbia University. Mr. Jablonski has been a columnist for the American Record Guide and a contributor to many magazines including Saturday Review and Theater Arts. He received a Bronze Battle Star after serving in the Army during World War II. The author has belonged to the American Aviation Historical Society and the Cross and Cockade, the society of World War I Historians. He has written for both adults and children. His juvenile books include: Ladybirds, Hawthorn, 1968; Wariors With Wings, Bobbs, 1966.   CA-2

JACKER, Corinne (Litvin) 1933-
Born in Chicago, Illinois, she attended Stanford University and received her B. S. and M. A. degrees from Northwestern University.   Corinne Jacker has been an editor in several publishing houses and a science teacher.   In 1959 she was a fellow of the MacDowell Colony. Her home has been in New York City.   Juvenile titles include: Black Flag Of Anarchy, Scribner, 1968; Window Of The Unknown, Scribner, 1967.   CA-19/20

JACKSON, Caary Paul 1902-
His pseudonyms are Colin Lochlons and Jack Paulson. He was born in Urbana, Illinois, grew up in Ohio and Michigan, and later made his home in Juno Beach, Florida.   He graduated from Western Michigan University in Kalamazoo and received his master's degree from the University of Michigan at Ann Arbor.   Mr. Jackson has been a teacher and a coach.   His articles and stories about sports have appeared in many publications.   Juvenile books include: All-Conference Tackle, Crowell, 1947; Barney Of The Babe Ruth League, (Colin Lochlons pseud.), Crowell, 1954; Bud Baker Racing Swimmer, Hastings House, 1962; Bullpen Bargain, Hastings House, 1961; Dub Halfback, Crowell, 1952; Midget League Catcher, Follett, 1966; Tim, The Football Nut, Hastings House, 1967.   CA-7/8

JACKSON, Jesse
Born in Columbus, Ohio, he studied at Ohio State University.   He also attended the Writers' Conference at Breadloaf, Vermont.   During college he learned to box and decided on a career as a professional boxer.   The author has also worked in camps and agencies associated with young people.   His juvenile books include: Call Me Charley, Harper, 1945; Tessie, Harper, 1968.

JACKSON, Mary Coleman
She has been a teacher in the school system of Los
Angeles, California. She wrote a book for boys and
girls after her class worked on a Social Studies Unit
which was about fishing. In order to teach her third
grade students about fishing, Mrs. Jackson made many
trips to the harbor area of Los Angeles and interviewed
various people in the fishing industry. Her book for
children was the result of this research and was entitled Climb To The Crow's Nest, Follett, 1957.

JACKSON, O. B.   see JACKSON, Orpha (Cook)

JACKSON, Orpha (Cook)
Her books are found in libraries under the name of O.
B. Jackson. She has written many books with her husband and author C. P. Jackson. She often was the
scorer for teams that her husband coached. Her knowledge of basketball enabled her to argue many technical
questions with him (arguments which she frequently
won). With Caary Paul Jackson she wrote: Basketball
Clown, McGraw, 1956; Freshman Forward, McGraw,
1959. She also wrote Basketball Comes To North Island, McGraw, 1963.

JACKSON, Robert Blake 1926-
He was born in Hartford, Connecticut, graduated from
Amherst College, and received his degree in library
science from Columbia University. Mr. Jackson has
been on the staff of the East Orange, New Jersey Public Library. He has been interested in sports cars
and photography. His books for young people include:
Road Race Round The World, Walck, 1965; Road Racing, U. S. A., Walck, 1964; Sports Cars, Walck, 1963;
Stock Car Racing, Walck, 1968.   CA-7/8

JACOBS, Beth
She was born in North Platte, Nebraska and graduated
from Chaffey College in Ontario, California. Her work
has appeared in newspapers including the Chaffey Press
and the Ontario Herald. She has also been a radio con-
continuity writer. The author has lived in San Loren-
zo, California. For boys and girls she wrote Look
To The Mountains (A Junior Literary Guild selection),
Messner, 1963.

JACOBS, Flora Gill 1918-
Author, editor, newspaper reporter, born in Washington, D. C. She has always liked to write, and at the age of ten she wrote a mystery story in longhand (193 pages). A collector of doll houses, Mrs. Jacobs and her family have lived in an old Victorian house similar to one in her collection. She wrote The Doll House Mystery (Coward, 1958) which told about an 1850 South Jersey doll house in her collection. She also wrote A World Of Doll Houses, Rand, 1965.   CA-1

JACOBS, Frank 1929-
Born in Lincoln, Nebraska, he has lived in New York. Mr. Jacobs has written for magazines in addition to his book for boys and girls which was called Alvin Steadfast On Vernacular Island, Dial, 1965.   CA-13/14

JACOBS, Helen Hull 1908-
Author, athlete, editor, born in Globe, Arizona. She began playing tennis at the age of thirteen. Later she won the American Singles Championship, Championship of the World at Wimbledon, and the American Doubles Championship. An additional honor was conferred on Miss Jacobs in 1962 when she was inducted into the Lawn Tennis Hall of Fame at Newport, Rhode Island. She served in the WAVES during World War II and again in the Korean War. She has been an editor on the staff of the Book Of Knowledge. Juvenile titles include: Better Physical Fitness For Girls, Dodd, 1964; Center Court, Barnes, 1950.   CA-9/10

JACOBS, Leland B.
He has been an elementary education professor at Teacher's College of Columbia University. He has written articles and given lectures on the subject of children's literature and has been recognized as an outstanding authority in this field. He wrote: Alphabet Of Girls, Holt, 1969; Just Around The Corner, Holt, 1964.

JAGENDORF, Moritz Adolf 1888-
Born in Bukovina, Austria, he came to America when he was a young man. He studied at Yale and Columbia Universities. He has been director of the Washington Square Players. His career in the theatre has included producing, translating, and directing. Mr. Jagendorf has also been interested in folklore and has been vice-

president of the International Folklore Congress and
president of the New York State Folklore Society.   With
Ralph Steele Boggs he wrote The King Of The Moun-
tains, Vanguard, 1960.   His books include: First Book
Of Puppets, Watts, 1952; Priceless Cats, And Other
Italian Folk Stories, Vanguard, 1956.   CA-5/6, MJA

JAMES, Norma Wood
She grew up in Brooklyn and attended the New York
schools and Pace College.   She married design engineer Edward H. James.   The author and her family
have lived in Freeport, Long Island.   For boys and
girls she wrote: Bittersweet Year, McKay, 1961;
Young Doctor Of New Amsterdam, Longmans, 1958.

JAMES, Will   1892-1942
Cowboy, author, artist, born in Montana.   Orphaned at
the age of four, he was adopted by his father's friend
who was a Canadian trapper.   He had no formal education, and he used charcoal from a branding fire to
make his first sketches.   His career as a writer and
illustrator began after Scribner's Magazine published
some of his work in 1924.   He was awarded the Newbery Medal in 1927 for Smoky, The Cowhorse, Scribner's, 1926.   Other books which he wrote and illustrated include: Cowboy In The Making, Scribner's, 1937;
Look-See With Uncle Bill, Scribner's, 1938; My First
Horse, Scribner's, 1940; Young Cowboy, Scribner's,
1935.   JBA-1, JBA-2

JAMESON, Malcolm   1891-1945
Born in Waco, Texas, the late Malcolm Jameson has
been referred to as "the science-fiction writer for
science-fiction writers. "   He studied art, architecture,
and engineering, but due to ill-health Malcolm Jameson
began a career in writing.   The author had ninety-three
books published from the one-hundred which he had
written during the last eight years of his life.   For
boys and girls he wrote Bullard Of The Space Patrol
(ed. by Andre Norton), World, 1951.

JANE, Mary Childs   1909-
Teacher and author.   She graduated from Bridgewater
State Teachers' College in Massachusetts and taught
school in Kentucky and Massachusetts.   The author has
been interested in creative writing and served as president of the Poetry Fellowship of Maine.   Mrs. Jane

has lived in Newcastle, Maine. Her juvenile books in-
clude: Indian Island Mystery, Lippincott, 1965; Mystery
At Dead End Farm, Lippincott, 1961; Rocking-Chair
Ghost, Lippincott, 1969.   CA-1

JANES, Edward C. 1908-
Editor and writer, born in Westfield, Massachusetts.
He studied at Deerfield Academy and Williams College.
Mr. Janes has been an enthusiastic hunter and fisher-
man since boyhood. He has written articles about
hunting and fishing and has been an Editor (Camping,
Fishing, and Associate Editor) of Outdoors Magazine.
He later became associated with Hunting And Fishing
Magazine as Travel Editor. With Oliver H. P. Rod-
man he wrote The Boys' Complete Book Of Fresh And
Salt Water Fishing, Little, 1949. He also wrote Boy
And His Gun, Barnes, 1951.

JANEWAY, Elizabeth (Hall) 1913-
Born in Brooklyn, she has lived in New York City with
her husband Eliot Janeway and two sons. She attended
Swarthmore and Barnard Colleges. Mrs. Janeway has
been a contributor of short stories and critical writing
to periodicals and newspapers. She has been a member of the Authors Guild of America and Judge of the
National Book Award in 1955. Books which she has
written for children include: Angry Kate, Harper, 1963;
Ivanov Seven, Harper, 1967.

JANICE see BRUSTLEIN, Janice Tworkov

JANSON, Horst Woldemar 1913-   Dora Jane (Heineberg)
Husband-wife team. Author, teacher, editor, Dr. Janson received his education at Harvard University and
in Europe. He has taught art appreciation, has edited
Art Bulletin book reviews, and has served New York
University (Washington Square College) as chairman of
its Fine Arts Department. His wife Dora Jane Janson
attended Radcliffe College and later did graduate work
at New York University's Institute of Fine Arts. She
has lectured at the St. Louis City Museum and the
Metropolitan Museum. The Jansons have lived in New
Rochelle, New York. Together they wrote The Story
Of Painting For Young People (first published 1952),
Abrams.   CA-1

JARRELL, Randall   1914-1965
     Poet, professor, born in Nashville, Tennessee. He
graduated from Vanderbilt University and has taught at
the University of North Carolina in Greensboro.   In
1961 his book of poetry entitled The Woman At The
Washington Zoo (Atheneum, 1960) received the National
Book Award.   Mr. Jarrell has been a chancellor of the
American Academy of Poets, member of the National
Institute of Arts and Letters, and Poetry Consultant of
the Library of Congress.   His books for boys and girls
include: Animal Family, Pantheon, 1965; The Bat-Poet,
Macmillan, 1964.   CA-7/8

JÁSZI, Jean Yourd
     She was born in Pennsylvania and has made her home
in Berkeley, California.   Prior to her marriage to a
professor at the University of California, Jean Jászi
had traveled and lived in nine states.   For boys and
girls she wrote Everybody Has Two Eyes, Lothrop,
1956.

JAUSS, Anne Marie   1907-
     Artist-author, born in Munich, Germany, the daughter
of painter George Jauss.   She studied at the State Art
School in Munich.   Her paintings have been exhibited
in Europe and America.   In 1946 she came to the United
States to live.   The New York Public Library has some
of her drypoints in its Print Collection.   She wrote and
illustrated The River's Journey, Lippincott, 1957.   She
selected and illustrated Wise And Otherwise, McKay,
1953.   CA-1

JAWORSKI, Irene D.
     Author and teacher, born in New York.   She graduated
from Hunter College and obtained her master's degree
from Columbia University and her doctor's degree
from Brown University.   Mrs. Jaworski has been a
teacher in New York City.   She and her family have
lived in Bethesda, Maryland.   She collaborated with
Alexander Joseph to write Atomic Energy, Harcourt,
1961.

JAYNES, Clara   see   MAYER, Jane (Rothchild)

JEFFERS, Harry Paul   1934-
     He was born in Phoenixville, Pennsylvania and studied
at Temple University.   He received his master's degree

from the University of Iowa. Mr. Jeffers has been a
linguist in the United States Army and has taught journalism at Boston University. He later became a producer and news writer for the American Broadcasting
Company. He also was a Fulbright lecturer in Thailand. With Senator Everett M. Dirksen he wrote Gallant Men, McGraw-Hill, 1967 and with Margaret Chase
Smith he wrote Gallant Women, McGraw-Hill, 1968.

JEFFRIES, Roderic (Graeme) 1926-
His pseudonym is Jeffrey Ashford. Attorney and writ-
er, born in England. He attended the University of
Southampton and was a cadet in the Merchant Navy.
He served in World War II. Roderic Jeffries gave up
his law practice to become a full-time writer. The
author has lived in Kent near London and has collected
Bentleys (cars) and enjoyed hunting as hobbies. His
juvenile books include: Against Time!, Harper, 1964;
River Patrol, Harper, 1969. CA-19/20

JENNINGS, Gary (Gayne) 1928-
A free-lance writer, the author has described himself
as "a Virginian by birth, a New Yorker by choice, and
a constant traveler by necessity." He served as an
Army correspondent in the Korean War. Mr. Jennings
has also been a newspaper reporter and has worked in
the advertising field. For boys and girls he wrote
Black Magic, White Magic, Dial, 1965. CA-7/8

JENNINGS, John Edward 1906-
He was born in Brooklyn, New York. John E. Jennings,
Jr., has written stories which have been published in
Cosmopolitan and the Saturday Evening Post magazines.
One of his stories appeared in serial form in Liberty
magazine. For young people he wrote Clipper Ship
Days, Random, 1952. CA-13/14

JENNISON, C. S. see STARBIRD, Kaye

JENNISON, Keith Warren
Although a Canadian born in Winnipeg, Mr. Jennison
has always claimed to be a Vermonter and has lived in
St. Albans, Vermont. He once said: "We are a Vermont family and my sons are the seventh generation in
the same house in St. Albans." He attended Williams
College at Williamstown, Massachusetts and the University of Toronto in Ontario. The author has worked in

JENSEN, David E.

the publishing field as a publishers' representative and
editor for many years. For boys and girls he wrote
From This To That (A Junior Literary Guild selection),
McKay, 1961.

JENSEN, David E.
Author and geologist, born in New York. After graduating from Cornell University he did further study at
the University of Rochester. A noted authority in
minerology and geology, David Jensen has been director
of Ward's Natural Science Establishment, Inc. , Geological Division. His articles have appeared in magazines. For young people he wrote My Hobby Is Collecting Rocks And Minerals, Hart, 1955.

JERR, William A.
Born in Massachusetts, he studied at Yale. When he
was in the Navy, he visited Central and South America
where he became interested in tropical wildlife. Mr.
Jerr has been associated with the National Audubon
Society and has conducted wildlife tours in Everglades
National Park and in the Florida Keys. He has also
served as a National Audubon Society Warden and has
been responsible for the protection of nesting sanctu-
aries on the coast of Texas. He wrote The Adventure
Book Of Birds, Capitol Pub. Co. , 1957.

JEWETT, Sarah Orne 1849-1909
She was born in South Berwick, Maine, the daughter of
a physician. Her Maine background provided the ideas
for many of her books. Sarah Orne Jewett began to
write at an early age, and at nineteen she sold her
first story to a magazine. A series of sketches which
she wrote appeared in the Atlantic Monthly and were
later published in a book. A small frail woman, Sarah
Jewett died in 1909 from a spine injury. Her juvenile
books include: Betty Leicester's Christmas, Houghton,
1899; . . . Play Day Stories, Houghton, 1914.   JBA-1

JOHANSEN, Margaret (Alison) 1896-
Alabama was her birthplace. After her marriage she
lived in Austin, Texas. Her husband's Danish background provided Mrs. Johansen with the incentive to
write about the Norsemen. She wrote Voyagers West
(A Junior Literary Guild selection), Washburn, 1959.
She collaborated with her sister (Alice Alison Lide) to
write Wooden Locket, Junior Literary Guild and Viking,

1953.

JOHNSON, Charles Frederick
He once served in the U. S. Marine Corps and has
written a book about the marines for young people.   He
served in the marines during World War II and was re-
called to duty in 1951.   Later he became an editorial
writer on the San Diego Union.   His first book was
Steve Fletcher, U. S. Marine, Winston, 1957.

JOHNSON, Crockett see LEISK, David Johnson

JOHNSON, Edgar 1901-   Annabel (Jones) 1921-
Husband-wife team.   She was born in Kansas City,
Missouri, and he was born in Washoe, Montana.   Both
attended the Art Students League in New York City.
They have traveled throughout the United States in order
to find material for their books.   In order to secure
first hand information for A Golden Touch (Harper,
1963), Mr. and Mrs. Johnson visited a gold mine and
panned gold.   They wrote: The Black Symbol, Harper,
1959; Count Me Gone, Simon, 1968.   CA-9/10

JOHNSON, Enid 1892-
Born in Indiana, she has studied music in New York
City.   Not only has she been an executive secretary,
but she has also worked with her sister in real estate.
After she began writing for boys and girls, Enid Johnson said: "No other job I have ever held gave me the
satisfaction I find in writing for young people. "   She
collaborated with Anne Merriman Peck to write Big
Bright Land, Junior Literary Guild and Messner, 1947,
and she wrote Garbage Dump Treasure, Melmond, 1964.

JOHNSON, Gerald White
Author and newspaperman, born in Riverton, North
Carolina.   He received his B. A. degree from Wake
Forest College in Winston-Salem, North Carolina.   He
has lived in Baltimore where he has been a newspaper-
man.   He has also been Professor of Journalism at the
University of North Carolina and a contributing editor
of The New Republic.   His juvenile books include:
America Grows Up, Morrow, 1960; America Is Born,
Morrow, 1959; America Moves Forward, Morrow, 1960;
The Cabinet, Morrow, 1966; Communism: An Ameri-
can's View, Morrow, 1964; The Congress, Morrow,
1963; The Presidency, Morrow, 1962; The Supreme

Court, Morrow, 1962.

JOHNSON, James Ralph 1922-
Author, illustrator, marine. He was born in Alabama
and graduated from Howard College in Birmingham.
Major Johnson was stationed in Japan, Lebanon, and
Iwo Jima during World War II. In the Korean Conflict
he was an intelligence officer. Prior to duty with the
Marine Corps School in Quantico, Virginia, Major Johnson studied in England and Japan at the Air Force Survival Schools. Juvenile books which he wrote and illustrated include: Animal Paradise, McKay, 1969; Ringtail, McKay, 1968; Utah Lion, Follett, 1962.

JOHNSON, Margaret Sweet 1893-
Her mother was an artist, and her father was interested in ornithology. She studied at the Academy of Design and the Art Students League in New York. She
married a man who had the same last name (Johnson).
Her name remained Margaret Johnson. The Johnsons
have lived in Yonkers, New York. With her mother
Helen Lossing Johnson she wrote Black Bruce (Harcourt,
1938). The author has written many animal books for
boys and girls. These include: Bright Flash, Morrow,
1961; Kelpie, Morrow, 1962. JBA-2

JOHNSON, Osa Helen (Leighty) 1894-1953
Author, explorer, wife of Martin Johnson. She was
born in Chanute, Kansas. Osa Johnson spent a great
part of her life in Africa and once acquired a baby
elephant as a pet. She has written books of authenticity
which have provided exciting reading for young people.
She and her husband have also made motion pictures.
Their film "Congorilla" took two years to produce, and
they lived with pygmies for over six months. She
wrote: Snowball, Random, 1942; Tarnish, The True
Story Of A Lion Cub, Follett, 1944.

JOHNSON, Robert E.
He was born in Yakima, Washington and graduated from
the University of Washington at Seattle. He has been
associated with the field of aviation since 1929. Although he was not a pilot, the author has flown thousands of miles as a passenger. He married an airline
stewardess who has shared his interest in aviation. For
boys and girls he wrote Flight Seven, Dodd, 1940.

JOHNSON, Siddie Joe   1905-
      She was born in Dallas, Texas and graduated from
      Texas Christian University at Fort Worth.   Prior to
      becoming a librarian, she taught school in Refugio.
      Miss Johnson obtained a degree in library science from
      Louisiana State University and later became children's
      librarian at the Dallas Public Library.   Juvenile titles
      include: Cat Hotel, Longmans, 1955; A Month Of
      Christmases, Longmans, 1952; New Town In Texas,
      Longmans, 1942; Texas, Random, 1943.   JBA-2

JOHNSON, William Weber   1909-
      Author and newspaperman, born in Illinois.   He re-
      ceived his education in Illinois and later made his home
      in California.   William Johnson has been both a war
      correspondent and a foreign correspondent.   When he
      was a student, he traveled in Mexico and later visited
      there as a foreign correspondent.   He once said: ". . .
      No other country holds as much fascination for me. "
      He later wrote Captain Cortés Conquers Mexico, Ran-
      dom, 1960.   He also was the author of Sam Houston,
      The Tallest Texan, Random, 1953.   CA-17/18

JOHNSTON, Johanna
      She has written for radio and has been on the staff of
      the Columbia Broadcasting System.   She married photo-
      grapher Martin Harris, and they have lived in New
      York City.   The family cat "Taffy" provided the ideas
      for her book Great Gravity The Cat, Knopf, 1958.   She
      also wrote A Special Bravery, Dodd, 1967.

JOHNSTON, Laurie
      Author and newspaperwoman, born in Pueblo, Colorado.
      She graduated from the University of Oregon at Eugene.
      She has been a correspondent for Reuters News Agency
      and was selected as one of the women correspondents
      authorized for the Navy and Army in the Pacific during
      World War II.   Her work has appeared in several
      newspapers including the Portland Oregonian and the
      New York Times.   For boys and girls she wrote Eliza-
      beth Enters, Scribner, 1953.

JOHNSTON, Louisa Mae
      She studied at Monmouth College and Northwestern Uni-
      versity and did graduate work in education at DePaul
      University.   Louisa Johnston has been editor-in-chief
      of an educational press in Chicago, Illinois.   She also

has written articles for magazines. She wrote Mystery Hotel, Whitman, 1964.

JOHNSTON, Ralph E. 1902–
Author and newspaperman, a westerner by birth. He studied at the University of Kansas and later entered the newspaper field in Greeley, Colorado where he worked on the Greeley Daily Forum. He became acquainted with the curator of the local historical museum whose stories led to Mr. Johnston's writing a book about the West. He also wrote Old Tangle Eye (A Junior Literary Guild selection), Houghton, 1954.

JONES, Elizabeth Orton 1910–
Author-illustrator, born in Highland Park, Illinois. She attended the University of Chicago, the Art Institute of Chicago, and did further study at Fontainebleau, France. She has lived in a house called "Book End" in Mason, New Hampshire. Her first book for children was Ragman Of Paris And His Ragmuffins (Oxford, 1937). Elizabeth Orton Jones has illustrated many books for other writers, and in 1945 she received the Caldecott Medal for Prayer For A Child (Macmillan, 1944) written by Rachel Field. She has also illustrated books written by her mother Jessie Mae (Orton) Jones. Books which Elizabeth Orton Jones wrote and illustrated include: Big Susan, Macmillan, 1947; Maminka's Children, Macmillan, 1940; Twig, Macmillan, 1942. JBA-2

JONES, Helen Hinckley see HINCKLEY, Helen

JONES, Lloid 1908– Juanita Nuttall 1912–
Husband-wife team. They met when they were both students at the University of Denver. After Lloid Jones graduated from the University, he taught school. He had also acquired some teaching experience between his junior and senior years at the University. Mr. and Mrs. Jones have enjoyed music in addition to their other interests. Their juvenile books include: Horseman Of Long Gone River, Westminster, 1956; Sentinel In The Saddle, Junior Literary Guild and Westminster, 1951.

JONES, Mary Alice 1898–
Educator, teacher, writer. She was born in Dallas, Texas and graduated from the University of Texas. She received her master's degree from Northwestern Uni-

versity and her doctor's degree from Yale University.
She has been children's editor for Methodist periodicals
and for many years served as Director of Children's
Work for the International Council of Religious Educa-
tion.   Mary Alice Jones has taught at several univer-
sities and was the first woman asked to teach at Yale
Divinity School.   Juvenile titles include: Bible Stories,
Rand, 1952; God Speaks To Me, Rand, 1961; His Name
Was Jesus, Rand, 1950; Know Your Bible, Rand, 1965;
Tell Me About Christmas, Rand, 1958.   CA-19/20,
MJA

JONES, Weyman 1928-
He was born in Tulsa, Oklahoma.   He has been interested in the Cherokee Indians since he was a boy in
Tulsa.   When he studied at Harvard, he wrote a thesis
on the folklore and mythology of the Cherokee.   He has
been Director of Information for the IBM Federal Sys-
tems Division and has lived in Chevy Chase, Maryland.
He wrote: Edge Of Two Worlds, Dial, 1968; The Talking Leaf, Dial, 1965.   CA-19/20

JORDAN, Philip Dillon 1903-
Professor and writer, he has lived in Minneapolis, Minnesota.   He has written many books, and his numerous
articles have appeared in such magazines as the New
York Folklore Quarterly, American Folklore Journal,
and Journal History Of Medicine.   Philip D. Jordan has
been on the staff of the University of Minnesota as a
professor of history.   For children he wrote Burro
Benedicto, And Other Folktales And Legends Of Mexico,
Coward, 1960.   CA-11/12

JORGENSON, Ivar see SILVERBERG, Robert

JORGENSEN, Mary Venn see VENN, Mary Eleanor

JOSEPH, Alexander 1907-
Author and teacher, born in Paris.   He came to the
United States in 1915.   After graduating from City Col-
lege in New York, he obtained his doctorate from New
York University.   He served in the Air Force and was
Director of Training at a French-American flying school
during World War II.   He was commended by the French
Ministry of Air for his translations of technical man-
uals into French.   Dr. Joseph has taught physics at
Harvard, the University of Connecticut, and at New

York University. He was awarded the Legion of Merit
by the President of the United States in 1946. In 1951
he received the Conspicuous Service Cross. The author collaborated with Irene D. Jaworski to write Atomic Energy, Harcourt, 1961.   CA-13/14

JOSLIN, Sesyle 1929-
She married author Al Hine, and they have lived in New
Milford, Connecticut. Prior to writing books for chil-
dren, Sesyle Joslin wrote book reviews, short stories,
and radio scripts. Her juvenile books include: Baby
Elephant Goes To China, Harcourt, 1963; La Fiesta,
Harcourt, 1967.   CA-15/16

JOY, Charles Rhind 1885-
Author and traveler. Since graduating from Harvard,
Dr. Joy has traveled extensively throughout the world.
His outstanding work in relief organizations has been
recognized by many foreign governments. He has been
awarded the Albert Schweitzer Medal and was made a
Life Fellow of the International Institute of Arts and
Letters. His juvenile books include: Getting To Know
Hong Kong, Coward, 1962; Young People Of Western
Europe, Meredith, 1967.

JUDSON, Clara (Ingram) 1879-1960
Teacher, lecturer, writer, born in Logansport, Indiana.
She grew up in Indianapolis and lived in Chicago and
Evanston, Illinois after her marriage to James McIntosh
Judson. Her career as a writer began when a national
syndicate of newspapers published her "Bedtime Tales. "
Mrs. Judson has also written many books about the
foreign-born in America. Her first biography was Abraham Lincoln, Friend Of The People (Wilcox & Follett, 1950). She has been the recipient of numerous
book awards and honors. The author died before she
could receive the Laura Ingalls Wilder Award in 1960.
Her juvenile books include: Andrew Carnegie, Follett,
1964; City Neighbor, Scribner, 1951; Green Ginger Jar,
Houghton, 1949; Lost Violin, Houghton, 1947; Mr. Justice Holmes, Follett, 1956.   JBA-2

JULIAN, Nancy R.
Teacher, author, born in Tennessee. She once taught
children of the American armed forces at an air base
near Frankfurt, Germany. Later she worked in advertising in Knoxville, Tennessee. Miss Julian's interests

have included: gardening, travel, and music. For young people she wrote: Peculiar Miss Pickett, Winston, 1951.

JUPO, Frank J. 1904–
He was born in Germany and spent his childhood there. Prior to coming to the United States in 1946, he had worked in London and Glasgow, Scotland. The author and his family have lived in Forest Hills, New York. He has been an illustrator and writer for Story Parade magazine. He has also been a political cartoonist and comic strip artist in addition to writing books for children. These include: Adventure Of Light, Prentice, 1958; Day Around The World, Abelard, 1968.   CA-7/8

JUSTER, Norton 1929–
Architect, teacher, author. He was born in New York City and has lived in Brooklyn Heights. The author attended the University of Pennsylvania and Liverpool University in England. Norton Juster has been an Assistant Professor of Design at Pratt Institute in Brooklyn. He has also worked as an architect. For children he wrote Alberic The Wise And Other Journeys, Pantheon, 1965.   CA-13/14

JUSTUS, May 1898–
Teacher and writer. She was born in Del Rio, Texas, attended the University of Tennessee in Knoxville, and has made her home in Tracy City, Tennessee. May Justus has taught school and at one time conducted classes for the handicapped in her home. The Tennessee mountains provided the background for many of her books. These include: Barney, Bring Your Banjo, Holt, 1959; Big Log Mountain, Holt, 1958; Children Of The Great Smoky Mountains, Dutton, 1952; The House In No-End Hollow, Doubleday, 1938; Lucky Penny, Aladdin, 1951; New Boy In School, Hastings House, 1963; A New Home For Billy, Hastings House, 1966. CA-9/10, JBA-2

K

KAHL, Virginia 1919–
She was born in Milwaukee, Wisconsin and graduated from Milwaukee-Downer College. She has been a librarian in Milwaukee and an army librarian in Berlin. She also worked in Salzburg, Austria which city pro-

vided the author with the incentive to write and illus-
trate picture books for boys and girls. These include:
Away Went Wolfgang!, Scribner, 1954; The Baron's
Booty, Scribner, 1963; Droopsi, Scribner, 1958; Duch-
ess Bakes A Cake (A Junior Literary Guild selection),
Scribner, 1955; Habits Of Rabbits, Scribner, 1957;
Maxie, Scribner, 1956.   MJA

KAHN, Roger
Sportswriter, editor.   At one time he was Sports Editor of Newsweek.   Prior to his association with Newsweek he wrote about the Dodgers baseball team for the
Herald Tribune.   Later he became a freelance writer
and lived in New York City.   For young people he
wrote Inside Big League Baseball, Macmillan, 1962.

KAKACEK, Gen
Author and lecturer, born in Naperville, Illinois.   She
has lived in California.   Her writing career has included: articles, religious books, and short stories.   The
author has been a member of the Catholic Press Association and the California Writers' Club.   She collaborated with Mary N. Dolim to write Four Hands For
Mercy (A Junior Literary Guild selection), Van Nostrand, 1965.

KALNAY, Francis
Author and teacher, born in Hungary.   He was selected
as a "professional storyteller" during his boarding
school days.   Mr. Kalnay came to the United States after World War I (he had been in the Hungarian Army).
He later served in the U. S. Army in World War II.
He has held such jobs as farmer, actor, journalist,
playwright, and teacher.   His hobbies have included
gardening and smoke cookery.   Francis Kalnay has resided in California and Mexico.   Juvenile books include:
Chúcaro: Wild Pony Of The Pampa, Harcourt, 1958;
Richest Boy In The World, Harcourt, 1959.

KALUSKY, Rebecca
Editor, teacher, writer, born in New York City.   A
graduate of Hunter College, she has taught school and
has been an editor for a publication at Scholastic Magazines.   For boys and girls she wrote Is It Blue As A
Butterfly?, Prentice, 1965.

KANE, Henry Bugbee 1902-
Nature photographer, artist, writer. He was born in
Cambridge, Massachusetts, grew up there and in Maine,
and later lived in Lincoln, Massachusetts. He received
his education at Phillips-Exeter Academy and the Massachusetts Institute of Technology (Cambridge). Well-
known as a nature photographer, he has specialized in
photographing the wild life of America. His photographs and drawings have appeared in both books and
magazines. Henry Kane has been in advertising, public relations, and has flown with the U. S. Navy.
Juvenile books which he has written and illustrated include: Four Seasons In The Woods, Knopf, 1968; Wild
World Tales, Knopf, 1949.

KANTOR, MacKinlay 1904-
Author and correspondent, born in Webster City, Iowa.
He served as a correspondent in England with the Royal
Air Force during World War II. He has always been
interested in the history of the Civil War. The author
was awarded a Pulitzer prize in 1956 for his book
Andersonville, World, 1955. His juvenile titles include:
Angleworms On Toast (new ed.), Putnam, 1969; Gettys-
burg, Random, 1952.

KAPLAN, Albert A.   Margaret (de Mille)
Mr. Kaplan graduated from Hofstra College (Long Island, New York) and received his master's degree from
New York University. Both he and his wife were very
active in the retailing field. Mrs. Kaplan studied at
Barnard College. Her family was a distinguished one
and included her sister Agnes de Mille who was a dancer and choreographer and her uncle, the late motion-
picture producer Cecil B. de Mille. Albert Kaplan was
consultant to the International Cooperation Agency.
Margaret de Mille Kaplan was Assistant General Manager and Director of Fashion in the Market Division of
the Associated Dry Goods Corporation. Mr. and Mrs.
Kaplan wrote Careers In Department Store Merchandis-
ing, Walck, 1962.

KAPP, Paul
Author and music publisher, born in Chicago, Illinois.
He graduated from Northwestern University at Evanston,
Illinois. Paul Kapp's father was a phonograph-record
dealer, and he was surrounded by music from early
childhood. At fifteen he played the piano for high

school dances. He later became president of a music
publishing company. He was the composer and anthologist of a collection of songs for children entitled Cat
Came Fiddling And Other Rhymes Of Childhood, Adapted
And Made Into Songs, Harcourt, 1956. Paul Kapp also
wrote Cock-A-Doddle-Doo! Cock-A-Doodle-Dandy!, Harper, 1966.

KAREN, Ruth 1922-
Correspondent and author, born in Nuremberg, Ger-
many. She graduated from high school in Jerusalem
and attended the New School for Social Research in the
United States. She returned to Nuremberg after the
war in order to write up the S. S. trial for the Toron-
to Star Weekly. She also wrote about the Korean War
for the Reporter magazine. The Toronto Star and the
North American Newspaper Alliance and Women's News
Service published her work about the United Nations.
The author later lived in Guatemala on Lake Amatitlan.
For boys and girls she wrote: The Land And People
Of Central America, Lippincott, 1965; Neighbors In A
New World, World, 1966. CA-19/20

KASSIRER, Norma
Author, playwright, teacher. She was born in Buffalo,
New York and has continued to make her home there.
She attended Western Reserve University at Cleveland,
Ohio and graduated from the University of Buffalo.
The author has taught English at the International Insti-
tute in Buffalo. She has also written children's plays
and directed them for the Buffalo Museum of Science.
Her first book for children was written for her two
daughters and was entitled Magic Elizabeth, Viking,
1966. She also wrote Doll Snatchers, Viking, 1969.

KÄSTNER, Erich 1899-
Author and poet, born in Dresden, Germany. He attended a university in Saxony and later lived in Munich.
Erich Kästner's books have been enjoyed by both adults
and children, and his prose and poetry have become
well-known throughout Europe. He received the Hans
Christian Andersen Prize in 1960 for his book When I
Was A Boy (tr. from the German by Isabel and Florence McHugh), Watts, 1961. Other juvenile titles include: Emil And The Detectives (tr. by May Massee),
Doubleday, 1930; The Little Man (tr. from the German
by James Kirkup), Knopf, 1966.

KAULA, Edna Mason 1906–
Author and illustrator, born in Australia. A graduate
of the Sydney (Australia) Technical College, she has
lived in Manhattan and Maine.   At the age of fourteen
she sold her first article.   Mrs. Kaula has traveled
in Europe and the Middle East and has lived in Holland, Java, Rhodesia, and New Zealand.   On a trip to
Ethiopia in 1964 she acquired a good background of the
country and its people and interviewed Haile Selassie I.
Her juvenile books include: African Village Folktales,
World, 1968; The Land And People Of Ethiopia, Lippincott, 1965.   CA-7/8

KAVALER, Lucy
A graduate of Oberlin College (Oberlin, Ohio), she was
born in Brooklyn, and has lived in New York City and
Washington, D. C.   Lucy Kavaler has written for both
adults and children.   Her work has appeared in such
publications as Business Week, McCall's, Medical Economics, Parents', and Today's Living.   For young
readers she wrote: Astors, Dodd, 1968; The Wonders
Of Fungi, Day, 1964.

KAY, Helen see GOLDFRANK, Helen Colodny

KEATING, Lawrence Alfred 1903–1966
His pseudonyms are John Keith Bassett and H. C.
Thomas.   Author and lecturer, born in Chicago, Illinois.   He received a degree in journalism from Mar-
quette University in Milwaukee, Wisconsin.   Mr. Keat-
ing served with the American Red Cross as Assistant
Director of Public Information in the Midwest during
World War II.   He has given lectures on writing at
universities and has enjoyed travel and music as hob-
bies.   His books for young people include: Freshman
Backstop, Westminster Press, 1957; Junior Miler (A
Junior Literary Guild selection), Westminster Press,
1958; Runner-Up (A Junior Literary Guild selection),
Westminster Press, 1961; Wrong-Way Neelen (A Junior
Literary Guild selection), Westminster Press, 1963.
CA-7/8

KEATING, Norma
She has written for both magazines and newspapers, and
several collections of her poetry have been published.
Norma Keating has also been associated with the New
York City Board of Education as a writer of stories for

the New Reading Material Program. She has lived in
Freehold, New Jersey. She wrote Mr. Chu, Macmillan, 1965.

KEATS, Ezra Jack 1916-
Artist, writer, born in Brooklyn, New York. He has
lived most of his life in the New York City area with
the exception of the time that he spent abroad in travel
and study. He served as a camouflage expert with the
U. S. Air Force during World War II. Mr. Keats has
been a teacher, magazine illustrator, and an illustrator
of many books. He received the 1963 Caldecott Medal
for The Snowy Day (Viking, 1962) which was the first
book that he wrote and illustrated. Other juvenile
books include: Jennie's Hat, Harper, 1966; John Henry,
Pantheon, 1965; Peter's Chair, Harper, 1967.   MJA

KEELER, Katherine (Southwick) 1887-
Born in Maine, the daughter of a doctor. She graduated
from Central State Teachers College at Stevens Point,
Wisconsin. She received her art training at the Chi-
cago Art Institute and the Pennsylvania Academy of
Fine Arts in Philadelphia where her husband, Burton
Keeler, also studied. Juvenile titles include: Apple
Rush, Nelson, 1944; In The Country, Abelard, 1953;
Winter Comes To Meadow Brook Farm, Nelson, 1949.

KEITH, Carlton see ROBERTSON, Keith

KEITH, Harold Verne 1903-
Native Oklahoman, he was born at Lambert and has
lived in Norman. The author attended Northwestern
State Teachers College at Alva and received his B. A.
and M. A. degrees in history from the University of
Oklahoma. His chief interests have been history and
sports. Mr. Keith has been director of sports publicity at the University of Oklahoma and in 1950 received
the Helms Athletic Foundation Award as the nation's
outstanding sports publicist. His interest in the Civil
War led to his Newbery Medal award book Rifles For
Watie (Crowell, 1957) in 1958. He also wrote: Ko-
mantcia, Crowell, 1965; Sports And Games (New rev.
ed.), Crowell, 1960.   CA-7/8, MJA

KELLER, Frances Ruth 1911-
She was born in Moab, Utah and later lived in California. Since her two small daughters shared her interest

in animals, Frances Keller created a story for them
entitled The Curious Little Owl, Platt, 1957.

KELLOGG, Jean 1916-
She has been interested in mythology. When she discovered that her own children enjoyed folklore, she decided to write about this subject for other young readers. She once said: "Even when the world was young,
people heard of the winged horses who sometimes came
to visit our earth . . ." She wrote about such a visit
in her book Hans And The Winged Horse, Reilly, 1964.
CA-9/10

KELLY, Eric Philbrook 1884-
He was born in Massachusetts, spent part of his childhood in Colorado, and attended high school in New
York. He later studied at Dartmouth College. Mr.
Kelly has been a newspaperman and teacher. While
he was teaching and studying at the University of Krakow in Poland, he wrote The Trumpeter Of Krakow
(Macmillan, 1928) which won the Newbery Medal in
1929. Following World War II, the United States government sent him to Mexico in order to be of assistance to Polish refugees. His books for young people
include: At The Sign Of The Golden Compass, Macmillan, 1938; In Clean Hay, Macmillan, 1953; Land Of
The Polish People, Stokes, 1943. JBA-1, JBA-2

KELSEY, Alice (Geer) 1896-
She was born in Danvers, Massachusetts, grew up in
Connecticut, and has lived in Ithaca, New York. After
graduating from Mount Holyoke College in Massachusetts, she continued her studies at Cornell University
in Ithaca. She married Lincoln David Kelsey who later
was on the staff at Cornell. She and her husband have
lived in Greece and Puerto Rico, and these experiences
have provided authentic material for several of her
books. For young people she wrote: Once The Mullah,
Longmans, 1954; Ricardo's White Horse, Longmans,
1948. CA-5/6, MJA

KENDALL, Carol Seeger 1917-
She was born in Bucyrus, Ohio and graduated from
Ohio University. Her husband, writer Paul Murray
Kendall, has been a member of the faculty at Ohio Uni-
versity. Mrs. Kendall has said that she could not re-
member a time when she wasn't interested in writing.

She wrote for school papers and once started a book in
the fourth grade.   The Kendalls have lived in Athens,
Ohio.   She wrote: Gammage Cup, Harcourt, 1959;
Whisper Of Glocken, Harcourt, 1965.   CA-5/6

KENNY, Hugh   Ellsworth Newcomb   1909-
Husband-wife team.   Hugh Kenny and his wife Ellsworth
Newcomb have lived in Washington, Connecticut.   They
have both enjoyed traveling and gardening.   Mr. Kenny
has contributed science articles to Coronet and Nation's
Business.   Miss Newcomb has written several books
for young people.   Together they wrote: Miracle Fabrics, Putnam, 1958; Miracle Plastics, Putnam, 1965.
CA-5/6

KENT, Louise (Andrews)   1886-
She was born in Brookline, Massachusetts.   She studied
library science at Simmons College in Boston.   Many
of her short stories have appeared in magazines, and
she has written editorials for the Boston Herald.   At
one time her work appeared in the Boston Traveler under the name of Teresa Tempest.   She married a publisher and editor, Ira Rich Kent.   Mrs. Kent has written many books with historical backgrounds which include: He Went With Hannibal, Houghton, 1964; He
Went With Magellan, Houghton, 1943.   CA-4, JBA-2

KENYON, Raymond G.   1922-
Teacher-writer.   Born in Gloversville, New York, he
has lived in New Paltz and Woodstock.   He graduated
from New York State University at Oswego and received
his master's degree from New York University.   He
also studied at the Munson William Proctor Art Institute.   Mr. Kenyon has been a school principal, college
professor, and a curriculum consultant.   He served
with the Third Army Combat Engineers during World
War II.   His articles about science and mathematics
have been published in educational journals.   For young
people he wrote and illustrated I Can Learn About Cal-
culators And Computers, Harper, 1961.

KEPES, Juliet   1919-
Born in London, England, she came to America in
1937.   She attended Askes Hatcham School in London,
Brighton School of Art, and the School of Design in
Chicago.   She married Gyorgy Kepes, a writer and
painter, and has lived in Cambridge, Massachusetts.

Juliet Kepes has received art awards and has had her
work exhibited in many museums and galleries. These
include the Art Institute of Chicago, Worcester Museum,
Baltimore Museum, and the Gropper Gallery in Cambridge. Juvenile books which she wrote and illustrated
include: Seed That Peacock Planted, Little, 1967; Two
Little Birds And Three, Houghton, 1960.

KERNER, Ben
Born in New York City, he attended the Art Students
League and the Master Institute of Arts. He also studied at Pratt Institute in Brooklyn. Prior to writing
for children, Ben Kerner had written a play and mystery story for adults. He has also written documentary
films which have won international awards. He has
contributed articles and reports to the National Mental
Health Board and other government agencies. His first
book for children was entitled Electricity, Coward,
1965.

KERR, Laura (Nowak) 1904-
She was born and grew up in Chicago where she attended the John H. Vanderpoel grade school. The paintings
of Mr. Vanderpoel's students were displayed in the
school, and children were asked to write about them.
Laura Kerr remembered this writing assignment as one
of her favorite ones. She later attended the University
of Chicago where she met her husband William Kerr.
For young people she wrote: Louisa: Life Of Mrs.
John Quincy Adams, Funk, 1964; Scarf Dance, Abelard,
1953.

KESSLER, Leonard P. 1921-
This author and his wife (Ethel) have created several
picture books based on experiences shared with their
children (Kim and Paul). Both have also worked with
children in summer camps as camp directors. Mr.
and Mrs. Kessler graduated from the Carnegie Institute
of Technology. They have lived in New City in Rockland County, New York. During World War II, Leonard
Kessler served in the United States Infantry. He wrote
Art Is Everywhere, Dodd, 1958. With his wife Ethel
he wrote: Peek-A-Boo (A Junior Literary Guild selection), Doubleday, 1956; Soup For The King, Grosset,
1969.

KETTELKAMP, Larry
He was born in Harvey, Illinois and graduated from the
University of Illinois. He also studied at Pratt Institute
in Brooklyn, New York. In addition to writing books
for boys and girls, he has also been an illustrator for
the magazine Highlights For Children. He has lived in
Honesdale, Pennsylvania. He wrote and illustrated:
Dreams, Morrow, 1968; Flutes, Whistles, And Reeds,
Morrow, 1962.

KEY, Alexander (Hill) 1904-
He served in Naval Intelligence during World War II.
Many of his articles and stories have been published
in Argosy, the Saturday Evening Post, and the American Mercury. He wrote his first space book (Sprockets
--A Little Robot, Westminster, 1963) after viewing a
Florida sky (". . . he and excited neighbors saw two
strange objects in the sky . . ."). Mr. Key has lived
in North Carolina. He also wrote Golden Enemy, Westminster, 1969.   CA-5/6

KEYES, Nelson Beecher 1894-
Author and publisher, born in New England. He has
traveled and lived in many parts of our country. An
authority on the Bible, Mr. Keyes has written factual
books about it for all age levels. He has also been
interested in our country's national parks and American
history. His books for young people include: Real
Book About Our National Parks, Garden City, 1957;
Story Of The Bible World, Hammond, 1959.

KIELTY, Bernardine
Columnist, editor, writer, New Englander. She has
been an editor of Story Magazine and has written a
column on books called "Under Cover" for the Ladies
Home Journal. Bernardine Kielty has also been a
book reviewer for the Book-Of-The-Month Club News.
She has enjoyed going to concerts, taking walks, and
reading. She has made her home in New York. Her
books for young people include: Fall Of Constantinople,
Random, 1957; Masters Of Painting, Doubleday, 1964.

KIENE, Julia
Author and home economics director. She organized
and directed over a thousand chapters of the Health-
for-Victory Club during World War II. Prior to her
retirement, Julia Kiene had been the director of the

Home Economics Institute at Westinghouse. She wrote
Step-By-Step Cook Book For Girls And Boys, Simon,
1956.

KINERT, Reed Charles 1912-
Author, illustrator, pilot. He grew up in Richmond,
Indiana and later became manager of the local airport.
At one time Mr. Kinert was associated with the U. S.
Weather Bureau as an airways observer. He has also
worked in advertising and was a flight instructor with
the Army. He has participated in numerous air races
and has combined his knowledge of aviation with his
actual experiences to write American Racing Planes
And Historic Air Races, Wilcox and Follett, 1952.
He also wrote and illustrated America's Fighting Planes
In Action, Macmillan, 1943.

KING, Martha Bennett
Writer, editor, playwright. She has entertained many
school children and adults with her folk songs and has
conducted folk song programs on radio. In addition she
has taught children's literature at the University of
Chicago. Martha Bennett King has also been children's
book editor of a newspaper in Chicago and has written
plays for children's theaters. Her books for young
people include: The Key To Chicago, Lippincott, 1961;
Papa Pompino, Rand, 1959.

KING, Seth S.
Newspaperman, author, born in Okmulgee, Oklahoma.
He graduated from the University of Oklahoma and en-
tered the newspaper profession when he worked for the
Oklahoma City Times. Later he traveled extensively
as a correspondent for the New York Times. As a
Times correspondent, he lived in Kuala Lumpur, Ma-
laysia. He also had assignments in London, Israel,
and Singapore. He wrote Getting To Know Malaysia,
Coward, 1964.

KINGMAN, (Mary) Lee 1919-
Author, designer, editor, born in Reading, Massachusetts. She attended Colby Junior College and graduated
from Smith College. In 1940 she won Vogue magazine's
Prix de Paris essay contest for her composition on
Mary Ellen Chase. She married Robert Natti, a teacher, and they have lived in Massachusetts. Her children's plays have been published in Plays magazine.

Juvenile books include: Magic Christmas Tree (A Junior Literary Guild selection), Ariel, 1956; Secret Journey Of Silver Reindeer, Doubleday, 1968.   CA-7/8,
MJA

KINGSLEY, Charles 1819-1875
British poet, clergyman, scientist, novelist, born in
Devonshire. He studied at King's College in London
and at Cambridge. He once served as chaplain to
Queen Victoria. He also taught modern history at
Cambridge, was rector of Eversley in Hampshire, and
was canon at Westminster and Chester. He retold the
Greek myths for boys and girls in his book The Heroes,
Dent, 1906. He also wrote The Water Babies (first
published in 1863), Watts, 1961; Westward Ho!, Scrib-
ner, 1920.   JBA-1

KIPLING, Rudyard 1865-1936
Author and poet, born in Bombay, India. He was educated in England but returned to India where he became
assistant editor of the Lahore Civil And Military Gazette. He also worked on the Allahabad Pioneer. He
married an American girl and lived in Brattleboro,
Vermont. He and his family later traveled to Africa
and finally settled in Sussex, England. Rudyard Kipling was awarded the Nobel Prize for Literature in
1907. His verse and poems have been published in his
Collected Verse, Doubleday, 1907. Other books include: All The Mowgli Stories, Doubleday, 1936; "Cap-
tains Courageous", Doubleday, 1897; Jungle Book,
Doubleday, 1932; Just So Stories, Doubleday, 1902;
Kim, Doubleday, 1901.   JBA-1

KIRK, Ruth (Kratz) 1925-
She grew up in Los Angeles and attended Occidental
College. Ruth Kirk visited Japan with her husband who
was a naturalist with the U. S. National Park Service.
He later was a naturalist at Olympic National Park
in Washington. In reference to her book Mrs. Kirk
wrote: ". . . I hope that from its pages American
teen-agers may glean at least a small awareness that
the people of Japan are people first, and Japanese
second--which is true of all people of all nations, including us. " Her book was entitled Japan: Crossroads
Of East And West (A Junior Literary Guild selection),
Nelson, 1966.   CA-15/16

KIRN, Ann
> Illustrator, teacher, writer, she grew up in Montgomery City, Missouri. She received her B. A. and M. A. degrees from Columbia University and attended William Woods College at Fulton, Missouri, the Chicago Academy of Fine Arts, the St. Louis School of Fine Arts, the University of California at Los Angeles, and the University of Missouri. At one time she was a fashion illustrator, an elementary school teacher, and on the staff at Florida State University in Tallahassee. Juvenile books which she wrote and illustrated include: I Spy, Norton, 1965; Peacock And The Crow, Four Winds, 1969; Tinkie, World, 1960.

KISER, Martha Gwinn
> She was born in Bloomfield, Indiana. The author attended night classes for six years after moving to Chicago. She has contributed regularly to trade periodicals and magazines for children. Mrs. Kiser has enjoyed cooking and bicycle riding. Her juvenile books include: Gay Melody, Longmans, 1949; Song Of Florence Marie, Reilly, 1967.

KISINGER, Grace Gelvin (Maze) 1913-
> She received a degree in music from the State Teacher's College at Indiana, Pennsylvania. Her stories have appeared in magazines. Grace Kisinger's first novel was written for teen-agers. Concerning this particular age group she once said: "I firmly believe the teens are a very important time in every girl's life, trying and turbulent, with many problems to be solved, and a multitude of far-reaching decisions to be made. If I can get across a constructive message to girls in their teens, I feel I will be accomplishing something worth while. " Her titles for young people include: Bittersweet Autumn, Macrae, 1960; More Than Glamour, Nelson, 1957.   CA-13/14

KJELGAARD, James Arthur 1910-1959
> Born in New York City, he spent his childhood on a farm in Pennsylvania and later lived in Galeton, Pennsylvania. He has held various jobs including: trapper, surveyor, and laborer. However, before the age of thirty, he decided to make writing his career. Mr. Kjelgaard has been interested in conservation and has enjoyed hunting and fishing as hobbies. Prior to his death in 1959, he lived in Milwaukee. His first book

was Forest Patrol, Holiday, 1941.   He also wrote:
Big Red, Holiday House, 1945; Dave And His Dog,
Mulligan, Dodd, 1966; Double Challenge, Dodd, 1957;
Fire-Hunter, Holiday House, 1951.   JBA-2

KLEIN, David 1919-
This author has been interested in the sea and boating
since boyhood.   During the war he served as a navigator on a twin-diesel harbor boat.   He has worked in a
publishing company, taught in a college, and has been
associated in a research foundation.   David Klein has
written articles about boating for magazines.   He has
lived in New York.   He wrote Beginning With Boats,
Crowell, 1962.   CA-4

KLEIN, H. Arthur
Publicist, teacher, writer.   He was born in New York,
graduated from Stanford University, and has lived in
Berlin and London.   He has worked for news services
as a feature writer and reporter.   Mr. Klein has been
interested in scientific phenomena and has been in complete agreement with Michael Faraday's words: "Nothing is too wonderful to be true!"   For young people he
wrote: Fuel Cells, Lippincott, 1966; Surf's Up, Bobbs,
1966.   CA-15/16

KLEIN, Leonore (Glotzer) 1916-
Librarian, author.   She received degrees from Barnard
and Wellesley Colleges.   She also studied library science at Columbia University.   While attending Barnard
she served as editor of the college's literary publication.   Leonore Klein has been a school librarian in
New York City and Pleasantville, New York.   At one
time she was reference librarian at Florida Southern
College at Lakeland, Florida.   Juvenile titles include:
Brave Daniel (A Junior Literary Guild selection), Scott,
1958; Just A Minute, Harvey, 1969.   CA-4

KNIGHT, Clayton 1891-
Author, illustrator, pilot.   He was born in Rochester,
New York, attended the Art Institute in Chicago, and
has lived in West Redding, Connecticut.   He served as
a pilot with the Lafayette Esquadrille in World War I
and was a correspondent during World War II.   Later
he flew around the world in order to collect material
for a history of the Military Air Transport Service.
For young people he wrote and illustrated: Big Book

Of Real Helicopters, Grosset, 1955; We Were There
At The Normandy Invasion, Grosset, 1956.   CA-9/10

KNIGHT, David C.
He was born in Glens Falls, New York, and graduated
from Union College in Schenectady, New York.   He also studied at the University of Paris in France.   Mr.
Knight has worked in Berlin as a civilian employee
with Military Intelligence and in New York as a science
editor with a publishing house.   He also has been a
contributor to the Book Of Knowledge encyclopedia.
The Knights have lived in Dobbs Ferry, New York.
For young people he wrote The Science Book Of Mete-
orology, Watts, 1964.

KNIGHT, Eric Mowbray 1897-1943
He was born in Yorkshire, England; however, when he
was a boy he came to America where he attended
school.   During the World War he served with the
Canadian Army.   At one time he wanted to be an artist, but he was forced to give up this ambition when
he discovered he was colorblind.   Many of his short
stories have been included in British and American
anthologies.   For boys and girls he wrote Lassie-
Come-Home, Winston, 1940.

KNIGHT, Hilary
He was born in New York and has traveled extensively.
Hilary Knight has visited Rome, Moscow, Paris, Madrid, and Panama City.   He has written and illustrated
many picture books for boys and girls.   His illustrations also gained renown when they appeared in the
"Eloise" books by Kay Thompson.   He wrote and illustrated: Christmas Nutshell Library, Harper, 1963;
Sylvia The Sloth, Harper, 1969.

KNIGHT, Peter
A free-lance journalist, the grandson of the noted landscape painter, W. H. Knight.   He attended London University and the Slade School of Art.   Peter Knight's
travels have taken him to India, Iran, and the Middle
East.   For young readers he wrote Shadow On Skjar-
ling, Coward, 1964.

KNIGHT, Ruth Adams (Yingling) 1898-
She was born in Defiance, Ohio.   Ruth Knight has
worked on newspapers and has written magazine articles

and radio scripts.   She married writer Dickson Jay
Hartwell, and they have lived on a farm in Connecticut.
One of her short stories has been included in an O.
Henry collection of best stories of the year.   She has
loved animals, and young people have enjoyed her books
about dogs which include Brave Companions, Doubleday,
1945.   She also wrote Halfway To Heaven, McGraw,
1952.   With Claud W. Garner she wrote Word Of Hon-
or, A Story About Thoroughbreds, Ariel, 1964   CA-
5/6, MJA

KNOX, Calvin M. see SILVERBERG, Robert

KOBAYASHI, Masako Matsuno see MATSUNO, Masako

KOCH, Dorothy (Clarke) 1924-
Teacher and writer, born in Ahoskie, North Carolina.
After graduating from Meredith College at Raleigh she
continued her education at the University of North Carolina.   She married a college professor and has lived
in Chapel Hill, North Carolina.   Mrs. Koch has taught
in the elementary schools of her native state, and her
experiences as a teacher provided her with the incentive to write.   Her juvenile books include: Gone Is
My Goose, Holiday, 1956; I Play At The Beach, Holiday, 1955; Let It Rain!, Holiday, 1959; Monkeys Are
Funny That Way, Holiday, 1962; Up The Big Mountain,
Holiday, 1964; When The Cows Got Out, Holiday, 1958.
CA-7/8

KOFFLER, Camilla d. 1955
Her pseudonym is Ylla.   Photographer, born in Austria.
She became well-known for her photographs of animals
and once said that the reason her photographs have
been popular is because she thinks every animal has a
personality of its own.   When she was on a photograph-
ic assignment in India, she died in an accident on
March 30, 1955.   Her books include: Animal Babies
(Story by Arthur Gregor), Harper, 1959; I'll Show You
Cats (Story by Crosby Bonsall), Harper, 1964; Polar
Bear Brothers (Story by Crosby Newell), Harper, 1960.

KOHL, Marguerite
She has written books for both adults and children.
Marguerite Kohl has been associated with General Foods
in White Plains, New York.   She collaborated with
Frederica Young to write: Games For Children, Wyn,

1953; <u>More Jokes For Children</u>, Hill & Wang, 1966.

KOHN, Bernice Herstein 1920-
A well-known writer of science books ("Junior Research
Books"), Bernice Kohn has done much research in this
field. She married a chemical engineer and has resided in New York City. Her books for children include: <u>Computers At Your Service</u>, Prentice, 1962;
<u>Ramps</u>, Hawthorn, 1969. CA-9/10

KOMROFF, Manuel 1890-
Lecturer, editor, author. Born in New York City, he
attended Yale University and for many years was a
lecturer at Columbia. Mr. Komroff has been a newspaperman and book editor. He has served as editor
of both the <u>Black And Gold Library</u> and the <u>Library Of
Living Classics</u> series. He has written adult novels,
biographies, and short stories. For young people he
wrote: <u>Mozart</u>, Knopf, 1956; <u>Thomas Jefferson</u>, Messner, 1961; <u>True Adventures Of Spies</u>, Little, 1954.
CA-4

KONIGSBURG, Elaine L.
Author-illustrator, born in New York City. She graduated from the Carnegie Institute of Technology (Pittsburgh, Pennsylvania) and did graduate work in chemistry at the University of Pittsburgh. She also studied
art at the Art Students League. Mrs. Konigsburg
taught science in a private school in Jacksonville, Florida. On January 13, 1968 she was notified that her
book <u>From The Mixed-Up Files Of Mrs. Basil E.
Frankweiler</u> (Atheneum, 1967) had been awarded the
Newbery Medal, and her book <u>Jennifer, Hecate, Mac-
beth, William McKinley, And Me, Elizabeth</u> (Atheneum,
1967) was the runner-up for the award.

KOOB, Theodora (J. Foth) 1918-
She was born in New Jersey and graduated from New
York University. As the wife of a regular Army officer, she has lived in many states throughout America
and also on Okinawa and in France. In addition to
teaching in France and Okinawa, Mrs. Koob has been
an Associate Professor at Shippensburg State College.
The Koob family has lived in Chambersburg, Pennsylvania. Her juvenile books include: <u>Benjy Brant</u>, Lippincott, 1965; <u>Deep Search</u>, Lippincott, 1969. CA-5/6

KOSTICH, Dragoš D.   1921-
Teacher and writer, born in Belgrade, Yugoslavia. In
1940 he joined the Yugoslav Air Force, and was later
a member of the Resistance. Mr. Kostich was captured and placed in a concentration camp. After his
escape, he lived in Rome and Paris before coming to
the United States. He received degrees from the University of Paris and has taught in New York City at
the New School for Social Research. Dragoš Kostich
has also been an expert on the history of the Balkans,
Poland, and Russia. His articles and book reviews
have appeared in many magazines. He collaborated
with Eric P. Kelly to write The Land And People Of
Poland, Lippincott, 1964. He also wrote The Land And
People Of The Balkans, Lippincott, 1962.   CA-5/6

KOVALIK, Nada
She studied at Stanford University where she served as
editor of the Stanford Daily. She later became a magazine writer and reporter on the Daily News in Anchorage, Alaska. She and Vladimir Kovalik wrote The
Ocean World (A Junior Literary Guild selection), Holiday House, 1966.

KRAHN, Fernando
Artist, cartoonist, writer. Born in Chile, he later
made his home in New York City. In addition to illustrating books, Fernando Krahn's work has appeared as
cartoons in The Reporter. His illustrations can be
found in The Furious Flycycle, Wahl, J., Delacorte,
1968. Juvenile books which he wrote and illustrated
include: Journeys Of Sebastian, Delacorte, 1968; Uncle Timothy's Traviata, Delacorte, 1967.

KRAMER, George
A native of New York, he has lived on Long Island.
George Kramer has always been a baseball enthusiast,
and his short stories about sports have been published
in magazines. For boys and girls he wrote Kid Battery, Putnam, 1968.

KRAMER, Nora
Author, editor, lecturer. She has been associated with
the Child Study Association of America and the National
Conference of Christians and Jews Committee on Chil-
dren's Books. At one time she was head of Macy's
Little Bookshop in New York. Nora Kramer's book

reviews have been published in trade journals and newspapers.   For children she wrote Nora Kramer's Storybook, Messner, 1956.   She also edited The Grandma
Moses Storybook, Random, 1961.

KRASILOVSKY, Phyllis 1926-
Born in Brooklyn, she attended Brooklyn College and
Cornell University where her husband studied law.   Following his graduation, the Krasilovskys lived in Alaska.
The idea for her book The Man Who Didn't Wash His
Dishes (A Junior Literary Guild selection, Doubleday,
1957) originated in a letter which she had written to
cheer up a small boy.   She has been a page girl at
the New York Stock Exchange and a secretary at
New Yorker magazine.   The author and her husband
have lived in Mamaroneck, New York.   Juvenile
titles include: Benny's Flag, World, 1960; Girl Who
Was A Cowboy, Doubleday, 1965; Scaredy Cat, Macmillan, 1959.   MJA

KRAUS, Robert 1925-
Author-illustrator, born in Milwaukee, Wisconsin.   Several covers of the New Yorker magazine have been
created by Mr. Kraus.   His drawings have also appeared in the New Yorker.   Robert Kraus and his family
have lived in Connecticut.   Books which he has written
and illustrated include: The Littlest Rabbit, Harper,
1961; Mouse At Sea, Harper, 1959.   As Eugene H.
Hippopotamus he wrote Hello, Hippopotamus, Simon,
1969.

KRAUSS, Ruth 1901-
Born in Baltimore, she studied at the Peabody Conservatory and Parsons School of Fine and Applied Art in
New York City.   Ruth Krauss married Crockett Johnson
(see Leisk, David Johnson) who has written and illustrated many books for boys and girls.   They have lived
in Rowayton, Connecticut.   She wrote Bears, Harper,
1948, and her husband Crockett Johnson illustrated her
book The Carrot Seed, Harper, 1945.   Together they
created Is This You?, Scott, 1955.   CA-3, MJA

KRISTOFFERSEN, Eva M. 1901-
Librarian and writer, daughter of a Danish inventor.
At twenty-one she came to America, became a citizen,
and has lived in Lincoln, Nebraska.   She studied at
Denmark's International Peoples College at Elsinore and

received her library degree from Drexel Institute of
Technology in Philadelphia. She has worked in college
and public libraries. The author married a librarian,
Magnus Kristoffersen who has served as librarian of
the Lincoln, Nebraska library. Her books for young
people include: Bee In Her Bonnet, Crowell, 1944;
Merry Matchmakers, Whitman, 1940.

KRUM, Charlotte 1886-
Author, playwright, teacher. She was born in Bloomington, Illinois. For many years she was associated
with the Avery Coonley School where she taught kindergarten and later served as school librarian. She has
written plays for boys and girls in addition to her
books which include: Four Riders, Junior Literary
Guild and Wilcox & Follett, 1953; Read With Me, Children's Press, 1946.

KRUMGOLD, Joseph 1908-
Film writer, producer, author, born in Jersey City.
After graduating from New York University, he began
his film career with Metro-Goldwyn-Mayer studios in
Hollywood. He has been both a writer and producer of
documentary motion pictures and television films. His
films have won many awards both here and abroad.
Mr. Krumgold has traveled throughout the United States,
Europe, and the Middle East, and at one time worked
in Jerusalem. It was in New Mexico that he made the
film about "Miguel Chavez" which later resulted in the
author writing his 1954 Newbery Medal award book
. . . And Now Miguel (Crowell, 1953). The Krum-
golds have lived in Hope, New Jersey which provided
the background for Onion John (winner of the 1960 Newbery Medal), Crowell, 1959. He also wrote Henry 3,
Atheneum, 1967.   CA-11/12, MJA

KRUSCH, Werner E.   1927-
He was born in Germany, spent several years in
France, and in 1951 came to Canada to live. Mr.
Krusch once said: "Photography and travel are my
major hobbies and since learning the English language
I have become interested in writing. " His home has
been in West Vancouver, British Columbia. With Ray-
mond Wohlrabe he wrote many books including: The
Key To Vienna, Lippincott, 1961; Land And People Of
Austria, Lippincott, 1956; Land And People Of Den-
mark, Lippincott, 1961; Land And People Of Germany,

Lippincott, 1957; Picture Map Geography Of Western Europe, Lippincott, 1967.   CA-7/8

KRÜSS, James
Editor, poet, writer, born in Helgoland (an island in the North Sea which belongs to West Germany). He attended schools in Lüneburg. At one time James Krüss was a newspaper editor and writer in Hamburg. He has also written poetry (which has appeared regularly in newspapers) and radio plays. The experiences of his own great-grandfather "formerly fisher of lobsters and a very talented storyteller" provided the ideas for his children's book My Great-Grandfather And I . . . (tr. from the German by Edelgard von Heydekampf Brühl), Atheneum, 1964.

KUBIE, Nora Gottheil Benjamin 1899-
She became interested in archaeology on a visit to Mexico and did additional study in this field at Columbia University. After a visit to Israel she became interested in the study of archaeology of the Near East. Mrs. Kubie has written several books for boys and girls on archaeology and once said: "Archaeology combines many things I like enormously: the study of history, particularly of ancient times; adventure in far places; and work in the open air . . . " Her juvenile titles include: First Book Of Archaeology, Watts, 1957; Israel (Rev. ed.), Watts, 1968.   CA-7/8

KUGELMASS, Joseph Alvin 1910-
Newspaperman and author, Mr. Kugelmass has lived on Long Island. He has traveled extensively on assignments for magazines and newspapers. When he worked on a newspaper in Washington, D. C. , his interest in the career of Ralph Bunche resulted in a biography for young people entitled Ralph J. Bunche: Fighter For Peace (Messner, 1962). On assignment for a Louisville paper he wrote about the American Printing House for the Blind which also resulted in the biography Louis Braille, Messner, 1951.   CA-7/8

KUMIN, Maxine (Winokur) 1925-
Author and teacher. Prior to her position as an English teacher at Tufts, Mrs. Kumin obtained her B. A. and M. A. degrees from Radcliffe College. Her poetry has been published in several magazines including Harper's and the New Yorker. The Kumin family has lived

in Newton Highlands, Massachusetts. Her books for
children include: The Beach Before Breakfast (A Junior Literary Guild selection), Putnam, 1964; When
Grandmother Was Young, Putnam, 1969.   CA-2

KUMMER, Frederic Arnold 1873-
His pseudonym is Arnold Fredericks. He has written
plays, novels, and books for boys and girls. Since he
has lived in Maryland, Frederic Kummer's research
on this part of the country for his book For Flag And
Freedom (Morrow, 1942) proved to be unusually rewarding. Mr. Kummer's great-grandmother used to
relate the story of the attack on Fort McHenry which
she watched when she was fourteen-years-old, and
this exciting episode was included in his book. He also wrote Leif Erikson, The Lucky, Winston, 1939.

KŮSAN, Ivan 1933-
Author and artist, born in Sarajevo, Yugoslavia. He
has made his home in Zagreb where he attended the
Academy of Fine Arts. He has written for both adults
and children. Ivan Kušan learned to paint and write
at an early age. Painting later became his hobby and
writing his career. For boys and girls he wrote The
Mystery Of Green Hill (tr. by Michael B. Petrovich),
Harcourt, 1962.   CA-9/10

KUSKIN, Karla Seidman 1932-
Author-artist. She was born in New York City, studied
at Antioch College, and graduated from the Yale School
of Design. The subject of her Yale thesis was children's books, and a sample book became her first publication Roar And More (Harper, 1956). The Kuskins
have lived in Brooklyn Heights. Juvenile books which
she wrote and illustrated include: ABCDEFGHIJKLMN-
OPQRSTUVWXYZ, Harper, 1963; Alexander Soames:
His Poems, Harper, 1962; All Sizes Of Noises, Harper, 1962; The Bear Who Saw Spring, Harper, 1961;
Square As A House, Harper, 1960; Watson, The Smart-
est Dog In The U. S. A. , Harper, 1968.   CA-3

KYLE, Elisabeth see DUNLOP, Agnes Mary Robertson

L

LA FARGE, Oliver 1901-
He was born in New York City, studied at Groton, and
graduated from Harvard. Mr. LaFarge has been interested in the American Indian and several times
served as president of the Association on American Indian Affairs. He was awarded the Pulitzer Prize for
his book Laughing Boy (Houghton, 1929) in 1929. Mr.
LaFarge served with the Department of Middle American Research at Tulane University and has been associated with the University of Pennsylvania Museum.
He has resided in Santa Fe, New Mexico. Juvenile
titles include: Cochise Of Arizona, Aladdin, 1953; The
Mother Ditch, Houghton, 1954.

LA FARGE, Phyllis
She graduated from Radcliffe College and has lived in
Brooklyn, New York with her husband Chester Johnson.
Phyllis LaFarge has translated French novels and plays
for several publishers. She also has written articles
for Harper's and Vogue magazines. She wrote: Kate
And The Wild Kittens, Knopf, 1965; Jane's Silver
Chair, Knopf, 1969.

LAFFIN, John
Explorer, soldier, teacher, writer. His books on mili-
tary history have been written with authority as the
author was in the Service for many years and served
in the Australian Imperial Force. He qualified for his
commission at the Royal Military College, Duntroon.
He has also been a member of the Royal Geographical
Society. John Laffin has lived in England. He wrote
Codes And Ciphers (A Junior Literary Guild selection),
Abelard, 1964.

LAMB, Harold 1892-
He was born in New York, attended Columbia University, and has lived in California. Mr. Lamb served
in both World Wars and has traveled extensively on the
continent of Asia. He once received a Guggenheim
Fellowship for further study. Many of his books have
been translated into different languages. The author
has enjoyed gardening, chess, and tennis as hobbies.
His books for young people include: Chief Of The Cos-
sacks, Random, 1959; Genghis Khan And The Mongol
Horde, Random, 1954. JBA-1, JBA-2

LAMBERT, Janet
    She was born in Crawfordsville, Indiana. After attend-
ing Ferry Hall near Chicago, she went to New York to
become an actress. She once played opposite Walker
Whiteside and was a member of the Northampton Players. When she married Army Officer Kent Lambert,
she lived on various army posts throughout the world.
The Lamberts later made their home on Long Beach
Island, New Jersey. Juvenile titles include: A Bright
Tomorrow, Dutton, 1965; Candy Kane, Dutton, 1943;
Dreams Of Glory, Dutton, 1942; Extra Special, Dutton,
1963; Five's A Crowd, Dutton, 1963; On Her Own, Dutton, 1964; Sweet As Sugar, Dutton, 1967.

LAMPMAN, Evelyn (Sibley) 1907-
    Lynn Bronson is her pseudonym. Born in Dallas, Ore-
gon, she graduated from Oregon State College and has
lived in Portland. At one time she worked in radio as
a continuity writer. After the death of her husband,
Mrs. Lampman returned to radio work and later became Educational Director of the local NBC radio station. Her stories have been published in magazines,
and she has received national recognition for several
radio scripts. Many of her juvenile books have been
Junior Literary Guild selections and include: The City
Under The Back Steps, Doubleday, 1960; Half-Breed,
Doubleday, 1967; Rock Hounds, Doubleday, 1958. Under
her pseudonym Lynn Bronson she wrote: Coyote Kid,
Lippincott, 1951; Darcy's Harvest (A Junior Literary
Guild selection), Doubleday, 1956; Popular Girl (A
Junior Literary Guild selection), Doubleday, 1957.
CA-15/16, MJA

LANDECK, Beatrice
    Music educator, author. She has taught music at the
Little Red School House in New York City and has also
been a member of the faculty at Mills College in California. She has lectured at many colleges and has conducted workshops. Her books for young people include:
Children And Music, Sloane, 1952; Echoes Of Africa In
Folk Songs Of The Americas, McKay, 1961.

LANE, Carl Daniel 1899-
    He was born in New York City and later made his home
in the state of Maine. He has also lived in Vermont
and Connecticut. The author has been interested in the
history of steamboats and has designed many boats in

which he sailed the North Atlantic.   Carl Lane has also been active in the Boy Scout program.   His books
for young people include: The Fire Raft, Little, 1951;
River Dragon, Little, 1948.

LANE, Neola Tracy
She has called Colorado her "home state" and has lived
in Denver.   She has studied at both Denver and Colorado Universities.   When her husband served in the Air
Force, the author traveled throughout the United States.
Her interests have been: painting, music, and photography.   She wrote Get Along, Mules, Lippincott, 1961.

LANG, Andrew 1844-1912
Journalist, historian, poet.   Born in Selkirk, Scotland,
he studied at Oxford in England and made his home in
London.   He acquired fame as an editor and translator
of folklore.   In England he has been called "editor-in-
chief to the British nation. "   Andrew Lang once said:
"Some are born soldiers from the cradle, some mer-
chants, some orators; nothing but a love of books was
given me by the fairies. "   Juvenile stories which he
collected and edited include: Arabian Nights, Longmans, 1946; Blue Fairy Book, Longmans, 1929; Crimson Fairy Book, Longmans, 1947; Rose Fairy Book,
Longmans, 1948.

LANGTON, Jane (Gillson) 1922-
She was born in Boston and attended Wellesley and Radcliffe Colleges.   Her book The Majesty Of Grace (Harper, 1961) began as an assignment at the Boston Museum School of Art.   She has written for both adults and
children.   The author married a physicist and has lived
in Lincoln, Massachusetts.   She also wrote The Diamond In The Window, Harper, 1962.   CA-4

LANIER, Sterling E.
Editor, sculptor, author.   Mr. Lanier, a professional
sculptor, has worked (in miniature) in silver, gold,
and bronze.   He once said: "Almost all of my ideas
on books and stories come while sculpturing. "   He has
also been a senior editor in publishing.   The author has
lived in Sarasota, Florida.   He was awarded the 1970
Charles W. Follett award for his book War For The
Lot, Follett, 1969.

LANSING, Elizabeth Carleton (Hubbard) 1911-
Her pseudonym is Martha Johnson. Author and librarian, born in Providence, Rhode Island. She received her library degree from Simmons College in Boston, Massachusetts and later made her home in Southport, Connecticut. Prior to being a children's librarian in a school library, Mrs. Lansing worked in the book department of a large store and in a publishing firm. She also wrote for Cue magazine. Her main interests have been gardening, politics, and reading. For young people she wrote: Ann Bartlett At Bataan, Crowell, 1943; Deer Mountain Hideaway, Crowell, 1953; House For Henrietta, Crowell, 1958; Jubliant For Sure, Crowell, 1954; Lulu Herself, Crowell, 1956; The Secret Of Dark Entry, Crowell, 1961.   CA-7/8

LAROM, Henry V.
Author and wrangler. Henry Larom's position as head dude wrangler at the noted Valley Ranch in Wyoming provided him with material for his horse stories. Preservation of wild life has always concerned him, and he once said: "The need for protecting elk, deer, and antelope is real and important. Every single man, woman, and child in the United States has a stake in conservation." His children's books include: Mountain Pony, Grosset, 1968; Ride Like An Indian!, McGraw, 1958.

LARRALDE, Elsa
She was born in Mexico. As a young girl she lived in Europe since her father was in the Mexican diplomatic service. In one of her books she told about the building of her house in Acapantzingo. She also wrote The Land And People Of Mexico (rev. ed.), Lippincott, 1964.

LARRICK, Nancy G. 1910-
Editor, author, teacher, born in Winchester, Virginia. Upon graduation from Goucher College in Towson, Maryland she taught school. She later received both her master's and doctor's degrees and taught at several universities. Nancy Larrick has been an editor of children's magazines and has served as president of the International Reading Association. She married Alexander L. Crosby and has lived near Quakertown, Pennsylvania. Juvenile titles include: Junior Science Book Of Rain, Hail, Sleet & Snow, Garrard, 1961;

Parent's Guide To Children's Reading, Doubleday, 1958;
Teacher's Guide To Children's Books, Merrill, 1960.
CA-1

LASCHEVER, Barnett D.   1924-
He has been travel editor of the New York Herald Tribune and at one time was a reporter for the United
States Army Stars And Stripes.   Mr. Laschever has
also written for the Hartford Times and the Detroit
Free Press.   His extensive travels have provided a
wealth of information for many of his books.   These
include: Getting To Know Cuba, Coward, 1962; Getting
To Know Hawaii, Coward, 1959.   CA-4

LASELL, Fen (Hegemann) 1929-
She was born in Berlin, Germany, grew up in America,
and has lived in Gloucester, Massachusetts.   She received her education in the schools of Vermont and
Massachusetts.   At one time she was a designer of
theater sets and costumes.   Fen Lasell's own desire
to own a horse resulted in her first book for children
Michael Grows A Wish, Houghton, 1962.   She also
wrote Kiya The Gull, Addison, 1969.   CA-7/8

LASSON, Robert 1922-
Author and editor.   He has been interested in animals,
cabinetmaking, and farming.   Robert Lasson has been
an editor with a publishing firm.   He has edited numerous manuals on various subjects (concrete and mason-
ry, flower arrangement).   The author has lived in
Philadelphia where he has been associated with an advertising agency.   For young people he wrote: Orange
Oliver: The Kitten Who Wore Glasses, McKay, 1957;
Which Witch? (A Junior Literary Guild selection), Mc-
Kay, 1959.

LATHAM, Jean Lee 1902-
Author and playwright, born in Buckhannon, West Vir-
ginia.   She received degrees from West Virginia Wes-
leyan College and Cornell University.   She also studied
at Ithaca College in New York.   Her home has been in
Coral Gables, Florida.   She has been a book editor and
trained Signal Corps inspectors during World War II.
Jean Latham has written plays for both stage and radio.
She has won many book awards and in 1956 received the
Newbery Medal for Carry On, Mr. Bowditch (A Junior
Literary Guild selection), Houghton, 1955.   Other juve-

nile titles include: The Chagres, Garrard, 1964; Drake: The Man They Called A Pirate, Harper, 1960; Man Of The Monitor, Harper, 1962; Retreat To Glory, Harper, 1965.   CA-7/8, MJA

LATHAM, Philip see ROBINSON, Robert Shirley

LATHROP, Dorothy Pulis 1891-
    Author-illustrator.   She was born in Albany, New York and attended Teachers College, Columbia University. After she had taught school for several years, she studied illustration at the Pennsylvania Academy of Fine Arts and later painted at the Art Students League. Dorothy Lathrop's mother was a painter, and her sister Gertrude was a sculptor.   She was the first person to receive the Caldecott medal in 1938 for her book Animals Of The Bible, Stokes, 1937.   Juvenile titles include: Angel In The Woods, Macmillan, 1947; Follow The Brook, Macmillan, 1960; Let Them Live, Macmillan, 1951; Littlest Mouse, Macmillan, 1955.   JBA-1, JBA-2

LATTIMORE, Eleanor Frances 1904-
    Author-illustrator, born in Shanghai, China.   At the age of sixteen she came to America and lived in Berkeley, California.   She attended the California School of Arts and Crafts and later studied at the Art Students League and the Grand Central School of Art in New York.   After her marriage to writer Robert Armstrong Andrews, she made her home on Edisto Island in South Carolina.   She has illustrated many of her own books and once said: "I only write about, or draw, the things I have actually seen or experienced."   Juvenile books which she wrote and illustrated include: Bayou Boy, Morrow, 1946; The Bittern's Nest, Morrow, 1962; The Bus Trip, Morrow, 1965; The Chinese Daughter, Morrow, 1960; Cousin Melinda, Morrow, 1961; First Grade, Harcourt, 1944; Little Pear, Harcourt, 1931; The Two Helens, Morrow, 1967.   JBA-1, JBA-2

LATTIN, Harriet (Pratt) 1898-
    She was born in Corning, New York, graduated from Smith College in Northampton, Massachusetts, and received her doctor's degree from Ohio State University at Columbus.   Mrs. Lattin has written many articles on medieval history and has been a member of the Mediaeval Academy of America and the American His-

torical Association. Her husband Norman D. Lattin
has been on the faculty of Western Reserve University.
The Lattins have lived in Cleveland, Ohio. She wrote
The Peasant Boy Who Became Pope, Schuman, 1951.

LAUBER, Patricia (Grace) 1924–
    Editor and writer, born in New York. After graduating
    from Wellesley College in Massachusetts, she returned
    to New York City to work and live. She has been a
    magazine editor and senior science editor of an ency-
    clopedia for young people. Miss Lauber has also
    served as editor-in-chief of Science World and has been
    on the staff of Look magazine. Her books for young
    people include: Adventure At Black Rock Cave, Ran-
    dom, 1959; All About The Ice Age, Random, 1959; All
    About The Planets, Random, 1960; Clarence, The TV
    Dog, Coward-McCann, 1955; The Congo, Garrard, 1964;
    The Friendly Dolphins, Random, 1963; The Mississippi,
    Giant At Work, Garrard, 1961; Our Friend The Forest
    (A Junior Literary Guild selection), Doubleday, 1959.
    CA-9/10

LAUGHLIN, Ruth
    After graduation from Colorado College at Colorado
    Springs, she studied in Rome and Paris. She once
    traveled to Guatemala as a member of an archaeologi-
    cal survey sponsored by the School of American Re-
    search. Ruth Laughlin has written for both the Chris-
    tian Science Monitor and the New York Times. She
 – has also been an officer in the Archaeological Society
    of New Mexico. She wrote Caballeros, Caxton, 1945.

LAVENDER, David (Sievert) 1910–
    Author, miner, mountain climber. He grew up on a
    Colorado cattle ranch, attended Princeton University in
    New Jersey, and later returned to Colorado to live.
    David Lavender's experiences as a gold miner, rancher,
    and mountain climber provided him with a good back-
    ground in order to write exciting stories for young peo-
    ple which include The Trail To Santa Fe, Houghton,
    1958.   CA-4

LAVINE, David 1928–
    A free-lance writer and teacher, native New Yorker.
    A graduate of DePauw University at Greencastle, Indi-
    ana, he did further study in political science at Colum-
    bia and New York Universities. David Lavine has been

a teacher in New York City and has worked in public
administration in New York state.   His articles have
appeared in magazines.   With Ira Mandelbaum he wrote
What Does A Peace Corps Volunteer Do?, Dodd, 1964.
He also wrote Under The City, Doubleday, 1967.   CA-
17/18

LAVINE, Sigmund Arnold   1908-
Newspaperman, teacher, writer.   Born in Boston, he
graduated from Boston University, and later made his
home in Milton, Massachusetts.   He served as feature
editor of his college paper and was both an actor and
stage manager of several school plays.   Sigmund Lavine has been a teacher and school principal, and at
one time taught children in a United States Government
Indian School at Belcourt, North Dakota.   He has also
been a newspaperman, sports correspondent, and a
literary critic.   For young people he wrote: Famous
Industrialists, Dodd, 1961; Handmade In America, Dodd,
1966; Kettering: Master Inventor, Dodd, 1960; Strange
Travelers (A Junior Literary Guild selection), Little,
1960; Wonders Of The Beetle World, Dodd, 1962.   CA-
3

LAWRENCE, Isabelle
She grew up in Cambridge, Massachusetts and graduated
from Radcliffe College.   She also studied with the Harvard 47 drama workshop.   She has lived in Chicago,
Illinois where she has taught history at the Latin School.
She has been the recipient of the Freedom Foundation
of Valley Forge Award ("Citizenship and the American
way of life, over and above the call of duty").   She
wrote: Drumbeats In Williamsburg, Rand, 1965; Spy
In Williamsburg (A Junior Literary Guild selection),
Rand, 1955.

LAWRENCE, Mildred Elwood   1907-
Newspaperwoman, author, born in Charleston, Illinois.
She has worked on the Flint Journal in Michigan.   Mil-
dred Lawrence studied at Lawrence College in Apple-
ton, Wisconsin and at Yale University.   Her husband
C. A. Lawrence also was on the staff of the Flint
Journal. The Lawrences have lived in Chambersburg,
Pennsylvania, and later made their home in Orlando,
Florida. Juvenile titles include: No Slipper For Cinder-
ella, Harcourt, 1965; Once At The Weary Why, Har-
court, 1969.   CA-1, MJA

LAWSON, Donald Elmer 1917-
Reporter, editor, writer. Don Lawson was born in
Chicago, graduated from Cornell College at Mt. Vernon, Iowa, and did graduate work at the University of
Iowa Writers' Workshop. Mr. Lawson received an
honorary degree from Cornell College for his achieve-
ments as a writer and an editor. He has served as
managing editor of Compton's Encyclopedia and in 1965
was appointed editor-in-chief. He served overseas
with the Air Force during World War II. His books
for young people include: Famous American Political
Families, Abelard, 1965; The United States In World
War II, Abelard, 1963; Youth And War, Lothrop, 1969.
CA-1

LAWSON, John
Native New Yorker, he graduated from Exeter and Harvard College. His home has been in Westchester, New
York. Mr. Lawson served in the Army during World
War II. The author has spent many summer months
in the mountains of Virginia, and these experiences
have provided authentic material for his books. Juvenile titles include: The Spring Rider, Crowell, 1968;
You Better Come Home With Me, Crowell, 1966.

LAWSON, Marie (Abrams) 1894-1956
Author-illustrator, born in Atlanta, Georgia. She attended schools in Georgia and Virginia. She spent her
childhood in North Carolina, and one of her fondest
memories was listening to songs sung by her grandfather who was an officer in the Confederate Navy.
She married writer Robert Lawson and lived near Westport, Connecticut. Mrs. Lawson wrote: Pocahontas
And Captain John Smith, Random, 1950; Sea Is Blue,
Viking, 1946.   JBA-2

LAWSON, Patrick see EBY, Lois Christine

LAWSON, Robert 1892-1957
Author-illustrator. He was born in New York, grew
up in Montclair, New Jersey and studied at the New
York School of Fine and Applied Art. He served with
the Army in the Camouflage Section during World War
I. He has lived near Westport, Connecticut on "Rabbit Hill" which provided the setting for his 1945 Newbery Medal winning book Rabbit Hill (Viking, 1944).
He also was awarded the Caldecott Medal in 1941 for

his illustrations in They Were Strong And Good, Viking, 1940.   Books which he wrote and illustrated include: Ben And Me, Little, 1939; Fabulous Flight,
Little, 1949; Great Wheel (A Junior Literary Guild selection), Viking, 1957; I Discover Columbus . . ., Little, 1941; Mr. Revere And I . . ., Little, 1953.
JBA-2

LAYCOCK, George Edwin 1921-
His boyhood was spent on a farm close to Zanesville,
Ohio, and he graduated from Ohio State University.
After graduation he served on the staff of Farm Quar-
terly as associate editor.   He also has contributed
articles to other magazines including: Sports Illustrat-
ed, Field And Stream, Nature, and Country Gentleman.
The Laycocks have lived in Cincinnati, Ohio.   He wrote:
Never Pet A Porcupine, Norton, 1965; Wild Refuge,
Doubleday, 1969.   CA-7/8

LEACH, Maria
She was born in New York.   She has been an authority
on folklore and as editor of Funk And Wagnalls Stan-
dard Dictionary Of Folklore, Mythology, And Legend,
spent over ten years in research.   Maria Leach has
been a member of the Modern Humanities Research
Association, the French Folklore Society, the American Dialect Society, and the American Anthropological
Association.   She also was a Councillor of the American Folklore Society.   Her books for young people include: The Luck Book, World, 1964; Soup Stone, Funk,
1954.

LEAF, Munro 1905-
Author-illustrator.   Born in Hamilton, Maryland (now
part of Baltimore), he graduated from the University
of Maryland, received his master's degree from Har-
vard, and has lived in Washington, D. C.   Munro Leaf
has been a teacher and a director in a publishing firm.
He has also lectured to children all over the world.
His first book written and illustrated for children was
Grammar Can Be Fun (Lippincott, 1934).   Both children
and adults have enjoyed his juvenile classic The Story
Of Ferdinand, Viking, 1936.   Other books include:
Arithmetic Can Be Fun, Lippincott, 1949; Being An
American Can Be Fun, Lippincott, 1964; Manners Can
Be Fun (Rev. ed.), Lippincott, 1958; Sam And The
Superdroop, Viking, 1948; Wee Gillis, Viking, 1938.

JBA-2

LEAR, Edward   1812-1888
Artist-writer, born in London, England. His first
book of nonsense appeared in 1846, and since that time
his verses have entertained generations of children.
At the start of his career Edward Lear painted birds and
animals. He once taught drawing to Queen Victoria. His
books include: The Jumblies, And Other Nonsense Verses,
Warne, 1910?, Edward Lear's A Nonsense Alphabet (pictures by Richard Scarry), Doubleday, 1962; Edward
Lear's Nonsense Book (A Junior Literary Guild selection),
(selected and illustrated by Tony Palazzo), Garden City
Books, 1956; Nonsense Omnibus, Warne, 1943.   JBA-1

LEAVITT, Jerome Edward   1916-
Professor and writer, born in Verona, New Jersey.
He graduated from New Jersey State Teachers College
and received his master's degree from New York University. He also studied at Northwestern, Arizona,
and Colorado Universities. Dr. Leavitt has been on
the staff at Northwestern and has been associated with
the Oregon State System of Higher Education as Assistant Professor of Education. He has written many
articles on education. The author has enjoyed gardening and the remodeling of old homes as hobbies. He
has lived in Portland, Oregon. His books for young
people include: America And Its Indians, Childrens
Press, 1962; True Book Of Tools For Building, Childrens Press, 1955. With John Huntsberger he wrote
Fun-Time Terrariums And Aquariums, Childrens Press,
1961.   CA-4

LECKIE, Robert (Hugh)   1920-
Marine, newspaperman, editor, born in Philadelphia.
He grew up in Rutherford, New Jersey, and later lived
with his wife and family in Mountain Lakes, New Jer-
sey. During World War II, he served with the First
Marine Division and received the Naval Commendation
Medal. In addition to writing for several newspapers,
Mr. Leckie has been the editor of MGM's theatre
newsreel and edited the Telenews Weekly. Juvenile
titles include: Great American Battles, Random, 1968;
The War In Korea, 1950-1953, Random, 1963.   CA-
13/14

LEE, Anne S.   see   MURPHY, Mabel Ansley

LEE, Manfred B.   1905-1971
His pseudonyms are Ellery Queen, Jr. , and Barnaby
Ross. Author-lecturer. Born in Brooklyn, he gradu-
ated from New York University, and has resided in
Roxbury, Connecticut. He has worked in the film in-
dustry in addition to writing Ellery Queen (pseudonym)
mystery stories with his counsin Frederick Dannay.
His special interest has been classical music. Manfred
Lee and Frederick Dannay began collaborating as mys-
tery novelists in 1928. Juvenile mysteries written by
Ellery Queen, Jr. , include: The Blue Herring Mystery,
Little, 1954; The Green Turtle Mystery, Lippincott,
1944. CA-1

LEE, Roy see HOPKINS, Clark

LEEKLEY, Thomas Briggs 1910-
Author and teacher, born in Parker, South Dakota. He
has been a high school teacher in his home state and
a Professor of English at the University of Pennsylvania. One of his main interests has been the study
of Indians. Mr. Leekley has worked for Newsweek
magazine and has lived in Ohio. For boys and girls
he wrote The World Of Manabozho, Vanguard, 1965.
CA-5/6

LEEMING, Joseph 1897-
He was born in Brooklyn and studied at Williams College.   Mr. Leeming has always been interested in the
sea and ships and at one time was in the shipping business. He also did publicity work. He has traveled
extensively including a visit to India. One of his books
was written with his daughter Avery Nagle, Kitchen
Table Fun, Lippincott, 1961. He also wrote: Card
Tricks Anyone Can Do, Appleton, 1941; . . . The Costume Book, Stokes, 1938; First Book Of Chess, Watts,
1953; Fun With Artificial Flowers, Lippincott, 1959;
Fun With Wire, Lippincott, 1956; Fun With Wood,
Stokes, 1942; Holiday Craft And Fun . . ., Lippincott,
1950.   JBA-2

Le GALLIENNE, Eva 1899-
British actress, director, translator. The daughter of
a writer, she was born in London and was educated in
Paris. Her home has been in Westport, Connecticut.
She has appeared in many plays and once directed and
starred in Chekhov's "The Sea Gull" while on tour with

the National Repertory Theatre. Miss Le Gallienne founded the well-known Civic Repertory Theatre in New York City in 1926. For children she has translated several stories of Hans Christian Andersen. These include: The Nightingale, Harper, 1965; Seven Tales, Harper, 1959.

LE GRAND see HENDERSON, Le Grand

LEIGHTON, Margaret (Carver) 1896-
The daughter of a college professor, she was born in Oberlin, Ohio. A graduate from Radcliffe College, she also attended schools in Massachusetts, France, and Switzerland. At one time she worked in a publishing firm and also did nursing in an Army hospital. After her marriage to Herbert Leighton, she made her home in Virginia. Since her husband's death, she has lived in California. Her juvenile books include: Bride Of Glory (A Junior Literary Guild selection), Farrar, 1962; Cleopatra, Farrar, 1969; Comanche Of The Seventh (Recipient of the Dorothy Canfield Fisher Memorial Award), Ariel, 1957. CA-9/10, MJA

LEISK, David Johnson 1906-
His pseudonym is Crockett Johnson. He was born in New York City. He studied at New York University and Cooper Union. For many years he created a popular comic strip known as "Barnaby." He married author Ruth Krauss, and they have lived in Rowayton, Connecticut. For boys and girls he wrote Frowning Prince, Harper, 1959. He illustrated, and his wife wrote The Carrot Seed, Harper, 1945. With his wife he wrote Is This You?, Scott, 1955. CA-9/10

LEMMON, Robert Stell 1885-
His study of nature began when he was a boy. Later he traveled throughout North America and into tropical countries south of the equator in his quest for information on birds, insects, and wildflowers. Mr. Lemmon's country home in Connecticut has provided him with many opportunities to pursue a career as naturalist and nature writer. His books for young people include: All About Monkeys, Random, 1958; All About Strange Beasts Of The Present, Random, 1957; All About Moths And Butterflies, Random, 1956; Junior Science Book Of Trees, Garrard Press, 1960.

L'ENGLE, Madeleine 1918-
Native New Yorker. She graduated from Smith College
at Northampton, Massachusetts and did further study
at Columbia. Madeleine L'Engle has been an actress,
teacher, and lecturer. She married actor Hugh Franklin who retired from the theater in 1952. In addition
to the theater, her main interests have been music and
travel. In 1963 she was awarded the Newbery Medal
for A Wrinkle In Time (A Junior Literary Guild selection), Farrar, 1962. Other juvenile titles include:
Camilla, Crowell, 1965; Meet The Austins, Vanguard,
1960; The Moon By Night, Ariel Bks., 1963; The Young
Unicorns, Farrar, 1968. CA-3, MJA

LENS, Sidney 1912-
He was born in Newark, New Jersey, attended schools
in New York, and later lived in Chicago. He has been
active in labor unions for many years and has lectured
at several universities including Roosevelt and DePaul
in Chicago. Mr. Lens has traveled extensively and
has written articles for Harper's, Nation, and Rotarian
magazines. The author has also been an active member in the Chicago Council on Foreign Relations. His
books for young people include: A Country Is Born,
Putnam, 1964; Working Men: The Story Of Labor, Putnam, 1960. CA-4

LENSKI, Lois 1893-
Artist and writer, born in Springfield, Ohio. After
graduating from Ohio State University at Columbus,
she attended the Art Students League in New York and
later studied at London's Westminster School of Art.
She married painter Arthur Covey and made her home
near Torrington, Connecticut. She later lived in Tar-
pon Springs, Florida. Her regional books have won
wide acclaim and many honors for the author. In 1946
she was awarded the Newbery Medal for Strawberry
Girl (Lippincott, 1945). She also received an Honorary
Degree of Doctor of Humane Letters from the Woman's
College of the University of North Carolina in 1962.
Juvenile books which she wrote and illustrated include:
Bayou Suzette, Stokes, 1943; Blueberry Corners, Stokes,
1940; Cowboy Small, Walck, 1949; Deer Valley Girl,
Lippincott, 1968. CA-13/14, JBA-1, JBA-2

LENT, Henry Bolles 1901-
He was born in New Bedford, Massachusetts, attended

Yale University, and graduated from Hamilton College
in Clinton, New York. Mr. Lent was associated with
the advertising profession for many years having served
as copywriter, supervisor, and vice president of a
large agency. He and his wife have lived in Woodstock, Vermont. Juvenile titles include: The Auto-
mobile-U. S. A. : Its Impact On People's Lives And The
National Economy, Dutton, 1968; The Bus Driver, Macmillan, 1937; Clear Track Ahead, Macmillan, 1932;
Eight Hours To Solo, Macmillan, 1947; Flight Overseas,
Macmillan, 1957; From Trees To Paper, Macmillan,
1952.   JBA-1, JBA-2

LEONARD, A. Byron 1904-
Author and professor, born in Manhattan, Kansas.
Prior to receiving degrees from the University of Kansas, the author attended Oklahoma City University and
Central Oklahoma State Teachers College. Dr. Leonard has written research papers on the fauna of Oklahoma and Kansas and has been associated with the
Dycke Museum of Natural History in those states. He
has also served on the staff of the University of Kansas as assistant professor of zoology. For boys and
girls he wrote Rufi, Caxton, 1942.

LERNER, Marguerite Rush 1924-
Physician and author. She has made her home in
Woodbridge, Connecticut with her husband who also was
a doctor. Prior to receiving her M. D. degree from
Western Reserve Medical School at Cleveland, Ohio,
Dr. Lerner graduated summa cum laude from the University of Minnesota. She also had pre-medical training at Barnard College and did further study at Johns
Hopkins Medical School. She has been Assistant Clini-
cal Professor of Dermatology in the School of Medicine
at Yale University. The medical books which she has
written for children include: Dear Little Mumps Child,
Minneapolis, Medical Books For Children, 1959; Who
Do You Think You Are? The Story Of Heredity, Prentice, 1963.   CA-13/14

LE SIEG, Theo see GEISEL, Theodor Seuss

LESSER, Milton 1928-
His pseudonyms are: Andrew Frazer, Jason Ridgway,
C. H. Thames, and Stephen Marlowe. Author, editor,
native New Yorker. After graduating from the College

of William and Mary in Williamsburg, Virginia, the
author traveled abroad. He has edited anthologies,
written for television, and contributed to magazines.
Milton Lesser has also served as a science fiction consultant. For young people he wrote Stadium Beyond
The Stars, Winston, 1960. CA-13/14

LESSIN, Andrew
He was born and grew up in Brooklyn; however, he
later lived in Merrick, Long Island, New York. Mr.
Lessin graduated from Long Island University and continued his studies in art education at New York University. Following service in the Army, he became art
director of Boys' Life magazine. He has enjoyed tennis and other sports. For young people he wrote Here
Is Your Hobby: Art, Putnam, 1963.

LESTER, Julius B. 1939-
He was born in St. Louis, Missouri and spent his childhood in Nashville, Tennessee. Mr. Lester has written
songs, recorded albums, and has been an editor for
Sing Out!. His articles and photographs have appeared
in: the Movement, the Guardian, the New York Free
Press, and the Village Voice. His book for young people To Be A Slave (Dial, 1968) was a runner-up for the
1969 Newbery Medal. CA-17/18

LEVIN, Marcia Obrasky 1918-
Author and teacher, she has lived in Rye, New York.
She attended Philadelphia Normal School and Temple
University. Mrs. Levin has been a teacher in the
public schools of Philadelphia. She has written for
both very young children and teen-agers. She collaborated with Jeanne Bendick to write: Pushups And
Pinups, McGraw, 1963; Take A Number, McGraw,
1961. CA-13/14

LEVINE, Israel E. 1923-
Native New Yorker, he has made his home on Long
Island. He served as a navigator with the U. S. Air
Force during World War II. After the war, he grad-
uated from New York's City College and later became
Director of Public Relations there. In addition to writ-
ing biographies for young people, Mr. Levine has writ-
ten books for adults and has contributed numerous arti-
cles to magazines. His juvenile books include:
Champion Of World Peace: Dag Hammarskjold, Mess-

ner, 1962; Inventive Wizard: George Westinghouse,
Messner, 1962; Miracle Man Of Printing: Ottmar Mer-
genthaler, Messner, 1963; Spokesman For The Free
World: Adlai Stevenson, Messner, 1967; Young Man
In The White House: John Fitzgerald Kennedy, Mess-
ner, 1964.   CA-3

LEVINE, Joseph
This writer was a former science teacher. He also
was the principal of a school in the Bronx, New York.
He collaborated with Tillie S. Pine to write the "All
Around" series books for children. Mr. Levine and
Mrs. Pine wrote the following books for boys and girls:
Electricity And How We Use It, McGraw, 1962; The
Eskimos Knew, McGraw, 1962.

LEVINE, Rhoda
Author and dancer, native New Yorker. She graduated
from Bard College (Annandale-on-Hudson, N. Y.).
Rhoda Levine has done choreography for television programs, the City Center Opera Company, Broadway
productions, the DuPont Show of the Month, and the
Festival of Two Worlds (Spoleto, Italy). Her books
for children include: Harrison Loved His Umbrella (A
Junior Literary Guild selection), Atheneum, 1964; Herbert Situation, Harlin Quist, 1969.

LEVINGER, Elma Ehrlich 1887-
She was born in Chicago, attended the University of
Chicago, and studied drama at Radcliffe. Mrs. Levinger has written plays, textbooks, and novels. Her son
has taught in the Physics Department at Cornell University, and his technical advice combined with her own
travel experiences in Europe helped Mrs. Levinger to
write Albert Einstein, Messner, 1949. She also wrote
Galileo: First Observer Of Marvelous Things, Messner, 1952.

LEWELLEN, John Bryan 1910-1956
Author and newspaperman. He was born in Gaston,
Indiana, attended Ball State Teachers College at Mun-
cie, and made his home in Chicago. At one time he
was a newspaper reporter and magazine photographer.
He worked for Fortune, Life, and Time magazines.
Mr. Lewellen also helped to write and produce radio
and television programs which included the "Quiz Kids."
In addition to his writing career, the author was an

airplane pilot. His juvenile books include: Atomic
Submarine, Crowell, 1954; Earth Satellite, Knopf, 1957;
Helicopters, Crowell, 1954; Tee Vee Humphrey, Knopf,
1957; Tommy Learns To Fly, Crowell, 1956; True Book
Of Airports And Airplanes (A Junior Literary Guild se-
lection), Childrens Press, 1956; True Book Of Farm
Animals, Childrens Press, 1954. MJA

LEWIS, Alfred
Editor and writer. He was born in Boston, Massachusetts, attended the University of California, and has
lived in White Plains, New York. He has written
many technical and scientific articles. At one time
Mr. Lewis was editor of International Management and
National Petroleum News. His juvenile books include:
Clean The Air!, McGraw, 1965; Treasure In The Andes, Abingdon, 1952.

LEWIS, Alice Hudson
Missionary, editor, writer. She and her husband were
both missionaries in China for many years. She has
also been associated with the Youth and Publications
Departments of the Presbyterian Board of Foreign Mis-
sions. Later she served as managing editor of the
YWCA Magazine. Mrs. Lewis has also written plays,
radio scripts, and articles for magazines. For young
people she wrote Day After Tomorrow, Friendship
Press, 1956.

LEWIS, Clive Staples 1898-1963
He was born in Belfast, Ireland, attended Oxford University in England, and served in the British Army in
World War I. C. S. Lewis served as Fellow and Tutor of Magdalen College, Oxford for over thirty years.
At the time of his death he was a Professor of Literature at Cambridge University. His stories of fantasy
include: Last Battle, Macmillan, 1956; The Lion, The
Witch And The Wardrobe, G. Bles, 1950; Magician's
Nephew, Macmillan, 1955; Prince Caspian, Macmillan,
1951; The Silver Chair, Macmillan, 1953. MJA

LEWIS, Elizabeth Foreman 1892-
She was born in Baltimore, Maryland, studied art at
Maryland Institute in Baltimore, and received special
training in religious education in New York. In 1917
she went to China where she taught at both the Huei
Wen School for Girls and at the Boys' Academy in

Nanking. It was also in Nanking that she married John
Abraham Lewis whose father had once served as Methodist Bishop of China. In 1933 the author was awarded
the Newbery Medal for her book Young Fu Of The Upper Yangtze, Winston, 1932. She also wrote: China
Quest, Winston, 1937; Ho-Ming, Girl Of New China,
Winston, 1934; To Beat A Tiger, One Needs A Brother's Help, Winston, 1956; When The Typhoon Blows,
Winston, 1942.   JBA-1, JBA-2

LEWIS, Mildred D.
Her pseudonym is James DeWitt. She was born in Battle Creek, Michigan and later studied at the University
of Michigan. She married Kent W. Lewis, a U. S.
Treasury Agent. Interested in history, the author has
searched for many rare books on this subject. Prior
to making writing her career, Mildred Lewis traveled
to Hawaii, Japan, and Hong Kong. She later made her
home in Phoenix, Arizona. For boys and girls she
wrote In Pursuit Of The Spanish Galleon, Criterion,
1961.

LEWIS, Milton   Mildred
Husband-wife team, native New Yorkers. Before their
marriage, Mr. Lewis was a reporter for the New
York Herald Tribune, and Mrs. Lewis was a public relations executive. Each was on an assignment when
they met. Milton Lewis later became a top general
assignment reporter for the Herald Tribune. His
specialty has been stories about crime. Mr. and Mrs.
Lewis have collaborated in writing articles and books.
For children they wrote Famous Modern Newspaper
Writers, Dodd, 1962.

LEWIS, Richard 1935-
Born in New York City, he graduated from Bard Col-
lege. Richard Lewis also attended Mannes College of
Music. He has taught at the Art Center of Northern
New Jersey and has been associated with Walden School.
At one time he was an assistant editor of Musical A-
merica magazine. Mr. Lewis has resided in New York
City. He edited In A Spring Garden, Dial, 1965 and
compiled Journeys, Simon, 1969.   CA-11/12

LEWIS, Roger   see   ZARCHY, Harry

LEWITON, Mina 1904-1970
    She was born in New York City and spent her childhood
    in Manhattan. Prior to her death in 1970, she had
    lived near Stanford, New York with her husband Ho-
    ward Simon. They also had a studio in New York City.
    Mina Lewiton wrote, and her husband illustrated Faces
    Looking Up, Harper, 1960. She also wrote Penny's
    Acres (A Junior Literary Guild selection), McKay,
    1955. MJA

LE WITT, Jan 1907-
    He has lived in London, England where he has designed
    sets and costumes for Sadler's Wells Ballet. Mr. Le
    Witt has also designed tapestries at Aubusson and glass
    sculptures in Italy. In 1954 he received a Gold Medal
    for book illustrations at the Milan Triennale and has
    been an honorary member of Venice's Centro Inter-
    nazionale nelle Arte del Vetro. He wrote and illustrat-
    ed The Vegetabull, Harcourt, 1956.

LEXAU, Joan M.
    Several of her books have been published under the
    name Joan L. Nodset. She was born in St. Paul,
    Minnesota and later lived in New York. In 1962 Joan
    Lexau was the recipient of the Child Study Association
    Book Award for her book The Trouble With Terry,
    Dial, 1962. Other juvenile titles include: Benjie,
    Dial, 1964; Crocodile And Hen, Harper, 1969. CA-
    19/20

LEY, Willy 1906-1969
    His pseudonym is Robert Willey. German author, lec-
    turer, teacher, born in Berlin. He attended the Uni-
    versities of Berlin and Koenigsberg. Willy Ley helped
    organize the German Rocket Society in 1927. He came
    to the United States in 1935, became an American citi-
    zen, and has lived in Jackson Heights, New York. He
    has lectured, taught, and written about science. The
    author has been a science editor and research engineer.
    He has also been a member of the American Associa-
    tion for the Advancement of Science, the Institute of the
    Aeronautical Sciences, and the American Rocket Soci-
    ety. For young people he wrote: Conquest Of Space,
    Viking, 1959; The Discovery Of The Elements, Dela-
    corte Press, 1968; Our Work In Space, Macmillan,
    1964; Space Travel, Simon & Schuster, 1958. CA-9/
    10

LEYSON, Burr Watkins 1898-
World War I fighter pilot, born in Medical Lake, Wash-
ington. He studied military aeronautics at Boston's
M. I. T. , Oxford and Lopcombe Corners, England, and
in Turnburry, Scotland. In addition to piloting many
types of aircraft, Captain Leyson has been qualified
for court testimony as an aeronautical expert in both
Connecticut and New York. Juvenile titles include:
It Works Like This, Dutton, 1942; Modern Wonders &
How They Work, Dutton, 1949; The Warplane And How
It Works, Dutton, 1943.

L'HOMMEDIEU, Dorothy (Keasbey) 1885-
The author has always lived in the country where she
has owned and raised a variety of animals. At an early age she developed a great love for dogs and later
became an authority on them. Dorothy L'Hommedieu
started the Sand Spring Kennel of Cocker Spaniels near
Morristown, New Jersey in 1920. Her juvenile dog
stories include: Leo, The Little St. Bernard, Lippincott, 1948; Macgregor, The Little Black Scottie, Lippincott, 1941; Nipper, The Little Bull Pup, Lippincott,
1943; Pompon, Ariel Bks. , 1955; Spot, The Dalmatian
Pup, Lippincott, 1950; Togo, The Little Husky, Lippincott, 1951; Tyke, The Little Mutt, Lippincott, 1949.

LICHELLO, Robert 1926-
Editor, writer, born in Parkersburg, West Virginia.
After several years of service in the Air Transport
Command when he was stationed in Japan, Robert
Lichello attended West Virginia University and was
feature editor of Moonshine, the campus humor magazine. Prior to his arrival in New York, he was a
radio disc jockey and news announcer. He once was
on the staff of the National Enquirer and has contributed
articles to many magazines. For young people he
wrote Ju-Jitsu Self Defense For Teen-Agers, Messner,
1961. CA-15/16

LIDE, Alice (Alison)
She was born in Alabama and has made her home there.
Her book Aztec Drums (Longmans, 1938) was the result
of much research which included visits to the Museum
of Natural History in New York City and the Garcia
Collection in the Library of the University of Texas.
Alice Lide also wrote Princess Of Yucatan, Longmans,
1939. She collaborated with her sister Margaret Alison

Johansen to write Wooden Locket, Junior Literary Guild
and Viking, 1953.

LIEB, Frederick George 1888-
Author, columnist, sports writer. Born in Philadelphia,
Pennsylvania, he has lived in Florida and St. Louis, Missouri. Mr. Lieb also spent over twenty years in New
York City where he was a newspaper editor, columnist,
and baseball writer. He has been considered an authority
on baseball and for many years attended all but one of the
World Series games. He reported on thirty-seven series
and was chief scorer for three of the series. His baseball articles have been published in the Sporting News
since 1935 and have also been featured in other magazines.
For young people he wrote Story Of The World Series,
Putnam, 1949.

LIERS, Emil Ernest 1890-
He grew up in Iowa and from early boyhood enjoyed wildlife and the out-of doors. In Minnesota Mr. Liers created the only otter sanctuary in the world. His observations
and study of otters resulted in his first book for boys and
girls entitled An Otter's Story (Junior Literary Guild and
Viking, 1953). He served as a technical adviser to the
late Walt Disney on his film "Beaver Valley" which won
an Academy Award. His juvenile books include: A Beaver's Story (A Junior Literary Guild selection), Viking,
1958; A Black Bear's Story, Viking, 1962.

LIETZ, Gerald S.
He was born in Illinois and graduated from the University
of Illinois with an M. D. degree. He spent the last year
of medical school in the Naval Training Program. It was
during his internship (as a Navy officer) that the new drug
penicillin was used by the armed forces. Dr. Lietz has
practiced medicine in Champaign, Illinois. His first book
for boys and girls was the Junior Science Book Of Bacter-
ia, Garrard, 1964.

LIFTON, Betty Jean 1926-   (see Addendum)

LILLIE, Amy Morris
Born in Elizabeth, New Jersey, she attended Teacher's
College, Columbia University, and the Philadelphia
Musical Academy. She has taught in a girls' school
in Philadelphia. Her stories have appeared in children's
magazines such as Story Parade and Child Life. The
author's interests have included: music, religious

activities, and working with young people.   Juvenile
titles include: Book Of Three Festivals, Dutton, 1948;
I Will Build My Church, Westminster Press, 1950;
Judith, Daughter Of Jericho, Dutton, 1951; Nathan, Boy
Of Capernaum, Dutton, 1945.

LINDGREN, Astrid (Ericsson) 1907-
Swedish author, born in Vimmerby, and later lived in
the city of Stockholm.   A noted writer of children's
books, Mrs. Lindgren was the first recipient of her
country's Nils Holgersson Plaque which is "the finest
mark of distinction in Sweden for any writer of books
for children and young people. " She also received the
Hans Christian Andersen Medal in 1958.   Astrid Lindgren has written motion picture and television scripts
and children's plays.   Her juvenile books include:
Bill Bergson And The White Rose Rescue (tr. by Florence Lamborn), Viking, 1965; Christmas In The Stable, Coward-McCann, 1962; Kati In Italy, Grosset, 1961;
Noy Lives In Thailand, Methuen, 1967; Pippi Long-
stocking (tr. by Florence Lamborn), Viking, 1950;
Springtime In Noisy Village, Viking, 1966.   CA-13/
14, MJA

LINDMAN, Maj Jan
She grew up in Örebro, Sweden and studied painting at
the Royal Academy of Arts.   The first book of her
series about "Snipp, Snapp, Snurr" was introduced to
young people in 1922.   Mrs. Lindman has made her
home in Djursholm, Sweden.   Juvenile titles include:
Dear Little Deer, Whitman, 1953; Flicka, Ricka, Dicka
And The Big Red Hen, Whitman, 1960; Flicka, Ricka,
Dicka And The Three Kittens, Whitman, 1941; Snipp,
Snapp, Snurr And The Big Farm, Whitman, 1946; Snipp,
Snapp, Snurr And The Reindeer, Whitman, 1957.
JBA-2

LINDQUIST, Jennie Dorothea 1899-
Editor, librarian, writer.   She was born in Manchester, New Hampshire and has made her home in Albany,
New York.   The author has been a children's librarian
in Manchester and Albany.   She has also served as
Consultant in Work with Children and Young People at
the University of New Hampshire Library.   Miss Lindquist has taught at the university and has served as
editor of Horn Book.   Her juvenile books include:
Golden Name Day, Harper, 1955; The Little Silver

House, Harper, 1959.

LINDQUIST, Willis 1908-
Attorney, photographer, writer. He was born in Win-
throp, Minnesota, attended the University of Minnesota
and George Washington University Law School (Washington, D. C.), and has made his home in New York.
Mr. Lindquist has worked with the U. S. Internal Revenue Service as a tax lawyer. An extensive traveler,
his photographs and articles have been published in the
National Geographic. During World War II, he served
in the Merchant Marine. During the winter the author
has enjoyed the study of arctic birds that migrate to
the area near Long Island. Juvenile books include:
Burma Boy, Junior Literary Guild and McGraw, 1953;
Call Of The White Fox (A Junior Literary Guild selection), McGraw, 1957. MJA

LINDSAY, Maud McKnight 1874-
Her father once served as the governor of Alabama.
Maud Lindsay has been the principal of the Florence
Free Kindergarten in Alabama. Her first book was
published in 1900. She also wrote for magazines. For
boys and girls she wrote Fun On Children's Street,
Lothrop, 1941.

LIONNI, Leo 1910-
Born in Holland, he came to the United States in 1939.
He has been head of the Design Department of the Parsons School of Design and has served as art director
on Fortune magazine. At one time Mr. Lionni also
served as President of the American Institute of Graphic Arts. His books for boys and girls include: Inch
By Inch, Obolensky, 1960; Little Blue And Little Yellow, Obolensky, 1959; On My Beach There Are Many
Pebbles, Obolensky, 1961; Swimmy, Pantheon Bks.,
1963; Tico And The Golden Wings, Pantheon Bks.,
1964.

LIPKIND, William 1904-
Author, poet, teacher, native New Yorker. After
graduating from New York's City College, he studied
for his doctorate at Columbia University. He served
in England with the Office of War Information during
World War II. After the war, Mr. Lipkind was associated with the American Military Government in Germany. Mr. Lipkind has taught anthropology at New

York University and writing at Hunter College. He
and Nicolas Mordvinoff formed the team "Will and Nicolas." He wrote, and Nicolas illustrated the 1952
Caldecott Medal award book Finders Keepers, Harcourt, 1951. William Lipkind also wrote: Boy Of The
Islands, Harcourt, 1954; Boy With A Harpoon, Harcourt, 1952; Days To Remember, An Almanac, Obolensky, 1961; Nubber Bear, Harcourt, 1966. MJA

LIPPINCOTT, Joseph Wharton 1887–
Publisher, naturalist, writer. Born in Philadelphia,
he graduated from the University of Pennsylvania's
Wharton School. He has served as chairman of the
board of the J. B. Lippincott Company. The author
has been interested in hunting, fishing, and exploring
and has contributed many articles on hunting to magazines. Juvenile titles include: Gray Squirrel (Rev.
ed.), Lippincott, 1954; Long Horn, Leader Of The
Deer, Lippincott, 1955; The Phantom Deer, Lippincott,
1954; The Red Roan Pony, Lippincott, 1951; Wahoo
Bobcat, Junior Literary Guild and Lippincott, 1950.
MJA

LISS, Howard
Born in Brooklyn, he has lived in New York City. He
served in the Army infantry and signal corps during
World War II. Howard Liss decided to write for children after he was requested to write an article for a
reference work. For boys and girls he wrote Heat,
Coward, 1965.

LISTON, Robert A. 1927–
Author, journalist, born in Ohio where he attended
Hiram College. Prior to residing in Westport, Con-
necticut, he lived in California, Iowa, and Texas.
Robert Liston edited an Army newspaper during the
Korean War. He has been on the staff of the Mans-
field, Ohio News-Journal, the Baltimore News-Ameri-
can, and the Marion, Ohio Star. He has contributed
to such magazines as Life, Saturday Evening Post, and
True. For boys and girls he wrote: Downtown: Our
Challenging Urban Problems, Delacorte, 1968; Your
Career In Law Enforcement, Messner, 1965. CA-19/
20

LITTEN, Frederic Nelson 1885–
Pilot and author. He has been interested in aviation

since his first solo flight in 1928. Many short stories
and several books have resulted from the author's own
flying experiences. Frederic Litten has flown with
pilots of the Marine Air Corps, the American Airlines,
and Colonel Cass Hough. For young people he wrote
. . . Rendezvous On Mindanao, Dodd, 1945.

LITTLE, Jean 1932-
Born on Formosa, the daughter of medical missionaries. Although Jean Little was blind when she was
born, she later gained partial vision. She graduated
from the University of Toronto in Canada. According
to Miss Little her preparation for becoming an author
was: ". . . The head librarian in our local children's
library (in Canada) told me recently that she was sure
that as a child I read literally every book on the
shelves. I read, I daydreamed, and so I prepared
myself for becoming a writer. " Her books for young
people include: Home From Far (A Junior Literary
Guild selection), Little, 1965; One To Grow On, Little,
1969.

LITTLE, Mary E.
Artist, author, librarian. Mary Little's first book
originated from her own experiences with puppets. The
illustrations which she made for the book were created
on rice paper. The author has been a children's librarian in New York City. For children she wrote and
illustrated Ricardo And The Puppets, Scribner, 1958.

LOBEL, Arnold Stark 1933-
Author-illustrator. He was born in Los Angeles, Cali-
fornia, grew up in Schenectady, New York, and has
lived in Brooklyn. After graduating from Pratt, he
began to illustrate children's stories and science books.
Arnold Lobel has also illustrated many of the "I Can
Read" series. Juvenile books which he wrote and illu-
strated include: The Bears Of The Air, Harper, 1965;
Giant John, Harper, 1964; The Great Blueness And
Other Predicaments, Harper, 1968; A Holiday For Mis-
ter Muster, Harper, 1963; Lucille, Harper, 1964;
Prince Bertram The Bad, Harper, 1963. CA-4

LOBSENZ, Amelia Freitag
She was born in Greensboro, North Carolina and grew
up in Atlanta, Georgia. She studied at Agnes Scott
College in Decatur, Georgia where she worked on the

school paper.   Her interest in ham radio led her to
receive a license in 1941 and the call letters, W20LB.
Mrs. Lobsenz has done public relations work for an
electronics firm and once taught the Morse code to
civil defense groups.   Her articles have appeared in
many magazines, and her husband has been managing
editor of Quick magazine.   She wrote Kay Everett Calls
CQ, Junior Literary Guild and Vanguard, 1951.   CA-
13/14

LOCKWOOD, Myna
Author-illustrator, born in Rome, Iowa.   She attended
the Chicago Art Institute before going abroad to study
in Italy and France.   Myna Lockwood has done portrait
painting in addition to writing as a profession.   Her
home has been on Long Island, New York.   For boys
and girls she wrote and illustrated: Free River, Dutton, 1942; Indian Chief, Oxford, 1943; Macaroni, An
American Tune, Oxford, 1939.

LOFTING, Hugh 1886-1947
He was born in Maidenhead, England and later came to
the United States where he attended the Massachusetts
Institute of Technology.   He completed his studies at
the London Polytechnic.   During World War I, he
served with the British Army in France and created
stories about animals in letters to his children.   These
stories later became books about the renowned character, Dr. Dolittle.   Mr. Lofting died at the age of six-
ty-one in Santa Monica, California.   He was the second
recipient of the Newbery Medal which was awarded in
1923 for The Voyages Of Doctor Dolittle, Lippincott,
1922.   Books in this series include: Doctor Dolittle
And The Green Canary, Lippincott, 1950; Doctor Dolittle In The Moon, Lippincott, 1928.   JBA-1, JBA-2

LOGSDON, Richard Henry 1912-   Lois Irene (Kupfer)
Librarians, husband-wife team.   He was born in Upper
Sandusky, Ohio, received his library science degree
from Western Reserve University, and his doctor's degree from the University of Chicago.   Irene Logsdon
was also born in Ohio (Scio), graduated from Western
Reserve University, and earned a master's degree in
library science from Rutgers University.   Dr. Logsdon
has been Director of Libraries and has taught library
science at Columbia University.   Mrs. Logsdon has
been a librarian in Demarest, New Jersey, at the

North Valley Regional High School. They have lived
in North Bergen County, New Jersey. Their book for
young people was called Library Careers, Walck, 1963.
CA-5/6

LOISY, Jeanne 1913-
French author, born in a village near Lyons. In addition to writing books, she has been both a teacher and
lecturer. Jeanne Loisy has received book awards including the 1956 Prix Jeunesse for the original French
edition of Don Tiburcio's Secret (tr. by James Kirkup),
Pantheon Bks., 1960. She also wrote Sierra Summer,
Follett, 1965.

LOMASK, Milton 1909-
He has written for both adults and children. In 1960
his adult book on the life of Andrew Johnson was pub-
lished, and this resulted in his writing a simpler ver-
sion for boys and girls entitled Andy Johnson: The
Tailor Who Became President (Ariel, 1962). Milton
Lomask has made his home in Washington, D. C.
Other juvenile titles include: John Quincy Adams,
Ariel, 1965; Old Destiny: Alexander Hamilton, Far-
rar, 1969. CA-3

LONDON, Jack 1876-1916
He was born in San Francisco, California. He wrote
novels and short stories and has been known as a
writer who believed in "the survival of the fittest. "
Mr. London has been a sailor, gold hunter in Alaska,
and war correspondent. His best-known novel was The
Call Of The Wild, Grosset, 1903. His other books include: The Star Rover, Macmillan, 1963; White Fang
And Other Stories, Dodd, 1963. JBA-1

LONERGAN, Joy 1909-
Pauline Joy MacLean Lonergan was born in Toronto,
Canada and came to the United States when she was
five-years-old. She studied at Syracuse and Denison
Universities. Mrs. Lonergan has been a teacher and
has worked in a bookstore. She married artist John
Lonergan and has lived in New York City. Juvenile
titles include: When My Father Was A Little Boy,
Watts, 1961; When My Mother Was A Little Girl,
Watts, 1961. CA-3

LONGFELLOW, Henry Wadsworth 1807-1882
This noted American poet was born on February 27 in
1807. At the age of eighteen he graduated from Bowdoin College where he later taught. Following his
teaching career at Bowdoin, he became Smith Professor
of Literature at Harvard University. His poem "The
Song Of Hiawatha" has been read and enjoyed by generations of young people. The meter in which it was
written was called trochaic tetrameter (Finnish epic
"Kalevala"). An unusual honor was bestowed upon
Longfellow when Great Britain placed his bust in the
Poet's Corner of Westminster Abbey (the only American
so honored). His juvenile books include: Paul Revere's
Ride (illustrated by Paul Galdone), Crowell, 1963; The
Skeleton In Armor (illustrated by Paul Kennedy), Pren-
tice, 1963.

LONGSTRETH, Joseph 1920-
Author, actor, critic, composer. Born in Indiana, he
has made his home in New York after living abroad for
sometime. He received his M. A. degree from Princeton, studied in London at the Royal Academy of Dramatic Art, and attended the St. Cecilia Conservatory in
Rome. Joseph Longstreth has been an Army Air Force
pilot. His books for young people include: Little Big
Feather, Abelard-Schuman, 1956; Penguins Are Penguins, Abelard-Schuman, 1955.

LONGSTRETH, Thomas Morris 1886-
He was born in Philadelphia and graduated from Haver-
ford College. He has been a teacher and was historian
of the Royal Canadian Mounted Police. His home has
been in Chester County, Pennsylvania. T. Morris
Longstreth has been interested in skiing and music.
His books for young people include: Bull Session, Mac-
millan, 1958; The Calgary Challengers, St. Martin's
Press, 1962; Camping Like Crazy, Macmillan, 1953;
Doorway In The Dark, Macmillan, 1956; Henry Thor-
eau: American Rebel, Dodd, 1963; The Scarlet Force,
Macmillan, 1953. CA-7/8, MJA

LONGSWORTH, Polly Ormsby
She grew up in New York in the town of Waterford.
She graduated from the Emma Willard School (Troy,
N. Y.) and Smith College (Northampton, Mass.). She
made her home in Amherst, Massachusetts, after her
husband became assistant to the president at Amherst

College. It was here that Mrs. Longsworth began her
biography of Emily Dickinson, Crowell, 1965. She also
wrote Exploring Caves, Crowell, 1959.

LOOMIS, J. Paul
Rancher and writer, born in Juneau, Alaska. He
studied at Kansas State College. Mr. Loomis has said
that he was born "under the sign of the Itching Foot"
because he has lived in so many places. These have
included the Mojave Desert, Canada, Siberia, and
California. The author has worked as a carpenter,
contractor, and boatbuilder. His main interests have
been horses and canoes. For young people he wrote
Salto, A Horse Of The Canadian Mounties, Dodd, Mead,
1950.

LOOMIS, Robert D.
Pilot, editor, author, born in Conneaut, Ohio. He
graduated from Duke University in Durham, North Carolina. Mr. Loomis was an Air Force cadet in World
War II and later flew Piper Tri-Pacers from New Jersey's Teterboro Airport. He has been an editor of a
large publishing house and has lived in New York City.
For young people he wrote: All About Aviation, Random, 1964; Great American Fighter Pilots Of World
War II, Random, 1961; Story Of The U. S. Air Force,
Random, 1959.   CA-19/20

LOPSHIRE, Robert Martin 1927-
Author and illustrator, born in Sarasota, Florida. He
attended the Vesper George School of Art and the
School of Practical Art in Boston, Massachusetts. He
has been an art director in New York and has also
operated his own advertising agency. Robert Lopshire
served in the U. S. Coast Guard and the Air Sea Rescue in World War II. He has made his home in Ser-
geantsville, New Jersey. His juvenile books include:
It's Magic, Macmillan, 1969; Put Me In The Zoo, Random, 1960.   CA-5/6

LORD, Bemen
Boys and girls in the third and fourth grades have enjoyed his books on sports. His book Our New Baby's
ABC (Walck, 1964) was inspired by his efforts to introduce his young son to a new baby sister. Bemen Lord
has lived in New York City. Other juvenile titles include: Look At Cars, Walck, 1962; Shot-Put Challenge,

Walck, 1969.

LORENZINI, Carlo 1826-1890
He has been known throughout the world as C. Collodi
who created the popular story of Pinocchio (Macmillan,
1926). He wrote Pinocchio at the age of fifty-four.
Collodi was the name of the town in Italy where his
mother was born, and he was born in the province of
Tuscany. He once was the editor of a newspaper and
served as a government official. After his retirement
he began to write for boys and girls. In the Attilio
Mussino illustrated edition, Carol Della Chiesa translated Pinocchio from the Italian.   JBA-1, JBA-2

LORING, Selden M.
Many of his relatives have been authors, and this inspired him to enter the writing field. He has written
magazine stories and plays. Mr. Loring has worked
in Boston, Massachusetts as Art Director for an advertising firm. For young people he wrote Mighty Magic, Holiday, 1964.

LOVEJOY, Bahija Fattouhi 1914-
Correspondent, teacher, writer, born in Iraq. She attended the American University in Beirut (Lebanon),
Radcliffe College in Cambridge, Massachusetts, and
Fouad University's Graduate School of Journalism. At
the UNESCO Conference in Beirut, Mrs. Lovejoy worked for the Baghdad Times as a correspondent. She
also was a teacher in the government schools of Iraq
before she arrived in the United States. The author
has continued her teaching career in this country and
has made her home in Somerset County, New Jersey.
She wrote The Land And People Of Iraq, Lippincott,
1964.   CA-5/6

LOVELACE, Delos Wheeler 1894-1967
Newspaperman and author, born in Brainerd, Minnesota.
He received his education at the University of Minnesota in Minneapolis and took further studies at Cambridge University in England and Columbia University.
After World War I, Delos Lovelace became a newspaperman with the Fargo Courier-News. He later worked
on the Minneapolis Tribune and the New York Daily
News. The author and his wife, writer Maud Hart
Lovelace, made their home on Long Island, New York
and in California. His books for young people include:

"Ike" Eisenhower, Crowell, 1952; That Dodger Horse, Crowell, 1956.   CA-7/8

LOVELACE, Maud Hart 1892-
She was born in Mankato, Minnesota and attended the University of Minnesota. She married Delos Lovelace, an officer in a machine gun battalion during the first World War. After the war her husband served on the staff of a large newspaper, and the Lovelaces lived in Garden City, Long Island. They later made their home in Claremont, California. Her books for young people include: Betsy And Joe, Crowell, 1948; Betsy And Tacy Go Over The Big Hill, Crowell, 1942; Betsy And The Great World, Crowell, 1952; Betsy-Tacy, Crowell, 1941; The Valentine Box, Crowell, 1966.   CA-7/8, JBA-2

LOW, Elizabeth Hammond 1898-
Prior to writing her first picture book, Elizabeth Low wrote several books for teen-agers (Hold Fast The Dream, Harcourt, 1955). Her summer house in Vermont (closed during the winter) provided the ideas for her children's book Mouse, Mouse, Go Out Of My House, Little, 1958.   CA-19/20

LOW, Joseph 1911-
Author-illustrator, born in Coraopolis, Pennsylvania. He attended the University of Illinois and the Art Students League in New York. Mr. Low has taught at Indiana University in Bloomington, operated Eden Hill (the name of his home) Press in Newton, Connecticut, and created drawings for magazines. Much of his work has been exhibited throughout the United States, South America, London, and Zurich. Juvenile books which he wrote and illustrated include: Adam's Book Of Odd Creatures, Atheneum, 1962; Smiling Duke, Houghton, 1963.

LOWREY, Janette (Sebring) 1892-
She was born in Orange, Texas and graduated from the University of Texas at Austin. Following graduation, she taught school and was also associated in the advertising profession. She later lived in San Antonio where her late husband practiced law. Margaret (Junior Literary Guild and Harper, 1950) was her first novel for older girls. She also wrote: Annunciata And The Shepherds, Harper, 1938; Lavender Cat, Harper, 1944;

Love, Bid Me Welcome, Harper, 1964.   CA-13/14

LUBELL, Cecil 1912-   Winifred (Milius) 1914-
Husband-wife team.   Born in Leeds, England, he graduated from Harvard and has done publicity and editorial
work.   He married author-illustrator Winifred A. Milius, and they have lived in Croton-on-Hudson, New
York.   Mrs. Lubell was born in New York City and
attended the Art Students League.   She has illustrated
numerous books for children and has been a teacher of
art.   Together the Lubbels wrote: In A Running Brook,
Rand McNally, 1968; Rosalie, Rand McNally, 1962;
Tall Grass Zoo, Rand McNally, 1960; Up A Tree (A
Junior Literary Guild selection), Rand McNally, 1961.
CA-9/10

LUM, Peter 1911-
Peter Lum (a woman) was born in the United States.
As a young girl she traveled in the Far East with her
mother who was an artist.   Her mother was interested
in Japanese and Chinese wood block prints.   Peter
Lum has also been interested in the art and culture of
China.   She wrote Great Day In China: The Holiday
Moon, Abelard-Schuman, 1964.   CA-9/10

LUMN, Peter
He has been a professor at Oregon State College in
Corvallis.   Mr. and Mrs. Lumn's two children were
born in Greenwich Village; however, "all the Lumns
prefer the wide open spaces of Oregon to life in a big
city." When another teacher, Faith Norris, at Oregon
State asked his help in writing a story for young people
about Korea, the result was Kim Of Korea (A Junior
Literary Guild selection), Messner, 1955.

LYMAN, Susan E.
Author and lecturer.   She has worked in New York in
the Educational Department of the City Museum.   An
authority on the history of New York, Susan Lyman has
written books about it and has given many lectures.
She has also written a textbook for children on the history of New York City.   She collaborated with Suzanne
Szasz to write Young Folks' New York, Crown [and]
Lothrop, 1960.

LYNN, Patricia see WATTS, Mabel Pizzey

LYON, Jessica see DE LEEUW, Cateau

M

MacAGY, Douglas
>   Author and teacher. He attended the University of
>   Toronto in Ontario, Canada and did further study in
>   England and the United States. At one time he acted
>   as Curator of the San Francisco Museum of Art and
>   Director of the California School of Fine Arts. He
>   served with the Propaganda Analysis Division of the
>   Far East Bureau of the OWI during World War II.
>   Since the war, Mr. MacAgy has been associated with
>   the Wildenstein Galleries as Director of Research. He
>   has also been on the staff of the Gazette des Beaux-
>   Arts and an art consultant. With Elizabeth MacAgy he
>   wrote Going For A Walk With A Line, Doubleday, 1959.

McALLISTER, Mariana Kennedy
>   Professor and writer, born in Cincinnati, Ohio. After
>   graduating from Butler University at Indianapolis, Indi-
>   ana, she obtained her B. S. degree in Library Science
>   from Columbia University. She was the editor of A
>   Basic Book Collection For High Schools published by
>   the American Association of School Libraries. Mrs.
>   McAllister has held several distinguished positions
>   which have included: acting Executive Secretary of the
>   American Association of State Teacher's College in New
>   Jersey and professor at the Universities of Texas and
>   British Columbia. With Geneva R. Hanna she wrote
>   Books, Young People, And Reading Guidance, Harper,
>   1960.

McBAIN, Ed see HUNTER, Evan

MacBEAN, Dilla Whittemore 1895-
>   Educator, librarian, born in Sioux City, Iowa. She
>   graduated from Northwestern University, received her
>   library degree from the Carnegie Institute of Technol-
>   ogy, and her master's degree from Chicago Teachers
>   College. She has served as director of the Chicago
>   Public School Libraries. With Ruth Harshaw she con-
>   ducted a weekly radio program entitled "The Battle of
>   Books." Dilla MacBean later made her home in Fort
>   Lauderdale, Florida. With Ruth H. Harshaw she wrote
>   What Book Is That?, Macmillan, 1948.   CA-5/6

McCAHILL, William P.
He studied at Marquette University's College of Jour-
nalism and later was a night editor in the Associated
Press Bureau at Milwaukee. He enlisted in the Marine
Corps in February 1941, became a public relations
officer in Washington, and was later stationed in San
Diego. For young people Captain McCahill wrote First
To Fight, McKay, 1943.

McCLINTOCK, Marshall 1906-1967
Author, editor, discoverer of the "Dr. Seuss" books.
Besides writing books, Mike McClintock has edited and
sold them. His books have varied from adventure to
science, and he has written several of the "Beginner
Books." A Fly Went By (Random, 1958) has been one
of his most popular books for young people. Other
juvenile titles include: Here Is A Book, Vanguard,
1939; Leaf, Fruit And Flower, Chanticleer Press, 1948;
Millions Of Books, Vanguard, 1941; Stop That Ball!,
Random, 1959; Story Of New England, Harper, 1941;
What Have I Got?, Harper, 1961.

McCLINTOCK, Theodore 1902-
He has enjoyed such hobbies as hiking, animals, and
bird watching. His nature articles have been published
in magazines, and he once created a special page about
science in World Youth magazine. For boys and girls
he wrote Animal Close-Ups (A Junior Literary Guild
selection), Abelard, 1958.

McCLOSKEY, Robert 1914-
He was born in Hamilton, Ohio and studied art in Boston and at the National Academy of Design in New York.
In 1964 he received an honorary degree of Doctor of
Literature from Miami University in Oxford, Ohio.
After serving in the Army during World War II, he
studied art in Rome. He married the daughter of au-
thor Ruth Sawyer (Margaret Durand), and they have
lived in Croton Falls, New York. Summers have been
spent on their own island off the coast of Maine. He
was awarded the Caldecott Medal twice: in 1942 for
Make Way For Ducklings, Viking, 1941 and in 1958 for
Time Of Wonder, Viking, 1957. Other titles include:
Blueberries For Sal, Viking, 1948; Burt Dow, Deep-
Water Man, Viking, 1963. CA-11/12, JBA-2

McCLUNG, Robert Marshall 1916-
Author-illustrator, born in Butler, Pennsylvania. He
graduated from Princeton, received his master's de-
gree from Cornell, and did further study at New York
University. At one time the McClung family lived in
Chevy Chase, Maryland but later made their home in
Amherst, Massachusetts. The author served in the
Navy during World War II. Mr. McClung worked in
advertising prior to his association with the Bronx
Zoo where he became Curator of Mammals and Birds.
Many years of study provided authenticity for his ani-
mal stories for children. These include: Black Jack,
Morrow, 1967; Bufo, Morrow, 1954; Caterpillars And
How They Live, Morrow, 1965; Ladybug, Morrow,
1966; Little Burma, Morrow, 1958; Possum, Morrow,
1963. CA-13/14, MJA

McCOLVIN, Lionel Roy 1896-
Librarian and author. He has been city librarian of
Westminster (England) and Past President of the Lib-
rary Association. Lionel McColvin has also been Vice-
President of the International Federation of Library
Associations. He wrote several books on libraries in-
cluding those of Australia and Great Britain. He also
wrote Libraries For Children, Phoenix House, 1961.

McCORMICK, Alma Heflin
Pilot, writer, born in Winona, Missouri. She graduated from Eastern Washington State College in Cheney
and studied aviation in Dallas, Texas. As a commercial pilot, she has flown not only throughout the United
States but also to Canada, Alaska, and Mexico. She
married Archie Thomas Edward McCormick. For
young people she wrote Merry Makes A Choice, Little,
1949.

McCORMICK, Wilfred 1903-
Author and lecturer, born in Newland, Indiana. After
graduating from the University of Illinois, he did further study at Washington and Lee University in Lexington, Virginia. He built his own home in Albuquerque,
New Mexico where he has enjoyed such hobbies as
campfire cooking and magic. Mr. McCormick has been
a lieutenant colonel in the Army. He later became a
Fellow in the International Institute of Letters, Arts
and Sciences and has taught creative writing at the University of New Mexico. His juvenile books include:

The Automatic Strike, McKay, 1960; Bases Loaded,
Putnam, 1950; First And Ten, Putnam, 1952; The Go-
Ahead Runner, McKay, 1965; One Bounce Too Many,
Bobbs-Merrill, 1967; Tall At The Plate, Bobbs-Mer-
rill, 1966.   CA-2

McCOY, Joseph Jerome 1917-
He graduated from the College of Agriculture at Pennsylvania State University. The author has been interested in the conservation of our country's natural resources and in the study of nature. His study of the
whooping crane began during World War II when he was
serving with the Army in Texas. Mr. McCoy has written many articles on animals, science, and conservation. For young people he wrote: The Hunt For The
Whooping Cranes, Lothrop, 1966; The World Of The
Veterinarian, Lothrop, 1964.   CA-13/14

McCRACKEN, Harold 1894-
He was born in Colorado Springs and grew up on a
ranch in Idaho. He studied at Drake University in
Des Moines, Iowa and later attended Ohio State University. Mr. McCracken has made airplane stunt films,
collected big game specimens, and conducted an Arctic
expedition for the American Museum of Natural History.
His books for young people include: Biggest Bear On
Earth, Stokes, 1943; Caribou Traveler, Lippincott,
1949; Flaming Bear, Lippincott, 1951; Great White Buffalo, Lippincott, 1946; Toughy, Lippincott, 1948; Winning Of The West, Garden City Books, 1955.   JBA-2

McCUE, Lillian Bueno see DE LA TORRE, Lillian

MacDONALD, Anson see HEINLEIN, Robert Anson

McDONALD, Barbara Guthrie
She was born in Brooklyn and studied at Hofstra University (Long Island, N. Y.). She once worked in a
public library and later operated a bookstore "McDonald's Book Ends. " The author has also worked with
young people in the Girl Scouts. She wrote Cooking
Fun, Walck, 1960.

MacDONALD, Betty (Bard) 1908-
Born in Boulder, Colorado, she grew up in Idaho, Montana, and Washington. She studied art at the University of Washington in Seattle. After her marriage,

Mrs. MacDonald lived on a chicken ranch on the Olympic Peninsula in Washington, and her experiences on the ranch provided the material for her best-seller The Egg And I (Lippincott, 1945). The author later returned to Seattle and worked in photography, modeling, and publicity. Her books for young people include: Hello, Mrs. Piggle-Wiggle, Lippincott, 1957; Mrs. Piggle-Wiggle, Lippincott, 1947; Mrs. Piggle-Wiggle's Farm, Lippincott, 1954; Nancy And Plum, Lippincott, 1952.

MacDONALD, George 1824-1905
He was born in Huntly, Scotland and attended King's College in Aberdeen. After receiving his degree, he became a tutor in London. Later he studied at London's Highbury College and became a Congregational minister. His fairy tales for boys and girls were published when Mr. MacDonald was thirty-four. He and his wife (Louisa Powell) were buried at Bordighera, Italy. Juvenile titles include: At The Back Of The North Wind, Macmillan, 1924; The Light Princess, Macmillan, 1926; The Princess And Curdie, Macmillan, 1927. JBA-1

MacDONALD, Golden see BROWN, Margaret Wise

McDONALD, Lucile (Saunders) 1898-
Author and reporter, born in Portland, Oregon. She received her education at Oregon, Washington, and Columbia Universities. She married H. D. McDonald and has lived in Washington where she has been a feature writer with the Seattle Times. Mrs. McDonald has also been on the staff of the Oregonian and the New York World. With Zola Helen Ross she wrote: Assignment In Ankara (A Junior Literary Guild selection), Nelson, 1959; Friday's Child (A Junior Literary Guild selection), Nelson, 1954; Pigtail Pioneer, Winston, 1956; Wing Harbor (A Junior Literary Guild selection), Nelson, 1957. Lucile McDonald also wrote: . . . Jewels And Gems, Crowell, 1940; Sheker's Lucky Piece, Oxford, 1941. CA-3

MacDONALD, Zillah Katherine 1885-
She was born in Halifax, Nova Scotia and studied at Dalhousie University. She later taught in the School of Business at Columbia University. In addition to writing plays, her stories and articles have appeared in many children's magazines including: Story Parade, Jack And

Jill, and Child Life.   She has lived in New York City
and has spent summers on Swan's Island off the coast
of Maine.   Juvenile titles include: Flower Of The For-
tress, Westminster Press, 1944; Rosemary Wins Her
Cap, Messner, 1955.   CA-9/10

McFADDEN, Dorothy Loa (Mausolff) 1902-
    She has worked closely with young people both as a
    writer and producer of television programs.   Dorothy
    McFadden instigated Junior Programs, Inc.   This com-
    pany toured the United States, and its shows were seen
    by many children.   She has traveled throughout Europe
    and once lived in Puerto Rico and Germany.   With
    Marjorie R. Carnahan she wrote Which Way, Judy?,
    Dodd, 1958.   CA-19/20

MACFARLAN, Allan A.
    Canadian author who has been an international camp
    director for both adults and children.   He acquired au-
    thentic material for his books after camping and living
    with the Indians of America and Canada as a Fellow of
    the Royal Geographical Society.   The author has intro-
    duced many Indian ceremonies to the programs of the
    Boy Scouts of America.   His books for young people
    include: Book Of American Indian Games, Association
    Press, 1958; Indian Adventure Trails, Dodd, 1953.

McFARLAND, Wilma
    Editor, author, born in Iowa.   She studied at Simpson
    College, Drake and Columbia Universities.   At the age
    of eight she achieved the distinction of having her first
    story published in a newspaper.   Many of her stories
    have appeared in magazines, and she has served as an
    editor on the staff of Child Life magazine.   She has
    also edited books for young people including For A
    Child, Junior Literary Guild and Westminster, 1947.

McGAVRAN, Grace Winifred
    Born in India, the daughter of missionaries, she has
    written stories, poems, and devotional materials for
    young people.   She graduated from Butler University
    and received her master's degree from Boston Univer-
    sity.   For young people she wrote: All Through The
    Year, Bethany Press, 1958; Ricardo's Search, Friend-
    ship Press, 1956; Stories Of The Book Of Books (rev.
    ed.), Friendship Press, 1960; They Live In Bible
    Lands, Friendship Press, 1950.

McGEE, Dorothy Horton
    Born at West Point, New York, she has spent most of
her life on Long Island. Her father was a West Point
graduate and later became a professor of law at the
Academy. The author attended schools in New York
and South Carolina. Her favorite sport has been sailing, and she has won recognition as a racing skipper.
For young people she wrote: Famous Signers Of The
Declaration, Dodd, 1955; Herbert Hoover, Engineer,
Humanitarian, Statesman, Dodd, 1959.

McGINLEY, Phyllis Louise 1905-
    This poet and author was born in Ontario, Oregon and
graduated from the University of Utah. After teaching
in New Rochelle, she lived in New York City where
she became a free lance writer. Her work has often
appeared in the New Yorker magazine. She married
Charles Hayden and has lived in Larchmont, New York.
In 1961 she was awarded the Pulitzer Prize for Poetry
for her collection entitled Times Three, Viking, 1960.
Her books for boys and girls include: All Around The
Town, Lippincott, 1948; Blunderbus, Lippincott, 1951;
Horse Who Had His Picture In The Paper, Lippincott,
1951; Plain Princess, Lippincott, 1945. CA-11/12,
JBA-2

McGOVERN, Ann
    Editor and writer. Mrs. McGovern has lived in New
York City and has written for both adults and children.
She has worked in a publishing firm as an editor and
production assistant. The author has also been asso-
ciated with Scholastic Magazines as Assistant Editor of
the Arrow Book Club. For boys and girls she wrote:
If You Lived In Colonial Times, Four Winds, 1966;
Little Wolf, Abelard, 1965; Too Much Noise, Houghton,
1967; Why It's A Holiday, Random, 1960; Zoo, Where
Are You?, Harper, 1964.

McGRAW, Eloise Jarvis 1915-
    Painter, author, born in Houston, Texas. She grad-
uated from Principia College in Elsah, Illinois and
studied sculpture and painting at Colorado and Oklahoma
Universities. The author has taught painting at Oklahoma City University and has also worked with marionettes. She married William Corbin McGraw and has
lived in Oregon. Her first book for young people was
Sawdust In His Shoes, Junior Literary Guild and Co-

ward-McCann, 1950.   She also wrote: Crown Fire,
Coward-McCann, 1951; Greensleeves, Harcourt, 1968;
Mocassin Trail, Junior Literary Guild and Coward-Mc-
Cann, 1952.   CA-7/8, MJA

McGRAW, William Corbin 1916-
    He writes under the name of William Corbin.   Born in
    Des Moines, Iowa, he graduated from Drake University.
    After graduate study at Harvard University, Mr. Corbin
    worked on newspapers in Ohio, Oklahoma, and Califor-
    nia.   His wife also has written books for young people
    (Eloise Jarvis McGraw).   They have lived on a ranch
    near Portland, Oregon.   His book High Road Home
    (Coward, 1954) received the Child Study Association
    Award and the medal from the Boys' Clubs of America.
    He also wrote Golden Mare (A Junior Literary Guild
    selection), Coward, 1955.   MJA

MacGREGOR, Ellen 1906-1954
    Librarian and writer, born in Baltimore, Maryland.
    She graduated from the University of Washington and
    did further study at the University of California at
    Berkeley.   Before her death in 1954, Miss MacGregor
    had lived in Chicago where she was a research librar-
    ian with a large implement company.   At one time she
    was a supervisor of school libraries in Hawaii.   Ellen
    MacGregor belonged to the Chicago Children's Reading
    Round Table and the Illinois Women's Press Associa-
    tion.   Her books for boys and girls include: Miss
    Pickerell Goes To The Arctic (A Junior Literary Guild
    selection), McGraw, 1954; Miss Pickerell Goes Under-
    seas, McGraw, 1953; Mr. Ferguson Of The Fire De-
    partment, McGraw, 1956; Theodore Turtle (A Junior
    Literary Guild selection), McGraw, 1955.   MJA

MacGREGOR-HASTIE, Roy 1929-
    Journalist, writer.   He has often visited Italy and once
    received the following citation: "for selfless dedication
    and extraordinary devotion as a volunteer in humanitar-
    ian service during 1961 and 1962 among the peasants
    of the depressed rural areas in NW Italy. "   In addition
    to books for adults, Mr. MacGregor-Hastie has also
    written documentary films.   For young people he wrote
    Africa, Criterion, 1968; Pope John XXIII, Criterion,
    1962.   CA-4

McGUIRE, Edna (Boyd) 1899–
   Author, lecturer, teacher, born in Sweet Springs, Missouri. She married publisher (now retired) John B.
   Boyd, and they have lived in Greencastle, Indiana. She
   received degrees from Central Missouri State College
   and the University of Missouri. The author did graduate study at the Universities of Missouri and Chicago.
   A noted writer of history books for boys and girls,
   she acquired a background for her books from her travels to foreign countries, Puerto Rico, and throughout
   the United States. Several of her books have been
   used in our country's elementary and junior high
   schools. Her juvenile books include: The Peace
   Corps, Macmillan, 1966; Puerto Rico, Bridge To Freedom, Macmillan, 1963. CA-7/8

McGUIRE, Frances
   Radio and television commentator, author, born in
   Crawfordsville, Indiana. She studied at Ferry Hall in
   Lake Forest, Illinois and received her degree from the
   University of Chicago. Frances McGuire has been Di-
   rector of Women's Activities at radio stations WIP and
   WPEN in Philadelphia. She later worked in television.
   Juvenile titles include: Arizona Hide-Out, Dutton, 1953;
   The Case Of The Smuggled Ruby, Dutton, 1956. CA-
   9/10

McILVAINE, Jane (Stevenson) 1919–
   Columnist, editor, author. She was born in Pittsburgh,
   Pennsylvania, graduated from Miss Porter's School in
   Farmington, Connecticut, and has lived in Middleburg,
   Virginia. The author has been on the staff of the Washington Times-Herald and Fortune Magazine. She has
   also been associated with the International News Service, lectured abroad, and visited Russia. She was
   the recipient of the 1949 Pennsylvania Women's Press
   Association Award. Her books for young people include: Cintra's Challenge, Macrae Smith, 1955; Copper's Chance, Junior Literary Guild and Macrae Smith,
   1951; Stardust For Jennifer, Macrae Smith, 1956.
   CA-2

MacKELLAR, William
   Born in Glasgow, Scotland, he came to America when
   he was eleven-years-old. During World War II, he had
   the opportunity to visit Scotland again, and this country
   provided the background for several of his books. He

has also contributed stories to magazines. Mr. and
Mrs. MacKellar have lived in Syosset, Long Island.
Juvenile titles include: A Dog Like No Other (A Junior
Literary Guild selection), McKay, 1965; Ghost In The
Castle, McKay, 1960; Two For The Fair, McGraw,
1958; Wee Joseph, McGraw, 1957; The Team That
Wouldn't Quit, McGraw, 1956.

McKELVEY, Gertrude Della
Author, teacher. She married a minister and has lived
in Jerusalem and Palestine. Mrs. McKelvey has been
interested in working with children and has taught
Christian Education for many years. Her Biblical
stories have been used in both home and church libraries. Juvenile titles include: Gertrude D. McKelvey's
Stories To Grow On, Winston, 1947; Stories To Live
By, Winston, 1943.

McKENNY, Margaret
She was born in Olympia, Washington. A lifelong interest in nature provided the author with the incentive
to write books on the subject. High school botony
courses led her to further study on birds, trees, mush-
rooms, and flowers. In addition to writing about trees,
the author has also photographed many of them throughout the country. She wrote Trees Of The Countryside,
Knopf, 1942 and with E. F. Johnston she wrote Book
Of Wayside Fruits, Macmillan, 1945.

MACKENZIE, Jeanette Brown
She has lived in Plymouth, Massachusetts where she
has collected a great deal of material for her books.
The author's stories have appeared in magazines for
children. For boys and girls Mrs. Mackenzie wrote:
Mystery At The Pilgrim Dig, Washburn, 1969; The
Puss In The Corner Mystery, Washburn, 1964.

McKINNEY, Roland Joseph 1898-
Art consultant and writer, born at Niagara Falls, New
York. He attended Niagara University, the Chicago
Art Institute, and studied abroad. At one time Roland
McKinney served as director of the Baltimore and Los
Angeles County Museums of Art. He has also acted
as Consultant to the Metropolitan Museum of Art in
New York City. In 1938 he was in charge of the se-
lection of American paintings to be shown at the first
Golden Gate International Exposition in San Francisco.

For young people he wrote: <u>Famous French Painters,</u>
Dodd, 1960; <u>Famous Old Masters Of Painting,</u> Dodd,
1951.

McKOWN, Robin
  She was born in Denver, Colorado and spent the summers of her childhood visiting grandparents in a ghost
  mining town called Ward. She studied at the University
  of Colorado, Northwestern University, and the University of Illinois where she won a drama prize. Following her marriage, she lived in New York and worked
  in publicity, wrote radio scripts, and a newspaper
  column on books and authors. Her book <u>Janine</u> (A
  Junior Literary Guild selection), Messner, 1960 received the 1961 Child Study Association Award. Juvenile titles include: <u>The Fabulous Isotopes,</u> Holiday,
  1962; <u>Giant Of The Atom: Ernest Rutherford,</u> Messner,
  1962; <u>Heroic Nurses</u> (A Junior Literary Guild selection),
  Putnam, 1966. CA-3

MacLEOD, Beatrice (Beach) 1910-
  Born in Brentwood, New York, she graduated from
  Pennsylvania's Swarthmore College and Yale Drama
  School. She has been an executive secretary of an
  educational fund, theater director, and college instructor. Beatrice MacLeod has lived in Ithaca, New York
  where her husband has been Sage Professor of Psychology at Cornell University. For young people she wrote
  <u>On Small Wings,</u> Westminster Press, 1961. CA-19/20

MacMANUS, Seumas 1869-1960
  He has been called the "dean of Irish storytellers."
  The author was born in County Donegal and grew up on
  a farm. After working on the farm during the day, he
  spent his evenings listening to ". . . the old men gathered around the fireplace telling ancient Irish fairy
  tales and folk tales." As a boy, Seumas MacManus
  could tell almost one-hundred of these Irish tales. He
  often visited America where he sold many of his stories
  to magazines and lectured at colleges and universities.
  He wrote <u>Hibernian Nights,</u> Macmillan, 1963. JBA-1

McMEEKIN, Clark see McMEEKIN, Isabel McLennan

McMEEKIN, Isabel McLennan 1895-
  She was born in Louisville, Kentucky and attended the
  University of Chicago. She married newspaperman Sam

McMeekin and has lived in Kentucky. Mrs. McMeekin
received the Julia Ellsworth Ford Award for her book
Journey Cake (Messner, 1942). At one time she taught
juvenile writing in a summer writers' conference at
Indiana University. She has written books with Dorothy
Park Clark under the pseudonym of Clark McMeekin
and has also written: Juba's New Moon, Messner,
1944; Kentucky Derby Winner, Junior Literary Guild
and McKay, 1949; Robert E. Lee, Knight Of The South,
Dodd, Mead, 1950. CA-5/6, MJA

McMILLEN, Wheeler
    Farmer, editor, reporter, author. Born on a farm in
    Ohio, he attended Ohio Northern University at Ada.
    He bought his own newspaper and managed the family
    farm before locating in the East. He served as editor
    of Country Home prior to editing the Farm Journal in
    Philadelphia. Mr. McMillen has been executive direc-
    tor of former President Eisenhower's Commission on
    Increased Industrial Use of Agricultural Products, trus-
    tee of Rutgers University and the Farm Foundation, and
    director of the Audubon Society. He has also served
    as vice-president of the Boy Scouts of America. For
    boys and girls he wrote: Fifty Useful Americans, Put-
    nam, 1965; Land Of Plenty, Holt, 1961.

McNALLY, E. Evalyn Grumbine see GRUMBINE, E. Evalyn

McNAMEE, James 1904-
    Born in Washington, he grew up in British Columbia.
    Mr. McNamee has been both a rancher and a member
    of the British Columbia Forest Service. He has also
    served in the Canadian Army. The author has written
    both novels and short stories. His book for young
    people was My Uncle Joe, Viking, 1963. CA-7/8

McNEER, May Yonge 1902-
    She was born in Tampa, Florida. Following high
    school May McNeer worked on a Tampa newspaper and
    later studied at the University of Georgia and at Colum-
    bia University's School of Journalism. When she mar-
    ried artist Lynd Ward, she accompanied him to Europe
    where he studied at the National Academy for Graphic
    Arts in Leipzig, Germany. They have lived in Cress-
    kill, New Jersey. With Lynd Ward she wrote: John
    Wesley, Abingdon, 1951; Little Baptiste, Houghton,

1954; <u>Martin Luther,</u> Abingdon, 1953; <u>My Friend Mac,</u> Houghton, 1960.   CA-7/8, JBA-1, JBA-2

McPHEDRAN, Marie (Green) 1904–
Born in Canada, she attended the University of Toronto.
She married Dr. Harris McPhedran who has been a
Professor of Medicine at the University of Toronto.
Her many trips on the Great Lakes aboard freighters
provided authentic material for her book <u>Cargoes On</u>
<u>The Great Lakes,</u> Bobbs, 1952.   Other juvenile titles
include: <u>David And The White Cat,</u> Aladdin, 1950;
<u>Golden North,</u> Macmillan, 1949.

MacPHERSON, Margaret L.
She was born in Scotland and later lived in New Zealand where she became a newspaper editor.   She has
also written articles for papers in Australia and lectured on the Antipodes.   A great deal of her time has
been spent on the eastern coast of the United States.
She wrote <u>New Zealand Beckons,</u> Dodd, 1952.

MacPHERSON, Thomas George 1915–
He has written for newspapers and has also worked on
publicity for his community's library.   Mr. MacPherson
at one time was executive editor of <u>Boys' Life</u> magazine.   He has also been a radio columnist.   One of the
books which he wrote for young people was called
<u>Great Racing Drivers,</u> Putnam, 1962.   CA-4

McSWIGAN, Marie 1907–1962
Reporter, author, born in Pittsburgh.   She graduated
from the University of Pittsburgh and did further study
at Columbia.   At one time she was a reporter for the
Pittsburgh <u>Press</u> and the Pittsburgh <u>Sun-Telegraph.</u>
Marie McSwigan has worked in public relations and
traveled extensively.   Her books for young people include: <u>All Aboard For Freedom!</u> (A Junior Literary
Guild selection), Dutton, 1954; <u>Five On A Merry-Go-</u>
<u>Round,</u> Dutton, 1943; <u>The News Is Good,</u> Dutton, 1952;
<u>Small Miracle At Lourdes,</u> Dutton, 1958; <u>Snow Trea-</u>
<u>sure,</u> Dutton, 1942.   MJA

MACE, Katherine (Keeler) 1921–
She was born in New York City and graduated from
Swarthmore College in Pennsylvania.   Her mother
Katherine Keeler was also an author of books for chil-
dren.   She married cartoonist Harry Mace and has

lived in Connecticut. She wrote, and her husband il-
lustrated: Chief Dooley's Busy Day (A Junior Literary
Guild selection), Abelard, 1954; Mr. Wiggington Joins
The Circus, Abelard Press, 1952. She wrote: Let's
Dance A Story, Abelard-Schuman, 1955; A Tail Is A
Tail, Abelard-Schuman, 1957.

MACE, Wynn
Athlete, author, Princeton graduate. He has been the
Southern California Tennis Champion four times and
with George Meyers Church won the 1912 Intercollegiate
Doubles Championship. He turned professional in
1922. Wynn Mace has been a tennis instructor at the
Annandale Golf Club in Pasadena, California and the
Los Angeles Tennis Club in Hollywood. His teaching
experiences provided the material for his book Tennis
Techniques Illustrated, Barnes, 1952.

MADIAN, Jon
A doctoral fellow in educational psychology at the University of California at Los Angeles, he has lived in
Santa Monica, California. His first book for young
people was Beautiful Junk, Little, 1968.

MALCOLMSON, Anne (Burnett) 1910-
Teacher and writer. She was born in St. Louis, Mis-
souri and graduated from Bryn Mawr College in Penn-
sylvania. She taught school in Chicago, Illinois, New
Haven, Connecticut, McLean, Virginia, and Washington,
D. C. She has also worked for a literary agency in
Washington, D. C. Her book Yankee Dooodle's Cou-
sins (Houghton, 1941) resulted from the tall tales which
she compiled for her fifth grade class in Chicago.
Other juvenile titles include: . . . Miracle Plays
(adapted by Anne Malcolmson), Houghton, 1959; Taste
Of Chaucer (chosen and edited by Anne Malcolmson),
Harcourt, 1964. MJA

MALKUS, Alida Sims 1895-
Author-illustrator Alida Wright was born in New York
and grew up in Michigan. During World War I, she
worked in the censor's office in Puerto Rico. Later
she became a reporter on a newspaper in Albuquerque,
New Mexico where she met her husband Hubert Malkus.
She has traveled extensively in Mexico and the Yucatan
and has been particularly interested in studying Mayan
ruins. She wrote: The Beloved Island (A Junior Liter-

ary Guild selection), Chilton Co., 1967; The Story Of
Jacqueline Kennedy, Grosset & Dunlap, 1967. She
wrote and illustrated: Along The Inca Highway, Heath,
1941; Constancia Lona, Junior Literary Guild and
Doubleday, 1947; The Sea And Its Rivers (A Junior Literary Guild selection), Doubleday, 1956.   CA-5/6,
JBA-1, JBA-2

MALONE, Mary
Librarian and author, born in Lambertville, New Jer-
sey. She graduated from Trenton State Teachers Col-
lege and Columbia University, and did further study at
Rutgers. She has made her home in Trenton, New
Jersey. Mary Malone has worked in both public and
school libraries. She has also reviewed books for the
Library Journal. Her first children's book was This
Was Bridget (Dodd, 1960), which won first place in the
Dodd, Mead Librarian Competition in 1959. Other juve-
nile titles include: Deenie's Coat, Dodd, 1963; Doro-
thea Dix, Garrard, 1968; Here's Howie, Dodd, 1962;
Three Wishes For Sarah, Dodd, 1961; Young Miss
Josie Delaney, Detective, Dodd, 1966.   CA-1

MALONEY, Pat see MARKUN, Patricia (Maloney)

MALOT, Hector Henri 1830-1907
He was born in the province of Normandy, France.
Although he studied law, in 1859 he gave up law for a
writing career. He once was a literary critic on
L'Opinion Nationale and a news correspondent in Lon-
don. He had an autobiography published before his
death, and two of his novels received recognition from
L'Académie Française. He died in Vincennes, France
at the age of seventy-seven. He wrote: Nobody's Boy
(tr. by Florence Crewe Jones), Platt & Munk, 1962;
Nobody's Girl (tr. by Florence Crewe Jones), Platt &
Munk, 1962.

MALVERN, Gladys
Author, actress, her early years were spent in New
Jersey. She later made her home in New York with
her sister, illustrator Corinne Malvern. Gladys Malvern at one time was an advertising manager for a
large store. She has enjoyed writing for young adults
whom she has considered "the most discerning and
critical audience. " Many of her books have been illustrated by her sister, and in 1943 the Julia Ellsworth

Ford Prize was awarded for Valiant Minstrel, Messner,
1943. Other titles include: Behold Your Queen, Longmans, 1951; Eric's Girls, Messner, 1949; The Foreign-
er (A Junior Literary Guild selection), Longmans, 1954;
Meg's Fortune, Messner, 1950; So Great A Love,
Macrae Smith, 1962; World Of Lady Jane Grey, Vanguard, 1964.   JBA-2

MAMMEN, Edward William 1907-
Born in Brooklyn, he received his doctor's degree from
Columbia University where he later became an instructor in dramatics and speech. He also has been on the
faculty of the City College of New York where he taught
public speaking. He wrote Turnipseed Jones, Junior
Literary Guild and Harper, 1950.

MANNING, Rosemary 1911-
Her pseudonym is Mary Voyle. She was born in Wey-
mouth, England and later made her home in London.
This author has written for both adults and children.
Besides working in the business field, she has taught
school. She wrote her first children's book about a
pirate who lived in England years ago. It is Arripay,
Ariel, 1964.   CA-3

MANTEL, S. G.
Editor and free-lance writer, born in New York City.
He received a B. S. degree in biology from Long Island
University and later obtained his M. A. degree from
Columbia University. Mr. Mantel has made his home
in Palo Alto, California. In addition to writing books,
the author has also been an advertising executive, editor, reporter, and sales manager for television programs. He has also been a merchant marine radio
officer. His juvenile books include: Explorer With A
Dream: John Ledyard, Messner, 1969; Youngest Conquistador (A Junior Literary Guild selection), McKay,
1963.

MANTON, Jo 1919-
British writer and editor, born in Hertfordshire, England. She attended Girton College and Cambridge University. After her marriage to poet Robert Gittings
she lived in Sussex. At one time Jo Manton worked
as editor and producer of the School Broadcasting Department of the British Broadcasting Company. She
served in the Women's Auxiliary Territorial Service of

England during World War II.   The author has always
enjoyed music and has been a member of the Bach
Choir.   She was awarded one of the five medals given
annually by the Boys' Clubs of America for The Story
Of Albert Schweitzer, Abelard, 1955.   She also wrote
Portrait Of Bach, Abelard-Schuman, 1957.   CA-5/6

MARABELLA, Madeline
Illustrator, author, art director.   She has enjoyed bird
watching since she was a small girl living in Mississippi and Louisiana.   She later studied birds in Wild Life
Refuges, at zoos, and in the mountains.   The author
attended art schools and has been both a commercial
artist and an advertising agency's art director.   She
has lived in Pennsylvania.   For boys and girls she
wrote and illustrated Birds At The Zoo, Westminster,
1965.

MARAIS, Josef 1905-
He was born and grew up in South Africa.   As a boy
he enjoyed hearing the stories and songs sung by the
Hottentot farm boys.   By the time he was nineteen he
had an extensive collection of African folk songs.
Prior to his arrival in the United States in 1939, Josef
Marais presented his folk songs over the British Broad-
casting Company's radio stations.   He has also been
heard over NBC in this country.   He wrote Koos, The
Hottentot, Knopf, 1945.

MARCUS, Rebecca (Brian) 1907-
Author, teacher, native New Yorker.   After graduating
from Hunter College, she continued her studies at the
City College of New York and Columbia University.
She married writer Abraham Marcus and has lived in
Flushing, New York.   Mrs. Marcus has been a science
teacher and has enjoyed cooking, hiking, and travel as
special interests.   Her juvenile books include: Antoine
Lavoisier And The Revolution In Chemistry, Watts,
1964; The First Book Of Glaciers, Watts, 1962.   CA-
5/6

MARIANA see FOSTER, Marian Curtis

MARINO, Dorothy (Bronson) 1912-
Author, illustrator, born in Oregon.   She graduated
from the University of Kansas in Lawrence where her
family owned a bookstore.   She later studied at the

Art Students League in New York.   Prior to living in
Brooklyn, the Marinos once spent two years in Middle-
bury, Vermont.   Most of her stories about "Buzzy
Bear" have been Junior Literary Guild selections and
include: Buzzy Bear And The Rainbow, Watts, 1962;
Buzzy Bear Goes South, Watts, 1961; Buzzy Bear's
Winter Party, Watts, 1967.

MARKS, Mickey Klar 1914-
She was born in Brooklyn, New York and attended New
York and Columbia Universities.   She married Nathan
H. Marks and has lived in Armonk, New York.   Her
interests have included: sculpturing, gardening, and
the theater.   Her sand sculptures have been sold in
America House in New York City.   She has been a re-
cipient of the Petry Prize.   Her books include: Fine
Eggs And Fancy Chickens, Holt, 1956; Painting Free:
Lines, Colors & Shapes, Dial, 1965; Sand Sculpturing,
Dial, 1962; Slate Sculpturing, Dial, 1963; Wax Sculp-
turing, Dial, 1963.   CA-2

MARKUN, Patricia (Maloney) 1924-
Her pseudonyms are: Sybil Forrest, Patricio Marroquin, and Pat Maloney.   She was born in Chisholm,
Minnesota and graduated from the School of Journalism
at the University of Minnesota in Minneapolis.   At one
time Patricia Markun worked in public relations, radio,
and on magazines and newspapers.   She married a lawyer and has made her home in Balboa Heights, Panama
Canal Zone.   Her husband has been Assistant General
Counsel for the Panama Canal Company.   Her books
for young people include: The First Book Of Central
America And Panama, Watts, 1963; First Book Of The
Panama Canal, Watts, 1958.   CA-5/6

MARLOWE, Stephen see LESSER, Milton

MAROKVIA, Mireille
French author, teacher, translator.   She studied at the
Sorbonne and attended Columbia University after coming
to the United States.   She has written poetry and short
stories and at one time was interested in fashion design.   Her first published book in English for children
was Jannot, Lippincott, 1959.   She also wrote: Belle
Arabelle, Lippincott, 1962; French School For Paul,
Lippincott, 1963.

MARRAN, Ray J.
He was born in New York City and grew up near Kansas City, Missouri. He later became a reporter on the Kansas City Star. He has also worked in advertising, both as a copywriter and a display manager in a department store. His books for young people include: Making Models Of Famous Ships, Appleton-Century, 1940; Playthings For Indoor And Outdoor Fun, Appleton-Century, 1940.

MARRIOTT, Alice Lee 1910-
Ethnologist-writer. She graduated from Oklahoma City University and the University of Oklahoma at Norman. Much of her time has been devoted to the study of the American Indian, and for many years she served in the Department of the Interior as a specialist on the Indian Arts and Crafts Board. Miss Marriott has been sponsored by the Santa Fe Laboratory of Anthropology and the Guggenheim and Rockefeller Foundations to conduct ethnological studies of the American Indian. For young people she wrote: Black Stone Knife, Crowell, 1957; The First Comers (A Junior Literary Guild selection), Longmans, 1960; Indians Of The Four Corners . . ., Crowell, 1952; Sequoyah: Leader Of The Cherokees, Random, 1956.

MARROQUIN, Patricio see MARKUN, Patricia (Maloney)

MARSH, Corinna
She was born in New York and graduated from Barnard College. She has been a playground supervisor for underprivileged children and a high school English teacher. Corinna Marsh was also editor of The Bookshelf For Boys And Girls. For boys and girls she wrote Flippy's Flashlight (A Junior Literary Guild selection), Dutton, 1959.

MARSH, Ngaio 1899-
New Zealander, writer, theater director. She was born in Christchurch, New Zealand. Although she has always lived in Christchurch, she has traveled throughout the Far East, Europe, and the United States. The author has been a theater director and a contributor of articles to magazines. Miss Marsh has written detective stories and plays in addition to books for young people. She wrote New Zealand, Macmillan, 1964.
CA-11/12

MARSHAK, Ilía Iákolevich 1895-
   His pseudonym is M. Ilin. He decided to write under
   a pen name to distinguish himself from his brother,
   poet S. Marshak. The author was born in Russia in
   the city of St. Petersburg (now known as Leningrad).
   M. Ilin graduated from Leningrad Technological Institute and became an engineer. Several books that he
   wrote originated from actual experiences. With E. Se-
   gal he wrote Giant At The Crossroads (tr. by Beatrice
   Kinkead), Progress Pub. Co., 1948.   JBA-1, JBA-2

MARSHALL, Catherine
   She was born in Yonkers, New York, and graduated
   from Mount Holyoke College in South Hadley, Massachusetts. She has been a secretary and has worked in
   advertising. Later she became a children's librarian
   in the Yonkers Public Library. Catherine Marshall has
   enjoyed sports, music, the theater, and ballet. Her
   first book was The Unwilling Heart, Longmans, 1955.
   She also wrote Julie's Heritage, Longmans, 1957.

MARSHALL, Dean 1900-
   She was born in Louisville, Kentucky and later lived in
   Connecticut. Dean Marshall graduated from Vanderbilt
   University in Nashville, Tennessee and did further
   study at the New York School of Social Work. She has
   worked with the New York Charity Organization Society
   and has also been a Case Supervisor in Hartford. Her
   books for young people include: House For Elizabeth,
   Dutton, 1941; The Silver Robin, Dutton, 1947.

MARSHALL, Samuel Louis Atwood
   Soldier, historian, author. General Marshall received
   many honors which have included: the Legion of Honor,
   the Bronze Star, and the Croix de Guerre. During
   World War II, he served as chief combat historian in
   the Pacific Area and during the Korean War was a
   Detroit News war correspondent. He wrote The Military History Of The Korean War, Watts, 1963 and the
   narrative for The American Heritage History Of World
   War I, American Heritage, 1964.

MARTIN, Charles Morris 1891-
   Rancher, columnist, author. Chuck Martin has lived
   on a ranch called "Boot Hill" in Oceanside, California.
   He has written newspaper columns and rodeo publicity
   in addition to books for children and adults. His hob-

bies have included: riding and training horses, raising cacti, and pistol and rifle shooting. For boys and girls he wrote: Cowboy Charlie, 4-H Champ, Viking, 1953; Monsters Of Old Los Angeles, Viking, 1950; Once A Cowboy, Viking, 1948; Orphans Of The Range, Viking, 1950.

MARTIN, George 1926-
Born in New York City, he graduated from Harvard and the University of Virginia Law School. He also studied at Trinity College, Cambridge, England. He has been a lawyer in New York and has served as a Director of the Metropolitan Opera Guild. He wrote The Battle Of The Frogs And The Mice, Dodd, 1962.   CA-9/10

MARTIN, Judith
She was one of the people who founded the Paper Bag Players. Judith Martin has also been in charge of a dance company and has worked with both children and adults in an experimental dance program. With Remy Charlip she wrote: Jumping Beans, Knopf, 1963; The Tree Angel, Knopf, 1962.

MARTIN, Patricia Miles
She has also written books as Miska Miles. Teacher, poet, author. She was born in Cherokee, Kansas, grew up in the Midwest (her first poem was accepted by the Monett, Missouri newspaper when she was seven), and has lived in San Mateo, California. She received her education in Denver and later taught school in Colorado and Wyoming. Newspapers have published her book reviews. Mrs. Martin has written poetry, fiction, and biography. She has collected old kerosene lamps as a hobby. For boys and girls she wrote: Abraham Lincoln, Putnam, 1964; Grandma's Gun, Golden Gate, 1968; John Fitzgerald Kennedy, Putnam, 1964; Jump Frog Jump (A Junior Literary Guild selection), Putnam, 1965; Pointed Brush, Lothrop, 1959; Trina's Boxcar, Abingdon, 1967; Woody's Big Trouble, Putnam, 1967.   CA-4

MARTIN, Ralph G. 1920-
He was born in Chicago, Illinois and graduated from the School of Journalism at the University of Missouri. During World War II, he was a war correspondent. Mr. Martin was a consultant on a television program called "The Valiant Years" which was about Winston

Churchill.   He also has been an editor for a magazine.
He has lived in East Norwich, New York.   He wrote
President From Missouri: Harry S. Truman, Mess-
ner, 1964.   CA-5/6

MARTINI, Teri 1930-
She was born and grew up in Teaneck, New Jersey
where her mother operated a bookstore.   She graduated
from Trenton Teachers College and received her master's degree from Columbia University.   The author
has taught young people in addition to writing for them.
She has lived in Leonia, New Jersey.   Juvenile titles
include: The Fisherman's Ring, St. Anthony Guild
Press, 1954; Mystery Of The Hard Luck House, Criterion Books, 1965; True Book Of Cowboys, Childrens
Press, 1955; What A Frog Can Do, Reilly & Lee, 1962.
CA-5/6

MARX, Robert F. 1934-
He has been interested in historical research and has
pursued this interest both in the archives of Europe and
on the high seas.   In 1962 he followed the route which
Columbus took to America and sailed on a ship which
was similar to Columbus' "Niña. " He has been associated with a magazine in America but later lived in
London.   He wrote The Battle Of The Spanish Armada,
1588, World, 1965.   CA-11/12

MASANI, Shakuntala
Author and newspaperwoman.   She graduated from India's Lucknow University and later attended Lucknow
Art School.   At one time she worked on a newspaper
in Bombay and also for an Indian publishing firm.
She married M. R. Masani who has been Indian Ambassador to Brazil.   For young people she wrote Neh-
ru's Story, Oxford University Press, 1949.

MASEFIELD, John (Edward) 1878-1967
The late John Masefield was born near Ledbury in
Herefordshire, England.   This author has been honored
as the 16th poet laureate of England.   In 1961 he was
the recipient of the Companions of Literature award.
He has been called "the poet of the people" since he
often sympathetically portrayed the poor in his poetry.
His juvenile books include: . . . Martin Hyde, The
Duke's Messenger, Little, 1924; Salt-Water Poems And
Ballads, Macmillan, 1942.   CA-19/20, JBA-1

MASON, Francis van Wyck   see   MASON, Frank W.

MASON, Frank W.   1901-
   His pseudonyms are Ward Weaver and Geoffrey Coffin.
   Born in New England, he spent part of his childhood in
   Europe where his grandfather served as a consul in
   Paris and Berlin.   He graduated from Harvard Univer-
   sity and became director of his own importing firm.
   He has also had a distinguished military career; begin-
   ning with service in the French Army, he later served
   as a Colonel in the United States Army.   He wrote
   Pilots, Man Your Planes!, Lippincott, 1944 and under
   the name of Francis van Wyck Mason he wrote: The
   Battle For Quebec, Houghton, 1965; The Battle Of Lake
   Erie, Houghton, 1960.   CA-5/6

MASON, George Frederick   1904-
   Author-illustrator, scientist, New Englander.   He grew
   up on a farm near Worcester, Massachusetts and later
   made his home in Princeton, Massachusetts.   After attending art school, he worked as a political cartoonist
   on a newspaper.   George Mason has served on the
   staff of New York City's American Museum of Natural
   History and later became Assistant Curator of its Department of Education.   Juvenile books which he wrote
   and illustrated include: Animal Baggage, Morrow, 1961;
   Animal Habits, Morrow, 1959; Animal Tails, Morrow,
   1958; Animal Teeth, Morrow, 1965; The Wildlife Of
   North America, Hastings House, 1966.   He also illustrated The Wildlife Of Australia And New Zealand (A
   Junior Literary Guild selection), Shuttlesworth, D. ,
   Hastings, 1967.

MASON, Miriam Evangeline   1900-
   She was born in Goshen, Indiana and grew up on a
   farm in southern Indiana.   She attended Indiana University and the University of Missouri.   Her first poem
   was published when she was in grade school and later
   her first story appeared in a farm magazine.   She has
   taught school, worked in advertising, and edited books
   for a publishing firm.   Her home has been in Bates-
   ville, Indiana.   Many books have been written by Miriam Mason for boys and girls including: Baby Jesus,
   Macmillan, 1959; Caroline And The Seven Little Words,
   Macmillan, 1967; Dan Beard, Boy Scout, Bobbs, 1953;
   Stevie And His Seven Orphans, Houghton, 1964.   CA-
   2, MJA

MASSIE, Diane Redfield
> Author-illustrator, oboist, born in Los Angeles, California. She attended Los Angeles City College where she studied art. She married a New York University mathematics professor and has lived in New York City. At one time Mrs. Massie was first oboist with the Pasadena (California) and Honolulu (Hawaii) Symphonies. In Hawaii she once acted, directed, and produced plays which she wrote. Juvenile books which she wrote and illustrated include: The Baby Beebee Bird, Harper, 1963; Tiny Pin, Harper, 1964; A Turtle And A Loon, And Other Fables, Atheneum, 1965.

MASTERS, Kelly Ray 1897-
> His pseudonym is Zachary Ball. This actor and writer was born in Missouri and grew up in Kansas along the Verdigris River. "I was still a boy when I first met Old Man River, and I got to know him well. Probably that's why a goodly portion of all my writing has had the big river for its setting." At the age of seventeen he joined a tent show and traveled throughout the United States. Many of his short stories have appeared in magazines. His book Bristle Face (A Junior Literary Guild selection; Holiday, 1962), was listed as one of the "Notable Books" of 1962 by the American Library Association, and it also won the Dorothy Canfield Fisher and William Allen White Awards. Other juvenile books include: Kep, Holiday, 1961; Young Mike Fink, Holiday, 1958. CA-3

MATSUNO, Masako 1935-
> A native of Japan, she attended Columbia University where she obtained a master's degree in library science. Masako Matsuno has enjoyed writing in the "beautiful rhythm of the English language." She has lived in Japan with her husband and son. For young readers she wrote: Chie And The Sports Day, World, 1965; A Pair Of Red Clogs, World, 1960. CA-5/6

MATTHEW, Eunice S.
> Author and teacher, born in New York City. Before receiving her Ph.D. degree from Cornell University, she graduated from Hunter College and obtained her M.A. degree from Columbia University. Dr. Matthew has been associated with experimental teacher training programs in Tennessee and later went to Thailand with the U.S. Point IV Program. As a result of her work

with this educational project, the International Cooperation Administration of the U. S. Department of State
awarded her a Citation of Meritorious Service. Dr.
Matthew has been on the staff of Brooklyn College (Department of Education). For children she wrote The
Land And People Of Thailand, Lippincott, 1964.

MATTHEWS, Herbert Lionel 1900-
He has had a distinguished career with the New York
Times. As a correspondent, he covered the Spanish
Civil War and the Italian campaign during World War
II. He also wrote about Fidel Castro when he was
fighting Batista (Fulgencio Batista Y Zaldívar) in the
Sierra Maestra. Herbert Matthews has received the
George Polk Memorial Award, the Newspaper Guild of
New York Page One Award, and the Maria Moors Ca-
bot Award. For young people he wrote Cuba, Macmil-
lan, 1964. CA-1

MATTHIESEN, Thomas
Author and photographer, born in Spokane, Washington.
At the age of fourteen he received a camera and became interested in the photography of insects. He
later lived in New York where he became a professional
photographer. Mr. Matthiesen has also been a graphic
artist and painter. His photographs have appeared in
Mademoiselle and other magazines. His book for boys
and girls was ABC, Platt, 1966.

MAULE, Hamilton Bee 1915-
Tex Maule was born in Ojus, Florida and graduated
from St. Mary's University of San Antonio and the University of Texas. He has been publicity director for
the Los Angeles Rams football team and associate editor of Sports Illustrated magazine. His interests have
included painting and sculpture. He wrote a novel
Jeremy Todd, Random, 1959, and these books for
young people: The Last Out, McKay, 1964; The Rookie, McKay, 1961; The Shortstop, McKay, 1962. CA-1

MAUROIS, André see HERZOG, Emile

MAXWELL, Gavin 1914-
Author and portrait-painter, born in Mochrum, Scotland.
He received his education at Stowe School in Buckinghamshire, England and Hertford College, Oxford University. The author has lived in London and Scotland.

He became a professional portrait-painter and a contributor of poetry and stories to British newspapers. Gavin Maxwell served in the Scots Guards and Special Forces during World War II. He has always been interested in nature and has been a member of both the American and Royal Geographic Societies. His experiments with commercial shark-fishing on his own island (Soay) in the Hebrides provided the material for his first book Harpoon Venture, Viking, 1952. He also wrote The Otter's Tale, Dutton, 1962.   CA-7/8

MAXWELL, William 1908-
He was born in Lincoln, Illinois. He taught freshman composition at the University of Illinois and later became an associate editor of the New Yorker magazine. In addition to the New Yorker his stories have appeared in Harper's Bazaar and the Atlantic Monthly. He has lived in New York City and Yorktown Heights, New York. When he was sixteen, he worked on a farm in Wisconsin. These memories furnished much of the material for his book The Heavenly Tenants, Harper, 1946.

MAY, Charles Paul 1920-
Author, editor, teacher, born in Bedford, Iowa. He received a B. A. degree from Drake University in Des Moines, Iowa and an M. A. degree from the Oklahoma Agricultural and Mechanical College (now Oklahoma State University). Mr. May has traveled throughout this country and in Canada, Africa, Asia, and Europe. He has taught English in several universities and lectured on creative writing. The author has been associated with the Grolier Society as a member of the editorial staff and has lived in New York City. For young people he wrote: Box Turtle Lives In Armor, Holiday, 1960; Central America, Nelson, 1966; Great Cities Of Canada, Abelard, 1967; High-Noon Rocket, Holiday, 1966; Veterinarians And Their Patients, Nelson, 1964; When Animals Change Clothes, Holiday, 1965.   CA-1

MAY, Julian 1931-
Science editor, author, born in Chicago, Illinois. She studied science at Rosary College in River Forest, Illinois and later became science editor for an encyclopedia and a publishing house. She married T. E. Dikty who has been a book designer and editor. They met at a science fiction convention. The author has been a

member of the Society of Midland Authors and has lived
in Chicago, Illinois. Juvenile titles include: There's
Adventure In Atomic Energy, Pop. Mechanics, 1957;
There's Adventure In Chemistry, Pop. Mechanics, 1957;
There's Adventure In Geology, Pop. Mechanics, 1959;
They Lived In The Ice Age, Holiday House, 1967.
CA-2

MAYER, Jane (Rothchild) 1903-
Clara Jaynes is her joint pseudonym with Clara Spiegel.
Born in Kansas City, Missouri, she has lived in Chi-
cago where she has done editorial work with the Field
Enterprises Educational Corporation. She graduated
from Vassar College in Poughkeepsie, New York. Mrs.
Mayer has always been interested in the welfare of
children and wrote a booklet "Getting Along In the
Family" for Encyclopedia Britannica, Jr. It was later
published by Teachers College, Columbia University.
Her books for young people include: Betsy Ross And
The Flag, Random, 1952; Dolly Madison, Random, 1954.
CA-9/10.

MAYNE, William 1928-
His joint pseudonym is James Dynely. He was born
in England and studied at the Canterbury Cathedral
Choir School. He has been interested in motor cars
and music and has made his home in a Yorkshire village named Leyburn. His book The Blue Boat (Dutton,
1960) was selected as a 1960 notable book by the A-
merican Library Association and Grass Rope (Dutton,
1962) was awarded England's Carnegie Medal. He also
wrote Earthfasts, Dutton, 1967.   CA-11/12

MEAD, Margaret 1901-
Author and anthropologist, born in Philadelphia, Penn-
sylvania. She graduated from Barnard College and re-
ceived her master's and doctor's degrees from Colum-
bia University. She has lived in New York where she
has been associate curator of ethnology at the American
Museum of Natural History. Dr. Mead was named the
"Outstanding Woman of the Year in Science" by the
Associated Press in 1949. In 1960 she was elected
President of the American Anthropological Association.
Her books for young people include: Anthropologists
And What They Do, Watts, 1965; People And Places,
World, 1959.   CA-3

MEADER, Stephen Warren 1892–
He was born in Providence, Rhode Island and grew up
in New Hampshire. Following graduation from Haverford College in Pennsylvania, he was associated with
the Newark, New Jersey's Children's Aid Society. He
later worked in a publishing house in Chicago and an
advertising firm in Philadelphia. His home has been
in Morristown, New Jersey. His many books for young
people include: Buffalo And Beaver, Harcourt, 1960;
The Muddy Road To Glory, Harcourt, 1963; Phantom
Of The Blockade, Harcourt, 1962; Sea Snake, Harcourt,
1943; Stranger On Big Hickory, Harcourt, 1964. CA-
5/6, JBA-1, JBA-2

MEADOWCROFT, Enid (La Monte) 1898–
Author, editor, teacher, born in New York City. After
graduating from Lesley College in Cambridge, Massachusetts, she taught school in New York and New Jersey. She later lived in Lakeville, Connecticut with her
husband Donald Wright. The author has been editor of
the "Signature Books" series of biographies. She has
also written radio scripts for "This Is America." Her
interests have included music and travel. Her books
for young people include: By Secret Railway, Crowell,
1948; Crazy Horse, Sioux Warrior, Garrard, 1965;
Land Of The Free, Crowell, 1961; On Indian Trails
With Daniel Boone, Crowell, 1947; Scarab For Luck,
Crowell, 1964; When Nantucket Men Went Whaling, Garrard, 1966. CA-17/18, JBA-2

MEANS, Florence Crannell 1891–
She was born in Baldwinsville, New York, the daughter
of a minister. She studied at the University of Denver.
She once lived in Kansas City where her father served
as president of the Kansas City Baptist Theological
Seminary. The author married Carleton Bell Means
who was a lawyer, and they have lived in Boulder,
Colorado. The Child Study Association of America
presented its 1945 award to her for the book The Moved
Outers, Houghton, 1945. She also wrote: Rainbow
Bridge, Friendship Press, 1934; The Rains Will Come,
Houghton, 1954; Reach For A Star, Houghton, 1957;
That Girl Andy, Houghton, 1962. CA-4, JBA-1, JBA-
2

MEEKER, Oden
He has written for both adults and young adults. One

of his books received the National Council of Christians
and Jews citation and the Anisfield-Wolf award. His
articles have been published in such magazines as Harper's and the New Yorker.   Oden Meeker has been a
world-wide traveler.   He has been associated with
CARE in several countries including Costa Rica, Hong
Kong, India, Israel, and Laos.   For boys and girls he
wrote Israel Reborn, Scribner, 1964.

MEEKS, Esther K.
Author and editor.   She has lived in Chicago, Illinois.
In addition to writing many books for boys and girls,
Mrs. Meeks has been Children's Book Editor for a
publishing firm.   Her fondness for animals resulted
in books about them which include: Bow Wow! Said
The Kittens, Wilcox, 1952; The Curious Cow, Follett,
1960; Jeff & Mr. James' Pond, Lothrop, 1962; Something New At The Zoo, Follett, 1957.

MEHDEVI, Anne (Marie) Sinclair
For many years Mrs. Mehdevi lived in Iran (her husband's country).   She studied Persian folk tales and
compared them to tales from other lands.   Her con-
clusion was that Persian tales possessed three unique
characteristics: irony, women were "saucy and flirta-
tious creatures, " visuality (". . . the quality which
can evoke complete and well-defined pictures in the
mind of the listener").   Her book was entitled Persian
Folk And Fairy Tales, Knopf, 1965.   She also wrote
Parveen, Knopf, 1969.   CA-5/6

MEIGS, Cornelia Lynde 1884-
Her pseudonym is Adair Aldon.   She was born in Rock
Island, Illinois and lived in Keokuk, Iowa.   She later
made her home in Brandon, Vermont.   Cornelia Meigs
studied at Bryn Mawr College in Pennsylvania and later
served as a member of its English department.   In
1934 she was awarded the Newbery Medal for her book
Invincible Louisa, Little, 1933.   Her other books include: Call Of The Mountain, Little, 1940; The Covered
Bridge, Macmillan, 1936; The Pool Of Stars, Macmillan, 1929.   She also edited Critical History Of Children's Literature [and others], Macmillan, 1953.   CA-
9/10, JBA-1, JBA-2

MEIGS, Elizabeth Bleecker 1923-
She studied at a convent in southern France and later

attended Cornell University where she studied animal
husbandry and veterinary medicine. Her book The Silver Quest (Bobbs, 1949) was based on real people who
lived on the Laredo Trail south of the Rio Grande.
Her interests have included: horses, music, and the
Greek language. For young people she wrote: Candle
In The Sky, Dutton, 1953; Crusade And The Cup, Dutton, 1952; Scarlet Hill, Bobbs, 1947; Sunflight, Dutton,
1951; White Winter, Bobbs, 1948.

MELBO, Irving Robert 1908-
He has been associated with the University of Southern
California in Los Angeles as Dean of the School of
Education. Dr. Melbo has been interested in our coun-
try's national parks. He has collected authoritative
material for his books by personal observation of the
parks, interviews with archaeologists, botanists, geo-
logists, zoologists, and working with the U. S. Park
Service. With his son Robert Irving Melbo he wrote
Our Country's National Parks, Bobbs, 1964.

MELLIN, Jeanne
Author-illustrator, born in Stamford, Connecticut. She
studied at the Rhode Island School of Design. Jeanne
Mellin has specialized in drawings of horses and once
said: ". . . Most influential has been owning and taking care of my own horse. Riding her in shows or
just pleasure riding has given me more inspiration than
anything else. " Her husband has also been an artist,
and they have lived in New Canaan, Connecticut. She
wrote and illustrated Horses Across America, Dutton,
1953.

MEMLING, Carl 1918-
Author, editor, native New Yorker, he graduated from
Brooklyn College. He served in the Army during World
War II. Mr. Memling has been both a writer and edi-
tor on the staff of the Bank Street College of Education
in New York. He has also written advertising for a
large firm. He married a school psychologist and has
lived in East Meadow, New York. His juvenile books
include: Barbie's Adventures At Camp, Random, 1964;
Gift-Bear For The King, Dutton, 1966; Happy-Go-Lucky
Skipper, Random, 1965; Life With Mindy, Dutton, 1966;
Seals For Sale, Abelard-Schuman, 1963.   CA-4

MERCER, Jessie see SHANNON, Terry

MEREDITH, David William   see   MIERS, Earl Schenck

MEREDITH, Nicolete 1896-
She was born in Des Moines, Iowa where she later graduated from Highland Park College. She has been interested in welfare work which included an appointment on the Governor's Board in Iowa in order to study and implement the welfare law. Her stories have appeared in magazines for both children and adults. The author has been a member of the Missouri Writer's Guild and the Gallery of Living Catholic Authors. Her home has been in Webster Groves, Missouri. Juvenile titles include: King Of The Kerry Fair, Crowell, 1960; Welcome Love, Lothrop, 1959.   CA-13/14

MERRIAM, Eve 1916-
Born in Philadelphia, Pennsylvania, she later made her home in New York. She attended Cornell University and graduated from the University of Pennsylvania. She did graduate study at Columbia and the University of Wisconsin. She has written many books of adult poetry including Family Circle (Yale University Press, 1946) which was awarded the Yale Series of Younger Poets Prize. Eve Merriam has written a column of verse for PM newspaper and has discussed poetry on a radio station in New York. Her juvenile books include: Funny Town, Crowell, 1963; Independent Voices, Atheneum, 1968.   CA-5/6

MERRILL, Jean Fairbanks 1923-
Author, editor, born in Rochester, New York. She graduated from Alleghany College in Meadville, Pennsylvania, received her master's degree from Wellesley College in Massachusetts, and attended the University of Madras in India on a Fullbright Grant. At one time Jean Merrill served both as a writer and editor for educational magazines. She has traveled throughout Europe and the Far East and has resided in New York City. The author received the Boys' Clubs of America Junior Book Award for The Pushcart War, Scott, 1964. Other juvenile books include: Elephant Who Liked To Smash Small Cars (with Ronni Solbert), Pantheon, 1967; The Superlative Horse (A Junior Literary Guild selection), Scott, 1961.   CA-1

METCALFE, Jane M.
She was born in Saskatchewan, Canada and became a

United States citizen in 1934. She has lived in Alaska,
Salt Lake City, San Francisco, and later made her
home in New York City. Mrs. Metcalfe has been an
associate member of the American Institute of Mining
and Metallurgical Engineers and a member of the Society of Woman Geographers. She has also been associated with Teachers College, Columbia University.
She wrote Mining Round The World, Oxford, 1956.

MEYER, Edith Patterson 1895-
Editor, librarian, writer. She has traveled throughout
the United States and Hawaii, and has made visits to
Greece, Ireland, Italy, and Scandinavia. Her varied
career has included being a children's book editor and
librarian. Mrs. Meyer has written for both adults and
children. Her books for young readers include: Meet
The Future, Little, 1964; That Remarkable Man, Little,
1967. CA-2

MEYER, Franklyn Edward 1932-
Author and teacher, born in St. Louis, Missouri. After graduating from the University of Missouri at Columbia, he served as a second lieutenant with the Marine Corps Reserve. Mr. Meyer has lived in Sarasota,
Florida where he has been a teacher and athletic director. He has also been a director of a summer camp
for boys. For young people he wrote Me And Caleb,
Follett, 1962. CA-4

MEYER, Gerard Previn
He was born and grew up in New York. Mr. Meyer
has taught English both in college and secondary
schools. In addition he has written scripts for radio
and television. One of his radio programs entitled
"How It Began" provided Mr. Meyer with the incentive
to write his first book for young people Pioneers Of
The Press, Rand McNally, 1961.

MEYER, Jerome Sydney 1895-
He was born in New York City and attended Columbia
University where he studied engineering. Mr. Meyer
has owned his own advertising agency, contributed articles to magazines, and produced the first radio quiz
program. He has also served as editor and president
of a publishing firm. His home has been in New York.
Juvenile books include: Engines, World, 1962; Fun
With Mathematics, World, 1952; Paper, World, 1960;

Prisms And Lenses, World, 1959; World Book Of Great
Inventions, World, 1956.   CA-2

MEYERS, Joan (Simpson) 1927-
Author and editor, born in Boulder, Colorado. She attended the University of Connecticut and won the
school's short story award and also was the recipient
of the Atlantic Monthly poetry prize. She later obtained her B. A. degree from the University of Michigan.
Joan Meyers has been an editor in a publishing firm
and literary editor for a record company. She collaborated with George Whitaker to write Dinosaur Hunt,
Harcourt, 1965.   CA-19/20

MEYNIER, Yvonne
Her books have been enjoyed by the boys and girls of
France (the author's birthplace).   The first book which
was translated into English was The School With A
Difference (Abelard, 1965).   This book won the Grand
Prix de la Literature pour les Jeunes and also received
the Enfance du Monde award.   She attended the Sor-
bonne, has been a kindergarten teacher, and also has
worked in radio in France.   She wrote The School With
A Difference (tr. by Patricia Crampton), Abelard, 1965.

MICHIE, Allan Andrew 1915-
Editor, war correspondent, reporter.   Allan Michie
graduated from Ripon College in Wisconsin and also attended the University of Chicago.   During World War
II, he was a correspondent for Life, Time, Fortune,
and the Reader's Digest.   Later he was associated with
Radio Free Europe.   He also became chief of the information section of the Ghana Embassy.   Prior to
serving with Education and World Affairs, he was managing editor of Current magazine.   The Michies have
lived in Briarcliff Manor (Westchester, New York).
He wrote The Invasion Of Europe, Dodd, 1964.

MIERS, Earl Schenck 1910-
Historian and writer, born in Brooklyn.   He graduated
from Rutgers University.   He has been interested in
the study of American history, and his books have re-
flected this interest.   Mr. Miers has become a noted
Lincoln scholar, and he was a member of the 1960
Lincoln Sesquicentennial Commission.   He also was
Founding Director and Editor of Rutgers University
Press.   His home has been in Edison, New Jersey.

Juvenile titles include: Abraham Lincoln In Peace And
War (by the editors of American Heritage, consultant:
Paul M. Angle), Am. Heritage, 1964; America And Its
Presidents, Grosset, 1959; Men Of Valor, Rand, 1965;
That Lincoln Boy, World, 1968.   CA-3

MILES, Betty 1928-
She graduated from Antioch College in Yellow Springs,
Ohio. Her husband has been on the staff of Columbia
University, and they have lived in New York City.
When she looked for books for her own children on
their age level (two and four-years-old), Mrs. Miles
decided to write books for children.   Her titles include:
A Day Of Autumn, Knopf, 1967; Having A Friend, Knopf,
1959.   CA-3

MILES, Miska see MARTIN, Patricia Miles

MILHOUS, Katherine 1894-
Author-illustrator, born in Philadelphia, she later attended the Philadelphia Academy of Fine Arts and the
Pennsylvania Museum of Industrial Art.   Miss Milhous
studied abroad on a Cresson traveling scholarship and
later served as head of a Federal Art Project.   In
1951 she was the recipient of the Caldecott Medal for
her story The Egg Tree, Scribner, 1950.   Other juvenile titles include: Appolonia's Valentine, Junior Literary Guild and Scribner, 1954; Herodia, The Lovely Puppet, Scribner, 1942; Through These Arches, Lippincott,
1964; With Bells On (A Junior Literary Guild selection),
Scribner, 1955.   JBA-2

MILLER, Donald George 1909-
He was born in Braddock, Pennsylvania and has lived
in Pittsburgh. He graduated from Greenville College
in Illinois and received his master's and doctor's degrees from New York University.   For several years
he taught at the Pyengyang Foreign School in Korea.
He has also served as Walter H. Robertson Professor
of New Testament at Union Theological Seminary in
Richmond, Virginia.   For young people he wrote Conqueror In Chains, A Story Of The Apostle Paul, Westminster Press, 1951.   CA-5/6

MILLER, Edna
When she was a young girl, she lived near the American Museum of Natural History in New York City and

often visited the various animal exhibits. She has continued to be interested in animals and has studied them both in this country and on her travels abroad. Edna Miller and her husband have lived in New York State near the Ramapo Mountains. Her books for boys and girls include: Mousekin's Christmas Eve (A Junior Literary Guild selection), Prentice, 1965; Mousekin's Family, Prentice, 1969.

MILLER, Eugenia 1916-
She grew up in Annapolis, Maryland where her writing career began at the age of eleven (she contributed stories in serial form to the local newspaper). She married Robert S. Mandelkorn, a naval officer, and has traveled throughout the world. She wrote about the bombing of Pearl Harbor which was later made into a radio script. Her work has also appeared in newspapers and magazines. The author and her family lived in Versailles near Paris when Captain Mandelkorn was associated with SHAPE. For boys and girls she wrote The Golden Spur, Holt, 1964. CA-11/12

MILLER, Helen Knapp see MILLER, Helen Markley

MILLER, Helen Louise
Teacher, playwright, author. In addition to teaching English in York, Pennsylvania, she has served as a consultant and lecturer for various educational organizations. The author has also been Director of Educational Radio and Television for the York City Schools. Her plays have been published in Plays, the drama magazine for young people, and civic groups in her community have also produced them. She married educator Samuel A. Gotwalt and has lived in York. Her juvenile books include: Easy Plays For Boys And Girls, Plays, Inc., 1963; Gold Medal Plays For Holidays, Plays, Inc., 1958; Modern Plays For Special Days, Plays, Inc., 1965.

MILLER, Helen Markley
Born in Cedar Falls, Iowa, she graduated from Iowa State Teachers College and received her master's degree from Western State College of Colorado. She has been an English teacher both before her marriage and after the death of her husband who had been an editor on a newspaper. Mrs. Miller once bought a trailer and lived in some of the ghost towns in Idaho. She

later lived in McCall, Idaho. Many of her books for young people have been Junior Literary Guild selections including: Dust In The Gold Sack, Doubleday, 1957; Kirsti, Doubleday, 1964; Westering Women, Doubleday, 1961. CA-2

MILLER, Helen (Topping) 1884-
This novelist once said: "To me the unchanging loveliness of the holy days is proof of the unchanging love of God. " Her series of books about Christmas in the lives of great Americans include: Christmas At Monticello, With Thomas Jefferson, Longmans, 1959; Christmas At Mount Vernon, With George And Martha Washington, Longmans, 1957; Christmas With Robert E. Lee, Longmans, 1958.

MILLER, Katherine
In order to introduce Shaespeare to her daughter, Katherine Miller produced one of his plays and followed this one with "A Midsummer Night's Dream" for other children. Her husband has been a psychologist at Harvard, and they have lived in Lexington, Massachusetts. For young people she wrote Five Plays From Shakespeare, Houghton, 1964.

MILLER, Lisa
She studied at Columbia University and has made her home in New York City. Miss Miller has worked in scientific research and has been a junior physicist with a large corporation. For young readers she wrote Wheels, Coward, 1965.

MILLER, Mark
He has worked on many newspapers including: the St. Paul Dispatch, Minneapolis Journal, Milwaukee Sentinel, Duluth News Tribune, and the Brownsville Herald. His experiences have ranged from reporter, editor, to publisher. Mr. Miller has been interested in Indian lore and stamp collecting. His books for young people include: The Singing Wire, Winston, 1953; White Captive Of The Sioux, Winston, 1953.

MILLER, Martha see IVAN, Gustave

MILLER, Mary Britton 1883-
Her pseudonym is Isabel Bolton. Author and poet, she was born in New London, Connecticut and has made her

home in New York. She received her education at the
Gilman School and has traveled abroad. The New York
Times once said of her books All Aboard (Pantheon,
1958) and Give A Guess (Pantheon, 1957): "Distinguished for the simplicity that comes with the passion for
perfection." Other juvenile books include: Jungle
Journey, Pantheon, 1959; Listen - The Birds, Pantheon, 1961.   CA-2

MILNE, Alan Alexander 1882-1956
A. A. Milne was born in London, England and studied
at Cambridge. He became assistant editor of Punch in
1906 and worked there until 1914. He married Dorothy de Sélincourt, and they lived in Chelsea, London.
Their son's name, Christopher Robin, was the one used
in Milne's books of poetry and his stories about Winnie-
the-Pooh. His books for young people include: House
At Pooh Corner, Dutton, 1928; Now We Are Six, Dutton, 1927; When We Were Very Young, Dutton, 1924;
Winnie-The-Pooh, Dutton, 1926.   JBA-1, JBA-2

MILNE, Lorus Johnson 1910-   Margery Joan (Greene)
1914-
Husband-wife team. Both have been teachers, photographers, and scientists. A naturalized American citizen, Lorus Milne was born in Toronto, Canada and attended the University of Toronto. He received his
M. A. and Ph. D. degrees at Harvard. Mrs. Milne was
born in New York and received her M. A. degree from
Columbia and Ph. D. from Radcliffe. The Drs. Milne
have lived in Durham, New Hampshire and have enjoyed
field trips as a favorite hobby. Together they wrote:
Because Of A Tree, Atheneum, 1963; Crab That Crawl-
ed Out Of The Past, Atheneum, 1965; Famous Natural-
ists, Dodd, 1952; Gift From The Sky, Atheneum, 1967.

MIMS, Sam 1887-
He was born on July 30, 1887 in Louisiana. He studied at Louisiana Polytechnic Institute, Ruston, Louisiana and at Louisiana State University in Baton Rouge.
During World War I, he served in the Marine Corps.
Following the war, he worked on a California ranch and
in municipal bond firms in Texas and New York. Later
he held a government position in Baton Rouge. For
young people he wrote Chennault Of The Flying Tigers,
Macrae Smith, 1943.

MINARIK, Else Holmelund
    Author, teacher.   Born in Denmark, she grew up in
    the United States and has made her home in Chatham,
    New York.   Her incentive to write the "I Can Read"
    series resulted from the shortage of books for begin-
    ning readers that she found as a first grade teacher.
    These include: Cat And Dog, Harper, 1960; Kiss For
    Little Bear, Harper, 1968; Little Bear's Friend, Har-
    per, 1960; Little Bear's Visit, Harper, 1961; No Fight-
    ing, No Biting!, Harper, 1958.   She also wrote: The
    Little Giant Girl And The Elf Boy, Harper, 1963; The
    Winds That Come From Far Away, And Other Poems,
    Harper, 1964.

MINER, Opal Irene (Frazine) Sevrey 1906-
    Author and teacher, born in Kewadin, Michigan.   She
    received degrees from Western Michigan University and
    the University of Michigan.   Her home has been in
    Muskegon Heights, Michigan.   She has been both a lib-
    rarian and science teacher in the schools of Michigan.
    In 1960 she was selected as the Greater Muskegon
    "Career Woman of the Year" award.   During World
    War II, she served in the WAC with the Fourth Air
    Force.   Her juvenile books include: The First Book
    Of The Earth, Watts, 1958; The True Book Of Com-
    munication, Childrens, 1960.   CA-5/6

MINTONYE, Grace
    Author-librarian.   In addition to writing books, Mrs.
    Mintonye has served as Children's Librarian and Assis-
    tant to the Director of Education of the William Rock-
    hill Nelson Gallery of Art in Kansas City, Missouri.
    She and writer James E. Seidelman collaborated to
    produce an art education program which has been de-
    signated by New York City's Metropolitan Museum of
    Art "as one of the best in the nation."   The National
    League of American Pen Women has awarded first prize
    for writing for children several times to Grace Min-
    tonye.   With James E. Seidelman she wrote: Creating
    Mosaics, Crowell-Collier Press, 1967; Creating With
    Clay, Crowell-Collier Press, 1967; Creating With Paint,
    Crowell-Collier Press, 1967; Creating With Paper, Cro-
    well-Collier Press, 1967; The Rub Book, Crowell-Col-
    lier Press, 1968.

MIRSKY, Reba Paeff 1902-
    Born in Boston, she attended Radcliffe College and did

graduate work at Harvard. She also studied at Basle's
Schola Cantorum and in Zululand, South Africa (on a
Guggenheim fellowship). Her husband Dr. Alfred Mir-
sky has been associated with Rockefeller Institute.
They have traveled extensively throughout the world.
Mrs. Mirsky, both a lecturer and teacher, has also
been a member of a concert ensemble. Her first bio-
graphy for young people was Beethoven, Follett, 1957.
She also wrote Mozart, Follett, 1960.   CA-2

MITCHELL, Isla
She was born in New York City, attended schools in
Florida, and later studied at Oxford University. For
fifteen years Isla Mitchell lived in London where her
children were born. Prior to moving to America, she
and her family spent seven years in Ireland. Her experiences in Ireland provided the background for her
children's book Irish Roundabout, Dodd, Mead, 1952.

MIZNER, Elizabeth Howard see HOWARD, Elizabeth

MOLLOY, Anne Stearns (Baker) 1907-
She was born in Boston where she studied at Brimmer
School. She later attended Mt. Holyoke College in
South Hadley, Massachusetts. Until his retirement, her
husband taught at Phillips Exeter Academy. They have
lived both in New Hampshire and Maine. The author
has enjoyed traveling, and one of her books resulted
from a visit to Peru. Juvenile titles include: . . . A
Bird In Hand, Houghton, 1945; Christmas Rocket, Hast-
ings House, 1958; The Girl From Two Miles High,
Hastings House, 1967; The Mystery Of The Pilgrim
Trading Post, Hastings House, 1964; Shaun And The
Boat (A Junior Literary Guild selection), Hastings
House, 1965.   CA-13/14

MONROE, Lyle see HEINLEIN, Robert Anson

MONTGOMERIE, Norah
Author and illustrator, born in London. She attended
art school, has worked in textile design, and has collected and recorded games, rhymes and tales of Scotland. She married Scottish poet and teacher William
Montgomerie. Together they have edited several collections of nursery rhymes. With Kathleen Lines she
compiled Poems And Pictures, Abelard-Schuman, 1959.
Norah Montgomerie also retold and illustrated Twenty-

Five Fables, Abelard-Schuman, 1961.

MONTGOMERY, Elizabeth (Rider) 1902-
She was born in Huarás, Peru, the daughter of a missionary. She studied at Western Washington Teachers
College and at the University of California. She has
been an elementary school teacher. In addition to her
books for young people she has written textbooks, plays,
and articles. Mrs. Montgomery's interests have included: rug-making, painting, and square-dancing.
She and her family have lived in Seattle, Washington.
Juvenile titles include: Old Ben Franklin's Philadel-
delphia, Garrard, 1967; Second-Fiddle Sandra, Dodd,
1958; Story Behind Great Books, McBride, 1946; Story
Behind Popular Songs, Dodd, 1958; Susan And The
Storm, Nelson, 1960.   CA-2

MONTGOMERY, Rutherford George 1896-
His pseudonyms are Al Avery and Everitt Proctor.
Born in North Dakota, he attended Colorado's Western
State College and later resided in Los Gatos, California. His flying experiences with the Air Corps in the
first World War provided the background for his stories about aviation, and his early experiences on a
ranch enabled him to write numerous animal stories
for young people. He received the 1956 New York
Herald Tribune Spring Book Festival Award and the
1957 Boys' Clubs of America Junior Book Award for
Beaver Water, World, 1956. Other juvenile titles include: Amikuk, World, 1955; Ghost Town Gold, World,
1965; The Golden Stallion And Wolf Dog, Little, 1958;
Jets Away!, Dodd, 1957; Kent Barstow Aboard The Dy-
na Soar, Duell, 1964; Thornbush Jungle, World, 1966.
CA-9/10

MONTRESOR, Beni 1926-
Designer, illustrator, born in Verona, Italy. He attended Verona Art School, the Academy of Fine Arts
in Venice, and was awarded a two-year scholarship to
the Centro Sperimentale di Cinematographia in Rome.
After his arrival in the United States, he illustrated
and wrote picture books. He also designed the sets
and costumes for the Broadway musical "Do I Hear A
Waltz?" and the Metropolitan Opera productions of
"The Last Savage" and "Centerentola" (Cinderella). In
1965 he was awarded the Caldecott Medal for his illustrations in Beatrice Schenk de Regniers book May I

Bring A Friend?, Atheneum, 1964. He wrote and illustrated: A For Angel, Knopf, 1969; House Of Flowers, House Of Stars, Knopf, 1962.

MOODY, Ralph Owen 1898-
He was born in East Rochester, New Hampshire and
grew up in Colorado. As a boy he enjoyed hearing
stories told by members of the Navaho, Ute, and A-
pache Indian tribes. He has been a rancher and cattle
trader. He later made his home near San Francisco,
California. Juvenile titles include: The Fields Of
Home, Norton, 1962; The Home Ranch, Norton, 1962;
Kit Carson And The Wild Frontier, Random, 1955; Little Britches, Norton, 1950; Wells Fargo, Houghton,
1961. CA-9/10

MOON, Grace Purdie 1883?-1947 Carl
Husband-wife team. Grace Moon was born in Indianapolis, Indiana. Her early interest in American Indians
continued after her marriage to "Indian" artist and
photographer Carl Moon. They collected authentic
material for their books when they lived with various
Indian tribes in Taos, New Mexico and Oklahoma. Together they wrote One Little Indian, Whitman, 1950.
She also wrote, and Carl Moon illustrated Chi-Weé,
Doubleday, 1925. JBA-1

MOORE, Anne Carroll 1871-1961
She was born in Limerick, Maine, the daughter of a
lawyer. She graduated from the Library School of
Pratt Institute where she served as Children's Librarian until 1906. She then became Supervisor of Work
with Children in the New York Public Library until
1941. Both Pratt Institute and the University of Maine
bestowed honors upon her in recognition of the contributions which she made in the field of children's literature. Anne Carroll Moore died January 20, 1961.
Her many books include: My Roads To Childhood, Horn
Bk. , 1961; Nicholas, Putnam, 1924; The Three Owls,
Macmillan, 1925. JBA-1, JBA-2

MOORE, David William
He was born on a farm near Highland, Ohio and has
lived in Florida and Michigan. He attended Ohio Wesleyan University at Delaware and later studied at Columbia University. Prior to devoting full-time to writing fiction, Mr. Moore had been an editorial writer

for magazines. His book The End Of Long John Silver
(Crowell, 1946) resulted from his son's class assign-
ment. For young people he also wrote The End Of
Black Dog, Crowell, 1949.

MOORE, Lamont 1909-
A well-known art educator, he started his career in
the Newark Museum in New Jersey. He became Director of Education at the National Gallery of Art in Washington, D. C., and he later served as Director of the
Yale University Art Gallery. During World War II, he
was an officer in the Monuments and Fine Arts Section
of Military Government and received membership in
the Legion of Honor awarded by the French government. For young people he wrote: The First Book Of
Architecture, Watts, 1961; First Book Of Paintings,
Watts, 1960; Sculptured Image, Watts, 1967.

MOORE, Lilian
Teacher, editor, author. She was born in New York
City and graduated from Hunter College. She did grad-
uate study at Columbia University. She has been asso-
ciated with the Bureau of Educational Research of the
New York City Board of Education and an editor of the
Arrow Book Club. She has also worked as a reading
consultant for both textbook and trade publishers. Her
juvenile books include: Bear Trouble, McGraw, 1960;
I Feel The Same Way, Atheneum, 1967; Little Raccoon
And The Outside World, McGraw, 1965; Once Upon A
Season, Abingdon, 1962; Papa Albert, Atheneum, 1964;
Wobbly Wheels, Abingdon, 1956. With Leone Adelson
she also wrote Old Rosie, Junior Literary Guild and
Random House, 1952.

MOORE, Nancy
She once was a professional actress and has also lectured on the theater. In addition to writing books, she
has written for both radio and television. Nancy Moore
has enjoyed traveling and on a trip around the world
was particularly impressed with the city of Ceylon.
Her hobbies have been the ballet and collecting antique
paper weights. Juvenile titles include: Ermintrude,
Vanguard, 1960; Unhappy Hippopotamus (A Junior Literary Guild selection), Vanguard, 1957. With Edward
Leight she also wrote Miss Harriet Hippopotamus And
The Most Wonderful, Vanguard, 1963.

MOORE, Patrick Alfred 1923-
British astronomer, author, lecturer. He was born in
Middlesex, England, attended private schools, and has
made his home in Northern Ireland. He served with
the Bomber Command of the Royal Air Force during
World War II. At the age of eleven, Patrick Moore
was a member of the British Astronomical Association
and later belonged to the Association of Lunar and
Planetary Observers, the Royal Society of Arts, and
many other astronomical societies. He received the
Lorimer Gold Medal for services to astronomy in 1962
and also served as editor of the Yearbook Of Astronomy. He was awarded the 1956 Boys' Clubs of America
book certificate for The Earth Our Home, Abelard,
1957. Other juvenile titles include: Exploring Maps,
Hawthorn, 1967; Peril On Mars, Putnam, 1965; The
Picture History Of Astronomy (new ed.), Grosset, 1967.
CA-13/14

MOORE, Vardine 1906-
Teacher, author. Prior to her marriage, she was a
kindergarten teacher in Evansville, Indiana. She also
conducted a story hour for boys and girls on radio.
Mrs. Moore later had her own nursery school. She
has written stories for many magazines including Child
Life and Jack And Jill. With Fleur Conkling she wrote
Billy Between, Westminster Press, 1951. She also
wrote Pre-School Story Hour, Scarecrow Press, 1966.

MORAN, Eugene Francis 1872-
Mr. Moran became President in 1906 of the Moran
Towing and Transportation Company which was founded
by his father in 1860. He later served as Chairman
of the Board. He has been Commissioner of the Port
of New York Authority and Chairman of the Rivers,
Harbors and Piers Committee of the Maritime Association of the Port of New York. His personal background enabled him to write Famous Harbors Of The
World, Random, 1953.

MORDVINOFF, Nicolas 1911-
His pseudonym is Nicolas. He was born in Leningrad
and graduated from the University of Paris. He spent
many years painting and writing on islands in the South
Pacific. After coming to the United States, he lived
on a farm in New Jersey. In 1952 he was awarded
the Caldecott Medal for his illustrations in William

Lipkind's Finders Keepers, Harcourt, 1951. In addition to illustrating many books for other authors, he also wrote Bear's Land, Coward-McCann, 1955. MJA

MORE, Caroline see CONE, Molly Lamken

MORENUS, Richard 1897-
Author and lecturer. At one time he was in the field of advertising. His home has been in Fennville, Michigan. Authenticity for his many children's books was acquired through travel in Canada and through "his six years of primitive bush living. " His juvenile books include: Dew Line (A Junior Literary Guild selection), Rand, 1957; Hudson's Bay Company, Random, 1956.

MOREY, Walt
He was born near the Olympic Mountains and has spent most of his life in the Pacific Northwest. At the end of World War II, he served as an Alaskan fish trap inspector. Mr. Morey has lived in Portland, Oregon but has looked forward to a return visit to the north where he can "travel for days and see no one; where the silence is a hundred miles deep and the sun hits you bang in the eye at 2:00 a. m. " His first book for children was Gentle Ben, Dutton, 1965. He also wrote Angry Waters, Dutton, 1969.

MORGAN, Alfred Powell 1889-
He was born in Brooklyn, New York and spent part of his childhood in Upper Montclair, New Jersey. He attended the Massachusetts Institute of Technology. During college he began writing books and articles for magazines. In addition to his career as an author, he has also been a manufacturer of electrical and electronic equipment. Juvenile titles include: Adventures In Electrochemistry, Scribner, 1959; Aquarium Book For Boys And Girls, Scribner, 1959; Boys' Book Of Engines, Motors, And Turbines, Scribner, 1946; A First Electrical Book For Boys, Scribner, 1963. MJA

MORISON, Samuel Eliot 1887-
Author, historian, teacher, born in Boston. The author has been a Professor of History at Harvard University where he received both his bachelor's and doctor's degrees. He has also been on the faculty at the University of California and at one time held the chair of American History at Oxford. During World War II,

Admiral Morison served as the official historian of the
U. S. Navy and was awarded the Legion of Merit with
Combat Clasp and seven battle stars. For young people he wrote Story Of The "Old Colony" Of New Plymouth [1620-1692], Knopf, 1956. CA-2

MORRIS, Richard Brandon 1904-
Historian, teacher, editor. He has been Professor of
History at Columbia University and has taught at City
College, New York. A member of Princeton Univer-
sity's Institute for Advanced Study, he also taught his-
tory in the school's graduate program. In addition Dr.
Morris has served as editor of the Encyclopedia Of
American History. Juvenile titles include: The First
Book Of The American Revolution, Watts, 1956; First
Book Of The Constitution, Watts, 1958; First Book Of
The Indian Wars, Watts, 1959.

MORROW, Suzanne Stark
She was born in California and studied at the University
of Oregon. She has worked in radio in addition to
writing for boys and girls. She decided to write about
the early history of man ("the first men inherited
nothing") in her book There Was A Time, Dutton, 1965.
She also wrote Inatuk's Friend, Little, 1968.

MOSCOW, Alvin 1925-
Author and reporter, born in New York. He studied in
New York at St. John's University and City College and
obtained a bachelor's degree in journalism from the
University of Missouri. His home has been in Santa
Monica, California. He served as a radioman with the
U. S. Navy during World War II. After the war, he
was a reporter for the Associated Press and was assigned to cover the "Andrea Doria" - "Stockholm"
hearings which resulted from a sea collision in 1956.
From his research he later wrote the best-seller Collision Course, Putnam, 1959. For boys and girls he
wrote City At Sea, Putnam, 1962. CA-2

MOSEL, Arlene
A native of Ohio, she has lived in Cleveland. Mrs.
Mosel graduated from Ohio Wesleyan University and
has been on the staff at Case Western University as
Assistant Professor of Library Science. Her own in-
terpretation of a tale she heard as a child resulted in
her first book for children entitled Tikki Tikki Tembo,

Holt, 1968.

MOSES, Anna Mary (Robertson) 1860-1961
Children and adults have known her as the artist called
"Grandma" Moses who started painting at the age of
seventy-eight.   She was born on a farm in New York.
Anna Mary Robertson began to earn her own living when
she was twelve-years-old.   In 1887 she married Thomas S. Moses, and they lived in Virginia.   Later Mr.
and Mrs. Moses bought a dairy farm in New York
State.   She received the New York State Prize for a
painting in 1941, and in 1949 was the recipient of an
award from the Women's National Press Club in Washington, D. C.   Her pictures vividly illustrate a children's book called The Grandma Moses Storybook (Nora
Kramer, ed., Random, 1961).   Her paintings illustrate
an edition of The Night Before Christmas by Clement
C. Moore, Random, 1961.

MOWAT, Farley 1921-
Born in Belleville, Ontario, Canada, he grew up in
Saskatchewan, and graduated from the University of
Toronto.   In 1940 he served overseas with the Canadian Army.   Following the war, he married and returned
to Toronto to live.   He and his wife traveled in the far
north; his wife being "the first white woman ever to see
the central Barrens."   Later Farley Mowat made his
home in a fishing outport in Newfoundland.   Juvenile
titles include: The Curse Of The Viking Grave (A
Junior Literary Guild selection), Little, 1966; Lost In
The Barrens (A Junior Literary Guild selection), Little, 1956; Owls In The Family, Little, 1961.   CA-3

MUEHL, Lois Baker 1920-
Born in Oak Park, Illinois, she graduated from Oberlin
College and later studied at the State University of
Iowa.   She married Siegmar Muehl, a professor at the
University of Iowa.   Besides writing, Mrs. Muehl has
taught school and worked in radio.   Her books for
young people include: The Hidden Year Of Devlin
Bates, Holiday, 1967; Worst Room In The School, Holi-
day, 1961.

MÜHLENWEG, Fritz
He has lived in Germany but has often visited Mongolia
where he has had many exciting experiences.   He was
once kidnaped, escaped through the desert, and finally

was saved by Mongolian cavalry. Besides painting in
Germany, Fritz Mühlenweg has accompanied expeditions
to Mongolia in order to set up meterorological stations.
He wrote Big Tiger And Christian (tr. by Isabel and
Florence McHugh), Pantheon, 1952.

MUKERJI, Dhan Gopal 1890-1936
Author and lecturer, born near Calcutta, India. Before
coming to America at the age of twenty, he attended
Calcutta University. After his arrival in the United
States, he studied at the University of California and
graduated from Stanford University. The author later
lectured on comparative literature throughout England
and the United States. Following his marriage to Ethel
Ray Dugan, he lived in Pennsylvania but later made
his home in New Milford, Connecticut where his writing
career began. Mr. Mukerji was the recipient of the
1928 Newbery Medal for Gay-Neck, The Story Of A
Pigeon, Dutton, 1927. Other juvenile titles include:
Fierce-Face, Dutton, 1936; Kari The Elephant, Dutton,
1922; Rama, The Hero Of India, Dutton, 1930.   JBA-1

MULCAHY, Lucille Burnett
Her pseudonym is Helen Hale. She was born in Albu-
querque, New Mexico and studied at New Mexico State
College. Her stories have appeared in many maga-
zines for boys and girls. Mrs. Mulcahy's interest in
Indian pottery resulted in her writing Magic Fingers
(A Junior Literary Guild selection), Nelson, 1958.
CA-5/6

MUNARI, Bruno
Italian author-artist, born in Milan. In addition to
book illustration, Mr. Munari has been a photographer,
sculptor, and toy designer. He has also worked on
projection slides and designed a fountain in Milan. His
work has been exhibited in New York City's Museum of
Modern Art. For children he wrote and illustrated:
ABC, World, 1960; Bruno Munari's Zoo, World, 1963.

MUNRO, Eleanor C. 1928-
Born in Brooklyn, New York, she graduated from
Smith College, and later studied at the University of
Paris on a Fulbright grant. She has been Associate
Editor of Art News and Managing Editor of Art News
Annual. She married editor and art critic Dr. Alfred
Frankfurter. Her articles have appeared in both Hori-

zon and Perspectives USA.   For young people she wrote
The Golden Encyclopedia Of Art, Golden Press, 1961.
CA-4

MUNSON, Gorham 1896-
He was born in Amityville, New York and graduated
from Wesleyan University at Middletown, Connecticut.
In addition to a career as a teacher and magazine edi-
tor, Mr. Munson has been an Assistant Professor of
English at Fairleigh Dickinson University in Madison,
New Jersey.   He also taught at the New School for
Social Research where he and the late Robert Frost
became good friends.   For young people he wrote Mak-
ing Poems For America: Robert Frost, Encyclopedia
Britannica, 1962.   CA-11/12

MURPHY, Mabel Ansley 1870-
Her pseudonym is Anne S. Lee.   She studied at Knox
College, Galesburg, Illinois, Columbia University, and
graduated from State Teachers' College, Indiana, Pennsylvania.   Mrs. Murphy once was in charge of a book
page for Holland's Magazine in Dallas, Texas.   Her
articles on religious education and travel have also appeared in other publications.   For boys and girls she
wrote They Were Little Once, Caxton, 1942.

MURPHY, Robert William 1902-
Author and editor.   He grew up in Virginia near the
Chickahominy Swamp.   He has always loved the outdoors, and the study of wildlife has been a lifetime interest.   Prior to writing full-time, Robert Murphy
served as senior editor of the Saturday Evening Post.
His books for children include: Heritage Restored, Dutton, 1969; The Pond (winner of the Dutton Animal book
award, 1964), Dutton, 1964; Wild Geese Calling (winner
of the Dutton Animal book award, 1966), Dutton, 1966.
CA-9/10

MURRAY, Don (Morison) 1924-
Author and newspaperman, born in Boston, Massachusetts.   A graduate of the University of New Hampshire,
he received his early education in the Quincy and Win-
throp schools in Massachusetts.   He was a paratrooper
in World War II.   Don Murray was awarded a Pulitzer
Prize for editorial writing when he worked for the Boston Herald newspaper.   His work has also appeared in
such magazines as the Reader's Digest and the Saturday

Evening Post. For young people he wrote The World
Of Sound Recording, Lippincott, 1965. CA-4

MURRAY, Gladys Hall
She studied at Vassar College where she stored up many
happy memories ("organ music in a dimly lighted chapel, a Christmas pageant in the snow, . . . picnics
and hikes along the country roads, and most important,
warm and lasting friendships"). She has worked in an
advertising agency and has written for magazines and
newspapers. Gladys Hall Murray has traveled many
times across the United States and has also visited A-
laska. Sitka, Alaska was the background for . . .
Mystery Of The Talking Totem Pole (winner of the Dodd,
Mead-Calling All Girls Prize Competition), Dodd, 1965.

MUSCIANO, Walter A.
He was born in New York City, attended Brooklyn Polytechnic Institute, and has made his home in River Edge,
New Jersey. In addition to writing books, Walter Musciano has been an engineering draftsman and model airplane designer. He has also designed and built model
boats and cars and has received many awards for his
models. His magazine articles about model construction have appeared in Mechanix Illustrated, Model Airplane News, and Air World. Juvenile books which he
wrote and illustrated include: Building And Operating
Model Cars, Funk, 1956; Model Plane Manual, Mc-
Bride, 1952.

MUSGRAVE, Florence 1902-
Teacher, librarian, author, born in Mount Clare, West
Virginia, the daughter of a Methodist minister. She
graduated from Fairmont State Teachers' College in
Fairmont, West Virginia and received her master's degree from New York University. She has taught both
in a rural school and in high schools. Following her
teaching experiences in South Orange, New Jersey, she
later taught English and Dramatics in the Willoughby-
Eastlake Public Schools near Cleveland, Ohio. Florence Musgrave has also served on the staff of the
Wheeling, West Virginia Public Library. She has lived
in Mentor, Ohio. Juvenile titles include: Catherine's
Bells, Ariel, 1954; Oh Sarah, Ariel, 1953; Two Dates
For Mike, Hastings House, 1964. CA-13/14

MYERS, Madeline Neuberger 1896-
    Author and teacher. She grew up in New York City
    and has lived in both New York and California. Mrs.
    Myers has been an instructor of occupational therapy
    and has also been associated with programs for under-
    privileged children. She has been interested in textile
    design and has created many hand-painted textiles. For
    young people she wrote: The Courting-Lamp Mystery,
    Holt, 1958; Pocketful Of Feathers, Westminster Press,
    1950.

MYLLER, Rolf 1926-
    He was born in Germany and graduated from Cornell
    University. He also studied at New York University.
    He has been an Assistant Professor of Architecture at
    Pratt Institute in Brooklyn, and he has also had his own
    architectural practice. Mr. Myller was awarded ten
    thousand dollars as one of six finalists in the Franklin
    D. Roosevelt Memorial Competition in Washington, D. C.
    His home has been in New York City. For boys and
    girls he wrote: How Big Is A Foot? (A Junior Liter-
    ary Guild selection), Atheneum, 1962; Rolling Round
    (A Junior Literary Guild selection), Atheneum, 1963.
    CA-7/8

MYRUS, Donald Richard 1927-
    Author and editor, born in Baldwin, New York. He at-
    tended the University of Chicago and received his A. B.
    degree from Muhlenberg College in Allentown, Pennsyl-
    vania. He began his career as a copy boy for the New
    York Daily News and was a reporter for the Schenec-
    tady (N. Y.) Union-Star. The author has also served
    as book editor for publishing houses. He was the foun-
    der and managing editor of American Gun. Donald My-
    rus has lived in New York City. In 1963 his book
    Keeping Up With The Astronauts (Grosset, 1962) was
    the winner of a Boys' Club of America book award.
    He also wrote I Like Jazz, Macmillan, 1964.   CA-4

N

NASH, Mary (Hughes) 1925-
    She lived in Seattle, Washington after she graduated
    from Radcliffe College. Her writing career began at
    the age of five when she reversed the usual procedure
    and told bedtime stories to her mother. Mary Nash
    has always enjoyed books and once said: "The great

unfailing pleasure in my childhood was my books, and
I have always felt a kind of debt to the authors who
wrote them for me. It would be a fine feeling, in my
turn, to pass this pleasure to other children today. "
Magazines such as Good Housekeeping, New Yorker,
and Pacific Spectator have published her stories. Her
juvenile books include: Mrs. Coverlet's Detectives,
Little, 1965; Mrs. Coverlet's Magicians, Little, 1961.
CA-5/6

NASH, (Frediric) Ogden 1902-1971
Author and poet, born in Rye, New York. He attended
St. George's School and Harvard University. Mr. Nash
and his family have lived in New York City and in
Boar's Head, New Hampshire. His two daughters are
also writers. In addition to writing fiction and poetry,
he collaborated with S. J. Perleman and the late Kurt
Weill to write "One Touch of Venus, " a Broadway musi-
cal. He has also written for the New Yorker. Ogden
Nash has been a member of the National Institute of
Arts and Letters. For boys and girls he wrote: The
Adventures Of Isabel, Little, 1963; The Animal Garden,
Lippincott, 1965; Custard The Dragon And The Wicked
Knight, Little, 1961; Girls Are Silly, Watts, 1962.
CA-13/14

NATHAN, Adele (Gutman)
Author, director, producer. She was the producer and
director of "Mr. Lincoln Goes To Gettysburg" which
was given by the Western Maryland Railroad Company.
This production was awarded the Freedom Foundation
Award at Valley Forge. Adele Nathan has also written
scripts and worked for the motion picture industry.
With William C. Baker she wrote Famous Railroad Sta-
tions Of The World, Random, 1953. She has also writ-
ten: Building Of The First Transcontinental Railroad,
Random, 1950; Major John Andre, Gentleman Spy,
Watts, 1969.

NATHAN, Daniel see DANNAY, Frederic

NEAL, Harry Edward 1906-
He was born in Pittsfield, Massachusetts. When he
retired from government service, he was Assistant
Chief of the United States Secret Service and was the
recipient of the Exceptional Civilian Service Medal.
His articles have appeared in many magazines, and he

has conducted workshops in fiction and nonfiction at
various writers' conferences including: Georgetown
University, La Salle College in Philadelphia, Pennsylvania, and the Christian Writers' and Editors' Conferences in St. Davids, Pennsylvania and Green Lake,
Wisconsin. He has lived in Rixeyville, Virginia. Juvenile titles include: Diary Of Democracy, Messner,
1962; Disease Detectives, Messner, 1959; The Protect-
ors, Messner, 1968.   CA-5/6

NEILSON, Frances Fullerton (Jones) 1910-
Born in Philadelphia, she lived in New York and Huntington, Long Island after her marriage to writer Winth-
rop Neilson. Her summers spent in Dorking, England
provided the background for her first book, and other
stories resulted from visits to British Guiana, South
America, and the West Indies. The Neilson family
have enjoyed sailing and deep-sea fishing as hobbies.
For young people she wrote: Bruce Benson On Trails
Of Thunder, Dutton, 1950; Look To The New Moon,
Junior Literary Guild and Abelard, 1953.

NELSON, Cholmondeley M. 1903-
He was born in London and attended the Royal Naval
College at Osborne and Dartmouth, England. After
coming to America he was associated with MGM studios. In 1939 he returned to England and joined the
British Army later serving as Assistant Adjutant General to Field Marshal Montgomery. Following the war,
he returned to America and became a United States
citizen. He has served as Director of the Los Angeles
World Affairs Council and U. N. Representative for the
Motion Picture Industry. His home has been in Pasadena, California. For young people he wrote With Nelson At Trafalgar, Reilly and Lee, 1961.   CA-5/6

NELSON, Marg
She was born in California and attended school there.
Marg Nelson has also lived in Bellevue, Washington.
Her stories have won acclaim for their social realism.
For boys and girls Mrs. Nelson wrote: A Girl Called
Chris, Ariel, 1962; Mystery On A Minus Tide, Ariel,
1964.

NEPHEW, William
He attended the University of California at Berkeley.
Mr. Nephew has been in charge of a missile research

team in an aircraft company.   The author has lived in
Palo Alto, California.   With Michael Chester he wrote
Planet Trip, Putnam, 1960.

NESBIT, E.   see BLAND, Edith (Nesbit)

NESBIT, Troy see FOLSOM, Franklin

NESS, Evaline (Michelow) 1911-
    Illustrator-author, born in Union City, Ohio.   When
    she was two-years-old, her family moved to Pontiac,
    Michigan.   Prior to attending art school she studied
    library science and took courses in education.   She at-
    tended the Art Students League in New York, the Art
    Institute in Chicago, and the Accademia di Belle Arti
    in Rome.   She has created illustrations for magazines
    and fashion drawings.   In addition to living in Rome,
    Evaline Ness has also visited Bangkok and traveled
    throughout the Orient.   Several of her book illustrations
    have been runners-up for the Caldecott Medal; however,
    in 1967 she received the Caldecott Medal for her book
    Sam, Bangs And Moonshine, Holt, 1966.   She also
    wrote and illustrated: A Double Discovery, Scribner,
    1965; Mr. Miacca, Holt, 1967; Pavo And The Prin-
    cess, Scribner, 1964.   CA-7/8

NEUFELD, John
    Author and playwright, Mr. Neufeld has lived and work-
    ed in New York City.   He received degrees from Phil-
    lips Exeter and Yale University.   In addition to writing
    books, the author has been active in the publishing
    field.   John Neufeld has also written plays, short sto-
    ries, and pieces for television.   The American Library
    Association named his first book for children Edgar
    Allan (Phillips, 1968) as one of its Notable Books of
    1969.   He also wrote Lisa, Bright & Dark, Phillips,
    1969.

NEVILLE, Emily Cheney 1919-
    She was born in Manchester, Connecticut and lived in
    New York's Gramercy Park after her marriage to news-
    paperman Glenn Neville.   She attended Oxford School
    in West Hartford, Connecticut and graduated from Bryn
    Mawr College in Pennsylvania.   At one time the author
    was on the staff of the New York Mirror and New York
    Daily News.   Mrs. Neville was the recipient of the
    1964 Newbery Medal award for It's Like This Cat (Har-

per, 1963).   Her book Berries Goodman (Harper, 1965)
was chosen as a 1965 ALA Notable Children's Book.
She also wrote: The Seventeenth-Street Gang, Harper,
1966; Traveler From A Small Kingdom, Harper, 1968.
CA-7/8

NEVINS, Albert J.   1915-
A Maryknoll priest, born in Yonkers, New York.   He
attended Cathedral and Venard Colleges and the Maryknoll Seminary.   Following his ordination in 1942, he
wrote for many publications, lectured, and produced
films.   Father Nevins has also served as a member
of the executive board of the Catholic Press Association
of the United States and the Catholic Institute of the
Press.   Juvenile titles include: Adventures Of Men Of
Maryknoll, Dodd, 1957; Away To Central America,
Dodd, 1967; Away To Mexico, Dodd, 1966; The Young
Conquistador, Dodd, 1960.   CA-5/6

NEWBERRY, Clare (Turlay) 1903-1970
Author-illustrator.   Born in Enterprise, Oregon, she
grew up in Vancouver, Washington.   She studied at the
University of Oregon in Eugene and attended art classes
at the Portland Art Museum and San Francisco School
of Fine Arts.   She also studied in Paris.   She married
Henry Trujillo and has lived in Las Vegas, New Mexico.   Juvenile books which she wrote and illustrated include: April's Kittens, Harper, 1940; Frosty, Harper,
1961; Herbert The Lion, Harper, 1956; Lambert's Bargain, Harper, 1941; Marshmallow, Harper, 1942; Wid-
get, Harper, 1958.   JBA-2

NEWCOMB, Covelle 1908-
She was born in San Antonio, Texas where she later
attended the Incarnate Word College.   She also studied
at Washington University in St. Louis, Hunter College
and Columbia University in New York.   She married
artist-author Addison Burbank, and they have lived in
Port Jefferson, Long Island, New York.   Covelle Newcomb received an honorary degree of Doctor of Letters
from Incarnate Word College in San Antonio, Texas.
Juvenile titles include: Black Fire, McKay, 1963;
Brother Zero, Dodd, 1959; Christopher Columbus, The
Sea Lord, Dodd, 1963; Red Hat, Longmans, 1941; Secret Door, Dodd, 1946.   CA-19/20, JBA-2

NEWCOMBE, Jack
He was born in Burlington, Vermont and graduated from
Brown University.   He also attended the Universities of
Missouri and California, Pomona College, and the A-
merican University at Biarritz.   Prior to being a text
editor of Life magazine, Jack Newcombe was managing
editor of Sport magazine.   His home has been in Rye,
New York.   For boys and girls he wrote The Firebal-
lers, Putnam, 1964.

NEWELL, Homer Edward 1915-
Dr. Newell has been associated with the U. S. space
programs.   He has served as Assistant Director in
charge of Space Science of the National Aeronautics
and Space Administration, Acting Superintendent of the
Atmosphere and Astrophysics Division, and Vice Chairman of the Technical Panel on Rocketry of the United
States National Committee for the International Geophysical Year.   He has also worked in the Naval Research Laboratory.   The Newell family has lived in
Kensington, Maryland.   He has written books for both
adults and children, and his juvenile titles include:
Express To The Stars, McGraw, 1961; Guide To Rockets, Missiles, And Satellites, McGraw, 1958; Space
Book For Young People, McGraw, 1960.

NEWELL, Hope (Hockenberry) 1896-
Nurse, author, born in Bradford, Pennsylvania, she
graduated from Columbia University.   During World
War I, she served in France with the U. S. Army
Nurse Corps.   Following the war, she married and
lived in Napa Valley, California.   Later she and her
family moved to New York City where she has worked
in public health nursing.   Juvenile titles include: The
Little Old Woman Carries On, Nelson, 1947; Mary
Ellis, Student Nurse, Harper, 1958; Steppin And Fam-
ily, Oxford, 1942; Story Of Christina, Junior Literary
Guild and Harper, 1947.   MJA

NEWMAN, Robert (Howard) 1909-
He was born in New York.   In addition to books, Mr.
Newman has written articles for magazines and plays
for radio, films, and television.   He has been interested in the country of Japan, archery, and fencing.
As a result of his interests, he wrote a book for young
people entitled Japanese, Atheneum, 1964.   CA-2

NEYHART, Louise Albright
     She has been active in civic, church, and educational
     projects in the community of Freeport, Illinois. As a
     teacher who has always enjoyed books and history,
     Louise Neyhart did thorough research for the stories
     which she has written for boys and girls. These in-
     clude: Henry Ford, Engineer, Houghton, 1950; Henry's
     Lincoln, Holiday, 1945.

NICKERSON, Jan see SMITH, Jan

NIC LEODHAS, Sorche see ALGER, Leclaire G.

NICOLAS see MORDVINOFF, Nicolas

NICOLAY, Helen 1866-
     She was born in Paris where her father John G. Nico-
     lay served as American Consul General. Mr. Nicolay
     also wrote with John Hay a ten-volume life of Abraham
     Lincoln. When her father died, Miss Nicolay finished
     a one-volume Lincoln biography which he had begun.
     She has lived in Washington, D. C. and has spent her
     summers in New Hampshire. Juvenile titles include:
     Born To Command, Appleton-Century, 1945; The Boys'
     Life Of Abraham Lincoln, Century, 1906; The Bridge
     Of Water, The Story Of Panama And The Canal, Apple-
     ton-Century, 1940; China's First Lady, Appleton-Cen-
     tury, 1944. JBA-1, JBA-2

NIEHUIS, Charles C.
     Author and editor, born in Buck Grove, Iowa. He
     worked in a variety of jobs in Arizona and Minnesota
     before his writing career began. His first story was
     published in Sports Afield, and he has contributed sto-
     ries about fishing and hunting to other magazines. Mr.
     Niehuis organized the Division of Information and Edu-
     cation for the Arizona Game and Fish Commission.
     He has also been editor of the Arizona Wildlife-Sports-
     man magazine. The author's main interest has always
     been the conservation of natural resources. For young
     people he wrote Trapping The Silver Beaver (A Junior
     Literary Guild selection), Dodd, 1956.

NIXON, K. see NIXON, Kathleen Irene (Blundell)

NIXON, Kathleen Irene (Blundell)
     Artist-author, born in London. Her pseudonym is K.

Nixon, and she married V. R. Blundell. She has lived
in India and has also made visits to America, Australia, Canada, China, and Japan. Her pictures of animals have been exhibited in many cities including: Melbourne, London, and Paris. The first story she wrote
was Pushti, Warne, 1956. She also wrote and illustrated Poo & Pushti, Warne, 1959.

NOBLE, Iris (Davis) 1922-
She was born in Calgary, Canada. Her family moved
to Oregon when she was eleven years old, and she attended school in Portland. After graduating from the
University of Oregon, she did further study at Stanford
University in California. Before her marriage to the
late author Hollister Noble, she had been a secretary
and publicity director. Mrs. Noble has contributed articles to magazines and has traveled abroad doing research for her biographies. Her home has been in
Point Arena, California. Her juvenile books include:
Clarence Darrow, Defense Attorney, Messner, 1958;
Courage In Her Hands, Messner, 1967; The Courage Of
Dr. Lister (A Junior Literary Guild selection), Messner, 1960; Labor's Advocate: Eugene V. Debs, Messner, 1966; Megan (A Junior Literary Guild selection),
Messner, 1965.   CA-3

NODSET, Joan L.   see   LEXAU, Joan M.

NOLAN, Jeannette Covert 1896-
Her pseudonym is Caroline Tucker. She was born in
Indiana where her grandfather served as one of the
state's first newspaper editors. Jeannette Nolan also
worked on a newspaper (the Evansville Courier) in
Evansville prior to her marriage. She has taught
creative writing at Indiana University and has conducted
juvenile workshops at the University of Colorado Writers' Conferences. In 1959 and 1961 she was presented
the Indiana University Award for the "Most Distinguished
Juvenile Book by an Indiana Author." She has lived in
Indianapolis. Juvenile titles include: Belle Boyd, Secret Agent, Messner, 1967; Gather Ye Rosebuds, Appleton, 1946; The Gay Poet, Messner, 1940.   CA-7/8,
JBA-2

NORDHOFF, Charles Bernard 1887-
He was born in London and was brought to the United
States by his American parents when he was three-

years-old. He grew up in Philadelphia, attended Stanford University in California, and graduated from Harvard. Charles Nordhoff met James Norman Hall during World War I when he served in the Lafayette Flying Corps. Following the war, the two men edited a
history of the Corps. Mr. Nordhoff has lived on the
island of Tahiti. His interests have been anthropology
and fishing. For boys and girls he wrote The Derelict,
Little, 1928. With James Norman Hall he wrote: Falcons Of France, Little, 1929; Mutiny On The Bounty,
Little, 1932. JBA-1

NORDSTROM, Ursula
Born in New York City, she attended Northfield School
for Girls and Scudder Preparatory School. In 1954 she
served as President of the Children's Book Council.
She has been Vice President and Director of the Department of Books for Boys and Girls in a publishing firm.
Miss Nordstrom has lived in Bedford Hills, New York.
She wrote The Secret Language, Harper, 1960. CA-
13/14

NORLING, Ernest Ralph 1892-   Josephine (Stearns) 1895-
Husband-wife team. Ernest Norling studied at Chicago's
Art Institute and Academy of Fine Arts. He has been
a free-lance artist and has been on the staff of the
Seattle Times. He has also been Art Director for an
airline company. Josephine (Jo) Norling graduated
from the University of Washington in Seattle. She has
been a teacher and at one time served with the Ameri-
can Red Cross. The Norlings have lived in Seattle.
Their juvenile books include: First Book Of Water,
Watts, 1952; Pogo's Farm Adventure, A Story Of Soil,
Holt, 1948; Pogo's Jet Ride, Holt, 1961; Pogo's Lamb,
Holt, 1947; Willie Skis, Holt, 1959. CA-2

NORMAN, Charles 1904-
He has been both a student and teacher at New York
University. When he was nineteen, he served as a
seaman on a freighter going to South America. He
later went to Europe and lived for several years in
Paris. During World War II, he served in the Army.
Mr. Norman has been a writer for Time magazine, the
Associated Press, and the Columbia Broadcasting Sys-
tem. His books for young people include: The Flight
And Adventures Of Charles II, Random House, 1958;
Orimha Of The Mohawks, Macmillan, 1961.

NORRIS, Faith Grigsby
Author-teacher. She grew up in the Orient and has
lived in Kobe, Tokyo, and Korea. She has been a
teacher at Oregon State College. Her correspondence
with friends in Korea provided the incentive to write a
book which would enable American children to understand Korea and its people. With author Peter Lumn
she wrote Kim Of Korea (A Junior Literary Guild selection), Messner, 1955.

NORTH, Sterling 1906-
Editor, author, born in Edgerton, Wisconsin, he studied
at the University of Chicago. St. Nicholas magazine
published his first poem at the age of eight. He has
been literary editor of the New York World Telegram
And Sun and also was General Editor of "North Star
Books." He and his wife have lived in Morristown,
New Jersey. His books for young people include: Abe
Lincoln, Random House, 1956; The First Steamboat On
The Mississippi, Houghton, 1962; Hurry, Spring!, Dut-
ton, 1966; Little Rascal, Dutton, 1965; Rascal, Dutton,
1963.   CA-5/6

NORTON, Alice Mary
Her pseudonyms are André Norton and Andrew Norton.
Author and librarian, born in Cleveland, Ohio. She attended Western Reserve University. In addition to
writing books, she has been a juvenile book editor and
once managed a bookshop. She has made her home in
Cleveland and at one time served as library assistant
in the children's department of the Cleveland Public
Library. Miss Norton has written science fiction stories, historical novels, and translated legends. For
young people she wrote: The Beast Master, Harcourt,
1959; Catseye, Harcourt, 1961; The Defiant Agents,
World, 1962; Key Out Of Time, World, 1963; Moon Of
Three Rings, Viking, 1966; Operation Time Search, Harcourt, 1967; Steel Magic, World, 1965.   CA-4, MJA

NORTON, André see NORTON, Alice Mary

NORTON, Andrew see NORTON, Alice Mary

NORTON, Mary
Actress, author, playwright. At one time she was a
member of the "Old Vic" Shakespeare Company. After
her marriage she lived in Portugal where her writing

career began.   Later she moved to London where she
lived in an eighteenth-century house in the Chelsea district.   Mrs. Norton received the British Library Association's Carnegie Medal for The Borrowers (Dent, 1952)
as the most distinguished book of 1952.   Other juvenile
books include: Bed-knob And Broomstick, Harcourt,
1957; Borrowers Afield, Harcourt, 1955; Borrowers A-
float, Harcourt, 1959; The Borrowers Aloft, Harcourt,
1961.

NOURSE, Alan E.   1928-
Science fiction writer, born in Iowa.   He took a pre-
medical course at Rutgers University, and graduated
from the School of Medicine at the University of Pennsylvania.   His stories have been published in many
magazines.   Prior to devoting full-time to writing, Dr.
Nourse practiced medicine in North Bend, Washington.
His medical background provided his science fiction
stories with authentic scientific detail.   Many of his
books have been Junior Literary Guild selections and
include: Psi High And Others, McKay, 1967; Raiders
From The Rings, McKay, 1962; Scavengers In Space,
McKay, 1959; Star Surgeon, McKay, 1960.   CA-1

NUGENT, Frances Roberts 1904-
Artist, author, teacher, born in New York.   She at-
tended Pratt Institute in Brooklyn, graduated from the
University of California at Los Angeles, and received
her master's degree from the University of Southern
California.   She also studied abroad.   Miss Norton la-
ter became an art instructor at UCLA and the Los
Angeles County Art Museum.   She also taught in the
Santa Monica grade schools.   Her main interests have
been sketching, reading, and travel.   For boys and
girls she wrote and illustrated Jan Van Eyck: Master
Painter, Rand, 1962.   CA-5/6

NURENBERG, Thelma
Author, editor, reporter.   Although New York City has
been her home, Mrs. Nurenberg has visited many for-
eign countries during her numerous travels abroad.
Her first book for young people was My Cousin, The
Arab, Abelard, 1965.

O

OAKES, Virginia Armstrong
She is also known as Vanya Oakes.   Born in Nutley,

New Jersey, she graduated from the University of
California at Berkeley. She has been a correspondent
for the United Press and the Christian Science Monitor
and has traveled throughout Indonesia, Burma, Siam,
and the Philippines. Vanya Oakes has lectured and
written on the Orient. She has also been on the faculty
of Los Angeles City College. Her books for young people include: By Sun And Star, Macmillan, 1948; Footprints Of The Dragon, Winston, 1949; Hawaiian Treasure, Messner, 1957; Willy Wong, American, Messner,
1951.

O'BRIEN, John Sherman 1898-1938
He has been known as Jack O'Brien to young readers.
Born in Duluth, Minnesota, he attended New York City's
Fordham University and the University of Minnesota in
Minneapolis. He served as chief surveyor with the
Byrd Antarctic Expedition and later lived in Canada.
The author belonged to the National Geographic Society
and Adventurers' Club. He died in New York City at
the age of forty. His last book Royal Red (Junior Lit-
erary Guild and Winston, 1951) was published after his
death. Other juvenile titles include: Rip Darcy, Ad-
venturer, Winston, 1938; Silver Chief, Dog Of The
North, Winston, 1933; Spike Of Swift River, Winston,
1942; Valiant, Dog Of The Timberline, Winston, 1935.
MJA

O'CLERY, Helen (Gallagher) 1910-
Author, nurse, born in County Donegal, Ireland. She
attended St. Vincent's, Dublin and Trinity College, University of Dublin. She has traveled in Japan, Australia, and the United States. She married Dermot O'
Clery, a civil engineer and has lived near Dublin. She
wrote The Mystery Of Black Sod Point, Watts, 1959.
CA-11/12

O'CONNOR, Patrick see WIBBERLEY, Leonard (Patrick
O'Connor)

O'DELL, Scott 1903-
Author, historian, newspaperman. Born in Los Angeles, California, he later made his home in Julian,
California. He attended Occidental College in Los Angeles, the University of Wisconsin, and Stanford Uni-

versity at Palo Alto, California. He also studied at the
University of Rome. Scott O'Dell has written books for
both adults and children, worked in the motion picture
industry, and contributed articles to newspapers and
magazines. His first book for boys and girls Island Of
The Blue Dolphins (Houghton, 1960) won the 1961 Newbery Medal. Other juvenile titles include: The Black
Pearl, Houghton, 1967; The Dark Canoe, Houghton,
1968; The King's Fifth, Houghton, 1966. MJA

ODENWALD, Robert Paul 1899-
He was born in Karlsruhe, Germany and studied at
many universities including Heidelberg and Frankfort
where he received his doctor's degree. Dr. Odenwald
has been a psychiatrist in Washington, D. C. He has
written articles for scientific and Catholic publications
and received the Family Catholic Action Award given
by the National Catholic Welfare Conference in 1952.
He has enjoyed stamp collecting and fishing as hobbies.
He wrote How You Were Born, Kenedy, 1963. CA-2

OFFORD, Lenore (Glen) 1905-
Born in Spokane, Washington, she later made her home
in Berkeley, California. She graduated from Mills College in Oakland, California and did further study at the
University of California. She has written for both
adults and children. Mrs. Offord has been associated
with the Mystery Writers of America, Inc. , and at one
time served as a reviewer of mystery stories for the
San Francisco Chronicle. Her books for young people
have received "technical advice" from her own daughter
and young friends. She wrote Enchanted August, Bobbs-
Merrill, 1956.

OGILVIE, Elisabeth 1917-
A noted novelist, she has written for both adults and
young people. She was born in Massachusetts and at-
tended schools there. When she was attending high
school, Elisabeth Ogilvie decided that someday she
would become a writer and live in the state of Maine.
She has lived on an island near Thomaston, Maine.
Her books for young people include: Blueberry Summer
(A Junior Literary Guild selection), McGraw, 1956;
Come Aboard And Bring Your Dory, McGraw, 1969.

OLATUNJI, Michael Babatunde
Author and musician, born in Nigeria. A graduate of

Morehouse College (Atlanta, Ga.), he attended New York
University where he worked toward a Ph. D. degree in
Public Administration. He has given lecture recitals
throughout the United States on African music, appeared on television, and made records. With Betty Warner Dietz he wrote Musical Instruments Of Africa, Day,
1965.

OLDEN, Sam
He was born near Yazoo City, Mississippi and studied
at the University of Mississippi where he also taught a
course in history. Later he was associated with the
Mobil International Oil Company's Office of Intergovern-
mental Affairs and lived in Nigeria. He has also served with the Navy and in foreign service in South America. For young people he wrote: Getting To Know
Africa's French Community, Coward-McCann, 1961;
Getting To Know Argentina, Coward-McCann, 1961;
Getting To Know Nigeria, Coward-McCann, 1960.

OLDRIN, John 1901-
Native of Connecticut. In addition to writing books, he
has been a banker and real estate broker. He served
as a major with the Air Transport Command during
World War II. He has been interested in antique cars.
For young people he wrote Eight Rings On His Tail,
Viking, 1956.

OLDS, Elizabeth 1897-
She was born in Minneapolis, Minnesota and studied at
the University of Minnesota, the Minneapolis Institute
of Art, and the Art Students League in New York. She
also received a Guggenheim fellowship to study painting
abroad. Her book Feather Mountain (Houghton, 1951)
was a runner-up for the Caldecott Medal in 1952. Her
illustrations have appeared in Fortune magazine. The
author has lived in Tamworth, New Hampshire. Her
books include: Big Fire, Houghton, 1945; Deep Treasure (A Junior Literary Guild selection), Houghton,
1958; Little Una, Scribner, 1963; Plop, Plop, Ploppie
(A Junior Literary Guild selection), Scribner, 1962.
CA-5/6

OLDS, Helen (Diehl) 1895-
Author-teacher. Born in Springfield, Ohio, she later
made her home in Little Neck, New York. She attended the School of Journalism at the University of Texas

and graduated from Ohio's Wittenberg College. In addition to a writing career, Mrs. Olds has conducted
courses in writing at several universities. She has also contributed articles to magazines. For young people
she wrote: Christmas-Tree Sam, Messner, 1952; De-
tour For Meg, Messner, 1958; The Little Ship That
Went To Sea, Reilly & Lee, 1962; Lyndon Baines Johnson, Putnam, 1965; What Will I Wear?, Knopf, 1961.
CA-4

OLIVER, Jane see REES, Helen Christina Easson (Evans)

OLNEY, Ross, R. 1929-
Writer and expert surfer, he has lived in Canoga Park,
California. Besides writing novels, Ross Olney has
contributed to many magazines including: Argosy,
Reader's Digest, Flying, and True. His experiences
as a surfer enabled him to write an authoritative book
for young people entitled The Young Sportsman's Guide
To Surfing, Nelson, 1965. He later wrote Kings Of
The Surf, Putnam, 1969. CA-15/16

OLSON, Gene 1922-
He was born in Montevideo, Minnesota. During World
War II, he interrupted his studies to serve in the Army
and later continued his education at the University of
Oregon. He received a master's degree from Pacific
University. He has been both a teacher and a newspa-
per editor. In addition to writing books, he has writ-
ten scripts for television. The Olsons have lived in
Los Angeles and in Grants Pass, Oregon. Juvenile
titles include: Bailey And The Bearcat (A Junior Liter-
ary Guild selection), Westminster Press, 1964; The
Ballhawks, Westminster Press, 1960; Between Me And
The Marshal, Dodd, 1964; Three Men On Third, Westminster Press, 1965.

O'MALLEY, Patricia
Author and flying enthusiast. She has been associated
with the Civil Aeronautics Administration and at one
served as Manager of the Public Information Department of an airline in Washington, D. C. Miss O'Malley helped to compile a government report "Survival
in the Air Age" as a member of a Presidential Commission. Her books for young people include: Faraway
Fields, Dodd, 1949; Happy Landings For Ann, Dodd,
1956.

ONCKEN, Clara
   She was born on a farm in Illinois. The author be-
   lieved that ". . . her real education came from the
   country itself, the woods and streams and fields of
   Illinois, and from the mudpies, circuses, green apples,
   ponies, and broken bones of her childhood. " Clara
   Oncken has enjoyed photography, travel, and music.
   Her book for boys and girls was entitled Hickory Sam,
   Holt, 1939.

O'NEILL, Hester 1908-
   During World War II, she was associated with the government information services in Washington. She has
   enjoyed travel, and her books have reflected Miss O'
   Neill's interest in people of other countries. Juvenile
   titles include: Picture Story Of Denmark, McKay, 1952;
   Picture Story Of Norway, McKay, 1951; Picture Story
   Of The Philippines, Junior Literary Guild and McKay,
   1948; Picture Story Of Sweden, McKay, 1953.

O'NEILL, Mary le Duc 1908-
   She was born in New York and grew up in Berea, Ohio.
   She received her education at Cleveland's St. Joseph
   Academy, Western Reserve University, and the University of Michigan.   At one time she served as vice-
   president of her own advertising firm. She has also
   contributed stories to magazines. Among her many interests have been travel, music, and the theatre. Her
   home has been in New York City. In 1961 the New
   York Times Book Review selected Mrs. O'Neill's book
   Hailstones And Halibut Bones (Doubleday, 1961) as one
   of the best books for children. Other juvenile titles
   include: Anna Amelia's Apteryx, Doubleday, 1966;
   People I'd Like To Keep, Doubleday, 1964; The White
   Palace, Crowell, 1966.   CA-5/6

OPPENHEIMER, Lillian
   She has written several books with Shari Lewis who has
   often appeared with her puppets on television.   Mrs.
   Oppenheimer has been interested in origami (the art of
   Japanese paper folding). She was the founder and
   President of the American Origami Center. With Shari
   Lewis she wrote Folding Paper Masks, Dutton, 1965.

ORCZY, Emmuska (Baroness) 1865-1947
   Author, illustrator, born in Hungary (Tarnaors). She
   received her education in Brussels, Paris, and London.

The Baroness did relief work in Monte Carlo during
World War II.   Her death came at the age of eighty-
two in London.   Her well-known work came out in both
book and play form and was entitled The Scarlet Pim-
pernel, Macmillan, 1964.

O'REILLY, John 1906-
Reporter, author.   He studied at Columbia University.
During World War II, he was a correspondent overseas
and wrote of the invasions of Italy and France.   Follow-
ing the liberation of Paris, he was chief of the Paris
Bureau of the New York Herald Tribune.   He later lived
in New York.   For young people he wrote The Glob,
Viking, 1952.

ORGEL, Doris
Born in Vienna, she graduated from Barnard College.
Her book Sarah's Room (Harper, 1963) was selected by
the New York Times in 1963 as one of the "100 Outstanding Children's Books. " She enjoyed hearing German fairy tales when she was a child and "once pro-
mised herself never to forget how she felt about things
as a child. " For young people she wrote Merry, Rose,
And Christmas-Tree June, Knopf, 1969.

ORMONDROYD, Edward
Author and librarian, born in Wilkinsburg, Pennsylvania.
He grew up in Ann Arbor, Michigan.   After World War
II (he served in the Pacific on a destroyer escort), Edward Ormondroyd continued his education at the University of California.   He has resided in Berkeley, California where he has been a librarian.   The author has
enjoyed playing the oboe and book collecting as hobbies.
His children's books include: Broderick, Parnassus,
1969; Time At The Top, Parnassus, 1963.

ORTON, Helen (Fuller) 1872-
Author and teacher, born in New York.   She received
her early education in "a little red schoolhouse. " After
her marriage to Professor Jesse F. Orton, she lived
in Ann Arbor where she continued her education at the
University of Michigan.   The Orton family later returned
to New York to live.   Her writing career resulted from
telling stories to her own children, and her first book
was published in 1921.   Juvenile titles include: A Lad
Of Old Williamsburg, Stokes, 1938; Mystery At The
Little Red Schoolhouse, Lippincott, 1941; Mystery In

The Apple Orchard, Lippincott, 1954; Prancing Pat,
Stokes, 1927; The Secret Of The Rosewood Box, Stokes,
1937.   JBA-1, JBA-2

OSBORNE, David see SILVERBERG, Robert

OSGOOD, William
    Librarian, author. He graduated from Simmons College
    in Boston, Massachusetts and the University of New
    Hampshire in Durham.   During World War II, he
    served with the 10th Mountain Division.   He has contri-
    buted articles to Vermont Life and the Vermonter maga-
    zines.   William Osgood has been the librarian of God-
    dard College in Plainfield, Vermont and has made his
    home in Northfield, Vermont.   With Leslie Hurley he
    wrote Ski Touring, Tuttle, 1969.

OSMOND, Edward 1900-
    Author, artist.   He was born in England, the son of a
    Curate.   He studied at the Regent St. School of Art in
    London and later received the National Diploma in
    Painting and Illustration and a University Extension Dip-
    loma in Art History.   In addition to writing and illus-
    trating books, Mr. Osmond has also been an art in-
    structor.   He married a sculptress (Constance Biggs)
    who has also written books for boys and girls.   They
    have lived in Middlesex, England.   Juvenile books in-
    clude: Animals Of Central Asia, Abelard, 1968; Ani-
    Of The World . . ., Oxford, 1956.   CA-13/14

OSTENDORF, (Arthur) Lloyd 1921-
    Photographer, artist.   Lloyd Ostendorf, Jr., has been
    interested in the study of history (Lincolniana) for many
    years and has also collected Civil War photographs.
    Concerning his interest in Abraham Lincoln, he once
    said: "A quarter of a century of collecting his pictures,
    and drawing his likeness for fun and for publication was
    bound to result some day in a book . . ." He illus-
    trated his book entitled A Picture Story Of Abraham
    Lincoln, Lothrop, 1962.   CA-2

OTTO, Margaret (Glover) 1909-
    The author and her husband have lived in Westport,
    Connecticut.   Prior to operating her own literary
    agency, Mrs. Otto had worked for a New York publish-
    ing firm and a Philadelphia bookstore.   Her books for
    young readers include: Little Brown Horse, Knopf,

1959; The Little Old Train, Knopf, 1960; The Man In
The Moon, Holt, 1957; Mr. Kipling's Elephant, Knopf,
1961; Mr. Magic, Holt, 1955; Syrup, Holt, 1956.

OURSLER, Fulton 1893-
Author and editor. Mr. Oursler has been associated
with radio, newspapers and magazines. At one time
he conducted "The Greatest Story Ever Told" radio program; he wrote the weekly "Modern Parables," and
was senior editor of Reader's Digest. For young people he wrote Child's Life Of Jesus, Watts, 1951.

OVINGTON, Ray
Author, editor, fisherman. His introduction to the
pleasures of fishing by his father formed a lifelong interest in this sport. Mr. Ovington has written a daily
sports column ("Hooks and Bullets") and has served as
outdoor editor of the New York World-Telegram And
Sun. He wrote The Young Sportsman's Guide to Fly
Tying, Nelson, 1962.

OWEN, Russell 1889-1952
Newspaperman, author. As a reporter for the New
York Times, he accompanied Admiral Byrd on his first
Antarctic Expedition. Later the Pulitzer Prize was
awarded (1930) to him for his articles about the Expedition. He has written books for adults, one of which
was written with thirteen Times correspondents; and
prior to his death, wrote for young people The Conquest
Of The North And South Poles, Random, 1952.

OWEN, Ruth (Bryan) 1885-
Author and traveler, the daughter of William Jennings
Bryan. She was born in Jacksonville, Illinois and attended Monticello Seminary and the University of Neb-
raska. The honorary degrees of Doctor of Law and
Doctor of Humane Letters were awarded to her. At
one time she represented Florida in Congress and later
served as United States Minister to Denmark. The author married Børge Rohde a former Captain in the
Danish Royal Guards. They made their home in New
York and West Virginia. Her main interests have been
travel and music. For young people she retold: The
Castle In The Silver Wood And Other Scandinavian
Fairy Tales, Dodd, 1939; Picture Tales From Scandinavia, Stokes, 1939.

P

PACK, Robert 1929-
Poet, author. He has been on the staff of Middlebury
College in Vermont as Assistant Professor in English.
The National Institute of Arts and Letters gave an A-
ward in Literature to him, and he has been a Fulbright
Scholar.   Robert Pack has written several volumes of
verse in addition to his books for boys and girls. These
books include: How To Catch A Crocodile, Knopf, 1964;
Then What Did You Do?, Macmillan, 1961.   CA-3

PACKER, Joy (Petersen) 1905-
Native of South Africa, the daughter of Dr. Julius
Petersen. She attended St. Cyprian's School and the
University of Cape Town. She lived in the Cape Peninsula with her husband, the late Admiral Sir Herbert
Packer. Prior to his retirement, Lady Joy Packer
accompanied her husband on assignments to many places
including the Mediterranean and the Orient. Books she
has written include: The Glass Barrier, Lippincott,
1961; The Moon By Night (A Junior Literary Guild selection), Lippincott, 1957.   CA-4

PAGE, Lou (Williams)
A recipient of a Ph. D. degree, she has served as Girl
Scout National Camp Counselor on Nature Study both at
Camp Andree in Briar Cliff Manor, New York and at
Great Lakes Regional Training Camp. She has also
been a member of Stephens College's Geology Department and on the staff of the University of Chicago. In
addition she has been managing editor of the Journal
Of Geology. She married Thornton Page. Her book
for young people was A Dipper Full Of Stars (rev. and
enlarged), Follett, 1959.

PALAZZO, Tony 1905-
Artist-author. He was born in New York and attended
Columbia and New York Universities. He has been an
art director of an advertising agency and of Coronet,
Collier's, Look, and Esquire magazines. His work has
been exhibited at many galleries and museums in the
United States. He and his wife have lived in Hastings-
on-Hudson, New York. He wrote and illustrated:
Amerigo: The Wandering Tortoise, Duell, 1965; A
Bird Alphabet, Duell, 1964; A Cat Alphabet, Duell, 1966;
Animals 'Round The Mulberry Bush (retold by Tony

Palazzo), Garden City, 1958; Did You Say Dogs, Garrard, 1964; Time For All Things, Walck, 1966.   CA-
7/8

PALMER, Helen Marion 1898-1967
    Author and teacher. She graduated from Wellesley
    College in Massachusetts and Oxford University in Eng-
    land. She married Theodor Seuss Geisel, author of
    the popular "Dr. Seuss" books. They made their home
    in La Jolla, California. Before her death in 1967,
    Helen Palmer had been an English teacher and a book
    editor. Her juvenile books include: Do You Know
    What I'm Going To Do Next Saturday?, Random, 1963;
    A Fish Out Of Water, Random, 1961; I Was Kissed By
    A Seal At The Zoo, Random, 1962.

PALMER, Robin 1911-
    She was born in New York and studied at Vassar. She
    married Dr. Douglas S. Riggs who has taught at Har-
    vard Medical School. Her stories have often appeared
    in Jack And Jill, Child Life, and Story Parade maga-
    zines. With Pelagie Doane she wrote Fairy Elves,
    Walck, 1964. She also wrote: Dragons, Unicorns,
    And Other Magical Beasts, Walck, 1966; Wise House,
    Harper, 1951.

PANOWSKI, Eileen Thompson see THOMPSON, Eileen

PARADIS, Adrian Alexis 1912-
    He was born in Brooklyn, New York and later made his
    home in Westport, Connecticut. He received a B. A.
    degree from Dartmouth and a degree in Library Science
    from Columbia University. In addition to writing books
    as a "hobby," Mr. Paradis has been a law librarian,
    hotel manager, and corporation secretary. His interest
    in the future careers of young people provided the in-
    centive for many of his books. These include: Busi-
    ness In Action, Messner, 1962; . . . Dollars For You
    (A Junior Literary Guild selection), McKay, 1958; Gov-
    ernment In Action, Messner, 1965; Labor In Action,
    Messner, 1963; Librarians Wanted, McKay, 1959; . . .
    The New Look In Banking, McKay, 1961.   CA-4, MJA

PARADIS, Marjorie Bartholomew
    She was born in Montclair, New Jersey and studied at
    Erasmus Hall and Columbia University. She has taught
    courses in writing at the Chautauqua Writers Workshop

and the YWCA. She and her husband Adrian F. Paradis have lived in Brooklyn and Westchester. Her hobbies have been portrait painting and hooking rugs. With
Adèle De Leeuw she wrote: Dear Stepmother, Macmillan, 1956; Golden Shadow, Macmillan, 1951. She wrote:
Jeanie, Westminster Press, 1963; Maid Of Honor, Dodd,
1959; Mr. De Luca's Horse, Atheneum, 1962.

PARISH, Margaret Holt see HOLT, Margaret

PARISH, Peggy
Author and teacher, born in Manning, South Carolina.
She later made her home in New York City where she
taught in a private school. She has also worked in advertising and at one time was a teacher in Texas. Her
books for children include: Amelia Bedelia, Harper,
1963; Key To Treasure, Macmillan, 1966; Let's Be Settlers With Daniel Boone, Harper, 1967; Let's Be Indians, Harper, 1962; Story Of Grains, Grosset, 1965;
Willie Is My Brother, Scott, 1963.

PARK, Thomas Choonbai
Author and educator, the son of a mathematics professor. He received his education in Seoul, Korea and
obtained his doctorate in education from the University
of Florida. Dr. Park has taught at Seoul National
University and at Florida Memorial College (St. Augustine). With Betty Warner Dietz he edited Folk Songs
Of China, Japan, Korea, Day, 1964.

PARKE, Margaret Bittner
Teacher, author. She was born in Mauch Chunk (now
called Jim Thorpe), Pennsylvania and has lived in New
York City. She has taught in schools and colleges and
later became Professor of Education at Brooklyn College. At one time she was affiliated with the University of Sydney as a Fulbright lecturer. She has been
a member of the Women's National Book Association
and the Women's Press Club. Juvenile titles include:
Getting To Know Australia, Coward-McCann, 1962; My
Second Book To Read: For Six-To-Eight-Year-Olds,
Grosset, 1957.

PARKER, Alfred Eustace
Author and educator. He has lived in Berkeley, California where he has been associated with the school
system. He has also served as a school counselor in

Burbank. The author collaborated with Los Angeles
police chief, the late August Vollmer to write about
crime and police for adult readers. For young people
Mr. Parker wrote Crime Fighter: August Vollmer,
Macmillan, 1961.

PARKER, Bertha Morris 1890-
    Teacher, author, editor. She was born in Rochester,
    Illinois and attended Oberlin College and Columbia Uni-
    versity. She received her master's and doctor's de-
    grees from the University of Chicago. Prior to teach-
    ing science in the Laboratory Schools of the University
    of Chicago, she taught in Springfield, Illinois. She has
    edited Science News Notes and was an associate editor
    of Science Education. At one time Miss Parker served
    as president of the National Council on Elementary Sci-
    ence. She has lived in Chicago. Juvenile titles include:
    The Golden Treasury Of Natural History, Simon and
    Schuster, 1952; . . . Gravity (checked for scientific
    accuracy by Clifford Holley), Row, 1942; . . . Living
    Things, Row, 1941; Science Experiences: Elementary
    School, Row, 1952.   CA-7/8, MJA

PARKER, Fania M. Pockrose
    She was born in Latvia and received her Ph. D. from
    Columbia University. Dr. Parker has been an Associ-
    ate Professor of Russian at Brooklyn College in New
    York. She has enjoyed European travel and has visited
    Russia several times. Her home has been in Rockville
    Center, New York. For young people she wrote The
    Russian Alphabet Book, Coward-McCann, 1961.

PARKER, Richard
    England has been the residence of this writer and jour-
    nalist. He has also been a librarian and teacher. On
    a trip to Australia's smallest state Tasmania, Richard
    Parker collected material to write several books includ-
    ing Voyage To Tasmania (A Junior Literary Guild se-
    lection), Bobbs, 1963. Other juvenile titles include:
    Lion At Large (A Junior Literary Guild selection), Nel-
    son, 1961; Sheltering Tree, Meredith, 1969.

PARLIN, John see GRAVES, Charles Parlin

PARR, Adolph Henry 1900-
    He lived in Nebraska when he was a boy. Prior to
    writing books for young people, Mr. Parr was the owner

and chief executive of a manufacturing business. He
also worked in the motion picture industry. After a
visit to Jerusalem, he wrote in one of his books:
"When I entered Jerusalem, I realized a lifelong dream
which had begun in my youth when I first heard the
story of Christmas. " For young people A. H. Parr
wrote The Open Door To Peace And Happiness, Fell,
1963.

PASCHAL, Nancy see TROTTER, Grace Violet

PATCHETT, Mary Elwyn 1897–
She was born in that part of Australia which is called
the "Outback" (backcountry of Australia or New Zealand). The author spent a great part of her childhood
in the wilderness and acquired a good background of
Australia and its animals which she later wrote about
in her books. Miss Patchett has traveled throughout
the world and later made her home in London. Her
books for children include: Brumby Come Home, Bobbs,
1962; Dingo, Doubleday, 1963. CA-7/8

PATON, Alan (Stewart) 1903–
He was born in Pietermaritzburg, South Africa and
graduated from the University of Natal. He has taught
school and once served as principal of Diepkloop Refor-
matory, an institution for African delinquent boys. He
has written magazine articles and books for adults including the well-known novel Cry, The Beloved Country,
(Scribner, 1948). He and his wife have lived in Kloof,
near Durban, South Africa. For young people he wrote
The Land And People Of South Africa (rev.), Lippincott,
1964. CA-15/16

PATTERSON, Lillie G.
Author, teacher, librarian. She has been a Specialist
in Library Services and a Chairman of the Elementary
Book Reviewing Committee for Baltimore, Maryland's
Department of Education. Miss Patterson has enjoyed
storytelling, and for boys and girls she wrote: Christmas Feasts & Festivals, Garrard, 1968; Francis Scott
Key: Poet & Patriot, Garrard, 1963; Frederick Douglas: Freedom Fighter, Garrard, 1965; Holiday Book:
Easter, Garrard, 1966; Holiday Book: Halloween, Garrard, 1963; Lumberjacks Of North Woods, Garrard,
1967.

PAULI, Hertha Ernestine 1909-
    Actress, author, born in Vienna, Austria. She studied
    at the Vienna Academy of Dramatic Arts.   Her mother
    was a journalist in Vienna, and Miss Pauli began writ-
    ing at the age of twelve.   She was one of a group of
    authors who came to America in 1940 under the spon-
    sorship of Eleanor Roosevelt.   She became an American
    citizen, and her home has been in Huntington, Long
    Island.   Juvenile titles include: Bernadette And The
    Lady, Farrar, 1956; Christmas And The Saints, Far-
    rar, 1956; The First Christmas Gifts, L Washburn,
    1965; Handel And The Messiah Story, Meredith, 1968;
    Lincoln's Little Correspondent, Doubleday, 1952.   CA-2

PAULL, Grace A. 1898-
    Author-illustrator, born in Cold Brook, New York. She
    received her education at Pratt Institute in Brooklyn,
    Grant Central Art School, and the Art Students League
    in New York.   Her early childhood was spent in Cana-
    da, New York, and New Hampshire.   One of her litho-
    graphs won a First Purchase Award at Laguna Beach,
    California, and another was purchased for the Library
    of Congress.   Several museums and galleries have ex-
    hibited her work.   Grace Paull has also operated her
    own art gallery called the "Old Mill" in Cold Brook.
    Juvenile books which she wrote and illustrated include:
    Come To The Country, Abelard-Schuman, 1956; Some
    Day, Abelard-Schuman, 1957.   JBA-2

PAYNE, Alma Smith
    Home economist, teacher, consultant.   At one time she
    was Supervisor of Emergency Nursery Schools for the
    California State Department of Education and was Super-
    visor of Parent Education, Parent Nursery Schools and
    Child Care Centers in the public schools of Berkeley.
    Mrs. Payne has also worked in the American Heart
    Association and served on the board of the Alameda
    County Heart Association.   With Robert Warner Cham-
    bers she wrote From Cell to Test Tube, Scribner,
    1960.   With Dorothy Callahan she wrote Great Nutrition
    Puzzle, Scribner, 1956.   CA-19/20

PAYNE, Emmy see WEST, Emily (Govan)

PEALE, Norman Vincent 1898-
    Clergyman, author, born in Bowersville, Ohio.   He
    studied at Boston University.   He has written several

popular adult books and has conducted a series of radio
programs.   He has also edited Guideposts magazine and
the newspaper column known as "Confident Living. "   He
was pastor of the Marble Collegiate Church in New York
City.   For children he wrote: Coming Of The King,
Prentice, 1956; He Was A Child, Prentice, 1957.

PEARCE, (Ann) Philippa
She was born in Cambridgeshire, England and studied
at Cambridge University.   She has worked in the School
of Broadcasting Department of the B. B. C. and in the
Education Department of a large publishing company.
Her books for young people include: A Dog So Small,
Lippincott, 1963; Mrs. Cockle's Cat, Lippincott, 1961;
Tom's Midnight Garden, Lippincott, 1958.   CA-7/8

PEARE, Catherine Owens 1911-
Author and teacher, born in Perth Amboy, New Jersey.
She received her B. A. degree from New Jersey's State
Teachers College in Montclair and did graduate work
at New York University.   Prior to a full-time writing
career, Catherine Peare had been a teacher and a
stockbroker on Wall Street.   She combined her main
interests of teaching and writing to produce books for
young people.   In 1962 she received the Sequoyah Children's Book Award for The Helen Keller Story, Crowell, 1959.   Other juvenile titles include: Albert Einstein, Holt, 1949; Charles Dickens, Holt, 1959; The
FDR Story, Crowell, 1962; The Herbert Hoover Story,
Crowell, 1965; Painter Of Patriots, Charles Willson
Peale, Holt, 1964; Rosa Bonheur, Her Life, Holt, 1956;
The Woodrow Wilson Story, Crowell, 1963.   CA-5/6,
MJA

PEARL, Richard Maxwell 1913-
He was born in New York and graduated from the University of Colorado.   He later received his master's
degree from Harvard University.   As a boy, he became interested in mineral collecting and later became
the second Certified Gemologist in the United States.
He has owned a mineral-supply store in Denver and has
worked for a large company in Tulsa.   Later he was a
Professor of Geology at Colorado College in Colorado
Springs.   He married a schoolteacher named Mignon
Wardell who has supplied drawings and photographs for
his books.   He wrote: Wonders Of Gems, Dodd, 1963;
Wonder World Of Metals, Harper, 1966.   CA-11/12

PEASE, Howard 1894-
Author, teacher. Born in Stockton, California, he
graduated from Stanford University, and has resided in
Livermore, California. He served in France with the
A. E. F. during World War I. At one time he was a
public school teacher. Mr. Pease has traveled throughout the United States, and his sea adventures aboard
cargo vessels enabled him to collect material for his
stories. He has received many book awards and in
1946 won the Award of the Child Study Association for
Heart Of Danger, Doubleday, 1946. Other juvenile
titles include: Black Tanker, Doubleday, 1941; High-
road To Adventure, Doubleday, 1939; Hurricane Weather, Doubleday, 1936; . . . Jungle River, Doubleday,
1938; Mystery On Telegraph Hill, Doubleday, 1961;
Shipwreck, Doubleday, 1957.   CA-7/8, JBA-1, JBA-2

PEASE, Josephine Van Dolzen
She was born in Au Sable, Michigan, the daughter of
a lumber dealer. Miss Pease has been a teacher in
Grosse Pointe, Michigan and has written not only
stories but also many poems for boys and girls. She
wrote This Is Our Land, Rand, 1961.

PEATTIE, Donald Culross 1898-
Author-editor. He attended Harvard University and has
been a "roving" editor for the Reader's Digest. His
home has been in Santa Barbara, California. He has
traveled throughout Europe and the United States. His
juvenile books include: A Child's Story Of The World,
From The Earliest Days To Our Own Time, Junior
Literary Guild and Simon and Schuster, 1937; Rainbow
Book Of Nature, World, 1957.

PECK, Anne Merriman 1884-
Born in Piermont, New York, this author-illustrator
was the daughter of a clergyman. She studied at the
Hartford Art School and the New York School of Fine
and Applied Art. She has lived in Tucson, Arizona.
Anne Merriman Peck has conducted classes in Children's Book Illustration and Writing for Children and
Young People in the Extension Division of the University of Arizona. She collaborated with Enid Johnson to
write Big Bright Land, Junior Literary Guild and
Messner, 1947. Books which Miss Peck has written
and illustrated include: Pageant Of Middle American
History, Longmans, 1947; Southwest Roundup, Dodd,

1950.   JBA-1, JBA-2

PECKINPAH, Betty
She attended the Castilla School for Girls on a poetry
scholarship. Mrs. Peckinpah has lived on a California
ranch. She has done volunteer work in children's hospitals and has also worked with migrant children. For
boys and girls she wrote Coco Is Coming, Lothrop,
1956.

PEDERSEN, Elsa Kienitz 1915-
She was born in Salt Lake City, Utah and later lived
in Alaska. She once said: "Being bred in the West,
I thought I knew about vast distances, but nothing com-
pares to Alaska. " The author and her husband lived
on a farm in Alaska, and the nearest town (Seldovia)
was approximately thirty miles from the farm. Juvenile titles include: Fisherman's Choice (A Junior Literary Guild selection), Atheneum, 1964; Mystery On
Malina Straits, Washburn, 1963.   CA-4

PEET, Creighton 1899-
He was born in New York City and graduated from
Columbia University. At one time he was a reporter
on the Philadelphia Evening Bulletin. He has also contributed articles to magazines. Mr. Peet has traveled
extensively but has made his home in New York City.
His books for young people include: Dude Ranch, Whitman, 1939; First Book Of Bridges, Watts, 1953; . . .
This Is The Way We Build A House, Holt, 1940.

PEET, William Bartlett 1915-
Author-illustrator, born in Grandview, Indiana. Bill
Peet attended the John Herron Art Institute in Indianapolis and later was the recipient of the school's citation for being an outstanding student. He has designed
greeting cards and for many years was associated with
the Walt Disney Studios. In 1967 he received recognition as "outstanding Hoosier author of children's literature. " The Bill Peet family has lived in Studio
City, California. Juvenile books which he wrote and
illustrated include: Buford, The Little Big Horn,
Houghton, 1967; Capyboppy, Houghton, 1966; Chester,
The Worldly Pig, Houghton, 1965; Ella, Houghton, 1964;
Farewell To Shady Glade, Houghton, 1966; Jennifer And
Josephine, Houghton, 1967.   CA-19/20

PELS, Gertrude Jaeckel
    Artist, puppeteer, teacher. She has taught drawing
    and painting to boys and girls in the Pels School of
    Art in New York which was conducted by her husband,
    artist Albert Pels. Mrs. Pels has also taught puppet-
    ry to adults for use in hospitals, to Girl Scout leaders,
    and in classes at New York's Hunter College Element-
    ary School and at Hessian Hills School. Her juvenile
    titles include: The Care Of Water Pets, Crowell, 1955;
    Easy Puppets, Crowell, 1951.

PENDER, Lydia Podger 1907-
    British writer and poet. She was born in London, at-
    tended English schools for girls, and later studied in
    Australia at Sydney University. Mrs. Pender has en-
    joyed gardening and acting. In addition to writing
    stories she has also had poetry published in Australian
    magazines. For young people she wrote: Barnaby And
    The Horses, Abelard, 1961; Dan McDougall And The
    Bulldozer, Abelard, 1963; Sharpur The Carpet Snake,
    Abelard, 1967. CA-5/6

PERKINS, R. Marlin 1905-
    Born in Missouri, he spent his childhood in Kansas and
    studied at the University of Missouri. An ardent ani-
    mal lover, his first job was at the St. Louis Zoo
    where he eventually became head of the reptile collec-
    tion. He has been director of the Buffalo Zoo and
    later was director of the Lincoln Park Zoo in Chicago.
    His television show, the recipient of many awards, was
    called "Zooparade." He later had a show entitled
    "Wild Kingdom" which utilized many photographs taken
    by his wife Carol Morse Perkins. With his wife he
    wrote "I Saw You From Afar", Atheneum, 1965. For
    young people he also wrote Marlin Perkins' Zooparade,
    Rand, 1954.

PERL, Lila
    A Home Economics major, Lila Perl continued her
    studies at Pratt Institute in Brooklyn and at New York
    and Columbia Universities. She has written several
    books on cooking, and her articles have appeared in
    many magazines. She married a writer, and they
    have lived in Buchhurst, New York. For young peo-
    ple she wrote: No Tears For Rainey, Lippincott, 1969;
    Red-Flannel Hash And Shoo-Fly Pie, World, 1965.

PERRY, John 1914-
Author and editor, born in Newark, New Jersey. He
attended Lehigh University at Bethlehem, Pennsylvania.
He and his wife, writer and economist Jane Greverus
Perry, and their children have lived in Washington,
D. C. He has contributed to magazines and professional journals. Mr. Perry has served as editor of Federal Science Progress and was a Senior Consultant in a
business firm. He has also been an executive in an
audio-visual design and production company. His books
for young people include: Exploring The Forest, Whittlesey, 1962; Our Polluted World (A Junior Literary
Guild selection), Watts, 1967. CA-5/6

PERSON, William Thomas 1900-
Author-teacher, born in Mt. Pleasant, Mississippi.
After graduating from Southwestern Presbyterian University, he entered the teaching profession and has
taught in Arkansas, Tennessee, and Mississippi. He
later became a high school teacher in Panama City,
Florida. In addition to writing books, Mr. Person has
contributed numerous stories to periodicals. His juvenile titles include: Bar-Face, Ariel Bks., 1953; Sedge-
Hill Setter (A Junior Literary Guild selection), Longmans, 1960.

PETERSHAM, Maud (Fuller) 1890- Miska 1889-1960
Authors-illustrators, husband and wife team. Mrs.
Petersham was born in Kingston, New York, the
daughter of a minister. Following graduation from
Vassar, she studied at the New York School of Fine
and Applied Arts. Miska Petersham was born in Hungary. He studied at the Royal Art Academy in Budapest and later attended an art school in London. After
coming to the United States, he became an American
citizen. In 1946 the Caldecott Medal was awarded to
their book The Rooster Crows (Macmillan, 1945). Mrs.
Petersham has continued to live in Woodstock, New
York following the death of her husband. Their books
include: America's Stamps, Macmillan, 1947; Box
With Red Wheels, Macmillan, 1949; Circus Baby, Macmillan, 1950. JBA-1, JBA-2

PETERSON, James see ZEIGER, Henry Anthony

PETERSON, Russell Francis
Author-illustrator, born in Montclair, New Jersey.

Before serving with a ski regiment in World War II, the author had attended Harvard University. After the war, he continued his studies at the College of Charleston in South Carolina. Mr. Peterson has been a mammalogist and has been on expeditions to New Guinea, Australia, the Arctic, and the South Seas. He has also been associated with the American Museum of Natural History in New York City. The author has belonged to the Explorers Club, American Society of Mammalogists, and Australian Mammal Society. His home has been in Locust, New Jersey. For young people he illustrated Rutherford Montgomery's King Of The Castle, World, 1961. He also wrote and illustrated The Story Of A Natural History Expedition, Doubleday, 1962.

PETRY, Ann Lane 1911-
She was born in Old Saybrook, Connecticut and graduated from the College of Pharmacy at the University of Connecticut. Following her marriage, she lived in New York but later returned to Connecticut. She has written adult novels in addition to these books for young people: Harriet Tubman, Conductor On The Underground Railroad, Crowell, 1955; Tituba Of Salem Village, Crowell, 1964. CA-7/8

PETTIT, Mary P.
Author and teacher. She was a teacher who always placed a special emphasis on nature and conservation. She attended Adelphi, Columbia, Fordham, and New York Universities. Her articles have appeared in such publications as Audubon and Travel magazines. For young people she wrote My Hobby Is Bird Watching, Hart, 1958.

PEYTON, K. M.
She was born in Birmingham, England. She married an artist and later lived in Essex. Prior to being an art instructor at Northampton High School, the author attended the Manchester School of Art. Mrs. Peyton has enjoyed music and gardening as hobbies. Her knowledge of the sea and sailing provided ideas for many of her books. Her work has been published both here and abroad. For young people she wrote: Fly-By-Night, World, 1969; The Plan For Birdsmarsh, World, 1966.

PHELAN, Josephine
Author-librarian. She has lived in Toronto, Canada
where she has been on the staff of the public library.
Miss Phelan has written for both adults and children
and has received several awards for her books about
Canada including a Governor-General's Medal in 1952.
For young people she wrote The Bold Heart, St. Mar-
tin's Press, 1956.

PHELPS, Margaret (Nelson)
She was born in Virginia and lived in Phoenix, Arizona
after her marriage to a lawyer.   Her husband became
Judge of the Supreme Court.   She has traveled throughout the United States and Mexico.   The author once
wrote to her publisher that she preferred mountains to
the sea.   She has written about her adopted state of
Arizona with the enthusiasm of one who might have
been born and raised there.   Her juvenile books include: Jaro And The Golden Colt (A Junior Literary
Guild selection), Macrae, 1954; Regular Cowboy,
Macrae, 1948.

PHILBROOK, Clem   1917-
Born in Oldtown, Maine, he studied at the University
of Maine.   He has had experience as a field accountant,
timekeeper in construction work, and later became
associated with a publishing firm in Sugar Hill, New
Hampshire.   The author has been interested in many
sports including: baseball, fly fishing, and skiing.
His books for young people include: Captured By The
Abnakis (A Junior Literary Guild selection), Hastings,
1966; Ollie's Team & Basketball Computer, Hastings,
1969.

PHILLIPS, Mary Geisler   1881-
She was born in Philadelphia and graduated from the
University of Pennsylvania.   She married Everett
Franklin Phillips who has been a noted authority on
bees and beekeeping.   Mrs. Phillips has been an instructor in a high school and a university, a radio
scriptwriter, and an editor.   She later became professor emeritus of Cornell University.   The author and
her husband have lived in Auburn, New York.   Her
books for young people include: Dragonflies And Dam-
selflies, Crowell, 1960; The Makers Of Honey, Crowell, 1956.   With Julia McNair Wright she wrote
Nature--By Seaside And Wayside . . . , Heath, 1936.

CA-5/6

PHIPSON, Joan   see   FITZHARDINGE, Joan Margaret

PHLEGER, Fred B.   1909-
   Author, teacher, born in Kansas City, Kansas.   He
   graduated from the University of Southern California,
   Harvard University, and the California Institute of
   Technology.   He has been both director and president
   of the Cushman Foundation.   He has been a Professor
   of Oceanography at Scripps Institution in La Jolla,
   California where he has made his home.   Dr. Phleger
   has been involved in scientific research and has studied
   the California Gray Whale.   He has belonged to many
   organizations including the Geological Society of America.   His juvenile books include: Ann Can Fly, Random, 1959; Red Tag Comes Back, Harper, 1961;
   Whales Go By, Random, 1959.   CA-2

PIATTI, Celestino
   Illustrator, designer, author.   His posters have received wide recognition.   The Swiss Federal Department of the Interior has bestowed annual awards on
   several of Mr. Piatti's posters.   He also was the
   winner of the poster competition for the Kieler Woche
   (1961) and the Foire Internationale de Lyon (1959).
   He married artist Marianne Piatti-Stricker, and they
   have lived near Basel, Switzerland in Riehen.   For
   boys and girls he created the picture book The Happy
   Owls, Atheneum, 1964.

PICARD, Barbara Leonie   1917-
   She was born in Richmond, Surrey, England and studied
   at St. Katherine's School in Berkshire, England.   She
   later lived in Lewes, Sussex, England.   She once said
   she was interested in: "Mythology and comparative
   religion.   Archaeology.   Ancient and medieval history.
   Folk culture of all kinds, particularly folk lore and
   legend and folk music. "   Her books for young people
   include: The Faun And The Woodcutter's Daughter (A
   Junior Literary Guild selection), Criterion Bks. , 1964;
   The Goldfinch Garden, Criterion Bks. , 1965; Hero-
   Tales From The British Isles, Criterion Bks. , 1963;
   The Lady Of The Linden Tree, Criterion Bks. , 1962;
   The Young Pretenders, Criterion Bks. , 1966.   CA-7/8

PIERCE, Mary Cunningham (Fitzgerald) 1908-
   Her pseudonym is Mary Cunningham. Author and
   teacher, born in Chicago, Illinois. She has taught
   teen-agers and has written plays and short stories.
   The U. S. Information Agency in Turkey translated
   and broadcast her play "The Lady Who Ate An Oyster. "
   The author has made her home in Hollywood, California. Her books for young people include: Paris Hat,
   Funk, 1958; Secret Of the Sea Witch, Funk, 1967.

PIERCE, Philip Nason
   Author and newspaperman. Both his books and magazine articles have been published here and abroad.
   Colonel Pierce has served at Marine Corps Headquarters in Washington, D. C. as Director of Media. He
   has become well-known as one of the Marine's contemporary writers. The author and Astronaut John Glenn
   have long been personal friends. With Karl Schuon he
   wrote John H. Glenn: Astronaut, Watts, 1962.

PIERSON, Sherleigh G.
   She has been closely associated with the United Nations
   since its beginning in San Francisco. She has been a
   member of the Secretariat and an executive officer
   with the Food and Agricultural Organization. Mrs.
   Pierson has also worked with Canadian Prime Minister
   Lester B. Pearson who was the originator of the first
   UN Peace Force. She has lived in Bangkok where her
   husband also worked for the UN. For young people
   she wrote What Does A UN Soldier Do?, Dodd, 1965.

PILGRIM, Anne   see   ALLAN, Mabel Esther

PILKINGTON, Roger Windle 1915-
   Born in Lancashire, England, Dr. Pilkington has been
   a research scientist at Cambridge University where he
   also received his degrees. He has written books on
   science and religion in addition to his books for young
   people. He and his family have enjoyed boating in
   several countries of Europe, and the author later wrote
   about their experiences in his books. The Pilkingtons
   have lived in London. His books include: The Eisen-
   bart Mystery, St. Martin's Press, 1963; In The Beginning, St. Martin's Press, 1957.   CA-3

PINE, Tillie Schloss
   Author and teacher. She has been a member of the

staff of the Bank Street College Workshop in New York.
Mrs. Pine collaborated with Joseph Levine to write
the "All Around" series books for children. With
Joseph Levine she wrote: Electricity And How We Use
It, McGraw, 1962; Gravity All Around, McGraw, 1963.

PINKERTON, Kathrene Sutherland (Gedney) 1887-
She was born in Minneapolis, Minnesota and later made
her home in New York. She received her B. A. degree
from the University of Wisconsin and did additional
work at the Chicago School of Civics and Philanthropy.
She married writer Robert Pinkerton, and they collaborated on magazine serials, short stories, and books.
Her juvenile titles include: Second Meeting, Harcourt,
1956; Silver Strain, Harcourt, 1946; . . . Windigo,
Harcourt, 1945; Year Of Enchantment, Harcourt, 1957.
CA-2

PISTORIUS, Anna
Artist, author. Her early years were spent in Chicago's Belmont Yacht Harbor area. The author spent
many hours on Lake Michigan; first in boats built by
her brothers and later in an old yawl owned by her
family. She once said: "We were a nature-loving
family and collected everything from beetles to snakes."
Juvenile books which she wrote and illustrated include:
What Bird Is It?, Wilcox & Follett, 1945; What Butterfly Is It?, Wilcox & Follett, 1949; What Dinosaur Is
It?, Follett, 1958; What Indian Is It?, Follett, 1956;
What Wildflower Is It?, Wilcox & Follett, 1950.

PIZER, Vernon 1918-
He was born in Boston, Massachusetts, grew up in New
York, and has resided in Fort Lee, Virginia. He has
lived and traveled in thirty countries. The author attended George Washington University. He served with
the Army during World War II. Colonel Pizer has
been a member of the Pentagon staff and a Public In-
formation Officer for the Supreme Headquarters Allied
Powers in Europe. He has also been a special assist-
ant to the Commanding General of the Army Ordnance
Missile Command at Redstone Arsenal in Alabama.
In addition to writing books, his work has been published in Esquire, Reader's Digest, and the Saturday
Evening Post. His juvenile books include: Glorious
Triumphs, Dodd, 1968; Rockets, Missiles, And Space,
Lippincott, 1962; World Ocean, World, 1967.   CA-4

PLACE, Marian Templeton 1910-
Her pseudonyms are Dale White and R. D. Whitinger.
She was born in Gary, Indiana and grew up in Minneapolis.   A graduate of Rollins College in Winter Park,
Florida, she received her degree in library science
from the University of Minnesota.   In addition to writing books, she has been a children's librarian and newspaperwoman.   Her husband was born in Montana where
the author has lived for many years.   The Places have
also lived in Portland, Oregon.   Her books have been
awarded the Spur Award twice (1958, 1959) for the best
western juvenile.   Her books for young people include:
The Copper Kings Of Montana, Random, 1961; Rifles
And War Bonnets, Washburn, 1968; The Yukon (A Junior Literary Guild selection), Washburn, 1967.   CA-1

PLATE, Robert 1918-
Author and editor.   He was born in Brooklyn, New
York, attended Duke and New York Universities, and
has made his home in New York.   He felt that his editorial work with a literary agency provided him with
good training for a writing career.   The author has
also performed such odd jobs as house painting, lum-
berjacking, and shipping books.   Mr. Plate's lifetime
interest in art and the American Indian resulted in his
juvenile book Palette And Tomahawk, McKay, 1962.
He also wrote: Alexander Wilson Wanderer In Wilderness, McKay, 1966; Charles Willson Peale, McKay,
1967; The Dinosaur Hunters, McKay, 1964.   CA-19/20

PLISS, Louise
She was born in Gowanda, New York and graduated from
the University of Michigan.   Following graduation, she
came to New York in order to go on the stage; however, she worked in a bookstore instead.   She later became a department head in a Chicago bookstore.   Teaching eventually became her career, and she has taught
in the Laboratory School of the University of Chicago.
Juvenile titles include: That Summer On Catalpa Street,
Reilly & Lee, 1961; The Trip Down Catfish Creek,
Reilly & Lee, 1962.

POHLMANN, Lillian (Grenfell) 1902-
She has worked with boys and girls as both a public and
a school librarian.   Lillian Pohlmann and her husband
have lived in a home on a hillside near San Francisco.
She wrote: Owls And Answers (A Junior Literary Guild

selection), Westminster, 1964; <u>Wolfskin</u>, Norton, 1968.
CA-11/12

POLITI, Leo 1908-
Author-illustrator, born in Fresno, California. He
lived and studied in Italy at the Institute of Monza located near Milan. He later returned to the United
States and made his home in Los Angeles. He was the
recipient of the 1950 Caldecott Medal for his picture
book <u>Song Of The Swallows</u> (Junior Literary Guild and
Scribner, 1949). He also was awarded the 1965 Catholic Library Association Regina Medal for continued distinguished contribution to children's literature. Other
juvenile titles include: <u>Boat For Peppe</u>, Scribner,
1950; <u>The Butterflies Come,</u> Scribner, 1957; <u>Lito And
The Clown,</u> Scribner, 1964; <u>Little Leo</u>, Junior Literary
Guild and Scribner, 1951; <u>Moy Moy</u>, Scribner, 1960;
<u>Piccolo's Prank</u>, Scribner, 1965; <u>Rosa</u>, Scribner, 1963.
CA-19/20, JBA-2

POLLAND, Madeleine Angela Cahill 1918-
She was born in County Cork, Ireland and grew up in
Hertfordshire, England. During World War II, she
served with the WAAF on England's southern coast.
She has also been a librarian in Letchworth, England.
After her marriage, Mrs. Polland lived in London and
Hertfordshire, England. Several of her books have re-
ceived honor awards by the New York <u>Herald Tribune</u>
Spring Children's Book Festival. Juvenile titles in-
clude: <u>Beorn The Proud,</u> Holt, 1961; <u>Children Of The
Red King,</u> Holt, 1959; <u>Chuiraquimba And The Black
Robes,</u> Doubleday, 1962; <u>Deirdre</u>, Doubleday, 1967;
<u>Stranger In The Hills,</u> Doubleday, 1968. CA-5/6

POND, Seymour Gates 1896-
During World War II, he served as an Intelligence Staff
Officer and held the rank of Lieutenant Colonel. His
stories have been published in many magazines. When
he was a boy, he became a crew member ("apprentice")
on schooners sailing off the California-Mexican coast.
He once said: "salt water has never entirely left my
bloodstream." Juvenile titles include: <u>African Explorer,</u> Dodd, 1957; <u>Ferdinand Magellan, Master Mariner,</u>
Random, 1957.

POOLE, Lynn 1910- Gray Johnson 1906-
Husband-wife team. Lynn Poole was born in Eagle

Grove, Iowa, graduated from Western Reserve University, and has been Director of Public Relations at the John Hopkins University in Baltimore, Maryland. He has also produced the school's television program "File Seven. " Gray Poole was born in Philadelphia, Pennsylvania, studied at John Hopkins University, and has been an industrial writer and magazine columnist. The Pooles have lived in Baltimore. Their juvenile books include: Balloons Fly High, McGraw, 1961; Danger! Icebergs Ahead!, Random, 1961; Doctors Who Saved Lives, Dodd, 1966; Fireflies In Nature And The Laboratory, Crowell, 1965; Men Who Dig Up History, Dodd, 1968; Scientists Who Work With Astronauts, Dodd, 1964; Volcanoes In Action, McGraw, 1962.   CA-7/8, MJA

POPE, Clifford Hillhouse 1899-
Herpetologist, author. He was born in Washington, Georgia, attended the University of Georgia, and graduated from the University of Virginia. He once served as president of the American Society of Ichthyologists and Herpetologists and has accompanied scientific expeditions to Mexico and China. He has been Assistant Curator of Herpetology at the American Museum of Natural History and Curator of the Division of Amphibians and Reptiles at the Chicago Natural History Museum. He has lived in Winnetka, Illinois and Escondido, California. His book for young people was Reptiles Round The World, Knopf, 1957.   CA-3

PORTER, Ella Blodwen (Williams)
Author and teacher, born in Iowa. After graduating from Coe College at Cedar Rapids, she taught music in the local public schools. At one time Mrs. Porter lived in Arizona but returned to Iowa where she worked with 4-H Clubs. Her juvenile books include: Prairie Shadows, Macmillan, 1952; A Song For Julie, Macmillan, 1951; Wind's In The West, Macmillan, 1950.

POSTON, Martha Lee
She was born in Shanghai, China, the daughter of a medical missionary. Following graduation from the Shanghai-American School, she taught in a girls' school in Wusih. She later came to America and graduated from Sweet Briar College in Virginia. For young people she wrote The Mystery Of The Eighth Horse, Nelson, 1949.

POTTER, Beatrix 1866-1943
Author-illustrator, daughter of an English barrister.
She grew up in London and spent her holidays in Scotland. She first wrote The Tale Of Peter Rabbit (Warne,
1903) in a letter to a five-year-old boy. In 1913 she
married lawyer William Heelis, and they lived in Saw-
rey, England at Hill Top Farm. After her death in
1943, her home has been visited by both young and old
admirers of her books. These include: Ginger & Pick-
les, Warne, 1909; The Pie And The Patty-Pan, Warner,
1905; The Roly-Poly Pudding, Warne, 1908; The Tale
Of Jemima Puddle-Duck, Warne, 1908; The Tale Of
Mr. Jeremy Fisher, Warne, 1906; The Tale Of Squirrel
Nutkin, Warne, 1903. JBA-1, JBA-2

POTTER, Miriam Clark 1886-
Author-illustrator. She was born in Minneapolis, and
she later graduated from the University of Minnesota.
She sold her first story to Youth's Companion when she
was only fourteen. Her husband was the late Zenas
Potter, a newspaperman. Mrs. Potter has lived in
Mexico, France, and India but later made her home in
Carmel, California. Juvenile titles include: The Gold-
en Book Of Little Verses, Simon and Schuster, 1953;
Goofy Mrs. Goose, Lippincott, 1963; Just Mrs. Goose,
Lippincott, 1957; No, No, Mrs. Goose!, Lippincott,
1962. CA-5/6

POTTER, Robert Ducharme 1905-
Author, scientist, teacher. He has taught at Duke and
New York Universities. The author has served as
president of the National Association of Science Writers
which he founded in 1934. He has also worked with
the Carnegie Institution in Washington and for distinguished science reporting was the first recipient of the
George Westinghouse Medal of the American Association
for the Advancement of Science. Robert Potter has
been a consultant to the U. S. Army Surgeon General
and at one time was a correspondent at the Bikini A-
bomb tests. His work has appeared in newspapers and
magazines, and he has been one of the few laymen who
has edited a medical journal. For boys and girls he
wrote Young People's Book Of Atomic Energy (Rev. ed.),
Dodd, 1948.

POTTER, Stephen
Lecturer and writer, born in London. He received his

education at Westminster and Merton College, Oxford.
He has served in the Coldstream Guards. In addition
to writing about English literature, Stephen Potter has
written for the British Broadcasting Company. His
first book for children was Squawky, Lippincott, 1964.

POUGH, Frederick Harvey 1906-
He was born in New York and studied at Harvard and
Washington Universities. He also attended the University of Heidelberg. Dr. Pough has been on the staff
of the American Museum of Natural History. An authority on volcanoes, he was sent to Mexico by the
Museum in order to study the volcano Parícutin when
it broke out in 1943. Dr. Pough has lived in New
York City. He wrote All About Volcanoes And Earth-
quakes, Random, 1953.

POWER, Effie Louise 1873-
Author, librarian, teacher, born near Conneautville,
Pennsylvania. After receiving an M. A. degree from
Allegheny College at Meadville (Pa.), she attended Carnegie Library School at Pittsburgh. Miss Power has
been an instructor of library science at several universities including Western Reserve and Columbia. She
has also been associated with public libraries in St.
Louis and Pittsburgh. She once said: "That I was the
first children's librarian in the Cleveland Public Library, under William Howard Brett, is my chief claim
to distinction." The author maintained a winter home
in Pompano, Florida. For young people she wrote
Work With Children In Public Libraries, A. L. A., 1943.
She also compiled: Bag O' Tales, Dutton, 1934; Stories
To Shorten The Road, Dutton, 1936. With Florence
McClurg Everson she wrote Early Days In Ohio, Dutton,
1928.

PRATT, Fletcher 1897-1956
He studied in Paris and later lived in New Jersey.
During World War II, he served as a Navy war correspondent. Mr. Pratt was one of the founders of the
American Interplanetary Society which became known
as the Rocket Society. His books have been written on
a variety of subjects including: The Civil War, Garden
City Bks., 1955; Monitor And The Merrimac, Random,
1951. With Jack Coggins he wrote: Rockets, Jets,
Guided Missiles And Space Ships, Random, 1951; Rockets, Satellites And Space Travel, Random, 1958.

PRESCOTT, Orville
> Book reviewer and author, born in Cleveland, Ohio.
> He later made his home in New Canaan, Connecticut.
> He graduated from Williams College where he also re-
> ceived an honorary doctor's degree in 1963. The au-
> thor has written daily book reviews for the New York
> Times. In addition to writing books, he has edited
> several anthologies which include A Father Reads To
> His Children, Dutton, 1965.

PREUSSLER, Otfried 1923-
> He was born in Reichenberg (Liberec) in Bohemia and
> has lived in Germany. Anthea Bell translated his book
> The Little Witch (Abelard, 1961) which was read and
> enjoyed by the children of Germany. He once wrote
> about this book's origin in these words: ". . . This
> story, then, is written for my three daughters--and
> for all children who want to know why it is that no one
> needs to be frightened of bad witches nowadays. " He
> also wrote The Little Ghost (tr. by Anthea Bell), Abe-
> lard, 1967.

PRICE, Christine Hilda 1928-
> British writer and illustrator, born in London. She
> came to the United States at the age of twelve and
> lived in Scarborough, New York. She attended Vassar
> College, the Art Students League, and the Central
> School of Arts and Crafts in London. Miss Price has
> traveled throughout Greece and other European countries.
> Her main interests have been chamber music and gar-
> dening. She has lived in Connecticut and Castleton,
> Vermont. Juvenile books which she wrote and illus-
> trated include: Made In Ancient Greece, Dutton, 1967;
> Made In The Renaissance, Dutton, 1963; Sixty At A
> Blow, Dutton, 1968; Valiant Chattee-Maker, Warne,
> 1965.   CA-5/6, MJA

PRICE, Olive M.
> She is also known as Anne Cherryholmes. She was
> born in Pittsburgh, Pennsylvania. At the age of eight-
> een she came to New York and was successful in hav-
> ing her first book of plays published. Some of her
> plays have been produced on radio and television. Her
> books for young people have been published in Italy,
> Denmark, and England. Mrs. Cherryholmes has lived
> in Westwood, New Jersey. Juvenile titles include: Dog
> That Watched The Mountain, Coward, 1967; The Island

Of The Silver Spoon, Coward-McCann, 1963; Mystery
Of The Sunken City, Westminster Press, 1962; Short
Plays From American History And Literature For
Classroom Use, S. French, ltd., 1925; Story Of Clara
Barton, Grosset, 1954.

PRICE, Willadene (Anton) 1914-
Author and editor, born in Omaha, Nebraska. After
her marriage to an army officer, she lived in various
parts of the United States and Europe. She later had
homes in Massachusetts and Michigan. In addition to
writing books, she has been a magazine editor and an
associate editor of a publishing firm. Mrs. Price was
the recipient of the 1960 First Prize for Research A-
ward presented by the National League of American
Pen Women for her book Bartholdi And The Statue Of
Liberty, Rand, 1959. She also wrote Gutzon Borglum:
Artist And Patriot, Rand McNally, 1961. CA-5/6

PRICE, Willard De Mille 1887-
Journalist and author, born in Canada. As a young man
he decided to see the world and journeyed to England.
After his return to the United States, he edited World
Outlook magazine. His career has taken him to many
countries throughout the world, and he has written articles for a geographic society, museum, and newspapers.
His juvenile books include: Gorilla Adventure, Day,
1969; South Sea Adventure, Day, 1952. CA-4

PRIDDY, Frances Rosaleen 1931-
She has lived in Decatur, Illinois. Frances Priddy has
always enjoyed animals, and her pets have included
dogs and a squirrel monkey. Miss Priddy has also
raised Afghan hounds. For boys and girls she wrote:
Sam's Country, McGraw, 1969; Shell Beach Mystery,
Westminster, 1963. CA-3

PRIESTLY, Lee Shore 1904-
Author and teacher, born in Iola, Kansas. She attended
schools in Kansas and Missouri and studied journalism
at the University of Oklahoma (where she met her husband). She later graduated from New Mexico State University. She and her husband have published newspapers
in Louisiana, Oklahoma, and New Mexico. Lee Priestly
has also taught school. She has lived in New Mexico
and has enjoyed cooking, gardening, cats, and travel as
hobbies. For young people she wrote Believe In Spring,

Messner, 1964.   CA-5/6

PRIETO, Mariana (Beeching) 1912-
She was born in Cincinnati, Ohio and received part of
her education in Cuba at Colegio Sagrada Corazon,
Havana. She also attended the Universities of Miami
and Florida. She has a Florida teacher's certificate
and has taught evening classes both at the University
of Miami and the Miami High School. During World
War II, she taught Spanish to members of the armed
forces and also wrote Spanish radio commercials. She
married Martin Prieto and has lived in Miami, Florida.
For young people she wrote El Gallo Sabio, Day, 1962.
CA-5/6

PROCTOR, Everitt see MONTGOMERY, Rutherford G.

PROUDFIT, Isabel (Boyd) 1898-
Born in Evanston, Illinois, she attended college in Boston, and has lived in both New York and Connecticut.
At one time the author worked as a reporter in New
York and London. She has traveled to many countries
in order to do research for her books. Many of her
stories have appeared in magazines. Her juvenile
books include: James Fenimore Cooper, Messner,
1946; Noah Webster, Messner, 1942; River Boy: The
Story Of Mark Twain, Messner, 1940; The Treasure
Hunter, Messner, 1939.   MJA

PRUD'HOMMEAUX, René
Born in Alexandria, Egypt, he lived in France until the
age of seven when he came to the United States. He
graduated from the University of North Carolina. When
he was in the Army, he was stationed in Brazil. Mr.
Prud'hommeaux married writer Patricia Gordon, and
they have lived on Fire and Mark Islands. Juvenile
titles include: Extra Hand, Viking, 1953; Hidden Lights,
Viking, 1956; Mystery Of Marr's Hill, Macrae Smith,
1958; Port Of Missing Men, Junior Literary Guild and
Viking, 1952; Sunken Forest, Junior Literary Guild and
Viking, 1949.

PUNDT, Helen Marie
Native of Rochester, New York, she graduated from
Iowa State University. She has been a teacher of feature writing at Iowa State, an assistant editor in the
extension division of the College of Home Economics at

Cornell University, and senior editor at General Foods
Corporation. Miss Pundt has lived in Yonkers, New
York. Her books for young adults include: Judge's
Daughters, Crowell, 1966; Mystery Of The Castle Coins,
Crowell, 1967.   CA-7/8

PURCELL, John Wallace
Author, correspondent, pilot. He graduated from Harvard where he studied anthropology. During his college
days John Purcell was editor of the Harvard Crimson,
a United Press "string" correspondent, and worked for
Time, Inc. He also served as a Life magazine correspondent during World War II in the Southwest Pacific.
He later reported on military affairs and was located
in Life's Washington Bureau. For young people he
wrote True Book Of Holidays And Special Days (based
on a text by the author), Childrens, 1955.

PURDY, Claire Lee 1906-
She was born in Chihuahua, Mexico, attended schools
in Georgia and the Midwest, and graduated from the
University of Colorado. She married artist Rudolf
Kohl, and they have lived in Green Verdugo Hills, California and in Mexico. Her husband has illustrated
some of her books about music. She has belonged to
Phi Beta Kappa, Chi Delta Phi, Delta Zeta, and the
American College Quill Club. Her association with
marionettes created the desire to write. She has received many book awards, including the Julia Ellsworth
Ford Foundation award in 1937. Juvenile titles include:
Gilbert And Sullivan, Messner, 1946; He Heard America Sing, Messner, 1940; Song Of The North, Messner,
1941; Victor Herbert, Messner, 1944.

PURDY, Susan Gold 1939-
Author-illustrator. Born in New York City, she grew
up in Ohio and Connecticut. Prior to study in Paris
at the Sorbonne and École des Beaux Arts, the author
attended Vassar College and New York University. She
also studied painting (M. Henri Goetz) in Paris. She
has been a textile designer and camp director in addition to writing and illustrating books. She married
Geoffrey H. Purdy and has lived in Wilton, Connecticut.
Her extensive travels throughout Europe have provided
many of the ideas and backgrounds for her books. These
include: Christmas Decorations For You To Make,
Lippincott, 1965; Festivals For You To Celebrate, Lip-

pincott, 1969.   CA-15/16

PYLE, Howard 1853-1911
    Noted painter, born in Wilmington, Delaware. He
    studied at the Art Students League in New York City.
    His pictures appeared in many magazines, and he also
    illustrated the books which he wrote for boys and girls.
    He taught at Drexel Institute in Philadelphia. Howard
    Pyle died at the age of fifty-eight in Florence, Italy.
    Juvenile titles include: Men Of Iron, Harper, 1904;
    The Merry Adventures Of Robin Hood, Scribners, 1946;
    The Wonder Clock, Harper, 1887.   JBA-1

PYNE, Mable Mandeville 1903-
    She was born in Mount Vernon, New York and studied
    at Pratt Institute Art School and Columbia University.
    In addition to writing books, she has been a secretary
    and fashion artist.   Her books have been translated in-
    to several languages for distribution by the United
    States Information Agency. Mrs. Pyne has made her
    home in Darien, Connecticut.   She wrote and illustrated:
    The Hospital, Houghton, 1962; The Little History Of
    The United States, Houghton, 1940; Story Of Religion,
    Houghton, 1954.   CA-4

                          Q

QUEEN, Ellery, Jr. ,   see DANNAY, Frederic

QUEEN, Ellery, Jr. ,   see LEE, Manfred B.

                          R

RABE, Olive (Hanson)
    Author and attorney. She has lived near Boulder, Colo-
    rado.   Olive Rabe attended the University of Chicago
    and for fifteen years (1916-1932) practiced law in Chi-
    cago.   Her legal articles have appeared in Reader's
    Digest, American Magazine, and Country Home.   She
    collaborated with Aileen Fisher to write: Patriotic
    Plays And Programs, Plays, 1956; We Dickinsons . . .
    (A Junior Literary Guild selection), Atheneum, 1965.
    CA-19/20

RADLAUER, Edward
    He was born in Louisville, Kentucky and graduated
    from the University of California at Los Angeles. He

received his master's degree from Whittier College and
in 1957 became Principal of Escalona Elementary
School in Norwalk, California. He married Ruth Shaw
who has also been his co-author. His interests have
included: photography, music, racing carts, and oriental cooking. He and his family have lived in La
Habra, California. For young people he wrote Drag
Racing, Abelard-Schuman, 1966.

RALSTON, Jan see DUNLOP, Agnes Mary Robertson

RAND, Addison 1896-
Newspaperman and author, born in Eau Claire, Wisconsin. He attended Eau Claire Teachers College,
served in the Navy during World War I, and graduated
from the University of Wisconsin. He spent eighteen
years as a copy reader, reporter, and managing editor
on newspapers in New York, Florida, California, Minnesota, and Wisconsin. His interests have always been
baseball and outdoor sports. Mr. Rand has written
biographies, westerns, and sports stories. For young
people he wrote Southpaw Fly Hawk, Junior Literary
Guild and Longmans, 1952.

RAND, Paul 1914-   Ann
Husband-wife team. Paul Rand was born in Brooklyn.
He has been a magazine art director and a teacher at
Pratt Institute and Yale University. He has received
awards from the British Royal Society for the Encouragement of Arts, the Art Directors Club, and the A-
merican Institute of Graphic Arts. Mrs. Rand was
born in Chicago and studied under Mies Van Der Rohe.
She and her husband designed their home in Connecticut.
The Rands have also lived in California. Together they
wrote: I Know A Lot Of Things, Harcourt, 1956; Little 1, Harcourt, 1962; Sparkle And Spin, Harcourt,
1957.

RANDALL, Blossom E.
She studied journalism at the University of Kansas at
Lawrence. She married an attorney and has lived in
Wichita, Kansas. Her husband has been her "favorite
critic," and her son was the model for Fun For Chris,
Whitman, 1956.

RANDALL, Janet 1919-
She was born in Lancaster, California and attended

UCLA. Both her father and her husband Robert W.
Young were newspaper editors. She learned to ride
horseback on a ranch in the Big Tujunga Canyon of the
Sierra Madres and once rode with a drill team in San
Diego. She and her husband have written articles for
magazines and have made their home in Whittier, California. Juvenile titles include: Pony Girl (A Junior
Literary Guild selection), McKay, 1963; Saddles For
Breakfast (A Junior Literary Guild selection), Longmans, 1961; The Seeing Heart (A Junior Literary Guild
selection), McKay, 1965. CA-5/6

RANDALL, Kenneth Charles
Sportsman and writer. He has been an Associate Professor of English at Michigan State College in East
Lansing, Michigan. Mr. Randall has always enjoyed
the outdoors with fishing and hunting as his main interests. His favorite hobby has been shotguns and
rifles. In addition to writing books, he has also contributed to such magazines as Field And Stream, Outdoor Life, and Sports Afield. For young people he
wrote Wild Hunter, Junior Literary Guild and Watts,
1951.

RANDALL, Robert see SILVERBERG, Robert

RANDALL, Ruth Elaine Painter 1892-
Born in Salem, Virginia, she graduated from Roanoke
College and Indiana University. Her father was a pro-
fessor, and she married Lincoln scholar James G.
Randall. She and her late husband made their home in
Urbana, Illinois. Recipient of many honorary degrees,
Mrs. Randall has written distinguished biographies for
young people. These include: I Elizabeth . . . . ,
Little, 1966; I Jessie, Little, 1963; I Varina . . . ,
Little, 1962; Lincoln's Sons, Little, 1955. CA-1

RANSOHOFF, Doris
Author, scriptwriter. Born in Cincinnati, Ohio, she
grew up in the Midwest, and attended schools here and
abroad. She married motion picture producer and director Leo Seltzer, and they have lived in New York.
Her career as a writer began when she won an essay
prize at Bryn Mawr College followed by a successful
one-act comedy produced by New York's Lambs Club.
Doris Ransohoff has been a reporter for the New York
Herald Tribune and has contributed articles to The

Californian. She and her husband have written documentary films and television programs for the USO,
American Cancer Society, United Nations, and other
agencies. She also wrote scripts for the films of the
late President John F. Kennedy's visit to Mexico in
1962. For young people she wrote Living Architecture:
Frank Lloyd Wright, Encyclopedia Britannica, 1962.

RANSOME, Arthur 1884-1967
English author, he attended Rugby, and at one time
wrote for the Manchester Guardian. His father was
Professor of History at Leeds. Arthur Ransome's
book Pigeon Post (Lippincott, c1937) was awarded the
British Library Association's first Carnegie Medal in
1936. Although he had traveled widely, Mr. Ransome's
favorite place was near the lakes and river where he
had spent his childhood. He enjoyed fishing in these
lakes and writing for boys and girls until he died at
the age of eighty-three. Juvenile titles include: Great
Northern?, Macmillan, 1947; Missee Lee, Macmillan,
1942; Secret Water, Macmillan, 1940; Swallows And
Amazons, Lippincott, 1931.   JBA-1, JBA-2

RANUCCI, Renato 1921-
His pseudonym is Renato Rascel. He was born in
Turin, Italy. He has appeared in films and on radio
in addition to having directed several musical shows.
He also wrote the popular song "Arrivederci Roma."
His first book for boys and girls was Piccoletto (tr. by
Mary Elizabeth Gemming), Pantheon Books, 1961.

RASCEL, Renato see RANUCCI, Renato

RAVIELLI, Anthony
Author-illustrator, son of a marine engineer. He attended Cooper Union and the Art Students League in
New York. In addition to writing books, he has done
magazine illustration and portrait painting. He has
also worked in advertising. His instructional murals
and visual training aids were used in the armed forces
during World War II. After the war, Mr. Ravielli began a career in medical illustration. He illustrated
Katherine Binney Shippen's book Men, Microscopes,
And Living Things, Viking, 1955. Other juvenile books
which he wrote and illustrated include: An Adventure
In Geometry, Viking, 1957; Elephants, Parents Magazine Press, 1965; The Rise And Fall Of The Dinosaurs,

Parents Magazine Press, 1963; The World Is Round (A
Junior Literary Guild selection), Viking, 1963.

RAY, Ophelia
Teacher and writer, born in Texas. When she was a
young woman ("before she was seventeen"), she taught
in West Texas in a one-room schoolhouse. Ophelia
Ray has always been interested in the history of Texas
and its people. For the young reader she wrote Daughter Of The Tejas, New York Graphic Society, 1965.

RAYMOND, John
He was born in Findlay, Ohio and spent his boyhood in
Southern Pines, North Carolina. The author obtained
a degree in journalism and at one time was sports editor on the Times in Gainesville, Georgia. He has also
worked with the Georgia Forestry Commission in publicity. He has been interested in Civil War history,
painting, and classical Spanish guitar. For boys and
girls he wrote The Marvelous March Of Jean François,
Doubleday, 1965.

RAYMOND, Margaret Thomsen
She was born in Baltimore, Maryland and graduated
from Philadelphia's Friends School. In addition to
writing, she has been interested in photography. Her
home has been in Chicago, Illinois. For young people
she wrote Linnet On The Threshold, Longmans, Green
and Co. , 1930.

RECHNITZER, Ferdinand Edsted 1894-
Born in Perth Amboy, New Jersey, the son of a Met-
hodist minister. As an R. A. F. pilot during World War
I and an aviation editor of the New York Telegram,
Mr. Rechnitzer's background enabled him to write about
flying for young people. He has also been interested
in dogs, and his books about them include: Bonny's
Boy Returns, Winston, 1953; Jinks Of Jayson Valley,
Junior Literary Guild and Winston, 1950. He also
wrote Captain Jeep, Winston, 1951; Midnight Alarm,
Holt, 1955.

RECK, Alma Kehoe 1901-
Librarian, author, born in Washington, Indiana. In
addition to writing books, she has also written advertising copy and stories for children's magazines. Her
home has been in Denver, Colorado. After reading

about Turkey's Candy Festival and the Befana Fair, she
interviewed people from other countries and wrote a
book about festivals for boys and girls called First
Book Of Festivals Around The World, Watts, 1957.
She also wrote The West From A To Z, Whitman, 1952.
CA-4

REDFORD, Lora Bryning
She was born in Olympia, Washington. Her work in
the foreign service and her marriage to a foreign service officer has taken her to many countries including
Belgium, Burma, Japan, Mexico, Nepal, and Turkey.
Mrs. Redford has also lived in Taiwan and Indonesia
before she located in Istanbul, Turkey. Her children's
books include: Getting To Know The Central Himalayas: Nepal, Sikkim, Bhutan, Coward, 1964; Getting
To Know The Northern Himalayas: Kashmir, Tibet,
Assam, Coward, 1964.

REED, Gwendolyn E.
A graduate of Radcliffe College, she was born in Louisville, Kentucky. At one time the author was Associate
Editor of the Book Of Knowledge. She has also been
associated with the Boston Museum of Fine Arts and
the Institute of International Education. With Sara
Hannum she compiled Lean Out Of The Window, Atheneum, 1965. She wrote The Sand Lady, Lothrop, 1968.

REEDER, Colonel Red see REEDER, Russell Potter

REEDER, Russell Potter 1902-
A graduate of West Point Military Academy in New
York, he was born at Fort Leavenworth, Kansas. His
distinguished Army career has included assignments
overseas in both the European and Pacific Theatres
during World War II. His active military service
ended when he was wounded at Normandy on D-Day in
1945. Colonel (Red) Reeder, Jr., has received many
awards including the Distinguished Service Cross, both
the Silver and Bronze Stars, and two French citations.
He later became Assistant Director of Athletics at
West Point. His many juvenile books include: Army
Brat, Duell, 1967; Dwight David Eisenhower, Garrard,
1968; Medal Of Honor Heroes, Random, 1965; On The
Mound: Three Great Pitchers, Garrard, 1966; The
Story Of The Mexican War, Meredith Press, 1967;
West Point Plebe (A Junior Literary Guild selection),

Duell; Little, 1955.   CA-3

REELY, Mary Katharine 1881-
She was born on a farm near Spring Green, Wisconsin
and graduated from the University of Minnesota. She
has been a teacher and also worked in a Unity Settlement House in Minneapolis. She began her career
with books in a publishing firm and later was associated with the Wisconsin Library Commission as head
of the Book Selection Department. Upon retirement
she lived near Minneapolis. Juvenile titles include:
The Blue Mittens, Grosset; Hale, 1935; Seatmates,
Watts, 1949. With Ada M. Randall she also wrote
Through Golden Windows, Hale, 1934.

REES, Ennis (Samuel) 1925-
Author, poet, teacher, Ennis Rees, Jr. , was born in
Newport News, Virginia. A graduate of the College of
William and Mary at Williamsburg, Virginia, he re-
ceived his master's and doctorate degrees from Har-
vard University. Dr. Rees has been Professor of
English at the University of South Carolina. At one
time he also taught at Duke and Princeton Universities.
The author and his family have lived in Columbia,
South Carolina. His books for children include: Pota-
to Talk, Pantheon, 1969; Riddles, Riddles Everywhere,
Abelard, 1964. CA-2

REES, Helen Christina Easson (Evans) 1903-
Her pseudonym is Jane Oliver. She was born on the
Scottish Border and later made her home in London.
Her interests have included history and flying. She
met her late husband (writer John Llewelyn Rees)
while learning to fly. Jane Oliver has held a pilot's
license. For boys and girls she wrote Queen Most
Fair, Macmillan, 1959. CA-7/8

REESE, John Henry
Author and newspaperman, born in Sweetwater, Nebraska. He attended schools in Kansas and Nebraska.
He later made his home in San Marino, California.
Prior to free-lance writing, Mr. Reese had worked
for the U. S. Department of Internal Revenue and was
a reporter on the Los Angeles Examiner. His early
interest in animals, especially dogs, later led him to
write about them. Juvenile titles include: Big Mutt,
Westminster, 1952; The Shouting Duke, Westminster,

1952.

REEVES, James   1909-
   Poet, lecturer, teacher.   He has lived in Lewes, Sussex, England.   James Reeves has written several collections of poetry for children and retold a selection
   of English fairy tales (English Fables And Fairy Stories, Oxford, 1954).   He has taught in a training college
   for teachers and has spoken on the radio.   Many young
   poets in Great Britain have received help and encouragement from him.   His books include: . . . Blackbird In The Lilac, Dutton, 1959; The Cold Flame,
   Meredith, 1969.

REGLI, Adolph Casper   1896-
   His childhood was spent in Eau Claire, Wisconsin, and
   he graduated from the University of Wisconsin in Madison.   He once served in the Navy and also was a
   newspaperman in Minnesota, Florida, Wisconsin, and
   New York.   Although his home has been in Minneapolis,
   Mr. Regli has traveled throughout the West and has
   written many stories for young people about it.   These
   include: Fiddling Cowboy, McKay, 1949; Fiddling Cowboy In Search Of Gold, Junior Literary Guild and Watts,
   1951.   He also wrote: The Mayos, Pioneers In Medicine, Messner, 1942; Real Book About Buffalo Bill,
   Garden City Bks. , 1952.

REID, Alastair   1926-
   Scottish poet and author, born in Whithorn, Scotland.
   His home has been in Barcelona, Spain.   Well-known
   for his poetry, Alastair Reid has also written many
   books.   He created one story from a notebook which
   he had kept on words.   He served with the Royal Navy
   during World War II.   At one time he was on the staff
   at Sarah Lawrence College in Bronxville, New York.
   His books for children include: Allth, Houghton, 1958;
   Supposing, Little, 1960.   CA-7/8

REILEY, Catherine Conway
   Girl scout executive and writer, born in Rumson, New
   Jersey.   She graduated from Manhattanville College in
   New York and received her M. A. degree from Columbia
   University.   Her chief interest has been in young peo-
   ple, and she has served in many capacities with the
   Girl Scout program.   She has been a camp counsellor,
   director, and volunteer leader.   Her articles have

appeared in American Girl and Girl Scout Leader magazines. Miss Reiley has also worked with the Girl Guide program in Denmark. Other interests have included music and photography. For boys and girls she wrote Group Fun, Dodd, 1954.

REINFELD, Fred 1910-1964
His pseudonym is Edward Young. Author of over seventy books, he attended New York University and City College of New York. He became interested in the game of chess as a teen-ager and later became intercollegiate champion, winner of the Manhattan and Marshall Club championships, and New York state champion. In addition to books on chess, he has written books on science and coin collecting. Juvenile titles include: The Biggest Job In The World: The American Presidency, Crowell, 1964; Chess For Children, Sterling, 1958; Chess For Young People, Holt, 1961; Coin Collectors' Handbook, Sterling, 1954; Creative Chess, Sterling, 1966; Rays, Visible And Invisible, Sterling, 1958.   CA-9/10

RENAULT, Mary
She was born in London and attended Oxford. During World War II, she served as a nurse. Later Mary Renault lived in South Africa near the Cape peninsula in a house called "Delos." She has been interested in the history of Greece. She wrote several books on this subject, and they received wide acclaim. For young people she wrote The Lion In The Gateway . . . (Ed. by Walter Lord), Harper, 1964.

RENDINA, Laura (Jones) Cooper 1902-
Born in Northampton, Massachusetts, she grew up near Boston, attended the Cambridge Latin School, Smith College, and the Yale School of Art. After traveling abroad, she made her home in Sarasota, Florida on the Gulf of Mexico. At one time the author also lived in Wayland, Massachusetts. In addition to writing teen-age books, Mrs. Rendina has contributed stories to such magazines as Seventeen and Senior Prom. Her books for young people include: Destination Capri, Little, 1968; Lolly Touchberry, Little, 1957; Roommates, Little, 1948; Trudi, Little, 1959; World Of Their Own, Little, 1963.   CA-11/12, MJA

RENICK, Marion (Lewis) 1905-
She was born in Springfield, Ohio where she later graduated from Wittenberg University. In addition to writing books about sports, she has conducted book broad-
casts on the Ohio School of the Air, taught at Ohio
State University, and was an editor of My Weekly Reader. Her home has been in Columbus, Ohio. Her
books for boys and girls include: Bats & Gloves Of
Glory, Scribner, 1956; The Big Basketball Prize, Scribner, 1963; Boy At Bat, Scribner, 1961; Champion Cad-
dy, Scribner, 1943; Football Boys, Scribner, 1967;
Heart For Baseball, Scribner, 1953; Jimmy's Own
Basketball, Scribner, 1952.   CA-3, MJA

RESNICK, Seymour
Authority on the Spanish language, teacher, editor. He
received his Ph. D. degree in Spanish from New York
University. Dr. Resnick has taught at the City College
of New York, Rutgers and New York Universities. He
also was a teacher in a high school on Long Island and
at Queens College (New York City). He edited Spanish-
American Poetry, A Bilingual Selection, Harvey House,
1964.

RESSLER, Theodore Whitson
He has worked with the Boy Scouts for many years and
has also been associated with the YMCA. At one time
Mr. Ressler served as Youth and Extension Secretary
of a YMCA in Perth Amboy, New Jersey. He has always been interested in Indian stories and wrote Treasury Of American Indian Tales, Association Press, 1957.

RESSNER, Philip 1922-
He was born in New York and has lived in Brooklyn.
The author attended Brooklyn College and the University
of Chicago. He has been an assistant editor in a publishing house. For boys and girls he wrote: August
Explains, Harper, 1963; Jerome, Parents, 1967. CA-
15/16

REY, Hans Augusto 1898-   Margaret Elizabeth (Waldstein)
Authors-illustrators, husband-wife team. Both were
born in Hamburg, Germany, married in Rio de Janiero,
Brazil, and became American citizens in 1946. They
lived in Greenwich Village for twenty-three years before moving to Cambridge. H. A. Rey received his
education at the Hamburg and Munich Universities and

later worked in Brazil.   Margaret Rey attended the
Bauhaus in Dessau, the Academy of Art in Duesseldorf,
and also studied art in Berlin.   Many of their books
have been published in other countries.   Juvenile titles
include: Curious George Goes To The Hospital, Houghton, 1966; Curious George Learns The Alphabet, Houghton, 1963; Elizabite, Harper, 1962; Find The Constell-
ations, Houghton, 1954.   CA-5/6, JBA-2

REYNOLDS, Marjorie Harris 1903-
She was born in Rochester, New York.   Before she and
her family settled in Avon, New York, Mrs. Reynolds
had lived in England, France, and Quebec.   She has
always enjoyed riding and has been interested in horses.
Her books for children include: The Cabin On Ghostly
Pond, Harper, 1962; Ride The Wild Storm, Macmillan,
1969.   CA-7/8

REYNOLDS, Quentin James 1902-1965
Newsman, author, born in Brooklyn, New York.   He
began his newspaper career as a sportswriter; however, in 1930 he received an assignment from International News Service to go to Berlin.   Later he wrote
for Collier's from London.   In 1965 he was in the
Philippines writing a biography of Philippine President
Diosdado Macapagal when he contacted pneumonia.   The
Air Force flew him to Travis Air Force Base where
he died.   His brother was Assistant Secretary of Labor
James Reynolds.   Juvenile titles include: Battle Of
Britain, Random, 1953; Custer's Last Stand, Random,
1951; The F. B. I. , Random, 1954; Life Of Saint Patrick, Random, 1955; Winston Churchill, Random, 1963.

RHOADS, Dorothy Mary 1895-
She was born in Pekin, Illinois, graduated from Wellesley College in Massachusetts, and later made her home
in Santa Fe, New Mexico.   In addition to writing books,
she has been a translator for the U. S. government,
a reporter, and society editor.   Miss Rhoads has
accompanied many archaeological expeditions to the
Yucatán and collected material about the Maya Indians
for her juvenile book The Corn Grows Ripe (runner-up
for the 1957 Newbery Medal), Viking, 1956.   CA-19/
20

RICE, Charles D.
He was born in Cambridge, Massachusetts and studied

at Harvard University.   He has written humorous novels
for adults in addition to his books for young people.
Mr. Rice has been an editor and writer on This Week
magazine in New York City.   His home has been in
Yorktown, New York.   For boys and girls he wrote
The Little Dog Who Wore Earmuffs, Dodd, 1957.

RICE, Inez
She grew up in the state of Oregon and once lived in
California and New Jersey.   Inez Rice once said about
a story she wrote for children: ". . . I feel a little
boy is a universally fascinating subject.   Little boys
have such deep convictions and such boundless experience to back them up.   They accept things at times
with simple faith . . . My story is just a moment of
a little boy's belief. "   Her book was The March Wind,
Lothrop, 1957.

RICH, Elaine Sommers 1926-
She grew up in Indiana in a rural Mennonite community.
Her experiences as a child later led to her first book
for children.   She has contributed many articles, poems,
and stories to magazines and journals.   She married
Dr. Ronald L. Rich, and they have lived in Arlington
Heights, Massachusetts.   For boys and girls she wrote
Hannah Elizabeth, Harper, 1964.

RICH, Josephine (Bouchard) 1912-
Nurse and writer, born in Tamora, Nebraska.   She
graduated from a school of nursing in Chicago and married physician and radiologist James Sears Rich.   Their
home has been in Lexington, Kentucky where Mrs. Rich
was the recipient of the "Outstanding Woman of 1958"
Beta Sigma Phi award.   She has written books for both
adults and children.   Her hobbies have been golf and
bridge.   Mrs. Rich has also enjoyed travel, and her
visits to homes of famous people have provided authentic material for many of her books.   Juvenile titles include: Doctor Who Saved Babies, Messner, 1961; Jean
Henri Dunant, Messner, 1956; Pioneer Surgeon, Messner, 1959; Women Behind Men Of Medicine, Messner,
1967.   CA-5/6

RICH, Louise (Dickinson) 1903-
She was born in Huntington, Massachusetts, the daughter
of a newspaper editor.   She graduated from Bridgewater
State Teachers College and became an English teacher.

When she married Ralph Rich, she lived in a camp in
the Maine wilderness which provided the background
for many of her stories. Juvenile titles include: The
First Book Of Lumbering, Watts, 1967; First Book Of
New England, Watts, 1957; Mindy, Lippincott, 1959;
Star Island Boy, Watts, 1968; Start Of The Trail, Lippincott, 1949.

RIDGWAY, Jason see LESSER, Milton

RIEDMAN, Sarah Regal 1902-
Professor, editor, camp director. Dr. Riedman has
been Assistant Professor of Physiology at Brooklyn
College and a member of Sigma Xi (honorary society
of scientists).   Besides writing science books and arti-
cles she was a children's camp director for over fif-
teen years.   She collaborated with her husband Elton
T. Gustafson to write Portraits Of Nobel Laureates In
Medicine And Physiology, Abelard, 1964. Other juve-
nile titles include: Let's Take A Trip To A Fishery,
Abelard, 1956; Water For People, Schuman, 1952.
CA-4

RIENOW, Leona Train
Her childhood was spent in northern Minnesota where
she developed her interest in geology.   This interest
also provided her with the incentive to make a study of
prehistoric man.   Leona Rienow has lived on a farm
near Albany.   In her "Note to the Reader" in the book
Bewitched Caverns (Junior Literary Guild and Scribners,
1948) she wrote: ". . . Because their blood flows in
our veins, and because they were such remarkable
people, we should all know about the Cro-Magnons.
That is the first reason this book was written." She
also wrote The Dark Pool, Scribners, 1949.

RIESENBERG, Felix 1913-
Editor and author, the son of the late writer and sea
captain, Felix Riesenberg.   He attended Columbia University.   He has sailed on various types of ships to
Europe, Africa, South America, and the West Indies.
Felix Riesenberg, Jr., also spent several years in the
American Merchant Marine.   At one time he served on
the editorial staff of the San Francisco News and was
a correspondent with the marine magazine Nautical Gazette.   The author's hobby has been model ship building, and he has sailed his own sloop "Skookum" around

the San Francisco Bay area. His books for young people include: Balboa: Swordsman And Conquistador, Random, 1956; Crimson Anchor, Dodd, 1948; Phantom Freighter, Dodd, 1944; Salvage, Dodd, 1942; Story Of The Naval Academy, Random, 1958; The Undercover Sloop, Westminster Press, 1962; Vanishing Steamer, Westminster Press, 1958.

RIETVELD, Jane 1913-
Author-illustrator. She married an artist, and they have lived in Milwaukee, Wisconsin. She became interested in drawing at an early age (she won a prize for her art work in the fifth grade). A teacher once gave her a sketchbook, and she later wrote about it: ". . . With the new sketchbook my interest really blossomed and ever since that time my art work has been a major activity. " She wrote and illustrated: Nicky's Bugle, Viking, 1947; Rocky Point Campers, Junior Literary Guild and Viking, 1950.

RIEU, Emile Victor 1887-
Editor, translator, born in London, England. He attended St. Paul's School and Balliol College, Oxford University. At one time he was manager of a publishing house in Bombay, India. He has also been an academic and literary advisor of a large company. The University of Leeds awarded him an honorary degree. His hobbies have been: petrology, mountains, and carpentry. For young people he wrote The Flattered Flying Fish, And Other Poems, Dutton, 1962. CA-4

RIFKIN, Lillian
Teacher and author, born in Wilkes-Barre, Pennsylvania. She attended school in Bloomsburg, Pennsylvania and later studied in New York at Teachers College. The author has enjoyed drawing and clay modeling as hobbies. Her travels abroad included a visit to Russia. Lillian Rifkin decided to write books of information for boys and girls when she found a need for them during her teaching career. She wrote When I Grow Up, I'll Be A Farmer (ed. by Frederick Grover and Paul Sears), Lothrop, 1944.

RIGGS, Ida Berry
She has lived on a ranch in Arizona. She wrote a book about a horse named Panchito which the author once owned. When she described Panchito, she said:

". . . never has there been such a cutting horse in all the South West!" Her book was entitled <u>Little Champion,</u> Macmillan, 1944.

RINK, Paul 1912–

He was born in San Jose, California and studied at San Jose State Junior College, the University of California, and the Inter-American University in Panama. During World War II, he did intelligence work in Panama followed by service in the South Pacific aboard an Army transport. He has written for <u>Esquire</u> and <u>American Heritage</u> and has also written scripts for the motion picture and television industries. The Rinks have lived in Monterey, California. For young people he wrote <u>Ernest Hemingway,</u> Encyclopaedia Britannica Press, 1962.

RINKOFF, Barbara Jean (Rich) 1923–

Author and social worker, native New Yorker. A graduate of New York University, she did further study at Columbia University. She has been a member of the national honorary sociological fraternity and was a medical social worker for a number of years. Mrs. Rinkoff has also worked on the International Relations Committee of the American Association of University Women. Some of her work has appeared in magazines and newspapers. The wife of a dentist, Barbara Rinkoff has made her home in Kisco, New York. She has enjoyed geology, stamp and foreign doll collecting, and wood carving as hobbies. Her books include: <u>The Remarkable Ramsey,</u> Morrow, 1965; <u>Sandra's View,</u> McGraw, 1969.   CA-19/20

RIPLEY, Elizabeth (Blake) 1906–

Author-illustrator, compiler, born in New Haven, Connecticut. She studied in Paris at the Sorbonne, the Art Students League in New York, and graduated from Smith College in Massachusetts. In addition to her art work, she has been interested in the theater. Following college, she lived several years in Europe. She later made her home in Connecticut and New Hampshire. Mrs. Ripley has done extensive research and travel to collect authentic material for her books. In addition to writing biographies, the author has also compiled and illustrated books of jokes and riddles for young readers. Her juvenile biographies include: <u>Botticelli,</u> Lippincott, 1960; <u>Copley,</u> Lippincott, 1967;

Dürer, Lippincott, 1958; Gainsborough, Lippincott, 1964;
Goya, Oxford, 1956; Rodin, Lippincott, 1966; Winslow
Homer, Lippincott, 1963.   CA-4

RITCHIE, Barbara Gibbons
She was born in Bemidji, Minnesota where she also
spent her childhood. She later made her home in Denver, Colorado. She has written books for boys and
girls which have their settings in neighboring countries.
Barbara Ritchie has endeavored to "open new vistas of
understanding between our children and their neighbors
in the West Indies. " The island of Martinique was the
setting for her book To Catch A Mongoose (the French
translation Pour attraper une mangouste, by Marie
Byrne), Parnassus, 1963. She also wrote Riot Report,
Viking, 1969.

RITCHIE, Rita (Krohne) 1930-
She was born in Milwaukee and graduated from the University of Wisconsin. Although she has been a camp
counsellor, library page, chemical technician, and
copywriter, she has always considered writing her main
interest. The author has traveled in Mexico and Europe. She married writer Jack Ritchie, and they have
lived on Washington Island, Wisconsin. Juvenile titles
include: Golden Hawks Of Genghis Khan (A Junior Literary Guild selection), Dutton, 1958; Pirates Of Samar-
kand, Norton, 1967; Rogue Whaler, Norton, 1966; Secret Beyond The Mountains (A Junior Literary Guild selection), Dutton, 1960.   CA-5/6

RIVERSIDE, John see HEINLEIN, Robert Anson

RIWKIN-BRICK, Anna 1908-1970
Photographer and author. She was born in Russia and
has made her home in Sweden. She has become well-
known for her photographs of children, people, and
places. Her photo-documentary books have been exhibited at the Museum of Modern Art in the Family of
Man show. The author has enjoyed traveling. For
young people she wrote: Dirk Lives In Holland, Macmillan, 1963; Eli Lives In Israel, Macmillan, 1965;
Elle Kari, Macmillan, 1952; Lilibet, Circus Child,
Macmillan, 1961; Nomads Of The North, Macmillan,
1962; Randi Lives In Norway, Macmillan, 1965.

ROBBINS, Ruth
    Illustrator, art director, author. She married Herman
    Schein and has resided in Berkeley, California. She
    retold the Russian folk tale Baboushka And The Three
    Kings (Parnassus, 1960) which was illustrated by Nicho-
    las Sidjakov who received the Caldecott Medal in 1961.
    Ruth Robbins also wrote: The Emperor And The Drum-
    mer Boy, Parnassus, 1962; Harlequin And Mother Goose
    Or Magic Stick, Parnassus, 1965.

ROBERTS, Catherine Christopher 1905-
    Author-illustrator. She has been associated with 4-H
    Clubs in Annandale, New Jersey. Her unusual interests
    have included: giving cooking lessons to teen-age farm
    boys, bricklaying, and building a family swimming pool.
    Mrs. Roberts has also contributed to fashion magazines.
    For young people she wrote and illustrated: First Book
    Of Sewing, Watts, 1956; The Real Book About Real
    Crafts, Watts, 1954.

ROBERTSON, Keith 1914-
    Carlton Keith is his pseudonym. He was born in Dows,
    Iowa and graduated from the U. S. Naval Academy.
    Following World War II, he worked in a publishing
    firm. When his first book was accepted, he decided
    to devote full-time to a writing career. He and his
    family have lived on a farm ("Booknoll Farm") in
    Hopewell, New Jersey. His books for young people
    include: Crow And The Castle, Viking, 1957; Henry
    Reed, Inc. (A Junior Literary Guild selection), Viking,
    1958; Henry Reed's Baby-Sitting Service, Viking, 1966;
    Henry Reed's Journey, Viking, 1963; The Pinto Deer,
    Viking, 1956.   CA-9/10, MJA

ROBINSON, Barbara Webb 1927-
    Author and librarian. She has made her home in Need-
    ham, Massachusetts. Prior to her marriage, Mrs.
    Robinson lived in Sewickley, Pennsylvania where she
    was a librarian. The author has spent her summer
    vacations in Massachusetts near Plymouth County which
    provided the background for her children's book Across
    From Indian Shore (A Junior Literary Guild selection),
    Lothrop, 1962. Other juvenile titles include: Fattest
    Bear In The First Grade, Random, 1969; Trace Through
    The Forest, Lothrop, 1965.   CA-3

ROBINSON, Charles Alexander 1900-
He was born in Princeton, New Jersey and later made
his home in Providence, Rhode Island. He attended
Princeton University and also studied in Rome and
Athens. Charles Robinson, Jr., has been Professor
of Classics at Brown University and has taught at the
American School of Classical Studies in Athens, Greece.
The author has belonged to the American Historical
Association and the Archaeological Institute of America.
His articles have appeared in newspapers and numerous
professional journals. Professor Robinson has written
many books about the ancient world for young people.
These include: The First Book Of Ancient Bible
Lands, Watts, 1962; The First Book Of Ancient Egypt,
Watts, 1961; First Book Of Ancient Rome, Watts, 1959;
The First Book Of Ancient Mesopotamia And Persia,
Watts, 1962. CA-1

ROBINSON, Ray
Editor, sportswriter. He graduated from Columbia
University where he continued his studies in law. He
has been on the staff of Good Housekeeping and Pageant
magazines and also was a senior editor of Coronet.
He has lived in Manhattan and has spent his summers
on Fire Island. His sports books for young people include: Stan Musial: Baseball's Durable "Man," Putnam, 1963; Ted Williams, Putnam, 1962.

ROBINSON, Robert Shirley 1902-
His pseudonym is Philip Latham. Author and astronomer, he has been associated with the Mount Wilson-
Palomar Observatories. Mr. Robinson has written a
college textbook about astronomy and has given technical advice and assistance to movie producers when they
have filmed stories on science fiction. For young people he wrote Five Against Venus, Winston, 1952.

ROBINSON, Thomas Pendleton 1878-
Architect, author, playwright, born in Calais, Maine.
He attended the Boston schools where he met his future
wife and later studied architecture at M. I. T. Mr.
Robinson has been associated with 47 Workshop at Harvard and has written several prize-winning plays. He
was the recipient of the Drama League-Longmans Green
Prize and the Morosco Prize. The Robinson family
made their home in Massachusetts. For boys and girls
he wrote: Buttons, Viking, 1938; Trigger John's Son,

Viking, 1949.   JBA-2

ROGERS, Cedric
Author-illustrator, born in Schenectady, New York. He
attended prep school and Dulwich College in England
ans also studied at Goldsmith's School of Art.   Mr.
Rogers and his family have lived in Bucks County,
Pennsylvania.   He served as a test pilot and flight instructor with the R. A. F. during World War II.   After
the war, the author drew cartoons for Punch magazine.
His interest in the hobby of collecting resulted in writing Rags, Bottles, And Bones, McKay, 1962.

ROGERS, William Garland 1896-
Teacher, critic, writer.   W. G. Rogers once taught at
Deerfield Academy and in the schools of Pittsburgh,
Pennsylvania and Springfield, Massachusetts.   He has
contributed articles to magazines and appeared on the
radio program "Invitation To Learning. " He wrote:
Mightier Than The Sword, Harcourt, 1969; A Picture
Is A Picture, Harcourt, 1964.   CA-11/12

ROJANKOVSKY, Feodor 1891-
Illustrator-author, born in Mitava, Russia.   He studied
at the Moscow Fine Arts Academy.   During World War
I, he served in the Russian army as an infantry reserve
officer.   Following the war, he lived in Poland where
he was art director of both the Opera in Pazan and a
Polish publishing firm.   He later worked in Paris and
came to the United States in 1941.   In 1956 he was
awarded the Caldecott Medal for Frog Went A-Courtin'
(retold by John Langstaff), Harcourt, 1955.   He has
illustrated books for many authors.   His books include:
Animals In The Zoo, Knopf, 1962; Animals On The
Farm, Knopf, 1967.   JBA-2

ROLLINS, Charlemae (Hill) 1897-
Author, librarian, teacher, born in Yazoo City, Mississippi.   Her home has been in Chicago.   The author
attended the University of Chicago and Columbia University.   Mrs. Rollins has taught at many colleges and
universities including Rosary College in River Forest,
Illinois and San Francisco State College in California.
She began her library career in 1927 at the Chicago
Public Library and retired in 1963.   The author has
contributed articles to ALA Bulletin, School Library
Journal, and other magazines.   She has been the recip-

ient of numerous awards and has also served as Chairman of the Children's Section of the Illinois Library
Association and of the Newbery-Caldecott Awards Committee of ALA.   For young people she wrote: Famous
American Negro Poets, Dodd, 1965; Famous Negro En-
tertainers Of Stage, Screen, & TV, Dodd, 1967.   CA-
11/12

ROOKE, Daphne 1914-
She was born in Transvaal, South Africa and grew up
on a cane plantation where she became acquainted with
the songs of the Afrikaans.   She later lived near the
Lebombo Mountains in northern Zululand.   In addition
to writing for young people, Mrs. Rooke has written
several adult novels.   Her juvenile books include:
Twins In Australia, Houghton, 1956; Twins In South
Africa, Houghton, 1955.

ROOS, Ann
Author and Girl Scout executive.   Born in Brooklyn,
New York, she grew up on Long Island, and graduated
from Syracuse University.   Her work with the Girl
Scouts led to extensive travel in both the United States
and England, and she has served as an executive with
the International Division of the U. S. A. Girl Scout program.   While studying Creative Writing at Columbia
University she wrote Man Of Molokai (Lippincott, 1943).
The author collaborated with Mary Alison Sanders to
compile Sing Noel, The Authors, 1948.   MJA

ROOSEVELT, Anna Eleanor (Roosevelt) 1884-1962
Writing books for boys and girls was also an accom-
plishment of this distinguished American.   She was the
niece of President Theodore Roosevelt and the wife of
President Franklin D. Roosevelt.   Eleanor Roosevelt
served as a delegate to the United Nations General
Assembly and once was chairman of the UN's Human
Rights Commission.   With Regina Tor she wrote Growing Toward Peace, Random, 1960.   With Helen Ferris
she wrote Partners, Junior Literary Guild and Doubleday, 1950.   She wrote Tomorrow Is Now, Harper, 1963.

ROSELLI, Luciana
Italian author and illustrator, born in Alessandria, Italy.
She attended the Universities of Pavia and Pisa in Italy.
She has made her home in New York City.   As an art-
ist, Luciana Roselli's work has been published in Gla-

mour, McCall's, Redbook, Harper's Bazaar, Seventeen,
and Vogue. Her juvenile books include: The Polka Dot
Child, Graphic Society Publishers, 1964; The Prin-
cesses' Tresses, Macmillan, 1963.

ROSENBURG, John M.
Sportswriter, teacher, he graduated from Ithaca College. He has been a baseball, basketball, and football
coach of several high schools in New York. In addition
to writing articles for Coronet and Colliers', he has
also been a correspondent for United Press International. Later he was associated with A. T. &T. and served
on its public relations staff. His books for young people include: Baseball For Boys, Oceana, 1960; The
Story Of Baseball, Random, 1962.

ROSS, Barnaby see DANNAY, Frederic

ROSS, Barnaby see LEE, Manfred B.

ROSS, Patricia (Fent) 1899-
She was born in Kansas and later lived in Mexico.
Patricia Ross has managed a dude ranch in New Mexico
and has also operated a hotel which was located in
Mexico. She once said: "For seven years I have lived
in Mexico, writing fiction and magazine articles . . .
The thing I want most is to give Americans a true pic-
ture of my Mexico. " Juvenile titles include: . . .
Made In Mexico, Knopf, 1952; Mexico, Fideler, 1962.

ROSS, Zola Helen (Girdey) 1912-
Author and teacher, born in Dayton, Iowa. She grew
up in Nevada and California and later made her home
on the West Coast. The author received her education
at MacMurray College for Women. In addition to writing, Zola Ross has also been an instructor at the University of Washington in Seattle. She has written for
both adults and children. With Lucile Saunders Mc-
Donald she wrote: Assignment In Ankara (A Junior
Literary Guild selection), Nelson, 1959; Friday's Child
(A Junior Literary Guild selection), Nelson, 1954; Pigtail Pioneer, Winston, 1956; Wing Harbor (A Junior
Literary Guild selection), Nelson, 1957.

ROTHERY, Agnes Edwards 1888-
Born in Brookline, Massachusetts, she studied at Wellesley College. She married Harry Rogers Pratt who

taught at the University of Virginia. During the summer months the author and her husband often visited
South America. She has also traveled to Scandinavia,
Central America, and Italy. Her interests have included: cooking, gardening, and painting. Juvenile
titles include: Central American Roundabout, Dodd,
1944; Iceland Roundabout, Dodd, 1948; Italian Roundabout, Dodd, 1950; Scandinavian Roundabout, Dodd, 1946;
South American Roundabout, Dodd, 1940; Washington
Roundabout, Dodd, 1942.

ROUNDS, Glen 1906-
Author-illustrator, born in the South Dakota Badlands.
He grew up on a ranch in Montana and received his
education at the Kansas City Art Institute and Art Students League in New York. He later made his home
in Southern Pines, North Carolina. At one time, the
author worked as a cowpuncher, logger, and baker.
He also was a sergeant in the Army. His career as
a writer and illustrator began in 1936 when he wrote
and illustrated Ol' Paul, The Mighty Logger . . . (5th
printing rev.), Holiday, 1949. Other juvenile titles
include: Beaver Business . . ., Prentice-Hall, 1960;
Blind Colt, Holiday, 1960; Casey Jones, Golden Gate
Junior Books, 1968; Lone Muskrat, Holiday, 1953;
Prairie Schooners, Holiday, 1968; Whitey And The Rust-
lers, Holiday, 1951. JBA-2

ROWE, Viola Carson
She was born in Melrose Park, Illinois. She began her
newspaper career on the Maywood Herald, the writer
of a column called "The Feminine Viewpoint." Later
she became associate editor of an affiliated paper. Following her marriage, she began writing fiction, and
her short stories have appeared in publications both
here and in Canada. She has lived in Elmhurst, Illinois. Juvenile titles include: Free For All, Longmans,
1959; Girl In A Hurry, Longmans, 1956; A Way With
Boys, Longmans, 1957. CA-2

RUBICAM, Harry Cogswell 1902-
Author and newspaperman, born in Denver, Colorado.
Before moving to the East, Harry Rubicam, Jr. had
been a reporter and editor for the Denver Post. He
later became associated with the advertising firm of
Young & Rubicam, Inc. in New York. After his retirement, he made his home in Grafton, Vermont. His

interests have included stamp collecting and photography.
For young people he wrote: Man At Work In The Great
Plains States, Putnam, 1961; Pueblo Jones, Knopf,
1939.   CA-17/18

RUCHLIS, Hyman 1913-
Teacher, author, born in New York. He graduated
from Brooklyn College and received his master's degree from Columbia University. For many years Mr.
Ruchlis taught mathematics and science in the New
York City School System. He has served as president
of the Science Federation of New York and of the Physics Teachers Association. In addition to writing a-
bout science, he has designed toys and created science
kits. His books for young people include: Bathtub
Physics, Harcourt, 1967; Clear Thinking, Harper, 1962;
Orbit: A Picture Story Of Force And Motion, Harper,
1958; Your Changing Earth, Harvey House, 1963.
CA-4

RUDOLPH, Marguerita
Author, educator, lecturer, born in Chernigov, Russia.
She received her early education there and later attended college in the United States. As an educator,
Mrs. Rudolph has lectured throughout our country. She
has said of her first book for children (about the Russian language): "I love the language because I was
brought up on it and had my first intellectual experiences through the Russian classics . . . I know the
excitement of learning and of sharing knowledge and
hope this will come across in the book. " Her book is
entitled You Can Learn Russian, Little, 1964. She also wrote I Am Your Misfortune, Seabury, 1968.

RUGH, Belle Dorman 1908-
She was born in Beirut, Lebanon, the daughter of an
American missionary doctor. She received her education in America at Vassar College and Columbia University. The author returned to Beirut and served on
the faculty at Women's College as an English instructor. She married an American professor in Shemlan
but later made her home in Wethersfield, Connecticut.
Her books for young people include: Crystal Mountain,
Houghton, 1955; Lost Waters, Houghton, 1967; Path
Above The Pines, Houghton, 1962.   CA-15/16

RUKEYSER, Muriel 1913-
   Poet, author, she was born in New York City.   She
   studied at Vassar and Columbia University.   Miss
   Rukeyser received many honors for her work including
   a National Academy Grant, a Guggenheim fellowship,
   and the Harriet Monroe prize.   She has also been a
   member of the Bollingen Award Committee.   She has
   lived in New York City.   Her books for young people
   include: Come Back, Paul, Harper, 1955; I Go Out,
   Harper, 1961.   CA-7/8

RUSH, William Marshall 1887-1950
   Forest ranger and author, born in West Virginia.   He
   received his education in Chanute, Kansas.   Mr. Rush
   was associated with the Forest Service in Montana,
   Oregon, and Wyoming for over twenty years.   His experiences as a ranger and game specialist later provided authentic material for his juvenile books.   These
   include: Rocky Mountain Ranger, Longmans, 1944;
   Wheat Rancher, Longmans, 1946; Wild Horses Of Rain-
   rock, Longmans, 1951; Yellowstone Scout, Longmans,
   1945.

RUSHMORE, Helen
   Librarian and author, born in Independence, Kansas.
   She attended schools in Missouri and later received
   both her bachelor's and master's degrees from the
   University of Tulsa in Oklahoma.   She was associated
   with the schools of Tulsa as a librarian.   Her earliest
   memories were of Tulsa when it was still part of the
   Indian Territory.   Her books for boys and girls in-
   clude: Cowboy Joe Of The Circle S, Harcourt, 1950;
   Look Out For Hogan's Goats, Garrard, 1969.

RUSKIN, Ariane 1935-
   Artist, dancer, writer, she has lived in New York
   City.   She graduated summa cum laude from Barnard
   College and received an Honours degree from Cambridge University.   Ariane Ruskin has traveled in Europe and South America, worked for the United Nations,
   and danced with the Marquis de Cuevas Ballet.   Her
   juvenile books include: Nineteenth Century Art, Mc-
   Graw, 1968; The Pantheon Story Of Art For Young People, Pantheon, 1964.   CA-15/16

RUSSELL, Franklin 1926-
   Author, naturalist, traveler, born in Christchurch,

Canterbury, New Zealand. He received his education
in New Zealand at Nelson College and Victoria University of Wellington. Franklin Russell has written for
both adults and children. The National Association of
Independent Schools named his book Argen The Gull
(Knopf, 1964) as one of the ten best adult books of
1964. The author was the recipient of a Guggenheim
Fellowship for the study of the Gulf of the St. Lawrence, its natural history. Mr. Russell has lived in
Frenchtown, New Jersey. For young readers he wrote
Hawk In The Sky, Holt, 1965. CA-19/20

RUSSELL, Solveig Paulson 1904-
She was born in Salt Lake City and attended the College
of Education in Monmouth, Oregon and the University
of Oregon. She taught in the Oregon rural schools
prior to teaching in a junior high school in Salem.
Mrs. Russell has contributed many stories and verses
to children's magazines. Her interests have included
camping and travel. She and her family have lived in
Salem, Oregon. Juvenile titles include: A Is For Apple, And Why, Abingdon, 1959; About Fruit, Melmont,
1962; All Kinds Of Legs, Bobbs, 1963; If You Were A
Cat, Childrens, 1967; Which Is Which? (A Junior Literary Guild selection), Prentice-Hall, 1966. CA-3

S

ST. JOHN, Philip
Author, editor, sports enthusiast. He has been a free-
lance writer. In addition to his career as a writer,
Philip St. John has also been an editor on Space Sci-
ence Fiction magazine. His juvenile books include:
Rocket Jockey, Junior Literary Guild and Winston, 1952;
Rockets To Nowhere, Winston, 1954.

SALTEN, Felix see SALZMAN, Siegmund

SALZMAN, Siegmund 1869-1945
This author's pseudonym is Felix Salten who became
famous for his stories about a deer named Bambi.
Austrian writer, critic, essayist. Mr. Salten was
born in Budapest, Hungary, but he spent a great part
of his life in Vienna, Austria. When the Nazis seized
Austria in 1938, Switzerland became Felix Salten's
home. Juvenile titles include: Bambi (tr. by Whittaker
Chambers), Simon and Schuster, 1929; Renni, The

Rescuer (tr. by K. C. Kaufman), Bobbs, 1940.

SAMACHSON, Dorothy (Mirkin) 1914-   Joseph 1906-
Husband-wife team. She was born in New York and
studied at Hunter College. She has been a professional
pianist and has played not only at the Metropolitan
Opera but also in a supper club on top of a Chicago
hotel. Dr. Samachson came from New Jersey where
he graduated from Rutgers University. He received
his Ph. D. degree from Yale. In addition to heading a
laboratory at the VA Hospital in Hines, Illinois, he has
been an Assistant Professor at the College of Medicine,
University of Illinois. The Samachsons have lived in
Oak Park, Illinois. Their books for young people include: The Fabulous World Of Opera (A Junior Literary Guild selection), Rand, 1962; Good Digging (A Junior Literary Guild selection), Rand, 1960; Masters Of
Music, Doubleday, 1967.   CA-11/12

SAMSTAG, Nicholas 1903-
He attended schools in New York where he was born.
Nicholas Samstag has written adult novels and his work
has appeared in such magazines as the New Yorker and
Serenade. In addition to his writing career, the au-
thor has enjoyed painting and reading as special inter-
ests. For children he wrote Kay-Kay Comes Home,
Obolensky, 1962.   CA-7/8

SAMUELS, Gertrude
Writer-photographer. She studied at George Washington University. She has been a staff writer for several newspapers, and her articles and photographs have
appeared in such magazines as Newsweek, Time, and
National Geographic. Miss Samuels has been the recipient of numerous awards for her newspaper work
including the George Polk Award from Long Island University for education reporting. She has also been
associated with UNICEF as a special observer. For
young people she wrote B-G: Fighter Of Goliaths,
Crowell, 1961.   CA-11/12

SANBORN, Duane see BRADLEY, Duane

SANDBURG, Carl (August) 1878-1967
Poet, collector of folk songs, biographer, born in
Galesburg, Illinois. He spent twenty years in the re-
search and writing of his biography on Abraham Lin-

coln. The part of the biography entitled The War
Years (4 vols. , Harcourt, 1939) was awarded the Pulitzer prize for history in 1940. He began to write
poetry when he was a student at Lombard College in
Galesburg, Illinois. He later was an editorial writer
on the Chicago Daily News. In 1951 he was awarded
a Pulitzer prize for poetry for his work entitled Complete Poems, Harcourt, 1950. His books for boys and
girls include: Early Moon, Harcourt, 1930; Rootabaga
Stories, Harcourt, 1922; Wind Song, Harcourt, 1960.
CA-7/8

SANDBURG, Charles see SANDBURG, Carl (August)

SANDBURG, Helga 1918-
Daughter of poet Carl Sandburg, she grew up in Michigan and later lived in North Carolina. Helga Sandburg
has always been interested in animals, and her books
for boys and girls have reflected this interest. She
has also written adult novels and stories for many
magazines. She has lived in Cleveland, Ohio and
Washington, D. C. For boys and girls she wrote:
Bo And The Old Donkey, Dial, 1965; Joel And The
Wild Goose, Dial, 1963. CA-4

SANDERSON, Ivan Terence 1911-
Writer, zoologist. He studied at Cambridge University
in England. Mr. Sanderson has been in charge of scientific collecting trips to Nigeria, Malaya, Guatemala,
and Dutch Guiana. His articles have often been published in scientific journals under the auspices of the
Chicago Museum of Natural History and the British
Museum. The author has also conducted a television
program. He and his wife have lived both on a farm
in New Jersey and an apartment in New York. His
books include: Abominable Snowmen: Legend Come
To Life, Chilton Co. , 1961; The Continent We Live
On (special ed. for young readers adapted by Anne
Terry White), Random, 1962.

SANDOZ, Mari (Susette) 1901-1966
Teacher, editor, author, born in Sheridan County,
Nebraska. She attended business college and the University of Nebraska who later awarded Miss Sandoz
a Doctor of Literature degree. Before her death in
1966, the author lived in Ellsworth, Nebraska. At one
time Miss Sandoz was a rural school teacher, proof-

reader, and magazine editor. She also served on the
staff of writers' conferences at several universities.
Her books for young people include: The Battle Of The
Little Bighorn, Lippincott, 1966; The Horsecatcher,
Westminster Press, 1957; The Story Catcher, West-
minster Press, 1963.   CA-2

SANGER, Frances Ella (Fitz)
Born in Summertown, Tennessee, she went to school
in Wisconsin and Colorado, and graduated from the
State Teachers College in San Diego.   Prior to her
marriage, she taught in Chula Vista, California. She
became interested in writing and took an extension
course from the University of Southern California. Her
book for young people was Silver Teapot, Westminster
Press, 1948.

SANTALO, Lois
She was born in Grand Rapids, Michigan. Lois Santalo
graduated from the University of Michigan and studied
at the University of California, Hunter College, and
Columbia University.   She has also done graduate work
at the University of Arizona in Tucson.   Mrs. Santalo
has worked in a library and has taught folk dancing.
Her husband has been a teacher at the University of
Arizona.   She wrote The Wind Dies At Sunrise, Bobbs,
1965.

SARASY, Phyllis Powell 1930-
Teacher and writer, born in Cleveland, Ohio. She received degrees from Miami University in Oxford, Ohio
and Hunter College in New York. She married real
estate broker Lewis Craigo Sarasy and made her home
in New York.   Phyllis Sarasy has taught school in
Connecticut, Ohio, and New York.   In her association
with International Seminars, the author helped to establish the first American Seminars in South America
between English and Spanish speaking people.   For boys
and girls she wrote Winter-Sleepers, Prentice-Hall,
1962.   CA-13/14

SARGENT, Shirley 1927-
She was born in Los Angeles and studied at Pasadena
City College.   She decided at the age of ten that she
would like to become a writer.   Shirley Sargent has
taught in a nursery school in Pasadena and has done
free-lance writing.   Her summers have been spent in

her cabin near Yosemite National Park in California.
For young people she wrote: Pat Hawly, Pre-School
Teacher, Dodd, 1958; Ranger In Skirts, Abingdon, 1966;
Yosemite Tomboy, Abelard, 1967. CA-4

SAUNDERS, Blanche 1906-1964
She was born in Easton, Maine, the daughter of a
clergyman. Before her death in 1964, she made her
home in Bedford, New York. The author received her
education in Massachusetts at Stockbridge School of
Agriculture. She was associated with obedience training programs for dogs for many years. She has shown
dogs, instructed trainers, and produced films. Her
articles have appeared in newspapers and magazines.
Blanche Saunders was chosen "Dog Woman of the Year"
both in 1946 and 1958. For young people she wrote
Dog Training For Boys And Girls, Howell Book House,
1962. CA-13/14

SAUNDERS, Caleb see HEINLEIN, Robert Anson

SAVERY, Constance (Winifred) 1897-
She was born in Wiltshire, England, the daughter of a
vicar. She graduated from Somerville College, Oxford
and taught school until her mother's death when she
returned home to assist her father in his East Anglian
parish. She has lived with a sister near Southwold.
She has contributed stories to American magazines.
Her books for young people include: Emeralds For
The King, Longmans, 1945; Magic In My Shoes (A Junior Literary Guild selection), Longmans, 1958; The
Reb And The Redcoats (A Junior Literary Guild selection), Longmans, 1961. CA-11/12, JBA-2

SAVITT, Sam 1917-
Author-illustrator, born in Wilkes-Barre, Pennsylvania.
He graduated from Pratt Institute in Brooklyn and
studied at New York City's Art Students League. He
has lived in North Salem, New York and has enjoyed
fox hunting and sculpture as hobbies. Mr. Savitt
served with the U. S. Army Engineers during World
War II. His illustrations have been published in numerous magazines. In 1958 he was the recipient of the
Boys' Clubs of America Junior Book Award for Midnight, Champion Bucking Horse, Dutton, 1957. He also
wrote and illustrated A Day At The LBJ Ranch, Random, 1965. Juvenile books which he illustrated for

other writers include: Dave And His Dog, Kjelgaard,
J., Dodd, 1966; Horse In Her Heart, Gray, P., Co-
ward-McCann, 1960; Patrick Visits The Zoo, Daly,
M., Dodd, 1963.   CA-4

SAVOLDI, Gloria Root
She was born in Birmingham, Alabama and attended
Howard College in Birmingham and American University
in Washington, D. C.   She has been both an editor and
a reporter and also has conducted classes in creative
writing.   She married an attorney, and they have lived
in West Middlesex, Pennsylvania.   She wrote Mystery
Of The Old Dutch Chest, Criterion, 1965.

SAWYER, Ruth 1880-1970
Born in Boston, Massachusetts, she attended Columbia
University.   She once taught school in South America
and Cuba and was a reporter on the New York Sun.
Ruth Sawyer started the first storytelling program for
boys and girls in the New York Public Library.   She
and her husband, a physician (Albert Durand), lived in
Hancock, Maine prior to her death on June 3, 1970.
She was awarded the Newbery Medal in 1937 for her
book Roller Skates, Viking, 1936.   Her other books include: Christmas Anna Angel, Viking, 1944; Cottage
For Betsy (A Junior Literary Guild selection), Harper,
1954; Daddles, The Story Of A Plain Hound Dog, Little,
1964; Journey Cake, Ho!, Viking, 1953.   JBA-2

SAXE, John Godfrey 1816-1887
Humorist, lawyer, politician.   He was born in Vermont
and graduated from Middlebury College.   In addition to
being an author, he was also a poet and lecturer.   His
career also included: newspaper editor and politician.
John Saxe was always "well armed with the light artillery of jest and epigram. "   For the young reader he
wrote The Blind Men And The Elephant, McGraw, 1963.

SAYERS, Charles Marshall 1892-
He was born in Kirkcudbright, Scotland, the son of a
cabinetmaker.   At the age of seven he began wood
carving and was teaching others by the time he was
fourteen.   He studied at the Royal Technical College
and the School of Art in Glasgow.   Following service
in the war, he came to America where he started his
School of Woodcarving in Carmel, California.   He has
taught in San Francisco, Des Moines, and at the

Colorado State College of Education at Greeley. He
later made his home in Walnut Creek, California.
His book for young people was The Book Of Wood Carving, A Text For Beginners, Caxton, 1942.

SAYERS, Frances Clarke 1897-
Author, librarian, storyteller. She was born in Tope-
ka, Kansas, grew up in Galveston, Texas, and later
made her home in Ojai, California. She studied at the
University of Texas and the Carnegie Library School
in Pittsburgh, Pennsylvania. Before her retirement
from library work, Mrs. Sayers had been Superintendent of Work with Children at the New York Public
Library and lectured on children's literature at UCLA.
Her articles have appeared in professional journals and
magazines. Mrs. Sayers was presented the 1965 Joseph W. Lippincott Award for distinguished service in
the profession of librarianship. The author was also
the recipient of the 1966 Clarence Day Award for Sum-
moned By Books (comp. by M. Blinn), Viking, 1965.
Other juvenile titles include: Ginny And Custard, Viking, 1951; Sally Tait, Viking, 1948.   CA-19/20, JBA-
2

SCARRY, Richard
Author and illustrator, born in Boston, Massachusetts.
He attended the Archipenko Art School (New York),
Boston Museum Art School, and the Water Color School
(Maine). In 1961 the Chicago Tribune said of his "Tin-
ker and Tanker" series: "The author-illustrator has a
classic children's series on his hands, in the best
Babar tradition. " Richard Scarry married an author,
and they have lived in Westport, Connecticut. He
wrote and illustrated: Tinker And Tanker And Their
Space Ship, Doubleday, 1961; The Supermarket Mystery,
Random, 1969.

SCHAEFER, Jack Warner 1907-
When his first novel came out in an illustrated edition
for young people (Shane, Houghton, 1954), the New
York Herald Tribune wrote: ". . . Both boys and
girls who want excitement to match that of TV and
movies will find it here, with a dimension added that
only words can give. " Jack Schaefer has enjoyed writing about the West and has lived on a ranch close to
Santa Fe, New Mexico. He also wrote: Mavericks,
Houghton, 1967; Old Ramon, Houghton, 1960.   CA-11/12

SCHEALER, John Milton 1920-
He was born in Boyertown, Pennsylvania and graduated
from the University of Pennsylvania. Following college
he worked in an auto body works and a print shop.
Later he became a founder and executive of a sound
and light corporation. Mr. Schealer has also created
games for both children and adults. Juvenile titles include: This Way To The Stars, Dutton, 1957; Zip-Zip
And His Flying Saucer, Dutton, 1956; Zip-Zip And The
Red Planet, Dutton, 1961; Zip-Zip Goes To Venus, Dutton, 1958. CA-5/6

SCHECHTER, Betty Goodstein 1921-
She was born in New York City, graduated from Smith
College at Northampton, Massachusetts, and has lived
in Kingston, Pennsylvania. After graduation from college, Mrs. Schechter was employed in the United Nations Information Office. In 1963 her children's book
The Peaceable Revolution (Houghton, 1963) received
the Thomas Alva Edison Award and was selected as an
American Library Association Notable Book. She also
wrote The Dreyfus Affair, Houghton, 1965. CA-7/8

SCHEELE, William Earl 1920-
Author-illustrator. He was born in Cleveland, Ohio,
graduated from Western Reserve University, and has
lived on a farm near Chardon, Ohio. William Scheele
has been associated with the Cleveland Museum of
Natural History as curator and director. He served in
the Army during World War II. The author has enjoyed
fossil hunting, gem cutting, and painting as hobbies.
His art work on natural history subjects has been exhibited in museums. Juvenile books which he wrote
and illustrated include: Ancient Elephants, World, 1958;
Cave Hunters, World, 1959; The Earliest Americans,
World, 1963; The Mound Builders, World, 1960; Prehistoric Animals, World, 1954.

SCHEER, Julian
He was born in Virginia and graduated from the University of North Carolina. Mr. Scheer has been Assistant
Administrator for Public Affairs of the National Aeronautics and Space Administration. He also was associated with the Charlotte, North Carolina News as a
reporter-columnist. With Marvin Bileck he wrote Rain
Makes Applesauce, Holiday, 1964.

SCHEIB, Ida
    She was born in Brooklyn and attended Hunter College,
    Cooper Union Art School, City College, and the Art
    Students League in New York. Prior to illustrating
    books, she made topographic maps for the U. S. Coast
    and Geodetic Survey. Writing books satisfied one of
    the author's childhood ambitions (to become a teacher)
    because in her books she felt "she was doing a little
    bit of teaching too. " She has illustrated science books
    for other authors and wrote and illustrated Elephants
    In The Garden, McKay, 1958.

SCHERMAN, Katharine 1915-
    Author, editor, native New Yorker. She graduated
    from Swarthmore College in Pennsylvania. Miss Sher-
    man married Axel G. Rosin and has lived in New York
    City near the Hudson River. She has been both a writer
    and editor for the Book-of-the-Month Club, Saturday
    Review, and Life. Her hobbies have been mountain
    climbing and music. For young people she wrote:
    Catherine The Great, Random, 1957; Slave Who Freed
    Haiti, Random, 1954. CA-5/6

SCHILLER, Barbara (Heyman) 1928-
    Author and editor, she has lived in New York. She
    received her degree from Syracuse University in Eng-
    lish and Journalism. She has worked for a publishing
    firm as a copywriter, editor, and reviewer. Her son's
    interest in stories about knights gave Mrs. Schiller the
    incentive to write her book for children entitled The
    Kitchen Knight (adapted and retold by Barbara Schiller),
    Holt, 1965. CA-17/18

SCHLEIN, Miriam 1926-
    She was born in Brooklyn, New York and graduated
    from Brooklyn College. Following college, she wrote
    advertising copy and later became secretary to an edi-
    tor of a publishing house. She married sculptor Har-
    vey Weiss who has illustrated many of her books for
    boys and girls. She and her husband have lived in
    Norwalk, Connecticut. Juvenile titles include: Amuny,
    Boy Of Old Egypt, Abelard-Schuman, 1961; Big Cheese
    (A Junior Literary Guild selection), Scott, 1958; Big
    Lion, Little Lion, Whitman, 1964; Billy, The Littlest
    One, Whitman, 1966; The Way Mothers Are, Whitman,
    1963. CA-4, MJA

SCHNEIDER, Herman 1905-   Nina 1913-
Husband-wife team. Both were born in Europe: he in
Poland, she in Belgium. Their home has been in New
York City where Herman Schneider has taught at New
York City College and at one time served as a grade
school science supervisor. He has also been a science
consultant. Nina Schneider has also been a teacher
and lecturer in addition to librarian, juvenile editor,
and editorial consultant. The Schneiders have contributed articles to magazines and have collaborated on
many books for children. These include: Follow The
Sunset, Junior Literary Guild & Doubleday, 1952; More
Power To You, Scott, 1953; Plants In The City, Day,
1951; Science Fun With Milk Cartons, McGraw, 1953.
MJA

SCHOLZ, Jackson Volney 1897-
Author and athlete, born in Buchanan, Michigan. He
attended schools in Colorado, California, and Missouri.
He received his degree in journalism from the University of Missouri. As a member of several Olympic
teams, Jackson Scholz had an excellent background in
order to write exciting books on sports for young people. These include: Bench Boss, Morrow, 1958;
Fullback Fever, Morrow, 1969.   CA-7/8, MJA

SCHOOR, Gene
Born in Passaic, New Jersey, he attended Miami Uni-
versity in Coral Gables, Florida. He reached the
1936 Olympic finals in boxing and was a coach at New
York University, City College, and the University of
Minnesota. Following service in the Navy, he became
active in radio and television. In addition to writing
and his work in radio, he has been director of a public
relations firm. With Henry Gilfond he wrote: Casey
Stengel, Messner, 1953; The Jack Dempsey Story,
Messner, 1954; The Jim Thorpe Story, America's
Greatest Athlete, Messner, 1951. He also wrote:
Roy Campanella, Putnam, 1959; Young John Kennedy,
Harcourt, 1963.

SCHRANK, Joseph 1900-
Playwright and author, born in New York. He has
lived in Erwinna, Pennsylvania. He has been associated with both the film and television industry as a
writer. His adaptation of "Beauty And The Beast"
proved to be a very popular television show. He has

credited his small daughter with being one of his "helpful critics. " He wrote The Plain Princess And The
Lazy Prince (A Junior Literary Guild selection), Day,
1958.   CA-5/6

SCHULTZ, James Willard 1859-1947
He was born in Boonville, New York, attended Peekskill Military Academy, and moved West at the age
of eighteen. He lived in Montana with the Blackfeet
Indians and married a girl of the Pikuni tribe. James
Schultz was one of the first white men to explore
Glacier National Park. His life among the Indians
combined with his visits in later years to his tribe
provided authentic material for his books. These include: Gold Dust, Houghton, 1934; Lone Bull's Mis-
take, Grosset, 1918; The Trail Of The Spanish Horse,
Houghton, 1960; With The Indians In The Rockies,
Houghton, 1911.   JBA-1, JBA-2

SCHULZ, Charles Monroe 1922-
He was born in Minneapolis, grew up in St. Paul, and
later lived on a ranch north of San Francisco, California. He received the Reuben award in 1956 from the
National Cartoonists' Society as Outstanding Cartoonist
of the Year for the comic strip "Peanuts. " After
graduating from high school, Mr. Schulz studied car-
tooning with Art Instruction, Inc. and later served
with the 20th Armored Division in World War II. He
married Joyce Halvorson. His books for young people
include: Happiness Is A Warm Puppy, Determined
Productions, 1962; I Need All The Friends I Can Get,
Determined Productions, 1964; Snoopy And The Red
Baron, Holt, 1966.   CA-9/10

SCHUON, Karl Albert 1913-
Author-illustrator, born in Allentown, Pennsylvania.
He later made his home in Annandale, Virginia. His
hobbies have included bowling and the opera. He
served in the Marine Corps during World War II and
wrote and illustrated for Leatherneck magazine. After
the war, Karl Schuon became Managing Editor of the
marine publication. In addition to writing books, he
has also written military stories and articles. For
young people he wrote Bowling, Watts, 1966. With
Philip N. Pierce he wrote John H. Glenn: Astronaut,
Watts, 1962. He also edited The Leathernecks (selected by Karl Schuon), Watts, 1963.   CA-15/16

SCHWALJE, Earl G.   1921-   Marjory C.
Husband-wife team, teachers. Both grew up on Long
Island, New York, and both graduated in 1943 from
State Teachers College in New Paltz, New York. Dur-
ing World War II, Mr. Schwalje was a pilot in the
U. S. Army Air Force. Following the war, he re-
ceived his master's degree from Columbia University.
The Schwaljes have lived in Bedford Village, New
York. For young people they wrote Cezar And The
Music-Maker, Knopf, 1951.

SCHWARTZ, Elizabeth Reeder 1912-   Charles Walsh 1914-
Husband-wife team. Mrs. Schwartz was born in Columbus, Ohio, received degrees from Ohio State and
Columbia Universities, and has been a biology and
zoology teacher. Charles Schwartz was born in St.
Louis, Missouri, graduated from the University of
Missouri, and has been a biologist and wildlife photographer for the Missouri Conservation Commission.
Their home has been in Jefferson City, Missouri. Mr.
and Mrs. Schwartz have contributed scientific articles
to journals and magazines and have collaborated on
stories and films about wildlife. They have received
numerous honors and awards for their motion pictures
of wildlife. Their juvenile books include: Cottontail
Rabbit, Holiday, 1957; When Animals Are Babies,
Holiday, 1964.   CA-13/14, CA-15/16

SCHWARTZ, Julius 1907-
Teacher, author. For many years he taught science
in the schools of New York City and also was an in-
structor of science education at Bank Street College.
He has served as Consultant in Science at the Bureau
of Curriculum Research, New York City schools and
was a science consultant to the Midwest Program on
Airborne Television Instruction. He and his family
have lived in New York City. Juvenile titles include:
The Earth Is Your Spaceship, McGraw, 1963; Go On
Wheels, McGraw, 1966; I Know A Magic House, Mc-
Graw, 1956; It's Fun To Know Why, McGraw, 1952.

SCHWEITZER, Byrd Baylor
She was born in San Antonio, Texas and grew up in
northern Mexico and the southwestern part of the United
States. She has lived in an adobe house near the
Arizona desert. The background for her story One
Small Blue Bead (Macmillan, 1965) was a cave on the

Papago Indian reservation which is located near Tucson.
She also wrote: Amigo, Macmillan, 1963; Chinese
Bug, Houghton, 1968.

SCOTT, Cora Annett (Pipitone)   see   ANNETT, Cora

SCOTT, Robert Lee   1908-
Born in Macon, Georgia, he later made his home in
Phoenix, Arizona.   After graduating from the U. S.
Military Academy and National War College, he became
a career officer with the U. S. Air Force.   Robert
Lee Scott, Jr. retired in 1957 as a brigadier general
after thirty years of service.   He received many a-
wards during his career including: two Silver Stars
and three Distinguished Flying Crosses.   He has enjoyed big game hunting as a hobby.   For young people
he wrote Samburu, The Elephant, Dodd, 1957.   CA-
11/12

SCRIMSHER, Lila Gravatt   1897-
She was born in Talmage, Nebraska, studied at Nebraska Wesleyan University, and graduated from the
University of Nebraska.   She also studied at the Chicago Art Institute.   She has worked in a library and
also taught at the Lincoln, Nebraska High School.   She
has written articles for magazines in addition to her
books for young people which include: The Pumpkin
Flood At Harpers Ferry, Reilly & Lee, 1962.   CA-4

SEAMAN, Augusta (Huiell)   1879-1950
A noted writer of mystery stories for young people,
Augusta Seaman's writing career began in 1914 with
the publication of her work in the St. Nicholas maga-
zine.   Her mystery-serials also appeared in American
Girl and Youth's Companion.   The author married
Francis P. Freeman and made her home in Seaside
Park, New Jersey where she died in 1950.   Her juve-
nile books include: Case Of The Calico Crab, Apple-
ton-Century, 1942; Charlemonte Crest, Doubleday,
1931; Crimson Patch, Century, 1919; The Half-Penny
Adventure, Appleton-Century, 1945; The Mystery Of
The Other House, Doubleday, 1947; The Vanishing Oc-
tant Mystery, Doubleday, 1949.   JBA-1, JBA-2

SEAMAN, David M.
Prior to his association with the American Museum of
Natural History in New York City, he served as Asso-

ciate Curator of Mineralogy at the Carnegie Museum
in Pittsburgh and at the Harvard Mineralogical Museum. At Harvard he worked under Dr. Clifford Fron-
del, Curator of the Museum. His book for young people was The Story Of Rocks And Minerals, A Guidebook
For Young Collectors, Harvey, 1956.

SECHRIST, Elizabeth (Hough) 1903-
Librarian, author, born in Media, Pennsylvania. She
received her education at the University of Pittsburgh
and Carnegie Library School. She later made her
home in York, Pennsylvania. In addition to writing
and compiling books, Mrs. Sechrist has been a librarian and lecturer. Several of her books have been
translated into braille and made into "Talking Books
for the Blind. " She collaborated with Janette Woolsey
to write: It's Time For Brotherhood, Macrae Smith,
1962; It's Time For Christmas, Macrae Smith, 1959;
It's Time For Easter, Macrae Smith, 1961; It's Time
For Story Hour, Macrae Smith, 1964. Elizabeth Sechrist also wrote and compiled Heigh-Ho For Halloween!, Macrae Smith, 1948.   CA-7/8

SEEGER, Ruth Porter (Crawford) 1901-1953
Musician, teacher, editor. She was born in East Liverpool, Ohio, the daughter of a minister. She studied
music in New York City and in Chicago at the American Conservatory of Music. Ruth Seeger was the first
woman composer to receive the Guggenheim Fellowship
in composition. Before her death in 1953, Mrs. Seeger lived in Chevy Chase, Maryland. Her experiences
with children and folk songs in the Silver Spring Cooperative Nursery School, the National Child Research
Center, Potomac School, and the schools near Washington, D. C. provided the author with material for her
books. These include: American Folk Songs For Children In Home, School, And Nursery School, Doubleday,
1948; Animal Folk Songs For Children, Doubleday,
1950. She compiled American Folk Songs For Christmas, Doubleday, 1953.

SEIDELMAN, James E.
He has been Director of Education of the Nelson Gallery in Kansas City, Missouri and later served as
Director of the Living Arts Science Center in Lexington, Kentucky. He has written and narrated art education films and has contributed articles to Arts And

Activities, Art Voices, Museum News, and Curator.
Mr. Seidelman has been editorial secretary of the A-
merican National Committee for Education and Cultural
Action and has served on a national jury to select out-
standing works by high school students for the 42nd
Annual National Scholastic Art Awards Exhibition. With
Grace Mintonye he wrote: Creating Mosaics, Crowell-
Collier Press, 1967; Creating With Clay, Crowell-Col-
lier Press, 1967; Creating With Paint, Crowell-Collier
Press, 1967; The Rub Book, Crowell-Collier Press,
1968.

SELDEN, George see THOMPSON, George Selden

SELDEN, Samuel 1899-
Teacher and writer, born in Canton, China. His home
has been in Santa Monica, California. He graduated
from Yale University, did additional study in drama at
Columbia, and received the degree of Doctor of Literature from Illinois College in 1952. In addition to
writing books, Mr. Selden has been a playwright and
teacher. He has served as Chairman of the Department of Dramatic Art at the University of North Carolina and of the Department of Theater Arts at the University of California. For young people he edited
Shakespeare: A Player's Handbook Of Short Scenes
(selected and arranged by Samuel Selden), Holiday,
1960.   CA-1

SELF, Margaret Cabell 1902-
Author-illustrator. She was born in Cincinnati, Ohio
and studied at the Parsons School of Design. In 1929
she started the Silvermine School of Horsemanship and
later was advisor-consultant of a Mexican riding school
(Escuela Ecusetre of San Miguel de Allende). She and
her family have lived on Block Island, near the coast
of Rhode Island and have spent winters in Mexico. Her
books for young people include: The Morgan Horse In
Pictures, Macrae Smith, 1967; Ponies On Parade, Dutton, 1945; Susan And Jane Learn To Ride, Macrae
Smith, 1965.   CA-7/8

SELKIRK, Jane see CHAPMAN, John Stanton

SELLEW, Catharine Freeman 1922-
After graduating from Wheaton College, she combined
her research in mythology with stories she heard as a

child to write myths for young readers.   She married
John Hinchman and has lived in New Jersey.   Her
stories from mythology include: Adventures With The
Giants, Little, 1950; Adventures With The Gods, Little,
1945; Adventures With The Heroes, Little, 1954. She
also wrote Adventures With Abraham's Children, Little,
1964.

SELSAM, Millicent (Ellis) 1912-
Born in New York City, she graduated from Brooklyn
College and received her master's degree from Columbia University.   She has taught biology in high schools
of New York City and at Brooklyn College.   She has
been a Fellow of the American Association for the Advancement of Science and a member of the Board of
Directors of the American Nature Study Society.   In
1964 she received the Eva L. Gordon Award of the
American Nature Study Society and in 1965 was the recipient of the Edison Foundation Award.   The Selsams
have lived in New York City and have spent summers
on Fire Island, New York.   Juvenile titles include:
All Kinds Of Babies And How They Grow, Scott, 1953;
Birth Of A Forest, Harper, 1964; Milkweed, Morrow,
1967.   CA-11/12, MJA

SENDAK, Jack
He has lived in Brooklyn, New York for many years
with the exception of that period of his life during
World War II when he served in the Army.   His brother, author-illustrator Maurice Sendak illustrated his
children's books which include: Circus Girl, Harper,
1957; The Happy Rain, Harper, 1956.

SENDAK, Maurice 1928-
Author-illustrator, born in Brooklyn, New York.   His
home has been in New York City where he attended
the Art Students League.   In addition to writing and
illustrating books for children, Mr. Sendak has worked
for a display house and comic book syndicate.   He has
illustrated numerous books for other authors, and
several of his illustrated books have been runner-ups
for the Caldecott Medal.   In 1964 he was awarded the
Caldecott Medal for Where The Wild Things Are, Harper, 1963.   Other juvenile stories which he wrote and
illustrated include: Higglety Pigglety Pop!, Or, There
Must Be More To Life, Harper, 1967; Kenny's Window,
Harper, 1956; Nutshell Library, Harper, 1962; The

Sign On Rosie's Door, Harper, 1960.   CA-7/8

SENTMAN, George Armor
He was born in Maryland and graduated from the University of Missouri.   His stories have been published in Redbook and Today's Woman, and he has also served as editor of several publications.   His book for young people was Drummer Of Vincennes, Winston, 1952.

SEREDY, Kate 1896-
Author-illustrator, born in Budapest, Hungary.   She received her education in Hungary at the Normal School and Academy of Art.   The author came to the United States in 1922 and has lived in Montgomery, New York.   Her career in book illustration began with painting greeting cards, then to fashion design, and finally to magazine illustrating.   Her illustrations have appeared in other author's books including Carol Ryrie Brink's Caddie Woodlawn (Macmillan, 1935) winner of the 1936 Newbery Medal.   Kate Seredy received the 1938 Newbery Medal for The White Stag, Viking, 1937. Other juvenile books which she wrote and illustrated include: A Brand-New Uncle, Viking, 1961; Gypsy, Viking, 1951; Listening, Viking, 1936; Tree For Peter, Viking, 1941.   CA-7/8, JBA-2

SETH, Ronald
He has lived in Kent, England.   Mr. Seth attended King's School, Ely, and Peterhouse, Cambridge University.   He later taught English Language and Literature at the University of Tallinn, Estonia.   During World War II, he served in the R. A. F.   Mr. Seth has also been founder and Chief of the BBC's Monitoring Intelligence Bureau.   He began writing full time in 1950. For young people he wrote Milestones In African History, Chilton, 1969.

SEUSS, Dr.   see   GEISEL, Theodor Seuss

SEVERN, Bill 1914-   Sue 1918-
He has also written under the names: William Irving and Nancy Irving.   William Irving Severn was born in Brooklyn, the son of a newspaper executive.   He began his writing career on a weekly Long Island newspaper and became news editor for the Associated Press in New York.   Mrs. Severn, born in Baltimore, has also been a writer and production supervisor of several

magazines. They have lived in New York City and also
have had a home in the Berkshire Hills of Massachusetts.
Their first collaboration was Let's Give A Show, Knopf,
1956. His titles include: Adlai Stevenson: Citizen Of The
World (A Junior Literary Guild selection), McKay, 1966;
Mr. Chief Justice: Earl Warren, McKay, 1968; People
Words, Washburn, 1966.   CA-4, CA-5/6

SEVERN, David see UNWIN, David Storr

SEWELL, Helen Moore 1896-1957
    Author-illustrator, born at Mare Island Navy Yard,
    California. She grew up in New York and on the
    island of Guam where her father was governor. She
    studied at Packer Institute and Pratt and Archipenko's
    Art Schools. In addition to illustrating her own books,
    she has illustrated books for other writers, and her
    work has appeared in both adult and children's books.
    Her drawings have also appeared in the New Yorker.
    Helen Sewell died in New York City in 1957.   For
    children she wrote and illustrated Blue Barns, Macmil-
    lan, 1933.   JBA-2

SEYFERT, Ella Maie
    Born in Pennsylvania, she later lived in Canada where
    her father served as American consul in Ontario. She
    once taught in the schools of Lancaster county, Penn-
    sylvania where she became interested in the Amish
    people. Her other interests have included the history
    of fine lace, and she has written articles on the sub-
    ject. Miss Seyfert has lived in New Jersey. Her
    books for young people include: Amish Moving Day,
    Crowell, 1942; Little Amish Schoolhouse, Crowell,
    1939.

SHANNON, Monica
    Author-librarian. She was born in Canada, grew up
    on a stock farm near the Rocky Mountains, and later
    lived in California. She worked in the Los Angeles
    Public Library after obtaining a degree in library sci-
    ence. In 1935 she was awarded the Newbery Medal
    for Dobry, Viking, 1934. She also wrote California
    Fairy Tales, Doubleday, 1926.   JBA-2

SHANNON, Terry
    Jessie Mercer, also known as Terry Shannon, was
    born in Bellingham, Washington and received her

schooling at Western Washington State College and the
Universities of Washington and California. She has
been a feature writer and motion picture columnist in
Hollywood in addition to writing books for young people.
She received the Boys' Clubs of America Junior Book
Awards in 1961 for About Caves, Melmont, 1960 and
in 1962 for A Trip To Mexico, Children's Press, 1961.
Her other titles include: About Ready-To-Wear Clothes,
Melmont, 1961; Among The Rocks, Sterling, 1956; A-
round The World With Gogo, Golden Gate Junior Books,
1964; Desert Dwellers, Whitman, 1958. CA-2

SHAPIRO, Irwin 1911-
Born in Pittsburgh, Pennsylvania, he attended Carnegie
Tech and studied painting at the Art Students League in
New York. He has been on the staff of Scholastic ma-
gazine and Facts On File. Mr. Shapiro has also work-
ed in the film industry. He has lived in Flushing, New
York. In 1947 the Julia Ellsworth Ford Foundation a-
ward was given to him for his book Joe Magarac And
His U. S. A. Citizen Papers, Messner, 1948. He also
wrote: John Henry And The Double Jointed Steam-
Drill, Messner, 1945; Tall Tales Of America, Simon,
1958. JBA-2

SHAPIRO, Milton J. 1926-
Newspaperman and author, born in Brooklyn. He completed his education at New York City College after
serving in the Air Force during World War II. Mr.
Shapiro and his family have lived in Merrick, Long
Island. At one time the author worked on a New York
newspaper as both a sportswriter and movie critic.
He later became sports editor of the National Enquirer
and executive editor of Gunsport magazines. Young
people have enjoyed his sports biographies which in-
clude: The Dizzy Dean Story, Messner, 1963; The Don
Drysdale Story, Messner, 1964; Mickey Mantle, Yankee
Slugger, Messner, 1962. He also wrote: Day They
Made Record Book, Messner, 1968; Heroes Behind The
Mask, Messner, 1968.

SHAPIRO, Rebecca
Artist, author, columnist. She has lived in Philadelphia
where she has been a columnist on the Philadelphia
Inquirer. Her interest in good cooking led Rebecca
Shapiro to collect recipes from people who had come
to America from other countries. For young people she

wrote and illustrated <u>Wide World Cookbook</u>, Little,
1962.

SHARFMAN, Amalie
    She was born in Baltimore, Maryland. She has been
active in radio work, and following her marriage to a
government lawyer she produced and moderated educational radio programs on child guidance in Washington,
D. C. Mrs. Sharfman has also taught in a nursery
school and has been active in the Mental Health Association. She and her family have lived in Worcester,
Massachusetts. Juvenile titles include: <u>A Beagle
Named Bertram</u>, Crowell, 1954; <u>Mr. Peabody's Pesky
Ducks</u>, Little, 1957.

SHAROFF, Victor
    Author and teacher, he was born and educated in New
York. He has taught children of all ages including
several groups in the New York ghettos. Mr. Sharoff
has been a veteran and world traveler in addition to
his career as a writer. He has enjoyed writing for
the very young reader "because he finds them the best
audience in the world." A special interest of the author's has been cooking. For boys and girls he wrote
<u>Garbage Can Cat</u>, Westminster, 1969.

SHARP, Adda Mai (Cummings)
    Author and storyteller. Her experiences in telling
stories to her nieces and nephews combined with her
story hour programs in Denton, Texas provided the
incentive and the background to write books for boys
and girls. Mrs. Sharp has enjoyed travel and music
as hobbies. The daughter of a naturalist, she has also
been interested in animal and plant life. Juvenile books
include: <u>Daffy</u>, Steck, 1950; <u>Gee Whillikins</u>, Steck,
1950; <u>Where Is Cubby Bear?</u>, Steck, 1950.

SHARP, Margery 1905-
    She has written many famous novels for adults. Early
in her career she contributed articles to <u>Punch</u>. Margery Sharp has also written plays in addition to her
stories for boys and girls. She has lived in London.
Her books for young people include: <u>Lost At The Fair</u>,
Little, 1965; <u>The Rescuers</u>, Little, 1959.

SCHECTER, Ben
    Author-illustrator. He received his education at the

Yale School of Drama and City College of New York.
Mr. Schecter has made his home in Brooklyn, New
York. His drawings have appeared in many books, and
he has been an outstanding set designer. The Wash-
ington Opera Company used his sets for the production
"Beatrice And Benedict. " In 1962 the author went to
Italy where he attended the Spoleto Festival of Two
Worlds. For boys and girls he wrote and illustrated:
Inspector Rose, Harper, 1969; Jonathan And The Bank
Robbers, Dial, 1964.

SHEEHAN, Ethna
Writer and librarian, born in Ireland. A graduate of
Hunter College in New York, she later attended Columbia University where she received her master's degree
in Library Science. Ethna Sheehan has been children's
librarian in a public library (Queens Borough, N. Y.).
She has also worked in the American and Catholic Library Associations. Miss Sheehan's stories have appeared in several publications, and she has been a reviewer for magazines. For children she edited A
Treasury Of Catholic Children's Stories, Lippincott,
1963.

SHELDON, Walter J.
He was born in Philadelphia, Pennsylvania. In addition to being an author, Mr. Sheldon has been an artist, TV director-producer, radio announcer, and a
continuity director for the Far East Network. He has
also served as a combat correspondent. For several
years he lived in Japan, and his knowledge of the
Japanese people resulted in his first book for young
people entitled The Key To Tokyo, Lippincott, 1962.

SHERBURNE, Zoa Morin 1912-
Her stories have appeared in many magazines such as
Seventeen and Catholic Miss. She has lived with her
husband and eight children in Seattle, Washington. In
1959 she received the Child Study Award. Her first
book for boys and girls was Almost April, Morrow,
1956. Other juvenile titles include: Evening Star,
Morrow, 1960; Girl In The Mirror, Morrow, 1966.
CA-3

SHERLOCK, Philip Manderson 1902-
He was born in Jamaica, British West Indies, the son
of a Methodist minister. He received his B. A. degree

from the University of London.   The author served as
Secretary of the Institute of Jamaica after teaching in
a boys' school.   He became associated with the University of the West Indies as Director of Extension
and later served both as Vice-Principal and Vice-
Chancellor.   Queen Elizabeth II conferred the honorary
title Commander of the British Empire upon him in
1952.   Sir Philip was knighted in 1967.   His special
interest in Caribbean history has resulted in writing
books about the subject.   Juvenile titles include: Anan-
si, The Spider Man, Crowell, 1954; The Land And
People Of The West Indies, Lippincott, 1967; West Indian Folk-Tales, Walck, 1966.   CA-5/6

SHERMAN, Allan 1924-
Comedian and writer, born in Chicago, Illinois.   When
he was a student at the University of Illinois, Allan
Sherman began his stage and writing careers.   His record albums have been best-sellers and have included:
"My Son, The Celebrity," "My Son, The Folksinger,"
and "My Son, The Nut."   Mr. Sherman has also produced television programs, performed on the stage as
a comedian, and written books, songs, magazine articles, and movie scripts.   The Shermans have lived in
Los Angeles.   For the young reader Allan Sherman
wrote: Hello Muddah, Hello Fadduh!, Harper, 1964;
I Can't Dance, Harper, 1964.

SHERMAN, Elizabeth see FRISKEY, Margaret (Richards)

SHIELDS, Karena
She grew up on a rubber plantation south of the Isth-
mus of Tehuantepec and has been interested in the
legends and tribes of the Central American Maya.   She
studied archeology at the University of Southern California and has often returned to Central America on
archeological explorations.   Mrs. Shields has also been
a pilot in the Civil Air Patrol and once taught navigation to Naval Air Cadets.   She has lived in Montrose,
California.   She wrote Three In The Jungle, Harcourt,
1944.

SHIELDS, Rita
Teacher and author, born in San Francisco, California.
She graduated from San Francisco State College and
taught in that city for a number of years.   Her first
book for young people was Norah And The Cable Car,

Longmans, 1960.   She also wrote Cecelia's Locket,
Longmans, 1961.

SHIPPEN, Katherine Binney 1892-
She was born in Hoboken, New Jersey, graduated from
Bryn Mawr, and received her master's degree from
Columbia University. Miss Shippen has been a history
teacher at the Beard School in Orange, New Jersey
and at the Brearley School in New York City. She also
has served on the staff of the Brooklyn Children's Museum and was headmistress of Miss Fine's School in
Princeton, New Jersey. Her home has been in Suf-
fern, New York. Juvenile books include: Andrew
Carnegie And The Age Of Steel, Random, 1958; Bridle
For Pegasus, Viking, 1951; Bright Design, Viking,
1949; Great Heritage, Junior Literary Guild and Viking,
1947; The Pool Of Knowledge (new and rev. ed.), Harper, 1965; Portals To The Past, Viking, 1963.   CA-
7/8, MJA

SHIRER, William Lawrence 1904-
Author and newspaperman, born in Chicago, Illinois.
He graduated from Coe College in Iowa and studied
European history at the College de France in Paris.
After twenty years spent in Europe, Mr. Shirer and
his family made their home in New York and Connect-
icut. His newspaper career has included: reporter
and foreign correspondent in Paris with the Chicago
Tribune, New York Herald Tribune, and Universal
News Service. He has also been a war correspondent
and worked with the CBS foreign news staff in Germany. The author has enjoyed the theater, chamber
music, and skiing as special interests. His books for
young readers include: The Rise And Fall Of Adolf
Hitler, Random, 1961; The Sinking Of The Bismarck,
Random, 1962.   CA-9/10

SHIRK, Jeannette Campbell 1898-
She was born in Middletown, Pennsylvania but has al-
ways lived near Pittsburgh. She graduated from the
Carnegie Institute of Technology and later attended
library school She worked in a high school library
prior to becoming librarian in the Henry Clay Frick
Fine Arts Department of the University of Pittsburgh.
The author received an Honorable Mention Award in
the Dodd, Mead Librarian Prize Competition for The
Little Circus, Dodd, 1955.

SHIRREFFS, Gordon Donald 1914-
His pseudonyms are Gordon Donalds and Stewart Gordon. He was born in Chicago, Illinois, attended Northwestern University and San Fernando Valley State College in California. His home has been in Granada Hills, California. The author was a captain with the U. S. Army during World War II. In addition to writing books, he has written television plays, movies, and magazine articles. Among his hobbies have been fishing, hunting, and travel. He was awarded the 1962 Commonwealth Club of California Silver Medal for The Gray Sea Raiders (A Junior Literary Guild selection), Chilton, 1961. Other juvenile books include: Action Front!, Westminster Press, 1962; Bolo Battalion, Westminster Press, 1966; Killer Sea, Westminster Press, 1968; Torpedoes Away!, Westminster Press, 1967. CA-15/16

SHORTER, Bani
She has been on the staff of the University Elementary School of the University of California at Los Angeles. Mrs. Shorter and her husband have lived and studied in India and Pakistan. Later they made their home in Princeton, New Jersey where Mr. Shorter taught economics at Princeton University. For young people she wrote India's Children, Viking, 1960.

SHULEVITZ, Uri 1935-
Artist and author, born in Warsaw, Poland. He grew up in Poland, France, and Israel where he studied at the Tel Aviv Academy of Art. After coming to the United States in 1959, he continued his studies at the Museum of Art in Brooklyn, New York. His work has received recognition from the American Institute of Graphic Arts and the Society of Illustrators. He married an artist and has lived in New York City. He was awarded the 1969 Caldecott Medal for The Fool Of The World And The Flying Ship, Ransome, A., Farrar, 1968. He wrote and illustrated The Moon In My Room, Harper & Row, 1963. He also illustrated The Carpet Of Solomon, Ish-Kishor, S., Pantheon, 1966. ICB-3, CA-11/12

SHUTTLESWORTH, Dorothy Edwards 1907-
Author and editor, born in Brooklyn, New York. Her Home has been in East Orange, New Jersey where her husband has been a high school principal. Mrs.

Shuttlesworth began her career at the American Museum of Natural History at the age of seventeen. She later founded and became editor of Junior Natural History magazine for young readers. Her many juvenile books include: ABC Of Buses, Doubleday, 1965; All Kinds Of Bees, Random, 1967; Clean Air - Sparkling Water, Doubleday, 1968; Dodos And Dinosaurs, Hastings, 1968; The Wildlife Of Australia And New Zealand, Hastings, 1967. CA-1

SIDJAKOV, Nicholas 1924-
He was born in Latvia and studied at the École des Beaux Arts in Paris. He has lived and worked in Italy, Germany, and Switzerland. Following his marriage to an American girl, he and his wife came to the United States in 1954. They have lived in Sausalito, California. In 1961 he was awarded the Caldecott Medal for his illustrations in Ruth Robbins' book Baboushka And The Three Kings, Parnassus, 1960. He also illustrated The Emperor And The Drummer Boy by Ruth Robbins, Parnassus, 1962. MJA

SIEGMEISTER, Elie 1909-
Musician and author, born in New York. His home has been in Great Neck, New York. This conductor and composer graduated from Columbia College and received diplomas from both the École Normale de Musique and Juilliard Graduate Schools. In addition to writing books, Mr. Siegmeister has collected folk music and has been a director of the American Ballad Singers. For young readers he wrote Invitation To Music, Harvey House, 1961. CA-3

SILLIMAN, Leland 1906-
Born in New York, he has been both a swimming coach and director of summer camps. During World War II, he was associated with the United States Navy's physical training program. His book The Scrapper (Winston, 1946) was awarded a certificate from the Boys' Clubs of America in 1947. He also wrote: Bucky Forrester, Winston, 1951; The Daredevil, Winston, 1948; The Purple Tide, Winston, 1949.

SILVERBERG, Robert
His pseudonyms are: Walter Drummond, Calvin M. Knox, Ivar Jorgenson, David Osborne, Robert Randall. He was born in New York, graduated from Columbia,

and has traveled extensively to collect authentic material for his books. He married an electrical engineer
and has resided in Riverdale, New York. The author
has written for both adults and children, and his science-fiction stories have appeared in many magazines.
He has been the recipient of many awards including
the 1956 World Science Fiction "Hugo. " For young
people he wrote: The Auk, The Dodo, And The Oryx,
Crowell, 1967; Four Men Who Changed The Universe,
Putnam, 1968; Frontiers In Archaeology, Chilton, 1966;
Ghost Towns Of The American West, Crowell, 1968;
Time Of The Great Freeze (A Junior Literary Guild
selection), Holt, 1964.   CA-3

SILVERMAN, Al 1926-
Graduate of Boston University, he was born in Lynn,
Massachusetts and later lived in Ardsley, New York.
Mr. Silverman has been editor-in-chief of Sport maga-
zine. He has been interested in baseball and has writ-
ten many articles about it. His work has appeared in
Saturday Review, TV Guide, Saturday Evening Post,
and Argosy magazines. Juvenile titles include: Heroes
Of The World Series, Putnam, 1964; Mickey Mantle:
Mister Yankee, Putnam, 1963; Sports Titans Of 20th
Century, Putnam, 1968.   CA-11/12

SIMBARI, Nicola 1927-
Painter and writer, born in St. Lucido, Calabria, Italy.
He has lived in Rome most of his life and attended
the Accademia Belle Arti. He later was a professor
at the school. His knowledge of the art treasures of
the Vatican resulted from his father's work there as a
builder. Mr. Simbari has worked in films, designed
stage sets, and has been an art director in Italy and
England. His paintings have been exhibited in America
and Europe. The author has enjoyed travel, and on a
visit to America he decided to write and illustrate his
first book for children entitled Gennarino, Lippincott,
1962.   CA-4

SIMON, Charlie May (Hogue) 1897-
She was born in Monticello, Arkansas and grew up in
Memphis, Tennessee. She attended Memphis State Uni-
versity, the Chicago Art Institute, and the Grande
Chaumière in Paris. She married poet John Gould
Fletcher, winner of the Pulitzer Prize. She has been
a teacher at the Japan Women's University in Tokyo.

Her honors include: an honorary LL. D. from the University of Arkansas and the Albert Schweitzer Book Award for A Seed Shall Serve (Dutton, 1958). Her home has been in Little Rock, Arkansas. Juvenile titles include: Art In The New Land, Dutton, 1945; Bright Morning, Dutton, 1939; Dag Hammarskjold, Dutton, 1967.   CA-9/10, JBA-2

SIMON, Hilda
Artist and author, born in California. She attended schools in Europe and later made her home in New York City. Miss Simon has had a lifelong interest in animal and insect life. She has collected sketches and drawings (including many of hummingbirds) which she has used in her books about nature. Juvenile books which she has written and illustrated include: Exploring The World Of Social Insects, Vanguard, 1962; Wonders Of Hummingbirds, Dodd, 1964.

SIMON, Norma (Feldstein) 1927-
Teacher and writer, born in New York. She received her B. A. degree from Brooklyn College, attended the Bank Street College of Education, and did graduate study at the New School for Social Research in New York. Mrs. Simon's experiences as a nursery school teacher and director later provided ideas for writing books for children. Her home has been in Norwalk, Connecticut where she organized and directed the Community Cooperative Nursery School. For boys and girls she wrote: Benjy's Bird, Whitman, 1965; Daddy Days, Abelard-Schuman, 1958; Hanukkah, Crowell, 1966; Passover, Crowell, 1965; Ruthie, Meredith, 1968; What Do I Say?, Whitman, 1967.   CA-7/8

SIMON, Ruth Corabel (Shimer) 1918-
Born in Orosi, California, she studied at Visalia Junior College, and graduated from San Jose State College. During World War II, she served with the American Red Cross at the Madigan General Hospital at Fort Lewis, Washington. Mrs. Simon was also an elementary schoolteacher. She and her husband have lived in Fort Wayne, Indiana. For boys and girls she wrote: Castle For Tess, Follett, 1967; Mat And Mandy And The Little Old Car, Crowell, 1952.

SIMONT, Marc 1915-
He was born in Paris and grew up in Barcelona, Spain.

He studied in Paris at both the Julien and Ranson Academies and at the André Lhote School. After coming to America he attended the National Academy of Design in New York. His home has been in West Cornwall, Connecticut. In addition to writing and illustrating children's books, Marc Simont has done caricatures, murals, and portraits. His illustrations have also appeared in magazines and books by other writers including Janice Udry's A Tree Is Nice (Harper, 1956) for which he received the 1957 Caldecott Medal. Marc Simont also wrote and illustrated How Come Elephants?, Harper, 1965. MJA

SIMS, Lydel
Author and newspaperman. He grew up in Louisiana and graduated from Northwest Louisiana State College (Natchitoches). Mr. Sims has worked on a Memphis, Tennessee newspaper, the Commercial Appeal, as a feature columnist. He received the National Headliners Award for his column. Many magazines have published his articles. Lydel Sims has enjoyed fishing and has been interested in Civil War history. He wrote Thaddeus Lowe: Uncle Sam's First Airman (A Junior Literary Guild selection), Putnam, 1964.

SINCLAIR, Upton Beall 1878-
Born in Baltimore, Maryland, he attended Columbia University and the College of the City of New York. At one time he was a Democratic candidate for governor of California. His book The Jungle (Doubleday, 1906) was about the Chicago meat-packing industry. This book was one of the factors which led to later enactment of pure-food laws. In 1943 Mr. Sinclair was the recipient of the Pulitzer prize for his novel Dragon's Teeth, Viking, 1942. For children he wrote The Gnomobile, Bobbs, 1962. CA-5/6

SINGER, Isaac Bashevis 1904-
He was born in Radzymin, Poland and attended a rabbinical seminary in Warsaw. The author came to the United States in 1935, and his first book in English was published fifteen years later. Mr. Singer has written for both adults and children. One of his short stories entitled "Dr. Beeber" (tr. from the Yiddish by the author and Elaine Gottlieb) appeared in the March 7, 1970 issue of the New Yorker. His first book for children Zlateh The Goat And Other Stories (tr. from

the Yiddish by the author and Elizabeth Shub), (Harper, 1966) was a runner-up for the 1967 Newbery Medal. He also wrote Mazel And Shlimazel (A Junior Literary Guild selection), (tr. by the author and Elizabeth Shub), Farrar, 1967.   CA-1

SLOBODKIN, Louis 1903-
He was born in Albany, New York and studied at the Beaux Arts Institute of Design in New York City.   He married Florence Gersh and had two sons (Michael who became a teacher and Larry, a scientist).   Mr. Slobodkin has been a sculptor in addition to illustrating children's books.   His work has been on display in many cities throughout America.   In 1944 his illustrations were awarded the Caldecott Medal in James Thurber's book Many Moons, Harcourt, 1943.   He wrote and illustrated: Amiable Giant, Macmillan, 1955; Circus, April 1st, Macmillan, 1953; Luigi And The Long-Nosed Soldier, Macmillan, 1963.   CA-13/14

SLOBODKINA, Esphyr 1909-
Author-illustrator, born in Russia.   She grew up in Siberia and Manchuria where she attended school.   After coming to the United States, she studied at New York's National Academy of Design.   Miss Slobodkina became an American citizen and has lived on Long Island, New York.   An accomplished storyteller, she has also been a lecturer, teacher, translator, and sculptor.   Her work has been exhibited in galleries and museums in this country.   For boys and girls she wrote and illustrated: Caps For Sale, Scott, 1947; Little Dinghy, Abelard-Schuman, 1958; The Long Island Ducklings, Lantern Press, 1961; Pezzo The Peddler & The Circus Elephant, Abelard, 1967; Pinky And The Petunias, Abelard-Schuman, 1959.   CA-1

SMARIDGE, Norah
The daughter of a sea captain, she spent her childhood in Liverpool, England.   She graduated from London University and did further study at Hunter College and Columbia University in New York.   Norah Smaridge has taught in a high school and junior college in the United States and also has worked in a publishing house. Her articles have appeared in magazines and newspapers, and she has translated several French books into English.   Her books include: Saint Helena, Saint Anthony Guild Press, 1962; Watch Out! (A Junior Liter-

ary Guild selection), Abingdon, 1965; World Of Chocolate, Messner, 1969.

SMITH, Agnes
She was born in Clarksburg, West Virginia and decided
at the age of sixteen to become a writer. She married Richard Parrish, editor of the West Virginian
published in Fairmont. The author's interests have
included: woodworking, ceramics, and furniture design. America House in New York have sold her
ceramics. She and her husband have lived on a farm
near Clarksburg. For young people she wrote Edge
Of The Forest (A Junior Literary Guild selection), Viking, 1959.

SMITH, Donald G. 1927-
Coach, newspaperman, born in New York. He attended
New York and Columbia Universities. Mr. Smith has
been director of public relations for the New York
Football Giants. He has lived in Flushing, New York.
With Lynn Burke he wrote The Young Sportsman's
Guide To Swimming, Nelson, 1962.

SMITH, Emma 1923-
She has lived in England. In her book Out Of Hand
(Harcourt, 1964) the author wrote about the countryside
of Wales where she has made her home. She also
based the descriptions of the children in the story upon
her own two children and their cousins; however, Emma
Smith said: ". . . The four children in the story are
really a good deal different from their prototypes.
Bellamy, the dog, is real and turned up in our lives
much as I have described in the book." She also
wrote Emily, The Traveling Guinea Pig, McDowell,
Obolensky, 1959.

SMITH, Eunice Young 1902-
Author-artist. Born in La Salle, Illinois, she studied
in Chicago at the Lake View Commercial Art School
and the Academy of Fine Arts. She also attended
Rosary College and Indiana University. Her home has
been in Mishawaka, Indiana. Prior to her career as
a writer and illustrator, Mrs. Smith designed Christmas cards. She has also exhibited her paintings and
illustrated magazine stories. Juvenile books include:
Denny's Story, Whitman, 1952; High Heels For Jennifer, Bobbs, 1964; The Jennifer Wish, Bobbs, 1949;

The Knowing One, Meredith, 1967; The Little Red
Drum, Whitman, 1961; Moppet, Whitman, 1951; To
Each A Season, Bobbs, 1965.   CA-13/14

SMITH, Fredrika Shumway
She has lived in the Chicago (Illinois) area all of her
life.   Fredrika Smith has always been interested in
American history.   She combined her interests (history
and the Midwest) in the books which she has written
for young people.   Her juvenile titles include: Fire
Dragon, Rand, 1956; Stanley, African Explorer, Rand,
1968.

SMITH, Imogene Henderson 1922-
This teacher and writer has spent most of her life in
Illinois.   After graduating from Carthage High School,
she attended college in Illinois and did graduate work
in Colorado.   Imogene Smith has contributed short
stories, articles, and poetry to magazines.   She has
taught both high school and college students.   The author married a former coach and has lived in St.
Charles, Illinois.   For boys and girls she wrote Egg
On Her Face, Lippincott, 1963.   CA-7/8

SMITH, Irene 1903-
Librarian, teacher, author.   She was born in Columbia, Kentucky and grew up in Indianapolis, Indiana
where she later worked in the library.   She received
her training from the University of Illinois.   Following
her work in Indianapolis, she became a children's librarian in the Brooklyn Public Library where she
eventually served as Superintendent of Work with Children for many years.   She has lectured in the library
school at Pratt Institute and contributed many articles
to periodicals.   She and her husband Louis William
Green have lived in Westchester.   Juvenile titles include: Down The Road With Johnny, McGraw, 1951;
History Of The Newbery And Caldecott Medals, Viking,
1957; Paris, Rand, 1961; Washington, D. C. , Rand,
1964.

SMITH, Jan
Her pseudonym is Jan Nickerson.   She was born in
Somerville, Massachusetts.   Miss Nickerson graduated
from Radcliffe College at Cambridge.   She has been
an actress and has also written books and poetry.   She
married Arthur Seymour Hall and made her home in

Quincy, Massachusetts. Her books for young people
include: Answer For April, Funk, 1963; Bright Promise, Funk, 1965; Circle Of Love, Funk, 1962; Double
Rainbow, Funk, 1966.   CA-4

SMITH, Jessie Wilcox 1863-1935
Author and artist, born in Philadelphia. She attended
the Philadelphia School for Design for Women, the
Pennsylvania Academy of Fine Arts, and later studied
art under Howard Pyle who was at Drexel Institute.
Her drawings appeared in the St. Nicholas magazine.
Miss Smith enjoyed portrait painting of children. She
was the recipient of numerous awards and medals.
She died at the age of seventy-two in Philadelphia.
Jessie Wilcox Smith compiled and illustrated A Child's
Book Of Old Verses, Dodd, 1952. She also illustrated
The Little Mother Goose, Dodd, 1918.   JBA-1, JBA-2

SMITH, Moyne Rice
Author and teacher, born in Oskaloosa, Kansas. Her
home has been in New Jersey where she has been on
the staff of Miss Fine's School in Princeton. She has
also taught high school and college English and dramatics. Mrs. Smith has also been an actress and director of her own summer theater. Her articles about
children's theater have appeared in Childcraft and The
Instructor. For young people she wrote: Plays & -
How To Put Them On, Walck, 1961; Seven Plays &
How To Produce Them, Walck, 1968.

SMITH, Philip M. 1927-
Author and glaciologist, born in Springfield, Ohio. He
graduated from Ohio State University. He has been interested in the exploration of caves (speleology). The
author served in the United States Army's Transportation Arctic Group. He was a member of the eleven-
man team which created the overland supply route between Little America and Byrd Station in Antarctica.
Phil Smith has lived in Washington, D. C. With Henry
S. Francis, Jr. , he wrote Defrosting Antarctic Secrets,
Coward, 1962.

SMITH, Ralph Lee 1927-
Author, editor, free-lance writer, born in Philadelphia.
He helped to establish the U. S. National Student Asso-
ciation when he was a student at Swarthmore College.
After serving in the Air Force during World War II, he

did graduate work at Columbia University. Ralph Smith
has been a contributor to many magazines including
Atlantic Monthly and Reader's Digest. At one time he
was publications editor for the National Better Business
Bureau. The Smith family has lived in Greenwich Village in New York. He wrote Getting To Know The
World Health Organization, Coward, 1963. CA-4

SMITH, Robert Paul
He was born in Brooklyn and has resided in Scarsdale,
New York. He received his degree from Columbia
University. Mr. Smith collaborated with Max Shulman
to write the play "The Tender Trap" which was later
made into a movie. He has also written for radio and
television. For children he wrote Jack Mack (A Junior
Literary Guild selection), Coward, 1960; Nothingatall,
Nothingatall, Nothingatall, Harper, 1965.

SNEDEKER, Caroline Dale (Parke) 1871-
This distinguished author's birthplace, New Hampshire,
Indiana, provided the background for several of her
books. She grew up in Mount Vernon, Indiana and in
Cincinnati. She married Charles H. Snedeker who was
dean of the Cathedral in Cincinnati. She has lived in
Mississippi, Nantucket, and on the Gulf of Mexico.
Her juvenile books include: The Beckoning Road,
Doubleday, 1929; Downright Dencey, Doubleday, 1927.
JBA-1, JBA-2

SNYDER, Dick
Photo-journalist, set designer, author. He has specialized in the photography of wild animals. One of his earliest photographs was of the Bengal tiger when he was on
an assignment in India. Later he became staff photographer for the Zoo at San Diego, California. He has lived in
La Jolla, California. For boys and girls he wrote: One
Day At The Zoo, Scribners, 1960; Talk To Me Tiger,
Golden Gate, 1965.

SNYDER, Louis Leo 1907-
He was born in Maryland and received his doctor's de-
gree from the University of Frankfort on Main, Ger-
many. He has been a history professor at the City
College of New York and an editor in a publishing
firm. He served in the Air Force during World War
II. Juvenile titles include: The First Book Of The
Soviet Union, Watts, 1959; First Book Of World War I,
Watts, 1958; Hitler And Nazism, Watts, 1961. CA-3

SNYDER, Zilpha Keatley 1927-
Born in Lemoore, California, she has lived in Ventura
and Whittier where she went to college. After her
marriage to Larry A. Snyder, she lived in New York,
Texas, and Alaska. The Snyders later returned to
California to live, and Mrs. Snyder taught student
teachers enrolled in the University of California. In
addition to writing, her interests have included children's dramatics and art. For boys and girls she
wrote: The Egypt Game, Atheneum, 1967; The Velvet
Room (A Junior Literary Guild selection), Atheneum,
1965. CA-11/12

SOBOL, Donald J. 1924-
Newspaperman and author, born in New York. He
graduated from Oberlin College. During World War II,
Donald Sobol served with the Combat Engineers and
was stationed in Europe and the South Pacific. He has
been a member of the editorial staff on the Long Island
Press. The author has lived in Coral Gables, Florida.
Juvenile titles include: Encyclopedia Brown, Nelson,
1963; Encyclopedia Brown Keeps The Peace, Nelson,
1969. CA-1

SOKOL, William 1923-
Illustrator-author. He came to New York from Poland.
At an early age he was encouraged to draw. He has
received recognition from museums in New York, the
Art Directors Club of New York, the American Insti-
tute of Graphic Arts, and Graphis magazine. Mr.
Sokol has been an Art Director for the New York
Times. The Sokol family has lived in Rutherford, New
Jersey. Juvenile books which he has written and illus-
trated include A Lion In The Tree, Pantheon, 1961.
His wife Camille wrote, and he illustrated Dis-moi,
Holt, 1963.

SOLOMON, Louis
He graduated from the City College of New York and
taught school in New York City. He has written for
television and was the co-author of the play "Snafu"
which was made into a movie. Louis Solomon married writer Wilma Shore, and they have lived in New
York City. His juvenile books include: Telstar, Mc-
Graw, 1962; Voiceway To The Orient, McGraw, 1964.

SOMMERFELT, Aimée   1892-
Norwegian author.   When her husband was a visiting
professor at Stanford University, she lived in Palo Alto, California.   Dr. Alf Sommerfelt was one of the
founders of UNESCO which resulted in the Sommerfelts'
visit to India.   She once wrote: "Indian children live
in a world where legends and fairy tales give a shim-
mer to the poverty of their daily lives . . . children
(Indian) are unlike any children I have met. "   Her experiences in India led her to write The Road To Agra
(Criterion, 1961).   Pat Shaw Iversen translated her
book Miriam (Criterion, 1963) which received the State
Prize in Norway.   She also wrote The White Bungalow
(translated by Evelyn Ramsden), Criterion, 1964.

SONI, Welthy H.
Although she was born in Ann Arbor, Michigan, the author lived in India for many years.   She studied at
Calcutta University where she was a member of the
debating team.   Her husband Davendra Kumar Soni was
once Assistant Harbor Master at the river port of Calcutta and also was employed by a company which owned
a fleet of paddle steamers on the Ganges.   Later Welthy
Soni lived in Ridgewood, New Jersey.   She wrote Getting To Know The River Ganges, Coward, 1964.

SOOTIN, Harry
Born in New York, he graduated from the City College
of New York.   Prior to being a teacher, Mr. Sootin
was a chemist.   He has taught in the High School of
Commerce in Manhattan and at Flushing High School on
Long Island.   He has been a member of many organi-
zations including: the History of Science Society, A-
merican Association for the Advancement of Science,
and Teachers Guild.   His home has been in Flushing,
New York.   Juvenile titles include: Experiments With
Heat, Norton, 1964; Experiments With Machines And
Matter, Norton, 1963; Light Experiments, Norton, 1963;
Science Experiments With Sound, Norton, 1964; 12
Pioneers Of Science, Vanguard, 1960.

SORENSEN, Virginia (Eggersten)   1912-
She was born in Provo, Utah, graduated from Brigham
Young University, and did graduate work at Stanford
University.   She also studied in Denmark and Mexico
on Guggenheim Fellowships.   She has lived in various
states including Alabama, California, Colorado, Michigan,

and Pennsylvania where she collected authentic material
for several of her books.   She has written for both
children and adults.   In 1957 she was awarded the
Newbery Medal for Miracles On Maple Hill, Harcourt,
1956.   Other juvenile books include: Curious Missie,
Harcourt, 1953; Lotte's Locket, Harcourt, 1964; Plain
Girl, Harcourt, 1955.   CA-15/16, MJA

SOUTHALL, Ivan (Francis) 1921-
He was born in Canterbury, Victoria, Australia and
attended Melbourne Technical College.   His house
"Hills End" provided the title for one of his books for
children.   He served as a pilot with the Royal Australian Air Force during World War II and was awarded
the Distinguished Flying Cross.   Ivan Southall has also
been a war historian.   After the war, he became a
newspaper engraver in Melbourne.   Many of his books
have been translated into foreign languages.   His titles
for young people include: Ash Road, St. Martin's,
1966; Curse Of Cain, St. Martin's, 1968; Fox Hole,
St Martin's, 1967; Hills End, St Martin's, 1963; Let
The Balloon Go, St Martin's, 1968; Sword Of Esau,
St Martin's, 1968; To The Wild Sky, St Martin's, 1967.
CA-9/10

SOWERS, Phyllis (Ayer)
She was born in Brooklyn, the daughter of an Army
officer.   Since her father was stationed in various
parts of the world, she has lived in the Philippine
Islands, Japan, Mexico, and Siam.   Phyllis Sowers
continued to live in the Orient after her marriage.
Following the death of her husband, she returned to
America and has made her home in Carlsbad, Califor-
nia.   She collaborated with Jean Bothwell to write
Ranch Of A Thousand Horns, Abelard, 1955.   Phyllis
Sowers also wrote Sons Of The Dragon, Whitman, 1942.

SPACHE, George Daniel 1909-
Author, teacher, psychologist, reading specialist.   Dr.
Spache has taught at Rutgers, New York University,
and the University of Maryland.   He also has been in
charge of the Reading Laboratory and Clinic at the
University of Florida.   In the reading field Dr. Spache
has been known for his work in producing the Spache
Readability Formula.   For young people he wrote Toward Better Reading, Garrard, 1963.   CA-7/8

SPEARE, Elizabeth George 1908-
She was born in Melrose, Massachusetts and graduated
from Boston University. After receiving her master's
degree, she taught in a high school. She married
Alden Speare, an engineer, and they have lived in Connecticut. Mrs. Speare has received the Newbery Medal
twice; in 1959 for The Witch Of Blackbird Pond, Houghton, 1958, and in 1962 for The Bronze Bow, Houghton,
1961. She also wrote: Calico Captive, Houghton, 1957;
Life In Colonial America, Random, 1963. CA-2,
MJA

SPEEVACK, Yetta
She was born in Romania and came to America when
she was quite young. She studied at Hunter College
and Columbia University. Mrs. Speevack has also
studied in Puerto Rico (on a Ford Foundation grant).
She has taught in the New York City schools for many
years and has lived in Morningside, New York. She
wrote The Spider Plant, Atheneum, 1965.

SPENCER, Cornelia see YAUKEY, Grace (Sydenstricker)

SPENCER, William 1922-
He has served as Assistant Editor of the Middle East
Journal, Program Specialist, U. S. Office of Information, and intelligence officer with the Department of
Defense. In 1954 he was the recipient of a binational
teaching fellowship to Turkey, and in 1958 he received
a Chamber of Commerce Distinguished Service Award.
Mr. Spencer has also been associated with UNESCO in
Paris and Morocco. His books for young readers include: The Land And People Of Algeria, Lippincott,
1969; The Land And People Of Morocco, Lippincott,
1965. CA-19/20

SPERRY, Armstrong W. 1897-
Writer-illustrator, born in New Haven, Connecticut.
He has lived in Hanover, New Hampshire and on a
farm in Vermont. He attended the Yale School of Fine
Arts and the Art Students League in New York. He
also studied in Paris, France. The author's main interest has been "islands," and his many travels to
Tahiti and the West Indies have resulted in new ideas
and authentic backgrounds for his stories. Armstrong
Sperry has received many awards for his books including the 1941 Newbery Medal for Call It Courage,

Macmillan, 1940. Other juvenile titles include: All
About The Arctic And The Antarctic, Random, 1957;
The Amazon, River Sea Of Brazil, Garrard, 1961;
Danger To Windward, Winston, 1947; Frozen Fire,
Doubleday, 1956; Great River, Wide Land, Macmillan,
1967; Rain Forest, Macmillan, 1947; Thunder Country,
Macmillan, 1952.   CA-9/10, JBA-2

SPICER, Dorothy Gladys
Author and folklorist. She has collected material for
her books during her travels throughout Europe and
the Orient. She has made her home in White Plains,
New York. The author has written many articles and
books about folk customs, festivals, and foods. Her
juvenile books include: 13 Ghosts, Coward, 1965; 13
Goblins, Coward, 1969.   CA-4

SPIEGEL, Clara   see   MAYER, Jane (Rothchild)

SPILKA, Arnold
Artist, author, sculptor, he has lived in Brooklyn, New
York. Many children's books have been illustrated by
him. Arnold Spilka has been "a firm believer in the
theory that art should be self-expression. Since the
young child's basic instincts are to express himself,
he need only be given paint, brush, paper and - quite
literally - a free hand." For boys and girls he wrote
and illustrated Paint All Kinds Of Pictures, Walck,
1963.

SPRAGUE, Gretchen (Burnham) 1926-
She grew up in Scottsbluff, Nebraska and attended the
University of Nebraska where she majored in English.
After her marriage to a Rhodes Scholar, Gretchen
Sprague lived in England. When she and her husband
returned to America, they lived in Arkansas and
Brooklyn, New York. Her interests have included:
the New York Mets, mountains, and books by J. R. R.
Tolkien. She wrote A Question Of Harmony, Dodd,
1965; White In The Moon, Dodd, 1968.   CA-15/16

SPRAGUE, Rosemary 1922-
Born in New York City, she graduated from Bryn Mawr
College in Pennsylvania and received graduate degrees
from Western Reserve University at Cleveland, Ohio.
Rosemary Sprague has also studied at the University of
London and at the Shakespeare Institute at Stratford-

upon-Avon, England. She has taught at Western Reserve University and at Fenn College in Cleveland. Later she was on the staff of Longwood College in Farmville, Virginia. For young people she wrote Forever In Joy, Chilton, 1965. She also edited Poems Of Robert Browning, Crowell, 1964. CA-19/20

SPYRI, Johanna (Heusser) 1827-1901
She was born in Hirzel, Switzerland, the daughter of Dr. and Mrs. Johann J. Heusser. She married Bernhard Spyri, and they lived in Zurich where her husband was town clerk. Her writing career began at the age of forty when she decided to raise money for war orphans following the Franco-Prussian War. Her best known book was Heidi (first published in 1880), Houghton, 1923. She also wrote The Pet Lamb, And Other Swiss Stories (tr. by M. E. Calthrop and E. M. Popper), Dutton, 1956. JBA-1, JBA-2

STACK, Nicolete see MEREDITH, Nicolete

STALL, Dorothy
Author and teacher, born in Thayer, Kansas. After graduating from the Kansas State Teachers College, she made her home in New York City where she has been a teacher at "The Little Red Schoolhouse." Miss Stall did further study in New York at the New School for Social Research, Columbia University, and the American Russian Institute. Her interest in the history of the American Indian led her to do research at the Arizona State Teachers College in Flagstaff. For young people she wrote Chukchi Hunter, Morrow, 1946.

STAMBLER, Irwin 1924-
Author, editor, engineer. He received a degree in aeronautical engineering from New York University. Irwin Stambler has been associated with Chase Aircraft and Republic Aviation. He has also been the engineering editor of Space/Aeronautics magazine. His articles about space programs have been published in many magazines. Mr. Stambler and his family have lived in Beverly Hills, California. He collaborated with Gordon Ashmead to write Find A Career In Engineering, Putnam, 1962. He also wrote Supersonic Transport, Putnam, 1965. CA-5/6

STAPP, Arthur Donald 1906–
Author and newspaperman, born in Seattle, Washington.
His career as a writer began when he worked on his
family's newspaper. At the end of World War II (he
served with the United States Air Force in Brazil), he
attended New York University. He has been a linotype
operator for a newspaper in New York. The author
married a children's librarian, and they have lived in
Irvington, New York. For the young reader he wrote:
Mountain Tamer, Morrow, 1948; Too Steep For Baseball, Harper, 1964. CA-4, MJA

STARBIRD, Kaye 1916–
Her pseudonym is C. S. Jennison. Author and poet,
she was born in Fort Sill, Oklahoma. Her father was
an army officer. She received her education at the
University of Virginia and attended writers' colonies
on various fellowships. She has been twice widowed
and has three daughters. The author has lived in
Burlington, Vermont and Washington, D. C. She has
written for both adults and children, and her poetry
has appeared in magazines. Miss Starbird has belonged to the Cercle Cultural in Paris, France. For
boys and girls she wrote The Pheasant On Route Seven,
Lippincott, 1968. CA-17/18

STARRETT, Vincent 1886–
Author and newspaperman, born in Toronto, Canada.
He has lived in Peking, Rome, London, Paris, New
York, and Chicago. Mr. Starrett has been a noted
authority on Sherlock Holmes. Prior to being a book
columnist on the Chicago Tribune, the author was a
police reporter and a war correspondent. Vincent
Starrett has written several volumes of essays and
verse and compiled bibliographies of Ambrose Bierce
and Stephen Crane. For children he wrote The Great
All-Star Animal League Ball Game, Dodd, 1957.

STEELE, Mary Quintard (Govan) 1922–
Her pseudonym is Wilson Gage. She married author
William O. Steele, and they have lived in Tennessee.
Her parents were authors Gilbert and Christine Noble
Govan. Her book Big Blue Island (World, 1964) re-
ceived the Aurianne Award for "the best children's
book of 1964 on animal life which develops a humane
attitude. " She also wrote: Dan And The Miranda,
World, 1962; Journey Outside, Viking, 1969. CA-4

STEELE, William Owen 1917-
He was born in Franklin, Tennessee and has continued
to live in that state in a house on a mountain near
Chattanooga. Mr. Steele studied at Cumberland University and did graduate work at the University of
Chattanooga. He married author Mary Govan whose
parents were also writers. The author served overseas in the armed forces during World War II. He
won the William Allen White Children's Book Award in
1960 for his book The Perilous Road (Harcourt, 1958)
which was the runner-up for the 1959 Newbery Medal.
In 1962 he was awarded the Thomas Alva Edison A-
ward. Other juvenile titles include: Buffalo Knife,
Harcourt, 1952; We Were There On The Oregon Trail
(Historical Consultant: Ray W. Irwin), Grosset, 1955.
CA-5/6

STEFANSSON, Evelyn (Schwartz) Baird 1913-
Native New Yorker, she has been in charge of the
Stefansson Arctic Library. She married explorer
Vilhjalmur Stefansson who has been Arctic Consultant,
Northern Studies Program at Dartmouth College. Mr.
and Mrs. Stefansson have worked together in geograph-
ical research. Mrs. Stefansson has lectured at the
University of Alaska. The authoritative book which
she wrote for young people was Here Is Alaska, Scrib-
ner, 1959.

STEFFERUD, Alfred Daniel 1903-
He was born in Kenyon, Minnesota, and graduated from
St. Olaf College. Mr. Stefferud also attended the
American Academy in Rome, the University of Berlin,
the University of Vienna, and Iowa State University.
He has been a high school teacher and a member of
the Associated Press. He also worked in the Office of
War Information during the war. He has been editor
of the U. S. Department of Agriculture's Yearbook and
wrote for boys and girls Wonders Of Seeds, Harcourt,
1956. CA-15/16

STEIG, William H.
Artist, cartoonist, writer. Born in New York City,
he later made his home in Greenwich Village. His
cartoons which have appeared in the New Yorker, and
his books of symbolic drawings have guided and in-
fluenced artists and cartoonists around the world. He
was awarded the 1970 Caldecott Medal for his illustra-

STEIN, Meyer Lewis   487

tions in Sylvester And The Magic Pebble (Simon, 1969)
which he also wrote. Other juvenile titles include:
Bad Island, Simon, 1969; CDB!, Simon, 1968.

STEIN, Meyer Lewis
    M. L. Stein was born in Escanaba, Michigan. He re-
ceived a degree in journalism from the University of
Missouri and an M. A. degree from Stanford University.
During his Army service in World War II, Mr. Stein
served as a part-time correspondent for the Army
newspaper, Stars And Stripes, and his stories appeared
in Yank magazine. After the war he worked in Royal
Oak, Michigan for the Daily Tribune, was a reporter
on the San Francisco Examiner, and also wrote for
Fortune, Life, and Time magazines. Mr. Stein resided in Port Washington, New York and has been an
associate professor in the Department of Journalism at
New York University. For young people he wrote
Your Career In Journalism (A Junior Literary Guild
selection), Messner, 1965. CA-17/18

STEINBERG, Alfred 1917-
    As a political writer, this author has been closely
associated with events which have taken place in our
nation's capital. He has worked with the Committee
for Equality in Immigration and the National Planning
Association. Alfred Steinberg has contributed articles
to many magazines including the Saturday Evening Post,
Nation's Business, Reader's Digest, and Harper's. He
has lived in Silver Spring, Maryland. Juvenile titles
include: Admiral Richard E. Byrd, Putnam, 1960;
The Kennedy Brothers, Putnam, 1969. CA-5/6

STEINER, Charlotte
    Author and illustrator. She was born in Czechoslovakia
and later came to the United States. She has studied
art in Prague, Paris, and Vienna. Very young readers
have enjoyed her colorful drawings and simple text.
Books which she has written and illustrated include:
Bobby Follows The Butterfly, Macmillan, 1959; Tomboy's Doll, Lothrop, 1969.

STEPHENS, Peter John
    Playwright, poet, writer, he attended schools in Lon-
don. He was associated with the Press Department of
the British Information Service in New York and wrote
many stories for American newspapers and magazines.

Poetry written by Peter Stephens has also appeared in
American poetry magazines. He also wrote documentary films, radio and television scripts, opera librettos,
and plays ("Men Like Kings" was awarded the AETA
Manuscript Play Project Prize as best play of the
year). Due to his interest in history Mr. Stephens
wrote several children's books which include: Battle
For Destiny, Atheneum, 1967; The Perrely Plight,
Atheneum, 1965.

STERLING, Dorothy 1913-
She was born in New York and studied at Wellesley
and Barnard Colleges. She has written many factual
books for children. At one time she worked for Time,
Inc. , and was a staff member of Life. The author
and her family have lived in Rye, New York. Her
books for boys and girls include: Sophie And Her Puppies, Junior Literary Guild and Doubleday, 1951; Story
Of Caves (A Junior Literary Guild selection), Doubleday, 1956. CA-9/10

STERLING, Helen see HOKE, Helen L.

STERN, Madeleine B.
She was born in New York City, graduated from Barnard College, and received her master's degree from
Columbia University. In addition to writing, the author has been interested in old and rare books. She
has visited many bookshops on her frequent trips to
Europe. For young people she wrote Queen Of Publishers' Row: Mrs. Frank Leslie, Messner, 1965.

STEVENS, Alden Gifford 1886-
When he graduated from high school, he decided to
"see the world. " He worked in New Mexico, Texas,
and Honduras (including a stint in the Honduran Army).
When he returned home, Alden Stevens graduated from
Yale. He later lived in Africa. For boys and girls
he wrote Lion Boy's White Brother, Junior Literary
Guild and Lippincott, 1951.

STEVENS, Carla
She graduated from New York University and later
taught at the Dalton School in New York City. She
married writer Leonard Stevens, and they have lived
in Connecticut. Her children's interest in nature provided the inspiration for her book Catch A Cricket,

Scott, 1961. She also wrote The Birth Of Sunset's
Kitten, Scott, 1969.

STEVENS, William Oliver 1878-
Author, illustrator, antiquarian, educator. He graduated from Yale University and Colby College. He has
been a contributor to many newspapers and magazines.
Mr. Stevens has had an illustrious career which has
included: Professor of English at the U. S. Naval
Academy, Dean of the School of Literature and Journalism at Oglethorpe University, and headmaster of the
Cranbrook School and the Roger Ascham School His
juvenile books include: David Glasgow Farragut, Dodd,
1942; Famous Men Of Science, Dodd, 1952.

STEVENSON, Augusta
Writer, teacher, lecturer, graduate of Indiana College.
She was born in Patriot, Indiana and later made her
home in Indianapolis. Her travels to historic locations
in this country and to Hawaii, Newfoundland, and Cent-
ral America provided the background for her books.
Miss Stevenson originated the idea for the popular
"Childhood of Famous American" series with her first
book Abe Lincoln: Frontier Boy (first published in
1932) Bobbs, 1959. Her other titles in this series in-
clude: Andy Jackson, Boy Soldier, Bobbs, 1942; Ben
Franklin, Printer's Boy, Bobbs, 1941; Israel Putnam,
Fearless Boy, Bobbs, 1959; John Fitch: Steamboat Boy,
Bobbs, 1966; Molly Pitcher, Bobbs, 1952; Squanto,
Young Indian Hunter, Bobbs, 1962; Wilbur And Orville
Wright, Bobbs, 1951. CA-2, MJA

STEVENSON, Robert Louis 1850-1894
He was born in Edinburgh, Scotland and died in Samoa
when he was only forty-four. He traveled a great deal
including a visit to the United States where he married.
His book Treasure Island (first published in 1882,
Scribner, 1911) was a result of his stepson's request
for an "interesting" book. His other titles include:
The Black Arrow, Scribner, 1916; A Child's Garden
Of Verses (illus. by Brian Wildsmith), Watts, 1966;
Kidnapped (first published in 1886), Scribner, 1913;
Prayers Written At Vailima, Macmillan, 1960. JBA-1

STEWART, Anna Bird
She was born in Cincinnati, Ohio and has lived in New
York. It was while she attended the University of

Cincinnati that Miss Stewart developed a deep interest
in David Garrick, the famed actor of the eighteenth
century. The author has visited the boyhood home of
the actor in Lichfield, England, and other places in
England where Garrick lived in order to collect material for her book Enter David Garrick, Lippincott, 1951.
She also wrote: Two Young Corsicans, Lippincott,
1944; Young Miss Burney, Lippincott, 1947.

STEWART, Elizabeth Laing
Author and editor, born in Colorado Springs, Colorado.
A graduate of Barnard College, she has worked for
publishing firms as an editor. Her books for young
readers include The Lion Twins, Atheneum, 1964.

STILLMAN, Myra Stephens 1915-
Teacher, librarian, social worker, author. She grad-
uated from New York State College for Teachers. Mrs.
Stillman has been associated with the Poughkeepsie Day
School and the County Welfare Department in Albany.
She has lived in New Paltz, New York. With Beulah
Tannenbaum she wrote: Isaac Newton, Pioneer Of
Space Mathematics, McGraw, 1959; Understanding Food,
McGraw, 1962.   CA-5/6

STINE, George Harry 1928-
Author, editor, lecturer. After he graduated from
Colorado College in 1952, G. Harry Stine worked in
New Mexico at the White Sands Proving Ground. His
duties at White Sands varied from rocket-engine testing
to head of the Range Operations Division of the U. S.
Naval Ordinance Missile Test Facility. He has also
been a lecturer on astronautics and a columnist for
Mechanix Illustrated magazine. Mr. Stine has been a
Fellow of the British Interplanetary Society, a member
of the Society for the Advancement of Space Travel,
the American Rocket Society, and the American Astro-
nautical Society. He has resided in Las Cruces, New
Mexico. For young people he wrote Rocket Power And
Space Flight, Holt, 1957.

STIRLING, Lilla
She was born and raised in Nova Scotia. After she
graduated from Dalhousie and Columbia Universities,
Lilla Stirling taught school. On a visit to northern
Ontario she found an idea for a story and said: "Sandy,
the grandson of a Presbyterian minister, had for his

friend the village priest. A common sight in the village was the tall black robed priest and the small boy
trudging along the snowy road together. " She wrote
about this village where people of all religious faiths
were friends and worked together. Her book for young
people was The Jolly Season, Scribners, 1948.

STIRLING, Nora Bramley
She was born in Atlanta, Georgia where she also attended schooL Nora Stirling continued her education
in Edinburgh, Scotland and New York City. She has
written for both television and radio. Her articles
have appeared in many publications including Argosy
and the New York Times Magazine. The author has
lived in New York City. For boys and girls she wrote:
Exploring For Lost Treasure, Garden City, 1960; You
Would If You Loved Me, M. Evans, 1969.   CA-7/8

STOCKTON, Frank Richard 1834-1902
He was born in Philadelphia, Pennsylvania. After
graduation from high school, Frank Stockton began
working as a wood-engraver. He later became assistant editor of the St. Nicholas magazine. His humorous book Rudder Grange (Scribner, 1907) originally began as a collection of stories which he wrote about a
maid who worked in his home at Nutley, New Jersey.
He gained a great deal of fame for his adult story
"The Lady Or The Tiger?" Prior to writing for adults,
he first became known for the fairy tales which he
wrote for children Ting-A-Ling (first published in
1870) Ting-A-Ling Tales, Scribner, 1955. Other juvenile titles include: The Bee-Man Of Orn (pictures by
Maurice Sendak), Holt, 1964; Buccaneers And Pirates
Of Our Coasts (new ed.), Macmillan, 1967.   JBA-1

STODDARD, Edward G. 1923-
His parents were missionaries, and he was born in
China. Mr. Stoddard has been an engineer for a
broadcasting station, promotion manager of a publish-
ing company, and has tested radar at Western Electric.
He has also acquired a first-class professional radio
operator's license. For young people he wrote: First
Book Of Magic, Watts, 1953; First Book Of Television,
Watts, 1955.   CA-11/12

STODDARD, Hope
Born in New Bedford, Massachusetts, she studied music

at the Institute of Musical Art (Juilliard School) and at
the University of Michigan. She has been on the staff
of Etude and served as associate editor of the International Musician. Her juvenile books include: From
These Comes Music, Crowell, 1952; Symphony Conduc-
tors Of The U. S. A., Crowell, 1957.

STOLZ, Mary (Slattery) 1920-
She was born in Boston, Massachusetts, grew up in
New York City, and attended Columbia University. She
and her husband Dr. Thomas Jaleski have lived in
Stamford, Connecticut. She has also lived in Pelham,
New York. In addition to teen-age novels, Mary Stolz
has written biographies and picture books. The author
has enjoyed cooking, reading, and traveling as hobbies.
She has been runner-up for the Newbery Medal two
times. Her juvenile titles include: And Love Replied,
Harper, 1958; Because Of Madeline, Harper, 1957;
Belling The Tiger, Harper, 1961; The Bully On Bark-
ham Street, Harper, 1963; Frédou, Harper, 1962; Hos-
pital Zone, Harper, 1956; A Love, Or A Season, Harper, 1964; Maximilian's World, Harper, 1966; Say
Something, Harper, 1968; A Wonderful, Terrible Time,
Harper, 1967.   CA-5/6, MJA

STONE, George K.
Teacher, amateur naturalist, author. He taught school
in New York and Ohio and has been on the staff of the
New York State Department of Education. He later
lived in Florida and had a laboratory workshop where
he conducted experiments which provided material for
his books. For boys and girls he wrote 101 Science
Projects, Prentice, 1963.

STONG, Philip Duffield 1899-1957
He was born in Keosauqua, Iowa and graduated from
Drake University in Des Moines. He began his career
as a newspaperman. He worked on the Des Moines
Register, was a wire editor in New York for the Associated Press, and later served on the staff of several
magazines. Phil Stong received several honorary degrees from Iowa's Parsons College and Drake University. His wife was reporter Virginia Maude Swain.
He wrote books for adults in addition to books for boys
and girls which include: A Beast Called An Elephant,
Dodd, 1955; Censored, The Goat, Dodd, 1945; Cowhand
Goes To Town, Dodd, 1939; Farm Boy, Doubleday,

1934; Honk: The Moose, Dodd, 1935.   MJA

STOUTENBURG, Adrien (Pearl) 1916-
Born in Minnesota, she attended the Minneapolis School
of Arts. Miss Stoutenburg has written serials and
short stories for many magazines including the Ameri-
can Girl, Calling All Girls, and Seventeen. She has
been a reporter for the Richfield, Minnesota News.
Adrien Stoutenburg has lived in Berkeley, California.
Many of her juvenile books have been Junior Literary
Guild selections. These include: In This Corner,
Westminster, 1957; River Duel, Westminster, 1956.
CA-7/8

STRATTON, William David 1896-   Lucille (Neville)
Midwestern husband-wife team.   The Strattons have
lived in North Dakota, Minnesota, and Idaho. Both of
them have been interested in wild life and have studied
the various water birds that lived in the marsh lands.
Prior to locating in California, the Strattons taught
school in the Middle West.   They wrote Wild Wings
Over The Marshes, Golden Gate, 1964.   CA-9/10

STRAUS, Jacqueline Harris
She was born in New York City and has resided in
Minneapolis, Minnesota with her husband and children.
She graduated from the University of Wisconsin where
she received a degree in sociology.   When her son
desired a chemistry set at a very early age, Mrs.
Straus wrote Let's Experiment! Chemistry For Boys
And Girls, Harper, 1962.

STREATFEILD, Noel
Book critic and writer, born in Sussex, England. Pri-
or to a writing career, she studied to be an actress
at the Royal Academy of Dramatic Art in London.
Miss Streatfeild has written adult novels in addition to
her books for children. She has served as a book
critic for Elizabethan magazine, and she has presented
book talks on the radio.   Most of her books have been
heard on BBC and translated into various languages.
A television film was made from her story The Magic
Summer (A Junior Literary Guild selection, Random,
1967).   Miss Streatfeild has enjoyed her hobby of growing wildflowers in her London flat.   Her many books
for young people include: The Family At Caldicott
Place (A Junior Literary Guild selection), Random,

1968; <u>Ballet Shoes</u>, Random, 1937; <u>The Children On</u>
<u>The Top Floor</u>, Random, 1965; <u>Traveling Shoes</u>, Ran-
dom, 1962. JBA-2

STRONG, Charles see EPSTEIN, Samuel

STRONG, Charles Stanley 1906-
    Author, explorer, and lecturer, born in Brooklyn. He
    attended Pace Institute and the Royal Frederick Univer-
    sity of Oslo, Norway. Mr. Strong has been an official
    observer for the Arctic Institute of North America.
    He was a member of the search party that was sent to
    rescue explorer Roald Amundsen. As a world-wide
    traveler he has acquired an excellent background which
    has enabled him to write books of authenticity. Mr.
    Strong has lived in Manhasset, Long Island. His juve-
    nile books include: <u>Real Book About The Antarctic</u>,
    Garden City, 1959; <u>We Were There With Byrd At The</u>
    <u>South Pole</u> (Historical consultant: Bernt Balchen),
    Grosset, 1956.

STYLES, (Frank) Showell 1908-
    British novelist, mountain climber. During World War
    II, he served as a lieutenant commander in the Reserve
    of the Royal Navy. He has enjoyed mountain climbing
    and has been a certified guide of the British Mountain-
    eering Council, a member of the Himalayan Club, and
    a Fellow of the Geographical Society. He has
    written about mountain climbing in addition to this book
    for boys and girls: <u>Greencoats Against Napoleon</u>, Van-
    guard, 1964. CA-4

SUGGS, Robert Carl 1932-
    Anthropologist and author, born in Portchester, New
    York. A graduate of Columbia University, Dr. Suggs
    has been an Associate Anthropologist with a research
    and consulting company. He has been on scientific
    expeditions in French Polynesia and the Marquesas
    Islands and has conducted anthropological research in
    Fiji and Tahiti. The author has also worked in the
    American Museum of Natural History. He served in
    the Marines during World War II. Dr. Suggs and his
    family have lived in Bridgeport, Connecticut and Alex-
    andria, Virginia. His books for young people include:
    <u>The Archaeology Of New York</u>, Crowell, 1966; <u>Lords</u>
    <u>Of The Blue Pacific</u>, N. Y. Graphic, 1962. CA-9/10

SULLIVAN, George Edward   495

SULLIVAN, George Edward 1927-
    Author and sportswriter, he graduated from Fordham
    University. He has written many books about sports
    including bowling, softball, and ice hockey. George
    Sullivan has also written a sports column which has
    appeared in many newspapers. He has resided in New
    York City. With Irving Crane he wrote The Young
    Sportsman's Guide To Pocket Billiards, Nelson, 1964.
    He also wrote They Flew Alone, Warne, 1969. CA-
    13/14

SUMMERS, James (Levingston) 1910-
    Born in Wisconsin, he studied at the University of
    California at Los Angeles. He has been a high school
    teacher in California. Mr. Summers received honor-
    able mention in the Martha Foley and O'Brien Collec-
    tions. The author has lived in Atascadero, California.
    He has written many books for young people and seve-
    ral of them have been chosen as Junior Literary Guild
    selections. These include: Gift Horse, Westminster,
    1961; The Karting Crowd, Westminster, 1961. CA-
    15/16

SURANY, Anico
    She was born in Paris and spent her childhood in El
    Salvador and Panama. She studied at Columbia Univer-
    sity in New York and at the Sorbonne in France. She
    has lived in New York City but has often visited Pan-
    ama where her family continued to live. Her books
    for boys and girls include: The Burning Mountain,
    Holiday, 1965; Lora, Lorita, Putnam, 1969.

SUTCLIFF, Rosemary 1920-
    She was born in Surrey, England and grew up in Devon-
    shire. She later lived in Sussex at Arundel. She
    studied art at the Bideford School of Art, and at the
    age of eighteen had her first miniature hung in the
    Royal Academy. When she was twenty-five, she gave
    up painting in order to write. In 1959 she was award-
    ed England's Carnegie Medal for her book The Lantern
    Bearers, Walck, 1959. Her other titles include:
    Dawn Wind, Walck, 1962; The Hound Of Ulster (retold
    by R. Sutcliff), Dutton, 1963; Knight's Fee, Walck,
    1960; The Mark Of The Horse Lord, Walck, 1965.
    CA-5/6, MJA

SUTTON, Felix
    He was born in West Virginia and graduated from the
    School of Journalism at West Virginia University. Mr.
    Sutton has been a sports reporter and has written copy
    for an advertising agency. A town was named Sutton
    in West Virginia for one of his ancestors who lived
    during the Revolutionary period of American history.
    He and his wife have lived in Wilton, Connecticut.
    Juvenile titles include: The Big Treasure Book Of
    Clowns, Grosset, 1953; Sons Of Liberty, Messner,
    1969.

SUTTON, Margaret Beebe 1903-
    She grew up near Austin, Pennsylvania. From her
    parents she learned to draw and how to make up
    stories and plays. Before her marriage and a writing
    career, Mrs. Sutton went to business school and be-
    came a stenographer. She also acquired a knowledge
    of the printing trade. Later she became a nurses'
    aide and said that she considers her hospital work one
    of the most rewarding experiences of her life. The
    cover for her book Gail Gardner Wins Her Cap (Dodd,
    1945) was designed by her daughter Peggy. She also
    wrote Jemima, Daughter Of Daniel Boone, Scribners,
    1942. CA-1

SUTTON, Myron Daniel   Ann (Livesay) 1923-
    Husband-wife team. Mrs. Sutton was born in Ashley,
    Illinois, and her husband was born in Arizona. She
    graduated from the University of Illinois and has been
    Curator of Geology at the Illinois State Museum in
    Springfield. She has also been a geologist with the
    U. S. Geological Survey. Myron Sutton has been asso-
    ciated with the National Park Service, Department of
    the Interior. The Suttons have lived in Alexandria,
    Virginia. They wrote Animals On The Move, Rand,
    1965.

SWANSON, Arlene Collyer 1913-
    Teacher, librarian, author. She graduated from Bar-
    nard College and attended Columbia University where
    she received a master's degree in English. Mrs.
    Swanson has been a high school librarian and teacher.
    She has also been Supervisor of Reading for the Junior
    and Senior High Schools in Ossining, New York. Her
    stories have been published in Senior Scholastic and
    American Girl magazines. For young people she wrote

Dulcy, Reilly & Lee, 1962.   CA-5/6

SWANSON, Neil Harmon 1896-   Anne (Sherbourne)
Husband-wife team. A historian and novelist, he was
born in Minneapolis and graduated from the University
of Minnesota. Neil Swanson has been a well-known
authority on the origin of our national anthem. The
General Society of the War of 1812 made him an honorary member and granted him the honor to wear the
medal. He served in World War I and has been a
newspaperman. Anne Swanson was born in Baltimore,
Maryland. She has been a newspaper columnist, a
radio and television commentator, and has worked in
fashion advertising. The Swansons have lived in Garrison, Maryland. Together they wrote Star-Spangled
Banner (A Junior Literary Guild selection), Winston,
1958.

SWARTHOUT, Glendon (Fred) 1918-   Kathryn (Vaughn)
Husband-wife team, teachers, authors. He was born
in Pinckney, Michigan, received degrees from the University of Michigan, and obtained his Ph. D. from
Michigan State University. He served with the U. S.
Army during World War II. Mr. Swarthout has been
a college professor, and his wife has been an elementary schoolteacher. Mrs. Swarthout has played tennis
as a hobby, and her husband has enjoyed trout fishing.
Their home has been in Scottsdale, Arizona. Together
they wrote: The Button Boat, Doubleday, 1969; The
Ghost And The Magic Saber, Randon, 1963.   CA-3

SWIFT, Helen Miller 1914-
She graduated from the University of Vermont and Simmons College. Her profession was retailing, and at
one time she was assistant training director of a department store. The author has also worked in a
specialty shop. She has written articles for many
magazines including Woman's Home Companion, Good
Housekeeping, and This Week. Her home has been in
Winchester, Massachusetts. For boys and girls she
wrote Chocolate Soda, Longmans, 1956.   CA-2

SWIFT, Hildegarde (Hoyt)
Author and teacher, born in Clinton, New York. She
attended New York's School of Social Work after graduating from Smith College in Northampton, Massachusetts. She married Arthur L. Swift, Jr., and has made

her home in New York.   Mrs. Swift has lectured both
here and abroad and at one time conducted a workshop
in writing for young people.   She has also taught children's literature.   The author has belonged to the Authors' League of America, New York's Pen and Brush
Club, and the Women's National Book Association. Her
books for young readers include: Edge Of April, Morrow, 1957; From The Eagle's Wing, Morrow, 1962;
Little Red Lighthouse And The Great Gray Bridge,
Morrow, 1942; The Railroad To Freedom, Harcourt,
1932.   JBA-2

SWINTON, William Elgin 1900-
He received both his B. Sc. and Ph. D. degrees from
the University of Glasgow in Scotland. Dr. Swinton
has been associated with the Natural History Museum
in London and served as Director of the Royal Ontario
Museum of Zoology and Palaeontology in Canada. He
has also been a Fellow of the Royal Society of Edinburgh.   The author has been interested in dinosaurs
and fossils.   For young people he wrote: Digging For
Dinosaurs, Doubleday, 1964; The Wonderful World Of
Prehistoric Animals, Garden City, 1961.   CA-13/14

SYKES, Jo
She was born in American Falls, Idaho and attended
school in Illinois and Montana. She studied at Mac-
Murray College in Jacksonville, Illinois and Rocky
Mountain College in Billings, Montana. She has worked
on a cattle ranch and in a fishing tackle shop. Jo
Sykes was also a children's librarian. Her hobbies
have been: music, photography, hiking, and swimming.
She has lived in Livingston, Montana. Juvenile titles
include: Leashed Lightning, Holt, 1969; Stubborn Mare
(A Junior Literary Guild selection), Winston, 1957.

SYME, (Neville) Ronald 1913-
He grew up in New Zealand and left school at the age
of sixteen to work on a Pacific cargo steamer. It was
during this time that Ronald Syme became interested
in writing.   During World War II, Mr. Syme served
with the British Merchant Service, the British Army
Intelligence Corps, and the Eighth Army in Africa.
In 1960 he married a Polynesian princess, and they
have lived in the Cook Islands. His children's books
include: Frontenac Of New France, Morrow, 1969;
John Smith Of Virginia, Morrow, 1954.   CA-9/10, MJA

SZASZ, Suzanne Shorr 1919-
  She was selected as one of the ten best women photographers in the United States in 1959. Many of her
  photographic essays have been published in magazines.
  When she created Young Folk's New York (Crown,
  1960) with Susan Lyman, she took over 2500 photographs and then selected 155 for publication. Her
  photographs were used in Now I Have A Daddy Haircut!
  (written by Clara and Morey Appell), Dodd, 1960.
  CA-5/6

SZE, Mai-Mai
  Born in Tientsin, China, the daughter of a Chinese
  Ambassador. Her father served as Ambassador in
  both London and Washington. She received her education at Wellesley College. In 1937 she organized the
  first Chinese War Relief group in New York and gave
  many lectures on China in the United States and Canada. She has also been a columnist and painter. For
  young people she wrote Echo Of A Cry, Harcourt,
  1945.

                              T

TALBERT, Ansel Edward McLaurine 1915-
  Author, correspondent, graduate of Columbia Univer-
  sity. He has been editor of aviation for the New York
  Herald Tribune and at one time was president of the
  Aviation Writers Association of North America. During
  World War II, Ansel Talbert served in England with
  Lt. General James H. Doolittle as an intelligence offi-
  cer and was a war correspondent during the Korean
  conflict. For young people he has written Famous Air-
  ports Of The World, Random, 1953.

TALLANT, Robert 1909-1957
  Author and editor. His entire life was spent in New
  Orleans where he was born. Robert Tallant wrote
  many books about his native city. In 1951 his book
  The Pirate Lafitte And The Battle Of New Orleans
  (Random, 1951) received the Louisiana Library Associ-
  ation Award. He died at the age of forty-eight. Mr.
  Tallant also wrote: Evangeline And The Acadians,
  Random, 1957; Louisiana Purchase, Random, 1952.

TALMADGE, Marian
  She has been a teacher at the University of Denver,

director of a Children's Theatre and marionette troupe, and a radio scriptwriter. In 1956 the Boys' Life-Dodd, Mead Prize Competition was awarded to the author and Iris Gilmore for their book Pony Express Boy (Dodd, 1956). Marian Talmadge has been interested in collecting antiques and historical facts about the West. With Iris Gilmore she wrote: Let's Go To A Truck Terminal, Putnam, 1964; Six Great Horse Rides, Putnam, 1968.

TAMBURINE, Jean 1930-
Artist and author, she attended the Art Students League in New York and the Traphagen School of Design. Her illustrations have appeared in many books for children. She married artist-designer Eugene Bertolli, and they have lived in Meriden, Connecticut. She wrote and illustrated I Think I Will Go To The Hospital, Abingdon, 1965. CA-9/10

TANNEHILL, Ivan Ray 1890-
Weatherman and author. When he was a boy, he bought a telescope to study birds and the stars. This hobby led to Mr. Tannehill's interest in the weather. He has studied the weather for more than thirty years. The author has been associated with the U. S. Weather Bureau as director of weather reporting and forecasting. He has also served as president of the International Commission on weather information. For young people he wrote All About The Weather, Random, 1953.

TANNENBAUM, Beulah Goldstein 1916-
Teacher, librarian, author. She received her master's degree from Columbia University and has lived in New Paltz, New York. She has been New York Science Consultant at the New York City Downtown Community School and Director of Educational Research in Cleveland, Ohio. Beulah Tannenbaum has also taught in a French normal school, and she has served on the staff of the Ethical Culture Schools as Science Specialist and Children's Librarian. With Myra Stillman she wrote: Isaac Newton, Pioneer Of Space Mathematics, McGraw, 1959; Understanding Maps, Charting The Land, Sea, And Sky, McGraw, 1957. CA-5/6

TANOUS, Helen Nicol 1917-
Author, designer, born in Minneapolis, Minnesota. She studied at the Minneapolis Institute of Art and later

attended the Jean Carol School of Dress Design in Los
Angeles. Following a career as a sportswear designer, Helen Tanous operated her own business (play-
clothes for children). Textile prints have also been
designed by her. When her younger daughter became
interested in sewing, Mrs. Tanous wrote Sewing Is
Easy!, Random, 1956.

TARRY, Ellen
Teacher and author, born in Birmingham, Alabama.
She later worked in Birmingham as a newspaperwoman
and teacher. She received a Bureau of Educational
Experiments scholarship which enabled her to be at
the Writers' Laboratory in New York. At one time
Ellen Tarry was known as the "Story Lady" in a Har-
lem Community Center. She collaborated with Marie
Hall Ets to write My Dog Rinty (new ed.), Viking,
1964. She wrote Young Jim, Dodd, 1967.

TATE, Elizabeth
She grew up in Richmond, Virginia and graduated from
Bryn Mawr College in Pennsylvania. Her first stories
appeared in the St. Nicholas magazine. Her husband
has been Dean of the Yale Law School, and they have
lived in New Haven. For children she wrote Little
Flower Girl, Lothrop, 1956.

TATHAM, Campbell see ELTING, Mary

TAVO, Gus see IVAN, Gustave

TAYLOR, Arthur
Author and painter, he attended the Philadelphia Museum College of Art. Mr. Taylor has been Art Director
of an advertising agency in Philadelphia. He has made
his home in New Jersey. The author and his wife have
lived on Cape May during the summers where he has
often photographed and painted the coastline. For children he wrote Mr. Fizbee And The Little Troop (A
Junior Literary Guild selection), Holt, 1962.

TAYLOR, Carl
He was born in New York and graduated from Harvard
University. He also studied at the Johns Hopkins
School of Advanced International Studies. The author
has been a member of the Experiment in International
Living and lived one summer with a German family in

Höxter.   He has written several articles for the Economist.   His juvenile books include: Getting To Know Burma, Coward, 1962; Getting To Know Indonesia, Coward, 1961.

TAYLOR, Margaret 1917-
Author, artist, teacher, born in Louisiana.   She has been an art teacher in Chicago where she has lived since childhood.   Her paintings have been exhibited in many places including the Library of Congress in Washington, D. C.   The author was a columnist for the Associated Negro Press during World War II.   She has also contributed poems to children's magazines. For boys and girls she wrote Jasper The Drummin' Boy, Viking, 1947.   She also compiled Did You Feed My Cow?, Crowell, 1956.

TAYLOR, Sydney Brenner 1904-
Dancer and author, born in New York.   She studied dramatics at New York University and dancing at the Martha Graham Dance Studio.   The author was awarded the Charles W. Follett award in 1951 for her book All-Of-A-Kind Family (Wilcox & Follett, 1951).   The author has been a member of a dance company and once was a director of dancing at a summer camp.   She married Ralph Taylor who was president of a firm of chemists and perfumers.   Other juvenile titles include: All-Of-A-Kind Family Uptown, Follett, 1958; Mr. Barney's Beard, Follett, 1961.   CA-5/6, MJA

TEALE, Edwin Way 1899-
Author, naturalist, photographer, born in Joliet, Illinois.   He attended Earlham College in Richmond, Indiana, the University of Illinois, and Columbia University.   Mr. Teale has been a teacher, lecturer, editorial assistant, and free-lance writer.   He has been on the staff of the Popular Science Monthly, New York Herald Tribune, and Audubon magazine.   The author received the John Burroughs Medal in 1943, and was once president of the New York Entomological Society. His books have been printed in Braille and in many languages.   His juvenile titles include: Bees, Childrens, 1967; Junior Book Of Insects . . ., Dutton, 1953.   CA-2

TEMKIN, Sara Anne Schlossberg 1913-
Librarian, author.   She has been Assistant Director of

the Cranford Public Library in New Jersey. Her husband was librarian of the McManus Junior High School in Linden, New Jersey. Sara Temkin has served in the WACs and later worked in the Army Medical Library in Washington, D. C. She collaborated with Lucy A. Hovell to write Jinny Williams, Library Assistant, Messner, 1962. CA-3

TEMPEST, Teresa see KENT, Louise (Andrews)

TENNYSON, Alfred Tennyson, 1st baron 1809-1892
English poet, born at Somersby, England. Alfred Lord Tennyson attended Trinity College, Cambridge. When he was eighteen, his first book of poetry was published. In 1850 he was made poet laureate by Queen Victoria to succeed William Wordsworth. When he died in 1892, he was buried in Poet's Corner in Westminster Abbey. His books for children include: Alfred Lord Tennyson's The Charge Of The Light Brigade (illus. by Alice and Martin Provensen), Golden, 1964; Poems Of Alfred Lord Tennyson (selected by Ruth Greiner Rausen), Crowell, 1964.

TENSEN, Ruth Marjorie
Teacher and writer, born in Rochester, New York. She received both her B. S. and M. A. degrees from Columbia University. She also studied at the Eastman School of Music. Her home has been in Rochester where she has taught primary grades in the public schools. Ruth Tensen has also been an exchange teacher in Hawaii. She has enjoyed music, travel, and hiking as special interests. For boys and girls she wrote: Come To See The Clowns, Reilly & Lee, 1963; Come To The City, Reilly & Lee, 1951; Come To The Farm, Reilly & Lee, 1949; Come To The Pet Shop, Reilly & Lee, 1954; Come To The Zoo!, Reilly & Lee, 1948. CA-7/8

TERHUNE, Albert Payson 1872-1942
Born in Newark, New Jersey, his father was a clergyman, and his mother was a writer. He received part of his schooling abroad and graduated from Columbia University. Prior to living in New Jersey ("Sunnybank") where he devoted his time to writing, the author spent some time in Egypt and Syria and also worked on a newspaper. Juvenile titles include: Buff: A Collie And Other Dog Stories, Grosset, 1921; Collie

To The Rescue, Grosset, 1928; Dog Of The High Si-
erras, Grosset, 1924; The Heart Of A Dog, Doran,
1924; His Dog, Dutton, 1922; Lad: A Dog, Dutton,
1926.   JBA-1

TERRELL, John Upton
Newspaperman and author.   He has also worked in
public relations.   Mr. Terrell has lived abroad and in
many cities in America including a period of fourteen
years which was spent in Washington.   Later Mr. and
Mrs. Terrell lived in California.   Juvenile titles include: The United States Department Of The Interior,
Duell, 1963; The United States Department Of Labor,
Meredith, 1968.

TERRY, Walter
Author, lecturer, dance critic, born in Brooklyn.   He
graduated from the University of North Carolina and
was in the Air Force during World War II.   Walter
Terry has lived in New Canaan, Connecticut.   Mr.
Terry has been a member of the dance panel for the
President's Special International Program for Cultural
Presentations.   At one time Mr. Terry was dance edi-
tor of the Encyclopaedia Britannica and has been editor
and dance critic of the New York Herald Tribune.   For
young people he wrote On Pointe! The Story Of Dancing
And Dancers On Toe, Dodd, 1962.

THAMES, C. H. see LESSER, Milton

THARP, Louise Hall 1898-
The daughter of a minister, she was born in Oneonta,
New York.   She attended the School of Fine Arts,
Crafts and Decorative Design in Boston.   She married
Carey E. Tharp, and they have lived in Darien, Con-
necticut.   Mrs. Tharp has been very active in the
Girl Scouts, and at one time was on the National
Brownie Committee.   Her books for young people in-
clude: Louis Agassiz, Adventurous Scientist, Little,
1961; Sixpence For Luck, Crowell, 1941.   CA-4, MJA

THAYER, Ernest Lawrence 1863-1940
Author and newspaperman, born in Worcester, Massa-
chusetts.   He attended Harvard and worked on the
Lampoon (student humor magazine) as editor-in-chief.
Ernest Thayer left school and joined former classmate
William Randolph Hearst in order to work on the San

Francisco Examiner (which in 1888 was the first to
print Thayer's famous poem "Casey At The Bat").
He later left the newspaper field and operated his
father's textile business but continued to write. The
author died at the age of seventy-seven in Santa Barbara, California. Numerous baseball players claimed
to be the real "Casey" Ernest Lawrence ("Phinney"--
his nickname) Thayer's famous poem, but he always
maintained that he had no special player in mind when
he wrote Casey At The Bat (illustrated by Paul Frame),
Prentice, 1964.

THAYER, Jane   see   WOOLLEY, Catherine

THEISS, Lewis Edwin
Athlete, author, teacher, horticulturist. He has worked with the Red Cross and was the recipient of the
Silver Beaver award for his outstanding service with
the Boy Scouts. Prior to his association with Bucknell
University as Professor of Journalism, Mr. Theiss
was a reporter on the New York Sun. Aviation has
also been one of his interests. For young people he
wrote Young Wireless Operator With The U. S. Secret
Service, Wilde, 1923.

THOMAS, Benjamin Platt   1902-1956
This author was born on Washington's birthday, and he
devoted a great part of his life to the study of Abraham
Lincoln. He was born in Pemberton, New Jersey and
graduated from Johns Hopkins University. At one time
he taught history at Birmingham-Southern College in
Alabama. He later served as executive secretary of
the Abraham Lincoln Association in Springfield, Illinois.
For boys and girls he wrote Abraham Lincoln, Knopf,
1952.

THOMAS, H. C.   see   KEATING, Lawrence Alfred

THOMAS, Lowell Jackson   1892-
Author, news commentator, world traveler. He was
born in Woodington, Ohio and has resided in Pawling,
New York. He has received degrees from the Chicago
Kent College of Law, Princeton, and the Universities
of Denver and Northern Indiana. Lowell Thomas has
been a teacher, explorer, editor, and radio reporter.
He also played an important part in developing "Ciner-
ama." For young people he wrote The Hero Of

Vincennes, Houghton, 1929.   JBA-1

THOMAS, Lowell Jackson Jr.   1923-
Author, lecturer, pilot, born in London. His job as
assistant cameraman on a South American naval voyage
at the age of fifteen was followed by similar expeditions to Canada and Alaska. He interrupted his studies
at Dartmouth to become an Air Force pilot in World
War II. Lowell Thomas, Jr., his wife, and children
have lived in Anchorage, Alaska. He organized the
Tibetan expedition for Lowell Thomas, Sr., in 1949,
and since 1957 he has written and produced the "High
Adventure" television series for his father. He wrote
The Dalai Lama, Duell, 1961.

THOMAS, Ruth
Author and columnist, she has lived near Little Rock,
Arkansas with her husband. For a number of years
Mrs. Thomas wrote a weekly column for the Arkansas
Gazette entitled "The Country Diarist." She wrote a
story about a bird which was published in the Audubon
Magazine and the Reader's Digest, and it later was
published in book form. Mrs. Thomas once bought a
brush goat which provided her with ideas for Brush
Goat, Milk Goat, Sterling, 1957.

THOMPSON, Eileen 1920-
A Nebraskan, she attended Miami University in Oxford,
Ohio and the Famous Writers School in Westport, Connecticut. She married a chemist, and they have lived
in Los Alamos, New Mexico. In 1962 she won the
short story first prize award given by the American
Association of University Women. Her books for
young people include: The Apache Gold Mystery, Abelard, 1965; Dog Show Mystery, Abelard, 1966.   CA-
5/6

THOMPSON, George Selden 1929-
He writes books under the name of George Selden. He
moved to New York City from Connecticut and has
lived in Greenwich Village. George Selden graduated
from Yale University and studied a year in Rome on a
Fulbright grant. He studied English and classical literature at Yale and has also been interested in archaeology. Juvenile titles include: The Cricket In Times
Square, Ariel, 1960; Sir Arthur Evans, Discoverer Of
Knossos, Macmillan, 1964; Tucker's Countryside,

Farrar, 1969.   CA-5/6

THOMPSON, Harlan H.   1894-
His pseudonym is Stephen Holt. He was born in Brewster, Kansas but grew up in Nebraska and Canada. Harlan Thompson developed a deep love and understanding of horses on his father's ranch in Alberta. He received his education at the University of Southern California in Los Angeles and later made his home in San Marino. In 1948 he was awarded the Boys' Club of America Gold Medal for Prairie Colt, Longmans, 1947. Other juvenile books include: Outcast, Stallion Of Hawaii, Doubleday, 1957; Spook, The Mustang, Doubleday, 1956; Whistling Stallion, Longmans, 1951. CA-9/10

THOMPSON, Hildegard (Steerstedter) 1901-
Born in De Pauw, Indiana, teacher, author. Hildegard Thompson was associated for many years with the U. S. Bureau of Indian Affairs. She was in charge of the government's Indian schools and also wrote primers which were read in these schools. At one time she taught school in Indiana and later in the Philippines where she also wrote textbooks for use in the schools. Her book for young people was Getting To Know American Indians Today, Coward, 1965.   CA-19/20

THOMPSON, Mary (Wolfe) 1886-
Born in Winsted, Connecticut, the daughter of author Theodore F. Wolfe. A graduate of the New York School of Fine and Applied Arts and the New Jersey State Normal School, she also attended Columbia University. The author married Charles D. Thompson and has lived in Arlington, Vermont. Mrs. Thompson has contributed short stories to magazines and has written vocational fiction for boys and girls. Her juvenile books include: Pattern For Penelope, Longmans, 1943; Snow Slopes (A Junior Literary Guild selection), Longmans, 1957.

THOMPSON, Vivian Laubach 1911-
Teacher and author, she graduated from Columbia University. She has taught in the New Jersey schools and in New York and California. Her interest in books for "beginners" was a result of teaching English and remedial reading. Her work has been published in many magazines including Child Life and Jack And Jill. Mrs.

Thompson has lived on a sugar plantation in Hawaii.
For children she wrote: Hawaiian Legends Of Trick-
sters And Riddlers, Holiday, 1969; The Horse That
Liked Sandwiches, Putnam, 1962.   CA-1

THOMSON, Peter 1913-
Photographer and author, born in the Philippine Islands.
Peter Thomson has loved the mountains since he was
a young man, and his father served as superintendent
of Yosemite.   He attended the University of California.
During World War II, he was a commander of an anti-
aircraft battery in Europe.   The author married Ellen
Schneider, and they have lived in San Francisco.   For
young readers he wrote: Cougar, Follett, 1968; Wonders Of Our National Parks, Dodd, 1961.   CA-7/8

THROCKMORTON, Peter
He has been a photographer and an underseas diver.
Peter Throckmorton has lived on the Greek island of
Kolymnos where he has worked with the sponge divers.
His background and experience enabled him to write
Spiro Of The Sponge Fleet (with Henry Chapin), Little,
1964.   CA-19/20

THRONEBURG, James
Teacher, author, born in North Carolina.   He grad-
uated from Duke University and continued his studies
at Columbia and the University of Florence.   He has
served as Science Coordinator for the Episcopal
Schools in the state of New York and has taught at St.
Luke's School in New York City.   James Throneburg
has been the author of several chapters in the "Heath
Elementary Science" series and has lived in New York
City.   He wrote Man On The Moon: Our Future In
Space, Knopf, 1961.   CA-5/6

THURBER, James 1894-1961
Author, illustrator, newspaperman.   He was born in
Columbus, Ohio and attended Ohio State University.
He began his newspaper career as a reporter with the
Columbus Dispatch in 1920.   He later worked in Paris
for the Chicago Tribune and has also been on the staff
of the New York Evening Post.   In 1926 he became
managing editor of the New Yorker magazine.   In later
years James Thurber lost his vision and had to give
up illustrating books.   Louis Slobodkin was awarded
the 1944 Caldecott Medal for Thurber's first children's

book Many Moons, Harcourt, 1943. Other juvenile titles include: Great Quillow, Harcourt, 1944; . . . The
White Deer, Harcourt, 1945. MJA

TITUS, Eve
Author and musician, born in New York City. A professional concert-pianist, Eve Titus has received piano
scholarships and honors in the National Music Week
competitions. She started the Storybook Writing Semi-
nar which has been conducted each summer. Mrs.
Titus has had both poems and stories published in
newspapers. She has lived in Miami Beach, Florida.
Her juvenile books include: Anatole, McGraw, 1956;
Anatole And The Thirty Thieves, McGraw, 1969.

TODARO, John
He has studied art at the Brooklyn Museum Art School,
New York City Community College, and the Art Students
League in New York. Mr. Todaro has traveled in Eur-
ope and at one time lived in Paris. He has been an
art director for an advertising agency and has lived in
Brooklyn, New York. With Barbara Ellen he wrote
Philip The Flower-Eating Phoenix, Abelard, 1961.

TODD, Anne Ophelia see DOWDEN, Anne Ophelia

TODD, Mary Fidelis
Born in Detroit, Michigan, she graduated from Stanford
University. She worked in her father's advertising
agency in Hollywood following the completion of her
college studies. She has lived in San Fernando Valley.
Her art work has been displayed in California schools,
libraries, and galleries. For young people she retold
and illustrated Juggler Of Notre Dame, McGraw, 1954.

TODD, Ruthven 1914-
Born in Scotland, his father was an architect. He
studied at the Edinburgh College of Art. Prior to coming to the United States, Mr. Todd lived in London
where he worked as a copywriter and teacher. In
1959 he became an American citizen and has lived in
Martha's Vineyard, Massachusetts. His books for
children include: Space Cat And The Kittens, Scribner,
1958; Space Cat Meets Mars, Scribner, 1957; Space
Cat Visits Venus, Scribner, 1955. MJA

TOLKIEN, John R. R. 1892-
John Ronald Reuel Tolkien was born in Bloemfontein,
South Africa and grew up in England. He graduated
from Oxford University and later taught there. His
teaching career began at the University of Leeds. In
1945 he became Merton Professor of English Language
and Literature and Fellow of Merton College. He
married Edith Bratt and wrote The Hobbit, Allen &
Unwin, 1937 for his children. He also wrote Farmer
Giles Of Ham, Houghton, 1950.   CA-17/18, MJA

TOLSTOY, Serge
Countess and writer, born in France. She studied at
the Sorbonne in Paris and at private schools in Eng-
land. She married a diplomat and has lived both in
France and New York. Countess Tolstoy's work has
appeared in the Social Spectator, and her stories for
children have been published in Canada and France.
For boys and girls she wrote: The Gold Fairy Book,
Random, 1962; Russian Stories & Legends (Reissue),
Pantheon, 1967.

TOMPKINS, Jane 1898-
She grew up in Westchester County, New York. She
married Burt M. McConnell who was a member of
Stefansson's last Arctic expedition. The McConnells
have owned an old house in Nantucket where they used
to spend their summers. For many years she prepared scripts for Kate Smith's radio program. Her
books for young people include: Beaver Twins, Stokes,
1940; Black Bear Twins, Lippincott, 1952; Cornelia,
Crowell, 1959; Moo-Wee, The Musk-Ox, Stokes, 1938.

TOMPKINS, Walker Allison 1909-
Newspaper reporter and author, born in Prosser,
Washington. He later made his home in Santa Barbara,
California. The author attended Modesto Junior College
and the Universities of Washington and Columbia. He
also studied in England and Egypt. Mr. Tompkins has
operated a ham radio station as a special interest.
His other hobbies have included golf and photography.
In addition to children's books, he has written many
western adult novels. Juvenile titles include: DX
Brings Danger, Macrae Smith, 1962; SOS At Midnight
(A Junior Literary Guild selection), Macrae Smith,
1957.   CA-7/8

TOOZE, Ruth (Anderson) 1892-
Born in Chicago, Illinois, she graduated from Oberlin
College and did graduate work at Columbia and Stanford
Universities. She has traveled and told stories through-
out the United States with her Children's Book Caravan.
Mrs. Tooze has also traveled to Cambodia as a mem-
ber of the education division of the State Department.
Her home has been in Evanston, Illinois. Juvenile
titles include: America, Viking, 1956; Cambodia:
Land Of Contrasts, Viking 1962; Nikkos And The Pink
Pelican, Viking, 1964; Silver From The Sea, Viking,
1962; Three Tales Of Turtle, Day, 1968; Your Children
Want To Read: A Guide For Teachers And Parents,
Prentice-Hall, 1957. CA-5/6

TOR, Regina
Author and poet, graduate of Skidmore College in Sara-
toga Springs, New York. She studied art at New
York's Art Students League and the University of Mexi-
co. The author also attended the New School for Social
Research in New York. She and her family have lived
in Dutchess County, New York where she has been
associated with the Community Children's Theatre.
Regina Tor has contributed poetry and stories to magazines. Her juvenile books include: Getting To Know
Canada, Coward-McCann, 1957; Getting To Know
Greece, Coward-McCann, 1959; Getting To Know Korea,
Coward-McCann, 1953; Getting To Know The Philippines, Coward-McCann, 1958. With Eleanor Roosevelt
she also wrote Growing Toward Peace, Random, 1960.

TOTTLE, John
Teacher, editor, author. He has been an editor of the
weekly magazine Young Citizens published by the Civic
Education Service of Washington, D. C. Mr. Tottle
has been a Lieutenant Colonel in the U. S. Army Re-
serves. He has also belonged to the National Press
Club. For young people he wrote Benjamin Franklin:
First Great American, Houghton, 1958.

TOUSEY, Sanford
Author-illustrator, born in Clay Center, Kansas. He
later made his home in New York City. He attended
high school in Anderson, Indiana and studied art in
Chicago. He grew up in the West on a ranch near a
Indian reservation which later provided authentic background for many of his stories. His drawings have

appeared in magazines, and he has illustrated stories
for other writers in addition to his own books. These
include: Bill And The Circus, Whitman, 1947; Bill
Clark, American Explorer, Whitman, 1951; Cowboys
Of America, Rand, 1937; Davy Crockett, Whitman,
1948; Horseman Hal, Doubleday, 1950; Pete And The
Old Ford, Ariel Books, 1954; Tinker Tim, Doubleday,
1946.   JBA-2

TRACHSEL, Myrtle Jamison
Born in Gower, Missouri, she studied at Hardin and
Oberlin Colleges. She has been interested in nature
and history and has often traveled to various parts of
the United States in order to visit gardens. Her
career in writing began when she sent a story about
nature to a farm magazine, and it was accepted. She
and her husband Louis Trachsel have lived in St.
Joseph, Missouri. For young people she wrote Elizabeth Of The Mayflower, Macmillan, 1950.

TRANTER, Nigel 1909-
He spent his boyhood near the famous Edinburgh castle
in Scotland and acquired a lasting interest in ancient
castles and Scottish history. During World War II,
the author served in the Army. He has been recognized as one of Scotland's outstanding writers. His
interest in mountains and climbing enabled him to
write the adventure story for boys and girls entitled
Smoke Across The Highlands, Platt, 1964.   CA-11/12

TRAVERS, Pamela L. 1906-
Author and poet, born in Queensland, Australia. Her
writing career began in England where she contributed
articles to the Irish Statesman and other British magazines, and it was in England where she wrote Mary
Poppins (Reynal & Hitchcock, 1934). This book has
been translated into several languages including Czech
and Swedish, and a Mary Poppins suite for orchestra
has been composed. The author has enjoyed gardening
as a special interest. She made her home in New
York during World War II. Her juvenile books include:
The Fox At The Manger, Norton, 1962; I Go By Sea,
I Go By Land, Norton, 1964; Mary Poppins Comes
Back, Reynal, 1935; Mary Poppins From A To Z, Harcourt, 1962; Mary Poppins In The Park, Harcourt,
1952.   JBA-2

TREASE, (Robert) Geoffrey 1909-
He was born in Nottingham, England and studied at
Oxford University.   Prior to devoting all of his time
to writing for young people, Mr. Trease was a journalist in London.   During World War II, he served in
the infantry and in the Army Educational Corps when
he was stationed in India.   He and his wife, the former
Marian Boyer, have lived in Worcestershire, England.
His books for young people include: Bent Is The Bow,
Nelson, 1967; Escape To King Alfred, Vanguard, 1958;
The Gates Of Bannerdale, Heinemann, 1956; . . . Mes-
sage To Hadrian, Vanguard, 1956; No Boats On Ban-
nermere, Norton, 1965; White Nights Of St. Petersburg, Vanguard, 1967; Young Traveler In India And
Pakistan, Dutton, 1956.   CA-7/8, MJA

TREAT, Roger L.
Sports columnist and author.   Roger Treat has been a
sportswriter for the Chicago Herald American and a
contributor to American Weekly.   His articles and
stories have also appeared in such magazines as
Coronet, Esquire, and Negro Digest.   In 1945 as a
member of a team of five writers selected by the Army he toured the African, European, and Mediterranean theatres in order to study service sport programs.
For young readers he wrote Walter Johnson, Messner,
1948.

TREECE, Henry 1911-1966
Born in Wednesbury, Staffordshire, England, he grad-
uated from Birmingham University and also received
his diploma from the University of Santander.   During
World War II, he served in the Army and in Air Force
Intelligence.   He has been a schoolmaster, magazine
editor, and poet.   Prior to his death in June 1966,
Henry Treece and his family lived in Barton-on-Hum-
ber, Lincolnshire, England.   Juvenile titles include:
Castles And Kings, Criterion, 1960; The Centurion,
Meredith Press, 1967; The Golden One, Criterion,
1962; Swords From The North, Pantheon, 1967; The
Windswept City (A Junior Literary Guild selection),
Meredith, 1968.   CA-1, MJA

TREGASKIS, Richard William 1916-
Newspaperman and author, born in Elizabeth, New Jersey.   He graduated cum laude from Harvard University.   His home has been in Honolulu, Hawaii.   Mr.

Tregaskis served as a war correspondent during World War II for the International News Service. He later traveled abroad on assignments for magazines. The author has also been a screen writer. His war and travel experiences have provided authentic material for his books. These include: Guadalcanal Diary, Random, 1955; John F. Kennedy And PT-109, Random, 1962. CA-3

TREICHLER, Jessie
Author, secretary, graduate of Montana State University at Bozeman. Prior to serving as secretary and assistant to the president at Antioch College in Yellow Springs, Ohio, Mrs. Treichler worked in the same capacity at both Montana State Normal College and Montana State University. She has also served as Director of Public Relations at Antioch College where her husband Paul Treichler has been director of the Antioch Area Theatre. Her articles and stories have appeared in magazines and college publications. For young people she wrote Educating For Democracy: Horace Mann, Encyclopaedia Britannica, 1962.

TRENT, Robbie 1894-
She was born in Wolf Creek, Kentucky and studied at the George Peabody College for Teachers and the Universities of Louisville and Wisconsin. Active in the field of religious education, she served for many years as Elementary Editor for the Sunday School Board, Southern Baptist Convention. Her home has been in Nashville, Tennessee. Juvenile titles include: Cubby's World, Story Of A Baby Bear, Abingdon, 1966; In The Beginning, Westminster Press, 1949; Jesus' First Trip, Broadman Press, 1961; To Church We Go, Follett, 1956; What Is God Like?, Harper, 1953. CA-9/10

TRESSELT, Alvin R. 1916-
Editor, author. Prior to becoming juvenile book editor of Parents' Magazine Press, Mr. Tresselt was Managing Editor of Humpty Dumpty magazine. He has also served as chairman of the Juvenile Writers Committee of the Authors Guild. He married author Blossom Budney and has lived in Redding, Connecticut. In 1948 his book White Snow, Bright Snow, Lothrop, 1947 illustrated by Roger Duvoisin received the Caldecott Medal. His other titles include: Autumn Harvest, Lothrop, 1951; A Day With Daddy, Lothrop, 1953; Hide And Seek

TREVINO, Elizabeth (Borton) de   515

Fog, Lothrop, 1965; A Thousand Lights And Fireflies,
Parents Mag. Press, 1965; The World In The Candy
Egg, Lothrop, 1967.

TREVIÑO, Elizabeth (Borton) de 1904-
She was born in Bakersfield, California and graduated
from Stanford University. She was once a member of
the staff of the Boston Herald. The author married
Luis Treviño and has lived in Cuernavaca, Mexico.
In 1966 she won the Newbery Medal for her book I,
Juan De Pareja, Bell Bks., 1965. She also wrote
Casilda Of The Rising Moon, Farrar, 1967.   CA-17/
18

TRIMBLE, Joe
Sportswriter and author, born in Brooklyn, New York.
He received his B. A. degree from St. John's College.
The author served in the Navy during World War II.
He began his newspaper career with the New York
Daily News and has been a city news reporter and
sportswriter. Joe Trimble was the official scorer of
the 1950 World Series (Yankees-Phillies) and has
served as Vice-President of the Baseball Writers As-
sociation of New York. His juvenile books include:
Phil Rizzuto, Barnes, 1951; Yogi Berra, Barnes, 1952.

TROTTER, Grace Violet
Her pseudonym is Nancy Paschal. She was born in
Dallas, Texas and attended school there. Her first
book for boys and girls ran as a serial in American
Girl magazine. Her interests have included nature
study and animals (particularly dogs). Juvenile titles
include: Emeralds On Her Hand, Ariel, 1965; Hillview
House, Westminster Press, 1963; Make Way For Laur-
en, Westminster Press, 1963; Name The Day, Westminster Press, 1959; No More Good-Bys, Westminster
Press, 1962; Song Of The Heart, Westminster Press,
1961.   CA-1

TUCKER, Caroline see NOLAN, Jeannette (Covert)

TUCKER, Ernest Edward
Native of Chicago, he attended the University of Illinois
at Champaign. He achieved the rank of Commander in
the U. S. Naval Reserve following service during the
war. Mr. Tucker has traveled in Europe, the Far
East, and Latin America as a newspaperman. He later

became city editor of the Chicago American. His
books for young people include: Soldiers And Armies:
Men At War Through The Ages, Lothrop, 1965; The
Story Of Knights And Armor, Lothrop, 1961.

TUDOR, Bethany
Artist-author, the daughter of writer and illustrator
Tasha Tudor. She grew up on a farm in New Hampshire surrounded by a sister, two brothers, and plenty
of animals (models for her drawings). Bethany Tudor
studied art with her mother and in Boston where she
later made her home. Books which she has written
and illustrated for children include: Gooseberry Lane,
Lippincott, 1963; Skiddycock Pond, Lippincott, 1965.

TUDOR, Tasha 1915-
She was born in Boston, Massachusetts, the daughter
of portrait painter Rosamond Tudor and W. Starling
Burgess, a yacht designer. She grew up on a farm
in Connecticut and studied at the Museum of Fine Arts
in Boston. Miss Tudor married Thomas L. McCready,
Jr., and has lived on a farm in Webster, New Hampshire. Her first book Pumpkin Moonshine (Walck,
1938) was written as a Christmas present for her husband's niece. Her other books include: A Is For
Annabelle, Oxford, 1954; Alexander The Gander, Oxford, 1939; Around The Year, Oxford, 1957; Becky's
Birthday, Viking, 1960; First Delights, Platt, 1966;
More Prayers, Walck, 1967. She also illustrated her
husband's book Increase Rabbit (A Junior Literary
Guild selection), Ariel, 1958.   JBA-2

TUFTS, Anne
Teacher and writer, born in Massachusetts near Boston.
She attended Radcliffe College in Cambridge and Columbia University in New York. She has made her home
in both New York and New Hampshire. Anne Tufts has
been a high school teacher in addition to writing books
for young people which include As The Wheel Turns,
Junior Literary Guild and Holt, 1952.

TUFTS, Georgia
She has lived in Oberlin, Ohio. When she was in high
school, she wrote and illustrated a story about Catrina's
cats, but she had been interested in such a project
since she was in the third grade. Her finished product
became the picture book Catrina And The Cats, Lothrop,

1959.

TUNIS, Edwin Burdett 1897-
Author-artist. He was born in Cold Spring Harbor,
New York and has lived near Shawan, Maryland. He
attended Baltimore City College and the Maryland Institute of Art and Design. His mural "The History Of
Spices" took two and a half years to complete and was
one hundred and forty-five feet long. Many galleries
have exhibited his works including the National Academy
of Design and the Society of American Etchers. Magazines have published his articles. He was the recipient
of the Thomas Alva Edison Foundation Children's Book
Award in 1958 for Colonial Living, World, 1957. CA-
7/8, MJA

TUNIS, John Robert 1889-
Sports announcer and writer, born in Boston, Massachusetts. He attended Harvard University and has
lived in Connecticut and Florida. A sportswriter for
the New York Evening Post, his articles and stories
have also appeared in various magazines. John Tunis
has announced many sports events including the first
broadcast via short wave in 1932 from Europe (the
Challenge Round of the Davis Cup in Paris). His radio
coverage of major sports events combined with personal
experiences as a champion tennis player later provided
an authentic background for many of his books. These
include: All-American, Harcourt, 1942; Buddy And
The Old Pro, Morrow, 1955; Champion's Choice, Harcourt, 1940; City For Lincoln, Harcourt, 1945; High-
pockets, Morrow, 1948; His Enemy, His Friend, Morrow, 1967; Young Razzle, Morrow, 1949. MJA

TURNBULL, Agnes Sligh 1888-
She was born in New Alexandria, Pennsylvania and
studied at Indiana State College, Indiana, Pennsylvania
and at the University of Chicago. Prior to her marriage to James L. Turnbull, she was a high school
English teacher. Mrs. Turnbull received an honorary
degree from Westminster College. Her home has
been in Maplewood, New Jersey. Juvenile titles include: George, Houghton, 1965; Jed, The Shepherd's
Dog, Houghton, 1957; The White Lark, Houghton, 1968.
CA-3

TURNER, Eloise Fain 1906-
Teacher and writer. She has been an elementary
school teacher in Clarksdale, Arizona, and she has
also done secretarial work. After the death of her
husband, Mrs. Turner completed her college education
and attended graduate school. She collaborated with
Carroll Lane Fenton to write Inside You And Me, Day,
1961. CA-5/6

TURNGREN, Annette 1902-
Her pseudonym is A. T. Hopkins. Born in Montrose,
Minnesota, she graduated from the University of Minnesota in Minneapolis, and later made her home in
New York. A former teacher and magazine editor,
the author has also been on the staff of the New York
Times. Her sister Ellen Turngren has also been an
author of children's books. Annette Turngren used
her mother's Swedish childhood memories in order to
write her first book Flaxen Braids (Nelson, 1937) and
traveled to Sweden to obtain material for The Copper
Kettle, Prentice, 1961. Other juvenile titles include:
Mystery Haunts The Fair, Funk, 1959; The Mystery
Of The Water Witch, Random, 1964; Mystery Walks
The Campus, Funk, 1956. CA-11/12, MJA

TURNGREN, Ellen
The daughter of Swedish immigrants, she was born in
Montrose, Minnesota. She grew up on a farm and
later taught school. She also served briefly as an
editor of a country newspaper. Her sister was author
Annette Turngren. She has lived near Minneapolis.
Ellen Turngren has been a member of the National
League of American Pen Women and the Minneapolis
Writers' Workshop. Her books include: Listen, My
Heart, Longmans, 1956; Shadows Into Mist, Longmans,
1958. CA-7/8

TUSIANI, Joseph 1924-
Poet, translator, born in Italy. He received a summa
cum laude doctorate from the University of Naples.
In 1956 he became an American citizen. Joseph Tusiani has been a director of the Catholic Poetry Society
of America and a vice-president of the Poetry Society
of America. He has been a member of the faculty at
the College of Mount Saint Vincent in New York. He
has published several books of poetry, has completed
several translations (poems of Machiavelli and

Michelangelo), and was the recipient of the Greenwood
Prize by the Poetry Society of England. His book was
Dante's Inferno (as told for young people by Joseph
Tusiani), Obolensky, 1965. CA-9/10

TUTT, Kay Cunningham
The idea for her book for boys and girls originated
when she was in college. Later she taught school and
continued to work on her story. She once said that
her teaching experience and getting to know children
helped tremendously in her composition of both story
and illustrations. Kay Tutt has lived in Dallas, Texas.
She wrote And Now We Call Him Santa Claus, Lothrop,
1963.

TWAIN, Mark   see   CLEMENS, Samuel Langhorne

U

UCHIDA, Yoshiko 1921-
Author-illustrator, born in Alameda, California, she
later lived in Oakland. After graduating cum laude
from the University of California, she received her
master's degree in education from Smith College at
Northampton, Massachusetts. In addition to writing
and illustrating books and magazine articles, Miss
Uchida has taught school. Her special interests have
included folk craft, and in Japan she became acquainted
with many leaders of the Folk Art Movement. Miss
Uchida's visits to Japan have provided authentic material for her books. She was the winner of the 1955
New York Herald Tribune Spring Book Festival award
for Magic Listening Cap, Harcourt, 1955. She also
wrote: The Forever Christmas Tree, Scribner, 1963;
Full Circle, Friendship Press, 1957; In-Between Miva,
Scribner, 1967; Mik And The Prowler, Harcourt, 1960;
Sumi's Prize, Scribner, 1964. CA-13/14, MJA

UDRY, Janice (May) 1928-
Born in Jacksonville, Illinois, she graduated from
Northwestern University. Following graduation, she
worked in a nursery school in Chicago. She and her
husband have lived in Garden Grove and San Luis Obis-
po, California and later made their home in Chapel
Hill, North Carolina. Her book A Tree Is Nice (Harper, 1956) illustrated by Marc Simont was awarded the
Caldecott Medal in 1957 and The Moon Jumpers (Harper,

1959) illustrated by Maurice Sendak was a runner-up
for the medal in 1960. Her other titles include: Alfred, Whitman, 1960; Danny's Pig (A Junior Literary
Guild selection), Lothrop, 1960; If You're A Bear,
Whitman, 1967. CA-5/6

ULLMAN, James Ramsey 1907-
He was born in New York City and later made his home
in Boston, Massachusetts. Prior to graduating from
Princeton University, he studied at Phillips Academy
in Andover, Massachusetts. In addition to a writing
career, Mr. Ullman has been a theatrical producer and
newspaperman. His stories have appeared in many
magazines including Life and Sports Illustrated. He
served with the British 8th Army in Africa during
World War II. The author has been a member of the
Authors Guild of America, Overseas Press Club, and
P. E. N. He has enjoyed travel and mountaineering as
special interests. He has written for both adults and
children, and several of his books have been made into
motion pictures. His books for young people include:
Banner In The Sky, Lippincott, 1954; Down The Colorado With Major Powell, Houghton, 1960. CA-3

ULRICH, (John) Homer 1906-
Born in Chicago, his father was one of the first piano
teachers there, and for many years various members
of his family have played in the Chicago Symphony
Orchestra. He studied at the Chicago Musical College
and received his master's degree from the University
of Chicago. Prior to teaching music at the University
of Texas, he was in charge of the music department
of Monticello College. Interested in photography and
woodworking, Mr. Ulrich later made his home in Silver Spring, Maryland. His book for young people was
Famous Women Singers, Dodd, 1953. CA-7/8

UNDSET, Sigrid 1882-
Nobel Prize winner and novelist, born in Kallundborg,
Denmark. She grew up in Oslo, Norway where her
father was an archaeologist. After the German invasion of Norway in 1940, Sigrid Undset came to America
where she began her career as a juvenile writer. After five years she returned to a free Norway. She was
the recipient of the 1928 Nobel Prize. For children
she wrote: Happy Times In Norway, Knopf, 1942;
True And Untrue, And Other Norse Tales (ed. by

Sigrid Undset), Knopf, 1945.

UNGERER, Tomi 1931-
Caricaturist, painter, sculptor, born in Strasbourg,
Alsace, France. After leaving college, he hitchhiked
through northern Europe and later worked for an advertising agency in Denmark. In 1956 he came to the
United States. His work has appeared in magazines,
and his paintings have been exhibited in both Europe
and the United States. He and his family have lived
in New York City. He wrote and illustrated: Ask Me
A Question, Harper, 1968; Crictor, Harper, 1958;
Emile, Harper, 1960; Mellops Go Spelunking, Harper,
1963; Moon Man, Harper, 1967; Zeralda's Ogre, Harper, 1967.

UNNERSTAD, Edith (Totterman) 1900-
She was born in Helsinki, Finland and attended art
school and Detthow College in Stockholm, Sweden. She
married an engineer and has lived in Djursholm, Sweden. Her books for both adults and children have been
translated into several languages. The author has enjoyed writing stories for young readers and once said:
"Writing children's books is a responsibility, for any
book that comes into the hand of a child may form his
future attitude toward literature. " Her juvenile books
include: The Ditch Picnic, Norton, 1964; Journey To
England, Macmillan, 1961; Little O, Macmillan, 1957;
Pysen, Macmillan, 1955; Saucepan Journey, Macmillan,
1951; Two Little Gigglers, Norton, 1968. CA-5/6

UNTERECKER, John 1922-
Biographer, literary critic, poet, teacher. He spent
his childhood in Buffalo, New York and later lived in
Leonia, New Jersey. He has been Associate Professor
of Contemporary Literature in Columbia University's
Graduate School. The author also was the recipient
of a Guggenheim Fellowship. A boyhood friend, George
Weinheimer, illustrated his children's book The Dream-
ing Zoo, Walck, 1965. CA-17/18

UNTERMEYER, Louis 1885-
Anthologist, critic, poet, born in New York City. At
the age of fifteen, he left school and entered his family's
jewelry firm. Later he became a vice-president of
the company. In order to write full-time, Mr. Untermeyer resigned his position and went to Europe to

study. He has edited numerous collections of poetry
and has been a poetry consultant for the Library of
Congress. Collections which he has edited include:
Rainbow In The Sky, Harcourt, 1935; Time For Peace,
World, 1969. He also wrote One And One And One,
Crowell, 1962. CA-5/6

UNWIN, David Storr 1918-
His pseudonym is David Severn. He was born in London, the son of publisher Sir Stanley Unwin. He
studied at schools in England and Germany. Prior to
entering his father's publishing firm, he was a printer
and bookseller. The author's home has been in Suf-
folk, England. His interests have included: winter
sports and mountain climbing. For young people he
wrote Burglars And Bandicoots, Macmillan, 1952.

UNWIN, Nora Spicer 1907-
Artist and writer. She grew up in England and graduated from the Royal College of Art in London. She
began her career as an illustrator when she was
eighteen. The author came to America in 1946 and
has lived in Wellesley, Massachusetts and Peterborough,
New Hampshire. In addition to writing and illustrating
books, Nora Unwin has taught at Wellesley College and
in Peterborough, New Hampshire. Her travels to
Mexico resulted in Poquito (A Junior Literary Guild selection), McKay, 1959. Other juvenile titles include:
Joyful The Morning, McKay, 1963; Midsummer Witch,
McKay, 1966; Proud Pumpkin, Junior Literary Guild
and Aladdin, 1953; Two Too Many, McKay, 1962.
MJA

UPDIKE, John (Hoyer) 1932-
Born in Shillington, Pennsylvania, he graduated from
Harvard College and studied at the Ruskin School of
Drawing and Fine Art in England. He later made his
home in Ipswich, Massachusetts. He has written for
the New Yorker magazine, adult novels, and poetry in
addition to children's books. In 1964 John Updike received the National Book Award for Fiction. His books
for young people include: A Child's Calendar, Knopf,
1965; with Warren Chappell he adapted both The Magic
Flute, Knopf, 1962 and The Ring, Knopf, 1964. CA-4

UPINGTON, Marion
She was born in Oregon and has lived in Klamath Falls.

The author has enjoyed books, walking, and rock collecting. She began to write during an illness, and her verses have appeared in magazines for boys and girls. Her first book for young people was entitled The Beautiful Culpeppers, Watts, 1963.

UTTLEY, Alison
English author, born on a farm in Derbyshire. She received an honors degree in physics from Manchester University. The author has lived in the county of Buckinghamshire. Her interest in science and literature was a predominant factor in her decision to become a writer. For boys and girls she wrote A Traveler In Time, Viking, 1964.

V

VAL BAKER, Denys
The author and his wife have operated a pottery in Cornwall. In addition to making pottery, Mr. Val Baker has been a professional writer. His wife has been a teacher. For young people he wrote The Young Potter, Warne, 1963.

VALENS, Evans G. 1920-
Newspaperman, author, and poet, born in State College, Pennsylvania. After graduating from Amherst College in Massachusetts, he continued his studies at California and Utah Universities. He also studied at San Francisco State and Stanford University. His home has been in Mill Valley, California. In addition to his writing career, Evans Valens, Jr., has been a U. S. wire-service correspondent and a reporter for the Herald-Post in El Paso, Texas. He has also been a film and television writer and producer. For young people he wrote: Cybernaut, Viking, 1968; Long Way Up, Harper, 1966; Magnet, World, 1964; Motion, World, 1965; Wildfire, World, 1963. With Wendell M. Stanley he also wrote Viruses And Nature Of Life, Dutton, 1961. CA-5/6

VANCE, Marguerite (Schlund) 1889-1965
Author and editor, born in Chicago, Illinois. She attended private schools both here and abroad. She married William Little Vance and made her home in Cleveland, Ohio. After his death in 1931, she moved to New York City where she became a children's book

editor in a publishing house. She retired in 1955 and
continued writing books, especially biographies, until
her death in 1965 in Camden, Maine. Her juvenile titles include: Ashes Of Empire, Dutton, 1959; The Beloved Friend, Holt, 1963; Courage At Sea, Dutton,
1963; Dark Eminence, Dutton, 1961; Esther Wheelwright, Indian Captive, Dutton, 1964; . . . Hear The
Distant Applause!, Dutton, 1963; Jared's Gift, Dutton,
1965; On Wings Of Fire!, Dutton, 1955; A Rainbow For
Robin, Dutton, 1966; Six Queens, Dutton, 1965; A Star
For Hansi, Dutton, 1936.   MJA

VAN COEVERING, Jack 1900-
Born in Herwynen, Netherlands, he studied at Calvin
College and graduated from the University of Michigan.
He has been a reporter and wildlife editor in addition
to writing books. Mr. Van Coevering has lived in
Orchard Lake, Michigan. His book for young people
was A-Hiking We Will Go, Lippincott, 1941.   CA-9/10

VAN COEVERING, Jan Adrian see VAN COEVERING, Jack

VANDER BOOM, Mae M.
She was born in South Dakota where she later taught
school. She has also been a teacher in Nebraska.
When she moved to California, she lived near a grove
of orange trees which provided the inspiration for her
book Our American Orange, Didier, 1951.

VAN DER HAAS, Henrietta
She was born in The Hague (Netherlands). After her
marriage to missionary John Kusch, she lived in Para-
maribo in South America. She later came to the United
States and became an American citizen. Her short
stories have been published both in this country and
abroad. For boys and girls she wrote Orange On Top,
Harcourt, 1945.

VAN DER VELDT, James A. 1893-
Franciscan priest and author, born in Amsterdam, Holland. After his ordination to the priesthood in 1919,
he attended Belgium's Louvain University and became
one among a select few to receive the school's Agrégé
degree. He also studied in Italy and at Nimwegen University in Holland. Father Van Der Veldt was appointed to the faculty at Pontifical University of the Propa-
gation of the Faith in Rome by the Holy See in 1928.

He came to the United States in 1940 and was associated with St. Joseph's Seminary in Dunwoodie, Yonkers, New York. He has also been a lecturer and contributor to magazines. For young people he wrote The City Set On A Hill, Dodd, 1944.

VAN DYNE, Edith see BAUM, Lyman Frank

VAN HORN, Grace
Librarian, farmer, author. She has been a librarian in Castle Rock, Washington. Prior to becoming a librarian, she lived on a farm and once said: ". . . Farm animals are individuals to us, and every cow, pig, and chicken has a distinct personality of its own. Perhaps that is why I enjoy writing about them." Her book for boys and girls was Little Red Rooster, Abelard-Schuman, 1961.

VAN LOON, Hendrik Willem 1882-1944
Author-illustrator, born in Rotterdam, The Netherlands. He graduated from Cornell and studied at the University of Munich. He came to the United States in 1902, became an American citizen, and made his home in Connecticut. Hendrik Van Loon served as a news correspondent in the Russian Revolution of 1905 and in World War I. In addition to a writing career, he has been a lecturer and historian. He was the first Newbery Medal recipient in 1922 for his book The Story Of Mankind, Liveright, 1921. He also wrote and illustrated: Life And Times Of Simon Bolivar . . ., Dodd, 1943; Thomas Jefferson . . ., Dodd, 1943. JBA-1

VAN RENSSELAER, Alexander 1892-
Author, editor, advertising manager. For many years Alexander Van Rensselaer was associated with the College Book Departments of publishing firms. He has written for both adults and children and has contributed to such magazines as the Bookman and St. Nicholas. Mr. Van Rensselaer has also worked for the old New York Sun and New York Telegram. A lifetime ambition to be a professional magician resulted in the author's study of: palmistry, puppetry, mind reading, and ventriloquism. His juvenile books include: Fun With Ventriloquism, Garden City, 1955; The Picture History Of America, Doubleday, 1961.

VAN STOCKUM, Hilda 1908-
She was born in Rotterdam, Netherlands where she
later attended school. She also studied at art schools
in Dublin, Amsterdam, Montreal, and at the Corcoran
School of Art in Washington, D. C. She married Er-
vin Ross Marlin and has lived in New York, Washington, D. C., and Montreal, Canada. Authenticity in
her books has resulted from experiences and activities
of her own family of six children. She wrote and illustrated: Andries, Viking, 1942; Canadian Summer, Viking, 1948; Cottage At Bantry Bay, Viking, 1938; Fran-
cie On The Run, Viking, 1939; Friendly Gables, Viking, 1960; Little Old Bear, Viking, 1962. CA-11/12,
JBA-2

VEGLAHN, Nancy Crary 1937-
She was born in Sioux City, Iowa and graduated from
Morningside College in Sioux City. Her husband was
the minister of Beach Memorial Methodist Church, and
they have lived in Howard, South Dakota. Mrs. Veglahn has enjoyed: writing, reading, and golf. For
young people she wrote: Peter Cartwright, Scribners,
1968; . . . The Tiger's Tail, Harper, 1964. CA-19/
20

VENN, Mary Eleanor 1908-
Her pseudonym is Mary Adrian. Born in Sewickley,
Pennsylvania, she attended New York University. She
has been the contributor of a column on nature in the
Boston Post and has written nature books and mysteries
for boys and girls. She married Henry Jorgensen and
has lived in Oregon. Juvenile titles include: Light Ship
Mystery, Hastings, 1969; The Skin Diving Mystery,
Hastings, 1964. CA-2

VENTURO, Betty Lou Baker see BAKER, Betty

VERMES, Hal G.
During World War II, he was a public relations writer
for the War Department. He has also served as copy
chief in several advertising agencies. In addition to
his books for young people, he has also written mystery stories and both magazine and newspaper articles.
His wife Jean C. has also been an author (The Girl's
Book Of Physical Fitness, Association Press, 1961;
Hobbies For Girls, Association Press, 1965). He
wrote: The Boy's Book Of Physical Fitness, Associa-

tion Press, 1961; Hobbies For Boys, Association Press, 1965.

VERMES, Jean C.
She married Hal G. Vermes, and they wrote a book on bowling. Her books on etiquette and health have been read and enjoyed by many young people. Her books include: The Girl's Book Of Physical Fitness, Association Press, 1961; Hobbies For Girls, Association Press, 1965.

VERNE, Jules 1828-1905
He was born in Nantes, France and later lived in Amiens. Since his father and grandfather were lawyers, Jules Verne left for Paris in order to study law; however, he pursued a writing career. He combined scientific facts with fantasy in his books. Readers throughout the world have enjoyed his books which have been translated into many languages. They include: Dr. Ox's Experiment (illustrated by William Pène Du Bois), Macmillan, 1963; Twenty Thousand Leagues Under The Sea, Grosset, 1917. JBA-1, JBA-2

VERNEY, John
Artist and author, born in London, England. He has lived in Surrey where he has enjoyed farming and writing. His interests have also included the making of pottery and painting. Mr. Verney has had several one-man shows in London. For boys and girls he wrote and illustrated: Friday's Tunnel, Holt, 1966; Seven Sunflower Seeds, Holt, 1969.

VERRAL, Charles Spain
His pseudonym is George L. Eaton. Author-artist, born in Highfield, Ontario, Canada. His home has been in New York. He studied at the Ontario College of Art and Canada College. Mr. Verral has written for both radio and newspapers. He has also been an editor of Harper's Encyclopedia Of Science and Reader's Digest. The author has served on several Chamber of Commerce aviation boards and also helped to organize junior aviation clubs. His juvenile books include: Champion Of The Court, Crowell, 1954; Go! The Story Of Outer Space, Prentice-Hall, 1962; Jets, Prentice-Hall, 1962; Robert Goddard: Father Of The Space Age, Prentice-Hall, 1963; Wonderful World Series, Crowell, 1956. CA-9/10

VICKER, Angus see FELSEN, Henry Gregor

VIERECK, Phillip R. 1925-   Ellen (Kingsbury)
Following college, Dartmouth for him and Vassar for
her, the Vierecks traveled to Alaska and worked with
the Alaska Native Service of the U. S. Bureau of Indian
Affairs. Born in New Bedford, Massachusetts, Phillip
Viereck and his wife later lived in North Bennington,
Vermont where he taught in the Bennington Junior High
School, and Mrs. Viereck taught in the Bennington Col-
lege Nursery School. She also taught at the Pine Cob-
ble School in Williamstown, Massachusetts, and he la-
ter served as principal of the Molly Stark School in
Bennington. He wrote, and she illustrated: Eskimo
Island, Day, 1962; Independence Must Be Won, Day,
1964. He edited, and she illustrated The New Land,
Day, 1967.   CA-7/8

VIGUERS, Ruth (Hill) 1903-1971
Editor, author, librarian, born in Oakland, California.
She graduated from Willamette University at Salem,
Oregon and received her degree in library science
from the University of Washington. Ruth Hill Viguers
has taught library science in Wuchang, China and has
been a librarian in Paris, France and Madrid, Spain.
She has also served as editor of the Horn Book magazine. She contributed to: Critical History Of Children's Literature (by Cornelia Meigs [and others]),
Macmillan, 1953; Illustrators Of Children's Books,
1744-1945 (compiled by Bertha E. Mahony, Louise P.
Latimer [and] Beulah Folmsbee), Horn Book, 1947.
She wrote Margin For Surprise, Little, 1964.   CA-15/
16

VIKSTEN, Albert 1889-
Author, editor, lecturer, born in Sweden. He attended
the Norrland Folkschool and received an honorary degree from the University of Uppsala. In addition to
writing books, he has been a playwright and newspaper
editor. He has traveled throughout Europe and went to
Columbia to write about the wildlife of the Andes for
a Swedish magazine, Folklet In Bild. Mr. Viksten has
also lectured in the United States. For young people
he wrote Gunilla (tr. by Gustaf Lannestock), Nelson,
1957.

VILLIERS, Alan John 1903-
Born in Melbourne, Australia, he later made his home
in Oxford, England. He has been a photographer, newspaper reporter, and sailor. During World War II, he
was a commander in the Royal Navy and was awarded
the Distinguished Service Cross. In 1957 he was Captain of the new "Mayflower" which crossed the Atlantic
from England to America. Captain Villiers also sailed
the "Joseph Conrad" around the world. His books for
young people include: The New Mayflower, Scribner,
1958; Whalers Of The Midnight Sun, Scribner, 1934.
CA-4

VINING, Elizabeth Gray see GRAY, Elizabeth Janet

VINTON, Iris
Author and teacher, born in West Point, Mississippi.
She grew up in Corpus Christi, Texas, lived in San
Antonio, and later moved to New York. Her early
years spent around the Gulf of Mexico combined with
teaching experiences in a two-room Texas schoolhouse
provided the author with many adventure stories. Her
work has appeared in both magazines and newspapers.
For young people she wrote: Flying Ebony, Dodd, 1947;
Look Out For Pirates, Random, 1961; The Story Of
John Paul Jones, Grosset, 1953; The Story Of Robert
E. Lee, Grosset, 1952; We Were There With Jean Lafitte At New Orleans, Grosset, 1957.

VITTENGL, Morgan J. 1928-
Born in Wilmington, Delaware, he graduated from Mary-
knoll Seminary in New York. He later received a
master's degree from Columbia University Graduate
School of Journalism. He has been Assistant Editor on
Maryknoll magazine and editor of Asia magazine. He
has also taught at the Maryknoll Seminary College in
Glen Ellyn, Illinois and later lived in Clarks Summit,
Pennsylvania at the Maryknoll Junior Seminary. He
has been a member of the Overseas Press Club of New
York City and has been interested in reading about the
Civil War as a hobby. For young people Father Vit-
tengl wrote All Round Hong-Kong, Dodd, 1963. CA-7/8

VOIGHT, Virginia Frances 1909-
She was born in New Britain, Connecticut, grew up in
New Haven, and later lived in Hamden. She attended
Yale School of the Fine Arts and also studied at Austin

School of Commercial Arts.   Many of her stories have
appeared in children's magazines.   Virginia Frances
Voight has enjoyed nature and the study of Indians.
Her juvenile books include: Mystery At Deer Hill,
Funk, 1958; Nathan Hale, Putnam, 1965; Patriots' Gold,
Macrae, 1969.   CA-7/8, MJA

VON HAGEN, Christine (Shields)
She married explorer and writer Victor W. Von Hagen
and has accompanied him on expeditions to the Amazon
and Galapagos Islands.   The Von Hagens have also explored Guatemala, Honduras, and Panama on explora-
tory trips.   She later lived in Lima, Peru.   Mrs. Von
Hagen used the name of a small boy in Central America in her book Pablo Of Flower Mountain, Nelson,
1942.

VON HAGEN, Victor Wolfgang 1908-
A recognized authority on the Indian cultures of this
hemisphere, Victor Von Hagen was born in St. Louis,
Missouri.   He undertook his first expedition (to Mexico) when he was twenty-three.   Mr. Von Hagen has
explored Guatemala, Honduras, and Panama.   Prior to
living in Rome, he made his home in Lima, Peru.
His juvenile books include: The Incas, People Of The
Sun, World, 1961; Maya, Land Of The Turkey And The
Deer, World, 1960; Riches Of Central America, Heath,
1942; Roman Roads, World, 1966.

VON SCHMIDT, Eric 1931-
He was born in Bridgeport, Connecticut.   He attended
the Farnsworth School of Art and the Art Students
League in New York.   The author married marine
biologist Kay Hornbogen, and they have lived in Sarasota, Florida and Henniker, New Hampshire.   He has
been a folk singer and guitar player.   Eric von Schmidt
was also a commercial artist.   He wrote a picture
book in verse and also created the illustrations for The
Ballad Of Bad Ben Bilge, Houghton, 1965.   He also
wrote Mr. Chris And The Instant Animals, Houghton,
1967.   CA-17/18

VORWALD, Alan
Teacher and writer.   He received degrees in mathematics from Queens College in Flushing, New York and
in mathematics education from New York University.
He has taught mathematics and has also served as a

school principal. Mr. Vorwald has been a recipient of
a National Science Foundation fellowship. He has lived
in Plainview, New York. With Frank Clark he wrote
Computers, Whittlesey House, 1964.

VOYLE, Mary see MANNING, Rosemary

W

WABER, Bernard 1924-
Born in Philadelphia, he studied at the University of
Pennsylvania, Pennsylvania Academy of Fine Arts, and
the Philadelphia College of Art. He served in the
U. S. Army during World War II. He has been a lay-
out artist for Life magazine in addition to creating picture books for boys and girls. The Wabers have lived
in Kew Gardens Hills, Long Island. His picture books
include: An Anteater Named Arthur, Houghton, 1967;
The House On East 88th Street, Houghton, 1962; How
To Go About Laying An Egg, Houghton, 1963; Just Like
Abraham Lincoln, Houghton, 1964; Lyle, Lyle, Crocodile, Houghton, 1965; Rich Cat, Poor Cat, Houghton,
1963; A Rose For Mr. Bloom, Houghton, 1968. CA-3

WAGNER, Frederick (Reese) 1928-
He was born in Philadelphia, Pennsylvania, grew up in
New Jersey, and later made his home in New York.
He received his master's degree in 1949 from Duke
University where he had graduated summa cum laude
the previous year. He served in the U. S. Army during World War II. Mr. Wagner has been an English
instructor both at Oklahoma and Duke Universities. He
has also been a copywriter and advertising manager
for publishing firms. He married actress and writer
Barbara Brady, and together they wrote Famous American Actors And Actresses, Dodd, 1961. His juvenile
titles include: Famous Underwater Adventurers, Dodd,
1962; Patriot's Choice: Story Of John Hancock, Dodd,
1964; Submarine Fighter Of The American Revolution,
Dodd, 1963. CA-7/8

WAGNER, Glenn A.
He was born in Buffalo, New York and graduated from
Fredonia State College and Oswego State Teachers Col-
lege. He also studied at Harvard University. He has
been a teacher in both elementary schools and colleges.
His hobbies have included: model railroading, furniture

building, and photography.   For young people he wrote:
The Book Of Hobby Craft, Dodd, 1952; Things To Make
Yourself, Dodd, 1957.

WAHL, Jan
It has been this author's belief that the years which he
spent as a boy on a farm in Ohio later provided the
ideas for his first children's book Pleasant Fieldmouse
(Harper, 1964).   Prior to attending the University of
Copenhagen on a Fulbright Scholarship, Jan Wahl graduated from Cornell and Michigan Universities.   He received the Avery Hopwood Award for Fiction.   Mr.
Wahl has lived in New York and has collected drawings,
old movies, and toys from around the world as a hobby.   For young readers he wrote: Cabbage Moon, Holt,
1965; How The Children Stopped The Wars, Farrar,
1969.

WALDECK, Theodore J.   1894-
Author and explorer, born in Brooklyn, New York.
Following the death of his parents, Theodore Waldeck
lived with his grandfather in Vienna.   When he was
eighteen-years-old, he traveled to Africa on an expedition.   Mr. Waldeck later led many expeditions to Africa, British Guiana, and South America.   His juvenile
books include: Lions On The Hunt, Viking, 1942; On
Safari, Viking, 1940.   JBA-2

WALDEN, Amelia Elizabeth   1909-
Teacher and novelist, born in New York City.   She
graduated from Columbia University and later attended
the American Academy of Dramatic Arts in New York.
After her marriage to the late John W. Harmon, she
lived in Westport, Connecticut.   In addition to her
writing career, Amelia Walden has been a theatrical
playwright, producer, and director.   She has also been
a high school teacher in Norwalk, Connecticut.   Her
juvenile books include: A Boy To Remember, Westminster Press, 1960; . . . Gateway, Morrow, 1946; A
Girl Called Hank, Morrow, 1951; In Search Of Ophelia,
McGraw, 1966; Name For Himself, Lippincott, 1967;
Race The Wild Wind, Westminster Press, 1965; A Spy
Called Michel-E, Westminster Press, 1967; Walk In A
Tall Shadow, Lippincott, 1968.   CA-1, MJA

WALDMAN, Frank   1919-
His pseudonym is Joe Webster.   Born in Chicago, Illin-

ois, he later studied at Harvard University. Prior to
becoming a sportswriter, he was a film writer on the
West Coast. He has also been sports director of a
television station in Chapel Hill, North Carolina. Mr.
Waldman has written for both the Christian Science
Monitor and the Los Angeles Times. He has visited
both Europe and Canada. Juvenile titles include: Bonus
Pitcher, Houghton, 1951; The Challenger, World, 1955;
Delayed Steal, Houghton, 1952; Lucky Bat Boy, World,
1956; Rookie From Junction Flats, Ariel, 1952.

WALKER, Kathrine Sorley
    She has written for several English publications which
    include the Dancing Times and the London Daily Tele-
    graph. Kathrine Sorley Walker has been interested in
    ballet since childhood. In addition to writing articles
    on the ballet, she has also been an editor of a dance
    encyclopedia. She wrote Eyes On The Ballet, Day,
    1965.

WALL, Gertrude Wallace
    Author and teacher. She grew up on a farm in New
    York and received her high school and college education
    in the state of California. Her home has been in
    Berkeley. In addition to writing books, Gertrude Wall
    has taught in the primary grades in Los Angeles. Her
    juvenile books include: Gifts From The Forest, Scrib-
    ner, 1958; Gifts From The Grove, Scribner, 1955.

WALLACE, John Adam 1915-
    Born in Lansdowne, Pennsylvania, he received degrees
    from the University of Pennsylvania. Prior to holding
    the position of Director of Undergraduate Studies of
    Boston University, he was on the staff of Beaver Col-
    lege. He has also served as director of foreign study
    programs at both schools. During World War II, he
    served as a paratrooper and later became a colonel in
    the U. S. Army Reserves. He has lived in Putney,
    Vermont. His books for young people include: Getting
    To Know Egypt, U. A. R., Coward-McCann, 1961; Get-
    ting To Know France, Coward-McCann, 1962; Getting
    To Know The Soviet Union, Coward-McCann, 1964;
    Getting To Know The U. S. S. R., Coward-McCann, 1959.
    CA-5/6

WALLACE, May Nickerson 1902-
    Born in Willimantic, Connecticut, she later made her

home in Scarsdale, New York. The author attended
schools in Florida and Wisconsin and also studied in
Alberta, Canada. Her work has appeared in many
magazines. For young people she wrote: The Mystery
Of The Old House, Abelard, 1953; The Plume Hunters
Mystery, McKay, 1956; A Race For Bill, Nelson, 1951.

WALLOWER, Lucille 1910-
Born in Waynesboro, Pennsylvania, she studied at the
Philadelphia Museum Art School. She also attended
New York's Traphagen School of Fashion and was fashion
artist in a department store. She has been both a
school librarian and assistant children's librarian in
the Harrisburg Public Library. Her books for boys
and girls include: Chooky, McKay, 1942; The Lost
Prince, McKay, 1963; The Morning Star, McKay, 1957;
Old Satan, McKay, 1956.

WALSH, Frances Waggener
Author and teacher, born in Clark County, Missouri.
After graduating from Northeast Missouri State Teachers College in Kirksville, Missouri, she did graduate
work at Columbia, Iowa, and Michigan Universities.
She also attended George Peabody College for Teachers
and the University of Missouri. Frances Walsh began
her teaching career in a rural school and later taught
in both elementary and high schools. Prior to her
position as assistant professor of children's literature
at Northeast Missouri State Teachers College, she had
been on the faculty at William Woods College in Fulton,
Missouri and Northern Michigan College. For young
people Mrs. Walsh compiled an anthology That Eager
Zest, Lippincott, 1961.

WALSH, Richard John 1886-1960
Born in Kansas, he received his education in New Eng-
land schools and at Harvard. He began his career as
a Boston newspaper reporter and later was editor of
Collier's and Asia magazines. In 1926 he became
president of the John Day publishing company. Mr.
Walsh was interested in the people and countries of
Asia. His wife was novelist Pearl S. Buck. His book
for young people was Adventures And Discoveries Of
Marco Polo, Random, 1953.

WALTERS, Hugh
Author and scientist, born in the county of Staffordshire,

England. He has been a member of the British Interplanetary Society and Chairman of the Juvenile Court
and Probation Committee in his district. Hugh Walters
has been interested in astronautics and astronomy. His
books for young people include: Journey To Jupiter,
Criterion, 1966; Terror By Satellite (A Junior Literary
Guild selection), Criterion, 1964.

WALTERS, Marguerite
Graduate of Boston University, she was born in Bridgewater, Massachusetts. After her marriage, she lived
in New York City. Prior to her writing career, Mrs.
Walters worked for a publishing house and taught
school. Her special interests have been cooking, painting, and sewing. She has also enjoyed animals as
pets. For boys and girls she wrote: City-Country
ABC, Doubleday, 1966; The Real Santa Claus, Lothrop,
1950; Small Pond, Dutton, 1967.

WALTNER, Willard Elma
Brother (photographer) and sister (writer) team, they
grew up on a farm in South Dakota. They both received early encouragement in handicraft from parents
". . . who believed there was more enjoyment in playing with something you had made yourself. " Their
projects in the field of craft have been written up for
many magazines. For young people their books include: Hobbycraft Around The World, Lantern Press,
1966; Hobbycraft For Juniors, Lantern Press, 1967;
Hobbycraft Toys & Games, Lantern Press, 1965; Wonders Of Hobbycraft, Lantern Press, 1962; Year Round
Hobbycraft, Lantern Press, 1968.

WARBURG, Sandol Stoddard 1927-
She was born in Birmingham, Alabama and later made
her home in Ross, California. She graduated magna
cum laude from Bryn Mawr College in Pennsylvania.
The author also attended San Francisco State College.
Her husband Felix M. Warburg has been an architect.
In addition to creating picture books for boys and girls,
she adapted the first book of Edmund Spenser's Faerie
Queen, and called the adaptation Saint George And The
Dragon, Houghton, 1963. She also wrote: Growing
Time, Houghton, 1969; I Like You, Houghton, 1965.
CA-7/8

WARD, Lynd Kendall 1905-
Author-illustrator.   Born in Chicago, he grew up in
Illinois, Massachusetts, and New Jersey.   He married
writer May McNeer, and they have lived in Cresskill,
New Jersey.   After graduating from Teachers College,
Columbia University, he attended the National Academy
of Graphic Arts in Leipzig, Germany.   Lynd Ward has
illustrated many books for both adults and children and
has collaborated with his wife in writing books.   His
many awards for book illustration include the 1951
Carteret Book Club Award for Book Illustration and the
1953 Caldecott Medal for The Biggest Bear, Houghton,
1952.   He also wrote and illustrated Nic Of The Woods,
Houghton, 1965.   CA-17/18, JBA-1, JBA-2

WARD, Nanda Weedon 1932-
Her parents were author May McNeer and artist Lynd
Ward.   She went to school in Leonia, New Jersey and
later attended Colorado College.   During college she
met her husband Robert Haynes.   He illustrated books
which she wrote with her father Lynd Ward, and these
include: The Black Sombrero, Ariel, 1952; High Flying
Hat (A Junior Literary Guild selection), Ariel, 1956.
She also wrote, and her husband illustrated: Beau,
Ariel, 1957; Mister Mergatroid, Hastings House, 1960;
Wellington And The Witch, Hastings House, 1959.

WARE, Leon Vernon 1909-
He was born in Plainview, Minnesota, grew up in Winnetka, Illinois, and has lived in Newport Beach, California.   He received a B. S. degree from Northwestern
University.   The author served with the U. S. Navy
during World War II.   He has conducted creative writing classes in addition to writing books.   His work has
appeared in magazines, and he has written for radio,
television, and the motion picture industry.   Mr. Ware
has enjoyed fishing and sailing as hobbies.   For young
people he wrote: The Mystery Of 22 East, Westminster Press, 1965; The Threatening Fog, Westminster
Press, 1962.   CA-2

WARNER, Gertrude Chandler 1890-
Born in Putnam, Connecticut, she attended summer
sessions at Yale University.   Prior to her retirement,
she was a grade school teacher.   Miss Warner has
been active in church work and has written publicity
for the National Cancer Society and the American Red

Cross.   Her hobbies have included: cooking, designing
flower arrangements, and playing the pipe organ.   Juvenile titles include: Blue Bay Mystery, Whitman,
1961; The Boxcar Children, Scott, 1942; Houseboat
Mystery, Whitman, 1967; The Lighthouse Mystery,
Whitman, 1963; Mountain Top Mystery, Whitman, 1964;
Snowbound Mystery, Whitman, 1968.   CA-4

WARREN, Billy see WARREN, William Stephen

WARREN, William Stephen 1882-
Author, cartoonist, cowboy.   He received his education
in Chicago at the Academy of Fine Arts and Art Institute.   Billy Warren's cartoons have appeared in such
newspapers as the Chicago Tribune and Cleveland News.
His early years spent as a cowboy in Colorado later
provided authentic background for his illustrated books
for boys and girls.   These include: Golden Palomino,
McKay, 1951; Headquarters Ranch, McKay, 1954; Ride
West Into Danger, Junior Literary Guild and McKay,
1953.

WASHBURNE, Heluiz Chandler 1892-
She was born in Cincinnati, Ohio and studied in Phila-
delphia at the School of Industrial Arts and Women's
School of Design.   Mrs. Washburne has traveled exten-
sively including a visit to the Orient where she saw
India's Vale of Kashmir.   These experiences resulted
in her book Rhamon, Whitman, 1939.   She also wrote:
Children Of The Blizzard (with Anauta), Junior Literary
Guild and Day, 1952; Little Elephant's Christmas, Whit-
man, 1938; Little Elephant's Picnic, Whitman, 1939.
CA-11/12

WASSERSUG, Joseph David 1912-
His pseudonym is Adam Bradford, M. D.   Author, physician, teacher, born in Boston, Massachusetts.   He
graduated cum laude from Harvard University and Tufts
Medical School.   His home has been in Quincy, Massachusetts where he has been associated with the Quincy
City Hospital and its school of nursing.   Dr. Wassersug has also been an instructor at Tufts University.
He has served as a consultant in various hospitals
throughout Massachusetts.   In addition to writing books,
he has contributed articles about health and medicine
to magazines and has conducted a newspaper column
"You're the Doctor. "   For young people he wrote

Hospital With A Heart, Abelard-Schuman, 1961.   CA-
19/20

WATSON, Helen Orr 1892-
Born in Pipestone, Minnesota, she graduated from
Carleton College.   She also studied at Boston and
Northwestern Universities.   She married Colonel James
T. Watson, Jr. , and has lived in Europe, South Amer-
ica, Puerto Rico, China, Japan, and the Philippines.
She was the First Vice-President of the National Lea-
gue of American Pen Women and has also served as
President of the Children's Book Club of Washington,
D. C.   Mrs. Watson has made her home in Washing-
ton, D. C. and Rumson, New Jersey.   Her books for
young people include: Beano, Circus Dog, Junior Literary Guild and Ariel, 1953; High Stepper, Houghton,
1946; Trooper, U. S. Army Dog, Houghton, 1943.
CA-7/8

WATSON, Sara Ruth   Emily
Both sisters were born in Cleveland, Ohio, the daughters of the late bridge engineer Wilbur Watson.   Prior
to receiving her master's and doctor's degrees from
Western Reserve University, Sara Ruth Watson graduated from Western Reserve's Flora Stone Mather College.   She later became an Associate Professor of
English at Fenn College in Cleveland.   Emily Watson
worked in her father's engineering firm after graduating
from Cleveland's Art Institute.   Both have traveled
abroad studying architectural and engineering structures
and have been lecturers and amateur musicians.   Together they wrote Famous Engineers, Dodd, 1950.

WATTS, Mabel Pizzey 1906-
She was born in London and attended schools in England
and Canada.   Her home has been in Burlingame, California.   Her book Something For You, Something For
Me (Abelard, 1960) was a selection of the Parents Magazine Book Club.   The author once said: ". . . As
soon as I get an idea for a story, I stack the dishes
in the sink, burn the carrots, sit in front of the type-
writer and think.   Chaos is everywhere, but I'm happy!" Other juvenile titles include: Everyone Waits
(A Junior Literary Guild selection), Abelard, 1959; The
Light Across Piney Valley, Abelard, 1965.   CA-4

WAYNE, Richard see DECKER, Duane Walter

WEART, Edith Lucie
Chemist, writer. She studied at Oberlin College and
has been a chemist at Mt. Sinai Hospital in Cleveland,
Ohio. Miss Weart's home has been in Jackson Heights,
New York. Her science books for young people in-
clude: The Story Of Your Bones, Coward, 1966; The
Story Of Your Brain And Nerves, Coward, 1961; The
Story Of Your Glands, Coward, 1963; The Story Of
Your Respiratory System, Coward, 1964.

WEAVER, John Downing 1912-
Author and newspaperman, born in Washington, D. C.
He later made his home in Los Angeles, California.
He attended Georgetown University and received de-
grees from George Washington University and the Col-
lege of William and Mary in Virginia. John Weaver
served with the U. S. Army Signal Corps during World
War II. He has worked for the federal government
and has been a reporter and book reviewer for the
Kansas City Star. He has also written for Holiday,
Collier's, and Harper's magazines. For young people
he wrote Tad Lincoln, Dodd, 1963. CA-11/12

WEAVER, Ward see MASON, Frank W.

WEBB, Cecil S.
He has been Curator-Collector to the Zoological Society
of London and Curator of Birds and Mammals at the
London Zoo. He has also served as Superintendent of
the Dublin Zoo. In the introduction to his book about
a pet hare he wrote: "Although my close association
with wild animals extends for over thirty years, it sur-
prises me that such a timid creature as the Irish hare
should make so delightful a pet." Children have enjoyed Cecil Webb's book A Hare About The House,
Houghton, 1957.

WEBB, Clifford Cyril 1895-
Author, artist, engraver. He was born in London and
attended the Westminster School of Art. His work has
been exhibited at the Royal Academy. Mr. Webb has
been a member of the Royal Society of British Artists
and the Royal Society of Painter-Etchers and Engravers.
The author has made his home in Surrey, England.
His juvenile books include: More Animals From Everywhere, Warne, 1959; Strange Creatures, Warne, 1964.

WEBB, Robert N.
    Author, editor, reporter, born in Dayton, Ohio. Mr.
    Webb has been a public relations expert and has writ-
    ten several books for adults. He has always been in-
    terested in history which has resulted in his popular
    "We Were There" series. The author has lived in
    Massachusetts near Boston. His juvenile books include:
    The Living JFK, Grosset, 1964; We Were There On
    The Nautilus, Grosset, 1961.

WEBER, Lenora (Mattingly) 1895-1971
    Born in Dawn, Missouri, she grew up in Colorado.
    She attended high school in Denver. In her senior
    year at high school she became captain of the basket-
    ball team which was coached by Al Weber whom she
    later married. Lenora Weber once won a silver
    trophy for riding in the Cheyenne Frontier show. The
    Webers have lived in Colorado. Juvenile titles in-
    clude: Come Back, Wherever You Are, Crowell, 1969;
    Happy Birthday, Dear Beany (A Junior Literary Guild
    selection), Crowell, 1957. CA-19/20

WEBSTER, Joe see WALDMAN, Frank

WEDDLE, Ethel Harshbarger 1897-
    Librarian, author. Her parents were Reverend Isaac
    Harshbarger and Martha Brubaker Harshbarger. She
    grew up in Illinois and later studied dramatics in Cali-
    fornia. After returning to Girard, Illinois she mar-
    ried a farmer. Mrs. Weddle once wrote: "In 1956
    my first book was published by the Brethren Press,
    Elgin, Illinois. It was the history of the wonderful
    community in which I was raised." She has been lib-
    rarian of the Girard Township Library. Juvenile titles
    include: Alvin C. York, Young Marksman, Bobbs,
    1967; Joel Chandler Harris: Young Storyteller, Bobbs,
    1964. CA-11/12

WEES, Frances Shelley (Johnson) 1902-
    Canadian and American author. Although Mrs. Wees
    was born in the United States, she has been a citizen
    of both the United States and Canada. She has also
    written for magazines of both countries. She has been
    interested in the study of genealogy which proved bene-
    ficial in writing Mystery In Newfoundland, Abelard,
    1965. CA-5/6

WEHEN, Joy De Weese 1926-
Born in Penang, Malaya, she attended St. Margaret's
School in Waterbury, Connecticut. She wrote an essay
on the subject of promoting Anglo-American friendship
and was awarded the $1000.00 national prize of the
English Speaking Union in 1948. She has traveled
throughout the world and has lived in Sausalito, California. She has had poetry and stories published in
newspapers and magazines. She wrote Tower In The
Sky (A Junior Literary Guild selection), Dutton, 1955.
CA-5/6

WEINGAST, David E. 1912-
Author and teacher, he received a Doctor of Philosophy
degree from Columbia University. He obtained a Ford
Foundation grant in 1953 and 1954 and did political research in Europe. David Weingast has been a history
teacher in Newark, New Jersey and has lectured on
political science at Rutgers University. His interests
have included: collecting antiques, swimming, and
music. For young people he wrote We Elect A President, Messner, 1962. CA-5/6

WEINSTOCK, Herbert 1905-
Editor and author, born in Milwaukee, Wisconsin. He
has been associated with the Little Orchestra Society
as an editor and program commentator for its Town
Hall concerts. Herbert Weinstock has also been an
executive editor of a publishing company. During his
travels to other countries, the author attended many
operas. With Irene Gass he wrote Through An Opera
Glass, Abelard, 1958. CA-4

WEIR, Rosemary 1905-
She has lived in England. The author has always been
fond of dogs and has enjoyed writing about them. Several have been pets at her cottage in Devonshire. Writing and gardening have also claimed the author's atten-
tion. Her juvenile books include: The Heirs Of Ashton
Manor, Dial, 1966; Mike's Gang, Abelard, 1965; Mystery Of The Black Sheep, Criterion, 1964. CA-13/14

WEISGARD, Leonard 1916-
Born in New Haven, Connecticut, he studied art at
Pratt Institute. His work has appeared in many magazines including: the New Yorker, Good Housekeeping,
and Harper's Bazaar. The sets and costumes which he

designed for "Nutcracker Suite" have been used by the
San Francisco Ballet.   In 1947 the Caldecott Medal
was awarded to Mr. Weisgard for his illustrations in
Little Island (Doubleday, 1946) written by Margaret
Wise Brown (Golden MacDonald, pseud.).   He has lived
in Roxbury, Connecticut where he has served as chair-
man of the board of education.   Juvenile titles include:
Life Long Ago: First Farmers, Coward, 1966; Ply-
mouth Thanksgiving, Doubleday, 1967; Silly Willy Nilly,
Scribner, 1953; Treasures To See, Harcourt, 1956.
CA-11/12, JBA-2

WEISS, Harvey 1922-
Author, illustrator, sculptor, born in New York City.
He attended New York University, the Art Students
League and National Academy School of Fine Arts in
New York, and the University of Missouri.   After serv-
ing in the Air Corps during World War II, the author
studied sculpture in Paris.   In 1954 he married writer
Miriam Schlein, and they have lived in Norwalk, Con-
necticut.   His wife wrote, and he illustrated The Pile
Of Junk (A Junior Literary Guild selection), Abelard,
1962.   Juvenile books which he has written and illus-
trated include: A Gondola For Fun, Putnam, 1957;
How To Be A Hero, Parents, 1968.   CA-5/6

WELDON, Martin 1913-
He was born in Brooklyn, New York and studied at
Brooklyn College.   He has written a sports column for
newspapers, and at one time was program director for
a radio station in Kingston, New York.   He was also
a radio announcer.   Later he became a member of the
staff of the Columbia Broadcasting System.   The author
has contributed articles to the New Yorker magazine.
His work also appeared in Yank magazine when he
served in the armed forces during World War II.   For
young people he wrote Babe Ruth, Crowell, 1948.

WELLMAN, Manly Wade 1905-
Born in Portuguese West Africa, his father was a medical missionary.   He graduated from Columbia University.   Mr. Wellman has been a newspaper reporter and
has had many stories published in magazines.   He has
been very interested in writing books on American history.   The author has lived in Chapel Hill, North Carolina.   His juvenile titles include: Appomattox Road,
Washburn, 1960; Frontier Reporter, Washburn, 1969.
CA-3, MJA

WELLMAN, Paul Iselin 1898-1966
Author and historian, born in Enid, Oklahoma. He was
once a reporter and later city editor on the Wichita
Beacon. Paul Wellman has written many books about
the West including his "North Star" series for children.
He has based his books on accurate historical research
and yet has provided exciting reading for young people
including his own grandchildren. Juvenile titles include: Indian Wars And Warriors: West, Houghton,
1959; Race To The Golden Spike, Houghton, 1961.
CA-2

WELLS, Helen Frances (Weinstock) 1910-
Author and social worker, born in Danville, Illinois.
She grew up in New York City where she later attended
Columbia and New York Universities. Her short stories have appeared in magazines and have been dramatized for the radio. Helen Wells worked with the Office of the Coordinator of Inter-American Affairs during the war. When she wrote A Flair For People
(Messner, 1955), the author consulted an outstanding
personnel worker and was temporarily employed in a
factory and department store in order to obtain additional information on personnel procedures. She also
wrote: Doctor Betty, Messner, 1969; Escape By Night,
Winston, 1953.

WELLS, Maie Lounsbury
Born in Fergus Falls, Minnesota, she received her
education at Northwestern University and the Sherwood
Music School in Chicago. She has been both a reporter
and an editor. Maie Wells has worked in the theatre
and once wrote a book of children's plays. With Dorothy Fox she wrote Boy Of The Woods, Dutton, 1942.

WELLS, Robert L. 1913-
Born in Illinois, he later made his home in New York
City. Robert Wells has been a Lieutenant Colonel in
the Army Signal Corps reserve and has belonged to the
American Rocket Society. The author visited space
centers and laboratories to acquire authentic material
for his books. He also accompanied a flight to the
South Pole to obtain first-hand information for Navigation In The Jet Age, Dodd, 1961. Other juvenile titles
include: Bionics, Dodd, 1966; Electronics, Key To Exploring Space, Dodd, 1964; Five Yard Fuller Of The
New York Gnats, Putnam, 1967; Messages, Men &

Miles, Prentice, 1958; What Does An Astronaut Do?,
Dodd, 1961; Wonders Of Flight, Dodd, 1962.

WENNING, Elisabeth
In addition to being a writer, she has been a librarian.
At one time she lived in Bavaria, Austria and Germany where she received the inspiration to write her
first picture book, a Christmas story for boys and
girls. It was called The Christmas Mouse, Holt, 1959.

WERNECKE, Herbert Henry 1895-
He received his A. B. degree from Mission House Col-
lege and studied at Milwaukee State Teachers College.
He also attended Western, Princeton (Th. M.), and
Southern Baptist (Ph. D.) Theological Seminaries.   Dr.
Wernecke has been a junior high school principal,
church pastor, professor, and librarian.   For boys
and girls he edited Celebrating Christmas Around The
World, Westminster, 1962.   He also wrote Christmas
Customs Around The World, Westminster, 1959.   CA-
5/6

WERNER, Pat
She has made her home in Van Dyne, Wisconsin with
her husband and twin sons.   Mrs. Werner has written
articles, poetry, and stories.   The curiosity of the
Werner children plus the family's love of nature and
thankfulness for "God's great abundance" inspired Pat
Werner to write How Many Angels In The Sky, Augs-
burg, 1965.

WERSBA, Barbara
She was born in Chicago, Illinois and has lived in a
150-year-old house overlooking the Hudson in Sneden's
Landing, New York.   A graduate of Bard College, Barbara Wersba has worked in advertising and has written
children's book reviews for the New York Times.   For
boys and girls she wrote: Dream Watcher, Atheneum,
1968; A Song For Clowns (A Junior Literary Guild selection), Atheneum, 1965.

WERSTEIN, Irving d. 1971
Author, newspaperman, native New Yorker.   He was
born in Brooklyn, attended New York University, and
has resided in New York City.   He has also lived
abroad.   The author served in the Army as a field
correspondent for Yank magazine during World War II.

After his discharge, he wrote articles and stories for magazines in addition to writing radio and television scripts. One of his main interests has been Civil War history. His juvenile books include: The Battle Of Midway, Crowell, 1961; The Battle Of Salerno, Crowell, 1966; Civil War Sailor, Doubleday, 1962; The Franco-Prussian War, Messner, 1965; I Accuse, Messner, 1967; The Many Faces Of The Civil War, Messner, 1961; Okinawa, Crowell, 1968; This Wounded Land, Delacorte, 1968; War With Mexico, Norton, 1965.

WEST, Betty see BOWEN, Betty

WEST, Emily (Govan)
Her parents were authors Gilbert and Christine Noble Govan. She has lived in Tennessee. Her sister Mary who wrote books under the name of Wilson Gage married author W. O. Steele. Emily West wrote Katy No-Pocket (Houghton, 1944) under the name of Emmy Payne. With her mother Christine Noble Govan she wrote many mysteries including: Mystery At Fearsome Lake, Sterling, 1960; Mystery At Ghost Lodge, Sterling, 1963.

WEST, James see WITHERS, Carl

WEYGANT, Sister Noemi
Photographer-writer. Born in Minnesota, she grew up on a homestead in Montana. She worked in advertising after graduating from the University of Minnesota. A convert to Catholicism, she became a Benedictine nun at the St. Scholastica Priory in Duluth. She studied photography and served as the convent's photographer. Sister Noemi has been the recipient of numerous awards from the Minnesota Professional Photographers Association and the Professional Photographers of America. Her work has been exhibited throughout this country. She has conducted classes in photography in the ghettos of Chicago and written poetry in addition to being an author. Her juvenile books include: It's Autumn, Westminster, 1968; It's Spring, Westminster, 1969; It's Winter, Westminster, 1969.

WHEELER, Post 1869-
He has been called "America's first career diplomat. " On an assignment to Tokyo he met writer Hallie Erminie Rives who became his wife. He has traveled

throughout the world and once served as Special Ambassador to Paraguay and Minister to Albania. He also
was editor of the New York Press. His books for
young people include: Albanian Wonder Tales, Doubleday, 1936; Hathoo Of The Elephants, Viking, 1943;
Russian Wonder Tales, Appleton, 1912.

WHEELER, Sessions S.
Biologist and conservationist, Sessions S. ("Buck")
Wheeler has always enjoyed the outdoors. He graduated from the University of Nevada and has taught
biology at Reno High SchooL He has also been an instructor in conservation during the summer at the
University of Nevada and the University of Southern
California. In 1963 he was the recipient of the Distinguished Nevadan Award from the University of Nevada. The author married a lady named Nevada who
has also been a teacher. For young people he wrote
Paiute, Caxton, 1965. CA-17/18

WHEELING, Lynn
Author and illustrator, born in Pennsylvania. Prior to
living in New York City, Lynn Wheeling traveled in
South America and Europe. At one time the author
was an airline hostess, free-lance artist, and greeting
card designer. For boys and girls she wrote and illustrated "When Is That?", Putnam, 1964.

WHEELWRIGHT, Jere Hungerford
Born in Baltimore, he has made his home in Montclair,
New Jersey. The author has written for both adults
and children. He served in the Navy during World
War IL Prior to this wartime assignment, sailing had
been one of his hobbies. Jere Wheelwright dedicated
his children's book with these words: "To those cheerful, loyal and stout-hearted gentlemen in blue dungar-
ees . . . Naval Air Base Tanapag, Saipan, Marianas
Islands." The book was entitled Gentlemen, Hush!,
Junior Literary Guild and Scribner, 1948.

WHITAKER, George O.
Paleontologist and writer, born in Valdosta, Georgia.
He studied at North Georgia College in Dahlonega.
During World War II, he served in the Army Medical
Corps. Since the war, George Whitaker has been as-
sociated with the American Museum of Natural History
in New York and has also been in charge of fossil

exhibits for other museums. He collaborated with
Joan Meyers to write Dinosaur Hunt, Harcourt, 1965.

WHITE, Anne Terry 1896-
Author and teacher, born in the Ukraine (Russia). She
grew up in America and has lived in New York City
and Stamford, Connecticut. She received a master's
degree from Stanford University after graduating from
Brown University in Providence, Rhode Island. Mrs.
White has been a teacher and social worker in addition
to writing books. She has also served as editor of
Young Citizen. Her books for young people include:
All About Archaeology, Random, 1959; Built To Sur-
vive, Garrard, 1966; Czar Of Water, Garrard, 1968;
First Men In The World, Random, 1953; Lost Worlds,
Random, 1941; Prehistoric America, Random, 1951;
When Hunger Calls, Garrard, 1966; Windows On The
World, Garrard, 1965.   CA-9/10, MJA

WHITE, Bessie (Felstiner) 1892-
She has lived in Washington, D. C. and Brookline,
Massachusetts. Mrs. White dedicated one of her books
to her brother John Felstiner who first heard her stories. She has also written and translated plays. Her
books for boys and girls include: A Bear Named
Grumms, Houghton, 1953; Carry On, Grumms!, Ariel,
1956.

WHITE, Dale see PLACE, Marian Templeton

WHITE, Elwyn Brooks 1899-
E. B. White was born in Mount Vernon, New York,
graduated from Cornell University, and has lived in
North Brooklin, Maine. He has been associated with
the New Yorker magazine both as a writer and editor.
At one time the author also worked in advertising.
Both adults and children have enjoyed his many books.
Juvenile titles include: Charlotte's Web, Harper, 1952;
Stuart Little, Harper, 1945.   CA-13/14, MJA

WHITE, Nancy Bean 1922-
She married author Theodore H. White, and they have
lived in New York City. She was born in Hartford,
Connecticut and attended Sweet Briar College in Virginia. Mrs. White has worked for the New York Times
and Life magazine. She also served with the United
States government in India. Her first book for boys

and girls was Meet John F. Kennedy, Random, 1965.
CA-15/16

WHITE, Percival 1887–   Pauline (Arnold)
Husband-wife team, market researchers. He was born
in Winchendon, Massachusetts, and she was born in
Galesburg, Illinois. Mr. White studied at Oahu College
in Honolulu and received his master's degree from
Harvard. Prior to her marriage, Pauline Arnold
headed Arnold Research Service which conducted sur-
veys for manufacturers. They have lived in Pound
Ridge, New York. Their books for young people in-
clude: The Automation Age, Holiday, 1963; Clothes
And Cloth, Holiday, 1961; How We Named Our States,
Criterion, 1966. CA-1

WHITE, Robb 1909–
Born in the Philippines, he later made his home in
Malibu, California. He received his early education in
Alexandria, Virginia prior to graduating from the U. S.
Naval Academy at Annapolis. Robb White has held the
rank of captain in the Naval Reserve since World War
II. In addition to writing books, he has also written
scripts for television. His story Up Periscope (A Jun-
ior Literary Guild selection), Doubleday, 1956 was
made into a movie. Other juvenile books include:
Candy, Doubleday, 1949; Flight Deck (A Junior Literary
Guild selection), Doubleday, 1961; Silent Ship, Silent
Sea, Doubleday, 1967; Surrender (A Junior Literary
Guild selection), Doubleday, 1966; The Survivor (A
Junior Literary Guild selection), Doubleday, 1964.
CA-2, JBA-2

WHITEHOUSE, Arch 1895–
He was born in England but came to the United States
to live when he was a boy of nine. He flew in the
Royal Flying Corps in World War I and was a war
correspondent during World War II. In addition to
writing books, he has also written for many magazines.
Mr. Whitehouse and his wife have lived in Montvale,
New Jersey. He wrote: Heroic Pigeons, Putnam,
1965; Laughing Falcon, Putnam, 1969. CA-5/6

WHITEHOUSE, Arthur George see WHITEHOUSE, Arch

WHITINGER, R. D. see PLACE, Marian Templeton

WHITNEY, Leon Fradley 1894-
Veterinarian, farmer, author. Both his father and son
have been veterinarians. He was born in Brooklyn,
New York, graduated from Massachusetts Agricultural
College, and did further study at Yale University and
Alabama Polytechnic Institute. Dr. Whitney's hobby
has been breeding bloodhounds. He has lived in
Orange, Connecticut where he has been associated with
the Whitney Veterinarian Clinic. He founded the Whitney collection of dogs at Yale University. For young
people he wrote The Wonders Of The Dog World, Dodd,
1959. CA-7/8

WHITNEY, Phyllis Ayame 1903-
Author, editor, teacher, born in Yokohama, Japan.
She later made her home in New York on Staten Island.
At one time she lived in California, Texas, China, and
the Philippines. Her writing career followed graduation
from high school in Chicago, Illinois. Phyllis Whitney
has been both a reviewer and editor of a children's
page for several newspapers in addition to writing
books. She has also taught writing courses at several
universities. She and her husband Lovell F. Jahnke
have collected material for her books during their
many travels. Juvenile titles include: Black Amber,
Appleton, 1964; Creole Holiday (A Junior Literary
Guild selection), Westminster Press, 1959; Sea Jade,
Appleton, 1965; Secret Of Goblin Glen, Westminster
Press, 1968; Secret Of The Spotted Shell, Westminster
Press, 1967. CA-4, JBA-2

WIBBERLEY, Leonard (Patrick O'Connor) 1915-
His pseudonyms are Leonard Holton and Patrick O'Connor. Born in Dublin, Ireland, he went to schools in
Ireland and England. Mr. Wibberley has worked on
newspapers as a copy boy, reporter, and later as an
editor of a Trinidad paper. In 1943 he came to the
United States as a foreign correspondent. Later he
was a columnist on the Los Angeles Times. He and
his family have lived in Hermosa Beach, California
where the author has enjoyed scuba diving and surfing.
His titles for young people include: Attar Of The Ice
Valley, Farrar, 1968; The Ballad Of The Pilgrim Cat,
Washburn, 1962; A Dawn In The Trees (A Junior Literary Guild selection), Ariel, 1964; Encounter Near Venus (A Junior Literary Guild selection), Farrar, 1967.
CA-7/8, MJA

WIDDEMER, Mabel (Cleland) 1902-1964
Author, librarian. She was a children's librarian at a
social service center in New York known as the Bowling Green Neighborhood Association. The September
1964 issue of the School Library Journal stated: ". . .
Mrs. Widdemer had seen the need for books that would
instruct the foreign-born on American culture. " Her
books include: Aleck Bell, Ingenious Boy, Bobbs,
1947; De Witt Clinton, Boy Builder, Bobbs, 1961.
CA-5/6

WIER, Ester (Alberti) 1910-
Author and poet, born in Seattle, Washington. She attended Southeastern Teachers College and the University
of California in Los Angeles. She married Henry
Robert Wier in Hankow, China, and they have lived and
traveled throughout the United States. In addition to
writing books, Ester Wier worked as a reporter for
the Chicago Tribune. She has also conducted a radio
show for women. The Wier family has enjoyed animals
and travel as hobbies. Her book The Loner (McKay,
1963) was the runner-up for the 1964 Newbery Medal.
It was also sold to Walt Disney Productions. Other
juvenile titles include: Action At Paradise Marsh,
Stackpole Books, 1968; The Barrel, McKay, 1966; The
Long Year, McKay, 1969; Wind Chasers, McKay, 1967;
Winners, McKay, 1968.   CA-11/12

WIESE, Kurt 1887-
Born in Minden, Germany, he came to the United
States in 1927 and later made his home in Frenchtown,
New Jersey. When he was a young man, he lived and
worked for six years in China. He has also lived in
Australia and Brazil. He wrote and illustrated: Cun-
ning Turtle, Viking, 1956; The Dog, The Fox And The
Fleas, McKay, 1953; Groundhog And His Shadow, Vik-
ing, 1959; Thief In The Attic, Viking, 1965; You Can
Write Chinese, Viking, 1945.   CA-11/12, JBA-1,
JBA-2

WILBER, Donald Newton 1907-
Author, architect, professor, born in Madison, Wisconsin. He graduated from Princeton University and following World War II received his Ph. D. degree. His
home has been in Princeton, New Jersey. In addition
to writing books, Donald Wilber has been on the staff
at the Asia Institute in New York City and the Univer-

sity of Chicago in Luxor, Egypt. He has also traveled
to foreign countries as a consultant for the government
and private industry. The author has been the recipient of numerous honors including the Social Science
Research Council fellowship. For young readers he
wrote The Land And People Of Ceylon, Lippincott,
1963. CA-5/6

WILCOX, Don
He was born in Lucas, Kansas and graduated from the
University of Kansas at Lawrence. He later received
his master's degree in Sociology from the University.
He has taught sociology, English, creative writing, and
history in high schools, at the University of Kansas,
and on the Chicago campus of Northwestern University.
Mr. Wilcox has written plays for television and articles
for Jack And Jill and Argosy magazines. His books
for young people include: Basketball Star, Little, 1955;
Joe Sunpool, Little, 1956.

WILDER, Alec
Author, composer, musician, born in Rochester, New
York. He received his education in New Jersey and
New York at the Eastman School of Music in Rochester.
Alec Wilder has composed chamber music (Alec Wilder
Octets), music for television, films, and radio. He
wrote the music for such television shows as "Hansel
And Gretel, " 'Omnibus, " and "Pinocchio. " Popular
songs have also been written and arranged by him.
An extensive traveler, Mr. Wilder has called New York
City his "home base. " For young people he wrote Lul-
labies And Night Songs, Harper, 1965.

WILDER, Laura (Ingalls) 1867-1957
She was born near Pepin, Wisconsin and spent her
childhood in Kansas, Minnesota, and the Dakotas. She
married Almanzo Wilder in 1885 and lived in Mans-
field, Missouri until her death at the age of ninety.
Their daughter, novelist Rose Wilder Lane, has lived in
Connecticut. Laura Ingalls Wilder began teaching at
the age of fifteen. Her writing career began in 1926.
Mrs. Wilder received many awards for her books, and
in 1938 her story On The Banks Of Plum Creek (Har-
per, 1937) was runner-up for the Newbery Medal.
Other titles in her "Little House" series include: Little
House In The Big Woods, Harper, 1932; Little House
On The Prairie (Williams, G. , illus.), Harper, 1953;

Little Town On The Prairie (Sewell, H. , and Boyle,
M. , illus.), Harper, 1941.   JBA-2

WILEY, Karla H.
Author and fashion designer. She attended Duke University at Durham, North Carolina and a school of
fashion in New York. Before her marriage, she designed teen-age clothes and later designed and manufactured clothes for children. The author has written
short stories and has been associated with the United
Nations as a Non-Governmental Observer and as a
U. N. correspondent and columnist. Her first book for
young people was Styles By Suzy, McKay, 1965.

WILKIE, Katharine Elliott 1904-
She was born in Lexington, Kentucky. She later studied
at the University of Kentucky where she met her hus-
band Raymond. Katharine Wilkie has been a Junior
High School teacher. Her hobbies have been gardening
and collecting antiques. John Sevier, Son Of Tennessee
(Messner, 1958) was her first book for young adults.
Her other titles include: Daniel Boone: Taming The
Wilds, Garrard, 1960; Father Of The Constitution:
James Madison (with Elizabeth R. Moseley), Messner,
1963; Mary Todd Lincoln, Girl Of The Bluegrass,
Bobbs, 1954.

WILKINS, Hugh Percival 1896-
British engineer and writer, born in Carmarthen, South
Wales, England. The recipient of an honorary Ph. D.
degree, he has also been a Fellow of the Royal Astronomical Society. Oxford University has sponsored him
as a lecturer in adult education, and he has been associated with the British Astronomical Association as
Director of its Lunar Section. He has also traveled
in Europe and the United States. For boys and girls
he wrote Clouds, Rings And Crocodiles, Little, 1955.

WILKINSON (John) Burke 1913-
He has written sea stories, adult novels, and books for
boys and girls. Mr. Wilkinson was Public Affairs Adviser to the Supreme Allied Commander, NATO, Paris,
France. He later lived in Washington. It was during
his assignment in Paris that the author became interested in Henry of Navarre (Henry IV of France) and
visited the castles and battlefields associated with this
historical figure. His research resulted in a book for

children entitled The Helmet Of Navarre, Macmillan,
1965. He also wrote Cry Spy!, Bradbury, 1969.   CA
-11/12

WILLEY, Robert see LEY, Willy

WILLIAMS, Edgar
Born in Lansdale, Pennsylvania, he graduated from
West Chester State Teachers College. Mr. Williams
has worked in radio and written stories for many magazines including: Boys' Life, Coronet, the Saturday
Evening Post, and Baseball Digest. He has also been
a feature writer on the staff of the Philadelphia Inquirer's Sunday magazine (Today). He has been a
member of the Philadelphia Basketball Writers Association. With Dave Zinkoff he wrote Around The World
With The Harlem Globetrotters, Macrae Smith, 1953.

WILLIAMS, Eric Ernest 1911-
Born in London, England, he studied at Christ's College in London. After serving with the Royal Air Force
in World War II, Eric Williams made his home in
South Devon. He has also lived on his yacht "Escap-
er" based in London. Mr. Williams has been a scriptwriter and interior architect in addition to writing
books. He has traveled to other countries to collect
authentic material for his books. These include: The
Tunnel, Abelard, 1961; Wooden Horse (A Junior Literary Guild selection), Abelard, 1958.   CA-11/12

WILLIAMS, Garth Montgomery 1912-
Born in New York City, he spent part of his childhood
in France, Canada, and England. He later studied in
art schools in London. He has designed textiles and
also has been a sculptor. He began his career in
America drawing for the New Yorker magazine. Mr.
Williams has made his home in Aspen, Colorado. In
1943 E. B. White asked him to illustrate his book
Stuart Little (Harper, 1945). In addition to illustrating
books for other authors, Mr. Williams wrote and illustrated: Adventures Of Benjamin Pink, Harper, 1951;
The Rabbits' Wedding, Harper, 1958.   MJA

WILLIAMSON, Joanne Small 1926-
Born in Arlington, Massachusetts, she has always been
interested in history and has enjoyed it as a hobby.
Her belief has been that "historical novels--if they're

good ones--make up one of the most important categor-
ies in reading for young people. " The author has lived
in Kennebunkport, Maine. For young people she wrote:
The Iron Charm, Knopf, 1964; To Dream Upon A
Crown, Knopf, 1967. CA-13/14

WILLIAMSON, Margaret 1924-
Author-illustrator.   She grew up on a farm near Quebec, Canada. She studied art following graduation
from McGill University in Montreal. The author and
her family have lived in a suburb of Detroit, Michigan.
Her interest in natural history led her to write and illustrate such books as: First Book Of Birds, Watts,
1951; First Book Of Bugs, Watts, 1949; First Book Of
Mammals, Watts, 1957.

WILLIS, Priscilla D.
She has lived on Chicago's North Shore.   The Willis
family have owned a farm in Indiana and a plantation
in Georgia where they raised beef cattle.   She has always been interested in horses and has owned a thor-
oughbred colt from Ireland.   Her books for young people include: Alfred And The Saint, Longmans, 1952;
The Race Between The Flags, Longmans, 1955.

WILLIS, Robert J.
He grew up in New York and later made his home in
Woodland Hills, California.   Prior to serving in the
U. S. Army, he studied art at Pratt Institute in Brook-
lyn, New York.   For boys and girls he wrote: Caesar's
Blue Ribbon, Follett, 1956; Model A Mule, Follett,
1959.

WILLSON, Dixie
Author and playwright, she was born in Mason City,
Iowa.   One of her brothers, Meredith Wilson, has been
a well-known composer and conductor.   Following graduation from college, she joined a touring theatrical
company.   She later worked in New York and Hollywood and married Charles Hayden.   Many of her stories were included in O'Brien's "best of the year" list.
In addition to writing plays and books, Dixie Willson
has also contributed stories to numerous magazines.
For boys and girls she wrote Mystery In Spangles,
Dodd, 1950.

WILSON, Charles Morrow   1905-
A native Arkansan, he graduated from the University
of Arkansas.   He has been associated with the State
Department, American firms in Latin America, and
served in the U. S. Army.   His articles have appeared
in such magazines as American Heritage, Atlantic
Monthly, and Harper's.   The author has made his
home in New England.   For boys and girls he wrote
Crown Point, The Destiny Road, McKay, 1965.   CA-
5/6

WILSON, Eleanore Hubbard
Born in Baltimore, she studied in New York at the
Art Students League and at the Chicago Art Institute.
She also attended a painting school in Michigan where
she met her husband Ronald Lee Wilson.   The Wilsons
have traveled extensively in Europe and the United
States and have made their home in New York City.
Her books for young people include: The Secret Three,
Lothrop, 1951; Treasures Three, Dutton, 1941.

WILSON, Hazel (Hutchins) 1898-
Librarian, professor, consultant, born in Portland,
Maine.   She graduated from Bates College in Lewiston,
Maine and Simmons College in Boston, Massachusetts.
Bates later awarded her an honorary degree of Master
of Arts.   In addition to working in libraries in this
country, she has also been a librarian in Paris,
France.   Her home has been in Washington, D. C.
Her books include: Herbert Again, Knopf, 1951; Her-
bert's Homework, Knopf, 1960; His Indian Brother,
Abingdon, 1955; . . . The Little Marquise: Madame
Lafayette (A Junior Literary Guild selection), Knopf,
1957.   CA-4

WILSON, Holly
Born in Duluth, Minnesota, she attended the University
of Michigan at Ann Arbor.   After her marriage to Dr.
Frederic W. Wilson who was with the Veterans Administration, she lived in various places including Kansas,
Pennsylvania, and Michigan.   Mrs. Wilson has written
both poetry and fiction.   She received the highest a-
ward in the Avery and Julie Hopwood Awards Contest
in fiction for a novel she wrote in college.   Her juvenile titles include: Caroline The Unconquered, Messner, 1956; Deborah Todd, Messner, 1955; The Hundred
Steps, Messner, 1958; Stranger In Singamon, Messner,
1959.

WILSON, Ruth
    She has lived in Philadelphia, Pennsylvania. In addi-
    tion to writing books, she has written poetry. One of
    her poems ("The Quiet Man") written to her husband
    was purchased by the New York Times. Her work
    has also appeared in magazines. She has enjoyed
    painting, and her work has been exhibited at the Phila-
    delphia Art Alliance. Her other interests have includ-
    ed music and cooking. For young people she wrote
    Outdoor Wonderland, Lothrop, 1961.

WINDER, Viola Hitti
    Of Lebanese descent, she was born in New York. She
    has often traveled to the Near East and once lived in
    Beirut, Damascus, and Cairo. The author received
    her education at Kent Place School and Connecticut
    College for Women. Her husband has taught at Prince-
    ton University. She wrote The Land And People Of
    Lebanon, Lippincott, 1965.

WINTER, Ginny Linville 1925-
    Author and artist, born in West Lafayette, Indiana.
    She received her art training in Chicago at the Art In-
    stitute and at the American Academy of Art. She also
    attended the Illinois Institute of Technology. She mar-
    ried Munroe Adams Winter and has lived in Lake
    Bluff, Illinois. Mrs. Winter has been a cartoonist
    and advertising artist in addition to her career as a
    writer. She has also been interested in the ballet.
    For young readers she wrote and illustrated The Ballet
    Book, Obolensky, 1962. CA-4

WINTER, William John 1912-
    He was an associate editor of Air Trails magazine and
    also a contributor of articles for industrial magazines.
    At one time Mr. Winter operated a model airplane
    hobby shop. His experience in building model air-
    planes provided useful material for his book Model Air-
    craft Handbook, Crowell, 1941.

WINWAR, Frances 1900-
    Author and poet, born Francesca Vinciguerra in Taor-
    mina, Sicily. She came to America when she was a
    young girl and later studied at Hunter College, City
    College, and Columbia University. In addition to
    writing poetry, novels, and non-fiction, Frances Win-
    war has reviewed books for the New York World. Her

juvenile books include: Elizabeth, World, 1957; Land Of The Italian People, Lippincott, 1951; Queen Elizabeth And The Spanish Armada, Random, 1954.

WIRT, Mildred (Augustine) 1905-
Journalist, author, she has lived in Toledo, Ohio. She began writing at the age of twelve when she was awarded a medal from St. Nicholas magazine. She received her master's degree in Journalism and has written serials and mystery stories for magazines. Mildred Wirt has also been a courthouse reporter for the Toledo Times. For young people she wrote Pirate Brig, Scribner, 1950.

WISE, William 1923-
He has lived in New York City where he was born. He graduated from Yale University after serving in the Army during World War II. Mr. Wise has written television scripts and contributed stories to magazines in addition to writing books for both adults and children. His book reviews have appeared in the Saturday Review and New York Times. For boys and girls he wrote: Aaron Burr, Putnam, 1968; Franklin Delano Roosevelt, Putnam, 1967; Sir Howard The Coward, Putnam, 1968; World Of Giant Mammals, Putnam, 1964. CA-15/16

WISE, Winifred E.
Graduate of the University of Wisconsin, she married mystery writer Stuart Palmer. She has been a staff editor of Compton's encyclopedia and an advertising executive of several department stores. Winifred Wise and her husband have lived in Laguna Beach, California. For young people she wrote: Fray Junipero Serra And The California Conquest, Scribner, 1967; Lincoln's Secret Weapon, Chilton Co. , 1961.

WISNER, William L.
Author, columnist, editor, a native of Long Island. He attended Columbia University. William Wisner has worked for a Long Island newspaper Newsday and the New York World-Telegram And Sun as an outdoor columnist. He has also served as managing editor of Sportsmen's Life. His articles about fishing have been used for radio programs. He collaborated with Joseph J. Cook to write The Phantom World Of The Octopus And Squid, Dodd, 1965.

WISSMANN, Ruth H.
　　Born in Lima, Ohio, she grew up in Colorado, Ari-
　　zona, and California. Her home has been in Colum-
　　bus, Ohio. She studied in Colorado at the Students'
　　School of Art in Denver and in California at the Pasa-
　　dena School of Fine Arts. Ruth Wissmann has been a
　　dancer and painter in addition to her career as a writ-
　　er. Her juvenile books include: Katy Kelly Of Cripple
　　Creek, Dodd, 1968; Scuba Divers Mystery, Dodd, 1966;
　　The Summer Ballet Mystery, Dodd, 1962.

WITHERS, Carl
　　His pseudonym is James West. Anthropologist, folk-
　　loriest, he was born on a Missouri farm in that part
　　of the country known as the Ozarks. He graduated
　　from Harvard and did graduate work at Columbia Uni-
　　versity. His interest in riddles was a result of
　　studies in social anthropology and the folklore of chil-
　　dren. Mr. Withers has done research in Venezuela,
　　Brazil, and Cuba. He has been a member of the
　　American Folklore Society and has been a Fellow of
　　the American Anthropological Association and has lived
　　in New York City. He wrote A World Of Nonsense,
　　Holt, 1968 and compiled: Counting Out, Oxford, 1946;
　　A Rocket In My Pocket, The Rhymes And Chants Of
　　Young Americans, Holt, 1948.

WITKER, Jim
　　Author and teacher, born in Pasadena, California. A
　　graduate of Harvard, he has taught English in Japan.
　　The author traveled to Scandinavia and other countries
　　after his marriage to a girl (Kristi) of Norwegian
　　descent. The Witkers have lived in New York City
　　and have planned a future home in the British Virgin
　　Islands. He has enjoyed archaeology, sailing, swim-
　　ming, and shooting as special interests. For young
　　people he wrote Getting To Know Scandinavia: Den-
　　mark, Norway And Sweden, Coward, 1963.

WITTE, Betty J.
　　She graduated cum laude from Valparaiso University
　　and taught in a high school in Indiana. She also edited
　　research reports of the Illinois Institute of Technology's
　　Armour Research Foundation. Her husband Dr. Henry
　　W. Witte has served on the staffs of the Chicago Oste-
　　opathic Hospital and the Chicago College of Osteopathy.
　　The Wittes have lived in Worth, Illinois. For boys

and girls she wrote Three Tales About The Hales,
Eerdmans, 1963.

WITTON, Dorothy
Born in Michigan, she grew up in Detroit, and attended
the University of Michigan at Ann Arbor. She also
studied in New York at the New School for Social Research. After her marriage to Luis Romero (who was
a forestry engineer in Mexico), she became a citizen
of Mexico. Her stories about Mexico have appeared
in both adult and juvenile magazines in various countries. She has enjoyed writing stories about Mexico
for young people because "she hopes that in those she
may have contributed a little to the understanding between young people of two nations who have so much
to offer each other. " In addition to her writing career, Dorothy Witton has been a newspaper reporter.
For teen-agers she wrote Treasure Of Acapulco (A
Junior Literary Guild selection), Messner, 1963.

WITTY, Paul Andrew   1898-
Author, editor, professor, born in Terre Haute, Indiana. After graduating from Indiana State Teachers'
College, he attended the University of Chicago and received his M. A. degree from Columbia. He served
in the U. S. Army as a Major during World War II.
Professor Witty has been on the staffs at Northwestern
and Kansas Universities. He has served on the board
of the National Society for the Study of Education and
has been President of the International Council for the
Improvement of Reading. He has also edited textbooks
and magazines. In addition to writing readers (including "Reading for Interest" series), he wrote True Book
Of Freedom And Our U. S. Family, Childrens Press,
1956. With Anne Coomer he also wrote Salome Goes
To The Fair, Dutton, 1953.

WOHLRABE, Raymond A. 1900-
He was born in Superior, Wisconsin. He graduated
from the University of Washington in Seattle and did
graduate work at Purdue and the University of Southern
California. He has been a teacher at West Seattle
High School in Washington. An avid traveler, Mr.
Wohlrabe has written travel articles for magazines in
addition to his books on other countries. His hobbies
have included art and photography. With Werner E.
Krusch he wrote: The Key To Vienna, Lippincott,

1961; <u>Land And People Of Austria</u>, Lippincott, 1956.
He also wrote <u>Exploring Electrostatics</u>, World, 1965.
CA-4

WOJCIECHOWSKA, Maia 1927-
Author, translator, tennis professional. Born in Warsaw, Poland, she studied in Poland, England, and
France, and has lived in the United States since 1943.
Maia Wojciechowska has visited Mexico, Spain, Haiti,
and Portugal. During visits to Spain, she became very
interested in bullfighting especially after watching the
great matador Manolete in the bullring. In 1965 she
received the Newbery Medal for her book <u>Shadow Of
A Bull</u> (Atheneum, 1964). In addition to her career
as a writer, the author has held such positions as:
translator for Radio Free Europe, editor, tennis instructor, private detective, and bullfighter. She has
lived in the New York City area with her daughter
Oriana. Other juvenile books include: <u>A Single Light</u>,
Harper, 1968; <u>Tuned Out</u>, Harper, 1968. CA-11/12

WOLCOTT, Carolyn Muller
A graduate of Brooklyn College and Hartford Seminary
Foundation, she was born in Brooklyn, New York. At
one time she was associated with churches in Pennsylvania as a director of children's work. After her
marriage to college professor and author Dr. Leonard
T. Wolcott, she lived in England. Later the Wolcotts
made their home in Nashville, Tennessee. Together
they wrote <u>Religions Around The World</u>, Abingdon,
1967. She also wrote: <u>I Can See What God Does</u>,
Abingdon, 1969; <u>Jesus Goes To The Market Place</u>,
Abingdon, 1963.

WOLCOTT, Leonard Thompson
Born in Buenos Aires, Argentina, he later lived in
Africa, Europe, and India. He married Carolyn Muller and has lived in Nashville, Tennessee. He received degrees from: Asbury College, Hartford Seminary Foundation, Drew University in Madison, New
Jersey, and Oxford University. Dr. Wolcott has been
a minister in India and a professor on the staff at
Scarrit College in Nashville. Most of his books have
been written for adults. For young readers he collaborated with his wife to write <u>Religions Around The
World</u>, Abingdon, 1967. CA-13/14

WOLFE, Louis 1905-
Born in Bound Brook, New Jersey, he graduated from
Rutgers University. He continued his studies at: New
York University, New School for Social Research, Col-
lege of the City of New York, and Columbia University.
Mr. Wolfe has been a teacher, a counselor in camps
for children, and a producer of radio programs for
children. Later he was associated with the Bureau of
Curriculum Research of the Board of Education in New
York City. His books for young people include: Indi-
ans Courageous, Dodd, 1956; Let's Go To The Louisiana Purchase, Putnam, 1963.

WOLFERT, Jerry
Newspaperman and author. During World War II, he
served as an army combat correspondent in Europe.
He has lived in Brooklyn, New York where he has been
a newspaperman. Many of his magazine serials and
short stories have been written from personal experiences as a seaman, traveler, and wild animal collector. Mr. Wolfert did research at the Buffalo Historical Society and in Ontario and Quebec, Canada in order to obtain authentic material for his book Brother
Of The Wind (A Junior Literary Guild selection), Day,
1960.

WOLLHEIM, Donald Allen 1914-
His pseudonym is David Grinnell. Born in New York,
he graduated from New York University. In addition
to editing magazines, Mr. Wollheim has been editor
of Ace Books (paperbacks) since 1952. His hobby has
been science fiction which he has both collected and
written. The author has lived in Rego Park, New
York. His books for young people include: One
Against The Moon, World, 1956; . . . Secret Of The
Ninth Planet (Cecile Matschat, ed. , Carl Carmer, Con-
sulting ed.), Winston, 1959. CA-4

WONDRISKA, William Allen 1931-
He was born in Chicago, Illinois where he later attended the Art Institute. He received his B. F. A. and
M. F. A. degrees from Yale University in New Haven,
Connecticut. In addition to his work as a designer, he
has taught art at the University of Hartford. His work
has been selected by the American Institute of Graphic
Arts to be represented in their exhibit of children's
books. His juvenile titles include: Mr. Brown And

Mr. Gray, Holt, 1968; Puff (A Junior Literary Guild
selection), Putnam, 1960.   CA-4

WOOD, Dorothy Carrico
Author and librarian, Mrs. Wood has lived in Madison,
New Jersey. She received a degree in library science
from the Carnegie Institute of Technology after grad-
uating from Duke University at Durham, North Carolina.
At one time she was an elementary school librarian in
Baltimore, Maryland. The author has also been asso-
ciated with the Boston Public Library and the Harvard
College Library. Juvenile titles include: Deer Fam-
ily, Harvey, 1969; This Nation, World, 1967.

WOOD, James Playsted 1905-
He was born in New York. He has written books for
both adults and children. Mr. Wood lived in New England and wrote about such famous New Englanders as
Henry David Thoreau and Ralph Waldo Emerson. His
books for boys and girls include: Colonial Massachusetts, Nelson, 1969; The Life And Words Of John F.
Kennedy (with editors of Country Beautiful magazine),
Doubleday, 1964.   CA-9/10

WOOD, Laura Newbold 1911-
She received her education in St. Louis, Missouri
where she was born. She also attended college in the
East and lived in New York. Married to a lawyer,
her home has been in Washington. In addition to writ-
ing books, Laura Wood has also done editorial work.
For boys and girls she wrote: Raymond L. Ditmars,
Messner, 1944; Walter Reed, Messner, 1943.

WOODWARD, Hildegard 1898-
Author-illustrator, born in Worcester, Massachusetts.
She studied at the School of the Museum of Fine Arts
in Boston where she later taught design. Hildegard
Woodward also taught at the School of Fine Arts and
Crafts in Boston. She has painted on her travels to
Europe, Haiti, and Mexico, and her work has been
exhibited often in the United States. Her home has
been in Brookfield, Connecticut. She illustrated
Great-Great Uncle Henry's Cats by Julia B. Bischoff,
Young Scott Bks. , 1965, and she wrote Time Was,
Scribner, 1962.   CA-5/6

WOODY, Regina Llewellyn (Jones) 1894-
She was born in Boston, Massachusetts and received
her education at Dana Hall in Wellesley. She married
physician McIver Woody and has lived in Elizabeth,
New Jersey. She has taught juvenile writing at New
York University and contributed articles to magazines
in addition to writing books for young people. Regina
Woody has also appeared on the stage as a professional
dancer. Her juvenile books include: One Day At A
Time, Westminster, 1968; TV Dancer, Doubleday, 1967;
Young Medics, Messner, 1968. CA-5/6, MJA

WOOLDRIDGE, Rhoda
Author and teacher, born in Buckner, Missouri. She
attended Stephens College at Columbia, Missouri. The
author has been a junior high school teacher in Independence, Missouri. Her interest in the history of
her home state has often inspired the author to visit
museums, libraries, and historical places in order to
collect material for her books. For young people she
wrote: Hannah's Brave Year, Bobbs, 1964; That's The
Way, Joshuway, Bobbs, 1965.

WOOLLEY, Catherine 1904-
Her pseudonym is Jane Thayer. She was born in Chicago and graduated from the University of California
at Los Angeles. She has worked in advertising and
sales promotion before she became an author of books
for boys and girls. Catherine Woolley has made her
home in Passaic, New Jersey where she has served on
the Board of Education and as president of the League
of Women Voters. Juvenile titles include: Andy And
The Runaway Horse, Morrow, 1963; The Cat That
Joined The Club, Morrow, 1967; Cathy's Little Sister,
Morrow, 1964; Chris In Trouble, Morrow, 1968. CA
-2, MJA

WOOLSEY, Janette 1904-
Author and librarian, born in Livingston Manor, New
York. She later made her home in York, Pennsylvania. After graduating cum laude from Middlebury College in Vermont, the author received her library degree from Pratt Institute in Brooklyn. She obtained
her master's from Columbia University. Janette Woolsey has been both a children's librarian and elementary
school librarian. She collaborated with Elizabeth
Hough Sechrist to write and compile: It's Time For

Brotherhood, Macrae Smith, 1962; It's Time For Story Hour, Macrae Smith, 1964; Terribly Strange Tales, Macrae Smith, 1967. CA-4

WORCESTER, Donald Emmet 1915-
Born in Tempe, Arizona, his childhood was spent on ranches in Arizona and California. He later lived in Gainesville, Florida. He attended the University of Arizona and received degrees from Bard College and the University of California. He served in the Naval Reserve and attained the rank of Commander. Often a visiting professor at many universities, the author has been head of the History Department at the University of Florida. His books for young people include: Lone Hunter's First Buffalo Hunt, Walck, 1958; Makers Of Latin America, Dutton, 1966; The Three Worlds Of Latin America, Dutton, 1963; War Pony, Walck, 1961. CA-2

WORLINE, Bonnie Bess
Born in El Dorado, Kansas, she grew up in Kansas City. She later graduated from the University of Chicago. Prior to her marriage to a minister (Irvill Courtner King), she worked in advertising and on the Chicago Daily News. She has taught journalism and English in several colleges and universities. She and her husband have lived in Kansas. For boys and girls she wrote Sod House Adventure, Longmans, 1956.

WORTH, Kathryn 1898-
Poet and author, born in Wilmington, North Carolina. She went to boarding school in Switzerland and attended Radcliffe College and Columbia University. She married Walter Clyde Curry, an English Professor at Vanderbilt University, and they have lived in Nashville, Tennessee. A daughter Josephine inspired Kathryn Worth to write children's poetry and books for girls. Juvenile books include: Middle Button, Doubleday, 1941; They Loved To Laugh, Doubleday, 1942.   JBA-2

WRIGHT, Dare
Author, illustrator, photographer. Born in Ontario, Canada, she grew up in Cleveland, and later made her home in New York City. She studied in New York at the American Academy of Dramatic Arts and Art Students League. She became a professional photographer after beginning her career as a photographer's fashion

model. She has worked in advertising, and her editorial photography has appeared in national magazines. Miss Wright's photographs of fashions have also been published in Harper's Bazaar and Vogue. Her juvenile books include: Edith & Big Bad Bill, Random, 1968; Edith & Mr. Bear, Random, 1964; The Lonely Doll (A Junior Literary Guild selection), Doubleday, 1957; Look At A Colt, Random, 1969.

WRIGHT, Enid Meadowcroft (LaMonte) see MEADOWCROFT, Enid (La Monte)

WRIGHT, Frances (Fitzpatrick) 1897-
Her childhood was spent in the country, and she later lived on a farm in Tennessee. Mrs. Wright's interests have been: cooking, gardening, and reading. She has also participated in a Great Books Community Group. Her juvenile books include: Bless Your Bones, Sammy, Abingdon, 1968; The Secret Of The Old Sampey Place, Abingdon, 1946. CA-13/14

WRIGHTSON, Patricia
Australian author. She grew up in the country which caused the author to receive some of her schooling by mail. The State Correspondence School sent lessons to her as they did to other children who lived in faraway places. She began to write in 1954, but she had desired to become a writer for many years. The first book which she wrote that was published in America was The Feather Star, Harcourt, 1963. She also wrote Racecourse For Andy, Harcourt, 1968.

WUNSCH, Josephine (McLean) 1914-
She graduated from the University of Michigan where her daughter Kay Wunsch also studied. Mrs. Wunsch has been a newspaperwoman and a free-lance writer. She has lived in Grosse Pointe Farms, Michigan. When her daughter Kay traveled with the University of Michigan Symphony Band to the Soviet Union, she kept a diary. This diary served as an inspiration for Josephine Wunsch's book Passport To Russia, McKay, 1965. She also wrote Summer Of Decision, McKay, 1968. CA-3

WYATT, Edgar
Historian, author, he has lived in Tucson, Arizona. Mr. Wyatt has done intensive research on the period

of the final Indian Wars. His biographies for young
people include: Cochise, McGraw-Hill, 1953; Geroni-
mo, McGraw-Hill, 1952.

WYATT, Geraldine (Tolman) 1907-
She was born in Hope, Kansas and later lived in Missouri where she married lawyer Roy A. Wyatt. She
attended business college, studied music, and took extension courses in creative writing from the University
of Missouri. For young people she wrote: Sun Eagle,
Longmans, 1952; Wronghand, Longmans, 1949.

WYATT, Isabel
Teacher, author. She was born in South Staffordshire,
England. During World War II, she worked with child
refugees in the southern part of England. In 1960 she
became Co-Director of Studies at Hawkwood College in
Gloucestershire. In her work she has become acquainted with students from various parts of the world. Her
book for young people was The Golden Stag, And Other
Folk Tales From India, McKay, 1962.

WYCKOFF, James M. 1918-
Author and editor, born in New York City. At one
time he was a cowboy, owner of a bookstore, and
soldier in the army (1942-46). He attended schools in
France, Switzerland, and England. When he was fifteen-years-old, James Wyckoff sailed across the Atlantic (19 days) in an 80-foot Dutch pilot boat. He has
written many short stories and has been an associate
editor of a publishing firm. His books for children
include Who Really Invented The Submarine?, Putnam,
1965.   CA-19/20

WYLER, Rose
Teacher and writer. She became a science instructor
after graduating from college. She married writer
Gerald Ames and has lived in New York City. In addition to writing books, Rose Wyler has written for radio
and the film industry. Her work has also appeared in
magazines. She collaborated with her husband to write:
First Days Of The World, Harper, 1958; Prove It!,
Harper, 1963. She also wrote: First Book Of Weather, Watts, 1956; Magic Secrets, Harper, 1967; Spooky
Tricks, Harper, 1968.

WYMER, Norman   1911-
Author and newspaperman, born in England. He received his education at Charterhouse (one of the leading
public schools of England).   His articles about the
British way of life were published in American newspapers during World War II.   Mr. Wymer has written
for both radio and television in addition to writing
books.   His home has been in Sussex near South Downs.
For young people he wrote Gilbert And Sullivan, Dutton, 1963.

WYNDHAM, Lee   1912-
Her pseudonym is Jane Lee Hyndman.   She was born
in Russia, came to the United States when she was a
young girl, and later became an American citizen.
Married to writer and editor Robert Hyndman, she has
lived in Morristown, New Jersey.   In addition to writing, Lee Wyndham has worked in a book shop and has
been a newspaper columnist.   Her interests have included ballet and opera.   Juvenile titles include: The
Family At Seven Chimneys House, Watts, 1963; Mour-
ka, The Mighty Cat, Parents, 1969; Thanksgiving, Garrard, 1963.   CA-7/8, MJA

Y

YATES, Brock Wendel   1933-
The son of writer Raymond F. Yates, he was born in
Buffalo, New York.   He graduated from Hobart College
at Geneva and has lived in both Castile and Perry,
New York.   A noted authority in the field of racing
cars and drivers, Brock Yates' articles have appeared
in racing publications and encyclopedias.   He has
served as an automotive columnist for Leisure.   He
collaborated with his father to write Sport And Racing
Cars, Harper, 1954.   He also wrote: Destroyers And
Destroyermen, Harper, 1959; The Indianapolis 500,
Harper, 1961; Plastic Foam For Arts And Crafts, Sterling, 1965; Racers And Drivers, Bobbs, 1968.   CA-
11/12

YATES, Elizabeth   1905-
Writer, lecturer, born in Buffalo, New York.   Follow-
ing her marriage to William McGreal, she lived in
London.   Later the McGreals made their home in
Peterborough, New Hampshire.   She has enjoyed cook-
ing, gardening, making hooked rugs, and exhibiting

Scotties.   In 1951 she was awarded the Newbery Medal
for her book Amos Fortune, Free Man, Aladdin, 1950.
She also wrote: Carolina's Courage, Dutton, 1964; An
Easter Story, Dutton, 1967; Someday You'll Write, Dut-
ton, 1962; With Pipe, Paddle, And Song, Dutton, 1968.
CA-2, JBA-2

YATES, Raymond Francis 1895-
Author, editor, newspaperman.   He was born in Lockport, New York, grew up in Niagara Falls, and has
lived in New York state.   His first articles were published before he was eighteen.   Mr. Yates has been a
radio columnist and radio editor of the New York Herald Tribune.   He has also served as contributing editor
of Science And Mechanics.   He has lectured throughout
this country and contributed articles to such magazines
as Life and Reader's Digest.   With his son Brock
Yates he wrote Sport And Racing Cars, Harper, 1954.
He also wrote: Atomic Experiments For Boys, Harper, 1952; Boy's Book Of Tools, Harper, 1957; Young
Inventor's Guide, Harper, 1959.   MJA

YAUKEY, Grace (Sydenstricker) 1899-
Her pseudonym is Cornelia Spencer.   Her sister was
Pearl S. Buck.   She was born in China, attended college in the United States, and returned to China where
she lived until 1935.   She has lived in Bethesda, Maryland.   Juvenile titles include: Made In Japan, Knopf,
1963; Three Sisters, Day, 1939.   CA-3, JBA-2

YEZBACK, Steven A. 1943-
Poet and author.   He has been an elementary schoolteacher in Detroit, Michigan where he was born.   Most
of his students have had similar backgrounds as the
main character in his first book for children entitled
Pumpkinseeds (A Junior Literary Guild selection),
Bobbs, 1969.

YOLEN, Jane H. 1939-
She studied at Smith College at which time her poetry
was published.   She married David Stemple, and they
have lived in New York.   In addition to writing children's books, she has edited books and has been in
charge of a creative-writing workshop.   Her interests
have included: skiing, guitar playing, and singing folk
songs.   She wrote: The Witch Who Wasn't, Macmillan,
1964; The Wizard Of Washington Square, World, 1969.
CA-15/16

YOST, Edna 1889-
Born in Pennsylvania, she graduated from Allegheny
College. She has written articles for many magazines
including: Harpers, Forum, and the North American
Review. She has also taught school. Edna Yost's
home has been in New York City. For young people
she wrote: Famous American Pioneering Women,
Dodd, 1961; Modern American Engineers, Lippincott,
1952; Modern Americans In Science And Technology,
Dodd, 1962. CA-2

YOUNG, Edward see REINFELD, Fred

YOUNG, Ella 1867-1956
Born at Fenagh, County Antrim, Ireland, she grew up
in Limerick and later lived in Dublin. She graduated
from Royal University. It was in 1925 that she came
to the United States. She gave lectures, told stories,
and held the Phelan Memorial Lectureship of Celtic
Mythology at the University of California in Berkeley.
Prior to her death in 1956, she lived in Oceana, California. Juvenile titles include: The Tangle-Coated
Horse And Other Tales, Episodes From The Fionn
Saga, Longmans, 1929; The Unicorn With Silver Shoes,
Longmans, 1932; The Wonder Smith And His Son, Longmans, 1955. JBA-1, JBA-2

YOUNG, Frederica
Author and teacher, she has written for both adults
and children. She has also been an elementary school
teacher in Westerly, Rhode Island. With Marguerite
Kohl she wrote: Games For Children, Wyn, 1953;
More Jokes For Children, Hill & Wang, 1966.

YOUNG, Jan see RANDALL, Janet

YOUNG, Janet Randall see RANDALL, Janet

YOUNG, John Richard
His father operated a ranch in Wisconsin. He graduated from Marquette University where he studied
journalism. The author has always been fond of
horses, especially the Arabian. He and his family
have lived in Milwaukee, Wisconsin. For young people he wrote: Arabian Cowhorse, Follett, 1966; Arizona Cutting Horse, Westminster Press, 1956; Olympic
Horseman, Westminster Press, 1957.

YOUNG, Miriam (Burt)
Author and playwright.   Prior to her marriage to commercial artist Walter Young, she worked as a fashion
artist in New York.   They have lived in Westchester
County and Goldensbridge, New York.   Her articles
and stories have appeared in Better Homes And Gardens, Humpty Dumpty, Mademoiselle, and Story Parade magazines.   She has worked on a newspaper, and
one of her adult novels was made into a motion picture.
Her juvenile books include: Bear Named George,
Crown, 1969; Billy And Milly, Lothrop, 1968; Jelly-
beans For Breakfast, Parents, 1968; Miss Suzy, Parents, 1964; Witch Mobile, Lothrop, 1969.

YOUNG, Patrick
Author and journalist.   He was born in Ladysmith,
Wisconsin, graduated from the University of Colorado,
and has lived in Silver Spring, Maryland.   His varied
career has included: movie projectionist, construction
worker, and radio announcer.   He selected journalism
as his profession and has been on the staff of the
National Observer.   As the great-grandson of a Civil
War captain, Patrick Young heard many "Old Abe"
stories when he was a boy.   He later wrote Old Abe:
The Eagle Hero (A Junior Literary Guild selection),
Prentice, 1965.

YOUNG, Percy Marshall 1912-
English author, composer, teacher.   He has made his
home in Wolverhampton, Staffordshire, England where
he has been associated with the College of Technology
as a Director of Music.   Dr. Young graduated from
the Universities of Cambridge and Dublin.   He has
been a well-known broadcaster in addition to a composer and teacher.   For young people he wrote: Stra-
vinsky, Ernest Benn/David White, 1969; World Con-
ductors, Abelard, 1966.   CA-15/16

YOUNG, Robert William 1916-
He was born in Chico, California, attended schools in
Sacramento, and graduated from the University of
Nevada at Reno.   He also studied in Los Angeles at
the University of California.   After serving with the
Army in World War II, Mr. Young made his home in
Whittier, California.   He married writer Janet Randall.
Together they wrote: Anza, Hard-Riding Captain,
Golden Gate, 1966; Empire Builder, Messner, 1967;

Frontier Scientist, Messner, 1968; Seven Faces West,
Messner, 1969.   CA-5/6

YOUNG, Stanley 1906-
Playwright, publisher, author.   His plays have been
produced on Broadway.   He married novelist Nancy
Wilson Ross, and they have lived on Long Island in
Old Westbury.   His books for young people include
Tippecanoe And Tyler, Too!, Random, 1957.

                           Z

ZACKS, Irene
She was born in Paris, France where she also attended
school.   She married artist Lewis Zacks who has illustrated many books for boys and girls.   Irene Zacks
has been a secretary and has managed a bookstore and
a bureau for speakers.   She and her husband have
lived in New York City.   She wrote Space Alphabet,
Prentice, 1964.

ZAFFO, George J.
Author-illustrator.   Born in Bridgeport, Connecticut,
he studied at Pratt Institute in Brooklyn, New York
and was also an apprentice to Norman Rockwell.   Dur-
ing World War II, Mr. Zaffo was in the Army Signal
Corps.   His hobbies have included hunting and model
railroads.   He has lived in Mount Vernon and later in
Tuckahoe, New York.   He wrote and illustrated: Big
Book Of Real Trains, Grosset, 1949; Big Book Of Real
Trucks, Grosset, 1950; Building Your Super Highways,
Garden City, 1957.

ZAGOREN, Ruby 1922-
Author and reporter, born in New Britain, Connecticut.
She married science teacher Samuel Silverstein, and
they have lived in Torrington, Connecticut.   Ruby Zagoren received her B. A. degree from Connecticut College at New London.   The author has been a reporter
for the Hartford Courant, and her work has appeared
in magazines and newspapers.   For young people she
wrote Venture For Freedom, World, 1969.   CA-17/18

ZAIDENBERG, Arthur 1903-
Artist, author, muralist.   He attended the Art Students
League and the National Academy in New York.   He
also studied in Munich and Rome and at the Beaux Arts

in Paris. A world traveler, Mr. Zaidenberg has
painted in such countries as Guatemala and Morocco.
His work has been included in the permanent collections
of art museums in this country. He has taught art at
New York University and illustrated numerous classics
of literature in addition to writing and illustrating
books for children. These include: How To Draw
Houses, Abelard, 1968; How To Draw Portraits, Vanguard, 1962; How To Paint With Water Colors, Vanguard, 1968; Your Child Is An Artist, Grosset, 1949.

ZARCHY, Harry 1912-
Native of New York, he studied at Pratt Institute and
New York University. He has been a commercial
artist, teacher, and musician. His hobbies have included: craftwork, target shooting, and ham radio
operation. The Zarchys have lived in Freeport, Long
Island. Juvenile titles include: Butterflies, World,
1966; Creative Hobbies, Knopf, 1953; Mobiles, World,
1966; Using Electronics, Crowell, 1958. CA-4, MJA

ZAREM, Lewis
Author and journalist, he graduated from the University
of Wisconsin. He served with both the Army and Air
Force during World War II. Mr. Zarem has devoted
much of his writing career to the sciences, especially
those about aeronautics and astronautics. He has
lived in Dayton, Ohio and has been associated with the
Wright-Patterson Air Force Base. His juvenile books
include: New Dimensions Of Flight, Dutton, 1959; New
Era Of Flight, Dutton, 1956.

ZEI, Alki
She was born and grew up in Greece, and at the age
of ten decided to become a writer. Following her
marriage to a stage director and writer, she lived in
France, Italy, Uzbekistan, and Russia. During her
stay in Moscow, Alki Zei studied scenario writing at
the Moscow Institute of Cinema. In 1967 she and her
family left Greece and moved to Paris. For young
people she wrote Wildcat Under Glass (tr. by Edward
Fenton), Holt, 1968.

ZEIGER, Henry Anthony 1930-
His pseudonym is James Peterson. Author, editor,
playwright, born in Brooklyn, New York. A graduate
from Kenyon College in Gambier, Ohio, he later

attended Columbia University and the Yale School of
Drama for advanced study. The author has served in
the Army, and he has continued to live in Brooklyn.
For young people he wrote Robert F. Kennedy, Meredith, 1968.

ZIEGLER, Ursina
Teacher, author. She attended the Gymnasium in
Chur, Switzerland and received a diploma in interior
design from the school for Innenarchitektur in Zurich.
Ursina Ziegler later taught at a school for girls in
Zurich. Her book for boys and girls was Squaps, The
Moonling (tr. by Barbara Kowal Gollob), Atheneum,
1969.

ZIM, Herbert Spencer 1909-
Born in New York, he attended City College of New
York and received degrees from Columbia University.
He has been a science teacher and an associate professor at the University of Illinois. In addition, he
once served as Educational Consultant for the United
States Fish and Wildlife Service. Dr. Zim has contributed articles and reviews on science and natural
history to magazines. Married to writer Sonia Bleek-
er, he has lived in Tavernier, Florida. With his wife
he wrote Life And Death, Morrow, 1970. His titles
include: Alligators And Crocodiles, Morrow, 1952;
Corals, Morrow, 1966; How Things Grow, Morrow,
1960; Sharks, Morrow, 1966; Waves, Morrow, 1967.
CA-15/16, JBA-2

ZIMELMAN, Nathan
He has lived in Sacramento, California. Mr. Zimelman has devoted all of his time to writing books since
he retired from business. For boys and girls he
wrote: A Good Mornings' Work, Steck, 1968; First
Elephant Comes To Ireland, Follett, 1969.

ZINDEL, Paul
Author and playwright, born in New York on Staten
Island. He has lived in New York State and in Houston, Texas where under a Ford Foundation Grant he
was Playwright-in-Residence at Nina Vance's Alley
Theater. In addition to writing for the theater, Paul
Zindel has also written plays for television ("The Ef-
fect of Gamma Rays on Man-in-the-Moon Marigolds"
and "Let Me Hear You Whisper"). For young people

he wrote Pigman, Harper, 1968.

ZINER, Florence (Feenie) Katz 1921-
Author and social worker, born in Brooklyn, New York.
After graduating from Brooklyn College, she received
her master's from the New York School of Social Work.
The mother of triplets (5 children in all), Mrs. Ziner
has lived in Dobbs Ferry, New York. At one time
she worked in Connecticut and Illinois as a caseworker
and psychiatric social worker. She also was instrumental in starting the "Trick or Treat for UNICEF"
program in Evanston, Illinois, and her articles have
appeared in magazines. With Paul Galdone she wrote
Counting Carnival, Coward-McCann, 1962. She also
wrote: Dark Pilgrim, Chilton, 1965; Wonderful Wheels,
Melmont, 1959. CA-3

ZINKOFF, Dave
He graduated from Temple University in Philadelphia.
Known as the "Voice of Philadelphia," he has announced
many sports events. During World War II, he was
with the Special Services and was instrumental in establishing a sports program for the young people of
Iceland. Mr. Zinkoff has also served as tour secretary of the Harlem Globetrotters. With Edgar Williams
he wrote Around The World With The Harlem Globetrotters, Macrae Smith, 1953.

ZION, Gene 1913-
Art director, author, designer. Born in New York
City, he graduated from Pratt Institute in Brooklyn,
and attended the New School in New York. He became
interested in the design and printing of books on a trip
to Europe. He designed training manuals and filmstrips for the Army during World War II. After the
war, Mr. Zion worked for Condé Nast Publications
and the Columbia Broadcasting System as an artist.
He married artist Margaret Bloy Graham who has illustrated many of his books for children. These include: All Falling Down, Harper, 1951; Dear Garbage
Man, Harper, 1957; Harry By The Sea, Harper, 1965;
The Meanest Squirrel I Ever Met, Scribner, 1962;
Sugar Mouse Cake, Scribner, 1964. MJA

ZIRBES, Laura
Educator and author. In 1948 she received recognition
as Woman of the Year in Education awarded by the

National Woman's Press Club.   Dr. Zirbes has been
a university professor and has served as Ohio State
Consultant in Elementary Education. Her articles have
often been published in educational journals. She has
lived in Columbus, Ohio.   For boys and girls she wrote
How Many Bears?, Putnam, 1960.

ZOLOTOW, Charlotte (Shapiro) 1915-
She was born in Norfolk, Virginia and studied at the
University of Wisconsin.   Following her marriage to
writer Maurice Zolotow, she lived in New York City.
At one time she served as an editorial assistant in a
publishing house.   The Zolotows later lived in Hastings-
on-Hudson. Juvenile titles include: Indian, Indian,
Simon, 1952; The Man With The Purple Eyes, Abelard,
1961; Mr. Rabbit And The Lovely Present, Harper,
1962; Someday, Harper, 1965; When I Have A Son,
Harper, 1967.   CA-5/6, MJA

LIFTON, Betty Jean   1926-
   She graduated from Barnard College.   Prior to living
   in the Far East with her husband Dr. Robert Jay Lifton, she worked in television in New York.   She has
   been interested in the folklore of Asia and has written
   several books for boys and girls that were based on
   ideas which she obtained in Japan.   The Liftons later
   lived in a former inn (180 years old) in Woodbridge,
   Connecticut.   Juvenile titles include: The Dwarf Pine
   Tree, Atheneum, 1963; Secret Cellar, Norton, 1968.
   CA-5/6

Caldecott Medal Winners

1970   Sylvester And The Magic Pebble, Steig, 486

1969   The Fool Of The World And The Flying Ship, Shulevitz, 469

1968   Drummer Hoff, Emberley, 157

1967   Sam, Bangs, And Moonshine, Ness, 381

1966   Always Room For One More, Hogrogian, 246

1965   May I Bring A Friend?, Montresor, 368

1964   Where The Wild Things Are, Sendak, 461

1963   The Snowy Day, Keats, 279

1962   Once A Mouse, Brown, 67

1961   Baboushka And The Three Kings, Sidjakov, 470

1960   Nine Days To Christmas, Ets, 161

1959   Chanticleer And The Fox, Cooney, 112

1958   Time Of Wonder, McCloskey, 330

1957   A Tree Is Nice, Simont, 473

1956   Frog Went A-Courtin', Rojankovsky, 440

1955   Cinderella, Brown, 67

1954   Madeline's Rescue, Bemelmans, 40

1953   The Biggest Bear, Ward, 536

1952   Finders Keepers, Mordvinoff, 371

1951   The Egg Tree, Milhous, 362

1950   Song Of The Swallows, Politi, 414

1949   The Big Snow, Hader, 217

1948   White Snow, Bright Snow, Duvoisin, 151

1947   The Little Island, Weisgard, 541

1946   The Rooster Crows, Petersham, 407

1945   Prayer For A Child, Jones, 271

577

1944	Many Moons, Slobodkin, 474
1943	The Little House, Burton, 78
1942	Make Way For Ducklings, McCloskey, 330
1941	They Were Strong And Good, Lawson, 304
1940	Abraham Lincoln, D'Aulaire, 129
1939	Mei Li, Handforth, 223
1938	Animals Of The Bible, Lathrop, 301

Newbery Medal Winners

1970	Sounder, Armstrong, 19
1969	The High King, Alexander, 10
1968	From The Mixed-Up Files Of Mrs. Basil E. Frankweiler, Konigsburg, 290
1967	Up A Road Slowly, Hunt, 254
1966	I, Juan de Pareja, Treviño, 515
1965	Shadow Of A Bull, Wojciechowska, 560
1964	It's Like This, Cat, Neville, 381
1963	A Wrinkle In Time, L'Engle, 309
1962	The Bronze Bow, Speare, 482
1961	Island Of The Blue Dolphins, O'Dell, 389
1960	Onion John, Krumgold, 293
1959	The Witch Of Blackbird Pond, Speare, 482
1958	Rifles For Watie, Keith, 279
1957	Miracles On Maple Hill, Sorensen, 480
1956	Carry On, Mr. Bowditch, Latham, 300
1955	The Wheel On The School, DeJong, 134
1954	And Now Miguel, Krumgold, 293
1953	Secret Of The Andes, Clark, 99
1952	Ginger Pye, Estes, 161
1951	Amos Fortune, Free Man, Yates, 567
1950	The Door In The Wall, DeAngeli, 132
1949	King Of The Wind, Henry, 234

1948   The Twenty-One Balloons, DuBois, 148

1947   Miss Hickory, Bailey, 24

1946   Strawberry Girl, Lenski, 309

1945   Rabbit Hill, Lawson, 304

1944   Johnny Tremain, Forbes, 177

1943   Adam Of The Road, Gray, 208

1942   The Matchlock Gun, Edmonds, 153

1941   Call It Courage, Sperry, 482

1940   Daniel Boone, Daugherty, 129

1939   Thimble Summer, Enright, 158

1938   The White Stag, Seredy, 462

1937   Roller Skates, Sawyer, 451

1936   Caddie Woodlawn, Brink, 64

1935   Dobry, Shannon, 463

1934   Invincible Louisa, Meigs, 357

1933   Young Fu Of The Upper Yangtze, Lewis, 314

1932   Waterless Mountain, Armer, 18

1931   The Cat Who Went To Heaven, Coatsworth, 103

1930   Hitty, Her First Hundred Years, Field, 170

1929   The Trumpeter Of Krakow, Kelly, 280

1928   Gay-Neck, Mukerji, 375

1927   Smoky, The Cowhorse, James, 263

1926   Shen Of The Sea, Chrisman, 97

1925   Tales From Silver Lands, Finger, 171

1924   The Dark Frigate, Hawes, 229

1923   The Voyages Of Doctor Dolittle, Lofting, 322

1922   The Story Of Mankind, VanLoon, 525